C L A S S I C

*H*OME
DESSERTS

C L A S S I C
HOME
DESSERTS

A treasury of heirloom and contemporary
recipes from around the world

Richard Sax

Photography by Alan Richardson

HOUGHTON MIFFLIN HARCOURT
BOSTON   NEW YORK
2010

2/11

Copyright © 1994, 2010 by Richard Sax
Photography © 1994, 2010 by Alan Richardson

For information about permission to reproduce selections from this
book, write to Permissions, Houghton Mifflin Harcourt Publishing
Company, 215 Park Avenue South, New York 10003
www.hmhbooks.com

Library of Congress Cataloging-in-Publication Data

Sax, Richard.
Classic home desserts : a treasury of heirloom and
contemporary recipes from around the world / Richard Sax ;
photography by Alan Richardson.
p. cm.
Reprint. Originally published: Shelburne, Vt. : Chapters Pub., c1994.
Includes bibliographical references and index.
ISBN 978-0-618-05708-5
1. Desserts. 2. Cookery, International. 3. Cookbooks.
I. Richardson, Alan. II. Title.
TX773.S3177 2010
641.8'6—dc22
2010025552

Printed and bound in China
SCP 10 9 8 7 6 5 4 3 2 1

Designed by Eugenie Seidenberg Delaney
Food styling by Anne Disrude
Prop styling by Betty Alfenito

Cover photograph by Alan Richardson:
Chocolate Cloud Cake, page 420

This is for
Michael Violanti
beloved friend
1948–1991

CONTENTS

FOREWORD BY DORIE GREENSPAN 9

INTRODUCTION 12

NOTES ON INGREDIENTS 21

DESSERT TECHNIQUES 24

KITCHEN EQUIPMENT 26

COOKWARE AND BAKEWARE 27

CHAPTER 1
THE EXTENDED FAMILY OF
COBBLERS AND CRISPS 32

CHAPTER 2
COMPOTES AND BAKED FRUIT 70

CHAPTER 3
CREAMS, FOOLS AND JELLIES 86

CHAPTER 4
CREAMY PUDDINGS, CUSTARDS AND SOUFFLÉS 120

CHAPTER 5
RICE, BREAD AND NOODLE PUDDINGS 170

CHAPTER 6
FRUIT PUDDINGS,
SWEET PANCAKES AND DUMPLINGS 212

CHAPTER 7
COOKIES 242

CHAPTER 8
PLAIN CAKES AND CAKES WITH FRUIT 297

CHAPTER 9
COFFEE CAKES 348

CHAPTER 10
LAYER CAKES, FANCY CAKES,
CHEESECAKES AND CHOCOLATE CAKES 380

CHAPTER 11
FRUITCAKES AND NUT CAKES 422

CHAPTER 12
PIE BASICS 441

CHAPTER 13
FRUIT PIES 452

CHAPTER 14
CUSTARD, CREAM AND ICE CREAM PIES 478

CHAPTER 15
NUT, SUGAR AND MINCEMEAT PIES 514

CHAPTER 16
TARTS 528

CHAPTER 17
THE WORLD OF PASTRIES 558

CHAPTER 18
FROZEN DESSERTS 590

CHAPTER 19
DESSERT SAUCES 608

HISTORICAL SOURCES 626

INDEX 634

FOREWORD

BY DORIE GREENSPAN

There's only one way I could be more thrilled about introducing you to Richard Sax's master-work, and that would be if I had written it my-self. And, now, almost two decades after *Classic Home Desserts* was first published, I can confess that for all those years I wished I'd written it.

I was a beginner cookbook author when *Classic Home Desserts* hit the stores and, while I had no idea what my future would be, when I bought Richard's book it became my ideal. It was that rare book that was both practical and pleasurable, a solid cookbook and a good read, and over the years I've shuttled it end-lessly between an easy-to-reach shelf in my kitchen and a just-as-easy-to-reach table next to my favorite chair.

I came to the book already a fan of Richard. I'd followed his work for years, clipping his travel articles, especially the ones from Paris, which appeared in *Gourmet*; cooking from his column in *Bon Appétit*; and baking from his *Cookie Lover's Cookie Book*.

He had talent to burn. He was trained as a chef (he was the founding chef-director of the *Food & Wine* test kitchen) and was as gifted—and as at home—with savory food as he was with sweet. All that and he was eloquently literate, too.

And while I may have wished I'd written this book, truly, I knew I couldn't have. No one else could have: It was Richard's book through and through—a book that grew out of a passion so strong it might just as well have been a quest.

This huge volume had its roots in a slim paperback called *Old-Fashioned Desserts* that Richard worked on in the early 1980s.

As he tells it, even after the book came out, he continued collecting recipes from around the world. He never ceased to be fascinated by them, by how home bakers kept them alive over generations, about what they meant to families and their communities and about the rituals that surrounded them. He loved heirloom recipes and what they told us about the people who made them, and he kept his finger on the pulse of what contemporary home bakers were making.

Whatever you do, don't skip Richard's introduction. Of course, it tells the story of how this book took shape, but it also gives voice to something I think all of us who bake at home have felt but might not have been able to express: the power of sharing something we make by hand, something that is always a gift because it is never a necessity.

No one else before Richard, or since, understood the subject of home baking as well, cared about it as deeply, or could tell us about it as beautifully. If he had simply collected the hundreds of quotations, stories, and journal entries that fill *Classic Home Desserts*, he'd have helped us understand how we home bakers are tied to a tradition that reaches back through centuries and across continents, and he'd have created a work to cherish. But this is also a cookbook to take into the kitchen, to use until its pages are spattered with butter and dusted with sugar, to keep in the kitchen until we've baked our way through it.

If there's a type of dessert not included in this book, I've never heard of it, or, as Richard explains, it's not a dessert that's made at home. When Richard says these are "home desserts," he means it: These are the recipes of moms, not chefs.

Starting with The Extended Family of Cobblers and Crisps, a large family with lots of branches, all of them delicious, Richard takes us through scores of recipes, so many of them based on fruit—there are fruit compotes and puddings, cakes and pies, tarts and pastries. There are cookies, of course, lots of them, and four full chapters on cakes: Plain Cakes and Cakes with Fruit; Coffee Cakes; Layer Cakes, Fancy Cakes, Cheesecakes and Chocolate Cakes; and Fruitcakes and Nut Cakes. Pies and tarts get as many chapters, and no one covers puddings and custards (and even pancakes and dumplings) as lusciously as Richard.

And on nearly every page, there's a story or a brilliant quotation—the amount of research Richard did is almost unfathomable—a historical recipe, a piece of fascinating background information, or a tip. On one page it might be instructions for making oatmeal puddings from Lady Anne Morton's handwritten manuscript dated 1693, and on another it might be a note from Richard telling us what the "short" in "shortbread" means. The great diarist Samuel Pepys chimes in on fritters; Jack Kerouac has his say on pies on the road; we learn the words to *The Hasty-Pudding: A Poem in Three Cantos*, and we are touched by the comments of bakers the world over.

Early in *Classic Home Desserts*, Richard includes a quote from Olene Garland (it comes from *The Foxfire Book of Appalachian Cookery*, 1984) that has haunted me for years, as much for what it says about a mother's love as for what it says about the meaning dessert holds in our lives: "There was ten children in my family, so it was a pretty big chore for Momma to make a dessert for so many, but she was always wanting to treat us."

This is the book for those of us who want to treat the people we love. For two decades, bakers have reached for it to bake for those they care about most. Now, with this new edition, it's your turn.

Richard died soon after giving us this treasure of a book. I can only imagine what it would have meant to him to know that, like his beloved home desserts, his work is passing from mother to child, from friend to friend, from generation to generation.

—DORIE GREENSPAN

Introduction

What is patriotism but the love of good things
we ate in our childhood?

Lin Yü-T'ang

*O*ver the past several years, while researching the material for this book, I spent much time leafing through the pages of old cookbooks. Some of the most interesting recipes had never been published or even printed but were found in the handwritten manuscripts, where housewives of various periods in various countries had recorded their own family recipes. Scattered among them were home remedies, friends' and relatives' addresses and other long-lost ephemera.

Sitting for hours in the wood-paneled recesses of the New York Public Library's rare book and manuscript collection, carefully turning pages copied out in the author's own hand, I became completely absorbed in these old notebooks—in their painstaking clarity, their graceful penmanship, the private notes of their owners. I felt as though I was being offered an intimate look into each person's home life and often, a glimpse into something deeper.

One day shortly before Christmas, while perusing a first edition of Mrs. Dalgairns' *The Practice of Cookery*, a seminal book of Scottish cooking published in 1830, I noticed a recipe for seed cake, a traditional fruitcake baked with caraway seeds. While the cake is not served specifically for Christmas in Scotland, it was remarkably similar to other fruitcakes featured at winter festivals. On returning home, I decided to try Mrs. Dalgairns' recipe in my own kitchen. I modified a few details, omitting the "comfits"—caraway seeds dipped in sugar that were strewn over the cake's surface—but otherwise, I obeyed her instructions to the letter.

The cake went into the oven, and as I watched it tease itself upward, its domed top rising and coloring gradually to a glorious gold, I felt as if Mrs. Dalgairns herself were looking over my shoulder. The cake came out perfectly, its rich pound-cake texture fragrant with orange and lavishly studded with candied fruit and nuts, and provided cheer through the holiday week. (See page 435 for Mrs. Dalgairns' recipe.) There was something miraculous to me about this: that I could take written instructions from someone long gone and, by following them, bake the same cake in my oven today. In so doing, I was continuing a process that she had set in motion two centuries ago.

As that rewarding experience shows, the world of home desserts is much more than just recipes. It's also a world of people and of the many ways food is woven into family life, whether it's a special layer cake that a mother bakes every year to celebrate her child's birthday, a pumpkin pie for Thanksgiving, a coffee cake for Easter, a nut cake for Passover or just a chocolate pudding that's an after-supper favorite.

Invariably, as soon as I mentioned my interest in home dessert traditions, people would say, "Oh, my grandmother used to bake an apple dessert that all of our cousins still make today" or, "Let me tell you about my mother's rice pudding—it's the best ever." Those recollections and the occasions on which these desserts were prepared and served—the people behind the food—are the heart and soul of this book.

Of all the foods that spur memories of childhood, few are as instantly evocative as old-fashioned home desserts. For Americans, just hearing those words conjures up images: of rice pudding, bread pudding, berry cobbler and lemon meringue pie. If you were raised elsewhere, a different flood of memories is unleashed: The French recall *oeufs à la neige*, puffy meringues afloat in a custard sea; Italians, frothy *zabaglione*; Hungarians, delicate jam-filled pancakes called *palacsinta* and flaky strudel, warm from the oven; Greeks think of buttery phyllo pastries drenched in honey-lemon syrup.

What is remarkable in all this diversity is how many parallels exist among the home desserts from all over the world. Rice may be flavored with vanilla and raisins in an English nursery, with kirsch in France, with candied fruits in China or with saffron and rose water in the Middle East, but the basic tradition—taking a leftover staple and transforming it into a simple, soothing dessert—is the same everywhere. Similarly, home cooks from

There was ten children in my family, so it was a pretty big chore for Momma to make a dessert for so many, but she was always wanting to treat us."

OLENE GARLAND
QUOTED IN *THE FOXFIRE
BOOK OF APPALACHIAN
COOKERY*
1984

It Started with the Fruitcakes . . .

The late Bill Neal, chef and author of several cookbooks, described the holiday cycle of his boyhood in North Carolina: "For us, Christmas was a process that started way before Thanksgiving; the main thing I remember as a child is everybody working together in the kitchen.

"It started with the fruitcakes, which I hated making, because I couldn't stand that candied fruit, but I did love the part where we poured bourbon over it or wine. The cakes were put away and aged for at least a week. And then you started giving them a little weekly dose, all in their own tins, a whole cabinet full, sitting there, pulling themselves together.

"After Thanksgiving, there was a series of candies and crystallized fruit peels, grapefruit, orange, lemon. I remember my sister and I rolling them through white sugar on the counter. And also stuffed dates—I love those to this day. Stuffed with a

places as far apart as Italy, America and Eastern Europe create delicious puddings from leftover bread and noodles, while warm desserts layering bread crumbs and apples show up with only slight variations throughout England, America, France and Sweden. The details change, but the essence remains universal.

Many cherished home desserts are served at a specific time of the year as part of a seasonal celebration. A chorus of voices tells the story:

Ron Popp of Omaha, Nebraska, remembers "a two-day orchestrated cookie event" every Christmas of his childhood. "There were three different cookie grades. My brother and sister and I would eat the rejects as we were baking. Then there were the ones we'd have around the house, for when people stopped in over the holidays. But the all-time perfect cookies were for taking from farmhouse to farmhouse."

Mary Codola, a superb home cook in Rhode Island, still carries on the traditions of Italy with her Easter baking: "We make the sweet bread, which I braid and also fashion into small loaves for the kids. I usually prepare *pasticciot´*, little tarts with yellow custard." She also makes rice pie, which, like the wheat-grain-and-ricotta-filled pie called *pastiera*, is traditional in southern Italy at Easter. (For her recipe, see page 510.)

Sometimes a dessert doesn't commemorate a holiday so much as it does a primal memory. During his frugal years as a university student away from home in Kolozsvár, Hungary, restaurateur Paul Kovi remembers his mother sending him parcels of his favorite strudel: ". . . so far as I was concerned, her poppy seed strudel guaranteed the perfect continuity of my ties to home and showed the only imaginable sign of a mother's concern for a hungry child."

The custom of serving a particular dessert to commemorate an important event is undoubtedly a holdover from earlier times when sweets had a ritual significance. Cakes were originally associated with religious festivals, serving as signs of thanksgiving for the earth's abundance at harvesttime or standing in for animal sacrifices to show gratitude for God's bounty. Christmas fruitcakes and cookies, too, were linked to agricultural festivals and marked the passage through the year's darkest days.

THE RISE OF DESSERTS IN HISTORY

*B*ut despite the primacy of desserts in memory and ritual, their rise to prominence in the development of the world's eating habits has been relatively recent. The history of our nourishment is one of grain and essential crops, with side ventures into produce, meat, fish and dairy products. It is a tale of bread and fermented drink, of royal tables and slavery, of uprisings and malnutrition.

The emergence of dessert as a separate course took place only during the past few centuries. Up to that point, distinctions between sweet and savory dishes were hazy. Basic preparations, such as pies and steamed puddings, frequently contained both meat and fruit. Though there is some evidence that fruits and other sweet dishes were served at the conclusion of banquets in ancient times, dessert as we know it today was not clearly defined. The menu for one banquet served in Pompeii, for example, included a final course of a molded cream and a selection of cakes, along with a wild boar's head, fricassee of wild duck and sow's udders.

Often, sweet creams and cakes were brought out early in the meal, together with meats and other savory dishes. At English banquets, a dessert course at meal's end did not evolve until the 16th century, when guests would move into another room to partake of an assortment of sweet wines, fruit tarts, marmalades and preserved fruits, marchpane (marzipan) and molded jellies.

In France, the banquet protocol gradually settled down into two principal courses. First, all the dishes (*mets*) were set out at once. Then came the *entremets*, with a staged spectacle. Only after the table was cleared—"de-served"—did desserts appear as an after-dinner refreshment.

In different cultures, desserts take on greater or lesser importance, based on a wild variety of factors, including agriculture, climate, religion, culinary traditions and what's best described, however nebulously, as the "national palate." The concept of dessert in the Far East is very different from ours, generally served with tea—as a snack, rather than at the end of the meal. In many other places, desserts are served outside the scope of meals. In the German *kaffeeklatsch*, still going strong in every village and in the still opulent baroque coffeehouses of Budapest and in Austria, cakes and other desserts play a central role all day through.

What does seem to be universal is that unlike salty foods, which spark the appetite, sweet flavors tend to shut it down. Thus, in much of the world, dessert assumed its place at the end of the meal, when we're not still actually hungry but may want "a little something" to cap things off.

pecan half, then sprinkled with bourbon or sherry and rolled through sugar until they were snowy white. Those were packed away to age.

"And I guess the next things were the cakes and pies made on the morning of Christmas Eve. Pecan pies, custard pies and ambrosia—orange and pineapple and fresh coconut. We would grate the coconut ourselves, and there were all those citrus flavors around—I was surrounded by a tropical atmosphere without really knowing it. I still can feel how it feels to hand-grate the coconut on a box grater, and I can still smell its headiness and the tropical flavors."

Bill Neal died at 41, leaving behind three children and a rich legacy of fine Southern cooking and baking.

WHAT IS—AND IS NOT— IN THIS BOOK

The roots of this project reach back into the early 1980s, when I wrote a little paperback cookbook called *Old-Fashioned Desserts*. Once I had finished it, I continued, without realizing it, to clip recipes and note down sources for other desserts until, about five years after, I had filled a file drawer with literally hundreds of ideas. Clearly, this was a subject I had not exhausted, nor was my enthusiasm dimmed.

Sometimes, what sounded like a wonderful idea came out terribly in the kitchen. In some cases, I would retest again and again (and again), until the dessert tasted as good as it had in my imagination. In other cases, I would realize that the recipe was never going to work or that the dish was more of historical interest than something you'd delight in eating.

Although this book aims to be a comprehensive collection of home desserts from all over the world, those included are *only the best in each category*—the things you can bring to your table and serve with confidence, knowing that they will be eaten to the last crumb. These are the desserts made at home by mothers and grandmothers rather than by professional pastry chefs. They include pies, cobblers and other fruit desserts; plain and fancy (but still uncomplicated) cakes; and yeast-raised baked goods like coffee cakes.

Crème brûlée, elegant and always up-to-the-moment, is here because this dessert with a long heritage is basically a simple (if rich) custard. Danish pastry, however, is not included; while old-fashioned in spirit, it is too "professional," too time-consuming and too technically demanding to fit in with homey pies and cobblers. Layer cakes are here, but not decorated birthday or wedding cakes; plenty of pies are found, but not precisely fashioned individual pastries; strudel is represented, but not mille-feuilles (Napoleons).

Within the realm of such home desserts, there's still plenty of room for innovative flourishes. Why not add a touch of grated fresh ginger to a plum crisp? Why not a bread pudding made with panettone, a sweet Italian yeast bread studded with raisins and citron, baked in caramelized individual molds (page 198)? Even though the white chocolate in the Buckhead Diner's White Chocolate Banana Cream Pie (page 486) is not a strictly traditional ingredient, this pie remains true in spirit to the old-fashioned versions we grew up with.

On the other hand, a chef's new takeoff on German chocolate cake wound up being omitted because, however delicious, the original cake had been totally transformed, with multiple mousse fillings precisely layered into a pastry crust. While the flavorings remained faithful to the traditional version, the finished product seemed too "concocted," too much the work of a chef. Home bakers are not likely to make three different fillings for a cake.

As Alfred Chadbourn, a contemporary artist, recently said of the Maine villages he likes to paint, "They haven't been gussied up or fallen victim to quaint gentrification. They retain an unadorned frankness." That unadorned frankness is the key to this collection, and it is that spirit which served as a guide, rather than precise or rigid categories.

The recipes came from several different types of sources. Some are heirlooms, handed down in a family. Although I have occasionally made minor changes for today's tastes, ingredients and kitchen equipment, I have tried to keep the recipes as much like the originals as possible. Other recipes are historical ones from old cookbooks or manuscripts and have been similarly adapted. Sometimes an idea was suggested by a description, by someone recalling his or her grandmother's baking, or by a name like "Strawberry Nonsense." Where I have used someone else's recipe but changed it more than incidentally, I have indicated that it was "based on" or "adapted from" that earlier recipe. Other desserts included in this book are of my own devising but reflect the manner and spirit of traditional home desserts.

In collecting them, the question of authenticity sometimes arose: What is the one true cobbler? Is it made with biscuit dough or pie crust? Is a pandowdy still a pandowdy if it uses bread dough instead of pastry? Which version is "real"? It's important to remember that food is folk culture, passed down orally. While there may be a general standard for a New England apple pie, if you go to several neighbors' kitchens, you may find one cook spicing apples with nutmeg instead of cinnamon or covering them with a crumb topping instead of a top crust, or serving the pie with a wedge of Vermont Cheddar instead of vanilla ice cream. The same dish, in the hands of three different cooks, will come out three different ways—even if they follow the identical recipe. Who's to say which one is the real Yankee apple pie? It's these individual touches that bring cooking to life and that make each of us remember our own mom's or grandma's bread pudding as the archetypal version.

Definitions, then, are hard to pin down. As far as possible, however, the desserts in this collection are authentic representatives of their various traditions, with respect to their countries of origin. But if you want to throw a handful of just-picked raspberries into a Southern peach cobbler, or use pecans or hazelnuts instead of almonds to top a crisp, who's to stop you?

The book begins with the cobblers and other easy-to-make fruit desserts. Smooth-textured, quivering desserts thickened with gelatin, cream or egg whites—jellies, creams and fools—compose the next category. Puddings and custards make up the next section, beginning with simple ones and ending with more complicated renditions.

The baked desserts are easier to categorize: cookies, cakes of several genres, pies, tarts and simple pastries. The book concludes with ice creams and other frozen confections and dessert sauces.

The Importance of Pure Flavors

I haven't called for esoteric ingredients in these dessert recipes. But using ingredients with pure flavors is crucial. I know people who bake dozens of cookies at holiday time, expending enormous effort to make everything by hand—and all for nothing, because they rely upon inferior ingredients like margarine, imitation vanilla extract and musty old spices. Cookies and virtually all baked goods should be made with pure unsalted butter—not with margarine.

Pure vanilla extract, too, is well worth its price. One whiff, whether of the bean or the extract, and you'll never bake with anything but the real thing. The imitation costs the manufacturer just pennies per gallon, but the flavor cannot compare to that of true vanilla. (For a mail-order source for extraordinary pure vanilla extract, see page 22.)

When adapting old recipes, the single most variable factor is the amount of sweetening, since most of us prefer desserts less sweet than did people a century or even 20 years ago. Therefore, I've reduced the sugar wherever possible. As a general rule, feel free to adjust the amounts of sugar to taste in puddings, fruit desserts and fillings for cobblers, pies and the like, depending on the sweetness of the fruit, other ingredients and your palate.

Where sugar is part of a cake or cookie batter, on the other hand, its composition in the finished product is less flexible. You can vary it slightly (up to about 20 percent), but in general, adjusting the amount can change the solid-to-liquid ratio or the overall bulk of the ingredients. So it's best to leave these quantities as is.

The important thing is to sweeten just enough to bring out the natural flavors; you'll learn to recognize when you've reached the optimal point. Any more, and the dessert will scream shrill sweetness instead of offering a delicate balance.

While I do not believe in making low-calorie imitations of old-fashioned desserts, in virtually all the recipes, I have also tried to reduce fat somewhat by using buttermilk or low-fat yogurt instead of milk or cream. Fat and cholesterol can be trimmed in other ways, too. For an early custard recipe that called for 8 egg yolks, I found that you can get almost as rich a flavor and texture with 3 whole eggs plus 2 yolks, or even fewer. Replacing sour cream with yogurt in baked goods also gives astonishingly good results, saving at least two-thirds the amount of fat, cholesterol and calories. Of course, not all homespun desserts are high in fat; some, like angel food cake and meringues, contain very little.

Keep in mind that when you decide to enjoy a dessert, it's far better to have one made with fresh ingredients than a low-fat one that's loaded with artificial flavorings and preservatives. An apple brown Betty made with fresh apples, good bread or cookie crumbs, spices and a little real butter has a lot more in common with a nutritious bowl of soup than it does with "junk food."

MEASURING CAREFULLY

*O*n the first day of a baking course in cooking school, our teacher told us, "Most of the mistakes you people will make will be in weighing and measuring ingredients." At the time, I thought he was crazy. But he was right.

In no other area of cooking is careful measuring as critical as in baking. With a soup or stew, you can "poke around" as it cooks, adding a dash of one ingredient or a spoonful of another, making it moister or chunkier and correcting the seasonings. But once you mix up a cake, pudding or pie and put it in the oven, that's it—there's no going back.

This may seem to contradict your experience if you were lucky enough to watch your mother or grandmother in the kitchen. Chances are you saw her throw in a little of this and a little of that, until it all "just felt right." But experienced bakers know when they can improvise freely and when they can't. Certain items, such as bread or pastry doughs, call for some discretion because flour varies depending on weather, humidity, age and other factors. You always have to add liquid to bread and pastry doughs "by feel," but for other items, such as cakes, cookies or gelatin-set creams, you should respect the integrity of the recipe's ingredients and measure carefully.

Because most home cooks use cup measurements instead of weighing ingredients as professional bakers do, quantities are a lot more variable. Spooning flour lightly into a measuring cup versus dipping a cup into a canister can give very different amounts—as much as 50 percent more by weight for the latter. (Unless other-

The desserts we just ate—they embody the qualities of lightness, gentleness, sweetness, and comfort—moral qualities because when you decide whether or not to have these things in your life, you make a moral choice.

MARY GAITSKILL
TWO GIRLS, FAT AND THIN
1990

wise specified, these recipes were tested by spooning the flour lightly into measuring cups without sifting it first.)

A friend once told me that she had watched her grandmother prepare a favorite cake many times and wanted to try making it herself. When she came to add the flour, she put in a cupful, just as her grandmother had told her to do. The cake was a failure. When she asked her grandmother why, the older woman opened her cupboard and pulled out an old cracked tea cup. "A cupful, yes—but it has to be *this* cup!"

Trust Your Instincts

A recipe should be a trusted guide, but it can tell you only so much. I have a friend who once called me as he was baking a cake. "I'm using your recipe," he said, sounding dismayed. "It says to bake the cake for 30 minutes, and the timer just rang. But I have a feeling something is wrong."

"What does it look like?"

"It's really pale, not browned at all, and it looks kind of soupy in the middle."

"Sounds like you need to bake it longer."

"But it said 30 minutes . . ."

Your oven may be off. Your apples may be larger, smaller, tarter or drier. Trust your instincts. Experiment with a different fruit, another spice, a different crust, a different topping.

Cooking, after all, should be high adventure.

Measure carefully. Measure carefully. Measure carefully.

NOTES ON INGREDIENTS

*Y*ou'll have best results if you use the same ingredients that were used to test the recipes. Follow these guidelines:

FLOUR means *all-purpose*. I generally use unbleached, but bleached all-purpose flour can be substituted successfully.

༺ **Don't sift** flour unless specifically directed to.
༺ **Measure** flour by *spooning it lightly* into the measuring cup and leveling the top with a table knife.

CAKE FLOUR: Use *regular*, not self-rising. If you can't find cake flour, you can improvise by placing 2 tablespoons cornstarch in a 1-cup measure and then spooning in all-purpose flour until you have 1 level cup. This mixture can be substituted for 1 cup cake flour.

SUGAR means *granulated*.

BROWN SUGAR: The recipes specify packed light or dark brown sugar. For some, you can use either or use "brownulated" (granular brown sugar). Do not substitute liquid brown sugar.

SUPERFINE SUGAR, also called bar sugar or instant-dissolving sugar, is available in supermarkets in small 1-pound boxes. It's rarely crucial, and you can make your own by whirling granulated sugar in a food processor.

SPICES aren't worth using unless they're *fresh*. If the ones on your shelf are more than a year old, replace them. If in doubt, smell them—if they're not fragrant, they're not going to contribute much to your baking.

BUTTER: Use *unsalted* for best flavor. (For greasing pans and baking sheets, either lightly salted butter or solid vegetable shortening is fine, as is flavorless nonstick cooking spray.)

EGGS: All recipes were tested with eggs graded "large." (See A Note on Egg Safety, page 23.)

CREAM: Look for cream that has not been ultrapasteurized. Unfortunately, this is not available everywhere. Ultrapasteurizing heats the cream to 280 degrees F for at least 2 seconds, extending its shelf life by at least 4 times—to up to 2 months. Unfortunately, it compromises the cream's fresh flavor and also makes it harder to whip. If ultrapasteurized is all you can find, it will work.

VANILLA EXTRACT: I've tasted vanilla extracts from all over the world. But nothing comes close to the double-fold vanilla extract made by the Penzey family at Penzeys Spices in Milwaukee, Wisconsin, source of extraordinary herbs and spices.

Pam Penzey explains that "over 250 chemical elements combine to form natural vanilla flavor; the outstanding one is natural vanillin. Artificial vanilla contains only one, synthetic vanillin, which is made from by-products of paper manufacture." Buy only *pure* vanilla extract.

VANILLA BEAN: When you've used a vanilla bean without scraping off the seeds, it can be reused. Remove it from the mixture, rinse and set on a paper towel to dry. Wrap the bean in plastic wrap and store at room temperature. It can be reused two or three times. After that, tuck the bean into a jar of granulated or confectioners' sugar and leave it there for vanilla-flavored sugar.

LEMON JUICE means *freshly squeezed*.

NUTS can quickly become stale or even rancid. To ensure freshness, store nuts, tightly wrapped, in the freezer (they don't need to be defrosted before you add them to a dough). Nuts always benefit by toasting. Spread them out in a cake pan, jellyroll pan or any other shallow baking pan. Toast in a 350- to 400-degree F oven until fragrant and slightly darker in color, usually 7 to 12 minutes.

FOR THE BEST SPICES BY MAIL

Penzeys Spices seeks out the best spices from all over the world. Don't miss the extra-fancy China Tung Hing cinnamon (the most fragrant I've ever found), Penang cloves, excellent pumpkin pie spice blend and double-fold vanilla extract. Write or call for Penzeys interesting catalogue:

Penzeys Spices, www.penzeys.com
(800) 741-7787

A Note on Egg Safety

*A*s much as we hate to admit it, it is an unfortunate fact that the American egg supply has a problem with *Salmonella enteritidis*, particularly in the northeastern states. Actually, recent figures show that the chances of contracting salmonella from an egg are very low. According to Dr. James Mason, head of the USDA's Salmonella Task Force, only one outbreak may occur for every 2 billion table eggs produced each year. And only one case of egg-related salmonella food poisoning may occur for every 250,000 eggs eaten. Most reported cases involve eggs improperly handled in restaurants and institutions, not in home kitchens.

Even with this low incidence, however, we are now advised to handle eggs as safely as possible in the kitchen. A contaminated egg is safe if it's thoroughly cooked. Recently revised guidelines say that cooking an egg at 140 degrees F for 3 minutes kills all bacteria.

Because raw eggs are to be avoided (especially raw egg yolks), many desserts that are made with uncooked beaten egg whites, such as mousses and Bavarian creams, are now questionable. Beaten raw egg whites are used in only a handful of recipes in this book. To guard against salmonella, buy fresh eggs, keep them well refrigerated and use them promptly, and you shouldn't have any problems. Keep all utensils, work surfaces and storage containers that come into contact with eggs scrupulously clean. You can, of course, simply avoid any recipes using raw egg yolks or whites, if egg safety is of particular concern.

You can adapt desserts made with raw beaten egg whites to make them safer by using the Swiss meringue method: Place the egg whites with at least ½ of the sugar in a large bowl. Whisk once or twice. Place the bowl in a saucepan in which it fits comfortably, over (but not in) barely simmering water. With a hand-held electric mixer or large whisk, beat the egg whites for 3½ minutes; they should be hot to the touch. Remove the bowl from the simmering water. With the mixer at medium speed, continue to beat until the egg whites cool to room temperature and increase slightly in volume, usually about 5 minutes (or less; do not overbeat). Fold the meringue into the other ingredients as directed in the recipe.

Note that babies, the elderly and anyone with a compromised immune system (such as those who are HIV-positive) should take extra care not to consume raw protein products. And let's hope that we'll soon see a safe egg supply.

Dessert Techniques
Tips and Common Mistakes

✑ **Egg whites are often overbeaten** so that they become grainy and do not rise to their maximum height. The phrase "stiffly beaten" is actually a misnomer; the beaten whites should *just* stand in tender peaks. To whip "stiff" egg whites correctly, start beating them fairly vigorously with an electric mixer, large balloon whisk or rotary egg beater. Keep whisking at medium-high speed and adding sugar and/or other ingredients as directed.

Perfectly beaten "stiff" egg whites will just hold a peak but will still be perfectly smooth. Check *before* you think they're done; you can always beat them a little longer. If the whites are stiff, but start to seem cottony—breaking up in cloud-like masses—you've gone too far. Beat just until they hold a peak, no longer.

✑ **Cream is often overwhipped.** Obviously, if you whip cream until it turns into butter, you've overbeaten. If whipped cream looks slightly "grainy"—that is, if you can see a slightly rippled effect in its texture—it has been overwhipped.

For perfect whipped cream, start with cold cream, especially in hot weather. Chilling the bowl and the beaters or whisk helps, too. Begin to whip slightly slower than you do for egg whites; gradually pick up speed.

Cream is perfectly whipped when it forms floppy peaks that droop slightly when spooned; it should not be completely stiff. It should still look perfectly smooth and white. Whipped cream can be held in the refrigerator for about an hour; whisk gently once or twice before serving. To hold whipped cream longer, spoon it into a fine-mesh sieve set over a bowl to drain any excess water, and then refrigerate.

✑ **To sift or not to sift?** Sifting lightens and aerates flour, removes lumps and helps blend the flour with leaveners, spices and salt. In some of the recipes in this book, sifting is called for, especially in delicate cakes like angel food cake or spongecake. But for many of these desserts, the dry ingredients are simply stirred together, without sifting.

As you may already know, sifting can mean a significant difference in the weight of the flour, though a cup of sifted flour will look the same as a cup of unsifted. For solid ingredients, weighing is much more precise than measuring by volume (cups). *Measure flour as follows: Spoon the flour lightly into the measuring cup, then level it off with a knife. Do* **not** *sift unless the recipe specifically tells you to.*

᠆ **Add flour to batters without toughening the dough.**
Whenever you beat or stir a batter or dough that contains flour, you're activating the flour's protein component to form gluten. The more you work a dough that contains flour, the tougher it will get.

Strong gluten formation is fine for bread dough, but it's exactly what you don't want in pie crust and other pastry doughs, biscuits, cakes and cookies. Therefore, *whenever you add flour to a cake, cookie dough, pastry or other tender product, use a low mixer speed and mix just until the ingredients are combined, no longer.* In fact, for best results, mix until the flour is not quite incorporated. Then turn off the electric mixer and finish blending the ingredients with a couple of quick swipes of a large rubber spatula.

᠆ **Add as little flour as possible to doughs.** In general, *resist the temptation to add more flour to these delicate doughs.* The flour will make them easier to handle, but it will also toughen them. Rolling out dough between sheets of wax paper (specified in some of the recipes) will help keep it manageable.

᠆ **When you're thickening fruit for pies, cobblers and other desserts,** first whisk the flour or cornstarch with the sugar. The sugar will break up all of the lumps in the starch before it is added to the fruit.

᠆ **If you forget to take the butter out of the refrigerator in advance,** just grate the cold butter into the mixing bowl, and it will warm up quickly. Or, do as French pastry chefs do: Cut the butter into pieces and place it in a heatproof bowl. Place the bowl on a stovetop burner over low heat. Break up the butter with a wooden spoon until it becomes warm, soft and creamy—but not melted (there will still be some solid pieces). When mixed with an electric mixer, it should soon become fluffy.

᠆ **Getting the most out of citrus zests:** It's best to add the lemon or orange zest when you cream the butter and sugar together. The sugar will act as an abrasive, releasing the fragrant citrus oils found in the zest.

᠆ **When grinding nuts in the food processor:** Always add a little of the sugar and/or flour in the recipe to the nuts before grinding them. The dry ingredients will prevent them from becoming oily, resulting in lighter baked goods.

KITCHEN EQUIPMENT

Throughout this book, no irregular pan sizes are called for. Frequently, you can substitute one pan for another with perfect results.

I should say at the outset that I'm not a gadget freak. My kitchen has exactly what I need in it to work effectively—no more, no less. I don't believe in cluttering up work space with equipment that gets used only once a year—or never.

But I'm very particular about what I do have. I believe in buying the best so that it performs well for years. I'm still using the same KitchenAid mixer I bought over 20 years ago, and it's been through catering, restaurant cooking and years of testing, working away all day long. Except for a couple of minor adjustments, it's still running happily, with all its original parts.

A few pieces of equipment are essential for dessert-making:

KitchenAid electric mixer: This heavy-duty, free-standing mixer blends ingredients energetically, and its clean, form-and-function design makes it beautiful to look at, too. This mixer does everything: blend (with the paddle attachment), whip cream and egg whites (with the large whisk attachment) and knead dough (with the dough hook).

Hand-held mixers are fine for all but the heaviest doughs. And you can always mix batters and doughs fairly quickly by hand, using a wooden spoon, a large mixing bowl and some elbow grease. If you do a lot of baking, however, the mixer is a wise investment that will help you out for years. Find space on your kitchen counter for it, so you don't have to haul it out every time you want to use it.

Food processor: You'll notice that a food processor is called for in many of these recipes. Food processors have become standard in most active kitchens. I use the food processor for anything pureed, for making pie pastry dough (though I process the ingredients only until they are partially combined, not until they form a cohesive ball), for grinding nuts and for similar operations.

If you don't own a food processor, an electric mixer and a blender can do everything it does. An inexpensive Mouli grater is excellent for grinding nuts, reducing them to a powder that's fluffy and never oily.

Nonstick-coated baking sheets: These are great for cookies; invest in two or three. They don't need to be greased, though a light coating ensures easy lift-off after baking. Nonstick-coated muffin tins save a lot of trouble, too.

❰ **Large work surface:** Although a cool marble work surface is ideal for rolling out pastry, I have never owned one. I have a wooden cutting surface installed on top of a kitchen counter for rolling out doughs to fit standard-size baking pans.

Scrape your work surface and cutting boards with a dough scraper (bench knife), and clean well after each use. Whatever your cutting surface, be sure that it's large enough for you to work comfortably.

❰ **Large, sturdy cooling racks** (with plenty of air space underneath): These are essential. Without them, your baked goods will become soggy.

COOKWARE AND BAKEWARE

Invest in the best cookware and bakeware. That means good, heavyweight pans for everything from skillets to pie plates. Flimsy aluminum bakeware is a bad investment—it's inexpensive but cooks unevenly and wears out quickly, too. A flimsy skillet or saucepan will wreak havoc when making caramel—the sugar on one side of the pan can burn before the other side has even melted.

I do not recommend going out and buying a whole battery of professional kitchen equipment. But if you keep your sights on the best, it will serve you well for years.

Every good dessert-maker's kitchen should contain the following:

❰ **Knives:** Invest in the best, preferably high-carbon stainless steel. They'll last for years. Have your knives sharpened professionally once or twice a year.

CHEF'S KNIFE: 8 or 10 inches (all-purpose)
PARING KNIFE: 3 or 4 inches (for trimming fruits and for other small cutting jobs)
SERRATED KNIFE (for cakes, bread and other soft foods): This should be stainless steel, since serrated edges are very difficult to sharpen.

❰ **Saucepans**—in several sizes, small, medium and large. When you see the term "nonreactive," it refers to any pan that will not react with acids in foods. Generally speaking, *uncoated*

27

aluminum or *unseasoned* cast-iron should not be used; however, nonstick-coated or anodized aluminum is fine, as is well-seasoned cast-iron.

◦ **Skillets**—large (10- to 12-inch) is good, as is cast-iron; buy at least one nonstick version. A small-to-medium (6- to 8-inch) nonstick skillet is great for crepes and dessert pancakes.

◦ **Baking pans:** Here are the basics:
ROUND CAKE PANS: 8-, 9-inch. For small families, 6-inch round cake pans, available in kitchenware shops, are nice. Half recipes of an 8- or 9-inch cake can be baked in them. I haven't called for 10-inch round pans, since they aren't standard. But a 9-, 9½- or 10-inch springform pan can be used if you have a recipe that calls for a 10-inch round cake pan. Because weight is not as crucial in round cake pans as it is in pie or tart pans, you can bake cakes in 8½-inch round foil pans. These are helpful for a cake you want to transport, give as a gift or freeze.
SQUARE CAKE PANS: 8-, 9-inch. Either metal or Pyrex works fine for cakes, cobblers and baked fruit desserts.
SPRINGFORM PANS are important for cheesecakes, ice cream cakes, fruitcakes and other cakes that you don't want to invert after baking. Standard sizes are 9-, 9½- and 10-inch; nonstick versions are a good idea; some are sold with a tube insert that can come in handy.
LOAF PANS: 8-x-4-inch and 9-x-5-inch sizes. Heavy metal, nonstick or Pyrex are all fine. I also use foil loaf pans (great for gifts or for freezing), both in the standard size (8 x 3¾ x 2 inches) and miniature (5¾ x 3¾ x 2 inches).
PIE PANS: 9-, 10- and deep 9½-inch Pyrex pans are standard and called for in these recipes. Heavy steel or aluminum pans also work well.
FLUTED TART PAN with a removable bottom (quiche pan): Buy at least one; I have 9- and 9½-inch pans in heavy steel or black steel. Recently, nonstick versions have become available.
TUBE, BUNDT AND KUGELHOPF PANS are among the most-used items in my kitchen. Have at least 2 on hand. I like the following:
Tube pan: 9 or 10 inches, for angel food and other smooth large cakes. (This can be made of inexpensive aluminum.)
Fluted Bundt or Kugelhopf pans: The most useful are the 8½-inch-wide and 10-inch-wide sizes. Because the fluting makes unmolding a potential problem, heavy nonstick pans

are a good idea. A German Bundform pan with double sili-con coating is also available in this country. For mail-order, contact Williams-Sonoma; (877) 812-6235.

BAKING SHEETS: At least one, preferably nonstick. One heavy black steel pan is useful (but not essential) for placing under tart or pie pans.

JELLYROLL PANS: Baking sheets with low sides all around. The most useful size is 15½ x 10½ x 1 inch.

MUFFIN TIN: Preferably a standard 12-cup tin, with non-stick coating.

RECTANGULAR BAKING DISH: 13 x 9 inches, for baking cakes and puddings and for a water bath for custards. Also useful: 11¾-x-7½-x-1¾-inch Pyrex pan.

GRATIN DISHES: These are among the most-used baking items I own, great for bread puddings, rice puddings and all sorts of other puddings and baked desserts. You can buy inexpensive white porcelain gratin dishes in several sizes (8-, 9- and 11-inch are common). There are also wonderful stoneware, spongeware and pottery gratin dishes that bake well and are homey for serving. Le Creuset and similar enameled cast-iron dishes are heavy and bake well. Small oval or round gratin dishes are handy for individual servings of gratins or crème brûlée.

RAMEKINS, CUSTARD CUPS AND SOUFFLÉ DISHES for individual custards, puddings and flan. Useful sizes are:

6- and 10-ounce Pyrex custard cups (which can replace ramekins).

Deep custard cups of brown earthenware, about 7 fluid ounces, are great for baked custards and rice puddings.

4- and 5-ounce ramekins (these are the standard sizes and widely available).

8- to 12-ounce white porcelain soufflé dishes (about 4 inches wide).

5-ounce porcelain pôts de crème cups (not necessary, since ramekins can be substituted, but nice to have).

Parchment paper: Also called "baking liners"or "nonstick parchment," for lining round cake pans, baking sheets and jellyroll pans. This paper doesn't need to be buttered or greased, and cakes, cookies and pastries will come right off without sticking. If you don't own parchment, butter the baking pan well. Some recipes will tell you to substitute buttered wax paper.

A FEW ESSENTIAL GADGETS

〜 **Large rubber spatula:** Professional-size spatulas clean out mixing bowls in a couple of quick strokes. Buy two or three; they're found in any good cookware shop.

〜 **Zester:** This handy tool, with several little holes, grates lemon, orange or lime zest quickly in long, thin strands, without taking your knuckles with it. (The zest is the colored part of the citrus skin, with none of the bitter white pith underneath.) Try to test the zester before buying (take a lemon with you to the store); you want the sharpest one you can find. Chop the long strands of zest with a chef's knife after zesting. If you don't have a zester, a vegetable peeler also removes zest in nice thin strips, which can then be chopped with a knife.

〜 **Sharp vegetable peelers:** I prefer the ones with stainless steel blades. Buy several, and toss them out the first time you think they are less than razor-sharp.

〜 **Dough scraper (bench knife):** Not strictly necessary, but lifts a whole batch of dough when rolling on a floured board and scrapes the board clean afterwards, too.

Equivalent Pan Sizes

Note that any shape pan of the same volume can be substituted for any other. Remember that because the depth of the batter may change, the baking time may need to be adjusted. All pans were filled to the top to determine the maximum capacity.

Round Cake Pans	6 x 2	3¾ cups
	8 x 1½	5 cups
	9 x 1½	6½ cups
Square Cake Pans	8 x 8 x 2	7 to 8 cups
	9 x 9 x 2	10 cups
Springform Pans	6 x 3	4 cups
	7 x 2½	5⅓ cups
	8½ x 2½	7½ cups
	9½ x 2½	9 cups
Bundt and Kugelhopf Pans	6½ x 3½	5½ cups
	8½ x 3½	7 cups
	10 x 3¼	12 cups

Tube Pans

narrow center funnel	9 x 3	10 cups
wide center funnel	9½ x 3	7 to 8 cups

Ring Mold	9 x 2¾	7½ cups

Loaf Pans

miniature disposable foil	5¾ x 3¼ x 2	1¾ cups
standard disposable foil	8 x 3¾ x 2	nearly 5 cups
metal	8 x 4 x 2	5 cups

Pie Pans	9 inches	4½ cups
	10 inches	6½ cups
	deep 9½-inch (Pyrex)	7 cups
Gratin Dishes	oval 11 x 2	7 cups
	oval 13 x 8 x 2¾	11 cups

Rectangular Baking Dishes

11¾ x 7½ x 1¾ (Pyrex)	10 cups	(2½ quarts)
13 x 9 x 3 (Le Creuset)	about 14 cups	(3½ quarts)

RECIPES

Mixed Fruit Cobbler

Southern-Style Peach and Raspberry Cobbler with Pecan-Crunch Topping

"Summer Riches"

New Hampshire "Plate Cake"

Virginia Blackberry Roll

Pear Pandowdy

Pear or Apple Brown Betty with Cake Crumbs

Cranberry Crumble with Fall Fruits

Rhubarb-Strawberry Crisp with Cinnamon-Walnut Topping

Apple Mush

Swedish Apple "Pie" with Vanilla Sauce

Danish Apple and Cookie Crumb Dessert

Black and Blueberry Grunt (or Slump)

Traditional Two-Berry Buckle

Lightened Down-East Berry Buckle

The Finamore Shortcake

Berry Shortcakes with Buttermilk-Almond Biscuits

Blueberry Shortcakes with Low-Fat Cornmeal-Yogurt Biscuits

CHAPTER 1

THE EXTENDED FAMILY OF COBBLERS AND CRISPS

ruit and dough—these are the essentials. Combine them in different ways (fruit on the bottom, fruit on top, fruit in between), vary the dough (biscuit dough, bread dough, pie crust, crumbs or crumbled streusel), and you've got the whole extended family that includes cobblers, crisps, brown Bettys, crumbles, pandowdies, even shortcakes.

The simplest of these sorts of desserts may be one put together by Appalachian housewives. Many people who grew up in the hills of Kentucky, Tennessee, the Carolinas and Georgia remember that when there wasn't pie, their mothers made what Ruth Holcomb, a rural cook quoted in *The Foxfire Book of Appalachian Cookery* (1984), calls "Applesauce Pie":

> Slice your biscuits left over from breakfast or last night's supper and lay them in the bottom of a baking dish. Spread applesauce on top of them. You may stir cinnamon into the applesauce, if you wish. . . . Make as many layers as you wish, ending with applesauce on top. Sprinkle brown sugar on the top layer. Put into the oven and warm. The brown sugar will melt and make a crust on top of the applesauce.

All-American Fudge-Chunk Brownies and White Chocolate–Macadamia Blondies

Down-East Cranberry Apple Pie

Cranberry-Raspberry Tart Pastiche

Berry Shortcake with Buttermilk-Almond Biscuit

Greek Custard-Filled Phyllo Pastry

Split-Level Lime Chiffon Pie

Summer Pudding of Four Red Fruits

Tiramisù

Edna Lewis's Chocolate Soufflés

Austrian Walnut Torte with Coffee Whipped Cream

Poached Plum and Raspberry Compote in Late-Harvest Wine Syrup

Southern Coconut Layer Cake with Divinity Icing

There is something touching about this effort to put together—with what precious little is on hand—something beyond strict necessity.

Homemade desserts like crisps and brown Bettys show more effort than just setting out a bowl of fruit after supper, but not as much as baking a pie. They are simple, unfussy, plain and homespun—made just by cutting up a few apples and strewing them with buttered crumbs. And therein lies their innate appeal.

Yet despite the deep feelings they evoke, old recipes for homey fruit desserts aren't all that easy to find. When you look back into old cookbooks, farm recipes and manuscript recipe notebooks handed down from mother to (usually) daughter, these perennials are often conspicuously absent.

Apple puddings are there, often with fruit incorporated into bread-and-custard puddings, but fruit topped with buttered crumbs or with a quilted biscuit blanket rarely appears. It seems that these fruit desserts are so simple that mothers assumed that recipes weren't needed. Cobblers and crisps (and pandowdies and brown Bettys, too) were just "something you did"—without relying on written instructions. So recipes for many of these desserts were never written down, and as a result, were easily lost or forgotten.

Fruit desserts finally begin to turn up in print in the late 19th century. By the 1920s, they appear in profusion, when cookbooks by home economists and those mass-produced by *Good Housekeeping* and the like began to define American cooking for a generation that had seen the rise of industrialization and the move away from life on the farm. But it's important to remember that, like pies, these desserts go back further than mere written records might suggest.

WHAT'S A COBBLER?
WHAT'S A CRISP?

*M*uch as we might like to be definitive, old-fashioned desserts are "folk food"— people's food—cooked at home, made with slight variations from kitchen to kitchen, and like all folk culture, the recipes are passed orally from person to person, often never written down.

For this reason, definitions are hard to agree upon. I think of a real cobbler as made with biscuit dough, but pie-crust dough is often used. For me, it's dough on top, fruit underneath. But plenty of Southern peach cobblers have bottom crusts or two crusts with fruit in between. Who is to say, in some attempt at academic codification, that these traditional Southern cobblers are not true cobblers?

Here, nevertheless, is the terminology, the distinctions sorted out as clearly as possible:

⌒ A **cobbler** is fruit baked with a crust. Most cobblers are made with a top crust of biscuit dough, which can be either a single solid layer or individual biscuits ("cobbles"). Pastry or bread dough is often substituted, and some cobblers are made with a bottom as well as a top crust.

⌒ A **crisp** refers to the most casual member of these fruit desserts (often made with apples or blueberries) in which the fruit is topped with a "rubbed" mixture of butter, sugar, flour and sometimes nuts. Buttered bread crumbs can be used, as can cookie crumbs, graham cracker crumbs, stale cake crumbs or even corn flakes. (When crumbs are layered in with the fruit instead of on top, it becomes a **brown Betty**.)

⌒ A **crumble** is an English cousin to our crisp. It has a crunchy shortbread-like topping of oats, butter, flour and brown sugar. Crumbles are often made with rhubarb, gooseberries or plums.

⌒ A **pandowdy** is made with sliced fruit (often apples), topped with a pastry crust that is cut up and pressed back into the fruit for the final few minutes of baking. Early versions of the pandowdy used bread dough as a crust, and some arranged the fruit on top and inverted the dessert before serving. The origin of this term is unknown, but a New England cookbook refers to "dowdying" as the process of breaking up the dough.

⌒ A **buckle** is generally made with berries, which are folded into (or scattered over) a tender yellow cake batter, usually topped with crumbs. The buckle is then baked and cut into squares.

⌒ A **grunt** or **slump** resembles a cobbler, but it is steamed on top of the stove (often in a cast-iron skillet) instead of being baked. The finished product resembles dumplings (also called "drop biscuits"), rather than crisp browned biscuits. "Grunt," they say, is the sound the fruit makes as it stews.

MIXED FRUIT COBBLER

The cobbler prototype: light buttermilk biscuit topping, "cobbled" (cut in individual biscuit rounds) and placed over fruit. The juices are left runny. Serve this warm in bowls, not plates, with a pitcher of cream or a scoop of ice cream (or frozen or chilled vanilla or plain yogurt).

Make this cobbler with any soft fruit, using similar quantities and adjusting for sweetness. Add a touch of grated fresh or minced crystallized ginger, ground spices or a few berries to a pear cobbler; add a sliced quince to an apple cobbler; add a handful of dried cherries, blueberries or cranberries to a peach cobbler.

Serves 4 to 6

FRUIT

4	firm-ripe nectarines
3	firm-ripe peaches
	Juice of 1 lemon
2	plums, halved, stoned and sliced
1½-2	cups blueberries or a combination of blueberries and blackberries, picked over
½	teaspoon minced or grated peeled fresh ginger
¼	cup packed light brown sugar
3	tablespoons sugar
1	tablespoon cornstarch
½	teaspoon ground cinnamon

LIGHT BISCUIT DOUGH

1½	cups all-purpose flour
⅓	cup sugar
1	teaspoon baking powder
½	teaspoon baking soda
½	teaspoon salt
¼	cup (½ stick) cold unsalted butter, cut into pieces
½	teaspoon pure vanilla extract
⅔	cup buttermilk (or ⅓ cup plain yogurt thinned either with ¼ cup skim milk or with cold water)
	Milk and sugar, for glaze

Ice cream, frozen yogurt or heavy cream, for topping

1. FRUIT: Peel the nectarines and the peaches by immersing them in a large pot of boiling water for about 30 seconds; rinse under cold water in a colander. The skins should slip off easily.

Raylene's Blackberry Cobbler

Raylene had brought some of her home-canned blackberries with her. She and Reese made a skillet cobbler the way Raylene said she had learned when she was with the carnival. She dropped lots of little butter slices on the bottom of the skillet, sprinkled brown sugar over that, then poured her blackberries, more butter, and a handful of white sugar over everything. Unsweetened biscuit dough made the top crust, and the cobbler was ready to eat in half an hour. It wasn't as good as Aunt Fay's pies, but Reese gorged on it, eating almost half the pan by herself. Afterwards, she leaned forward lazily on the table, almost asleep, her blue-stained lips slightly parted.

DOROTHY ALLISON
BASTARD OUT OF CAROLINA
1993; 1992

Halve the fruit, remove the stones and cut into thick wedges, letting them fall into a mixing bowl and tossing them with the lemon juice to prevent discoloration. Pour off any excess liquid, leaving the fruit somewhat moist. Add the plums, berries and ginger; toss.

2. In a small bowl, stir together the brown and white sugars, the cornstarch and the cinnamon with a fork or small whisk until free of lumps. Sprinkle this mixture over the fruit and toss gently with your fingers or 2 large spoons until thoroughly mixed. Transfer the mixture to an 8-inch square baking pan, oval gratin dish or other shallow baking dish with a capacity of about 2 quarts.

3. **Light Biscuit Dough:** In a food processor, combine the flour, sugar, baking powder, baking soda and salt, pulsing once or twice. Add the butter and process, pulsing, until the mixture is crumbly. Add the vanilla and dribble most, but not all, of the buttermilk or yogurt mixture over the dry mixture; pulse to combine. If necessary, add the remaining buttermilk; the dough should hold together and should be moist, but not sticky. Gather the dough onto a floured sheet of plastic wrap or wax paper, patting it together to form a cohesive disk. *(The dough can be made several hours in advance; wrap and refrigerate until needed.)*

4. Preheat the oven to 400 degrees F. Pat out the dough on a lightly floured sheet of wax paper to about ¾ inch thick. Cut with a biscuit cutter or glass dipped in flour; reroll and cut the scraps. Brush the biscuit rounds with milk; then arrange them over the fruit. Lightly sprinkle the biscuits with sugar.

5. Place the cobbler in the oven with a sheet of foil underneath to catch any drips. Bake the cobbler until the biscuits are golden and the fruit is bubbly, 30 to 35 minutes. Cool briefly on a wire rack. Serve warm, with ice cream, frozen yogurt or cream.

⌒ *Variations*

Summer
blueberries/blackberries
blackberries/nectarines/plums
raspberries/peaches/red currants
sweet and sour cherries/nectarines
Winter
cranberries/apples/pears
pears/dried cherries/ginger
pears/bananas/mangoes

KITCHEN HINTS FOR COBBLERS AND CRISPS

A word about thickening . . .
Too many cobbler and other fruit dessert recipes overthicken the fruit. And in doing so, they miss the point of capturing all the glorious juice that flows together with cream or ice cream, just waiting to be sopped up with a bite of biscuit. I like a very slight thickening, though—rather than none—so the cobbler isn't awash in runaway juices.

Vary the amount of sugar in all of these fruit mixtures to taste, based on the fruit you buy. In many heirloom recipes, you can reduce sugar by up to half.

For light-textured biscuits for cobblers, make the dough slightly wetter than for baking biscuits, but not sticky. They'll come up tender and light when baked. Don't overknead or overhandle the dough at any stage of preparation.

If you don't have buttermilk on hand, substitute plain (or vanilla) yogurt thinned with low-fat milk or cold water.

A Peach Pot-Pie

A peach pot-pie, or cobler, as it is often termed, should be made of clingstone peaches, that are very ripe, and then pared and sliced from the stones. Prepare a pot or oven with paste, as directed for the apple pot-pie, put in the prepared peaches, sprinkle on a large handful of brown sugar, pour in plenty of water to cook the peaches without burning them, though there should be but very little liquor or syrup when the pie is done. Put a paste over the top, and bake it with moderate heat, raising the lid occasionally, to see how it is baking. When the crust is brown, and the peaches very soft, invert the crust on a large dish, put the peaches evenly on, and grate loaf sugar thickly over it. Eat it warm or cold. Although it is not a fashionable pie for company, it is very excellent for family use, with cold sweet milk.

LETTICE BRYAN
The Kentucky Housewife
CINCINNATI, 1839

38

SOUTHERN-STYLE PEACH AND RASPBERRY COBBLER WITH PECAN-CRUNCH TOPPING

Peach cobbler is both a home and restaurant mainstay down South, where the sweet tooth has been refined into a regional cultural institution.

When you can't find good peaches, whether for cobbler, shortcake or pie, try using nectarines.

Serves about 6

FRUIT
10 large firm-ripe peaches (4-5 pounds)
Juice of ½ lemon
½ pint raspberries, picked over

SYRUP
½ cup sugar
3 tablespoons cornstarch
½ teaspoon ground cinnamon
Pinch fresh-grated nutmeg
Pinch salt
2 tablespoons peach schnapps or liqueur, or amaretto (optional)

LIGHT BISCUIT DOUGH
1⅓ cups all-purpose flour
¼ cup sugar
1¼ teaspoons baking powder
1 teaspoon baking soda
¼ teaspoon salt
¼ cup (½ stick) cold unsalted butter, cut into pieces
½ cup buttermilk (or equal parts plain yogurt and skim milk or water)
Milk, for glaze

PECAN-CRUNCH TOPPING
½ cup coarsely chopped pecans (or almonds)
3 tablespoons packed light brown sugar
½ teaspoon ground cinnamon

Ice cream, frozen yogurt or heavy cream, for serving

1. **Fruit:** Peel the peaches by immersing them in a large pot of boiling water for about 30 seconds; rinse under cold water in a colander. The skins should slip off easily. Halve the fruit, remove the stones and cut the fruit into wedges, letting the slices fall into a mixing bowl and tossing them with the lemon juice to prevent discoloration. Pour off any excess liquid, leaving the fruit somewhat moist. Add the raspberries; toss to combine.

2. **Syrup:** In a small bowl, stir together the sugar, cornstarch, cinnamon, nutmeg and salt. Add the optional liqueur and stir with a fork or small whisk until free of lumps. Drizzle this mixture over the fruit and toss gently with your fingers or 2 large spoons until thoroughly mixed. Transfer the mixture to an 8-inch square baking pan, oval gratin dish or other shallow baking dish with a capacity of about 2 quarts.

3. **Light Biscuit Dough:** In a food processor, combine the flour, sugar, baking powder, baking soda and salt, pulsing once or twice. Add the butter and process, pulsing, until the mixture is crumbly. Dribble most, but not all, of the buttermilk over the dry mixture; pulse to combine. If necessary, add the remaining buttermilk; the dough should hold together and should be moist, but not sticky. Gather the dough onto a floured sheet of plastic wrap or wax paper, patting it together to form a cohesive disk. *(The dough can be made several hours in advance; wrap and refrigerate until needed.)*

4. Preheat the oven to 375 degrees F. Pat out the dough on the lightly floured sheet of plastic wrap or wax paper to a little more than ¼ inch thick. With a star-shaped cutter or a fluted round cutter, cut out the biscuits. Reroll and cut the scraps. Gently place the biscuits over the fruit, arranging them fairly close together, or overlapping them slightly. Brush the biscuits with milk.

5. **Pecan-Crunch Topping:** In a small mixing bowl, stir together the pecans or almonds, brown sugar and cinnamon. Scatter the topping over the dough.

6. Place the cobbler in the oven with a sheet of foil underneath to catch any drips. Bake the cobbler until the biscuits are golden and the fruit is bubbly, usually about 35 minutes. (If the biscuits begin to brown before the fruit is bubbly, lay a sheet of foil loosely over the dough and continue to bake until done.) Cool the cobbler briefly on a wire rack. Serve warm, with ice cream, frozen yogurt or cream.

"SUMMER RICHES"
(CHERRY AND NECTARINE COBBLER WITH RICH PASTRY DOUGH)

Capture the momentary height of summer in this deep ruby-colored dessert, bursting with cherries and nectarines. This is basically a cobbler, but topped with a lid of pastry dough instead of biscuits, and baked in a deep casserole instead of a shallow dish.

You can use either sweet cherries or sour ones here. The deep red cherries you find in the supermarket are sweet cherries, usually Bing cherries. Other sweet varieties, not as commonly grown, are Rainiers (golden with a pink blush) or dark Lamberts. Queen Annes are also golden, but the crop is used almost exclusively to manufacture maraschino cherries. Sour cherries such as Montmorency are often found at farmers' markets; they work beautifully in cobblers and pies, as long as you sweeten them accordingly. (See also Spiced Sour Cherry Compote for Ice Cream on page 619.)

~~ Serves about 6

2	pints sour or sweet cherries, stemmed, pitted and juices reserved (about 4 cups)
4	large firm-ripe nectarines, blanched (see step 1, page 39), skinned, halved, stoned and thickly sliced
	Juice of ½ lemon
2-3	tablespoons amaretto or Grand Marnier (optional)
½-¾	cup packed light brown sugar (depending on the cherries' sweetness)
1½	tablespoons cornstarch
¾	teaspoon ground cinnamon
	Pinch salt
1	tablespoon unsalted butter
	Rich Tart Dough (page 451) or Basic Pie Dough (page 449), for a 1-crust pie or 1-shell tart
	Cream or milk and sugar, for glaze
	Ice cream, frozen yogurt or heavy cream, for serving (optional)

1. Preheat the oven to 425 degrees F. In a large bowl, combine the cherries, nectarine slices, lemon juice and optional amaretto or Grand Marnier. Add the brown sugar, cornstarch, cinnamon and salt and toss until well blended. Pile the fruit mixture in a deep 1½- to 2-quart casserole. Dot the fruit with the butter.

2. Roll out the pastry on a lightly floured surface about ⅛ inch thick. Gently transfer the pastry to the dish, so that it covers the surface with a ¾-inch overhang on all sides. Tuck the edges under and flute them, if desired. Brush the dough with cream or milk; sprinkle with sugar. Cut 4 or 5 slashes in the crust for steam vents.

3. Bake until the pastry is golden and the filling is bubbly, 40 to 45 minutes. Cool briefly. Serve warm, topped with ice cream, frozen yogurt or cream, if you like.

MAKE-AHEAD STRATEGY FOR FRUIT DESSERTS

Like shortcakes, cobblers should be served warm from the oven, preferably shortly after they're baked. (Baking too far ahead guarantees sludge.) But you can make it easy for yourself. Here's how:

⌒ Put the biscuit dough together ahead of time.

⌒ Press it out on a sheet of lightly floured wax paper, and fold the paper over the dough or cover with a second sheet. If you like, the dough can be cut into rounds ahead of time, too.

⌒ Refrigerate for up to several hours until needed.

⌒ Streusel and crumb mixtures can also be made ahead and refrigerated or frozen in a sealed plastic bag. In summer, make a double or triple batch of streusel; keep it on hand in the freezer, and scatter as much as you need over fruit desserts and pies.

⌒ Fruit fillings can be readied in advance, too; cover the filling with plastic wrap, right in its baking dish.

When ready to bake, just preheat the oven, arrange the dough over the fruit and you're there.

To Pit a Cherry

Tucking into a cherry dessert, a friend suddenly looked up and asked, "How do you get the pits out of the cherries?"

"With a cherry pitter," I answered. He had never heard of such a thing. (It's like a big pair of tweezers, with a pin to push the pit clean through.)

Devices like these were once standard in every home kitchen. Even with all the high-tech gadgetry now available, there's still nothing better for getting cherry pits out quickly, without mangling the cherries. (If you don't own one, use a chopstick to push the pits straight through.)

NEW HAMPSHIRE "PLATE CAKE"

This is something unusual—the cobbler components are first baked, and then turned upside-down. Based on a New Hampshire recipe from early in the 20th century, this dessert tops fruit (in summer, berries or peaches; in winter, pears or apples with a splash of cider added) with a disk of biscuit dough. When it's inverted after baking, the fruit drips its juices down over the biscuit "plate."

I've added a little cornmeal to the dough for crunch, plus a little spice, including pepper, an old touch. Try this with Rhode Island white jonnycake meal for a subtle but fragrant corn flavor (see page 310 for mail-order information). Bake this shortly before serving.

⟋⟍ Serves 6

SPICED BISCUIT DOUGH

1	cup all-purpose flour
⅓	cup white jonnycake meal or other cornmeal
3	tablespoons sugar
2¼	teaspoons baking powder
½	teaspoon ground ginger
½	teaspoon ground allspice
¼	teaspoon ground cardamom (optional)
¼	teaspoon ground cinnamon
	Pinch *each* salt and freshly ground pepper
¼	cup (½ stick) cold unsalted butter, cut into pieces
½	cup milk

FRUIT

1½	cups blackberries or blueberries or ¾ cup of each
½	pint red or golden raspberries
1-2	small plums, halved, stoned and sliced (optional)
⅓	cup sugar, or to taste, depending on the berries' sweetness

Vanilla ice cream or frozen yogurt, for topping (optional)

1. **SPICED BISCUIT DOUGH:** In a food processor, combine the flour, jonnycake meal or cornmeal, sugar, baking powder, spices, salt and pepper, pulsing once or twice. Add the butter and process, pulsing, until the mixture is crumbly. Dribble most, but

not all, of the milk over the mixture; pulse to combine. If necessary, add the remaining milk; the mixture should hold together and should be moist, but not sticky. Gather the dough onto a floured sheet of plastic wrap or wax paper, patting it together to form a cohesive disk. *(The dough can be made several hours in advance; wrap and refrigerate until needed.)*

2. **FRUIT:** Preheat the oven to 400 degrees F. Generously butter just the sides of a 9- or 9½-inch pie pan. Combine all of the berries. Place ½ of the berries and the optional plums in the pan; sprinkle with ½ of the sugar. Repeat with the remaining fruit and sugar; set aside.

3. On the floured sheet of plastic wrap or wax paper, gently pat or roll out the biscuit dough to the same size as the pie pan. The edges can be rough; that's fine. With both hands, place the round of dough over the berries. Cut a few slits in the dough with a small knife.

4. Bake until the dough is golden and fruit is bubbly, about 30 minutes. Let the pan stand on a wire rack for about 5 minutes. Run the tip of a knife around the edge of the dough and quickly invert the pan onto a serving platter, so the fruit is on top, with the juices dripping down the sides. Serve immediately, cutting the "plate cake" into wedges. Top with ice cream or frozen yogurt, if you like.

VIRGINIA BLACKBERRY ROLL

Here the cobbler components are rearranged—instead of biscuit dough topping the fruit, it's rolled out and used to line a Pyrex loaf pan. Ripe summer blackberries are piled inside, and the dough is gathered up and over the top and decorated with leaf cutouts made with scraps of the dough. This delightful variation on the berries-and-biscuit theme is a family heirloom recipe from Eileen Proctor Rowe, who enjoyed this as a child in Goochland County, Virginia.

⌒ *Serves 8*

BERRIES

½-⅔ cup sugar (depending on the berries' sweetness)
3 tablespoons quick-cooking tapioca
Pinch salt
4 cups blackberries, picked over
Juice of ½ lemon

BUTTERMILK BISCUIT DOUGH

3 cups all-purpose flour
3 tablespoons sugar
1 tablespoon baking powder
1½ teaspoons baking soda
Pinch salt
½ cup (1 stick) cold unsalted butter, cut into pieces
¾ cup buttermilk (or equal parts yogurt and low-fat milk or cold water)
1 large egg, lightly beaten
2 teaspoons milk or cream

Sugar, for topping
Vanilla ice cream, for serving

1. **BERRIES:** Stir together the sugar, tapioca and salt in a mixing bowl. Add the berries and lemon juice and toss to combine. Set aside.

2. **BUTTERMILK BISCUIT DOUGH:** Place the flour, sugar, baking powder, baking soda and salt into a food processor and pulse briefly to blend. Add the butter and pulse briefly, just until crumbly. With the machine running, add the buttermilk, just until the dough almost comes together. The dough should be quite soft; if it is still dry, add another tablespoon or two of buttermilk.

3. Transfer the dough to a large sheet of floured wax paper and gently knead once or twice to blend the ingredients. Gently pat or roll out the dough into a rectangle about 11 x 14 inches. Neatly trim; set aside the trimmings.

4. Generously butter a loaf pan, preferably a Pyrex loaf pan about 9½ x 2½ inches. Very gently invert the sheet of wax paper over the pan, flipping the dough into the pan without stretching it. The dough should cover the bottom and 2 long sides of the pan with a slight overhang and come to the top of the short sides. Cut off and set aside any excess dough; repair any tears in the dough by gently pressing together.

5. Preheat the oven to 400 degrees F, with a rack in the center and a sheet of foil underneath to catch any running juices.

6. Pour the berry mixture into the dough-lined pan. Carefully fold one long side of the dough over the fruit. Lightly beat the egg together with the milk or cream and gently brush some of the glaze over the folded surface of the dough. Gently fold in the other long side of the dough and press lightly to seal. Tuck in the dough at the short ends of the pan. Brush the dough again with the glaze. Cut attractive shapes from the reserved dough (flowers, leaves and a stem; fruit shapes, diamonds or other shapes) and lay them on the surface. Brush the pastry cutouts with the glaze.

7. Bake until the roll is nearly golden, 50 to 60 minutes. Sprinkle the top with sugar and bake for 10 minutes longer, until golden. Cool briefly on a rack. Serve warm directly from the pan, cutting the roll into slices and spooning up the berries. Top each serving with vanilla ice cream.

Going a-Blackberrying

I have also seen this made in a square pan, or in little packets but these are not official 'rolls.' My mother always made hers in the 'roll' style. We only had this old-fashioned dessert a few times each summer, so they were special. People who knew we loved blackberries would bring us some, or tell us where the good picking was.

Now, I am fortunate to have a good supply in a vacant lot next to a shopping mall nearby. My 6-year-old daughter and I go early in the morning or at dusk to pick berries, wearing our bandannas and long sleeves so as to avoid ticks and chiggers."

EILEEN PROCTOR ROWE

Rye 'n Injun

Cover [sweetened] apples with this [dough of rye flour and cornmeal, an early American combination called "rye 'n Injun"], bake slowly for five hours, then break the crust down into the apples, cover and bake for two hours longer. Serve with sugar and cream. Half a cupful of molasses can be used instead of the sugar.

OLIVE GREEN
EVERYDAY DESSERTS
1911

ABOUT PANDOWDY

Pandowdy is American, not English—no-frills Yankee fare. It consists of a dish of fruit (usually apples), sweetened with molasses or maple syrup, topped with a pastry crust (or bread dough) and baked until the dough starts to brown. The pastry is then cut up into squares ("dowdied") and pressed back down into the fruit. The dish is returned to the oven, and everything finishes baking together, the fruit juices thoroughly saturating the dough.

Like so many other key old-fashioned desserts, pandowdy recipes are conspicuously absent from old cookbooks. The word, says the *Oxford English Dictionary*, is "of obscure origin," though there is a Somerset word *pandoulde*, meaning custard, now lost.

But while there are few references to pandowdy in 19th-century cookbooks, the dessert does date back at least that far. In *The Blithedale Romance* (1852), New Englander Nathaniel Hawthorne writes: "Hollingsworth [would] fill my plate from the great dish of pandowdy." Later in that century, author Charles Leland refers to "pan-dowdy, a kind of coarse and broken-up apple pie."

One of the first published recipes for pandowdy, featuring a cut-up crust—to me, the dish's distinctive mark—appeared in about 1880. The apple dessert was baked overnight in the waning embers of a wood fire. Like pie, pandowdy was often served for breakfast: "In the morning cut the hard crust into the apple," this recipe concluded. "Eat with yellow cream or plain."

While pandowdy had clearly been around earlier, published recipes begin to show up in the early 20th century, and they veer all over. Many don't mention cutting up the crust at all. A Maine apple pandowdy simmers the fruit in a kettle with salt pork and molasses. Imogene Wolcott, whose 1938 *Yankee Cook Book* is one of the best regional American cookbooks, says that "apple brown Betty is made according to the modern recipe for pandowdy," with bread crumbs standing in for the crust.

Pear Pandowdy

This pandowdy is kept simple; I like it made with pie crust instead of biscuit dough, which bakes up crisper once it's soaked with the fruit juices. The pears add a more intense fruit presence than most apples.

~ *Serves 8*

6 firm-ripe juicy pears (such as Anjou), peeled, cored, halved and sliced ½ inch thick (about 2½ pounds; 6½ cups sliced)
2 tablespoons fresh lemon juice
½ cup pure maple syrup
¼ teaspoon ground cloves
¼ teaspoon fresh-grated nutmeg
1 tablespoon unsalted butter
   Basic Pie Dough for a 1-crust pie (page 449)
1 tablespoon cream or milk, for glaze
   Sugar, for topping
   Ice cream, heavy cream or whipped cream, for serving

1. Preheat the oven to 400 degrees F. Butter a 9- or 9½-inch pie pan or other shallow baking dish.

2. Toss the sliced pears with the lemon juice in a mixing bowl to prevent discoloration. Add the maple syrup, cloves and nutmeg; toss to combine. Place the pears in the pie pan; dot with the butter.

3. Roll out the pastry on a lightly floured surface to an even thickness of about ⅛ inch; lay it gently over the pears. Trim it flush with the edges of the dish. Brush the pastry with the cream or milk; sprinkle it with sugar. Cut several steam vents in the pastry.

4. Bake until the pastry is lightly golden, about 30 minutes. Lower the oven temperature to 350 degrees. Remove the pandowdy from the oven and cut the pastry into 1-inch squares. Use a spatula to press the squares into the pear filling (this is called "dowdying").

5. Return the pandowdy to the oven and bake until golden brown, about 30 minutes longer. Serve warm, in bowls, with ice cream, heavy cream or whipped cream.

"Shoo-fly pie and Apple Pan-Dowdy, Makes your eyes light up and your stomach say howdy."

Old Song

Popular Betty

As with cobblers, recipes for brown Bettys don't show up often in American cookbooks before this century. British crisps and crumbles are clearly related, but the brown Betty seems to be American and rises in popularity at about the same time as the cobbler, in the late 1800s.

There is no brown Betty recipe in Fannie Farmer's 1896 *Boston Cooking-School Cook Book*, but she does include a recipe for "Scalloped Apples" baked with bread crumbs that's virtually identical. By the 1930 revision, the same recipe is called "Brown Betty (Scalloped Apples)."

Brown Betty has appeared in an even more upscale way: as a stuffing for roast pheasant, at Guy Abelson's Café in the Barn in Seekonk, Massachusetts, now closed.

48

⤳ Variation
APPLE PANDOWDY: Substitute sliced apples for the pears, adding ½ cup cider or water to the fruit in step 2. Then proceed as directed.

PEAR OR APPLE BROWN BETTY WITH CAKE CRUMBS

Say the words "warm fruit dessert," and this brown Betty is what comes to mind—ripe seasonal fruit, baked with spices, butter and a few crumbs to soak up juices and crisp the surface. You usually find this made with apples; pears are, to my taste, even more interesting.

This is a basic formula; quantities are given for both moist pears (Anjou or Bartlett), or drier pears (Bosc) or apples. This should come to the table in its baking dish, topped with a thick blanket of buttery crumbs. Stale cake crumbs instead of bread crumbs make brown Betty even better.

⤳ Serves 6

1¼	cups stale plain cake crumbs (from spongecake, pound cake or angel food cake), or use soft fresh bread crumbs, white or whole-wheat
⅓	cup packed light or dark brown sugar
¼	cup sugar
1½	teaspoons ground cinnamon
½	teaspoon ground allspice
¼	teaspoon ground ginger
	Pinch ground cloves
2-2½	pounds firm-ripe Bosc pears or apples (about 6 medium), peeled, quartered, cored and sliced about ½ inch thick
	Fresh lemon juice
⅓	cup cider or water (reduce liquid to 2 tablespoons if using moist pears, such as Bartletts or Anjous)
3-4	tablespoons cold unsalted butter, cut into pieces
	Ice cream or heavy cream, for serving

1. Preheat the oven to 375 degrees F. Butter a shallow baking dish, such as a 9-x-6-inch rectangular baking dish (or other baking dish with 3½-to-4-cup capacity); set aside.

2. In a small bowl, combine the crumbs, brown and white sugars and spices. Prepare the pears or apples, dropping the slices into a second bowl and tossing with a little lemon juice.

3. Scatter 1 to 2 tablespoons of the crumb mixture into the bottom of the baking dish. Top with ½ of the fruit. Pour the cider or water over, and scatter slightly less than ½ of the crumbs on top. Dot with about ½ of the butter. Top with the remaining fruit, the remaining crumbs and the remaining butter.

4. Bake until the crumbs are nicely browned and fruit is bubbly and tender, about 35 minutes. Cool briefly on a wire rack. Serve warm, with ice cream or cream. This dessert can be re-warmed at 300 degrees.

Ulysses saw in the glorious garden of Alcinoüs "pears and pomegranates, and apple-trees bearing beautiful fruit."

HENRY DAVID THOREAU
WILD APPLES
1862

Native Sweets

One of only three fruits native to North America (the others are blueberries and Concord grapes), the cranberry was called *Sasemin* by the Wampanoag ("People of the Dawn") Indians in New England. They used it not only as food but as a curative for scrapes, cuts or "even arrow wounds," says Ocean Spray.

Paula Marcoux, former Foodways Manager at Plimoth Plantation, points out that cranberries and other berries were incorporated into many savory dishes to add a sharp edge of flavor. There was no way to sweeten dishes in pre-colonial days, since honeybees were not native to North America and cane sugar production came later.

For natural sweetening, the native cranberries and blueberries, and also others such as bearberries and chokecherries—whether fresh or dried on mats in the summer sun—were indispensable. Blueberries and other berries were added to "boiled breads," mixtures that resembled dumplings. To make them, fine cornmeal was mixed

CRANBERRY CRUMBLE WITH FALL FRUITS

If you were to ask me which *one* recipe to try from this book, this might be it. I've baked it every year for Thanksgiving; it goes great with pumpkin pie, as well as with the next day's leftover turkey.

A variation on a crisp, with a nubbly golden topping made with oats, this is a family recipe from England, where it is made with plums, gooseberries and other berries.

After gradually evolving the recipe through several versions, I've eliminated the fruit thickening entirely. (The topping absorbs some of the excess juices.) The result is whole cranberries, glistening in clean, clear juices, their tartness offset by sweet pears and apples—a song to autumn. Instead of the Ginger Cream topping, you may serve this crumble with vanilla ice cream.

⌒ *Serves 8*

1½	pounds (7-8 cups) fresh or frozen (not thawed) cranberries, rinsed, drained and picked over
1½	cups sugar
	Grated zest and juice of 1 large orange
2	Golden Delicious or other sweet apples, peeled, quartered, cored and thickly sliced
2	firm-ripe Bosc pears, peeled, quartered, cored and thickly sliced

OAT CRUNCH TOPPING
¾	cup old-fashioned or quick-cooking oats (not instant)
¾	cup all-purpose flour
¾	cup packed dark brown sugar
½	cup (1 stick) cold unsalted butter, cut into pieces

GINGER CREAM (OPTIONAL)
1	cup heavy cream, well chilled
2-4	tablespoons minced crystallized ginger, to taste

1. Preheat the oven to 375 degrees F, with a rack in the center and a large sheet of foil on the rack. Butter a large, shallow baking dish, such as a 12-inch oval gratin dish; set aside.

2. In a large, heavy saucepan or casserole, bring about ½ of the cranberries and all of the sugar to a boil; the berries will pop and the sugar will melt. Remove from the heat and stir in the

remaining cranberries, orange zest and juice, apples and pears. Spoon the fruit mixture into the baking dish and set aside.

3. **OAT CRUNCH TOPPING:** In a food processor, combine the oats, flour, brown sugar and butter. Pulse until the mixture is crumbled to the size of peas; do not overprocess. (You can also cut the mixture together with 2 knives or with your fingers.) Scatter the topping mixture evenly over the fruit.

4. Bake until the fruit is bubbly and the topping is nicely browned, 50 to 60 minutes. If you'd like to brown the top further, very briefly run it under the broiler. Cool the baking dish on a wire rack until warm.

5. **GINGER CREAM** (optional): Whip the cream until not quite stiff. Gently fold in crystallized ginger to taste; transfer to a glass serving bowl.

6. Serve the crumble warm, spooning some of the fruit and topping into each bowl. Top each portion with a spoonful of Ginger Cream, and pass the remaining cream separately.

⌒ *Variation*

For a quince version, use ¾ pound cranberries, 4 to 5 apples and 2 quinces.

with boiling water to form a sticky paste, rolled into balls, dropped into boiling water and simmered. Dried berries, pulverized fruits, crushed nutmeats or sunflower seeds were all optional additions.

In 1677, when King Charles II was annoyed with the Massachusetts Bay Colony for minting its own coins, the colonists hastily offered him a mollifying gift of their three most important crops: codfish, corn, and "tenn barrells of cranburyes."

RHUBARB-STRAWBERRY CRISP WITH CINNAMON-WALNUT TOPPING

For the first 200 years in America, rhubarb pies were almost as popular as apple or mince. In fact, so strong was the connection that for years people called rhubarb "pie plant." Technically a vegetable, rhubarb makes as good a crisp as it does a pie. Not only does the old rhubarb-and-strawberries combination play sour against sweet, but the two arrive in the garden at the same time in spring.

~ *Serves about 6*

FRUIT

1½	pounds rhubarb, stalks trimmed, cut into ¾-inch pieces (about 3 cups)
1	pint strawberries, hulled, and halved, if large
¼	cup sugar
¼	cup packed light brown sugar
	Juice of ½ lemon
¼	cup cold water

CINNAMON-WALNUT TOPPING

3	tablespoons cold unsalted butter, cut into pieces
¼	cup all-purpose flour
¼	cup packed light brown sugar
3	tablespoons sugar
1	teaspoon ground cinnamon
⅔	cup coarsely chopped walnuts

Ice cream or frozen yogurt, for serving (optional)

1. **FRUIT:** Preheat the oven to 375 degrees F. Butter an 8-inch pie pan or other shallow baking dish. In a mixing bowl, combine the rhubarb, strawberries, white and brown sugars, lemon juice and water. Transfer the mixture to the buttered pan.

2. **CINNAMON-WALNUT TOPPING:** In a small bowl, combine the butter, flour, brown and white sugars and cinnamon. Cut together until the mixture forms large crumbs. Crumble in the walnuts. Scatter the topping over the fruit, pressing it in lightly.

3. Bake until the topping is golden brown, about 35 minutes.

Cool briefly. Serve warm, topped with ice cream or frozen yogurt, if you like.

⌒ Variation

WARM PLUM CRISP: Plums work well in warm desserts. I often slice a couple of plums into berry and nectarine desserts, just to deepen the flavor. Substitute about 1¾ pounds plums for the rhubarb and strawberries, add 3 tablespoons of flour and a little cinnamon to the fruit, and eliminate the water. Proceed as directed.

APPLE MUSH

These homespun desserts were often named by kids, and the family names stuck. This one features apples piled high in a pie plate, topped with a cake-like batter that bakes up crunchy and irresistible, trapping all the fragrant apple juices inside. It is an old family recipe from Pamela Cohen, a producer at ABC Television. It's also one of the best in this collection.

⌒ Serves about 6

TOPPING

½	cup all-purpose flour
½	cup sugar
1	teaspoon baking powder
1	large egg, beaten

FRUIT

4	large Granny Smith apples, peeled, quartered, cored and sliced ¼ inch thick
	Fresh lemon juice
¼	cup sugar
¼	cup packed dark brown sugar
1½	teaspoons ground cinnamon
3	tablespoons cold unsalted butter, cut into pieces
	Vanilla ice cream or whipped cream, for serving (optional)

1. **TOPPING:** In a bowl, combine the flour, sugar and baking powder. Stir in the egg until the mixture forms a smooth dough (the mixture will be quite stiff). Set aside for about 30 minutes.

2. Preheat the oven to 450 degrees F. Lightly butter a 9-inch pie pan; set aside.

3. **FRUIT:** Toss the apples with the lemon juice. Combine the sugar, brown sugar and cinnamon in a small bowl. Place about ⅓ of the apples in the pan. Sprinkle with ⅓ of the cinnamon mixture, and dot with ⅓ of the butter. Make 2 more layers in the same way, mounding the apples quite high in the center of the pan. With your fingers, break off tablespoon-size dabs of the topping mixture and scatter them over the apples.

4. Place the pie pan on a baking sheet or a sheet of foil and bake for 10 minutes. Lower the oven heat to 350 degrees and continue to bake until the topping is nicely browned and the apples are soft, about 45 minutes longer. Cool on a wire rack. Serve warm, topped with vanilla ice cream or whipped cream, if you like.

SWEDISH APPLE "PIE" WITH VANILLA SAUCE

This old Swedish dessert from the province of Scania is called a pie, but with the apples baked with butter and crumbs until they meld together, it belongs with crisps and brown Bettys. The apple flavor permeates the buttery crumbs. This recipe was shared by Barry Judd, owner of Min Lilla Trädgård, a restaurant in Stockholm.

Serves 6 to 8

5 large apples, peeled, cored, quartered and very thinly sliced
1 cup dry bread crumbs
½ cup plus 1 tablespoon sugar, or to taste (depending on the apples' sweetness)
3 tablespoons cold unsalted butter, cut into pieces

SWEDISH VANILLA SAUCE

1 cup heavy cream
3 large egg yolks
¼ cup sugar, or more to taste
¾ teaspoon pure vanilla extract
Juice of 1 orange, tangerine or lemon

1. Preheat the oven to 350 degrees F. Butter a 10-to-12-inch oval gratin dish or other shallow baking pan; set aside.

2. Cover the bottom of the baking dish with a layer of the apple slices. Sprinkle with some of the bread crumbs and sugar; dot with some of the butter. Continue layering until all of the ingredients are used, finishing with a layer of crumbs, sugar and butter.

3. Bake for 1 to 1¼ hours, or until the apples are very soft and about to disintegrate.

4. **SWEDISH VANILLA SAUCE:** Scald ⅓ cup of the cream in a small, heavy saucepan. In a small bowl, beat the egg yolks, sugar and vanilla until well combined. Gradually add the hot cream to the egg yolk mixture, mixing constantly. Return the mixture to the saucepan and reduce the heat to very low. Cook, stirring constantly, just until the custard thickens slightly, usually 2 or 3 minutes. Do not allow to boil. Remove from the heat and transfer the

custard to a bowl; place a sheet of wax paper or plastic wrap directly on the surface and chill thoroughly. Whip the remaining ⅔ cup cream until it forms soft peaks; fold into the egg yolk mixture. Add the orange, tangerine or lemon juice to taste. Cover and refrigerate until serving time.

5. Cool the pie to lukewarm or room temperature. Turn the pie out onto a serving platter, or serve directly from the dish (I like it best this way). Serve with the Vanilla Sauce.

DANISH APPLE AND COOKIE CRUMB DESSERT

("PEASANT GIRL WITH VEIL")

In this Danish dessert, apples are layered with cookie crumbs and baked until they meld together, with a crisped top layer (the "veil").

This is actually an amalgamation of two similar apple-and-crumb recipes from unrelated sources: a Danish dessert made with rye bread crumbs and Vincent La Chapelle's 1744 dessert, made with a spiced apple "marmalade" and crumbled "biskets."

This is one of the simplest and best of the crisp/brown Betty genre.

Serves 6 to 8

2　pounds apples, peeled, quartered, cored and coarsely chopped (about 5 cups)

½　cup sugar, or to taste, plus more for topping

1　teaspoon ground cinnamon

¼　cup (½ stick) unsalted butter

1¾　cups coarsely crushed (about the size of mini chocolate chips) amaretti (crisp Italian macaroons) and/or mixed cookie crumbs

⅛　teaspoon salt

　Ice cream, frozen yogurt or heavy cream, for serving

1. Cook the apples with the sugar and cinnamon over low heat in a covered heavy saucepan, stirring and mashing them occasionally as they cook, until they are reduced to a coarse, chunky puree, usually about 15 minutes. Remove from the heat and cool slightly.

2. Preheat the oven to 375 degrees F. Butter an 8-inch round cake pan or other shallow baking dish. Melt the butter in a saucepan, and stir in the cookie crumbs and salt until combined. Layer the crumbs and apple mixture alternately in the baking pan, beginning and ending with the crumbs. Sprinkle the top layer of crumbs with a spoonful of sugar.

3. Bake until golden brown, 35 to 40 minutes. Cool briefly on a wire rack. Serve warm with ice cream, frozen yogurt or cream. This can be reheated gently at 300 degrees.

Black and Blueberry Grunt (or Slump)

Similar to cobblers in that they combine fruit with nubs of biscuit dough, both slumps and grunts are simmered on top of the stove rather than baked. Do the berries actually "grunt" as they simmer? That's what some say. Do the biscuit dumplings "slump" down into the fruit as they bubble away? Maybe.

The biscuit dough is made slightly softer than for a cobbler, then spooned over the fruit—these are actually "drop biscuits" or dumplings. When simmered, tightly covered—you're actually steaming them—the dumplings set but don't color.

The terms "slump" and "grunt" are thrown around as carelessly as "crisp" and "cobbler." Some say that grunts are steamed (usually with apples), while slumps are baked (usually with berries). Others contend that "grunt" is the name of the dumpling on top, or the satisfied sound you make when you eat one.

Yankee magazine, which has been chronicling these things since 1935, concludes, "The Brown Betty Rule of slumps and grunts is: There Is No Rule!"

Serves about 6

Berries

1	generous pint blueberries, picked over
1	generous pint blackberries, picked over
¾	cup sugar, or more to taste
¼	cup water
1	tablespoon fresh lemon juice
	Pinch *each* ground cinnamon and freshly ground pepper (optional)

Dumpling (Drop Biscuit) Dough

1	cup all-purpose flour
2	tablespoons sugar
1	teaspoon baking powder
½	teaspoon baking soda
⅛	teaspoon salt
2	tablespoons unsalted butter, melted
½	cup buttermilk (or a mixture of plain yogurt and skim milk or water), plus more as needed
2	tablespoons cinnamon sugar, for topping
	Heavy cream or vanilla ice cream, for serving

1. **BERRIES:** The grunt can be simmered in a well-seasoned 8-inch cast-iron skillet or a shallow heatproof casserole (such as Le Creuset enameled cast-iron) of similar size. Place the berries in the skillet or casserole; add the sugar, water, lemon juice and optional spices and toss gently to combine. Set aside.

2. **DUMPLING (DROP BISCUIT) DOUGH:** In a mixing bowl, stir together the flour, sugar, baking powder, baking soda and salt. Stir in the melted butter. Add enough of the buttermilk to form a soft, sticky dough that is slightly wetter than a biscuit dough.

3. Cover the skillet with the berries in it and bring to a boil. Lower the heat to a steady simmer, uncover, and spoon the dough over the fruit, forming small dumplings with a soup spoon. Sprinkle the dumplings lightly with the cinnamon sugar. Tightly cover the skillet with the lid or a sheet of foil and steam the mixture over medium-low heat, without opening the lid, until the dumplings set and the surface is dry when touched with a fingertip, usually about 15 minutes.

4. Spoon the grunt into serving bowls, with some of the berries and dumplings in each portion. Pass the heavy cream separately, or top each portion with vanilla ice cream.

"Apple Slump" was what Louisa May Alcott named her home in Concord, Massachusetts.

TRADITIONAL TWO-BERRY BUCKLE

This is the traditional, crumb-topped coffee-cake-style buckle; you can make it with any type of berries in season. The berries, not the cake, are its essence, for a buckle is almost a berry batter pudding. It's said to "buckle" as it bakes, but I've never seen that happen.

This recipe was adapted from a dessert from the former Joe's Bar and Grill in Greenwich Village. At Joe's, the buckle would be cut out into neat rounds with a cocktail glass and precisely arranged over a pool of custard. You can cut it into squares and serve right from its dish.

Serve this warm; New Englanders like buckle with a warm lemon sauce.

Serves about 8

CAKE BATTER
¾ cup (1½ sticks) unsalted butter, softened
¾ cup sugar
1 teaspoon pure vanilla extract
3 large eggs
1 cup all-purpose flour
1½ teaspoons baking powder
¼ teaspoon salt
2 cups blueberries, picked over
1 cup raspberries, picked over

CRUMB TOPPING
¼ cup (½ stick) cold unsalted butter, cut into pieces
½ cup sugar
⅓ cup all-purpose flour
½ teaspoon ground cinnamon
½ teaspoon fresh-grated nutmeg
1 teaspoon grated lemon zest

Low-Fat Custard Sauce (page 610) spiked with bourbon, John's Mother's Lemon Sauce with Lemon Slices (page 612), Cider-Lemon Sauce (page 611) or vanilla ice cream, for serving

1. Preheat the oven to 375 degrees F. Butter an 8-inch square baking dish or a 10- or 11-inch gratin dish; set the dish aside.

2. **CAKE BATTER:** Cream the butter, sugar and vanilla with an electric mixer at medium-high speed until light. Add the eggs, one at a time, and beat until incorporated. Meanwhile, stir together the flour, baking powder and salt in a small bowl; add to the creamed mixture and mix just until blended, no longer. Gently fold in the berries until well coated with the batter. Scrape the batter into the baking dish.

3. **CRUMB TOPPING:** In a food processor or with 2 knives, cut together the butter, sugar, flour, cinnamon, nutmeg and lemon zest until the mixture is coarsely crumbled. Scatter the mixture evenly over the cake batter.

4. Bake the buckle until the topping is lightly golden brown and the cake has set, usually 45 to 50 minutes. Cool on a wire rack. Cut into large squares and serve lukewarm or at room temperature, topped with a sauce or ice cream.

LIGHTENED DOWN-EAST BERRY BUCKLE

This new two-berry buckle is less substantial than traditional versions. It's a deep panful of raspberries and blackberries, topped with a layer of the lightest butter cake, studded with sliced almonds. The cake batter is spooned over the fruit, with the center left uncovered, so that the berries gleam through.

Serve this buckle warm, and try it with different berry combinations. Top it with ice cream or yogurt, and let it run down into the crimson berry juices. This is high summer pleasure.

Serves 6

BERRIES

1	pint blackberries, picked over
½	pint raspberries, picked over
⅓	cup sugar
3	tablespoons cold water

ALMOND CAKE TOPPING

6	tablespoons (¾ stick) unsalted butter, softened
½	cup sugar
	Grated zest of ½ small lemon
1	cup all-purpose flour
1	teaspoon baking powder
	Pinch salt
1	jumbo egg (or 1½ large; beat the second egg, then add ½ of it)
1½	teaspoons pure vanilla extract
⅛	teaspoon almond extract
3	tablespoons milk
¼	cup sliced almonds
	Ground cinnamon (optional)
	Vanilla frozen yogurt, ice cream or heavy cream, for serving (optional)

1. **BERRIES:** Preheat the oven to 350 degrees F. Place the blackberries and raspberries in a 9½- or 10-inch deep-dish pie pan or baking dish. Sprinkle with the sugar and pour in the water, combining gently and turning the berries over with your fingers.

2. **ALMOND CAKE TOPPING:** Beat the butter with an electric mixer at medium speed until very soft. Add the sugar and lemon

zest and continue beating until very light. Meanwhile, stir together the flour, baking powder and salt. Add the egg or eggs and both extracts to the butter mixture, beating until smooth. Add the flour mixture alternately with the milk, beginning and ending with the flour. Do not overmix.

3. Drop the cake batter in large spoonfuls about 1 inch from the edge of the pan, leaving the berries uncovered in the center. Sprinkle the batter with the almonds, then lightly with cinnamon, if you like.

4. Bake until the cake is golden and a toothpick emerges clean, 35 to 40 minutes. Cool briefly on a wire rack. Serve warm, with vanilla frozen yogurt, ice cream or cream, if you like.

BRINGING OUT
THE FLAVOR OF RIPE BERRIES

*G*et the most flavor out of ripe berries with a natural light sugar syrup, whether you plan to serve them on their own, over ice cream or with shortcake. Here's how:

Toss hulled fresh strawberries or other berries, whole, sliced or quartered, in a small amount of sugar, preferably superfine.

Let the berries stand at room temperature for 30 to 60 minutes, tossing them from time to time. The sugar will help draw out some of the berry juices, forming a light syrup and concentrating the berry flavor.

ABOUT SHORTCAKE

*S*hortcake! What better celebration of summer? Strawberry shortcake took the country by storm during the "Strawberry Fever" of the 1850s and soon rose to its eminent position in the American dessert pantheon. Historians look to its New England origins; wild strawberries were available and preferred there.

A somewhat rough version of strawberry shortcake was described in 1636 by Roger Williams, who founded Rhode Island: "The Indians bruise [wild strawberries] in a morter and mix them with meal and make strawberry bread."

Settlers here found strawberries growing wild among a profusion of other berries: blackberries, whortleberries, elderberries, mulberries and the native blueberries and cranberries. Captain John Smith found "fine and beautifull Strawberries, foure times bigger and better than ours in England."

Made with buttered split biscuits, shortcake continued to be popular in the decade after the Civil War. By the 1870s and 1880s, when a tidal wave of American cookbooks was published, recipes for strawberry and peach shortcakes with biscuits were standard and were frequently included with breakfast and tea items.

Real shortcake is made with biscuit dough. It can be made as one large round of biscuit-like cake or in individual biscuits. There are, of course, other ways to make shortcake; if your mother made hers with spongecake or pie crust, chances are that that's what "real" shortcake is for you.

You can layer ripe strawberries with tender spongecake and real whipped cream; New Yorkers have fond memories of Lindy's mountainous layer-cake version with giant berries. Others remember their mothers tucking lots of berries between two rounds of pastry dough. But to purists, neither is the real thing.

Contemporary restaurant pastry chefs cradle fruit between layers of puff pastry, phyllo dough and meringue.

All of these are good eating. But for a "real American strawberry shortcake," biscuit it should be.

"Strawberries! Strawberries! Fine, ripe, and red!"

FRUIT VENDOR'S CALL, AS PORTRAYED BY PAINTER NICOLINO CALYO IN 1840

The World's Best Lemon Tart

Southern-Style Peach and Raspberry Cobbler with Pecan-Crunch Topping

Cranberry Upside-Down Cake

Double Chocolate Pudding, Butterscotch Pudding, Coffee Cup Crème Caramel

Coiled Yeast Coffee Bread with Nut Filling

Free-Form Pear Galette

Chef Andrea's Breakfast Polenta Cake

Warm Baked Apples with Macaroon Soufflé and Cool Custard

Carême's Hazelnut Pithiviers with Orange

Crinkly Baked Pears, Trattoria-Style

THE FINAMORE SHORTCAKE

This is a tender round of not-too-sweet biscuit cake, with a buttery flavor and clean crumb. It's named for my friend, cookbook editor Roy Finamore, who adapted this from a recipe of cooking teacher Helen Worth.

Serve this shortcake still warm from the oven (I prefer a single layer to the original double). Slather it with ripe berries or peaches and a little cream or vanilla ice cream, and let the flavors take you away.

⌒ Serves about 6

1½-2	pints ripe strawberries or mixed berries, picked over and hulled (you can also use a combination of berries and sliced, peeled peaches)
⅔	cup sugar, preferably superfine
⅓	cup (5⅓ tablespoons) unsalted butter, softened
1	large egg
1	cup all-purpose flour
2	teaspoons baking powder
	Pinch salt
⅓	cup milk
1	cup chilled heavy cream, whipped, or vanilla ice cream, for topping

1. Butter an 8- or 8½-inch round cake pan; set aside. Toss the berries with ⅓ cup sugar and let stand for about ½ hour.

2. Preheat the oven to 350 degrees F. With an electric mixer at medium-high speed, cream the butter with the remaining ⅓ cup sugar until very light, 4 or 5 minutes. Add the egg and continue to mix for about 2 minutes. Meanwhile, sift the flour, baking powder and salt onto a sheet of wax paper. Lower the mixer speed and add the dry ingredients to the butter mixture alternately with the milk, beginning and ending with the dry ingredients. Do not overmix. With a large rubber spatula, gently spread the batter in the pan.

3. Bake until lightly golden, about 20 minutes. Cool on a wire rack for about 5 minutes. Invert the cake onto a serving platter. Top with the berries and their juices. Cut into wedges and serve warm, topping each serving with whipped cream or a scoop of ice cream.

Della Lutes's Mother Bakes Shortcake

... try as I may, I cannot persuade my palate that a shortcake made today using exactly the same component parts tastes *quite* as did those so inextricably mingled in memory with the rare, sweet Junes of my childhood. Perhaps it was the berries—my father was a master hand at raising berries. None nowadays taste nearly so sweet or have such *strawberry* flavor. Perhaps it was because my father said it was good— for when my father said a thing was good you could take his word for it. It *was* good. And—perhaps it was because my mother made it! When your cake is done (and "shortcake" in my kind of recipe doesn't mean "biscuits"), proceed after this fashion: have your strawberries (dead ripe) washed, hulled, mashed and sweetened, in a bowl. And be sure there are plenty of them.

Turn your hot cake out on a platter and split it in two, laying the top half aside while you give your undivided attention to the

66

BERRY SHORTCAKES WITH BUTTERMILK-ALMOND BISCUITS

These are tender biscuits, with a little egg yolk and vanilla to make them cakey. They're baked in individual rounds, each topped with a crunchy almond-and-sugar glaze. You can make the biscuit dough ahead, cut out rounds, arrange them on a baking sheet, glaze them and refrigerate until dinnertime. Get the berries ready, too, tossing them with sugar so they form their own light syrup.

As you finish your main course, pop the panful of biscuits into a hot oven, bake quickly, split them while warm and fill with berries and a spoonful of vanilla ice cream or whipped cream. Then replace the almond-crusted lids and let their warmth make the cream dribble down through the berries in thick rivulets. Serve at once.

⌇ *Serves 6*

2	generous pints ripe fresh strawberries, picked over, hulled and sliced (or a combination of berries; see variations below)
⅓	cup sugar, preferably superfine (or to taste, depending on the berries' sweetness)

BUTTERMILK-ALMOND BISCUITS

2¼	cups all-purpose flour
½	cup plus 1 tablespoon sugar
1½	teaspoons baking powder
¾	teaspoon baking soda
¼	teaspoon salt
6	tablespoons (¾ stick) cold unsalted butter, cut into pieces
⅔-1	cup buttermilk (or use equal parts plain yogurt and low-fat milk or water)
1	large egg yolk
½	teaspoon pure vanilla extract
⅛	teaspoon almond extract
	Milk or cream, for glaze
⅓	cup sliced almonds
1¼	cups heavy cream (or vanilla ice cream—easier and just as good)
1	teaspoon pure vanilla extract (if using heavy cream)

1. Place the sliced berries in a large bowl and toss them with the sugar. Use the back of a large wooden spoon to crush some of the berries into the sugar. Let stand at room temperature for at least ½ hour, stirring occasionally, until the berries form a light, natural syrup. Chill.

2. **BUTTERMILK-ALMOND BISCUITS:** Preheat the oven to 425 degrees F. Butter a baking sheet (do not use a black steel sheet). Place the flour, ½ cup sugar, baking powder, baking soda and salt in a food processor and pulse briefly to combine the ingredients. Add the butter and pulse briefly until the mixture is crumbly. Place ⅔ cup of the buttermilk or yogurt mixture in a measuring cup; stir in the egg yolk and the vanilla and almond extracts. With the processor running, add the buttermilk mixture and turn off the machine. Add enough extra buttermilk, pulsing briefly after each addition, to form a slightly sticky but manageable dough. Transfer the dough to a floured sheet of wax paper; do not overhandle.

3. Sprinkle the dough with flour. With your fingertips, gently pat out the dough to an even thickness of about ¾ inch. Use a 3- or 3¼-inch fluted round biscuit cutter to cut out biscuits and transfer them gently to the buttered baking sheet. Gather the scraps of dough, pat out again and cut out the remaining biscuits. With your fingers or a pastry brush, coat the tops of the biscuits with a light film of milk or cream. Scatter the almonds over the tops; sprinkle the biscuits with the remaining 1 tablespoon of sugar. *(The biscuits can be made ahead to this point. Cover them with plastic wrap and refrigerate until ready to bake.)*

4. Bake the biscuits until pale golden, 11 to 14 minutes (watch carefully, as timing can vary; do not overbake). Transfer the biscuits to a wire rack and cool for about 2 minutes. Using a serrated knife and a gentle sawing motion, slice the biscuits horizontally in half.

5. Whip the cream with the vanilla (adding a little sugar, if you like), until nearly, but not quite, stiff. Place the bottoms of the biscuits on serving plates. Spoon the berries generously over the biscuits, dividing them evenly and spooning the juices over. Spoon some of the whipped cream over the berries (or top them with a small spoonful of vanilla ice cream); replace the almond biscuit lids. Serve immediately, passing the remaining whipped cream or additional ice cream separately.

lower. Spread this most generously with butter just softened enough (but never melted) to spread nicely, and be sure to lay it on clear up to the very eaves. Now slosh your berries on, spoonful after spoonful— all it will take.

Over this put the top layer, and give it the same treatment, butter and berries, and let them drool off the edges—a rich, red, luscious, slowly oozing cascade of ambrosia. On the top place a few whole berries—if you want to— and get it to the table as quickly as you can. It should be eaten just off the warm, and if anybody wants to deluge it with cream, let him do so. But the *memory* of a strawberry shortcake like this lies with the cake and not with cream.

DELLA T. LUTES
HOME GROWN
1937

⌒ *Variations*

PEACH MELBA SHORTCAKES: Use a combination of 4
peaches, peeled, stoned and thickly sliced, and ½ pint fresh
raspberries. Proceed as directed above.

OTHER BERRY COMBINATIONS FOR SHORTCAKE:
Strawberries and raspberries
Strawberries, raspberries and blackberries and/or blue-
berries
Raspberries, blueberries and red currants

BLUEBERRY SHORTCAKES WITH LOW-FAT CORNMEAL-YOGURT BISCUITS

This is my version of a recipe from Sonia Malikian, a Lebanese-
born pastry chef who now runs a café in Brussels.

There's almost no fat in these biscuits—yogurt is used to
replace both the butter and the liquid of traditional biscuit recipes.
They bake up crisp and nicely browned outside, moist within. This
is a good dough, not too soft or hard to handle. It is from Sidney
Burstein, a talented cook and food stylist who died far too young.

⌒ *Serves 6*

LOW-FAT CORNMEAL-YOGURT BISCUITS

1¾	cups all-purpose flour
1	cup low-fat plain yogurt
2	tablespoons sugar, plus more for sprinkling on biscuits
½	cup cornmeal
2	teaspoons baking powder
½	teaspoon baking soda
½	teaspoon ground cardamom (optional)
½	teaspoon ground cinnamon
½	teaspoon salt
	Milk, for glaze
3	tablespoons thinly sliced blanched almonds (optional)

BERRIES IN LIGHT SYRUP

> 3   cups blueberries (or use a combination of blueberries, raspberries and blackberries)
>
> ¼   cup sugar, preferably superfine, or more to taste
>
> Vanilla low-fat frozen yogurt, ice cream or whipped cream, for serving
>
> Confectioners' sugar, for serving

1. **LOW-FAT CORNMEAL-YOGURT BISCUITS:** In a bowl, stir together 1 cup of the flour and the yogurt until smooth; sprinkle the sugar on top, cover and let stand in a warm place for at least 3 hours or overnight.

2. **BERRIES IN LIGHT SYRUP:** At least 30 minutes before serving, toss the berries with the sugar, mashing them slightly. Cover and chill, tossing once or twice. The berries will form a light, natural syrup as the sugar draws out their juices.

3. **MIXING AND BAKING THE BISCUITS:** Preheat the oven to 425 degrees F. Lightly butter a baking sheet. In a bowl, combine the remaining ¾ cup flour, the cornmeal, baking powder, baking soda, optional cardamom, cinnamon and salt. Stir this mixture into the yogurt mixture, just until it blends into a cohesive dough.

4. Turn the dough out onto a lightly floured surface, and pat into a rectangle about 8 x 4 inches. Cut the dough into 2-inch squares and place 2 inches apart on the baking sheet. Brush the biscuits lightly with milk, sprinkle with the optional sliced almonds and lightly sprinkle with more sugar. *(The biscuits can be made ahead up to this point; cover them with plastic wrap and chill until ready to bake.)*

5. Bake the biscuits until golden and crusty, about 12 minutes (do not overbake). Cool briefly on a wire rack.

6. Horizontally split the still warm biscuits with a serrated knife; place the bottoms on dessert plates. Spoon some of the berries and their juices over each bottom, and add a spoonful of frozen yogurt, ice cream or whipped cream. Top with the biscuit lids, sprinkle with the confectioners' sugar and serve immediately.

RECIPES

*Poached Plum and Raspberry
    Compote in Late-Harvest
    Wine Syrup*
Chilled Citrus Platter
Marie's Fall Fruit Compote
Honey-Stewed Quinces
*Dutch Mennonite Dried
    Fruit Compote in Creamy
    Syrup*
*Madeira Dried Fruit
    Compote*
Ruby Baked Apples
*Crinkly Baked Pears,
    Trattoria-Style*
*Pears Poached in Mint Tea
    with Dark Chocolate Sauce*
*Broiled Pears with Warm
    Caramel Sauce*
*Warm Baked Apples with
    Macaroon Soufflé and Cool
    Custard*
Pavlova
Forgotten Pudding

CHAPTER 2

COMPOTES AND BAKED FRUIT

*Al cafone non far sapere
Quant' e' buon formaggio e pere.*
(Don't let the peasant know
How good are cheese and pears.)
ITALIAN FOLK SAYING

ince biblical times, fruit has been part of the conception of joyous abundance. The simplest dessert, of course, is simply fresh fruit. But from there, it isn't much of a stretch to cook the fruit quickly, resulting in a wide variety of compotes and baked desserts. I remember watching both my mother and grandmother, dishcloths in hand, taking panfuls of baked apples from the oven. (To my child's sense of things, baked apples were a Jewish dessert.)

Enter just about any trattoria in Italy, and you're greeted by a ceramic dish of baked pears, their skins crinkled and bronzed, standing in a pool of winy syrup. Fruit compotes, fruits served in syrup, are made everywhere in the world, highlighted by the flavors characteristic of their cuisines—rose water and honey in the Middle East, cassia and ginger in Asia.

The simplest compotes are made by cooking a single fruit in sugar or honey syrup. Historically, these were part of the world of preserves rather than of desserts. Preserving was, in fact, the primary way that fruits figured in old cookbooks. Long sections, even entire books, gave directions for putting up "abricocks in syrup" or preserving "orringes and Leamons" or making a "marmalet of Mullberries or raspberies."

A good example is *The Queens Closet Opened*, published in 1655, and apparently a best-seller, which went through 12 reprintings between 1655 and 1698. Transcribed from "the true Copies of the receipt books" of Queen Henrietta Maria, the wife of Charles I of England, "by W. M. one of her late servants," the book offers a rainbow of fruits in syrup, jellies and marmalades, plus candied flower petals, gingerroot and stalks of angelica. Another favorite method of preserving fresh fruits was by making fruit pastes, or *gelées*. To make these pastes, fruit was cooked down and mashed into a thick, sweetened paste, which was then dried in a slow oven. Kept on hand, fruit pastes were used as sweetmeats—cut in fanciful shapes, dredged in sugar and used to decorate cream desserts. Later, they adorned such composed desserts as trifles and floating islands.

In the 1700s, cookbooks such as Hannah Glasse's *The Compleat Confectioner* (1762) featured diagrams of the well-set dessert table, including such preserved fruits as a "Compote of Pears" and "Morella Cherries in Brandy."

The desserts that follow are gently cooked fruits—fresh, dried and in combination. Also represented are a few uncooked preparations that qualify as compotes because they are moistened with liquid. Pavlova and forgotten pudding, meringue desserts that exist solely to showcase a combination of fresh fruits, are here as well. They can be topped with any of the compotes in this chapter.

One thing I haven't included is the glitzy world of flaming fruit like cherries jubilee and bananas Foster—hallmarks of an era. Tasting more of singed alcohol than fruit, they were designed to impress—and often seduce—rather than, as these desserts are, to nourish and delight.

Exotic Fruit

George Jackson Eder, a retired economist and lawyer, remembered his first tastes of exotic fruit in New York City, early in the 20th century:

"Bananas were a penny, but down at the United Fruit Pier near the Fulton Fish Market, there were always some bananas that fell off the bunch and those could be picked up for free. And pineapples! My father remembered when they were $5 each, but could be rented as the centerpiece for a fancy banquet at $1 a night. There was a grocer, Madden's, opposite where the Stock Exchange is now, and they sold exotic fruits from South America— mangoes, alligator pears, grapefruit. I remember when Father came home with a grapefruit (perhaps 20 cents—expensive!) and peeled it, giving a section to each of us. It was sour, and we all said we liked oranges better."

POACHED PLUM AND RASPBERRY COMPOTE IN LATE-HARVEST WINE SYRUP

Nothing complicated: just a cool blend of summer fruits in dessert-wine syrup. This late-harvest wine syrup is basic; you can use it for any combination of fresh fruits in season.

Serves 4

1   cup sweet dessert wine, such as late-harvest Riesling or Gewürztraminer, Muscat de Beaumes-de-Venise or Sauternes (or substitute ½ cup each dry white wine and water, plus ⅓ cup sugar)
¼   cup cold water
½   vanilla bean, split lengthwise
4   quarter-size slices peeled fresh ginger
½   cinnamon stick
1   pound Italian prune plums (12-16), rinsed, stems removed, halved and stoned, or 1 pound purple or red plums, quartered and stoned
½   pint fresh raspberries, picked over
    Fresh lemon juice
    Vanilla or plain yogurt or ice cream, for serving

1. Place the wine, cold water, vanilla bean, ginger and cinnamon stick in a nonreactive saucepan. (If you want to go to the trouble, tie the vanilla, ginger and cinnamon stick in a piece of cheesecloth.) Cover and bring to a boil, stirring to dissolve the sugar, if using. Uncover and simmer to reduce slightly, about 3 minutes.

2. Add the plums, cover and simmer gently, turning them over once or twice, until they are tender, but not mushy, about 5 minutes. Remove the pan from the heat and gently stir in the raspberries and a squeeze of lemon juice. Let stand for at least 20 minutes. Remove the cinnamon stick and vanilla bean.

3. Serve the compote warm or cool, drizzling a spoonful of yogurt or ice cream into the syrup in each serving.

"Frutto proibito, più saporito."
(Forbidden fruit is tastier.)

ITALIAN PROVERB

Chilled Citrus Platter

In this light, refreshing dessert, the oranges are sprinkled with orange liqueur, garnished with candied citrus zest and glazed sprigs of fresh rosemary.

Serves 12

Fruit

7-8	blood oranges or other oranges
12	tangerines
3	pink or ruby-red grapefruits
	Grand Marnier or Cointreau (optional)

Syrup for Candied Zest

1	cup sugar
1½	cups water

Glazed Rosemary Sprigs (optional, for garnish)

4-5	fresh rosemary sprigs
	Fresh lemon juice
	Sugar, as needed

1. **Fruit:** Wash 3 oranges and 2 tangerines well. With a zester, remove their zest in long, thin strips. If you don't have a zester, use a vegetable peeler to remove the strips of zest, and cut them in long, fine julienne with a chef's knife. Set the zest aside.

2. Place a small cutting board on a tray with a lip to catch the juices, such as a jellyroll pan. (You can also work over a bowl.) With a sharp paring knife, cut off the peel and white pith from all of the citrus fruits, discarding the peels. Slice the fruits into neat rounds about ⅜ inch thick and arrange them attractively, overlapping slightly, on a serving platter. Pour the collected juices over the fruit. If you like, sprinkle the fruits with a little Grand Marnier or Cointreau. Cover the fruit loosely with plastic wrap and chill well.

3. **Candied Citrus Zest:** Bring a saucepan of water to a boil, add the reserved strips of citrus zest and blanch for 2 minutes. Drain and repeat, blanching the zest again in fresh water. Drain.

4. **Syrup for Candied Zest:** In a saucepan, bring the sugar and water to a boil, stirring to dissolve the sugar. Add the drained strips of zest and simmer gently until the zest is translucent, 8 to 10 minutes. Remove from the heat and let the zest cool in the syrup.

5. **GLAZED ROSEMARY SPRIGS** (optional): You can glaze the rosemary sprigs as is, or break them in pieces about 1½ inches long. Dip each one in lemon juice and turn gently in a shallow dish of sugar until it is lightly coated. Place on a sheet of wax paper (leave at room temperature if not using immediately).

6. Just before serving, drain the candied zest, reserving the syrup. Scatter the zest over the fruit; drizzle a little of the syrup on top. Arrange the optional rosemary sprigs around the edges of the platter and serve.

MARIE'S FALL FRUIT COMPOTE

In this compote, fresh and dried fruits are combined in a way that lets you taste the layers of fruit flavor. The compote can also serve as the filling for a fall shortcake (see page 66 for the recipe for Buttermilk-Almond Biscuits). The recipe is from Marie Simmons, my former collaborator on *Bon Appétit*'s "Cooking for Health" column, and a true cook.

Serves 6

3	cups unsweetened apple juice or cider
1	¼-inch-thick slice peeled fresh ginger
2	firm-ripe Comice or Anjou pears (about 8 ounces each)
2	Golden Delicious apples
1	tablespoon fresh lemon juice
⅓	cup (about 2 ounces) dried apricots
6	pitted prunes
½	cup low-fat plain yogurt
1	tablespoon molasses, preferably dark, or honey
2	tablespoons sliced unblanched almonds
	Julienne strips of lemon zest

1. Combine the apple juice or cider and the ginger in a large, shallow nonreactive saucepan; bring to a simmer. Meanwhile, peel, quarter and core the pears and apples, toss with the lemon juice and add to the saucepan. Cover and cook over low heat until the pears are just tender, about 10 minutes. Add the apricots and prunes, cover and cook over low heat for 5 minutes longer.

2. With a slotted spoon, transfer the fruit to a shallow serving bowl; discard the ginger. Raise the heat and boil the apple juice, uncovered, until reduced to 1¾ cups. Cool the liquid slightly; pour over the stewed fruits. *(The fruit mixture can be prepared ahead; cover and refrigerate up to 8 hours. Remove from the refrigerator at least 30 minutes before serving to return the fruit to room temperature.)*

3. In a small bowl, stir together the yogurt and molasses or honey; set aside. Toast the almonds in a small, dry skillet over low heat until pale golden, about 2 minutes. Drizzle the fruit with a spoonful of the yogurt mixture. Garnish each serving with a few strips of lemon zest and a sprinkling of the toasted almonds.

HONEY-STEWED QUINCES

From my friend, chef Ralph Stieber. A good basic method for cooking quinces, which turn a rosy gold color as they cook. This mixture also works well as a filling for tarts.

Makes 2½ pints

3	pounds (about 9 medium) quinces
½	cup (1 stick) unsalted butter
2	tablespoons sugar
1½	cups dry white wine
¾	cup light-flavored honey
	Juice of ½ lemon
	Pinch salt

1. Peel the quinces. Halve, core and slice ¼ inch thick.

2. Melt the butter in a wide nonreactive skillet over medium heat. Add the sugar and the quince slices and toss to coat. Cook until the sugar is melted and the slices are well coated, 5 to 7 minutes. Stir in the wine, honey, lemon juice and salt. Cover the pan and cook over medium heat for 25 minutes.

3. Uncover the pan and cook, stirring frequently, until the quinces are just tender, 20 to 25 minutes more. Cool. Serve warm or chilled. Store in the refrigerator.

DUTCH MENNONITE DRIED FRUIT COMPOTE IN CREAMY SYRUP
(*PLUMA MOOS*)

This is an unusual compote of dried fruits that cooks up plump and tender in a smooth, saucy spiced syrup. The recipe is an old Dutch-German one from Vivian Schellenberg, owner of The Prune Tree in Dallas, Oregon, whose orchards were planted more than a century ago.

The compote is best served warm; try it also over a slice of spongecake or spooned over warmed crepes.

⟶ Serves 8

2	cups raisins
1	pound pitted prunes, halved if desired (see note)
½	pound dried peaches or apricots
1	small cinnamon stick
2-3	pieces of star anise
2	quarts cold water
¼	cup plus 2 tablespoons all-purpose flour
1	cup sugar
1	cup heavy cream

1. In a large nonreactive saucepan, combine the raisins, prunes, dried peaches or apricots, cinnamon stick, star anise and water. Bring nearly to a boil; lower the heat and simmer until the fruit is tender but not mushy, usually 10 to 15 minutes.

2. In a small bowl, whisk together the flour and sugar (the sugar will help eliminate lumps in the flour). Gradually whisk in the cream until the mixture is smooth. Gently stir this mixture into the simmering fruit syrup. (If there are any small lumps of flour, strain the cream mixture into the syrup, pushing it through the strainer with a rubber spatula.)

3. Return the mixture to a gentle boil; cook, stirring once or twice, until the mixture is thickened and smooth, 2 to 4 minutes. Remove from the heat and cool briefly.

4. Remove the cinnamon stick and the star anise. Transfer the compote to a serving dish and serve warm or cool.

NOTE: To order especially moist prunes by mail-order, write to Myrna and Wayne Simmons at Orchard Crest Farms, www.orchardcrestfarms.com; (503) 362-4381; (800) 362-4381.

MADEIRA DRIED FRUIT COMPOTE

Fruit compotes can be found all over the world—they are an almost obligatory conclusion to Jewish holiday meals. "You can use almost any fruit, as long as you cook it within an inch of its life," says my friend Jonathan.

With its concentrated fruit and wine flavors, this is delicious with Ricotta Bavarian (page 110), or with a plain cake or cookie.

About 6 cups; serves about 6

1	cinnamon stick
12-16	black peppercorns
12-16	white peppercorns
12	allspice berries
1	3-inch strip orange zest (removed with a vegetable peeler)
1	2-to-3-inch strip lemon zest
¾	pound (about 2 cups) pitted prunes
½	pound (about 1¾ cups) dried apricots
½	pound (about 1⅓ cups) small dried figs
1¼	cups dry Madeira or dry sherry
½	cup water
¼	cup honey

1. Tie the cinnamon stick, black and white peppercorns, allspice and citrus zests in a piece of cheesecloth. Combine the spice bag with all of the remaining ingredients in a large nonreactive saucepan. Bring to a boil over medium heat, stirring occasionally. Reduce the heat, cover and simmer gently until the fruit is nearly tender, about 5 minutes. Do not overcook.

2. Transfer the compote to a serving dish and let cool. Discard the cheesecloth bag, gently pressing out all possible liquid. Serve the compote at room temperature.

"For the Lord, your God is bringing you to a good land, a land of wheat and barley, and vines, and fig trees, and pomegranates; a land of olive oil, and honey . . ."

DEUTERONOMY
8: 7-8

Heirloom Revival

In 1900, over 8,000 varieties of apples were available in America. At that time, fresh fruits were grown seasonally (no strawberries and peaches in January), and apples were likely to be blemished because they were grown without pesticides.

By the 1980s, the apple market had narrowed to Delicious apples (perfect-looking, but all crunch and no flavor), McIntosh, Granny Smith and pallid-tasting Golden Delicious.

Recently, however, interest in fresh food, nutrition awareness and responsible agriculture have joined to make better and more varied produce available. Farmers are beginning to offer such apples as Roxbury Russet, Black Twig and Cox's Orange Pippin at farmers' markets, and you can now buy seeds for "heirloom" fruits and vegetables in breathtaking variety. Even more encouraging is the fact that these apples are also showing up in supermarkets.

RUBY BAKED APPLES

When I walked into cooking teacher Anna Amendolara Nurse's sunny Brooklyn kitchen, sitting on the stove was a wide copper pan full of huge apples, gleaming outrageously, redder than red. Rome apples are a longtime favorite for baking; Anna buys hers by the bushel from an orchard in upstate New York.

Her secret in the following recipe is pomegranate syrup—grenadine, available in bottles in the "cocktail-supplies" section of the supermarket. These are quick and easy to make, and the sweet-tart pomegranate flavor marries nicely with the apples.

◦───◦ *Serves 6*

6	Rome apples
3	tablespoons sugar, plus more as needed
¼	teaspoon ground cinnamon, or as needed
½	cup grenadine or raspberry syrup

1. Preheat the oven to 375 degrees F. With a paring knife, cut out the core from the bottom of each apple, without cutting all the way to the center. Hollow out the core at the top of each apple, leaving a little of the core in the middle to help the apples hold their shape. Neatly peel the top half of each apple, leaving the lower halves unpeeled. Place the apples in a gratin dish or other shallow baking dish in which they will fit without crowding.

2. Sprinkle the peeled parts of the apples lightly with the sugar and cinnamon. Drizzle the grenadine or raspberry syrup over and around the apples; there should be a shallow pool of syrup in the bottom of the dish. Bake the apples until tender but not mushy, anywhere from 35 to 60 minutes, depending on the apples. During the last 10 or 15 minutes, baste the apples once or twice with the syrup in the dish. Remove the pan from the oven and turn on the broiler.

3. Spoon some of the syrup over the tops of the apples. Run them under the broiler, watching carefully, until the syrup just begins to caramelize, usually about 2 minutes. Cool to room temperature before serving.

CRINKLY BAKED PEARS, TRATTORIA-STYLE

In the autumn of 1976, two dear friends and I traveled through Italy for several weeks, spending as much time in small country towns as we did in cities. We explored, excavated, devoured.

Every day we'd pile disheveled out of our car and into a trattoria for lunch. As we were being welcomed and led to a table, I'd notice a shallow ceramic dish of whole baked pears, stems on. Everywhere we'd see them, skins crinkled and shiny in a pool of amber syrup, and I'd wonder how they could be baked for so long without turning mushy, their flavor concentrated into pear essence. Here's how.

Serves 6

1	cup dry Marsala or dry red wine
⅔	cup sugar
2	cloves
1	cinnamon stick
1	strip lemon zest, removed with a vegetable peeler
½	vanilla bean, split lengthwise, or ¼ teaspoon pure vanilla extract
6	firm-ripe pears, preferably Bosc (unpeeled)

1. Preheat the oven to 300 degrees F. Place all of the ingredients except the pears in a shallow gratin or baking dish in which the pears will fit; stir to combine. Stand the pears in the liquid.

2. Bake, basting now and then with the pan juices, for about 2 hours. When the pears are done, they will be tender but not mushy, the skins wrinkled and crinkly and the liquid syrupy. Cool the dish on a wire rack.

3. Remove the spices and lemon zest. Serve the pears warm or at a cool room temperature, spooning a little syrup over them.

PEARS POACHED IN MINT TEA WITH DARK CHOCOLATE SAUCE

The simplest of desserts, with the surprising hint of fresh mint. The idea is from restaurant consultant and author Rozanne Gold. The pears can be served in just a little of their syrup or napped with chocolate sauce.

∽ *Serves 8*

2	quarts water
6	mint tea bags or 2 tablespoons loose mint tea
3	tablespoons honey
4	fresh mint sprigs, torn
6	quarter-size slices peeled fresh ginger, smashed with the side of a knife
1	lemon, halved
8	firm-ripe pears: Bartlett, Anjou or Bosc
	Schrafft's Hot Fudge Sauce (page 613)
	Fresh mint sprigs, for garnish

1. Bring the water to a boil in a wide saucepan or casserole. When it comes to a full boil, turn off the heat and add the tea, honey, mint and ginger. Add the ½ lemon to the water. Let the tea steep for 5 minutes.

2. Peel the pears, rubbing them with the cut side of the other ½ lemon as you peel them. Halve them lengthwise and core them, leaving the stems on. Slip the pear halves into the tea; cover with a round of parchment or wax paper. Bring the tea nearly to a boil. Reduce the heat to low and gently simmer until the pears are just tender but not mushy (the timing varies according to the ripeness of the pears; it can range from 5 to 18 minutes). Let the pears cool in the cooking liquid. Refrigerate if not serving immediately.

3. The pears should be served at a cool room temperature. With a slotted spoon, place 2 pear halves beside one another on each serving plate, the stem end of one next to the rounded bottom of the other. Pour 3 or 4 tablespoons of chocolate sauce over the pears, garnish with mint sprigs and serve.

Lattice-Topped Peach-Berry Pie

Cranberry Crumble with Fall Fruits

Neapolitan Easter Pie

Molded Rice Pudding with Caramel Sauce

Ice Cream Social Peach Ice Cream, Grandmother's Lemon Custard Ice Cream,
Espresso-Cinnamon Ice Cream

Lemon-Molasses Marble Cake

Polish Apple Tart

Caramelized Panettone Bread Pudding

Prune-Filled Pecan-Caramel Sticky Buns

Oven-Steamed Figgy Pudding

Dried Fruit Strudel with Pear-Brandy Custard Sauce

Citrus Wine Jelly

BROILED PEARS WITH WARM CARAMEL SAUCE

An amazingly quick fruit dessert, with full, mellow flavor. If you want to make it even quicker, serve it without the sauce.

Serves 4

Warm Caramel Sauce (page 614)
2   large, firm-ripe pears, preferably Anjou or Bartlett
    Fresh lemon juice
2   tablespoons melted butter
2   tablespoons sugar, or as needed

1. Preheat the broiler, with the rack about 4 inches from the heat. Line a baking sheet with foil; butter the foil lightly. Warm the caramel sauce.

2. Peel the pears. Halve them lengthwise and carefully remove their stems and cores. Rub all of the exposed surfaces with lemon juice to prevent discoloration. With a paring knife, score the rounded sides of the pears in a series of parallel crosswise lines, without cutting all the way through. Arrange the pears, rounded sides up, on the baking sheet. Brush with the melted butter and sprinkle generously with the sugar.

3. Broil the pears just until very lightly golden, 3 to 7 minutes. Spoon a pool of the warm caramel sauce on each of 4 warm plates. Place a pear half, browned side up, on each plate and serve immediately.

WARM BAKED APPLES WITH MACAROON SOUFFLÉ AND COOL CUSTARD

Several years ago, a friend mentioned baked apples stuffed with marzipan and served with vanilla custard. I never tasted them but always remembered the idea. Using crushed amaretti (crisp Italian macaroons available in gourmet shops and Italian markets) adds a haunting flavor.

⌒ *Serves 4*

> 4   Rome or other baking apples
>   Juice of ½ lemon
> 2   tablespoons melted butter
>   Sugar, as needed
> 1½   cups (3 ounces) amaretti
> 2   large egg whites
>   Eggnog Custard Sauce (page 609) or Low-Fat Custard Sauce (page 610)

1. Preheat the oven to 350 degrees F. Peel the apples neatly halfway down, leaving the skin on the bottom halves. Working with a paring knife from the stem end of each apple, carefully cut out the top ⅔ of the core, leaving the bottoms intact. Enlarge the opening in the top until it is 2 or 3 inches wide and very stuffable. Brush the cut surfaces of the apples inside and out with the lemon juice. Brush the cut surfaces of the apples with melted butter; roll the outside edges and tops in sugar, coating lightly. Place the apples in a shallow baking dish; set aside.

2. In a food processor, grind the amaretti to coarse crumbs. Add 1 of the egg whites and pulse just to combine. In a mixing bowl, beat the remaining egg white until nearly stiff. Add the amaretti mixture to the beaten egg white and gently fold together. Spoon this mixture into the apple cavities, dividing it evenly and mounding it slightly. Sprinkle the filling lightly with sugar.

3. Place the baking dish in the oven; pour a small amount of water around the apples to prevent sticking. Bake until the apples are tender and the filling is puffed and lightly browned, about 45 minutes (the timing can vary). Cool slightly. Transfer the apples to a serving bowl and serve warm, surrounded by a pool of the cool custard sauce.

PAVLOVA

This is Australia's contribution to the dessert world: a crunchy meringue shell filled with whipped cream and a rainbow of cut-up fresh fruits that soften the meringue slightly. In England, Pavlova is served everywhere, frequently at dinner parties. The name honors the Russian ballerina Anna Pavlova, legendary for her role in *Swan Lake*. Helen Mayer, a good cook who grew up in New Zealand and now lives in La Jolla, California, shared this recipe.

Serves 6

MERINGUE SHELL

4   large egg whites (about ½ cup), at room temperature
       Pinch salt
½   cup sugar
1   teaspoon balsamic vinegar
½   teaspoon pure vanilla extract
1   tablespoon cornstarch

1   cup heavy cream, well chilled
       Sliced or cut-up assorted fresh fruits (see next page)

1. **MERINGUE SHELL:** Preheat the oven to 400 degrees F. Using a plate as a guide, trace an 8-inch circle onto a sheet of parchment or wax paper. Invert the paper onto a baking pan, and butter the paper lightly; set aside.

2. With an electric mixer or a whisk, beat the egg whites with the salt on medium-high speed until foamy. Gradually beat in the sugar; beat in the vinegar and vanilla. Continue beating until the meringue forms stiff peaks. Sift the cornstarch over the meringue and fold in gently.

3. Heap the meringue onto the parchment paper, swirling it out with the back of a spoon to fill the 8-inch circle, forming high sides around the edge and leaving a wide indentation in the center.

4. Place the baking pan with the meringue in the oven and immediately lower the temperature to 250 degrees. Bake, undisturbed, for 1½ to 2 hours, or until set but still somewhat soft when pressed lightly with a fingertip. Cool the shell completely on a wire rack, about 30 minutes. *(You can bake the meringue early in the day and leave it, loosely covered, at room temperature.)*

Helen Mayer makes several Pavlovas as dessert for her family's first Passover seder, using potato starch instead of cornstarch.

"Necessity is the mother of invention," Helen wrote to me. "The original recipe called for white-wine vinegar to stabilize the foam. I had nothing but balsamic vinegar in my kitchen, and since then, I've continued to use it for its mellow flavor."

5. Shortly before serving, whip the cream in a chilled bowl until nearly stiff. Top the meringue with the whipped cream; arrange the fruit attractively over the top. Serve immediately.

⌒ *Good fruit combinations for Pavlova*
Nectarines, blueberries, kiwis, and raspberries
Peaches, plums, golden raspberries, and blackberries
Mangoes, bananas, oranges, and pink grapefruit
Red currants, blackberries, plums, and strawberries
Apples, pears, grapes, and dried cranberries
Pineapple, passion fruit, and grated coconut

FORGOTTEN PUDDING

In her spacious but comfortable kitchen in Barrington, Rhode Island, Dorothy McCulloch told me about this pudding, which her mother made for years. "Forgotten" is a good name for it—egg whites are beaten into a meringue, spread gently in a large roasting pan and left overnight in a slow oven. This is similar to Pavlova, but the meringue turns out soft and smooth and is cut into puffy squares.

Serves 12

12	large egg whites (about 1½ cups)
1	teaspoon salt
2½	cups sugar
1	teaspoon cream of tartar
1	teaspoon pure vanilla extract
1	cup heavy cream, well chilled
	Sliced fresh fruits, such as strawberries and peeled peaches, for serving

1. Preheat the oven to 450 degrees F. Butter a shallow 13-x-11-inch (or 13-x-9-inch) baking pan.

2. Place the egg whites and salt in a large bowl. With an electric mixer, beat on high speed until foamy. Gradually add the sugar, and then the cream of tartar and vanilla, and continue beating until the egg whites are stiff but not dry.

3. Transfer the meringue to the buttered pan, spreading it evenly with a large rubber spatula. Place in the oven, close the door and immediately turn off the oven. Leave the pan in the oven overnight. Do not peek.

4. To serve, whip the cream until stiff. Spread the cream over the meringue. Refrigerate the pudding for up to 2 hours. Cut into squares and serve with fresh fruit.

Kindred Desserts

Desserts from radically different sources can share close kinship. At Comme Chez Soi in Brussels, Belgium, chef Pierre Wynants makes a signature dessert that's close in spirit, miles away in detail. On my first night of a several-month stay in Europe to hunt for kitchen work, I concluded an unforgettable feast with Wynants' *Ile maison en surprise*: a pillow of soft meringue glazed with caramel, with a rainbow of fresh fruits set like jewels in pools of custard and berry puree. What I ate that night, in a state of solitary rapture, was, in essence, a combination of meringue and fruit similar to Dotty McCulloch's mother's homey Forgotten Pudding.

RECIPES

*Light Cannoli Cream for
  Fresh Fruit*
Plum Fool
Apricot-Amaretto Fool
Lime Syllabub
Cranberry-Raspberry Kissel
Pear Snow
Raspberry Flummery
Apricot Sponge
Citrus Wine Jelly
Jefferson's Tea Cream
Sherry Velvet Cream
Spanish Cream
Modern Almond Blancmange
*Panna Cotta and Poached
  Pears in Merlot Syrup*
Ricotta Bavarian
Mont Blanc
Frozen Scottish Atholl Brose
*Warm Amaretto-Cognac
  Zabaglione*
Strawberry Nonsense
Marie's Vanilla Spongecake
Charlotte Russe

CHAPTER 3

CREAMS, FOOLS AND JELLIES

*L*ike visiting cards and the dodo, dessert creams and jellies have nearly vanished. What links items as disparate as syllabubs (frothy spirit-infused whipped cream), fruit fools (crushed fruit folded into whipped cream), homemade gelatins and Bavarian creams is that they all set, that is, they jell or firm up in some way. (The late novelist Laurie Colwin called these "desserts that quiver.") Many, such as the clean, alabaster white panna cotta from the Piedmont region of Italy, are set with gelatin; others are lightly bound with cornstarch or even oats. Cornstarch holds fruit purees together, without making them "tight" enough to set firmly. All of these desserts are served cold.

All, that is, except one: zabaglione (sabayon), in which eggs are frothed with wine or spirits. Though it can be chilled, zabaglione is best when it's just been whipped and served airy and warm. Its only thickener is eggs, beaten to a foam over simmering water until they trap enough air to triple their original volume.

Quivery creams and crystalline jellies, presented on pedestaled platters and shimmering with the faceted patterns of fancy molds, figured prominently on tables from the 16th century until the early part of the 20th. "Clouted Cream," "Virgin Cream," "Plumb" or "Apricock Cream"—the recipes for cream desserts in early manuscripts and cookbooks go on and on, in endless variety.

So why have we lost them?

One reason is that they too often have been over-gelatinized. No dessert, regardless of how wonderful its flavor, appeals when it's been rubberized to death, especially as our tastes have lightened over the years. But when properly prepared—with lively flavorings and just enough gelatin to set it—a cream dessert, jelly or cake-and-cream assembly, like charlotte russe, can soothe and delight, just as they did in former times.

These dessert creams were brought to America in 1789 by Thomas Jefferson, who returned from his post as Minister to France just two months before the storming of the Bastille set off the French Revolution. (He also brought vanilla beans, macaroni, olive oil, anchovies and several French wines that remain among the best today.)

Jefferson's recipes, some recorded by his chef Julien, and many gathered by his daughter, Martha Jefferson Randolph, who ran his household at Monticello, are so carefully written that you still can cook from them with complete success.

Desserts favored by Jefferson include ice cream, meringues, macaroons, "Blanc Manger" and "Biscuit de Savoye" (the original ladyfingers). Jefferson's tea cream and his wine jelly, both included here, will surprise with their clean, refreshing flavors and voluptuous textures.

The simplest of all of these desserts is Cannoli Cream, nothing more than ricotta cheese whipped until smooth and served over fresh fruit. The fruit selections range from fools and syllabubs, both dating from the 16th century, to berry kissel and flummery, which are both lightly thickened, translucent purees. Purees lightened with beaten egg whites are called fruit snows (now nearly forgotten) or sponges, much like molded fruit puddings.

Molded jellies, another branch of these nearly lost desserts, date back to medieval times. Flavored with wine and/or citrus fruits, they became popular at 16th-century English banquets, when they were served as a dessert course along with preserved fruits and fruit tarts. (Before packaged gelatin mixes were available, these dessert jellies were set with plain gelatin, which, until surprisingly recently, had to be rendered at home. The history of the rise of commercial gelatin is fascinating; see page 100.)

The creams in this chapter progress from straightforward little cupfuls flavored with tea, sherry or almonds to others that are aerated with egg whites (Spanish or snow cream) or, in the case of Bavarian cream, set with gelatin and lightened and enriched with whipped cream.

Many of these desserts are "airy nothings" with fanciful, silly names: Fool is the most common example, but others include

Snow Eggs

Separate 5 eggs and beat the whites until you can turn the vessel bottom upwards without their leaving it. Gradually add 1 tablespoonful of powdered sugar and ½ teaspoonful of any desired flavoring [Jefferson used orange flower or rose water].

Put 2 cups of milk into a saucepan, add 3 tablespoonfuls of sugar, flavoring, and bring slowly to a boil. Drop the first mixture into the milk and poach until well set. Lay them on a wire drainer to drain.

Beat the yolk of 1 egg until thick, stir gradually into the milk. Add a pinch of salt. As soon as the custard thickens pour through a sieve. Put your whites in a serving dish and pour the custard over them. A little wine stirred in is a great improvement.

JAMES
COOK AT MONTICELLO
CA. 1794

A Rum Jelly

At the end of the meal appeared a rum jelly. . . . It was rather threatening at first sight, shaped like a tower with bastions and battlements and smooth slippery walls impossible to scale, garrisoned by red and green cherries and pistachio nuts; but into its transparent and quivering flanks a spoon plunged with astounding ease. By the time the amber-colored fortress reached Francesco Paolo, the sixteen-year-old son, who was served last, it consisted only of shattered walls and hunks of wobbly rubble. Exhilarated by the aroma of rum and the delicate flavor of the multicolored garrison, the Prince enjoyed watching the rapid demolishing of the fortress beneath the assault of his family's appetites.

GIUSEPPE DI LAMPEDUSA
THE LEOPARD
TRANSLATED BY
ARCHIBALD COLQUHOUN
1958; 1960

flummery, slip, whim-wham, tipsy parson or kickshaws (from *quelque chose*, French for "something").

For centuries, they represented the height of culinary artifice, disguised to look like other things. Today's devilishly clever cookbook authors who mold chocolate in the shape of furled cabbage leaves might be surprised to realize they are perpetuating a long-held tradition. For example, "Cabbedg-Cream," a curiosity in which a creamy froth of milk flavored with rose water, nutmeg and musk is gathered in 10 small earthen pans or bowls, then piled "that it may lie round and high like a cabbage," was described in great detail in 1673 by Hannah Woolley in London.

In *The Experienced English Housekeeper* (London, first published 1773), Elizabeth Raffald gives instructions for molding a starch-thickened flummery into "Gilded Fish," "Hen and Chickens," "Cribbage Cards" and "Eggs and Bacon."

This art of disguised desserts finds its most convoluted expression in the work of Alexis Soyer, the French-born chef of The Reform Club in England. Soyer detailed instructions for trompe-l'oeil dessert creams masquerading as Leg and Chops of Mutton and, his crowning glory, Wild Boar's Head.

LIGHT CANNOLI CREAM FOR FRESH FRUIT

This probably holds the record as the quickest of all recipes in the book. In a food processor, it takes less than 30 seconds. It's so luxuriously smooth that no one will suspect that it's made with ricotta cheese, which is what renders it remarkably low in fat.

The idea, a radically lightened version of the filling of the deep-fried Sicilian pastry called cannoli, originally came from my friend Johanne Killeen, co-owner of Al Forno restaurant in Providence, Rhode Island. When I ran a restaurant on Martha's Vineyard, I served this cream over mixed ripe berries. It quickly became our most popular dessert, and we made it in several-gallon batches. It's also good over a slice of plain cake, a mixture of berries or a mixture of cut-up pears, bananas and grapes tossed with a splash of orange juice.

If you can get freshly made ricotta, leave out the liqueur and flavor the cream with just a touch of sugar, orange zest and vanilla—and let the sweet, clean flavor of the ricotta shine through.

✎ *Makes about 2 cups*

1   pound (2 cups) ricotta cheese, preferably freshly made
     (available at cheese shops and Italian markets)
2   tablespoons milk or cream, if needed
⅓   cup sugar, or to taste
1½   teaspoons pure vanilla extract
     Grated zest of ½ orange
2   tablespoons amaretto, Cointreau or Frangelico (optional)

1. Place the ricotta cheese in a food processor and pulse briefly. If the ricotta seems dry, add the milk or cream and pulse until the cheese is nearly smooth. Add the sugar and vanilla and process, scraping the mixture from the sides of the bowl, until perfectly smooth and satiny. Add the orange zest and the optional liqueur; taste and adjust all of the flavorings.

2. Transfer the cannoli cream to a glass serving dish. Cover and refrigerate until thickened, at least 1 hour. Serve with fresh fruit.

✎ *Variation*

BLACK AND WHITE CANNOLI CREAM: Once the ricotta is smooth, add 2 tablespoons coarsely chopped semisweet chocolate or chocolate morsels and pulse until the chocolate is broken up.

ABOUT FOOLS

*F*ool—does it mean "nitwit"? While dessert names veer towards frivolity, some origins aren't as clear as they might seem. Take the fool, for example, an English dessert with references dating back to before 1600. It's been suggested that the word may not connote "foolish" but may be derived from the French *fouler*—to crush. It seems to make sense: A fool is a puree or mash of stewed fresh fruit, often gooseberries or other berries, folded into whipped cream.

But all it takes to dispel this oft-repeated etymological explanation is a quick check in the *Oxford English Dictionary*. This supposed "derivation from *fouler* to crush," says the OED, "is not only baseless, but inconsistent with the early use of the word." The word must have been in the foolish spirit after all.

The first surviving recipes for fools contained no fruit—these fools were creams: A 1598 description mentions "a kinde of clouted creame called a foole or a trifle." A 1685 recipe for "Norfolk fool" is made with cream, egg yolks, bread crumbs and cinnamon, but no crushed fruit—a far cry from the weightless, cool fruit-and-cream in a glass that fools later became and still are.

An interesting side note is that creamy desserts like fools and trifles, so popular in the 15th and 16th centuries, were considered strictly rural fare, not worthy of a sophisticated table. But the 18th century saw the fashionable rise of dishes rich with butter and cream.

Heady froth that's as much fruit as cream, fools are still a popular English dessert. Aside from the traditional fruits—gooseberries, greengage plums, raspberries—fools can be made with any fruit that can be mashed or crushed: blueberries and blackberries, purple plums, apricots, mangoes, rhubarb. If you'd like to try a streamlined version, the cream can be replaced with yogurt or with yogurt lightened with just a touch of whipped cream.

"My Mother . . . could have taught thee how to a made . . . fritters, pancakes . . . and the rarest fools."

JOHN DAY
THE BLIND-BEGGAR OF BEDNAL-GREEN
(CA. 1600)

PLUM FOOL

This fool layers the fruit and cream in goblets, instead of folding them together.

Serves 6 to 8

    2   pounds ripe red or purple plums (9-12 plums), stoned
        and sliced
    ½   cup red currant jelly
  ⅓-½   cup packed light or dark brown sugar, depending on the
        plums' sweetness
    1   long strip orange zest
    1   cinnamon stick
    1   cup heavy cream, or 1 cup crème fraîche (page 624)
        plus 2 tablespoons milk, chilled
    ½   teaspoon pure vanilla extract
        Toasted almonds, for garnish

1. Place the plum slices in a heavy nonreactive saucepan with the currant jelly, brown sugar, orange zest and cinnamon stick. Bring the mixture to a boil, stirring occasionally. Boil gently over low heat, mashing some of the slices against the side of the pan as they cook, until the plums are very tender, about 15 minutes. Remove the pan from the heat. Allow to cool slightly.

2. Mash some more of the slices so that only about ¼ of them remain intact. Cool the fruit completely; remove the orange zest and cinnamon stick. (Put the fruit through a food mill if you'd like a smoother fool.) Cover and chill.

3. Up to 2 hours before serving, whip the cream and vanilla until thick but not stiff. Layer the plum mixture and cream alternately in a glass serving bowl, wine glasses or goblets, beginning with a layer of plums and ending with a layer of cream. Chill. Sprinkle with the almonds just before serving.

A Norfolk-Fool

Take a quart of thick Sweet Cream, and set it a boiling in a clear scoured Skillet, with some large Mace, and whole Cinamon; having boiled a little while, take the yolks of five or six Eggs beaten well, and put to it; being off the fire take out the Cinamon and Mace, the Cream being pretty thick, slice a fine Manchet [light French bread] into thin slices as many as will cover the bottom of the Dish, and then pour on the Cream; trim the Dish with carved Sippets, and stick it with Sliced Dates; and scrape Sugar all over it.

HANNAH WOOLLEY
*The Gentlewoman's
Companion; or, A Guide
to the Female Sex*
LONDON, 1673

APRICOT-AMARETTO FOOL

Simmering dried apricots results in a more concentrated puree than using the fresh fruit, which can often be slightly bitter.

⤳ *Serves 6*

½	pound (about 1½ cups, fairly loosely packed) dried apricots
2⅓	cups cold water
¾	cup sugar
1¼	cups heavy cream, well chilled
¼	cup plus 1 tablespoon confectioners' sugar
¼	cup amaretto, or to taste
¼	teaspoon almond extract (optional)
¼	cup sliced almonds, lightly toasted, for serving

1. Combine the apricots, water and sugar in a heavy nonreactive saucepan; bring to a boil over medium heat. Cover, reduce the heat to low and simmer until the apricots are tender, about 10 minutes. Remove from the heat; set aside to cool slightly.

2. Puree the apricots and syrup in 2 batches in a food processor or blender. Press the puree through a sieve into a large mixing bowl, pressing the mixture with the back of a spoon or a large rubber spatula to extract as much puree as possible. Cover and refrigerate until slightly chilled but not cold.

3. Beat the cream until thickened. Add the confectioners' sugar and continue to beat until the cream forms soft peaks. Gently fold in the amaretto and the optional almond extract.

4. Stir the apricot puree once or twice to loosen it. Gently fold the whipped cream into the puree, leaving clearly visible streaks of the apricot and cream; do not blend thoroughly. Carefully transfer to a glass serving bowl, 6 wine glasses or 6 goblets. Cover and refrigerate until chilled, at least 1 hour. Serve the fool garnished with the toasted almonds.

ABOUT SYLLABUB

This is the Deep South dessert that is supposed to start Southern beaux and belles on their drunken downfall, since it is so mild that children are allowed to have it, thus acquiring a taste for the flavor of all liquors. The idea is silly, and the syllabub is delicious. The moral damage is negligible.

MARJORIE KINNAN RAWLINGS
CROSS CREEK COOKERY, 1942

*T*ake one milking paill" begins a handwritten recipe for syllabub in a 17th-century Englishwoman's collection. When new warm milk was added directly to a basin or a syllabub bowl full of cider, ale or wine and left to settle, a frothy curd would rise to the top. Sometimes topped with cream, this potent concoction was drunk from a glass.

Syllabub peaked in popularity in England in the 17th and 18th centuries, when it was the spirited drink of choice at festive country occasions. When made with a higher proportion of cream, the dessert version of syllabub stayed solid without separating.

Generally called "everlasting syllabub," this heady cream dessert was not only served on its own but was also used, instead of meringue, as the frothy topping for floating island (see page 155), or as the halo over a bowlful of trifle, which eventually eclipsed syllabub in popularity as England's favorite party dessert.

To Make a Sillybub

*T*ake one quarter of a pound of currans beinge well washed and picked, you must boyle them in a little more than one quarter of a pint of white wine, and when they go plump gett them away till very go cold, you must boiyle them in a sylver spollott, and then you may put them out into your syllabub pott, put in your sugar and a litle more white-wine and one spoonfull or two of sack, when you are a milkinge of your milk in a syllabub pott then you must go still a stiringe of it up with rosemary and leammon-peale about it.

ANONYMOUS
*COLLECTION OF MEDICAL
AND COOKERY RECIPES*
HANDWRITTEN FOLIO
ENGLAND, 17TH CENTURY

Lime Syllabub

This cream is at once light and frothy, yet tart with wine and citrus—a delicate balancing act of textures and flavors. It's based on Eliza Acton's "Very Superior Whipped Syllabub" from *Modern Cookery* (London, 1878); she notes that syllabubs are "considered less wholesome without a portion of brandy."

⌒ *Serves 4*

Grated zest and juice of 2 limes
½   cup dry sherry
3   tablespoons brandy
½   cup sugar
1   cup heavy cream, well chilled
Additional lime zest, cut into fine julienne strips, for garnish

1. Combine the grated lime zest, lime juice, sherry, 1 tablespoon of the brandy and the sugar in a bowl. Allow to steep for at least 1 hour.

2. Begin to beat the mixture with a whisk or an electric mixer; very gradually add the cream in a thin stream. Continue to beat, until the mixture thickens and becomes light and fluffy. When the mixture is very thick and forms soft peaks (but is not completely stiff), beat in the remaining 2 tablespoons brandy.

3. Spoon the syllabub into tall parfait or wine glasses and chill. Serve garnished with the julienne strips of lime.

⌒ *Variations*

Lemon or Tangerine Syllabub: Substitute an equal amount of lemon or tangerine juice and zest and proceed as directed.

The delicious syllabub . . . a familiar childhood treat . . . the fragile whip of cream in a little glass, concealing within its innocent white froth a powerful alcoholic punch . . ."

Elizabeth David
"Syllabubs and Fruit Fools"
From *An Omelette and a Glass of Wine*
1969; 1984

CRANBERRY-RASPBERRY KISSEL

The name for this dessert is derived from the Russian word *kislyi*, or "sour." A thickened, translucent fruit pudding, this is deep scarlet, refreshingly sweet-tart, with intense berry flavor, and it's quick and easy to do.

⌒ *Serves about 6*

1	bag (12 ounces; about 3 cups) fresh or frozen (not thawed) cranberries, picked over
¾-1	cup sugar, to taste
	Grated zest of 1 large orange
1	cup fresh orange juice
2	teaspoons cornstarch
1	tablespoon cold water
½	pint raspberries
	Heavy cream or sour cream, for serving (optional)

1. Combine the cranberries, sugar, orange zest and orange juice in a nonreactive saucepan over medium heat. Cover and bring the mixture to a boil, stirring occasionally. Simmer the cranberries, covered, until they pop open, about 20 minutes.

2. Press the cranberry mixture through a medium sieve into a bowl, pushing all of the pulp through. Rinse out the saucepan, return the mixture to the pan and bring back to a boil.

3. In a small cup, dissolve the cornstarch in the cold water. Add to the saucepan and simmer, stirring, until the mixture thickens slightly, 2 to 3 minutes. Stir in the raspberries and remove the pan from the heat. Let cool, stirring now and then. Spoon the mixture into wine glasses or sundae dishes and refrigerate.

4. Serve the kissel cold, with a little cream poured over each serving or with sour cream as an accompaniment, if you like.

PEAR SNOW

A fruit snow is a smooth blend of pureed fruit (usually apple-sauce), folded together with beaten egg whites and served chilled. Apple snow recipes appear in most 19th-century American cookbooks. The origins of this dessert are probably English.

More elaborate is "Apple Floating Island," in which a pool of custard is topped with apple snow. A German version is called *Apfelschnee*, a direct translation of "apple snow."

Why have we lost fruit snows? This version, made with ripe pears, is cool and light, one of the airiest of all puddings and creams, and packed with the flavor of fresh fruit. It's low in fat, too.

⌒ *Serves 4 to 6*

3   ripe pears or 4 apples, well washed (leave the peels on), cored and coarsely chopped
½   cup pear or apple cider (pear cider is available at farmers' markets) or apple juice
¾   teaspoon ground cinnamon
¼   teaspoon ground cardamom, or to taste
2   teaspoons (slightly less than 1 envelope) unflavored gelatin
¼   cup cold water
3   large egg whites (for a note on egg safety, see page 23)
     Pinch salt
     Juice of ½ lemon, or to taste

1. Place the fruit, cider or apple juice, cinnamon and cardamom in a nonreactive saucepan. Cover and bring to a boil. Boil very gently, stirring occasionally, until the fruit is very tender, usually 25 to 30 minutes.

2. Meanwhile, in a small bowl, sprinkle the gelatin over the cold water and stir until combined; set aside.

3. When the fruit is tender, force the hot mixture through a food mill or strainer into a mixing bowl, forcing as much pulp through as possible. Discard the peels. Immediately scrape the gelatin mixture into the hot puree, stirring until the gelatin dissolves. Set aside to cool to lukewarm.

4. Whisk the egg whites and salt until nearly stiff but not dry. Fold the lemon juice and about ¼ of the beaten egg whites into the fruit mixture; gently fold in the remaining whites. The heat of

the puree will cook the egg whites slightly. If the mixture doesn't fold together evenly, chill the bowl for a few minutes and fold gently with just a few more strokes.

5. Spoon the snow into goblets or custard cups and chill before serving.

NOTE: You can also cover the goblets or cups and freeze the snow. Let it soften in the refrigerator for about 15 minutes before serving. Frozen, this is a very airy, refreshing dessert, with grainy crystals that burst with fruit flavor.

ABOUT FLUMMERY

"I know you too well to be deceived by your fine flummery tales . . ."

MRS. ELIZA PARSONS
MYSTERIOUS VISIT, 1802

Flummery is a generic term for early, simple starch-thickened puddings. In the tradition of desserts with silly names, the word means "mere flattery or empty compliment; nonsense, humbug, empty trifling." More substantial cousins to syllabubs and creams, flummeries are thickened variously with oatmeal, flour, ground almonds, hartshorn or isinglass (both early forms of gelatin).

Later flummery recipes are something else—thickened fruit puddings. Usually made in America with blackberries, blueberries or raspberries, fruit flummeries are lighter than their predecessors, bound with either cornstarch or gelatin (or some precursor thereof).

Fruit porridges like this have been known since medieval times. According to Scandinavian food authority Beatrice Ojakangas, fruit soups, whipped berry puddings and porridges comprise most of the everyday desserts in Finland. The German dessert *rote grütze* ("red grits"), a combination of red currants and red raspberries (and sometimes other red fruits) is a kind of flummery, as is the Danish *rød grød med fløde* ("red grits with cream").

Raspberry Flummery

This is a dessert of real delicacy; it's light and cool on the palate, with a clear ruby color and deep berry flavor. I've made it with strawberries, too; this preparation seems to heighten their flavor. The recipe is a reinterpretation of a handwritten English manuscript, a personal recipe collection typically kept by women of the upper classes. It represents a radical lightening of the flummery tradition.

Serves 4

1	pint raspberries or hulled strawberries (about 2⅔ cups whole berries)
½	cup sugar, or to taste, depending on the berries' sweetness
1¼	teaspoons (½ envelope) unflavored gelatin
2	tablespoons cold water
	Heavy cream, whipped cream, vanilla yogurt or vanilla frozen yogurt, for serving

1. In a bowl, combine the raspberries or strawberries with the sugar, stirring to crush slightly; let stand for about 15 minutes. Sprinkle the gelatin over the cold water in a small saucepan; let stand until softened, about 5 minutes.

2. Place the berry mixture in a nonreactive saucepan and bring to a boil, stirring to dissolve the sugar. Boil, stirring constantly, until softened and juicy, 3 to 4 minutes.

3. Heat the gelatin mixture over low heat, stirring until the gelatin dissolves.

4. With a slotted spoon, remove ¼ to ⅓ of the berries and set them aside. Stir the gelatin mixture into the remaining berry mixture. Strain the mixture, pushing all possible pulp through a fine sieve into a bowl. Stir in the reserved berries. If you'd like to serve the dessert unmolded, rinse the custard cups or ramekins with cold water before filling them with the flummery; I prefer to serve it in individual glass dishes or wine glasses. Spoon into the dishes or glasses and chill until cold.

5. Serve the flummery cold, passing cream to pour over it or with a spoonful of whipped cream or yogurt on top.

Raspberry Flummery

Put on the fire a pint of raspberries (or if not in season a pound of preserved ones) with half a pint of vinegar. Let them boil 3 or 4 minutes, stirring them constantly. Then strain it through a hair sieve. Dissolve one ounce of Isinglass in half a pint of water, and sweeten it with ¾ pound of sugar; mix the whole together, set it in the fire and when it comes to a boil, strain it through a sieve—when nearly thick, put it into a shape.

Maria Forde
Memorandum Book
Containing
Cookery Recipes
England, ca. Late 18th-
Early 19th Century

APRICOT SPONGE

This light, molded dessert sings with clear fruit flavor; it's refreshing and low in fat. Fruit "sponges," "fluffs," "flips" and "whips" are all genteel niceties that we've pretty much lost. A sponge is a molded dessert lightened with beaten egg whites. These and other molded desserts were sometimes called "shapes." You can unmold this, but I like it better served in parfait glasses.

⌒ Serves 6 to 8

1½	cups (about ½ pound) dried apricots
1½	cups water
1¼	teaspoons (½ envelope) unflavored gelatin
½	cup cold water
¼	cup sugar
12	gratings nutmeg
¼	teaspoon almond extract
1-2	tablespoons amaretto (optional)
3	large egg whites (for a note on egg safety, see page 23)

1. In a nonreactive saucepan, bring the apricots and the 1½ cups water to a boil. Lower the heat, cover and simmer the apricots until soft, about 10 minutes. Set aside for 30 minutes.

2. Puree the mixture in a food processor or blender until smooth. Transfer the puree to a bowl.

3. Sprinkle the gelatin over the cold water in a small saucepan; set aside to soften for 5 minutes. Add the sugar and stir over medium-low heat until the sugar and gelatin dissolve. Add this warm mixture to the apricot puree and let cool, stirring occasionally, until the mixture begins to thicken, without setting, usually about 20 minutes.

4. Add the nutmeg, almond extract and optional amaretto and beat briefly with an egg beater or a whisk until the mixture becomes slightly opaque and paler in color, almost white, several minutes.

5. In a bowl, beat the egg whites until stiff. Add the whites to the puree and fold them together just until blended. Pour the mixture into a lightly oiled mold or, preferably, into parfait or wine glasses, and refrigerate. Unmold (if in a mold) and serve the dessert icy cold.

Peach Sponge

1½	cup peach puree
½	ounce gelatin in ½ cup water
¼	cup granulated sugar
	Whites 3 eggs
6	drops extract of bitter almonds
12	gratings nutmeg

Put sugar and gelatin in a ... kettle and stir over fire until dissolved, put peaches in a bowl and add hot mixture, add nutmeg and almond after it is slightly congealed, beat with Dover egg beater until almost white, then beat whites stiff and add to mixture, beat again till well mixed, rinse mould with cold water and pour in mixture, serve it icy cold and serve with whipped, plain cream or vanilla sauce.

MRS. HENRY W.
DARLING
HANDWRITTEN
MANUSCRIPT
SCHENECTADY, NEW
YORK, CA. 1882–93

To Make Jelly

Take out the great Bones of four Calves Feet, and put the Feet into a Pot with ten Quarts of Water, three Ounces of Hartshorn, three Ounces of Isinglass, a Nutmeg quarter'd, four Blades of Mace; then boil this till it comes to two Quarts, and strain it through a Flannel-Bag, let it stand twenty-four Hours, then scrape off all the Fat from the Top very clean, then slice it, and put to it the Whites of six Eggs beaten to Froth, boil it a little, and strain it again through a Flannel-Bag, then run the Jelly into little high Glasses . . . You must colour Red with Cochineal, Green with Spinage, Yellow with Saffron, Blue with Syrup of Violets, White with thick Cream, and sometimes the Jelly by itself. You may add Orange-flower Water, or Wine and Sugar, and Lemon if you please, but this is all Fancy.

HANNAH GLASSE
*THE ART OF COOKERY,
MADE PLAIN AND EASY*
LONDON, 1747

ABOUT MOLDED JELLIES

Too many over-gelatinized desserts ("It's alive!!") and artificially flavored packaged versions have given gelatin-set desserts a bad name. But as long as today's easy-to-use gelatin is used with discretion, these desserts can be delicate and tasty. Just a little too much, though, can turn a limpid, quivering jelly or softly set cream to rubber.

In the days before you could sprinkle granulated gelatin from an envelope (which became available only around the turn of this century), gelatin had to be rendered at home, a culinary process possibly unmatched for sheer labor intensity. First, the home cook had to extract the gelatin from calves' feet or other natural sources, a process that required many hours of slow simmering. (Gelatin was also rendered from another natural source, hartshorn, or shavings from the horns of stag red deer.) The resulting viscous liquid was then clarified with egg whites and strained through muslin. To make a dessert jelly, the gelatin was then combined with wine, sugar, lemon and orange juice and spices.

Medieval jellies, like puddings, might contain both meat and fruit flavors in the same dish. Jellies didn't split into separate sweet (often layered in variegated colors) and savory (generally meat) versions until the days of Tudor or Stuart banquets in the 16th century. At this time, dessert jellies emerged as the third and final course of a formal dinner, served along with fruit tarts, marmalades and preserved fruits and marchpane (marzipan).

Over the years, desserts have been stabilized with other naturally jelling substances. One was isinglass, the pure gelatin extracted from the bladders of fish, especially sturgeon. Others, many of them still used today, include agar-agar, Irish moss, Iceland moss and *kanten*, Japanese seaweed. American cookbook author-teacher Mrs. Sarah Tyson Rorer, writing in 1917, advised that agar-agar "has a decided advantage over animal gelatin in the fact that it congeals quickly without ice and is less liable to contamination." While agar-agar has the benefit of being free of meat products (welcome to vegetarians and those who keep kosher, who cannot use animal-derived gelatin), it has never caught on for widespread use. You can find it at health food stores.

The story of commercially available gelatin for dessert-making starts in 1845, when Peter Cooper, inventor of the locomotive "Tom Thumb" and founder of Cooper Union in New York City, which still provides free college education, obtained the first patent for a gelatin dessert. He described his dessert as a

transparent, concentrated substance containing all the ingredients fitting it for table use in a portable form, and requiring only the addition of hot water to dissolve it, so that it may be poured into moulds and when cold will be fit for use.

Cooper didn't do much with marketing his gelatin, however, and it wasn't until 1897 that Jell-O, an instant flavored gelatin, appeared on the market. Only in 1902 did sales of Jell-O take off.

In the meantime, unflavored gelatin became widely available in 1889 when Charles B. Knox founded the Knox Gelatine Company in Johnstown, New York. Knox was a tireless promoter of his "pure, plain and sparkling" product, and his booth at the 1904 St. Louis World's Fair helped make Knox gelatin a household name. The manufacturing process was similar to one used when making stock, in which bones are simmered to extract the gelatin from their collagen, a protein substance.

On a commercial scale, the collagen is first stripped of its mineral salts, lime and acids and is diluted and filtered twice to purify and clarify it. It is then evaporated, concentrated and formed into thin strips or "noodles" of pure gelatin. These are chilled, dried and milled to produce the granulated gelatin we use today.

With the perfection of commercial gelatin and the appearance of artificially flavored mixes, the from-scratch jellies suddenly became history.

Remember? "What's for dessert? What's for dessert? What's for dessert? J-E-L-L-O!"

TELEVISION
COMMERCIAL
1950s

Antiwar Jello

At a party in Cambridge, Massachusetts, in the fall of 1967, I met the well-known songwriter Tom Lehrer . . . We discussed the war in Vietnam, of course, and that got him reminiscing over his experiences in the Army from 1954 to 1956, during which he said his greatest accomplishment was to find a way around the Army regulation that forbids alcoholic beverages at the noncommissioned officers' annual Christmas party.

This he did by perfecting alcoholic Jell-O. He tried various flavors and liquors and settled on orange Jell-O and vodka. You mix the package with one cup of hot water, as you would to make ordinary Jell-O; stir in one cup of cold vodka, and refrigerate. On Christmas Mr. Lehrer and his comrades carried 17 trays of it past the guards.

As it is not a beverage, you cannot be properly said to get drunk on it. But as it is 40- or even 50-proof Jell-O, you can quickly get quite wiggled.

MICHAEL FERBER
LETTER TO
THE NEW YORK TIMES
1991

CITRUS WINE JELLY

Rediscover how refreshing a molded dessert jelly can be with this recipe adapted from one of Thomas Jefferson's. Gleaming on a pedestaled stand, a wine jelly was once the centerpiece of the finale to a grand table; they're included in all 19th- and early 20th-century cookbooks.

You can make this jelly with white wine instead of red; choose one with some fruitiness, such as a Riesling. And you can suspend thin lemon and orange slices in the jelly; slip them in when the jelly has thickened but not yet set.

Makes about 4 cups; serves 6 to 8

2	envelopes (about 5¼ teaspoons) unflavored gelatin
1	cup cold water
½	cup sugar, or to taste, depending on the wine
2	cups full-bodied dry red wine
⅓	cup Madeira (optional, but good)
¾	cup fresh orange juice
	Juice of 1 lemon
	Thin orange or lemon slices (optional)

1. In a nonreactive saucepan off the heat, sprinkle the gelatin over the cold water. Let stand until softened, about 5 minutes. Stir over low heat until the gelatin dissolves.

2. Stir in the sugar, wine and optional Madeira and bring to a simmer, stirring to dissolve the sugar. Transfer the mixture to a bowl and stir in the citrus juices; set aside to cool to lukewarm.

3. Rinse a 4- to 5-cup mold with cold water; pour the gelatin mixture into the mold; chill until set, at least 2 hours. If you'd like to suspend citrus slices in the jelly, do so when it is thick, but not yet set, usually after less than 1 hour in the refrigerator.

4. To unmold, run the tip of a knife around the edge of the gelatin to loosen the seal. Invert onto a serving plate sprinkled with a few drops of cold water and serve.

JEFFERSON'S TEA CREAM

For the past few years, chefs have been using tea to flavor desserts like sorbets and custards and to poach pears and other fresh fruits. This is actually a revival of an old practice from the days before commercial extracts were available, when tea was widely used as a dessert flavoring.

This tea cream is based on a dessert from Monticello, which was itself modeled after a French recipe. It's extraordinary: The cream has a beautifully smooth texture, with a lucid, shimmering surface that looks almost liquid and quivers when you spoon it up. With just a suspicion of tea flavor, it's pleasantly astringent and not too sweet. By serving tea cream in individual cups the way this one is, you can use less gelatin than in creams that are unmolded.

Black currant, jasmine or Earl Grey teas all work well here.

Serves 4

    3   cups milk
    1   envelope (about 2½ teaspoons) unflavored gelatin
    1   rounded tablespoon tea leaves or 3 tea bags
    ¼   cup plus 2 tablespoons sugar
        Pinch salt

1. Bring 2¾ cups of the milk to a boil in a nonreactive saucepan. Meanwhile, place the remaining ¼ cup cold milk in a small cup or bowl and sprinkle the gelatin over it. Set aside until the gelatin softens, about 5 minutes.

2. When the milk comes to a boil, stir in the tea. Add the softened gelatin, sugar and salt; stir to dissolve the gelatin and sugar. Let the tea steep for 3 to 5 minutes, tasting until it is as strong as you like it.

3. Strain the mixture through a very fine sieve (preferably lined with a double layer of dampened cheesecloth) into a measuring cup or pitcher with a spout. Cool the mixture to room temperature.

4. Pour the cream into four 6- to 8-ounce goblets or ramekins, or into a 1-quart glass serving bowl. Cover and refrigerate until the cream sets, at least 2 hours. Serve cold.

SHERRY VELVET CREAM

This simple cream, adapted from an old English recipe, with both the gelatin and wine reduced to a minimum, is very light, with a silky texture, clean on the spoon. There's just enough sherry to make it interesting and "adult" and just enough lemon to lift the flavor. Serve this with a crisp cookie, such as Brown Sugar Shortbread Wafers (page 258).

Sherry was one of the principal dessert flavorings before the days of readily available extracts (vanilla extract wasn't widely sold in American markets until the late 1840s to 1850). Like other fortified wines, sherry was referred to as "sack" (from the Spanish word *saca*, literally, "removed"), meaning an exported wine.

For years, sherry was overused in trifles and other desserts. That's a shame, because its golden, toasted nuances can grace desserts with a fragrant depth of flavor. You can use dry (fino) or medium-dry (amontillado) or sweet cream sherry in this recipe; Madeira or Port also work fine. Adjust the sugar to taste.

∽ *Serves 6*

1	cup dry or medium-dry sherry
1	envelope (about 2½ teaspoons) unflavored gelatin
⅔	cup sugar
	Strips of zest and juice of 2 lemons
1	cup heavy cream
1	cup milk

1. Place ½ cup of the sherry in a nonreactive saucepan, and sprinkle the gelatin over it. Set aside until the gelatin softens, about 5 minutes. Stir over medium-low heat until the gelatin dissolves. Add the remaining ½ cup sherry and the sugar and bring to a simmer, stirring. Simmer, uncovered, stirring, for 3 minutes. Add the lemon zest and juice and set aside until cool to room temperature.

2. Strain the mixture into a mixing bowl; whisk in the cream and milk until combined. Transfer the mixture to a measuring cup or pitcher with a spout. Pour into six 4-ounce goblets or ramekins, or into a 1-quart glass serving bowl. Cover and refrigerate until the cream sets, at least 2 hours. Serve cold.

To Make a Sack Creame

Set a quart of Cream on the fire, when it is boyled, drop in a spoonfull of Sack, and stirre it well the while that it curd not, so do till you have dropped in six spoonfulls, then season it with Sugar, Nutmeg, and strong water.

W. M.
A SERVANT TO QUEEN
HENRIETTA MARIA,
WIFE OF CHARLES I
OF ENGLAND
*THE QUEENS CLOSET
OPENED*
LONDON, 1655

SPANISH CREAM
(SNOW CREAM)

Spanish cream is a delicious white custard that separates as it cools into a fluffy layer on top and a smooth, glassy one underneath. The cream is good on its own, or you can set off its whiteness with colorful fruit.

⁓ Serves 6

2	envelopes (about 5¼ teaspoons) unflavored gelatin
2½	cups milk
3	large eggs, separated (for a note on egg safety, see page 23)
½	cup sugar
	Pinch salt
1	teaspoon pure vanilla extract
	Fresh fruit, Raspberry Sauce (page 617) or Madeira Dried Fruit Compote (page 77), for serving (optional)

1. In a small cup, sprinkle the gelatin over ½ cup of the milk and let stand until softened, about 5 minutes.

2. Bring the remaining 2 cups milk to a simmer in a heavy nonreactive saucepan. In a bowl, whisk the egg yolks with the sugar and salt just until well blended. Gradually beat in the hot milk. Return the mixture to the saucepan and cook over low heat, stirring, until the custard thickens slightly and coats the back of a spoon, about 7 minutes. Do not allow to boil.

3. Remove the pan from the heat; stir in the softened gelatin mixture and the vanilla until very smooth. Strain the mixture through a sieve into a bowl.

4. Beat the egg whites until nearly stiff; fold the beaten whites into the custard mixture. Pour the mixture into a 1-quart dessert mold rinsed with cold water. Cover and chill until set, at least 2 hours.

5. Run the tip of a knife around the edge of the cream. Unmold onto a serving plate and serve cold, with fresh fruit, fruit sauce or compote, if you like.

NOTE: If you prefer a smooth cream throughout, in step 3, chill the custard mixture, stirring now and then, until it is cool and starts to thicken. Fold in the beaten egg whites and continue as directed.

What's in a Name?

Recipes for Spanish cream show up everywhere in old English and American cookbooks, including Shaker recipe collections.

The name is a mystery: There is nothing Spanish about this dessert. Similar creams are named variously "Charleston Snow Cream" and "New England Quaking Custard."

This Spanish cream is based on a Shaker recipe from the late Eldress Bertha Lindsay; she credits the recipe to *Pictorial Review Standard Cookbook.*

MODERN ALMOND BLANCMANGE

This blancmange is pure white, wonderfully airy and richly flavored with almonds. It's firm enough to unmold, but still creamy. Make this in ½-cup ramekins or other individual molds, unmold and serve, surrounded with fresh fruit. The fruit should be a little tart to cut the richness of the almonds and cream: A combination of sliced peaches, raspberries and a few blackberries or blueberries is ideal.

Jean-Louis Gerin, a native of Annecy in the French Alps, adapted this recipe from one of Escoffier's and served it in celebration of the Bicentennial of the French Revolution at his Restaurant Jean-Louis in Greenwich, Connecticut.

Serves about 8

⅓ cup plus 1¼ cups heavy cream or crème fraîche (which adds a slightly tarter taste; page 624)

¼ cup cold water

1 envelope (about 2½ teaspoons) unflavored gelatin

1½ cups (about 4½ ounces) blanched, sliced or slivered almonds

⅔ cup sugar

4 teaspoons kirsch or amaretto, or to taste
  Fresh fruits, for serving

1. In a small saucepan, combine the ⅓ cup cream or crème fraîche and the cold water. Sprinkle the gelatin over the surface; let stand until the gelatin softens, about 5 minutes.

2. Stir the mixture over low heat until the gelatin dissolves; set aside.

3. Meanwhile, pulse the almonds and sugar in a food processor until the almonds are very finely ground. When the gelatin mixture has cooled slightly, stir in the kirsch or amaretto and the ground almond mixture.

4. Whip the remaining 1¼ cups cream or crème fraîche until it forms soft peaks (do not overbeat). Fold the cream into the almond mixture, about ⅓ at a time. Rinse a 6- to 8-cup mold or eight 4-ounce ramekins in cold water; pour in the mixture. Cover with plastic wrap (the wrap shouldn't touch the cream mixture) and refrigerate for 2 hours or overnight.

5. To serve, run the tip of a knife around the edge of the mold. Dip the mold quickly in and out of hot water. Invert the mold onto a moistened plate and unmold. Serve the blancmange surrounded with the fruit.

ABOUT BLANCMANGE

*B*lancmange is a molded custard thickened with ground almonds. As with creams and jellies, once the old-fashioned versions are lightened, the result is delectable. With a food processor, you can put one together in a flash.

Blanc-manger (the earlier term; literally, "to eat white") probably has a longer history than any other dessert, except fruit picked right from the tree. Recipes for it appear in medieval manuscripts, when the dish was not sweet and was made with a pulverized capon breast and almonds.

Making blancmange involved intense manual labor, blanching almonds by hand (the word *blanch* means to whiten), grinding them to a paste in a mortar (again, by hand), while gradually moistening them with milk, and simmering the mixture to extract the flavor. The milk was then squeezed through a cloth to extract all of the almond essence.

By the 17th century, blancmange had become a dessert; an English jellied version arrived in the 18th century. Blancmange recipes appear everywhere, in virtually every old French, English and American cookbook, with variations in color and thickening. In fact, the term blancmange is often used generically for such starch-thickened pudding as vanilla and chocolate custards.

"Then, my mother would fill a bowl about half full of wine gelatin, flavored with lemon juice, sugar and Sauternes or other wine. And she'd let it jell . . . She'd make a nest in the bed of gelatin by taking julienned orange and grapefruit peels, and she'd cook them in sugar syrup, put them out to cool and roll them in granulated sugar.

"She'd form the strips of candied peel into a nest, and when ready to use them, she'd carefully peel the shells from around the cream eggs and lay the eggs in the nest, with the strips all around the edge of the gelatin. Each person would ask for whichever flavor he or she liked and had it with cream poured over. We still make the dessert—my sister and myself."

PANNA COTTA AND POACHED PEARS IN MERLOT SYRUP

Panna cotta—the name literally means "cooked cream"—is a smooth, alabaster white, rich molded custard. After years of being unknown outside of its native Piedmont in northern Italy, panna cotta is turning up on restaurant menus all over this country. In its simplest form, it is sweetened heavy cream, flavored with lemon and vanilla and sometimes rum, set with gelatin (not baked) and unmolded in individual servings.

I first enjoyed this beautifully composed panna cotta as the conclusion to an unforgettable fall feast at the guest house of Livio Felluga, whose wines are among the best in Friuli, the region northeast of Venice. The custard's gleaming surface was counterpointed by a warm poached pear half, sliced but still joined at the stem, both fruit and panna cotta perfumed by a heady syrup made with Merlot wine. This recipe is from Leda and Claudio Della Rovere, the brother and sister who own Ristorante Romea in nearby Manzano.

I've cut back on the fat of this custard a little; the proportions below are a happy compromise, clean but just rich enough. You can also serve panna cotta without the pears and syrup; just scatter a few berries alongside.

༄ *Serves 6*

PANNA COTTA
2⅓ cups milk
⅔ cup heavy cream
1 vanilla bean, split lengthwise, or 1 teaspoon pure vanilla extract
Strips of zest of 1 lemon
1½ envelopes (3¾ teaspoons) unflavored gelatin
⅓ cup sugar

PEARS AND MERLOT SYRUP
2¼ cups Italian or American Merlot wine
⅓ cup plus 1 tablespoon sugar
3 firm-ripe pears, such as Bosc, Bartlett or Anjou, peeled with stems left on, halved and cored

1. **PANNA COTTA:** In a saucepan, combine 2 cups of the milk, the cream, vanilla bean and lemon zest. (If using vanilla extract, do not add it now.) Set the pan over medium-high heat, cover and

bring just to a boil. Remove from the heat and let steep, covered, for about 1 hour.

2. Sprinkle the gelatin over the remaining ⅓ cup milk. Return the milk and cream mixture to a simmer. Remove from the heat and whisk in the dissolved gelatin and sugar until smooth. Strain the mixture into a pitcher; if using vanilla extract, add it now. Scrape the vanilla seeds out of the bean and stir them into the cream. Pour into six ½-cup ramekins or other small molds. Chill until set, at least 2 hours.

3. **PEARS AND MERLOT SYRUP:** Bring the wine and sugar to a simmer in a wide nonreactive sauté pan; stir to dissolve the sugar. Gently slip the pear halves into the syrup. Cover and poach them gently over low heat until tender, 10 to 20 minutes, depending on the pears. Remove the pears with a slotted spoon; arrange in a layer on a plate. Cover and set aside.

4. Boil the poaching liquid over high heat until lightly syrupy, about 10 minutes or slightly longer. Remove from the heat and set aside.

5. To serve, rewarm the pears in the Merlot syrup. Run the tip of a knife around each ramekin of cream; unmold onto a serving plate. Gently place a warm pear next to each cold cream. Make 4 or 5 lengthwise cuts in each pear half, leaving the pear joined at the stem end. Spoon some of the warm syrup over and around the pear and serve immediately.

RICOTTA BAVARIAN

This is a Bavarian cream—a custard that's gently set with gelatin and lightened and enriched with whipped cream. Bavarians are "presentation desserts," served unmolded, and can be flavored with all sorts of fruits, liqueurs and nuts. This one is kept simple to bring out the sweet, milky flavor of the ricotta cheese. Although freshly made ricotta, found in Italian markets and in cheese shops, is especially delicious, supermarket ricotta will work fine.

This is a very "white" dessert, designed to be served with Madeira Dried Fruit Compote (page 77), ripe berries, a tart fruit sauce such as a blackberry puree (try Chunky Double-Berry Sauce, page 617, substituting blackberries for the raspberries and strawberries) or just a cookie.

⌒ Serves 8 to 10

3	tablespoons milk
1	envelope (about 2½ teaspoons) unflavored gelatin
2	large eggs
2	large egg yolks
½	cup sugar
1	pound (about 2 cups) ricotta cheese, at room temperature
1½	teaspoons pure vanilla extract
	Pinch *each* ground cinnamon and fresh-grated nutmeg
1	cup heavy cream, chilled

1. Place the milk in a small saucepan; sprinkle the gelatin over the surface and set aside to soften.

2. Meanwhile, in the top of a double boiler, whisk the eggs, egg yolks and sugar with an electric mixer until combined. Set over barely simmering water and whisk vigorously, without stopping, until the mixture triples in volume and is very pale, frothy and thick, 10 minutes or longer. The mixture should hold soft mounds when dropped from the whisk.

3. Meanwhile, as you are whisking the egg mixture, place the pan of gelatin over low heat and stir until completely dissolved. When the egg mixture is ready, remove the top of the double boiler from the heat and whisk in the gelatin mixture. Continue to whisk or beat with an electric mixer, until the mixture cools to room temperature, 5 to 10 minutes.

4. Quickly process the ricotta in a food processor, pulsing on and off just until smooth. Transfer to a mixing bowl. (If you do not own a processor, just whisk the ricotta; do not use a blender.) Stir in the vanilla, cinnamon and nutmeg. Fold about ¼ of the beaten egg mixture into the ricotta; gently fold in the remaining egg mixture.

5. Whip the cream until it thickens and holds very soft peaks (do not whip until stiff). Gently fold the whipped cream into the ricotta mixture. Generously oil a 6-cup fluted mold (such as a kugelhopf mold). Pour the mixture into the mold. Cover the mold and chill until set, at least 2 hours.

6. To unmold, dip the sides of the mold very briefly into a bowl of hot water. Invert a serving platter over the mold and in-vert the two. If the bavarian doesn't slip out easily, dip again briefly. Chill to firm briefly or until serving time. Serve, spooning a colorful fruit or sauce next to each portion.

112

MONT BLANC
(CHESTNUT AND CREAM DESSERT)

This dessert is a fragile mound of sweetened vanilla-scented chestnut puree, put through a potato ricer and topped with whipped cream (hence, Mont Blanc). It's an Old-World favorite meant to be eaten with tiny silver spoons.

The best way to form the mounds is to let them fall from the ricer right onto individual serving plates. If you don't have a ricer, you can push the chestnut puree through the holes of a colander; a food mill with large holes also works, though not as well.

Serves 4

1½	cups cooked peeled chestnuts or 20-25 large fresh chestnuts (see note)
¾	cup milk
1	vanilla bean, split lengthwise
3	tablespoons plus 1 teaspoon sugar, preferably superfine
2	teaspoons cognac (optional)
½	teaspoon pure vanilla extract
½	cup heavy cream, well chilled, for serving

1. Place the chestnuts in a small saucepan with the milk and the vanilla bean. Cover and simmer over low heat, stirring occasionally, until the chestnuts are softened and infused with the vanilla, for 15 to 20 minutes. Drain, reserving the milk. Remove the vanilla bean; scrape the seeds into the milk.

2. Puree the chestnuts with 2 tablespoons of the reserved milk in a food processor until completely smooth. (The puree should have the consistency of stiff mashed potatoes; add more of the milk as needed.) Scrape the puree into a bowl and stir in the sugar, optional cognac and the vanilla extract.

3. Force the puree through a potato ricer or colander onto individual serving plates, letting the mixture fall in a loose pile of strands. Whip the cream until floppy (not stiff), and spoon some over each mound of chestnut. Serve immediately; eat slowly.

NOTE: Cooked chestnuts can be purchased frozen, vacuum-packed or packed in brine; drain in a sieve, rinse, drain again and proceed as above. Whole chestnuts in syrup can also be used (they're wildly expensive); drain and reduce the amount of sugar in the recipe to taste.

To use fresh chestnuts, cut an X in the flat side of the shell of each; blanch in boiling water for 10 minutes. Drain, rinse with cold water and peel off the skins with a paring knife. Simmer in milk with the vanilla bean as directed in step 1, but increase the cooking time to about 45 minutes, or until the chestnuts are very tender. Proceed as directed.

To mail-order frozen peeled chestnuts, from Michigan or Spain, contact Earthy Delights, www.earthy.com. Chestnuts are sold in 1-pound and 2.2-pound packages; chestnut flour is also available.

FROZEN SCOTTISH ATHOLL BROSE

Served frozen but still soft, this untraditional version of Atholl Brose has the texture of a semifreddo or tortoni. The recipe is adapted from one served at The Airds Hotel in Port Appin, Argyll, Scotland.

～ Serves 6 to 8

1	scant cup steel-cut, old-fashioned or quick-cooking oats (not instant)
1	cup heavy cream, well chilled
¼	cup honey, preferably heather
1-2	tablespoons Scotch whisky, preferably a single malt

1. Preheat the oven to 350 degrees F. Scatter the oats over a jellyroll pan or other shallow pan and toast, stirring once or twice, until crisp and golden brown, about 15 minutes. Transfer the toasted oats to a plate and let cool on a wire rack.

2. In a bowl, whip the cream until it has thickened quite a bit but has not yet formed soft peaks. With a large rubber spatula, fold in the honey and whisky until not quite blended. Add the cooled oats and gently fold until blended. Spoon the mixture into decorative serving goblets or custard cups. Freeze until lightly frozen but not firm, about 1 hour. Serve cold.

Potent Tradition

A Scottish tradition since the 1400s, Atholl Brose is the name for both a potent drink made with toasted oats, heather honey and plenty of the local malt whisky, and also for a dessert in which the same ingredients are folded into softly whipped cream.

According to author Theodora Fitzgibbon, the Duke of Atholl captured his enemy, the Earl of Ross, by causing him to drink the potent draft unwittingly.

WARM AMARETTO-COGNAC ZABAGLIONE

Eggs, cognac and sugar, whipped to a vaporous froth, become a warm topping for berries or other summer fruits. Either zabaglione or zabaione is correct; the French version is called sabayon.

You can also make zabaglione with another fortified wine, like sherry or Madeira, or with a dessert wine—Quady Essencia, Muscat, Italian Picolit or a late-harvest Riesling.

Serves 4

2	large eggs
2	large egg yolks
⅓	cup sugar
¼	cup cognac or brandy
¼	cup amaretto, or more to taste
	Ripe berries, for serving

1. In the top of a double boiler or in a bowl, off the heat, whisk the eggs, egg yolks and sugar until the mixture begins to become frothy.

2. Place over briskly simmering water and add the cognac or brandy and the amaretto. Whisk constantly until the mixture is fluffy and flops in soft peaks when dropped from the whisk, usually about 8 minutes. Taste and add more amaretto if needed.

3. Serve the warm zabaglione immediately in large goblets, preferably over ripe berries.

Starting the Day Right

"Did you know," asked cookbook author Anna Teresa Callen, a native of Abruzzo, Italy, looking up at me one afternoon over tiny cups of espresso, "that we had zabaglione for breakfast every day?

"As a matter of fact, my uncle Filippo would kid me that he was going to count the eggs used to make all the zabaglione I ate, and I would owe him when I started to earn my own money.

"You see, we Italians really had no breakfast. But you gave the children zabaglione in the morning—without the Marsala. But I think maybe we had it *with* Marsala."

STRAWBERRY NONSENSE

I found this recipe in an old Southern collection, and the name drew me in. The dessert is as good as its name—it's a quick, chilled assembly of cubes of cake and summer-ripe strawberries, suspended in a cool custard, much like a bread pudding, but lighter.

I've since played around with several versions. This one uses cubes of leftover spongecake, along with an eggless custard that's nothing but lightly sweetened milk set with a little gelatin—white custard, yellow cake, crimson berries.

This is best made with small strawberries. At my local farmers' market in Manhattan's Union Square, there are fragrant little strawberries that almost resemble wild ones; if you can't get small ones, slice larger berries.

⌒ *Serves 6*

> Marie's Vanilla Spongecake (page 117), cooled, trimmed and cut into ½-inch cubes (you'll need 3½-4½ cups cubes, probably not the whole cake; you can also use angel food cake)

1½ tablespoons (about 1¾ envelopes) unflavored gelatin
3 cups milk
⅔ cup sugar, plus more, depending on the berries' sweetness
1½ teaspoons pure vanilla extract
1-1½ pints ripe strawberries, hulled, halved or quartered, if large

> Whipped unsweetened heavy cream, for serving (optional)

1. Scatter the cubes of cake over a work surface and leave out to dry slightly.

2. Sprinkle the gelatin over ½ cup of the cold milk; let stand until softened, about 5 minutes. Meanwhile, heat the remaining 2½ cups milk and ⅓ cup of the sugar until nearly boiling; remove from the heat. Stir in the gelatin and whisk until the gelatin dissolves completely; stir in the vanilla.

3. Choose a deep serving dish, preferably glass, about 1½ quarts in size; a soufflé dish works fine. Line the bottom of the dish with a layer of about ¼ of the spongecake cubes. Ladle on a little of the milk mixture. Top with a thick layer of strawberries,

using about ⅓ of them (set aside a few small berries for garnish); sprinkle the berries with about 1 tablespoon of sugar to taste. Add another layer of cake cubes, top with a layer of berries and about 1 tablespoon of sugar. Add a third layer of cake cubes, the remaining berries and about 1 tablespoon sugar. Scatter the remaining cake cubes on top. Pour the remaining milk mixture over all. Cover and refrigerate until the custard sets, about 2 hours.

4. Spoon the optional whipped cream around the edge of the dish, leaving the middle of the pudding exposed. (Or pipe the whipped cream from a pastry bag.) Arrange the reserved berries on top, and serve, spooning the pudding from the dish.

"Strawberries and cream are many a rural man's banquet, we have known such banquets to put men in jeopardy of their lives."

QUOTED BY
DOROTHY HARTLEY
LOST COUNTRY LIFE
1979

MARIE'S VANILLA SPONGECAKE

This is a good basic recipe from my friend Marie Simmons. It's useful in any dessert that needs a light cake base.

Makes one 8- to 9-inch cake (about 8 ounces baked)

4   large eggs, separated
     Pinch salt
¼   cup sugar
1   teaspoon pure vanilla extract
¼   cup sifted all-purpose flour
¼   cup sifted cornstarch

1. Preheat the oven to 375 degrees F, with a rack in the center. Lightly butter a 9-inch square baking pan or an 8- to 9-inch springform pan. Line the bottom of the pan with wax paper cut to fit; lightly butter and flour the paper; set aside.

2. In a bowl, beat the egg whites with the salt until they form soft peaks; gradually beat in the sugar until the whites are just stiff, no longer.

3. In another bowl, whisk the egg yolks and vanilla until blended. Fold in about ¼ of the beaten whites. Pour the egg yolk mixture into the beaten whites; sprinkle the sifted flour and cornstarch through a strainer over the egg whites. Fold together thoroughly, without overmixing. Spread the batter in the prepared pan, tilting gently so the batter spreads to the edges.

4. Bake until the edges are set and the cake is golden, 25 to 30 minutes. Cool the cake in the pan for a few minutes. Invert the cake onto a wire rack and carefully peel off the paper, or remove the sides of the springform pan. Cool completely on the rack. *(The cake can be prepared in advance; wrap in plastic and store at room temperature.)*

CHARLOTTE RUSSE
(ICEBOX CAKE)

Charlotte russe or icebox cake are both names used for desserts that consist of a mold neatly lined with pieces of spongecake or ladyfingers and filled with whipped cream. When chilled, the cream sets and the dessert is unmolded and served cut into wedges. Credit for the invention of charlotte russe is generally given to French pastry chef Antonin Carême, who cooked at the court of the Russian Czar Alexander.

To judge from cookbook authors like Mrs. Rorer and the tireless Mrs. Ida Bailey Allen, American housewives were whipping themselves into an icebox-cake frenzy beginning sometime in the 1920s.

My version of icebox cake is simple and tasty. The filling sets just enough to be unmolded but is still soft, reminiscent of the ice cream cakes served at childhood birthday parties. (If you like, before lining the mold with the cake, brush one side of each piece with a little sherry or other spirits, and place the pieces in the mold as directed, soaked side in.) You can also fold some sliced strawberries or other fruit into the cream before filling the mold.

Serves about 8

	Marie's Vanilla Spongecake (page 117) or other plain cake, preferably baked in a round pan, cooled, edges trimmed and cut horizontally into 3 layers
¼	cup milk
1	envelope (about 2½ teaspoons) unflavored gelatin
¼	cup sherry, preferably sweet, plus more for brushing on cake, if desired, or Marsala, Madeira or 3 tablespoons Grand Marnier (optional)
2	cups heavy cream, well chilled
½	cup confectioners' sugar, plus more for sprinkling
1	teaspoon pure vanilla extract
	Grated zest of ½ lemon
	Whipped cream, for serving (optional)
	Strawberry slices or whole raspberries, for serving

1. Cut a round of wax paper to fit the bottom of a charlotte mold 6½ inches wide and 3½ inches high, or use a 1½-quart soufflé dish. Using the paper as a guide, cut a neat round from one layer of cake; cut the round into wedges. Line the bottom of the pan with the wax paper, then with the cake wedges, points toward the center and yellow side down, against the paper.

2. Cut the 2 remaining cake layers into triangles. Line the sides of the mold with the wedges, alternating point end up, then point end down, and so on. With a serrated knife, carefully trim the wedges flush with the rim of the pan. Set the cake-lined mold aside.

3. Place the milk in a small saucepan and sprinkle the gelatin over the surface; set aside to soften for about 5 minutes. Stir over low heat until the gelatin dissolves. Remove the pan from the heat and stir in the optional sherry or other spirit.

4. In a bowl, whip the cream with the ½ cup confectioners' sugar and the vanilla until thickened and floppy. Strain the gelatin mixture into the cream, add the lemon zest and continue to whip until the cream forms soft peaks (do not overbeat). Gently pour the mixture into the lined mold, without disturbing the arrangement of the cake pieces. Place the mold in the refrigerator.

5. After a few minutes, lay a sheet of wax paper or plastic wrap on the surface of the cream filling. Chill until the cream sets, at least 2 hours.

6. To serve, gently remove the wax paper from the surface of the cream. Invert the charlotte onto a serving plate by giving the mold a sharp downward shake. Gently remove the round of wax paper on the top and sprinkle the charlotte with confectioners' sugar. If you like, you can pipe a little extra whipped cream around the top edges. Garnish with strawberry slices or whole raspberries.

RECIPES

Double Chocolate Pudding
Butterscotch Pudding
South American Caramel
Pudding
Banana Pudding
Grape-Nuts Pudding
Lemon Pudding Cake
Italian Ricotta Pudding
Warm Chocolate-Hazelnut
Pudding
Fluffy Baked Tapioca
Pudding
Asian-Style Coconut Tapioca
Pudding
Durgin-Park's Indian
Pudding
Colonial Cup Custard
Pôts de Crème
Coffee Cup Crème Caramel
Jasper White's Maple Sugar
Crème Caramel
Mexican Chocolate Flan with
Kahlúa
Cuban Caramel Custard
Brazilian Coconut Custards
Classic Crème Brûlée
Bert Greene's Pumpkin
Crème Brûlée
Oeufs à la Neige with
Raspberries
Floating Island
Luli's Trifle
Cabinet Pudding
Tiramisù
Thomas Keller's Molten
Chocolate
Blintz "Soufflé"
Little Pear Soufflés
Salzburg Little Mountain
Soufflés
Edna Lewis's Chocolate
Soufflé

CHAPTER 4

CREAMY PUDDINGS, CUSTARDS AND SOUFFLÉS

It is [a] paltrie cap,
A custard coffin, a bauble, a silken pie.
WILLIAM SHAKESPEARE, *THE TAMING OF THE SHREW*, CA. 1593

She had a strong sweetish odor that all her
rose water and soap could not subdue, an odor I loved
because it made me think of warm custard.
ISABEL ALLENDE, *EVA LUNA*, 1987

*M*ilk and eggs, gently baked until they set—
could anything be simpler, more soothing to
the palate, to the stomach, to the soul? Because they are so easy to digest, custards have
long been spooned to children, to babies in the nursery and to in-
valids. (One early-American recipe is called "a sick-bed custard"—
the original comfort food.) That's a clue to these desserts' appeal:
There is something inherently nurturing about them. Unlike
desserts with more "texture," custards offer no challenge, no resis-
tance—you can just glide on in with the spoon.

While each has its own characteristic consistency, simple puddings, custards and soufflés are actually variations on a theme. The
simplest puddings are starch-thickened mixtures (usually made
with milk and sometimes with eggs) that are stirred in a saucepan

until smooth. A true custard, on the other hand, is set by eggs alone and baked (usually protected by the gentle heat of a water bath). Custard that is cooked on top of the stove and thickened by eggs alone with no starch is called crème anglaise or custard sauce. It is a sauce rather than a spoon dessert; see Eggnog Custard Sauce (page 609) and Low-Fat Custard Sauce (page 610). And despite all the mystique that surrounds the soufflé, it is nothing more than a flavored custardlike base that's lightened with beaten egg whites, baked and served immediately.

Once you have the basics, you can elaborate, enriching and flavoring a basic cup custard so that it becomes a pôt de crème. Or coat individual baked custard molds with caramel for flan or crème caramel; when they are unmolded, the caramel glazes them with an instant sauce. Or you can sprinkle the surface of a baked custard with sugar, then brown it under a flame to make crème brûlée (the name means "burned cream"), which originated much earlier than you might think. Taking the theme still further, custard can be used as part of an assembly, layered in a bowl with cake, fruit and liqueur for a trifle, a special-occasion dessert. Topped with poached meringues, a cool custard becomes oeufs à la neige, also called "snow eggs."

Not surprisingly for food of such primal comfort, custards are a very old preparation. Originally a corruption of *crustade* (other forms are *crustarde* and *custad*), which was an open pie, the word first appeared in 1390 in *The Forme of Cury*, as "Crustardes of Flesch, also of Fysche." Custards of the 15th and 16th centuries were usually baked in a crust—Shakespeare's "custard coffin." In 1628, Brother John Earle refers to "Quaking Tarts, and quiuering Custards, and such milke sop Dishes."

We've come to expect custard to taste of vanilla. But vanilla extract wasn't widely available in American grocery stores until sometime between 1847 and 1850. Before that, from the early 1800s, tincture of vanilla, an extract-like concoction in an alcohol base, was sold mainly through druggists. (The first vanilla beans were brought to this country from France by Thomas Jefferson just before the turn of the 19th century.) Before vanilla, custards were flavored with wine—usually fortified wines like sherry, Madeira or Malaga; or with brandy, tea or spices and often with peach leaves or kernels, which imparted an almond-like flavor.

Contrary to Mrs. Rorer's warning, in the context of a healthy diet, there's no reason to avoid these desserts. Eat them after dinner or, at my favorite time for them, just before going to bed.

"Don't eat desserts made from eggs and milk after a meat dinner. . . . Why harden the arteries while still young?"

SARAH TYSON RORER
MRS. RORER'S
KEY TO SIMPLE COOKERY
PHILADELPHIA, 1917

DOUBLE CHOCOLATE PUDDING

If there is a single dessert that conjures up childhood to me, it is chocolate pudding: served in a tall glass sundae dish, topped with homemade whipped cream and a cherry, with "skin," please.

As with all favorite childhood foods, there was a definite strategy to eating chocolate pudding. The cherry was saved for the end. The first few bites were just pudding; you'd break a crater in the surface and eat around the whipped cream. Then, a dab of whipped cream was piggybacked on each mouthful of pudding. As the bottom became visible, the mouthfuls became smaller, to try to make the pleasure last.

My mother was and is a good, simple cook, and the taste of freshly whipped cream and real vanilla brings me back to the desserts she made for us in the 1950s.

This chocolate pudding is made with both cocoa and chocolate, plus some vanilla to round out the flavor. Do not "refine" it with cognac or rum. Do not "enhance" it with espresso, orange zest, cinnamon or mint.

⟿ *Serves 4*

2¼	cups milk
½	cup sugar
	Pinch salt
3	tablespoons unsweetened cocoa powder
2	tablespoons cornstarch, sifted
1	large egg
2	large egg yolks
5	ounces best-quality semisweet chocolate, finely chopped
2	tablespoons unsalted butter
1	teaspoon pure vanilla extract
	Lightly whipped cream flavored with vanilla extract, for serving

1. Place 2 cups of the milk, ¼ cup of the sugar and the salt in a heavy nonreactive saucepan. Bring to a boil over medium heat.

2. Meanwhile, mix together the remaining ¼ cup sugar, the cocoa and the cornstarch in a bowl. Whisk in the remaining ¼ cup cold milk until smooth and free of lumps.

3. Slowly whisk the hot milk mixture into the bowl; return the mixture to the saucepan. Slowly bring to a boil over medium

heat, stirring very frequently. Boil gently, stirring constantly, until the mixture is fairly thick, about 2 minutes.

4. In a small bowl, whisk the egg and egg yolks together. Slowly whisk in 1 cup of the hot cocoa mixture. Whisk the egg mixture back into the hot cocoa mixture. Cook over medium-low heat, whisking constantly, until the mixture becomes slightly thicker, 3 to 5 minutes. Do not allow the mixture to boil or over-cook. Transfer the pudding to a clean bowl and lay a sheet of wax paper or plastic wrap directly on the surface. Cool slightly on a wire rack.

5. Melt the semisweet chocolate with the butter in a small saucepan. Stir until smooth and cool slightly; the chocolate should remain pourable.

6. Whisk the chocolate into the thickened egg mixture; stir in the vanilla. Pour the pudding into 4 glass sundae dishes or ramekins. Refrigerate until cold, 2 to 3 hours. (If you'd like to prevent a "skin" from forming, lay a sheet of wax paper or plastic wrap directly on the surface of each serving before chilling.)

7. Serve the pudding chilled, topped with vanilla-flavored whipped cream.

BUTTERSCOTCH PUDDING

If you love pudding, then the dessert flavor trinity wasn't vanilla, chocolate and strawberry but vanilla, chocolate and butterscotch.

This pudding has that marvelous real butterscotch flavor you just can't get from a boxed mix.

⌒⌐ *Serves 4*

    3   cups milk
    4   large egg yolks
    ¾   cup packed dark brown sugar
    ¼   cup cornstarch, spooned lightly into a measuring cup
         (do not pack tightly)
    2   tablespoons cold unsalted butter, cut into pieces
    2½   teaspoons pure vanilla extract
         Whipped cream flavored with vanilla extract, for serving
         (optional)

1. Rinse a heavy nonreactive saucepan with cold water, and shake out the excess water (this helps prevent the milk from scorching). Bring 2½ cups of the milk nearly to a boil.

2. Meanwhile, in a mixing bowl, whisk together the remaining ½ cup milk, the egg yolks, brown sugar and cornstarch until smooth.

3. Pour about ½ cup of the hot milk into the egg yolk mixture and whisk vigorously. Repeat the process 2 more times. Pour the warmed yolk mixture into the pan of hot milk and bring to a boil, whisking over medium heat. Boil, whisking almost constantly (be sure to stir at the edges of the pan), for 2 minutes. Remove from the heat and whisk in the butter and vanilla.

4. Strain the pudding through a fine sieve into a clean bowl. Transfer the pudding to 4 individual serving dishes, preferably glass sundae dishes. If you want to prevent a pudding "skin" from forming, lay a sheet of wax paper or plastic wrap directly on the surface of the pudding. Chill for 2 to 3 hours. Serve topped with vanilla-flavored whipped cream, if you like.

SOUTH AMERICAN CARAMEL PUDDING

(*DULCE DE LECHE*)

When my assistant Luli was growing up, her family cook Elisa, an Argentinian of Italian descent, used to spread a baked pie shell with this superrich caramelized pudding, then top it with a rum-flavored custard. She'd use it to fill cakes, too, and to spread on toast (they called it "milk jam"). It also works nicely over cinnamon toast, as a dip for cut-up fresh apples or bananas or over ice cream.

This is rich stuff.

Serves 4

1   can (14 ounces) sweetened condensed milk

1. **OVEN METHOD:** Preheat the oven to 425 degrees F. Pour the condensed milk into a 9-inch pie pan; cover with foil. Place the pie pan in a roasting pan. Place in the oven. Pour in enough hot tap water to reach halfway up the sides of the pie pan. Bake until thick and caramel-colored, about 1½ hours. Remove from the water bath and stir until smooth.

STOVETOP METHOD: Pour the condensed milk into the top of a double boiler over simmering water. Cover and simmer until thick and caramel-colored, 1 to 1½ hours. Stir until smooth.

MICROWAVE METHOD: Pour the condensed milk into a 2-quart glass measuring cup with a handle or another glass container. Cook at medium (50% power) for 4 minutes, stirring every 2 minutes, until smooth. Then cook at medium-low (30% power) for 12 to 18 minutes, stirring every 2 minutes, or until thick and caramel-colored.

2. Cool and serve the pudding in 4 demitasse cups or ramekins.

BANANA PUDDING

Banana pudding is a favorite down South, but it turns up all over the country. This version is lightened a bit—the pastry cream base is made with low-fat milk and fewer egg yolks than most traditional recipes.

Serves about 4

2½	cups low-fat or whole milk
⅓	cup plus 3 tablespoons sugar
2	large eggs
1	large egg yolk
¼	cup cornstarch
1	tablespoon unsalted butter
2	teaspoons pure vanilla extract
2	firm-ripe bananas (3, if small)

1. Pour ½ cup of the milk into a bowl; add the ⅓ cup sugar, the eggs, egg yolk and cornstarch and whisk until smooth; set aside.

2. In a small, heavy saucepan, combine the remaining 2 cups milk with the remaining 3 tablespoons sugar. Bring almost to a boil over medium heat.

3. Whisking constantly, slowly pour the hot milk into the egg mixture. Return the mixture to the saucepan, and bring to a boil, whisking constantly. Lower the heat and boil gently, whisking constantly, until thickened and smooth, about 2 minutes. Immediately remove the pan from the heat.

4. Strain the hot custard into a clean bowl; whisk in the butter and vanilla until the butter melts.

5. Spoon a little of the custard into an attractive 1-to-1½-quart glass bowl or soufflé dish. Peel and slice the bananas and scatter a layer of banana slices over the custard. Continue alternating layers of custard and banana slices, ending with a smooth layer of custard. Place a sheet of wax paper or plastic wrap directly on the surface of the custard. Refrigerate until cold, at least 2 hours. Serve cold.

Variation

BANANA PUDDING WITH VANILLA WAFERS: I like this pudding as is, but if you'd like to add vanilla wafers, scatter 1 or 2 layers of vanilla wafers (20 to 24, or about ¼ of a 12-ounce package) as you layer the pudding in step 5. The wafers soften and get puffy as they absorb the custard.

GRAPE-NUTS PUDDING

If you were raised in New England, you're likely to have childhood memories of this smooth, straightforward Yankee custard pudding. It's flecked with Grape-Nuts, the wheat-and-barley cereal that softens in baking. If you grew up anywhere else, chances are you're baffled by the idea, but it's delicious.

Serves 6 to 8

4	cups (1 quart) whole milk
¾	cup Grape-Nuts cereal
3	large eggs
⅔	cup sugar
1½	teaspoons pure vanilla extract
	Fresh-grated nutmeg

1. Preheat the oven to 325 degrees F. In a saucepan, scald the milk with the cereal; set aside to cool slightly. Meanwhile, in a bowl, beat the eggs with the sugar and vanilla; whisk in the warm milk mixture.

2. Stir the custard to redistribute the Grape-Nuts, and pour the custard into a buttered 1½-quart casserole or buttered 1-cup custard cups or ramekins.

3. Bake the casserole or cups for 10 to 15 minutes. Stir the pudding very gently to redistribute the Grape-Nuts; sprinkle the surface of the pudding lightly with the nutmeg. Continue to bake until set but still slightly wobbly, 45 to 50 minutes for the large baking dish, or 25 to 30 minutes for the small custard cups. (The timing can vary; do not overbake.)

4. Cool the pudding(s) on a wire rack. Refrigerate or serve at a cool room temperature.

Lemon Pudding Cake

Sponge puddings separate into two layers as they bake: Light "cake" comes to the top, while a custardy "sauce" forms below. It's the high proportion of milk to eggs and flour in the custard mixture that separates the pudding.

This is Nashville food stylist Ginger Walsh's recipe, and it's one of the best—tart with lemon, beautifully golden, almost soufflé-like. Try it warm.

Serves 4

¾	cup sugar
¼	cup all-purpose flour
¼	teaspoon salt
3	large eggs, separated
1	cup milk
1	tablespoon grated lemon zest
¼	cup fresh lemon juice

1. Preheat the oven to 325 degrees F, with a rack in the center. Butter a 1- to 1½-quart shallow baking dish, such as a 9-inch oval gratin dish or an 8-inch square baking dish; set aside.

2. In a bowl, combine the sugar, flour and salt. In another bowl, beat the egg yolks, milk, lemon zest and lemon juice; pour the milk mixture over the flour mixture and stir until blended.

3. Beat the egg whites with an electric mixer at medium-high speed until they form soft peaks. Fold a little of the egg whites into the lemon mixture; gently fold in the remainder.

4. Pour the batter into the buttered baking dish. Place the baking dish in a slightly larger roasting pan; set on the center rack of the oven. Pour in enough hot tap water to reach about halfway up the sides of the baking dish.

5. Bake until the surface of the pudding is lightly golden, about 35 minutes. (The bottom layer will still be quite liquid.) Cool in the pan on a wire rack for about 30 minutes.

6. Serve the cake warm or at room temperature, spooning up some of the top and "sauce" from the bottom for each portion.

Sponge Pudding

Put in a kettle of water on the stove or in a rice cooker 1 pint of milk add 2 ounces of flour made smooth with cold milk 2 ounces sugar 2 ounces butter. Let it cook 5 minutes stirring the while. Take from the stove and let cool. [Add] The yolks of 6 eggs and stir in when partly cold. Lastly add the whites beaten nice flavor to taste set in a pan of water and bake one hour. Serve with hard or wine sauce.

Mrs. Henry W. Darling
Handwritten
Manuscript
Schenectady, New York
ca. 1882–93

Panna Cotta and Poached Pears in Merlot Syrup

Peanut Butter Pie with Fudge Topping

Mary's Pignoli (Italian Pine Nut Macaroons), Alsatian Christmas Cinnamon Stars, Cornmeal-Almond Biscotti

Rhubarb-Strawberry Crisp with Cinnamon-Walnut Topping

Oeufs à la Neige with Raspberries

Reuben's Legendary Apple Pancake

Marie's Rich Gingerbread with Candied Ginger and Lemon Glaze

Chocolate Cloud Cake

Schrafft's Hot Fudge Sauce, Warm Caramel Sauce, Chunky Double-Berry Sauce, Pot-au-Feu Praline Sauce, Spiced Sour Cherry Compote for Ice Cream

Warm Pear Charlotte

Mother Church's Spirited Dark Fruitcake

Apple-Pecan Upside-Down Pie Baked in a Skillet

ITALIAN RICOTTA PUDDING
(*BUDINO DI RICOTTA*)

This pudding has a good creamy texture, similar to light cheesecake, and is not too sweet. Coating the mold with crumbs gives a nice crunchy crust.

∽ *Serves 6 to 8*

	Fine, dry bread crumbs, for coating the mold
1	pound (about 2 cups) ricotta cheese
3	large eggs, separated
1	tablespoon all-purpose flour
⅓	cup sugar
	Grated zest of 1 lemon
	Grated zest of 1 orange
3	tablespoons candied orange rind and/or citron, cut into short, thin slivers
1	teaspoon pure vanilla extract
¼	teaspoon ground cinnamon
	Pinch salt
	Cinnamon sugar, for sprinkling

1. Preheat the oven to 350 degrees F, with a rack in the center. Butter a charlotte mold or a 1-quart soufflé dish. Dust the mold with a fine coating of bread crumbs, shaking out the excess; set aside.

2. Pulse the ricotta and egg yolks in a food processor just until smooth, no longer; transfer to a mixing bowl. Sift the flour over the mixture; add the sugar, zests, candied orange rind or citron, vanilla and cinnamon; mix gently until incorporated.

3. Beat the egg whites with the salt to nearly stiff peaks; fold a little of the whites into the ricotta; fold in the remainder. Transfer the mixture to the prepared mold.

4. Bake until the pudding is set when you shake the pan gently, usually 45 to 50 minutes (the timing can vary based on the size and depth of the baking dish; do not overbake).

5. Cool the pudding on a wire rack until lukewarm. Unmold onto a platter, sprinkle with cinnamon sugar and serve. According to Italian tradition, this is "best not hot, not cold."

Local Pudding

All over Italy, wherever ricotta is made from the whey that remains from making mozzarella and provolone, simple ricotta puddings are found. These puddings are flavored with lemon, or sometimes with cinnamon and ground almonds. Actually a form of simple cheesecake, this very old dessert dates back to Roman times, when cakes were made by sweetening curd cheeses with honey and spices.

WARM CHOCOLATE-HAZELNUT PUDDING

This is a straightforward chocolate-hazelnut pudding topped with whipped cream. Based on the Viennese *Mohr in hemd* ("Moor in a shirt," a racist reference to the black-and-white scheme), it has a deep chocolate flavor and a molten dark center.

The pudding can be made in a ring mold or in individual molds, custard cups or ramekins. The timing will vary based on the depth of the mold; don't overbake, as the warm, fluid center is what makes this.

Serves 8 to 10

- 1 scant cup unblanched hazelnuts
- 8 ounces best-quality bittersweet or semisweet chocolate, coarsely chopped
- 10 tablespoons (1 stick plus 2 tablespoons) unsalted butter, softened
- 1 cup sugar
- 6 large egg yolks
- 8 large egg whites
  Confectioners' sugar, for sprinkling
  Whipped cream flavored with vanilla extract, for serving

1. Preheat the oven to 350 degrees F, with a rack in the center. Generously butter a 4-cup (about 8-inch) ring mold or eight 1-cup pudding molds, custard cups or ramekins; set aside.

2. Scatter the hazelnuts over a baking pan and toast until lightly browned, about 10 minutes. Cool slightly, then rub gently in a kitchen towel to remove some of the loosened skins. Finely grind the nuts in a Mouli grater or food processor. Do not over-process, or the nuts will become oily; set aside.

3. Melt the chocolate in the top of a double boiler over hot, not boiling, water, stirring until smooth. Set aside to cool slightly.

4. In a large bowl, beat the butter until light. Add the sugar and beat until light and fluffy. Beat in the egg yolks, one at a time, beating well after each addition. Stir in the cooled chocolate and ground hazelnuts.

5. In a large bowl, beat the egg whites until stiff but not dry. Fold ¼ of the whites into the chocolate mixture; fold in the

remainder. Carefully pour the pudding into the prepared mold(s), filling about ¾ full.

6. Place the mold(s) in a roasting pan; place on the center rack of the oven. Pour in enough hot tap water to reach about halfway up the sides of the mold(s). Cover the mold(s) with a large sheet of buttered foil, buttered side down. Bake until the edges of the pudding(s) are almost firm to the touch and the center is slightly moist, usually about 35 minutes for the ring mold, 12 to 16 minutes for individual puddings. (The timing will vary depending on the mold used.) Check frequently to prevent overbaking.

7. Carefully remove the pudding(s) from the water bath to a wire rack; let cool for several minutes. Carefully unmold the warm pudding(s) onto a platter or serving plates. Sprinkle lightly with confectioners' sugar. Serve while still warm, with a spoonful of whipped cream next to each serving. Pass the remaining whipped cream separately.

ABOUT TAPIOCA

*W*hy don't we see tapioca more often? Clearly, all of its "fish-eye," "frog-eye" and "freshman's tears" nicknames don't help improve tapioca's reputation. But despite generations of derision, tapioca is as comforting as a pudding can be, the equal of rice pudding in innate appeal and even gentler on the palate.

Tapioca is ground from the root of the starchy cassava plant, which is also called manioc and sometimes "tapioca plant." Native to Africa, where cassava is a staple starch, the plant grows in several tropical regions.

There are two types of tapioca available:

Whole (or Pearl) Tapioca—This form of tapioca requires soaking in cold liquid until it softens, often overnight, before cooking.

Quick-Cooking Tapioca—Ground into smaller pellets than whole tapioca, the best-known is Minute brand; it needs no presoaking and literally cooks in minutes. (Note that this is not "instant" tapioca, which is available in presweetened and flavored mixes.) Quick-cooking tapioca is used for puddings and as a thickener for fruit pie fillings, where it is less starchy than cornstarch or flour. Its slightly nubbly texture, however, works best with berry pies, such as blackberry or blueberry, or with other fruits whose texture is more compatible with tapioca's grain.

The process of running whole tapioca through a commercial-size coffee grinder to make it less lumpy when cooked was developed in the mid 1890s. It was first sold as "Tapioca Superlative" and later as "Minute Tapioca." The company that produced it took on the name Minute Tapioca Company in 1908, which became part of General Foods that same year.

We shouldn't let tapioca get lost; it makes one of the best of the simple puddings.

Tapioca

*W*ash the tapioca well, and let it steep for five or six hours, changing the water three times. Simmer it in the last water till quite clear, then season it with sugar and wine, or lemon juice.

ELIZA LESLIE
DIRECTIONS FOR COOKERY
PHILADELPHIA
1848; 1837

FLUFFY BAKED TAPIOCA PUDDING

Here is the lightest tapioca ever—soft and fluffy, like a vanilla-scented cloud. It is first simmered on top of the stove and then baked just until it puffs up and turns gold. The interior remains soft and holds its shape tremulously.

Serves 4 to 6 (or 1 or 2 night owls)

¼	cup quick-cooking tapioca
⅔	cup sugar
	Pinch salt
3	cups milk
1	tablespoon unsalted butter
3	large egg yolks
2	teaspoons pure vanilla extract
2	large egg whites

1. Butter a 1½- to 2-quart soufflé dish, and place the dish in a roasting pan; set aside. Preheat the oven to 375 degrees F, with a rack in the center.

2. In a nonreactive saucepan, whisk together the tapioca, sugar and salt. Whisk in the milk and place over medium heat. Bring to a boil, whisking once or twice. Lower the heat and simmer for 6 minutes, whisking occasionally to prevent burning. Remove from the heat and whisk in the butter, egg yolks and vanilla.

3. In a bowl, beat the egg whites until nearly stiff; do not overbeat, or the pudding will be less smooth. Whisk a large spoonful of the egg whites into the pudding; fold in the remaining whites. Pour the mixture into the prepared soufflé dish. (The pudding will fill the dish completely.)

4. Place the roasting pan that holds the pudding in the oven. Pour in enough hot tap water to reach about halfway up the sides of the soufflé dish. Bake until the top is puffed and golden but the inside is still somewhat liquid, about 35 minutes.

5. Remove the soufflé dish from the water bath; cool to lukewarm on a wire rack. Serve warm, spooning the pudding directly from its dish. Or chill the pudding and remove it from the refrigerator a few minutes before serving.

Tapioca Reborn

This tapioca is based on a recipe that appears in Charles Elmé Francatelli's *The Modern Cook* (London, 1865). Francatelli uses about six times the quantity of tapioca as I do for the same amount of milk, and he steams the pudding for over an hour, resulting in a much firmer pudding than this one. Francatelli then poured his into a mold, chilled it and unmolded it for serving.

ASIAN-STYLE COCONUT TAPIOCA PUDDING

This unusual and delicious vanilla-and-coconut-infused tapioca pudding is from David Lebovitz, who was pastry chef at Bruce Cost's Monsoon restaurant in San Francisco. He got his start at Chez Panisse. David's desserts integrate both Eastern and Western influences. He presents this pudding with an elaborate arrangement of freshly grated coconut and colorful caramelized fruits: pineapple, banana and mango. At home, it's just as tasty without the fruit garnish.

David recommends using small pearl tapioca, available at Asian markets. If that's hard to find, however, regular quick-cooking tapioca works fine.

⌒ *Serves 6 to 8*

3⅓	cups store-bought unsweetened coconut milk (preferably Chaokoh brand, available in Asian markets)
⅔	cup small pearl tapioca or quick-cooking tapioca
⅔	cup sugar
1	vanilla bean, split lengthwise
	Pinch salt
1	large egg, separated (for a note on egg safety, see page 23)

1. In a heavy nonreactive saucepan, combine the coconut milk, tapioca, sugar, vanilla bean and salt over low heat. Stir constantly with a wooden spoon until the tapioca pearls are translucent, about 10 minutes; be careful not to let the pudding scorch as it cooks. If the mixture looks lumpy, whisk it a few times to break up the lumps.

2. Vigorously stir in the egg yolk; remove the saucepan from the heat. Cover and let stand until lukewarm, 30 minutes to 1 hour.

3. Remove the vanilla bean from the pudding; scrape the seeds into the pudding and stir to combine. In a small bowl, beat the egg white until it forms stiff peaks. Fold the egg white into the lukewarm pudding. Cover and chill or serve warm.

ABOUT HASTY
AND INDIAN PUDDINGS

*H*eady with cornmeal and molasses, coaxing itself together during a long, slow baking and served while still warm, topped with vanilla ice cream, which runs down the sides, Indian pudding is arguably the most American of desserts.

Its beginnings lie in what was called "hasty pudding," a cornmeal mush that could be spooned up hot, or left to cool and solidify, and then cut in pieces and fried. Despite its name, hasty pudding was really neither pudding nor dessert, but a staple, the oatmeal or "instant breakfast" of its day. From these simple mushes to Indian pudding as we know it was simply a matter of adding the plentiful and cheap molasses and baking it all together slowly in a crock.

Both cornmeal and molasses were colonial staples; settlers learned how to use cornmeal from the native Americans. Molasses, cruder and far cheaper than sugar, was the usual sweetener in colonial dessert recipes.

But misconceptions abound when it comes to Indian pudding. First, the term "Indian" means Indian meal—cornmeal—and doesn't necessarily mean that the dish in question was eaten by, borrowed from or even known by the native Americans. Any dish that used cornmeal was given the name "Indian"; see page 301 for an Indian Pound Cake, which, but for its cornmeal crunch, is thoroughly English in provenance. "Most English settlers had little interest in learning the cultural habits of the native American Indians," says Paula Marcoux, former foodways manager of Plimouth Plantation, "and that includes their cooking."

There are both boiled and baked Indian puddings; most old recipes call for as long as 5 hours of baking time to cook the cornmeal thoroughly. Some New England versions add sliced apples, but the pudding is smoother without them.

The Hasty-Pudding

. . . I sing the sweets I know, the charms I feel,
    My morning incense, and my evening meal,
    The sweets of Hasty-Pudding. Come, dear bowl,
    Glide o'er my palate, and inspire my soul.
. . . .
    But man, more fickle, the bold license claims,
    In different realms to give thee different names.
    Thee the soft nations round the warm Levant
Polenta call, the French, of course, *Polente*;
    Ev'n in thy native regions, how I blush
    To hear the Pennsylvanians call thee Mush!
    On Hudson's banks, while men of Belgie spawn
    Insult and eat thee by the name of *Suppawn*.
    All spurious appellations, void of truth;
    I've better known thee from my earliest youth,
    Thy name is *Hasty-Pudding*!

JOEL BARLOW
THE HASTY-PUDDING:
A POEM IN THREE CANTOS
1793

Durgin-Park's Indian Pudding

For smoothness and haunting, old-fashioned flavor, you can't beat the Indian pudding served at Durgin-Park, in Boston's Faneuil Hall Marketplace. The last time I ate there, our waitress warned as we sat down: "Don't give me a hahd time." We didn't.

⁓ *Serves 6 to 8*

3½	cups cold milk
½	cup yellow cornmeal
¼	cup molasses
2	tablespoons unsalted butter
2	tablespoons sugar
1	teaspoon ground cinnamon
1	teaspoon ground ginger
½	teaspoon fresh-grated nutmeg
¼	teaspoon salt
⅛	teaspoon baking soda
1	large egg
	Vanilla ice cream, for serving

1. Bring 2½ cups of the milk to a boil in a heavy saucepan. Meanwhile, place ½ cup of the milk in a small bowl, and gradually whisk in the cornmeal. Add the cornmeal mixture to the boiling milk and boil gently, whisking frequently, until lightly thickened, about 15 minutes.

2. Preheat the oven to 275 degrees F, with a rack in the center. Generously butter a 1½-quart ceramic crock, soufflé or baking dish; set aside.

3. Remove the cornmeal mixture from the heat and stir in the molasses, butter, sugar, spices, salt and baking soda. Beat the egg in a small bowl; stir in a little of the hot cornmeal mixture to warm it. Return the egg mixture to the pan and whisk vigorously to blend. Pour the mixture into the baking dish and set aside for about 3 minutes.

4. Gently pour the remaining ½ cup milk over the top of the pudding; do not stir in. Bake until set, 2¾ to 3 hours.

5. Cool the pudding to lukewarm. Serve warm with the ice cream.

A Boston Favorite

This recipe has been adapted slightly from the one served at Durgin-Park for almost 170 years.

Food has been served to market men and ship crews in this warehouse adjoining Faneuil Hall almost since that landmark was built in 1742. In 1826, John Durgin, a commission merchant, and Eldrige Park, who owned a livery stable nearby, in partnership with John Chandler, opened Durgin-Park. To this day, Bostonians come here for the Bunyanesque portions of chowder, Boston baked beans, New England boiled dinner, apple pandowdy, hot corn bread and this Indian pudding.

MAKING PERFECT CUSTARDS

Custard's utter simplicity calls for care in cooking. More involved dishes can be "tricked out" to success, but custard needs just the right amount of egg and/or yolks, just the right richness of milk and/or cream and the right baking temperature and time. With gentle heat, custard comes together so that it spoons up smooth, not curdled, not droopy or milky, soggy or bland. The perfect custard is a simple masterpiece of eggy integrity, of substance mellowed by tenderness.

The key to a perfect custard: *Don't overcook it.* Just a few moments beyond perfection—the point at which the eggs set the milk—and the custard will break into weeping, watery curds. Those curds are a sure sign of overcooking or of too high a heat.

For dessert custards, the liquid is usually milk, cream or any combination thereof. Sometimes, sugar syrup is used, which results in a sugary translucence. Savory custards can be made with water, various juices and broths.

While many early recipes are made with a combination of half milk and half cream, I've used milk in most of the recipes for this collection because it is lower in fat. Sometimes, however, for custards with particularly silken textures, part or all cream is preferable. While using milk or cream does affect texture, it generally doesn't change the way custards set or alter their baking time significantly. Feel free to add a little cream to a recipe where you'd like a richer result, or even to substitute low-fat milk for whole milk.

You can set a custard with whole eggs, egg yolks or egg whites, in any combination. Because egg whites set before the yolks (the protein coagulates at a lower temperature) custards made with whole eggs (or with all whites) will set more quickly than those made with egg yolks. A good general formula for velvety custards is 1 egg plus 2 egg yolks per cup of liquid. For a lower-fat dessert, you can substitute 1 whole egg for each 2 yolks. To lower the fat further, substitute 2 egg whites for each whole egg, but watch carefully to prevent overcooking.

In baking custards, gentle heat is the watchword. Usually, this means cooking in:

🍥 **a water bath** (*bain-marie*), which surrounds the custard with hot water to insulate it against direct heat and cook it more evenly (otherwise, the direct heat will toughen the edges before the center has set), or

🍥 **a crust**, as in a custard pie. Like the water bath, the crust protects the custard from direct heat.

Notes on Doneness— Please Read This

*A*s a general rule, to ensure perfect results, take a custard away from the heat when it's still slightly wobbly (but not soupy) in the center. The custard will continue to cook briefly once you've removed it from the oven and will thicken further ("set up") as it cools.

If, on the other hand, a custard is left in the oven until it is quite firm, it will continue to cook—making the surface crack once it cools. Perfect smoothness is what you want.

I've tested baked custards made with cold milk alongside those in which the milk was scalded first and then beaten into the eggs, a traditional technique that hastens the setting process and is supposed to prevent the eggs from curdling during long baking. Frankly, there's little appreciable difference in the finished product, so I've omitted the scalding step in the recipes that follow.

To Make a Custard

Breake your egges into a bowle, and put your Creame into an other bowle, and streine your egges into the creame, and put in saffron, cloves, and mace, and a litle synamom and ginger, and if you will, some suger and butter, and season it with salt, and melt your butter, and stirre it with the ladle a good while, and dubbe your Custard with dates or currants.

Thomas Dawson
*The Good Huswifes
Iewell [Jewel]*
London, 1587

COLONIAL CUP CUSTARD

Except for the addition of vanilla, this custard follows Eliza Leslie's 1828 recipe from *Seventy-five Receipts* for "Plain Custards" exactly. It's still one of the best.

⌒ *Serves 6*

3	large eggs
1	large egg yolk
2	cups milk
¼	cup sugar
1½	tablespoons pure vanilla extract
	Fresh-grated nutmeg (optional)

1. Preheat the oven to 325 degrees F, with a rack in the center. Set six 6-ounce ramekins or custard cups in a roasting pan; set aside.

2. In a bowl, whisk the eggs and egg yolk until blended. Whisk in the milk, sugar and vanilla. For extra-smooth results, strain the mixture into a large measuring cup or pitcher.

3. Pour the custard into the ramekins, dividing evenly. If you like, sprinkle the tops with nutmeg. Place the roasting pan on the center rack of the oven. Pour in enough hot tap water to reach halfway up the sides of the ramekins.

4. Bake until the custards are set but still quite jiggly, usually 30 to 35 minutes (the timing can vary depending on the depth of the ramekins). Remove the custards from the water bath and let cool on a wire rack. Chill until serving time.

PÔTS DE CRÈME

Made with egg yolks and cream, these little French-style custards are rich, rich, rich. The spoon glides through their quivering, eggy density, and the intense flavor—whether vanilla, caramel, coffee or bittersweet chocolate—cascades over the palate.

The caramel version, which plays off the richness of the custard itself, may be my favorite of these. The caramel is incorporated into the cream, not used to coat the mold, as in a flan or crème caramel.

Like all custard desserts, pôts de crème are easy to make ahead of time, ideal to serve for a dinner party dessert.

∼ *Serves about 6*

1	cup heavy cream
1	cup milk
1	vanilla bean, split lengthwise, or 1½ teaspoons pure vanilla extract
2	large eggs
2	large egg yolks
⅓	cup sugar

1. Bring the cream, milk and vanilla bean (if using) to a boil in a heavy saucepan over medium heat. (If you have time and are using the vanilla bean, set aside, off the heat, for at least 30 minutes to steep. Return to a near-boil before proceeding.)

2. Preheat the oven to 300 degrees F, with a rack in the center. In a bowl, whisk the eggs, egg yolks and sugar until well mixed. Slowly whisk in the hot cream mixture; if you are using vanilla extract, stir it in now. Strain the mixture into a large measuring cup or a pitcher. Scrape the seeds from the vanilla bean into the custard and stir to combine.

3. Place 6 pôts de crème cups, custard cups or ramekins in a roasting pan. Carefully pour in the custard, dividing evenly. Place the roasting pan on the center rack of the oven. Pour in enough hot tap water to reach about halfway up the sides of the cups.

4. Bake until the custards are set but still slightly wobbly in the center, usually 25 to 30 minutes. Carefully remove the custards from the water bath and cool to room temperature on a wire rack. Cover and chill the custards in the refrigerator.

How to Bake Custards

Take to every pinte of Creame: fiue Egges, and put in no whites, and straine your Creame and Egges togither, season it with Cloves and Mace: and Sugar. And when your paste is well hardened in the Oven, having small Raisins and Dates: put in your stuffe, and let it not bake too much, for muche baking will make your custard to quaile, or els to fall.

A.W.
A BOOK OF COOKRYE
LONDON, 1587

⌐ *Variations*

CHOCOLATE PÔTS DE CRÈME: Add 4 ounces chopped semisweet chocolate to the milk and cream in step 1 as it heats, stirring as the mixture comes to a simmer, until the chocolate is smooth. Proceed as directed.

CARAMEL PÔTS DE CRÈME: To make the caramel, combine ¾ cup sugar with 2 tablespoons cold water in a small, heavy saucepan. Cook over medium-high heat, stirring occasionally, until the sugar melts. Continue to cook, without stirring, until the syrup turns medium-dark amber, 6 to 7 minutes; the timing can vary. Carefully add 2 tablespoons hot water; the caramel will sputter wildly. Add the caramel to the hot cream–milk mixture in step 1 and continue to cook, whisking constantly over low heat, until the caramel dissolves and is smooth. Proceed, combining the caramel mixture with the eggs, egg yolks and sugar in step 2.

COFFEE PÔTS DE CRÈME: In a small cup, dissolve 2 tablespoons instant coffee, preferably espresso powder, in a little of the hot milk and cream in step 1. Stir it into the remaining hot cream–milk mixture and proceed as directed.

MOCHA PÔTS DE CRÈME: Melt 2½ ounces chopped semisweet chocolate in the hot cream–milk mixture in step 1. Dissolve 2 teaspoons instant coffee, preferably espresso powder, in a little of the hot cream mixture, then stir this mixture into the remaining hot liquid. Proceed as directed.

COFFEE CUP CRÈME CARAMEL

Every restaurant in Spain offers flan, the traditional custard baked in caramel-coated cups. As crème caramel, the same dessert is a standby in every bistro in France, in much the same way that every American restaurant serves cheesecake.

Too many crèmes caramel, however, are made indifferently, the custard pocked with holes and weeping watery liquid and without enough egg yolks to give it that sweet, gelid essence on the tongue. Which is why, when you find a crème caramel as perfect as that of Stephen Lyle, chef of the Odeon restaurant in New York City, you sit up and take notice. Lyle bakes his crème caramel in thick restaurant coffee cups; any ramekins or heatproof custard cups will work fine. The caramel stays liquid as it bakes and is then poured over and around the custard as it is unmolded.

~ Serves 6 (or more, if you use smaller ramekins)

CARAMEL
1½	cups sugar
¼	cup cold water

CUSTARD
3	cups milk
2	vanilla beans, split lengthwise
¾	cup sugar
3	large eggs
6	large egg yolks

1. **CARAMEL:** Place 6 heavy coffee cups, ramekins or custard cups in a roasting pan. Cook the sugar and water in a heavy saucepan or skillet, stirring, until the sugar dissolves. Raise the heat and bring the syrup to a full boil. Cook, without stirring, until the syrup caramelizes to a medium-dark amber color, 8 to 10 minutes; the timing can vary. Immediately immerse the bottom of the pan in cold water to stop the cooking. Pour the caramel into the cups, swirling to coat the bottoms. Set aside.

2. **CUSTARD:** Preheat the oven to 325 degrees F, with a rack in the center. In a heavy saucepan, bring the milk and vanilla beans to a boil; let steep, off the heat, for about 15 minutes. Remove the vanilla beans; scrape the seeds from the pods into the milk.

3. In a bowl, whisk the sugar, eggs and egg yolks; gradually

whisk in the hot milk mixture. Strain the mixture into a pitcher or large measuring cup; pour the custard into the caramel-lined cups, using about ¾ cup for each.

4. Place the roasting pan on the center rack of the oven. Pour in enough hot tap water to reach halfway up the sides of the cups. Bake until the custards are just set but still slightly wobbly in the center, 50 to 60 minutes (the timing can vary; do not overcook). Carefully remove the custards from the water bath and cool to room temperature on a wire rack. Cover and chill until cold, at least 2 hours.

5. To serve, run the tip of a knife gently around the edge of each cup; invert the crème caramel onto a dessert plate. Serve, spooning the liquid caramel over the tops.

JASPER WHITE'S MAPLE SUGAR CRÈME CARAMEL

At the former Boston restaurant bearing his name, Jasper White made a crème caramel that's flavored with maple sugar, which imparts its stalwart character to this suave dessert. Maple sugar is granular and pale golden but drier and more free-flowing than light brown sugar.

You can order maple sugar by mail; see the next page for a source.

Serves 8

2	cups granulated maple sugar
½	cup cold water
1	tablespoon unsalted butter
4	large eggs
2	large egg yolks
2½	cups milk, heated

1. Preheat the oven to 325 degrees F, with a rack in the center. Place 8 custard cups or 6-ounce ramekins in a roasting pan; set aside.

2. Heat 1 cup of the maple sugar with the cold water in a

Virtuous Maple

Food historian Richard J. Hooker notes that in the 18th century, making and using maple sugar was a way to subvert the slave trade that produced refined cane sugar. "Sugar made at home," insisted one almanac, "must possess a sweeter flavor to an independent American of the north, than that which is mingled with the groans and tears of slavery."

small, heavy saucepan. Boil, uncovered, until the mixture reduces by about ½, about 12 minutes. Remove from the heat and whisk in the butter. Carefully pour the caramel into the custard cups, dividing evenly. Set aside to cool briefly.

3. In a bowl, whisk the eggs, egg yolks, warm milk and the remaining 1 cup maple sugar until smooth. Pour about ⅔ cup of this mixture into each cup. Place the roasting pan on the center rack of the oven. Pour in enough hot tap water to reach halfway up the sides of the cups.

4. Bake until the custards are set but still quite jiggly in the center, 25 to 30 minutes. Carefully remove the custards from the water bath and cool on a wire rack.

5. Cover the custards and chill for at least 2 hours.

6. To serve, run the tip of a knife gently around the edge of each custard cup, and invert the custard onto a serving plate, pouring the maple caramel over and around the custard.

MAIL-ORDER SOURCE FOR GRANULATED MAPLE SUGAR
Butternut Mountain Farm, www.butternutmountainfarm
.com; (800) 828-2376.

MEXICAN CHOCOLATE FLAN WITH KAHLÚA

(*FLAN DE CHOCOLATE CON KAHLÚA*)

Since chocolate is native to Central America and was used by the Aztecs for centuries, combining it with a dessert from the Spanish settlers makes sense. In this smooth custard, caramel and chocolate mingle to give a sharp, double-edged flavor. Mexican chocolate includes cinnamon and frequently almonds; you can approximate its flavor with semisweet chocolate and cinnamon, as directed below. This recipe is from Rick and Deann Bayless, owners of Chicago's Frontera Grill and Topolobampo and authors of *Authentic Mexican*.

Serves 10 or more

CARAMEL

1	cup sugar
⅓	cup water

CUSTARD

2	cups half-and-half, or 1½ cups milk plus ½ cup heavy cream
2	cups milk
2½	3-ounce tablets Mexican chocolate (see note) or 7 ounces semisweet chocolate, very finely chopped
1	cinnamon stick
⅔	cup sugar
10	large eggs
1½	tablespoons Kahlúa or other coffee liqueur
1	teaspoon pure vanilla extract
½	teaspoon almond extract

1. Set out 10 small custard cups, plus a roasting pan large enough to hold the cups.

2. **CARAMEL:** Combine the sugar and water in a small, heavy saucepan. Bring to a boil over medium heat, washing down the sides of the pan with a brush dipped in water, until the sugar completely dissolves. Continue to cook, without stirring, until the syrup turns an even, deep amber color, about 8 minutes; the timing can vary.

3. Working carefully, divide the caramel among the custard

cups, tilting the cups to coat the bottom and sides. Set the caramelized cups in the roasting pan.

4. **Custard:** Pour the half-and-half or milk and cream mixture and the milk into a large saucepan. Add the chocolate, cinnamon stick and sugar. Bring to a simmer over medium heat, stirring occasionally. Remove the pan from the heat, cover and set aside to steep for 20 minutes. Meanwhile, preheat the oven to 350 degrees F, with a rack in the center.

5. In a large bowl, beat together the eggs, Kahlúa, vanilla and almond extract. Slowly beat in the hot milk mixture. Strain through a fine-mesh sieve into a pitcher or large measuring cup; discard the cinnamon stick. Pour the mixture into the caramelized molds, dividing evenly.

6. Place the roasting pan on the center rack of the oven. Pour in enough hot tap water to reach halfway up the sides of the cups. Loosely cover the pan with foil. Bake just until the custards are set but still slightly wobbly in the center, usually 20 to 25 minutes; do not overbake.

7. Remove the custards from the water bath. Refrigerate until they are well chilled, at least 2 hours. Cover with plastic wrap.

8. To unmold the custards, run the tip of a knife gently around the edge of each custard cup. Place a serving plate over the mold and invert the two, shaking gently until the flan slips out. Spoon any remaining caramel onto the flan and serve immediately.

Note: Mexican Ibarra chocolate is available at many specialty stores and by mail-order from Dean & DeLuca, www.deandeluca .com; (800) 221-7714.

CUBAN CARAMEL CUSTARD
(*TOCINO DEL CIELO*)

If you love eggy puddings, this dense, caramelized custard will make you swoon. The translucent pudding uses sugar syrup instead of milk as the liquid element. I've cut back on both the sugar and the egg yolks in this version, but this is still no diet dessert.

⤳ *Serves 6 to 8*

1¼	cups sugar
⅓	cup water
	Juice of ½ lemon
4	large eggs
4	large egg yolks
1	teaspoon pure vanilla extract

1. Combine the sugar, water and lemon juice in a nonreactive saucepan and cook, stirring, until the sugar dissolves. Boil the syrup, uncovered, without stirring, until it thickens slightly and reaches 225 degrees F on a candy thermometer, usually about 7 minutes. Pour all but about ¼ cup of the syrup into a heatproof bowl; set aside to cool. Meanwhile, preheat the oven to 350 degrees F, with a rack in the center.

2. Continue to cook the reserved ¼ cup syrup, without stirring, until it turns medium amber, 3 to 5 minutes. Immediately pour the caramel into an 8-inch square or 10-x-6-inch rectangular baking dish, tilting the dish to coat the bottom evenly. Set aside.

3. Add the eggs, egg yolks and vanilla to the bowl of cooled syrup; whisk until blended. Place the baking dish in a roasting pan; pour the custard mixture into the caramel-lined dish.

4. Place the roasting pan on the center rack of the oven. Pour in enough hot tap water to reach halfway up the sides of the baking dish. Bake until the custard is almost set but still quite liquid in the center (it will firm as it cools), about 25 minutes. Remove from the water bath and cool the custard on a wire rack.

5. Chill the custard until cold, at least 2 hours. Run the tip of a knife along the edge of the custard and unmold onto a serving plate, so the caramel side is up. Serve in small portions.

"Bacon from Heaven"

This pudding, whose Spanish name means "bacon from heaven," is originally from Spain and is a favorite home dessert in Cuba.

Reflecting the belief that using a lot of eggs shows prosperity, early Spanish and Portuguese dessert recipes call for 12, 14, 18 or even more egg yolks.

BRAZILIAN COCONUT CUSTARDS
(QUINDIN DE YA-YA)

From Brazil, here's a sweet coconut custard that's almost as dense as fudge, golden on top, with a gelatinous bottom layer. The custards are most often served with afternoon tea. I have reduced the number of egg yolks in this one from the original 16.

⤙ Makes 6 puddings

1	large egg
6	large egg yolks
1	cup sugar
½	cup (1 stick) unsalted butter, softened
1	teaspoon orange flower water, or to taste (see note)
½	teaspoon ground cinnamon
½	teaspoon ground cloves
1½	cups shredded sweetened or unsweetened coconut

1. Preheat the oven to 350 degrees F, with a rack in the center. Generously butter 6 custard cups or ramekins and place them in a roasting pan.

2. In a bowl, beat the egg and egg yolks with an electric mixer at medium-high speed. Gradually add the sugar and beat until the mixture is pale and thick and forms a ribbon when the beater is lifted, about 8 minutes.

3. Beat in the butter, orange flower water, cinnamon and cloves. Turn off the machine; fold in the coconut just until blended. Spoon the mixture into the cups, dividing evenly.

4. Place the roasting pan on the center rack of the oven. Pour in enough hot tap water to reach about halfway up the sides of the cups. Bake until the custards are lightly golden and set when pressed gently with a fingertip, 30 to 35 minutes. Remove the cups from the water bath and let cool to room temperature on a wire rack. Serve at room temperature, directly from the cups.

NOTE: Orange flower water is available in specialty stores or by mail-order from Dean & DeLuca, www.deandeluca.com; (800) 221-7714. Rose water is also available.

Eggs as Status Symbol

This dessert, like others rich in sugar and egg yolks, reflects Brazil's Portuguese influence. Traditional Portuguese desserts can be summed up by two ingredients: egg yolks and sugar—custard lover's heaven.

"Yaya" or "Iaia" was the slaves' way of addressing the young girls of the Big House, the home of the owner and his family on the sugar plantations in the North of Brazil. "Sinha"— a contraction of Senhora— was used to address the mistress. This sweet confection was popular in the Big House.

ABOUT CRÈME BRÛLÉE

Before the 1980s, crème brûlée was virtually unknown to most Americans or was seen as a quaint English dessert. But suddenly, this smooth, rich custard topped by a sheer layer of crisply caramelized sugar became one of the signatures of that decade's self-indulgence and the darling of the restaurant boom.

The source of crème brûlée is usually considered to be a Trinity College recipe for "Cambridge Burnt Cream," dating from the 1860s. But this custard turns up in both French and English cookery books at least two centuries earlier—often enough that it was probably widely made considerably before that.

In England, in *The Modern Cook*, published in the early 18th century, Vincent La Chapelle includes a "Crackling Cream," directing the cook to glaze a boiled custard with a "fire-shovel red-Hot," then "Let it dry a little more in the Oven, till it be much diminished and crackling." From that time on, this dessert became "the phoenix dish of our [British] cookery," according to the late author Jane Grigson, "that rises again and again in popularity."

Like so many desserts, crème brûlée may have been borrowed from the French, brought over to England by a working chef. But a more critical connection is to Catalonia in northeastern Spain, where a similar dessert called *crema catalana* is served. This custard of cream and egg yolks flavored with lemon zest and cinnamon is poured into ramekins, topped with sugar and caramelized with a hot poker (or under a broiler). Although slightly different in texture and flavor, it's crème brûlée in spirit, down to its brûléed surface.

Originally called *crema de Sant Josep*, the catalan custard was traditionally served on Saint Joseph's feast day, March 19th. It didn't acquire its burned surface until much more recently, in recipes printed during this century.

To Make Burnt Cream

Boil a pint of cream with sugar, and a little lemon peel shred fine, then beat the yolks of six and the whites of four eggs separately, when your cream is cooled, put in your eggs, with a spoonful of orange flower water, and one of fine flour, set it over the fire, keep stirring it till it is thick, put it into a dish; when it is cold sift a quarter of a pound of sugar all over, hold a hot salamander over it till it is very brown, and looks like a glass plate over your cream.

ELIZABETH RAFFALD
THE EXPERIENCED ENGLISH HOUSEKEEPER
PHILADELPHIA, 1818;
LONDON, 1773

Crema Catalana

One litre of milk, 100 grams of sucre, four or five egg yolks, 125 grams of cooking starch. Mix everything together, filter through a colander and bring to a boil on a slow fire with a lemon peel and a stick of cinnamon. Stir continuously, always in one direction, until it comes to a good point. Take out the lemon and the cinnamon, put the cream on a plate and let it cool.

When cold, and moments before serving, pour good fine sugar mixed with some powdered cinnamon, burn it without letting it melt, with a palette knife or a grill [a special grill with a handle, similar to an iron]. If the plate is large and you only have one palette or grill, only use the amount of sugar that can be burned [caramelized at once] without having to reheat the grill.

The question is that the sugar shouldn't melt into the cream.

FERRÁN AGULLÓ I VIDAL
*LIBRE DE LA CUINA
CATALANA*
1931

150

CLASSIC CRÈME BRÛLÉE

Crème brûlée can be made in a single large pan or, for neater, more luxurious presentation, in individual ramekins. The wide, shallow white porcelain ramekins used in restaurants are perfect—little depth, all surface. The crucial part, of course, is the crackly sugar surface, but the custard is important, too—this is the time to pull out all the stops and use real cream.

This recipe is based on one from Dieter Schorner, a gifted pastry chef who occasionally taught at New York City Community College when I was a student there. Dieter was the pastry chef at New York's Le Cirque, the epicenter from which crème brûlée hysteria swept the nation.

Serves 8

4	cups (1 quart) heavy cream
1	vanilla bean, split lengthwise
8	large egg yolks
½	cup sugar
¾	cup packed light brown sugar, or to taste

1. In a small saucepan, scald the cream with the vanilla bean over medium heat. Remove from the heat. (If you have time, let the vanilla bean steep in the milk for 30 to 60 minutes. Reheat before proceeding.) Place eight 6-ounce ramekins in a roasting pan; set aside.

2. Preheat the oven to 300 degrees F, with a rack in the center. In a small bowl, whisk the egg yolks just until blended. Slowly whisk in the sugar. Remove the vanilla bean from the hot cream and scrape the seeds into the cream. Slowly beat the hot cream into the yolks, whisking all the time. Strain the mixture through a fine sieve into a large measuring cup or pitcher. Pour the custard into the ramekins.

3. Place the roasting pan on the center rack of the oven. Pour in enough hot tap water to reach about halfway up the sides of the ramekins. Bake until the custards are just set, about 30 minutes (the timing can vary based on the depth of the ramekins). Remove the custards from their water bath and place on a wire rack until cooled.

4. Refrigerate until very cold, at least 3 hours.

5. Shortly before serving, preheat the broiler with the rack

about 3 inches from the heat. Sieve a thin, even layer of the brown sugar over the custards. Place under the broiler just until the sugar melts, usually less than 1 minute (watch carefully to prevent burning). Serve immediately.

BERT GREENE'S PUMPKIN CRÈME BRÛLÉE

While I generally like crème brûlée's rich vanilla egginess unadorned by other flavors, this one melds soft pumpkin with gentle spices, topping it with crackly caramel. The recipe is the late cookbook author Bert Greene's version. I first made this dessert for Thanksgiving in 1981, when I gave thanks daily for returning to the U.S. from England, and I've made it for almost every Thanksgiving since.

Serves 8

- 3 cups heavy cream
- ½ cup sugar
- 6 large egg yolks
- ⅔ cup pumpkin puree (fresh, page 496, or canned unsweetened)
- ½ teaspoon ground cinnamon
- ¼ teaspoon *each* ground ginger, fresh-grated nutmeg and ground cloves
- 1 tablespoon dark rum
- 1 teaspoon pure vanilla extract
- 3 tablespoons packed light brown sugar

1. Preheat the oven to 325 degrees F, with a rack in the center. Heat the cream with the sugar in a saucepan, stirring frequently, until the sugar dissolves. Turn off the heat.

2. In a bowl, whisk the egg yolks until light and fluffy; gradually whisk in the pumpkin, cinnamon, ginger, nutmeg and cloves. Slowly whisk in the hot cream mixture; stir in the rum and vanilla.

3. Pour the mixture into a 1½-quart soufflé dish; place the dish in a roasting pan. Set the pan on the center rack of the oven and pour in enough hot tap water to reach halfway up the sides of the dish.

4. Bake until the custard is set but still slightly wobbly in the center, usually about 1½ hours. Remove the dish from the water bath; cool to room temperature on a wire rack.

5. Cover and refrigerate for 6 hours or overnight.

6. About 15 minutes before serving time, preheat the broiler and adjust the broiler rack so that the top of the soufflé dish will be about 3 inches from the heat.

7. Sieve the brown sugar evenly over the surface of the custard. Broil until the sugar melts and turns brown, 2 to 3 minutes; watch carefully to prevent burning. Serve immediately.

About Oeufs à la Neige and Floating Island

*I*n both oeufs à la neige and floating island, custard and soft, sweet meringue conspire to make two of the most soothing of the extended family of custard desserts.

For purposes of clarity, oeufs à la neige are generally considered to be individual egg-shaped meringues—"snow eggs"—while floating island is a single large meringue afloat in a custard sea. Countless cookbooks, mainly in the 19th and 20th centuries, ignore or mangle these distinctions, however. For example, Mrs. Sarah Tyson Rorer's floating island recipe of 1886 is made with individual "meringues piled onto a custard," while *Larousse Gastronomique* translates oeufs à la neige simply as "floating islands." Early French versions of floating island aren't meringue at all, but layers of spongecake or brioche moistened with liqueur and filled with nuts and raisins, served in a custard sauce or a pool of berry puree.

These sorts of desserts were frequently elaborate, as is the floating island from *The Experienced English Housekeeper* by Elizabeth Raffald, also published in the 1700s, in which the egg whites are decorated to simulate a pastoral winter landscape:

beat the white of an egg to a strong froth, and roll a sprig of myrtle in it to imitate snow . . . when your dish is full to the brim; let it stand till it is quite cold and stiff, then lay on rock candied-sweetmeats upon the top of your jelly, and sheep and swans to pick at the myrtle; stick green sprigs in two or three places on the top of your jelly, amongst your shapes; it looks very pretty in the middle of a table for a supper. You must not put the shapes on the jelly till you are going to send it to the table.

Although not nearly as fanciful as Raffald's creation, floating island and oeufs à la neige still make a striking conclusion to a meal.

OEUFS À LA NEIGE WITH RASPBERRIES

These meringues are quite large and puff up further as they poach. You can make them ahead; keep them refrigerated on the custard (or in a bowl of milk) for several hours. The dessert has always been fairly light because of the meringues, and this version uses a low-fat custard with plenty of flavor and body.

For garnish, you can scatter toasted sliced almonds or a few raspberries over the meringues. At restaurants, oeufs à la neige is often topped with caramel. To do this, make the caramel following step 1 in the recipe for Warm Caramel Sauce (page 614); while it is still hot, use a fork to drizzle it in thin strands over the meringues.

Serves 6

CUSTARD SAUCE
2½ cups low-fat (1%) milk
1 vanilla bean, split lengthwise
1 strip orange zest
2 large eggs
⅓ cup sugar

POACHED MERINGUES
1 cup low-fat (1%) milk
4 large egg whites

¼   cup sugar, preferably superfine
½   teaspoon pure vanilla extract

24   small ripe strawberries or raspberries, for garnish

1. **CUSTARD SAUCE:** Rinse a heavy saucepan with cold water; shake dry. Add the milk, vanilla bean and orange zest and bring nearly to a boil. Cover and set aside to steep for at least 30 minutes.

2. Return the milk to a simmer. In a bowl, whisk the eggs and sugar until smooth but not fluffy; gradually add a little of the hot milk to warm the eggs. Pour all of the egg mixture into the simmering milk. Cook over low heat, stirring constantly, until the mixture thickens enough to coat the back of a spoon, usually 7 to 8 minutes; do not boil. Strain the custard into a clean bowl. Scrape the seeds from the vanilla bean into the custard and stir in. Cover the bowl and refrigerate until cold. *(The sauce can be prepared 1 to 2 days ahead; cover and refrigerate.)*

3. **POACHED MERINGUES:** Place the milk in a wide sauté pan, and add enough water to bring the liquids to a depth of about 2 inches; bring to a simmer. Meanwhile, beat the egg whites until they form soft peaks; gradually add the sugar and the vanilla and continue to beat until the meringue is stiff but not dry. With 2 large spoons dipped in cold water, form 6 large 3-inch egg-shaped ovals of meringue, gently dropping them into the simmering liquid as they are formed. (Work in batches; the meringues should not touch as they poach.) Poach the meringues on one side for about 8 minutes. Gently turn over and poach the second side for about 4 minutes. Lift the meringues from the liquid and drain briefly on a kitchen towel; form and poach the remaining meringues in the same manner.

4. Spoon the cold custard sauce into a wide, shallow tureen or other serving dish. Gently arrange the meringues on the pool of custard. Cover and chill if not serving immediately.

5. Spoon about ¼ cup of the custard sauce into each shallow serving bowl. Carefully place a meringue on the sauce in the center of the bowl. Scatter 4 berries around each meringue and serve.

FLOATING ISLAND

This is a beauty—a large molded soft meringue on a custard sea. It is based on a great idea from chef-author Pierre Franey. Instead of fussing with forming and poaching individual meringues, you simply pile the beaten egg white mixture into a buttered kugelhopf pan or ring mold to make one large meringue. Then the meringue is oven-poached in a water bath.

Not only does this technique make for easy work, but with the meringue rising impressively over the rim of the mold and inverted effortlessly onto its pool of custard, it makes a spectacular presentation.

Serves 10 to 12

10	large egg whites
½	teaspoon cream of tartar
1	cup sugar
	Eggnog Custard Sauce (page 609) or Low-Fat Custard Sauce (page 610)
12	large strawberries, hulled, for garnish
	Caramel (optional; see note)

1. Preheat the oven to 350 degrees F, with a rack in the lower third. Generously butter a 12-cup (8½-x-3-inch) kugelhopf or other fluted tube pan or ring mold; set aside.

2. Beat the egg whites with an electric mixer at medium-high speed until frothy. Add the cream of tartar. Gradually beat in the sugar and continue beating until the meringue is quite stiff and shiny.

3. With a large spatula, lightly pack the meringue into the prepared mold; smooth the top. Tap the mold on a counter several times to deflate any air pockets. Lightly butter a sheet of foil and lay it, buttered side down, without crimping, on top.

4. Place the mold in a roasting pan and set the dish on the oven rack. Pour enough hot tap water into the roasting pan to reach ⅓ to ½ the way up the sides of the mold.

5. Bake the meringue until it is set and puffed above the rim of the mold, about 15 minutes. Remove the mold from the water bath and remove the foil. Let cool completely on a wire rack. (*If the meringue is being made a day ahead, refrigerate it in its mold at this point.*)

Flooting Island

Take a Soop Dish . . . a pretty deep Glass Dish is best, and set it on a China Dish, first take a Quart of the thickest Cream you can get, make it pretty sweet with fine Sugar, pour in a Gill of Sack, grate the yellow Rind of a Lemon in, and mill the Cream till it is all of a thick Froth, then as carefully as you can, pour the thin from the Froth into a Dish; take a French Role . . . cut it as thin as you can, lay a Layer of that as light as possible on the Cream, then a Layer of Currant-jelly, then a very thin Layer of Role, and then Hartshorn-jelly, then French Role, and over that whip your Froth which you have saved off the Cream . . . and lay at Top as high as you can heap it; and as for the Rim of the Dish set it round with Fruit or Sweetmeats according to your Fancy, this looks very pretty in the middle of a Table with Candles round it . . .

HANNAH GLASSE
THE ART OF COOKERY,
MADE PLAIN AND EASY
LONDON, 1747

6. To assemble, unmold the meringue onto a large round platter and spoon 1 cup of the custard sauce around and in the center of the meringue. Place the strawberries around the meringue. Serve in slices, each garnished with a strawberry, and pass the remaining custard sauce separately.

NOTE: If you'd like to garnish the floating island with caramel, make a batch of caramel following step 1 in the recipe for Warm Caramel Sauce (page 614). Let the caramel cool for about 10 minutes; it should still be fluid. With a fork, drizzle thin, random lines of caramel over the top of the floating island.

LULI'S TRIFLE

Trifle is the centerpiece of countless English celebrations. It allows for all sorts of variations; try different fruit and liqueur combinations. This is my friend Luli's recipe, which she whips up for birthdays and holidays. To serve a crowd, you can double or triple the quantities; 1 to 1½ cups of cream is usually plenty for the topping, even when you multiply the recipe.

 Serves 6

	Marie's Vanilla Spongecake (page 117), cooled, or pound cake
2	tablespoons sweet or medium-dry sherry
2	tablespoons dark rum or brandy
1	pint fresh or dry-frozen, thawed raspberries
½	cup best-quality raspberry jam or other jam of choice
2	cups Eggnog Custard Sauce (page 609) or Low-Fat Custard Sauce (page 610)
1	cup heavy cream, well chilled
2	teaspoons confectioners' or superfine sugar
½	teaspoon pure vanilla extract
⅓	cup slivered almonds, for garnish

1. Trim the edges of the cake with a serrated knife and cut the cake into 1-inch triangular wedges or slices. Fit the pieces of cake into the bottom of a 1½-quart glass bowl or soufflé dish, making a fairly solid layer. (You probably won't need all of the cake, but that depends on the size of the bowl you're using.) Sprinkle the sherry and rum or brandy over the cake.

2. In a bowl, mix the berries (reserving a few for decoration) with the jam, stirring them to bruise the berries a bit. Spread the berry mixture over the soaked cake, so that it reaches all the way to the sides of the dish. Pour the custard sauce over the berries. Cover the dish with wax paper or plastic wrap and refrigerate for 2 hours or longer to allow the ingredients to soak together and combine their flavors.

3. Up to about 1 hour before serving, whip the cream with the sugar and vanilla until it forms soft peaks. With a spatula, spread the cream over the trifle. If you like, reserve a little of the cream and pipe rosettes around the edges of the cream. Decorate the top with the reserved raspberries. Chill for at least 2 hours.

4. Just before serving, sprinkle the almonds over the top and serve, spooning up the trifle from the bottom.

Whim Wham

Sweeten a quart of cream, and mix with it a tea-cupful of white wine, and the grated peel of a lemon; whisk it to a froth, which drain upon the back of a sieve, and put part into a deep glass dish; cut some Naples biscuit as thin as possible, and put a layer lightly over the froth, and one of red currant jelly, then a layer of the froth, and one of the biscuit and jelly; finish with the froth, and pour the remainder of the cream into the dish, and garnish with citron and candied orange-peel cut into straws.

MRS. DALGAIRNS
THE PRACTICE OF COOKERY
EDINBURGH, 1830

CABINET PUDDING

For a cabinet pudding, a mold is lined with spongecake, filled with custard and baked in a water bath until set. For trifle, a near relative, cake and boiled custard are layered in a bowl, with no baking.

Though simplified, this recipe stays fairly true to the 19th-century cabinet pudding of Charles Elmé Francatelli in *The Modern Cook* (London, 1865). Cake, studded with macaroons and brandy-soaked dried fruit, is covered with custard and baked. Custard sauce is the traditional accompaniment, but it isn't necessary.

Serves 8

¼ cup dried cherries or dried currants
2 tablespoons candied orange rind
3 tablespoons brandy or Grand Marnier
4 ounces (½ of a cake) Marie's Vanilla Spongecake (page 117), cooled, edges trimmed
2 ounces (about 1 cup) miniature or regular-size amaretti (crisp Italian macaroons)
5 large eggs
2 large egg yolks
⅔ cup sugar
1 teaspoon grated lemon zest
½ teaspoon grated orange zest
4 cups (1 quart) milk
Eggnog Custard Sauce (page 609) or Low-Fat Custard Sauce (page 610), for serving (optional)

1. In a small bowl, combine the dried cherries or currants, orange rind and brandy or Grand Marnier; set aside to macerate for about 15 minutes. Butter a 2-quart soufflé dish; set aside.

2. Using a long serrated knife, cut the cake into ¼ inch-thick slices. If the amaretti are miniature, use them as is; if they are regular size, coarsely crumble. Arrange ½ of the cake and ½ of the macaroons in the buttered dish. Sprinkle about ½ of the macerated fruits on top, along with some of the soaking liquid. Repeat, arranging the remaining cake and amaretti in a layer, and sprinkling with the remaining macerated fruit and liquid.

3. Preheat the oven to 325 degrees F, with a rack in the center. In a bowl, whisk together the eggs, egg yolks, sugar and citrus zests until blended. Whisk in the milk until blended. Pour the mix-

ture into the mold, gently press the cake with a spatula, and pull it away from the sides a bit, so that the custard mixture soaks down into the mold. Let the pudding stand for about 10 minutes.

4. Place a folded dish towel in a large roasting pan. (It will prevent the bottom of the pudding from overcooking.) Set the pudding on the towel and place on the center rack of the oven. Pour enough hot tap water into the roasting pan to reach halfway up the sides of the soufflé dish. Bake until the custard is set but still trembles slightly in the center, usually about 1 hour and 25 minutes.

5. Carefully remove the pudding from the water bath. Cool to room temperature on a wire rack. Refrigerate until cold, at least 3 hours.

6. Serve the pudding cold, spooning it out of the soufflé dish, and accompany it with custard sauce, if you like.

Diplomat Pudding

Cabinet pudding, also called diplomat pudding or *diplomate*, is a baroque affair from the hands of Victorian-era chefs: Candied cherries and citron are arranged in jewel-like patterns to ornament the mold, followed by crushed biscuits, brandy, preserved ginger—all are fair game here. There are also frozen versions, such as Alexis Soyer's *pouding de cabinet glacé*.

Later recipes (particularly American ones) bastardize cabinet pudding, transforming it into a gelatinized dessert; even, in one instance, lining the mold with canned peaches.

TIRAMISÙ

Who could have predicted that this Italian family dessert of Venetian origin (actually, from the nearby town of Treviso), whose name literally translates as "pick me up," would become the toast of chic restaurants on several continents? It's nothing but a simple spoon dessert: ladyfingers or spongecake soaked in coffee and piled in a dish with a custard made with mascarpone cheese.

This version is from Johanne Killeen, co-owner of Al Forno restaurant, in Providence, Rhode Island. Johanne adapted it from a recipe that her good friend, Becky More, got from Mercedes Zezza in Naples. I've tried lots of versions of tiramisù, but the composition of this one—the relative amounts of cake, custard and coffee—is pitch-perfect.

⤳ *Makes one 9-inch cake; serves about 8*

Marie's Vanilla Spongecake (page 117), baked in an 8½- to 9-inch springform pan until golden and set, about 30 minutes
2 cups milk
¾ cup sugar
6 large egg yolks
¼ cup all-purpose flour
¼ cup (½ stick) unsalted butter, cut into pieces
¼ cup light rum or cognac
2 teaspoons pure vanilla extract
¾ cup (about 6 ounces) mascarpone cheese (available in cheese shops and at Italian markets)
About 2 cups strong-brewed espresso, for moistening cake, or less
3-4 tablespoons unsweetened cocoa powder, for sprinkling

1. Cool the spongecake in the pan on a wire rack for 20 minutes. Remove the sides of the pan and carefully invert the cake onto the rack. Turn right side up; cool completely. *(Wrap the cake in plastic and store at room temperature if preparing in advance.)* Wash and dry the springform pan; reassemble the pan.

2. While the cake is cooling, prepare the custard: In a non-reactive saucepan over medium heat, scald all but 2 tablespoons of the milk with the sugar, stirring until the sugar dissolves. In a bowl, beat the egg yolks with the reserved cold milk and the flour. Gradually pour about ½ of the hot milk into the yolk mixture and whisk constantly. Return the mixture to the saucepan and cook

over medium heat, stirring constantly, until it comes to a boil. Boil, stirring constantly, for 2 minutes. Remove from the heat and strain the custard into a clean bowl. Whisk in the butter, rum or cognac and vanilla. Cover with wax paper or plastic wrap pressed directly on the surface to prevent a "skin" from forming. Refrigerate until cold, at least 2 hours.

3. In a bowl, lighten the mascarpone by folding it over itself a few times with a rubber spatula and mashing gently, if necessary. Gradually fold in the cold custard. Cover and chill until you are ready to assemble the cake.

4. With a serrated knife, cut the cake horizontally into 3 equal layers. Place the bottom layer in the springform pan. Drizzle and brush it with part of the espresso, soaking it generously. Gently top the cake with ⅓ of the custard. Repeat with another layer of cake, more espresso and more custard. For the top layer, moisten the cut surface of the cake with espresso. Invert it, browned side up. Gently spread with the remaining custard, smoothing the surface. Sift some of the cocoa in an even layer over the top of the cake. Refrigerate for at least 1 hour so the cake will be well chilled and the layers will set.

5. Sprinkle a little more cocoa over the top before serving in wedges.

THOMAS KELLER'S MOLTEN CHOCOLATE

This is the ultimate in chocolate: a warm, baked-to-order individual hot soufflé-like mousse with a crackled, brownie-like exterior enclosing a molten chocolate center.

This dessert is so good, so essence-of-chocolate, that it evokes the timeless chocolate puddings, moist cakes and warm soufflés that linger in memory. It's the creation of the amply gifted Thomas Keller, whose restaurant, French Laundry, is in Napa Valley, California. Though Keller calls it a tart, it has no crust.

The baking dishes are frozen before they go into the oven, so the dessert comes out creamy. It should be baked just before serving. The recipe has been adapted slightly for the home kitchen. Keller serves his dessert with a cool pear puree and vanilla ice cream. I like to accompany it with either a small scoop of ice cream or a spoonful of cool vanilla-scented whipped cream.

Serves 6

4	ounces best-quality imported semisweet chocolate, finely chopped
1½	ounces unsweetened chocolate, finely chopped
10	tablespoons (1 stick plus 2 tablespoons) unsalted butter, softened
½	cup sugar
3	large eggs
½	cup plus 2 teaspoons all-purpose flour
¾	teaspoon baking powder
1½	tablespoons unsweetened cocoa powder
	Vanilla ice cream or vanilla-flavored whipped cream, for serving

1. Lightly butter six 1-cup ramekins or custard cups; set aside. Place the semisweet and unsweetened chocolate in the top of a double boiler or in a bowl set over a saucepan of hot water over low heat (the bottom of the bowl should not touch the water). Stir occasionally until the chocolate melts; remove from the heat.

2. When the chocolate is smooth, stir in the butter and sugar until smooth. Add the eggs, flour, baking powder and cocoa. Beat with an electric mixer at medium-high speed until the mixture is pale and has a thick, mousse-like consistency, about 5 minutes.

3. Fill the ramekins ½ full, cover each with plastic wrap. Freeze for at least 3 hours. *(The ramekins can be filled and frozen up to 3 days in advance.)*

4. Just before serving time, preheat the oven to 375 degrees F, with a rack at the center. Bake the cold desserts until the outer edges of the tops are set, but the centers are still moist and shiny, usually 10 to 11 minutes. Invert each portion onto a serving plate and serve warm, with a small scoop of the vanilla ice cream or a spoonful of vanilla-flavored whipped cream. Alternately, serve directly from the ramekins.

ABOUT SOUFFLÉS

*P*eople are afraid of making soufflés—but they shouldn't be. The base of a dessert soufflé is simple: It can be a cooked, starch-thickened mixture, a pastry cream, a thick fruit puree, or just egg yolks beaten with sugar until they've doubled in volume. Well-beaten (but not overbeaten) egg whites are gently folded into the base, and the soufflé is popped into the oven. The oven's heat expands the air that's trapped in the beaten egg whites with ethereal results.

Your soufflé will rise more reliably if you use a straight-sided soufflé dish or other baking dish. I find that 1½ quarts is a good all-purpose size; 1- and 2-quart soufflé dishes are also nice to have on hand. (Soufflé dishes can be used as general-purpose baking dishes, as bowls or containers for vegetable and fruit salads.) My favorites are made of white porcelain, but glass soufflé dishes work well, too. I have several small ones—about 1 cup in capacity—that are great for individual soufflés—always a treat.

The soufflé base can be made ahead, with the beaten whites added just before it goes in the oven. Once you've whipped up a couple of perfect soufflés, look out—you'll acquire a reputation as a magician in the kitchen.

BLINTZ "SOUFFLÉ"

Blintzes are the Jewish pancakes that are rolled and folded around a sweetened cheese filling, then browned in butter. They're served for breakfast or for a dairy (nonmeat) supper. Russian *blinchiki* are close cousins.

This innovative spin on tradition takes the same flavors and ingredients and transforms them into a creamy "soufflé"—capturing all the buttery flavor of traditional blintzes, but without the hassle of rolling and frying, or even of beating egg whites. This luscious dessert is from Ilene Fields Stein of Rock Springs, Wyoming.

✑ Serves 6 to 8

1	pound cottage cheese (Ilene uses creamed; I use low-fat)
3	ounces (¼ cup plus 2 tablespoons) cream cheese
¼	cup (½ stick) unsalted butter, melted
¼	cup plus 2 tablespoons sugar
½	cup all-purpose flour
3	large eggs
½	teaspoon fresh lemon juice
½	teaspoon baking powder
½	teaspoon ground cinnamon
	Sour cream, for serving
	Strawberry, raspberry or black currant jam, for serving

1. Preheat the oven to 350 degrees F, with a rack in the center. Butter an 8- to 9-inch baking dish; set aside.

2. In a bowl, stir together the cottage cheese, cream cheese, butter and sugar until blended. Gently stir in the flour, eggs, lemon juice and baking powder. Spoon the batter into the prepared pan; sprinkle with the cinnamon.

3. Bake until the soufflé is set and the edges are just beginning to turn light gold, 40 to 45 minutes. Cool briefly on a wire rack.

4. Serve warm, spooning the soufflé from the dish (or cut it into squares or wedges), and passing the sour cream and jam at the table.

LITTLE PEAR SOUFFLÉS

Because these soufflés are made from pears with only some beaten egg whites to lighten them, they have an intense flavor.

Serves 4

1½	pounds (5-6) ripe Bosc pears, peeled, cored and cut into coarse chunks
1½	tablespoons fresh lemon juice
½	teaspoon ground cinnamon
½	teaspoon ground allspice
1	vanilla bean, split lengthwise
¼	cup cold water
2½	tablespoons pear eau-de-vie, Armagnac or amaretto
4	large egg whites
	Pinch salt
2½	tablespoons sugar
	Confectioners' sugar, for sprinkling

1. Butter four 1-cup ramekins or soufflé dishes; sprinkle the interiors with granulated sugar. Refrigerate until serving time.

2. Combine the pears, lemon juice, spices, vanilla bean and water in a heavy nonreactive saucepan. Cover and cook over medium heat, stirring, until the pears are soft, 7 to 10 minutes.

3. Uncover the pan and continue to cook, stirring and mashing the pears, until the mixture has reduced to a thick, chunky puree, about 5 minutes longer. Add the pear eau-de-vie or other liqueur and heat for a few moments. Remove from the heat. Remove the vanilla bean and scrape the seeds into the pear puree. Set aside to cool to lukewarm.

4. Shortly before serving, preheat the oven to 400 degrees F, with a rack in the lower third. Beat the egg whites with the salt until they form soft peaks; gradually add the sugar and continue beating until not quite stiff. Fold a large spoonful of whites into the pear mixture; gently fold in the remaining whites. Place the ramekins on a baking sheet; fill with the soufflé mixture. Smooth the tops with a spatula, and run your thumb around the batter inside the rim to help the soufflés to form a "high hat" as they bake.

5. Bake the soufflés until they are puffed and brown, 10 to 12 minutes.

6. Sprinkle the tops with confectioners' sugar. Quickly transfer the dishes to serving plates (lined with doilies, if you like) and serve immediately.

SALZBURG LITTLE MOUNTAIN SOUFFLÉS
(*SALZBURGER NOCKERL*)

On my first trip through Europe, two friends and I ordered this local specialty in a Salzburg wine bar, without having any idea what it was. It arrived, a big panful of puffed pillows of egg white, fragrant with vanilla, with just enough yolk folded in to give a melting, unctuous texture. I would up eating almost the whole thing.

It is sometimes eaten there as a light supper. This version comes from Andy Kistler, Austrian-born chef at Vienna '79, a New York restaurant that is no longer.

∽ *Serves 4*

4	tablespoons heavy cream or milk
4	teaspoons currant or other jelly
4	teaspoons unsalted butter, cut into 4 pats
6	large egg whites
¼	cup sugar
1	teaspoon pure vanilla extract
	Grated zest and juice of ½ large lemon
3	large egg yolks, lightly beaten
¼	cup sifted all-purpose flour
	Confectioners' sugar, for sprinkling

1. Preheat the oven to 450 degrees F, with a rack in the center. Place 4 shallow baking dishes, such as 7- or 8-inch oval gratin dishes, on a baking sheet. Pour 1 tablespoon of the cream or milk into each dish; spoon 1 teaspoon of the jelly over it, trying to distribute it fairly evenly, and then add 1 pat of the butter. (You can also bake this in a 10- to 12-inch gratin dish or shallow baking pan.)

2. With an electric mixer at medium-high speed, beat the egg whites until they form soft peaks. Gradually add the sugar, and then the vanilla, lemon zest and juice and beat until stiff and shiny.

3. Gently fold the egg yolks into the beaten egg whites. Sprinkle the flour over the mixture and fold together gently. Using a large rubber spatula, place 3 large mounds of the mixture in each of the prepared gratin dishes, gently smoothing each with the spatula.

4. Bake until puffed and golden, about 8 minutes. Sprinkle with confectioners' sugar and serve immediately.

*Edna Lewis,
National
Treasure*

Edna Lewis is the
author of several
cookbooks that convey
her unique voice, honesty
and good humor.

She grew up in
Freetown, Virginia, a
community of freed slaves,
where the seasons were
marked by hog-butchering
and sausage-making,
picking spring greens and
putting up summer fruits.

One afternoon over
coffee and pound cake,
Edna Lewis recalled when
she first came to New
York. "I was 18. I had
been to Washington the
summer after I finished
school. But at that time,
Washington was very
segregated. It was hard to
break through. But when I
got to New York, you
could do anything!"

Edna supported herself
by doing everything from
reproducing Dior gowns
from a magazine photo to
creating clothes for Bonwit
Teller's Christmas windows
(including one outfit with
500 hand-sewn peacock
feathers). One morning,
she "whipped up clothes—
real whory clothes—for a

EDNA LEWIS'S CHOCOLATE SOUFFLÉ

It's hard to think of a soufflé, that loftiest of desserts, as a homely pudding. But what is a soufflé, but a pudding lightened with beaten egg whites and baked until inflated to momentary glory?

Soufflés have been made for centuries. Antonin Carême gave detailed instructions for dozens of dessert soufflés, many thickened with ground rice. He also spins wild variations on the basic theme: mocha, hazelnut, pistachio, saffron and rose.

Still fondly remembered by New Yorkers, this was Edna Lewis's signature dessert during the heyday of Café Nicholson.

Serves 4 to 6

SOUFFLÉ
1	cup milk
½	vanilla bean or 1 teaspoon pure vanilla extract
2	tablespoons unsalted butter
2	tablespoons all-purpose flour
4	ounces unsweetened chocolate, grated
⅓	cup hot water
3	tablespoons sugar
¼	teaspoon salt
2	large egg yolks
5	large egg whites

HOT CHOCOLATE SAUCE
1½	ounces unsweetened chocolate, grated
1	cup water
2	tablespoons sugar
	Small piece vanilla bean or ½ teaspoon pure vanilla extract

Confectioners' sugar, for sprinkling
Whipped cream, for serving

1. **SOUFFLÉ:** Preheat the oven to 450 degrees F, with a rack in the center. In a small saucepan, scald the milk with the vanilla bean. (If using the vanilla extract, do not add it now.) Turn off the heat; set aside.

2. In a heavy-bottomed saucepan, melt the butter. Add the flour and cook over medium heat, stirring for 3 minutes, until

opaque but not brown. Remove the vanilla bean and add the milk, whisking vigorously. Cook the mixture, whisking occasionally, until thick and smooth, about 5 minutes.

3. Add the chocolate and whisk until melted and smooth. Remove the pan from the heat. If using the vanilla extract, add it now.

4. Whisk in the hot water, sugar and salt until blended. Add the egg yolks, stirring vigorously until smooth and satiny. Cover the chocolate base with wax paper, pressing it directly on the surface; set aside in a warm place.

5. In a medium bowl, beat the egg whites until they are stiff but not dry. Fold a little of the egg whites into the chocolate base; gently fold in the remainder. Spoon gently into a 2-quart unbuttered soufflé dish or four to six 1-cup ramekins. In either case, the dish(es) should be about ¾ full.

6. Bake until puffed and browned, 20 to 25 minutes for a large soufflé; 12 to 13 minutes for individual ones.

7. **HOT CHOCOLATE SAUCE:** Meanwhile, in a small heavy-bottomed saucepan, combine the chocolate, water, sugar and vanilla bean, if using. (If using the vanilla extract, do not add it now.) Simmer, stirring occasionally, for 15 to 20 minutes. Remove the pan from the heat, remove the vanilla bean and keep the sauce warm until needed. Stir in the vanilla extract, if using, just before serving.

8. Sprinkle the soufflé with confectioners' sugar and serve immediately with the hot chocolate sauce and whipped cream.

young model, real cute, for the cover of *True Story* magazine." It turned out to be Marilyn Monroe.

In 1948, Edna started cooking at New York City's Café Nicholson, still remembered as a unique blend of smart, East Side sophistication and down-home comfort that attracted a lively mixture of neighborhood regulars, society types and leading writers and artists. William Faulkner, Carson McCullers, Truman Capote, Marlon Brando— Edna fed them all.

Only one or two dishes were served each evening. "We wanted the kind of place where truck drivers eat, where the food isn't fancy, but it's good." Her signature dish was a chocolate soufflé, baked and served in small soup bowls, with hot chocolate sauce and a heaping bowl of whipped cream. Laughing shyly, Edna unfolded a yellowed clipping from the long-gone *New York Herald Tribune*, in which Clementine Paddleford wrote that Edna Lewis's soufflé was "as light as a dandelion seed in a wind."

RECIPES

Luli's Simplest Rice Pudding

Creamy Diner-Style Rice Pudding

Baked Custard-Style Rice Pudding

Sandy's Citrus Rice Pudding

Wild Rice Pudding with Honey and Dried Cherries or Cranberries

Marie's Brown Rice Pudding with Maple Syrup

Molded Rice Pudding with Caramel Sauce

The Coach House Bread-and-Butter Pudding

Challah Bread Pudding with Raisins

Buttermilk Corn Bread Pudding

Bon Ton's New Orleans Bread Pudding with Whiskey Sauce

Omaha Caramel Bread Pudding

Commander's Palace Bread Pudding Soufflé

Chocolate Silk Bread Pudding

Santa Fe Bread Pudding with Wine and Cheese

Italian Chocolate Bread Pudding

Caramelized Panettone Bread Pudding

Warm Pear Charlotte

Summer Pudding of Four Red Fruits

Gingerbread Custard

Mom's New Noodle Kugel

Hungarian Cheese-Noodle Dessert

Czech Noodle and Apple Soufflé

New England Oatmeal Pudding with Warm Maple Syrup

CHAPTER 5

RICE, BREAD AND NOODLE PUDDINGS

Rice and bread puddings, and other puddings based on noodles, starches and grains, collectively form one of the twin pillars that hold up the entire edifice of old-fashioned desserts. (The other is the family of warm fruit desserts that includes cobblers, crisps and brown Bettys.)

Probably no other type of homemade dessert shows so many cross-cultural parallels. All over the world, leftover bread and rice are turned into simple desserts by adding a little sugar or honey, plus milk and an egg or two.

Grains were the basis of the most ancient puddings, dating back to the times when wheat and oats were sweetened with honey and spices and transformed into primitive mushes or gruels—the forerunners of the puddings we know today. In the first century A.D., Pliny described cooking "black oats" to "form excellent creams," and two centuries before Christ, the Roman statesman Cato the Elder explained in detail how red wheat flour was stewed slowly with white cheese, honey and an egg to make "Carthaginian pudding."

It may seem surprising to see a simple rice pudding grouped with a Czech noodle soufflé, but in each case, a culture's staple grain is the dessert's starting point. In India, Africa, the Middle East and throughout the Far East, it's rice; in Japan, red azuki beans; in Eastern Europe, fresh egg noodles. In India, ground rice is made into a pudding called *firni*; split peas and mung beans are simmered in coconut milk to make *payasam* for weddings, and farina is formed into balls served in cool rose-water-scented syrup. *Sholezard*, a Persian rice pudding tinted yellow with saffron, is traditionally served on the anniversary of the death of a member of the Prophet Muhammad's family. A Spanish rice pudding called *arroz con miel* is of Arabic origins, brought to the Iberian peninsula during the days of the Moorish occupation that began in the 8th century A.D.

By taking that little bit of last night's rice or some day-old bread—the staples that nourish and keep us alive—and making something sweet out of them, mothers and grandmothers offer us something "extra" to end a meal—not because we need it, but because it tastes good. And that's the first step in transforming food from something that simply keeps us alive to a source of pleasure. Maybe that's why rice and bread puddings evoke childhood memories so vividly.

CHOOSING RICE FOR PUDDING

There are now over 25 different types of rice available, with several new hybrids. In general, short- and medium-grain rices work well for rice puddings, since the starch in them breaks down and helps to thicken the pudding. Long-grain rice can also be used for rice pudding, if you cook it enough.

Experiment with other rices—basmati and Texmati add surprising flavor. Both wild rice (not a true rice) and brown rice also make delicious puddings (see the recipes on pages 178 and 179).

Old-Fashioned Spirit

Remembering the French dessert called *Riz à l'Impératrice*, writer M.F.K. Fisher says that when this pudding was tipped out upon its platter, "there was, magically to a hungry child, red currant jelly on the top, which flowed down over the rich creamy pudding."

That phrase, "magically to a hungry child," kept wandering and playing through my mind as I worked on this book. It seems to me to sum up the essential spirit of old-fashioned desserts and their perennial appeal.

LULI'S SIMPLEST RICE PUDDING
(*ARROZ CON LECHE*)

This is the starting point for rice puddings: rice simmered in sweetened milk until it thickens, with no eggs and no baking. The recipe is from my dear friend Luli Gray, a chef and novelist whose family took her to live in Argentina as a child, and who now lives in Chapel Hill, North Carolina. (Luli says you can add the raisins, "if the children have been *very* good.")

Serves 6

4	cups cold water
¼	teaspoon salt
1	cup long-grain white rice
3	cups milk
¼	cup raisins (optional)
½	cup sugar
⅛	teaspoon ground cinnamon (optional)
1½	teaspoons pure vanilla extract
	Heavy cream, for serving (optional)

1. Bring the water to a boil in a heavy saucepan; add the salt and stir in the rice with a fork. Cover and simmer over the lowest possible heat, stirring now and then, until the rice is very tender, about 35 minutes.

2. Add the milk, optional raisins, sugar and optional cinnamon and simmer, uncovered, stirring frequently, until most of the milk is absorbed, usually about 20 minutes.

3. Remove from the heat, and stir in the vanilla. Serve with or without cream poured over the top.

Comfort Food

Though she can generally pass up dessert, Luli Gray recalls being fed this rice pudding in the nursery: "Elisa, our cook, who was an Argentinian of Italian descent, was with my family for about 40 years or so. When we were really little, she made children's food for us like *arroz con leche*. I still make it when I'm feeling sad or have a cold or something. And it brings Elisa back. I remember sitting in a rocking chair, on her lap, and her singing a song about *arroz con leche*."

CREAMY DINER-STYLE RICE PUDDING

This is the quintessential creamy rice pudding—softly cooked, not baked. Its delightful texture comes from a pastry cream that is made separately and folded into the warm rice.

Cook the rice until it's very tender—to the point where it seems overcooked: This is important. No matter how creamy the pudding, you don't want to chew through al dente rice.

This recipe is adapted from one made by Naomi Uman, a former assistant of mine. Whether or not to add the raisins and cinnamon is up to you. This recipe can be doubled (I would, if I were you).

Serves 6 to 8

1	cup long-grain white rice
2	cups low-fat milk, plus more, if needed
1	cup sugar
1½	teaspoons salt
2	tablespoons cornstarch
1	large egg
2	large egg yolks
1	tablespoon pure vanilla extract
⅓	cup raisins (optional)
	Ground cinnamon, for sprinkling

1. Bring a large pot of salted water to a boil. Stir in the rice with a fork and boil, uncovered, until the rice is very tender, about 35 minutes—it should be overcooked, almost mushy. Drain in a large sieve and rinse with hot water to remove the excess starch. Transfer to a large bowl; set aside.

2. Rinse a heavy nonreactive saucepan with cold water; shake dry (this helps prevent the milk from scorching). Add 1½ cups of the milk, ¼ cup of the sugar and the salt and bring to a boil. Meanwhile, in a bowl, whisk the remaining ½ cup milk, the remaining ¾ cup sugar, the cornstarch, egg and egg yolks until pale and light, about 1½ minutes.

3. Remove the saucepan from the heat, and add 3 or 4 ladlefuls of the hot milk to the egg yolk mixture, whisking vigorously after each addition. Scrape the egg mixture into the saucepan with the milk, and whisk until boiling. Whisking constantly, boil for about 1 minute. Remove the pastry cream from the heat, whisk in

the vanilla, and strain through a fine sieve into a clean bowl. Place a sheet of wax paper or plastic wrap directly on the surface of the pastry cream to prevent a skin from forming. Refrigerate until thoroughly chilled, at least 2 hours.

4. Fold together the rice and pastry cream; add the optional raisins and stir in up to ½ cup more milk to bring the pudding to a consistency that feels right. Transfer to a glass serving dish or individual sundae dishes or custard cups. Top with a little of the ground cinnamon and serve right away or chill before serving.

BAKED CUSTARD-STYLE RICE PUDDING

The result of many tests in the kitchen, this ultimate baked rice pudding is custardy but still soft and tender on the spoon.

✐ *Serves 6 to 8*

6	cups (1½ quarts) milk
1	cup sugar
¼	teaspoon salt
1	vanilla bean, split lengthwise, or 2 teaspoons pure vanilla extract
⅔	cup long-grain white rice
1	large egg
2	large egg yolks
½	cup raisins
	Ground cinnamon, for sprinkling

1. Rinse a heavy saucepan with cold water; leave wet. Place 4 cups of the milk, the sugar, salt and vanilla bean in the pan (if using vanilla extract, do not add it now). Cover and bring slowly to a boil. Stir in the rice with a large fork. Cover and simmer gently, stirring occasionally, until the rice is quite tender, about 40 minutes. Remove the vanilla bean; scrape the seeds into the rice mixture and stir in.

2. Preheat the oven to 400 degrees F, with a rack in the center. Butter a 12-inch oval pudding or gratin dish or other large shallow baking dish. In a bowl, beat the egg, egg yolks and the remaining 2 cups milk until combined (if you are using vanilla

I still have a special weakness for [rice] served as it was at home: boiled in salted water and presented in a heaping mound on a dinner plate in a puddle of warm milk, generously seasoned with brown sugar and cinnamon. We often made a meal of it. I have cooked the dish for my own children, but they, alas, find it disgusting.

PAUL GRUCHOW
"BREAD AND ETHICS"
THE JOURNAL OF
GASTRONOMY
1990

extract, add it now). Add this mixture and the raisins to the rice and stir to combine. Pour into the prepared baking dish. Set the baking dish in a roasting pan, and place in the oven. Pour enough hot tap water into the roasting pan to reach about halfway up the sides of the baking dish.

3. Bake for 25 minutes. Stir the pudding gently with a fork to redistribute the rice. Bake for another 25 minutes. Stir again; lightly sprinkle the surface of the pudding with the cinnamon. Bake until the top of the pudding has crusted over lightly and is spotted with gold; the pudding should still be slightly liquid, another 25 minutes. (The total baking time is about 1¼ hours. The timing can vary based on the depth and size of the baking dish; do not overbake.)

4. Remove the pudding from the water bath and cool on a wire rack. Serve lukewarm or slightly chilled.

What is the matter
with Mary Jane?
She's perfectly well and she
hasn't a pain,
*And it's lovely rice pudding
for dinner again!—*
What *is* the matter with
Mary Jane?

A.A. MILNE
"RICE PUDDING"
*WHEN WE WERE
VERY YOUNG*
1924

SANDY'S CITRUS RICE PUDDING

This simmered rice pudding, with a whisper of citrus as a high note, is from Sandy Gluck, a chef and dear friend. Sandy's cooking is distinguished by its full, true flavor, and this rice pudding is no exception. The caramel sauce, made with a base of fresh citrus juice instead of water, is optional, but it's a delicious touch. Any leftover sauce can be kept refrigerated for a month; serve it warm, over ice cream.

Serves 6

PUDDING

1	orange
1	lemon
1	lime (optional)
4	cups (1 quart) milk, plus more as needed
2	tablespoons unsalted butter
⅔	cup sugar
1	vanilla bean, split lengthwise, or 1½ teaspoons pure vanilla extract
⅛	teaspoon salt
⅔	cup long-grain white rice
2	large egg yolks
3	tablespoons heavy cream (or use additional milk)

CARAMEL SAUCE (OPTIONAL, BUT DELICIOUS)

1	cup sugar
¼	cup fresh orange juice
½	teaspoon fresh lemon juice
⅓	cup very hot water, or as needed
1	tablespoon unsalted butter

1. **PUDDING:** Wash the citrus fruits well, and pat dry. With a vegetable peeler, peel the zest from the orange, lemon and optional lime in long strips, making sure the peels have no white pith attached. (Reserve the orange and lemon for the optional caramel sauce; reserve the lime for another use.) Place the strips of zest in a double layer of cheesecloth and tie with string.

2. Combine the milk, butter, sugar, vanilla bean (if you are using the vanilla extract, add only ½ teaspoon now) and salt in a heavy nonreactive saucepan. Add the bundle of citrus zests. Bring the mixture to a simmer. Stir in the rice, cover and simmer gently

over low heat, stirring occasionally, for 45 minutes. Remove and discard the cheesecloth bag.

3. Continue to simmer the pudding gently, stirring occasionally and checking to maintain a gentle simmer, until the rice is very tender and almost all of the milk has been absorbed, about 45 minutes longer.

4. Combine the egg yolks and cream or milk in a cup or small bowl. Stir into the pudding and cook very gently, stirring constantly, until the pudding thickens slightly, 2 to 3 minutes longer. Remove from the heat and set aside to cool slightly. Remove the vanilla bean and scrape the seeds into the pudding (if using vanilla extract, add the remaining 1 teaspoon now).

5. **CARAMEL SAUCE** (optional): While the pudding is cooking, combine the sugar, orange juice and lemon juice in a heavy nonreactive saucepan. Stir constantly over medium heat until the sugar dissolves. Continue cooking, stirring occasionally, until the mixture colors to a medium golden brown, about 8 minutes. Turn off the heat; carefully stir in the hot water and the butter. Set the sauce aside. *(The sauce can be made in advance. Rewarm gently before using.)*

6. Serve the pudding warm or at room temperature, drizzling a little of the sauce over each portion, if you like. (If the sauce is too thick, thin it with additional hot water.)

Rice Creame

Take a quart of Cream, 2 good handfull of Rice flower, a quarter of a pound of Sugar, butter beaten very small, mingle your Sugar and flower together, put it into your Cream, take the yelk of an Egg, beat it with a spoonfull or two of Rosewater, then put it to the Creame, and stir all these together, and set it over a quick fire, keeping it continually stirring till it be a thick as water Pap.

W.M.
A SERVANT TO QUEEN
HENRIETTA MARIA,
WIFE OF CHARLES I
OF ENGLAND
*THE QUEENS CLOSET
OPENED*
LONDON, 1655

Wild Rice Pudding with Honey and Dried Cherries or Cranberries

Wild rice adds its distinctive flavor to this honey-sweetened pudding, and the dried fruit contributes additional sweetness. Cooking the rice in a lot of water, as you would pasta, results in clearly separate grains that are not mushy.

➺ *Serves 6*

½   cup dried cherries, dried cranberries or raisins
½   cup hot tap water
1½ teaspoons salt
¾   cup (4 ounces) wild rice
2   cups milk
2   large eggs
⅓   cup honey, or to taste
3   tablespoons packed light or dark brown sugar, or to taste
½   teaspoon fresh-grated nutmeg, or to taste
1½ teaspoons pure vanilla extract
     Fresh blueberries, cherries or other fruit, for serving (optional)
     Heavy cream, for serving (optional)

1. Bring a large pot of water to a boil. Plump the dried cherries, cranberries or raisins in the hot tap water; set aside. Add the salt to the boiling water; stir in the wild rice. Cover and boil gently until quite tender, usually 45 to 50 minutes (the timing can vary). Drain in a colander, rinse with cold water and drain again.

2. In the bottom of a double boiler (or in the same pot used to cook the rice), bring about 2 inches of water to a simmer. In the top of the double boiler or in a heatproof mixing bowl, off the heat, beat the milk, eggs, honey, brown sugar and nutmeg until blended. Stir in the wild rice and the dried fruit with its liquid.

3. Place over the simmering water and cook, stirring almost constantly, until it thickens just enough to coat a spoon lightly, usually about 7 minutes. Do not allow the mixture to begin to curdle or come anywhere near a boil. As the mixture thickens, taste and add a pinch of salt, if needed, plus more honey, sugar and/or nutmeg to taste.

Native Grain

Not a rice, but a wild grass, wild rice is harvested by hand in canoes by native Americans in Minnesota. It has been cultivated there and in California for more than 25 years and is the only grain native to North America. Flavored with nuts and berries, wild rice is a traditional ingredient in native American cooking.

4. As soon as the mixture thickens slightly, remove from the simmering water and stir in the vanilla. Transfer the pudding to a 1½-quart glass or ceramic serving dish. Press a sheet of wax paper or plastic wrap directly on the surface to prevent a skin from forming. Serve warm or cold. If you like, scatter some fresh blueberries or other fruit over the pudding and drizzle on a little heavy cream.

MARIE'S BROWN RICE PUDDING WITH MAPLE SYRUP

When my friend Marie Simmons raved about this rice pudding while feverishly working on her book, *Rice: The Amazing Grain*, I pestered her for weeks to get the recipe.

On the very day the recipe arrived in the mail, I made a batch of this pudding and nipped at little bowlfuls of it while on a three-day solitary retreat, eventually putting away all eight servings. It's a simple, creamy rice pudding, not too sweet, but the toasty brown rice and maple flavors give it real character.

Short-grain brown rice is best for this pudding; you can find it in Asian grocery stores (or, in New York City, at any Korean market). Long-grain brown rice, more readily available in supermarkets, works fine, too, becoming creamy as it cooks long and slowly. This pudding isn't quick, but the cooking doesn't need much watching. Plan ahead by making additional brown rice when you're preparing a meal; that way, you will have cooked rice on hand for the recipe.

Serves 6 to 8

2½	cups cooked short- or long-grain brown rice (see note)
4	cups (1 quart) milk
¼	teaspoon salt
½	cup pure maple syrup
1½	teaspoons pure vanilla extract
½	cup raisins, preferably golden
¾	cup heavy cream
	Ground cinnamon or fresh-grated nutmeg, for sprinkling

1. Combine the cooked rice with the milk and salt in a large, heavy saucepan. Cover and bring to a boil over medium heat. Uncover, lower the heat and simmer, stirring frequently, until the

mixture thickens, about 30 minutes. Stir in the maple syrup and simmer, stirring, for 15 minutes longer. Stir in the vanilla. *(The recipe can be prepared in advance to this point. If you are proceeding with it immediately, let the mixture stand for about 15 minutes as you preheat the oven.)*

2. Preheat the oven to 350 degrees F, with a rack in the center. In a small bowl, soak the raisins in boiling or very hot tap water to cover for about 10 minutes. Generously butter an 8-inch square Pyrex baking dish, a deep 9½-inch pie pan or other shallow baking dish.

3. Drain the raisins; stir them into the rice mixture, transfer the rice mixture to the baking dish and smooth the top. Drizzle the top evenly with the cream. (The dish can be made with as little as ½ cup cream; just be sure to coat the entire surface of the pudding.) Sprinkle lightly with the cinnamon or nutmeg.

4. Bake until the cream is bubbly and browned, 30 to 40 minutes. Serve the pudding warm or chilled.

NOTE: If you're starting with raw rice, bring 2 cups cold water to a boil in a heavy saucepan. Stir in ¾ cup raw brown rice and a generous pinch of salt. Lower the heat to maintain a simmer, cover, and simmer until the rice is tender and the liquid has been absorbed, usually about 45 minutes. Transfer the rice to a bowl, stir once to release the steam, and cool slightly before beginning to assemble the pudding.

MOLDED RICE PUDDING WITH CARAMEL SAUCE
(LIGHTENED *RIZ À L'IMPÉRATRICE*)

R*iz à l'Impératrice*—Rice in the Empress's Style—is one of the most traditional French desserts and, as the name suggests, a luxurious one. It is traditionally molded in a low smooth-sided ring mold called a savarin ring, with a Bavarian cream base—custard set with gelatin and lightened with whipped cream. Here's a new version, inspired by the traditional one, but radically simplified and lightened. The caramel sauce is clear and deeply flavored.

Serves 8 to 10

PUDDING
¾	cup dried currants
3	tablespoons cognac, brandy or Grand Marnier
¾	cup long-grain white rice
1⅔	cups milk
⅓	cup sugar
	Pinch salt

CRÈME ANGLAISE
1	envelope (about 2½ teaspoons) unflavored gelatin
⅓	cup cold water
2	cups milk
5	large egg yolks
½	cup sugar
2½	teaspoons pure vanilla extract
¾	cup heavy cream, well chilled

THIN CARAMEL SAUCE
1	cup sugar
¼	cup cold water
½	cup fresh orange juice or hot water

1. **PUDDING:** Soak the currants in the cognac, brandy or Grand Marnier; set aside.

2. In a large saucepan of boiling water, boil the rice for 5 minutes. Drain and rinse.

3. Bring the milk and sugar to a simmer in a heavy saucepan.

Stir in the rice and salt. Cover and simmer until the rice is quite tender, 35 to 40 minutes. Set aside to cool.

4. **CRÈME ANGLAISE:** In a cup, sprinkle the gelatin over the cold water; set aside. In a heavy nonreactive saucepan, heat the milk over medium heat until bubbles appear around the edges. Whisk together the egg yolks and the sugar in a bowl until blended. Gradually whisk the hot milk into the yolk mixture. Pour the mixture into the pan and stir constantly over medium heat until the custard thickens, about 7 minutes; do not boil.

5. Remove the custard from the heat, add the vanilla and softened gelatin and stir thoroughly to dissolve the gelatin. Strain the custard into a clean bowl. Cool, uncovered, in the refrigerator, stirring often, until thickened, but not set, 1 hour or longer. Stir the rice and the currants with their soaking liquid into the crème anglaise; continue to stir in the refrigerator, until syrupy.

6. Whip the heavy cream until it forms soft (not yet stiff) peaks. Fold the cream into the custard until just partially blended. Place the bowl in the refrigerator for 5 minutes. Finish folding the cream and the custard together quickly, distributing the rice and the currants. Pour the pudding into a well-oiled 6- or 7-cup mold, preferably a kugelhopf mold. Cover the mold and chill well, at least 2 hours.

7. **THIN CARAMEL SAUCE:** In a small, heavy saucepan, stir together the sugar and the cold water. Bring to a boil over medium heat, stirring and brushing down any crystals from the sides of the pan with a brush dipped in warm water until the sugar dissolves completely. Boil, without stirring, until the mixture turns deep amber, 8 to 10 minutes. Remove from the heat. Carefully add the orange juice or hot water; the mixture will sputter violently. Swirl the pan gently until the syrup is smooth. Cool to room temperature.

8. To unmold the pudding, run the tip of a knife around the edge. Dip the mold into hot water for about 3 seconds. Place a round serving plate over the mold, invert the plate and the mold and carefully lift off the mold. Chill the pudding again briefly, until set up, 5 to 10 minutes.

9. Drizzle some of the caramel sauce over the top so that it runs down the sides of the pudding and around the edges. Pass the extra sauce separately.

Flavor Restored

Three conclusions—a rice pudding must be flavored with a vanilla pod or cinnamon stick, it must be cooked long and slowly, it must be eaten with plenty of double cream. Like so many other English dishes, it has been wrecked by meanness and lack of thought.

JANE GRIGSON
ENGLISH FOOD
1974

ABOUT BREAD PUDDINGS

Not too many years back, bread pudding was something you remembered being fed while visiting your grandmother's house, something quaintly passé. Then came the 1980s, and old-fashioned standbys like bread pudding exploded onto restaurant menus on several continents and in various incarnations:

- Challah bread pudding
- Gingered pumpkin bread pudding
- Whole-wheat bread pudding
- Croissant bread pudding with apples
- Blueberry bread-and-butter pudding
- Souffléed brioche pudding with caramelized pears
- Cinnamon-raisin bread pudding
- Apricot bread pudding
- Chocolate bread pudding
- White chocolate bread pudding
- Bourbon bread pudding
- Lemon meringue bread pudding
- Bread pudding soufflé with whiskey sauce
- Date and nut bread pudding
- Biscotti bread pudding

In old cookbooks from all over the world, but especially from England, you find similar instructions: take stale bread ("grate a penny loaf or manchet"), soak in milk and beaten egg, add a few raisins (or not), and bake.

In America, the frequency of recipes for bread pudding, from Amelia Simmons' *American Cookery* in 1796 through the late 20th century, attests to its continuing comfort.

Desserts to Remember

It was raining when I arrived at the Coach House at 9:30 to meet Susan Lowenstein for dinner.

A good restaurant freed me from the desolate narrowness, the definitive thinness of experience, that is both the vainglory and the dead giveaway of a provincial man. Above the perfect napery, I could purchase my own place in the city for the night and compose a meal that I would remember with unstinted pleasure for the rest of my life.

. . . "What's good to eat here, Tom?" she said . . . "I'm utterly famished."

"Everything is good here, Lowenstein," I said as the waiter brought us a bottle of cold Chablis I had ordered brought to the table when my guest arrived.

. . . "Desserts are simply ambrosial here."

PAT CONROY
THE PRINCE OF TIDES
1986

THE COACH HOUSE BREAD-AND-BUTTER PUDDING

Leon Lianides, who welcomed his guests personally at the Coach House restaurant in New York City for over 40 years ("and I don't want to tell you how many hours"), is one of the last thriving gentlemen of the old school. Leon was and is dedicated to one thing: quality. Although this landmark has now closed, it won't soon be forgotten.

Back when "American cuisine" meant burgers and fries, Leon (who grew up in Corfu, Greece, and who was a professor of mathematics earlier in life) served the finest American products with pride, including a mostly American wine list—unheard of at the time.

Despite other considerable temptations from the dessert table there, I always came back to this plain bread-and-butter pudding served with raspberry sauce. (It's equally good unsauced.) This is bread pudding perfected.

Serves 10

12	thin slices day-old French bread, crusts trimmed
3-4	tablespoons unsalted butter, softened
4	cups (1 quart) milk
1	cup heavy cream
5	large eggs
4	large egg yolks
1	cup sugar
⅛	teaspoon salt
1	teaspoon pure vanilla extract
	Confectioners' sugar, for dusting
	Raspberry Sauce (page 617; optional)

1. Preheat the oven to 375 degrees F, with a rack in the center. Butter one side of each slice of bread; set aside. Butter a 2-quart soufflé dish or baking dish.

2. In a heavy nonreactive saucepan, simmer the milk and cream over medium heat until small bubbles appear around the edges. Meanwhile, in a large bowl, beat the eggs, egg yolks, sugar and salt until well blended.

3. Gradually stir the scalded milk and cream into the egg mixture; stir in the vanilla.

4. Arrange the bread slices, buttered side up, in the prepared dish. Strain the custard mixture over the bread. Set the baking dish in a roasting pan, and place the pan in the oven. Pour enough hot tap water to reach about halfway up the sides of the dish.

5. Bake the pudding until barely set in the center, about 45 minutes. Remove the baking dish from the water bath.

6. Preheat the broiler. Sift a generous coating of confectioners' sugar over the surface of the pudding. Place briefly under the broiler until the top is glazed (watch carefully to prevent burning). Transfer to a wire rack to cool to room temperature.

7. Serve the pudding at room temperature or chilled, alone or with Raspberry Sauce.

⌒ *Variation*

For a richer pudding, replace the French bread with leftover slices of pound cake, leaving on the crust and omitting the butter.

CHALLAH BREAD PUDDING WITH RAISINS

R ich with eggs, challah (Jewish egg bread) makes as good a bread pudding as it does French toast. This is another basic bread pudding.

⌒ *Serves about 6*

3½	cups (4-5 ounces) cubed (¾-inch) day-old challah or other egg bread, crusts partially trimmed
5	large eggs
2	large egg yolks
⅔	cup sugar
3	cups milk
2½	teaspoons pure vanilla extract
½	cup raisins or dried currants

1. Preheat the oven to 375 degrees F, with a rack in the center. Let the bread cubes stand at room temperature to dry out slightly.

2. In a large bowl, whisk together the eggs, egg yolks and sugar. Whisk in the milk and vanilla. Add the bread cubes and raisins or currants and stir gently to combine without breaking up the bread.

3. Pour the mixture into a large shallow baking dish; I use an oval ceramic gratin dish about 11 inches long; any 7- or 8-cup casserole or baking dish will work fine. Set the dish in a roasting pan and place in the oven. Pour in enough hot tap water to reach about halfway up the sides of the baking dish.

4. Bake until the pudding is just set in the center, usually about 1 hour. (The timing can vary based on the depth of the baking dish; do not overbake.)

5. Carefully remove the pudding from the water bath and cool to lukewarm on a wire rack. Chill until very cold, about 2 hours. If possible, remove the pudding from the refrigerator about 10 minutes before serving.

Variation
APPLE BREAD PUDDING: You can also use chunks of pear, peaches or other fresh fruits.

1	tablespoon unsalted butter
1-1½	cups peeled, cored, coarsely chopped apples

In a large skillet, preferably nonstick, heat the butter over medium-high heat. Add the apples and sprinkle with about 2 tablespoons of the ⅔ cup sugar. Let sizzle for a few moments, then cook, tossing frequently, until the apples begin to brown, about 4 minutes. Remove from the heat and set aside. Add the apples to the pudding with the bread cubes and raisins or currants in step 2; proceed to bake as directed.

BUTTERMILK CORN BREAD PUDDING

This unusual bread pudding is based on the Southern custom of crumbling last night's leftover corn bread into a glass, pouring buttermilk over it and eating it with a spoon. The buttermilk and cornmeal meld together with a taste almost like cheesecake, but much lighter on the palate.

Serves 6

3	cups buttermilk
¾	cup sugar
4	large eggs
2	large egg yolks
2	teaspoons pure vanilla extract
1	cup coarsely crumbled corn muffins or leftover corn bread (about 3 ounces)
½	cup raisins

1. Butter an 8- or 9-inch gratin dish, square Pyrex dish or other shallow baking dish.

2. In a large bowl, whisk together the buttermilk, sugar, eggs, egg yolks and vanilla. Add the crumbled corn muffins or corn bread to the buttermilk mixture; add the raisins and stir gently to blend. Pour the mixture into the buttered baking dish. Let stand while you preheat the oven to 375 degrees F, with a rack in the center.

3. Set the baking dish in a roasting pan and place the pan in the oven. Pour in enough hot tap water to reach about halfway up the sides of the baking dish.

4. Bake until the pudding is lightly golden and nearly set, but is slightly soft in the center, usually about 45 minutes. Remove the pudding from the water bath and cool on a wire rack.

5. Serve the pudding lukewarm, at room temperature or chilled.

Muffin Pudding

Pare off the crust of 2 muffins; split and halve them, put into a tin shape a layer of any sort of preserves—apricot is the best—then a layer of muffin, then a layer of fruit, and then the remainder of the muffin, and pour over it a pint of warm milk; in which 4 well-beaten eggs have been mixed. Cover the shape, and place it in a sauce-pan with a small quantity of boiling water. Keep on the cover; and let it boil 20 minutes; turn it out, and serve it with pudding sauce.

Light white bread may be substituted for the muffins. The pudding will be better if it is prepared three or four hours before it is boiled.

MRS. DALGAIRNS
THE PRACTICE OF COOKERY
EDINBURGH, 1830

BON TON'S NEW ORLEANS BREAD PUDDING WITH WHISKEY SAUCE

Southerners didn't need the 1980s revival to rediscover old favorites like bread pudding and peach cobbler. They had never stopped enjoying them. Food stylist Ginger Walsh gave me this recipe when we worked together in Nashville on a series of television specials on cooking.

This is a straightforward Southern-style bread pudding, based on one from Bon Ton Restaurant in New Orleans. You can serve it with or without the whiskey sauce—good stuff—which can also be used with any of the other bread puddings in this section.

～ Serves 8

BREAD PUDDING

½	cup raisins
¼	cup bourbon
4	cups cubed stale French bread with crusts (4 ounces)
2	cups milk
¾	cup sugar
2	large eggs
1	tablespoon pure vanilla extract
2	pinches fresh-grated nutmeg
1½	tablespoons unsalted butter

WHISKEY SAUCE

½	cup sugar
1	large egg
½	cup (1 stick) unsalted butter, melted
¼	cup bourbon

1. **BREAD PUDDING:** In a small bowl, combine the raisins with the bourbon. Let stand for at least 30 minutes or longer, preferably overnight.

2. In a large bowl, combine the bread cubes and the milk. Let stand while you prepare the remaining ingredients.

3. Preheat the oven to 350 degrees F, with a rack in the center. In a bowl, whisk together the sugar, eggs, vanilla, nutmeg and the raisins with their soaking liquid. Add the egg-raisin mixture to the bread mixture and fold together.

A Boiled Loaf

Take a Penny-loaf [ordinary bread, milled from coarse flour], pour over it half a Pint of Milk boiling hot, cover it close, let it stand till it has soaked up the Milk, then tye it up in a Cloth, and boil it a quarter of an Hour. When it is done, lay it in your Dish, and pour melted Butter over it, and throw Sugar all over, a Spoonful of Wine, or Rosewater, does as well in the Butter, or Juice of Seville Orange. A French Manchet [bread of the finest quality] does best; but there are little Loaves made on purpose for the Use. A French Role, or Oat-cake, does very well boiled thus.

HANNAH GLASSE
*THE ART OF COOKERY,
MADE PLAIN AND EASY*
LONDON, 1747

4. Place the butter in a 1-quart shallow baking dish (such as a 9-inch gratin dish) and put the dish in the oven until the butter melts. Carefully pour the bread mixture on top. Bake until the pudding is firm and a knife inserted into the middle emerges clean, about 35 minutes. Cool to room temperature on a wire rack.

5. **WHISKEY SAUCE:** In a small bowl set over simmering water, whisk the sugar and egg together until warm to the touch and beginning to fluff up. Whisk in the melted butter; whisk in the bourbon.

6. Cut the pudding into individual servings. Pour some of the warm whiskey sauce over each serving. Serve the remaining sauce separately.

OMAHA CARAMEL BREAD PUDDING

Late one morning, when I was in Omaha, Nebraska, I wandered into the Garden Café, where a neon sign at the door read: "We Love Food." Bakery cases were filled with freshly baked cinnamon rolls, pastries and pies. Looking past the counter, I watched two cooks keeping an eye on several pans of omelets and pancakes, giving a quick flip at just the right instant. I knew immediately that I'd found the breakfast hangout of my dreams.

On the counter was a round pan the size of a manhole cover, topped with a thick cloak of molten caramel. It was cooling so it would be ready in time for the lunch crowd. "What's that?" I called to the cooks. "Oh, that's our caramel bread pudding—don't miss it." I didn't, and here's owner Ron Popp's recipe, "Omaha's favorite dessert," adapted from one given to him by a happy customer. (You can halve this recipe and bake it in an 8-inch square pan.)

◡◠ *Serves 12 to 16*

BREAD PUDDING

8	cups loosely packed cubed (½-inch) cinnamon rolls, raisin bread or French bread
3	cups milk
2	cups heavy cream
9	large eggs
¾	cup packed dark or light brown sugar
¾	cup sugar
1½	teaspoons ground cinnamon
2	tablespoons pure vanilla extract
¾	teaspoon salt

CARAMEL TOPPING

30-40	caramel candies, such as Kraft, usually 8-13 ounces
1½	teaspoons pure vanilla extract
	Heavy cream, for serving (optional)

1. **BREAD PUDDING:** Place the bread cubes in a 13-x-9-inch baking dish; set aside. Heat the milk and cream in a large saucepan until hot.

2. In a large bowl, whisk the eggs, brown and white sugars, cinnamon, vanilla and salt. Slowly whisk in the hot milk mixture.

Pour the mixture over the bread cubes and let stand for 10 to 20 minutes so that the bread absorbs the liquid. Press the bread cubes into the custard with a spatula once or twice.

3. Meanwhile, preheat the oven to 350 degrees F, with a rack in the center.

4. Bake the pudding until the custard is set but still slightly wobbly in the center, usually about 40 minutes. Cool on a wire rack.

5. CARAMEL TOPPING: While the pudding is cooling, melt the caramels in a heavy saucepan over low heat, stirring until smooth. Remove from the heat and stir in the vanilla. While the pudding is still warm, drizzle a random pattern of thin lines of the hot caramel, Jackson Pollock–style, over the surface of the pudding. (At the Garden Café, the pudding is topped with a thick, even coating of caramel; I like it drizzled lightly, but you decide. To make an even coating like the café's, use about 40 caramels.) Do not touch or disturb the surface of the pudding, or you will tear it. If the caramel in the pan gets too hard as you are working, rewarm it over low heat.

6. To serve, rewarm the pudding in a 325-degree oven before serving, to soften the caramel. You can also cut squares of the pudding and warm them in individual ovenproof serving dishes. If you like, drizzle each serving with a little cream.

How to Make Yr Custard Puddinge

Take a stale manchett [light French bread] and slice it as thinn as a wafer, lay your slices in yr bottome of a deep pewter dish, then take a quarter of a pound of raisons stoned, strow your raisons all about the bottome of your dish, then lay in some pieces of marrow aboutt ye bignesse of a nuttmegg then take a quart of thick creame, it must be very good, sett it overe the fire to boyle and putt in a little mace and nuttmegg, then beat yr yolks of 18 eggs very well, and let them be strayned . . . then put in some sugar and your eggs, when your creame is a little cold; stirr all very well together, and putt it over yr fire, stirr in till it is prtty thick . . . then putt it in your dish . . . then some pistacho nutts . . . if your oven is too hott it will make your puddinge whey and not cleare.

ANONYMOUS
COLLECTION OF MEDICAL
AND COOKERY RECIPES
HANDWRITTEN FOLIO
ENGLAND, 17TH CENTURY

191

COMMANDER'S PALACE BREAD PUDDING SOUFFLÉ

A signature recipe from the jewel in the Brennan family crown of restaurants in New Orleans. At first, I wondered why anyone would take a simple thing like bread pudding and go to all the trouble of baking it, just to cut it up and rebake it in a soufflé batter.

Try it—it's worth it. The soufflé is light and luscious—like inhaling vanilla-scented air. This is what you'll be spoon-fed in the nursery in heaven—but why wait?

At Commander's Palace, it is served with whiskey sauce. If you'd like to sauce it, use the Whiskey Sauce on page 188.

Serves 6 to 8, with some left over

BREAD PUDDING
- 5 large eggs
- 2 cups milk
- ¼ cup (½ stick) unsalted butter, melted
- ¾ cup sugar
  Pinch ground cinnamon
- 1½ tablespoons pure vanilla extract
- ¼ cup raisins
- 12 slices (1 inch thick) French bread with crust

SOUFFLÉ
- 6 large eggs, separated
- ¼ cup sugar, plus additional for coating the dish
- 1 teaspoon pure vanilla extract
- ½ cup confectioners' sugar, plus additional for serving

1. **BREAD PUDDING:** Preheat the oven to 350 degrees F, with a rack in the center. In a bowl, whisk the eggs until blended; add the milk, butter, sugar, cinnamon, vanilla and raisins and mix until combined.

2. Pour the mixture into a 9-inch square baking pan. Arrange the bread slices over the custard mixture in a single layer, and let stand until softened slightly, about 3 minutes. Turn the bread slices over and let stand for 3 minutes longer. With a spatula, gently press the slices down into the custard, so they are nearly covered. Cover the pan with foil. Set the pan in a roasting pan and place in the oven. Pour in enough hot tap water to reach halfway up the sides of the baking dish.

3. Bake for 25 minutes; the custard should be not quite set. Remove the foil and bake until the custard is nearly set but still quite jiggly, about 10 minutes longer. Remove the pudding from the water bath and cool on a wire rack. Refrigerate the pudding until shortly before serving time. *(The pudding can be made 1 to 2 days in advance and chilled until needed.)*

4. SOUFFLÉ: Preheat the oven to 375 degrees F, with a rack in the center. Butter a 1½-quart soufflé dish and coat it with sugar. (You can also bake this in a shallower pan, such as a 15-x-10-inch rectangular baking dish or a large shallow gratin dish. I prefer the soufflé baked in a dish with a lot of surface area.) With a large spoon, measure 2½ to 3 cups of the bread pudding (about ⅔ of the pudding); place in a mixing bowl and set aside. (Refrigerate the rest of the bread pudding and eat cold at another time.)

5. Bring about 1 inch of water to a simmer in the bottom of a double boiler or saucepan. Place the egg yolks and sugar in the top or in a bowl and place over the simmering water. Whisk until frothy and shiny, usually 3 to 4 minutes. Fold this mixture into the bread pudding along with the vanilla. The mixture may seem lumpy, but that's all right.

6. In a bowl, beat the egg whites until frothy. Gradually add the confectioners' sugar and beat until the meringue stands in not-quite-stiff peaks. Gently fold the beaten egg whites into the pudding.

7. Bake until the soufflé is lightly golden brown and set, but still slightly wobbly in the center, usually 35 to 40 minutes in a soufflé dish or about 25 minutes in a shallow baking dish. Sprinkle the soufflé with additional confectioners' sugar and serve immediately, spooning out some of the crust and soft interior for each serving.

CHOCOLATE SILK BREAD PUDDING

Now this is something else altogether—more a deep chocolate pudding than a bread pudding—pure dark silk. It's an old family recipe from Judith Dern in San Francisco.

The bread crumbs (used in many older versions of bread pudding) dissolve and melt into the eggs and chocolate as the dessert bakes, forming a smooth custard that's rich without being heavy. Use only the best chocolate for this pudding.

Serves 6

4	cups (1 quart) milk
¼	cup (½ stick) unsalted butter, cut into pieces
4	ounces best-quality unsweetened chocolate, chopped
2	large eggs
½	cup sugar
1	teaspoon pure vanilla extract
½	teaspoon ground cinnamon
¼	teaspoon salt
2	cups soft fresh bread crumbs
	Whipped cream or vanilla ice cream, for serving (optional)

1. Preheat the oven to 325 degrees F, with a rack in the center. Butter a 1½-quart shallow baking dish.

2. In a medium saucepan, combine the milk, butter and chocolate. Bring to a boil over medium-low heat, stirring occasionally, until the butter and chocolate melt.

3. Meanwhile, in a large bowl, whisk the eggs, sugar, vanilla, cinnamon and salt. Add the bread crumbs; stir in the hot milk mixture. Pour into the prepared baking dish.

4. Bake until the pudding is set and slightly wobbly, but not liquid in center, usually 45 to 60 minutes; do not overbake. Let cool on a wire rack.

5. Serve the silk pudding lukewarm or cold, with whipped cream or vanilla ice cream, if you like.

My mother made this for years," Judith Dern says. "My job was to take fresh bread and tear it apart, then rub it between the palms of my hands into crumbs. By the way, you can also toss ¼ cup of Kahlúa into the custard mixture before baking."

SANTA FE BREAD PUDDING WITH WINE AND CHEESE
(*CAPIROTADA*)

Originally a Lenten dish (without the wine) made by the Spanish settlers in New Mexico, this bread pudding is called a *sopa* ("soup"). Made without eggs or milk but flavored with wine and cheese, it is an unusual version. The recipe is based on one generously shared with me by Huntley Dent, whose book, *Feast of Santa Fe* (Simon and Schuster, 1985; Fireside, 1993) gives a vivid look at the food and the people in that magical place.

〜 *Serves 6 to 8*

8	ounces good French bread or rolls
1	cup sugar
1¾	cups water
1	teaspoon ground cinnamon
¼	cup (½ stick) unsalted butter
1	cup sweet wine, preferably Madeira, Marsala or sweet sherry
¾	cup pine nuts, blanched slivered almonds or chopped pecans
¾	cup raisins
1	cup (about 4 ounces) shredded Monterey Jack cheese Sweetened whipped cream, for serving (optional)

1. Preheat the oven to 350 degrees F, with a rack in the center. Butter an 11-inch oval gratin dish or other large shallow baking dish.

2. Tear the bread into rough bite-size pieces; you should have 4 to 5 cups. Place the bread on a baking sheet and toast lightly in the oven, about 10 minutes.

3. Meanwhile, combine the sugar and ¼ cup of the water in a heavy saucepan over medium heat. Cook, stirring, until the sugar dissolves completely. Raise the heat slightly and cook, without stirring, until the sugar begins to caramelize to a medium-dark amber color, 8 to 10 minutes; the timing can vary. Remove the pan from the heat and gradually pour in the remaining 1½ cups water; the mixture will sputter violently. Return the syrup to low heat and cook, swirling the pan occasionally, until the mixture forms a thin, smooth caramel syrup.

4. Add the cinnamon and butter to the hot caramel. Place the toasted bread in the prepared baking dish; drizzle the sweet wine over it. Sprinkle with the nuts and raisins; top with an even layer of the cheese. Pour the caramel syrup over the mixture, being sure to coat all of the bread pieces.

5. Cover the pan with foil and bake for 15 minutes. Uncover and bake until the surface is lightly browned, about 15 minutes more. Cool on a wire rack.

6. Serve warm or cold, topped with the whipped cream, if you like.

ITALIAN CHOCOLATE BREAD PUDDING
(*BUDINO NERO*)

B lack pudding" is how the name translates. In this Italian rendition, cubes of bread are baked in a chocolate custard; they rise to the top, forming a cobbled surface that's crusty and irresistible.

This light, not-too-sweet pudding is adapted from a recipe in *Antichi Dolci di Casa* ("Home-Style Desserts of the Past") by Silvia Tocco Bonetti. In the original recipe, the pudding was unmolded after baking, but I like to bake it in a springform pan, so the nubbly surface comes out on top.

Serves 4

	Fine dry bread crumbs, for coating the pan
3½	ounces semisweet chocolate, chopped
1	cup whole milk
2	large eggs
¼	cup sugar
4	cups (about 3 ounces) cubed (½-inch), day-old French or Italian bread, crusts removed (semolina bread works well)
	Confectioners' sugar, for serving
	Softly whipped cream, for serving

1. Preheat the oven to 350 degrees F, with a rack in the center. Butter an 8-inch springform pan or a 6-cup ring or other mold; coat with the bread crumbs, shaking out the excess. Wrap

the exterior bottom and sides of the springform pan in foil, forming a tight seal where the sides join; set aside.

2. Combine the chocolate and milk in a small saucepan over
medium heat. Stir occasionally until the chocolate is partially
melted. Remove from the heat and stir until completely smooth.

3. In a bowl, whisk the eggs and sugar until combined.
Whisk in the chocolate mixture; fold in the bread cubes. If the
bread is quite dry, let the mixture stand for 5 to 10 minutes, so the
bread absorbs some of the liquid.

4. Transfer the mixture to the prepared pan. Cover the top
with a buttered sheet of foil, buttered side down. Set the pan in a
roasting pan and place in the oven. Pour in enough hot tap water
to reach about halfway up the sides of the pan.

5. Bake until the pudding is nearly set, but still slightly wobbly, about 35 minutes (the timing can vary based on the size and
depth of the pan; do not overbake).

6. Carefully remove the pan from the water bath and cool to
lukewarm on a wire rack. Run the tip of a knife around the edges
of the pudding; remove the sides, if you are using a springform
pan. Serve on a platter—without inverting. (If using a ring mold,
invert the pudding and lift off the mold.) Sprinkle with confectioners' sugar, and serve warm, with softly whipped cream.

CARAMELIZED PANETTONE BREAD PUDDING

Panettone is the traditional Italian Christmas bread; it originated in Milan but is now found throughout Italy during the holiday season. The egg-rich yeast dough, studded with raisins and candied orange peel, has a characteristic aroma and flavor that work beautifully in a bread pudding. The caramel offsets the pudding perfectly.

This is the invention of Susan Rosenfeld, owner with her husband, Peter Hoffman, of Savoy, a New York City restaurant that is one of my favorite places to share a quiet afternoon or evening with a friend. Susan developed this for New Year's Eve when she was the pastry chef at New York's Le Madri; now her customers at Savoy insist that she bring this dessert back for the holidays.

At the restaurant, Susan pops each ramekin into the oven until the caramel starts to bubble, then unmolds it. It's equally good served cold.

Serves 6 to 8

1	cup plus 3 tablespoons sugar
2	tablespoons cold water
3-4	cups cubed (1 inch), day-old panettone, challah, brioche or other egg bread, crusts left on
2¼	cups milk
1	cup heavy cream (or substitute an equal amount of milk)
½	vanilla bean, split lengthwise, or 1 tablespoon pure vanilla extract
3	large eggs
3	large egg yolks

1. Butter 6 to 8 ramekins, custard cups, heavy coffee cups or disposable foil baking cups. Place the ramekins or cups in a large roasting pan.

2. In a small, heavy saucepan, combine the 1 cup sugar and water over medium heat and stir to dissolve the sugar completely. Wipe down any crystals from the sides of the pan with a brush dipped in cold water. Bring the mixture to a boil. Cook, without stirring, until the sugar caramelizes to a medium amber color, 5 to 7 minutes; the timing can vary. Carefully pour about ¼ inch hot caramel into each ramekin or cup; set aside to cool.

3. In a large bowl, combine the bread cubes with 1 cup of the milk. Set aside, stirring occasionally, until needed. Meanwhile, in a heavy saucepan, scald the remaining 1¼ cups milk with the cream or milk and vanilla bean (if using vanilla extract, do not add it now). Cover and set aside.

4. Preheat the oven to 300 degrees F, with a rack in the center. In a bowl, whisk the eggs, egg yolks, the remaining 3 tablespoons sugar and the scalded cream mixture until smooth. Scrape the vanilla seeds from the pod into the custard (or add the vanilla extract now). Strain this mixture over the soaked bread mixture and stir gently to combine.

5. Ladle the pudding mixture into the ramekins, filling them nearly full. Place the roasting pan in the oven. Pour in enough hot tap water to reach halfway up the sides of the ramekins. Lay a sheet of buttered foil, buttered side down, directly over the puddings.

6. Bake for 30 minutes. Very carefully rotate the roasting pan, back to front. Continue to bake until the custards are just set and a toothpick emerges clean, usually about 10 minutes longer (the timing can vary based on the size of the ramekins; do not overbake).

7. Carefully remove the ramekins from the water bath to a wire rack to cool for about 15 minutes. Chill until cold, at least 2 hours.

8. Gently run the tip of a knife around the edge of each pudding and invert each onto a serving plate, letting the caramel drip over the top and sides of the pudding. (If you'd prefer serving these warm, place on a baking sheet in a 350-degree oven until the caramel bubbles around the edges.)

NOTE: Panettone is available by mail-order from Todaro Brothers, 555 Second Avenue, New York, New York, 10016; (212) 532-0633; www.todarobros.com.

To Make a Green Pudding

Take a penny loafe of stale bread, Grate it, put to halfe a pound of Sugar, a grated Nutmeg; as much salt as will season it, three quarters of a pound of Beef suet shred very small, then take sweet Herbs, the most of them Marrigold, eight Spinage, shred the Herbs very small mix all well together, then take two eggs and work them up together with your hand, and make them into round Balls, and when the water boyles put them in, serve them, Rosewater, Sugar, and Butter for sauce.

W. M.
A SERVANT TO QUEEN
HENRIETTA MARIA,
WIFE OF CHARLES I
OF ENGLAND
*THE QUEENS CLOSET
OPENED*
LONDON, 1655

WARM PEAR CHARLOTTE

The name charlotte is, like a lot of traditional dessert names, a matter of dispute. There is some speculation that the dessert was named for Queen Charlotte, the wife of George III of England, since charlottes appear during his reign at the end of the 18th century. But charlottes are probably older than that.

Warm charlottes, actually a form of bread pudding filled with fruit, are characteristically made in a fez-shaped metal mold that is first lined with strips of buttered bread and then filled with apples or other fruit bound with apricot jam. The charlotte is baked until the bread is toasted golden and crisp, unmolded and served warm.

This one is not seen much anymore, but never fails to satisfy.

Serves 8 to 12

7	firm-ripe medium-size pears, such as Bartlett or Anjou (about 3 pounds), peeled, cored and cut into coarse chunks
	Juice of 1 lemon
¾	cup (1½ sticks) unsalted butter, melted
¼	cup sugar
1	teaspoon fresh-grated nutmeg
	Grated zest of 1 lemon
12-16	slices whole-wheat or white bread, crusts removed
1	12-ounce jar (1½ cups) good-quality apricot preserves
4-6	tablespoons brandy or pear eau-de-vie, to taste
	Lightly whipped cream, for serving

1. Place the pears in a bowl and toss with the lemon juice to prevent discoloration; set aside.

2. Heat 2 tablespoons of the melted butter in a large skillet over medium heat. Add the pears (work in batches, if necessary) and toss. Cover and steam until the pears soften, about 6 minutes. Uncover, add the sugar, nutmeg and lemon zest and cook, tossing, until the pears are soft, dry and chunky, about 4 minutes. Remove the pan from the heat.

3. Choose a 1½-quart charlotte mold, soufflé dish or other round, deep baking dish. Using the mold or baking dish as your guide, cut 6 slices of the bread into long, thin triangles; cut the remaining slices into long, thin rectangular strips. Dip one side of the bread triangles in the remaining melted butter and arrange them, side by side, buttered side down and points to the center,

over the bottom of the mold. Dip one side of the rectangular strips in the butter and arrange them upright, buttered sides against the sides of the mold, overlapping slightly.

4. Preheat the oven to 400 degrees F, with a rack in the center. Place ½ of the pear mixture in the mold, pressing the bread against the sides of the mold as you do so. Add about ½ cup of the apricot preserves; sprinkle on 1 tablespoon of the brandy or eau-de-vie. Add the remaining pears, another ½ cup of the preserves, and another 1 tablespoon or so of brandy. Dip one side of the remaining bread triangles in the remaining butter; arrange on top of the mold, buttered sides up, points in, and sprinkle the bread with another tablespoon of brandy.

5. Set the mold on a baking sheet; put in the preheated oven and immediately lower the temperature to 375 degrees. Bake for 35 minutes. If after 15 or 20 minutes, the pieces of bread on the top are browning too quickly, cover the mold loosely with foil.

6. Meanwhile, in a small nonreactive saucepan, melt the remaining ½ cup preserves over low heat. Strain and stir in the remaining 3 tablespoons brandy. Strain into a small bowl.

7. When the top of the charlotte is golden brown, remove to a wire rack. Let cool for 10 to 15 minutes. Gently invert the charlotte onto a serving platter and let it cool for about 10 minutes longer. Carefully remove the mold, and brush the charlotte with the warm strained preserves. Serve lukewarm, cut into wedges; pass the whipped cream separately.

SUMMER PUDDING OF FOUR RED FRUITS

Summer pudding is one of England's favorite traditional desserts. A dome-shaped pudding basin is lined with slices of white bread; berries and red currants serve as the filling; the mixture is weighed down, and the whole thing melds together in the refrigerator, with the crimson juices soaking through the bread. Served with plenty of whipped double cream or heavy cream as it is in England, this beautiful dessert cools the palate and lifts the spirits on a sluggish hot day.

⌒ *Serves about 6*

8-9   slices firm-textured white bread (such as Pepperidge Farm), preferably 2 days old, crusts removed, cut diagonally in half
½   generous pint red currants, stemmed (or substitute another berry, decreasing the sugar accordingly)
½   generous pint raspberries, picked over
½   generous pint blackberries, picked over
⅔   cup sugar, or to taste
2   tablespoons cold water
½   generous pint strawberries, hulled, halved or quartered if large
Heavy cream, for serving

1. Choose a 1-quart bowl, soufflé dish or charlotte mold. Line the bottom with the triangles of bread, arranging the points toward the center so that the pieces fit closely together. Line the sides with more bread triangles. Carefully cut out scraps of bread and fit them into any open spaces; the bowl should be completely lined with bread. Set the bowl and the remaining bread triangles aside.

2. In a nonreactive saucepan, stir together the red currants, raspberries, blackberries, sugar and water. Cover and bring to a boil. Lower the heat, partially cover and simmer until the fruits are giving up their juices, but are still partially intact, about 5 minutes. Remove the pan from the heat; stir in the strawberries. Taste and add more sugar if needed.

3. With a slotted spoon, spoon the fruit into the bread-lined bowl. Spoon some of the juice, but not all, over the fruit; reserve the remaining juice. Strain the remaining juice and add the solids to the bowl. Cover and refrigerate the reserved juice.

4. Cover the fruits in the bowl with a neat, flat layer of bread triangles, points toward the center. Patch any open spaces carefully with the bread scraps; trim any edges of bread that protrude above the sides of the bowl with a serrated knife.

5. Invert a plate that is slightly smaller than the bowl directly on the bread inside the rim. Place the bowl in a pan to catch any drips. Weigh down the plate with a heavy can or other weight; refrigerate the pudding overnight. After several hours, check to see if any parts of the bread are still dry and white; if so, spoon a little of the reserved berry juice over them so that all parts of the bread are soaked with juice.

6. To serve, remove the weight and plate. Run the tip of a knife all around the sides of the bowl, and invert the pudding onto a serving plate. Serve cold, cut into wedges, with plenty of cream poured over each serving. (Melted vanilla ice cream will do nicely in a pinch.)

Boston Cream

½ cup Boston brown bread
    grated fine
1   "   milk
½ ounce gelatin soaked in
    extra ½ cup milk
little more than ¼ cup
    gran. sugar
½ pint whipping cream
2 tablespoons orange juice
1 teaspoon vanilla

Put together gelatin and
sugar in double boiler. Stir
till g. is dissolved, turn
into brown bread crumbs
and milk, let stand to cool,
whip cream add to it
slowly the mixture of
brown bread stirring
constantly, add orange
juice and vanilla and stir
till bears impression of
spoon; turn into cold
mould to cool for a time.

Mrs. Henry W. Darling
Handwritten
Manuscript
Schenectady, New York
ca. 1882–93

GINGERBREAD CUSTARD

Why not use gingerbread as the basis for a bread pudding? Quite by accident, I found an old recipe with this title in a popular "middlebrow" cookbook from early in the 20th century.

This pudding separates into layers as it bakes; the bottom layer is almost cake-like, with a toffee-colored custard on top.

⁓ *Serves about 6*

1   cup crumbled stale gingerbread or gingersnap cookies
2   cups milk
2   large eggs
¼   cup sugar
½   cup raisins
½   teaspoon pure vanilla extract
2   tablespoons minced crystallized ginger

1. Preheat the oven to 350 degrees F, with a rack in the center. Combine the crumbled gingerbread or gingersnaps and 1 cup of the milk in a large bowl; let stand until the gingerbread dissolves slightly into the milk and is quite soft. Add the remaining 1 cup milk, the eggs, sugar, raisins, vanilla and crystallized ginger; whisk until well combined.

2. Transfer to a 1-to-1½-quart soufflé dish or deep baking dish; set the dish in a roasting pan. Place the pan in the oven. Pour in about 1 inch of hot tap water.

3. Bake for 30 minutes. Stir the pudding gently to redistribute the ingredients. Bake until the pudding is set but still slightly wobbly in the center, about 30 minutes longer. Remove from the water bath and cool on a wire rack. Serve lukewarm or cold.

⁓ *Variation*
Meringue Topping: If you'd like to top the pudding with meringue, whip 2 egg whites until frothy. Gradually add ⅓ cup sugar and ½ teaspoon pure vanilla extract and whip until stiff. Spread the meringue over the baked pudding, sealing completely. Bake in a 350-degree oven until lightly golden, about 15 minutes longer. Cool on a wire rack; serve lukewarm or cold.

ABOUT NOODLE PUDDINGS

*I*n Jewish-American families with roots in Eastern Europe, particularly in Russia, Poland, Lithuania and Romania, no Jewish meal—from brunch to midnight snack to wedding banquet—is complete without a big, heavy panful of noodle kugel. The word *kugel* means pudding in Yiddish and refers generically to dishes made variously with noodles, bread, rice and potatoes. Made with eggs and sugar, and sometimes fruit, and topped with nuts or corn flakes—a sort of casserole pudding—Jewish noodle puddings clearly belong in the dessert category. In practice, though, they are often served alongside meat dishes, even though they are sweet. Certain other Eastern European kugels, like Czech Noodle and Apple Soufflé (page 209) and Hungarian Cheese-Noodle Dessert (page 207) are reserved exclusively for dessert.

In keeping with the kosher separation of meat and dairy products, there are dairy and nondairy kugels. When served with meat dishes, they're made with eggs, chicken or goose fat (not butter), sugar and raisins and candied fruit or fresh fruits, such as apples and pears. Dairy versions include butter, cottage cheese and/or sour cream.

But while the Jews and Eastern Europeans have raised noodle puddings to the level of a folk art, the dessert is almost universal. As early as 1747, Hannah Glasse gave instructions for an English "Vermicella Pudding," layering cooked noodles with butter, eggs, bread crumbs and seasonings. "If you lay a good thin Crust round the Bottom of the Dish and Sides," she suggests, "it will be better." A French *crème soufflée de vermicelle* from the mid-18th century is made along the same lines, though elaborated with praline and crushed macaroons. In the Middle East, noodles are combined with honey, oil and chopped nuts.

Does my mother's noodle pudding belong with these dessert puddings? Or is it more properly considered a side dish?

You're asking me?

MOM'S NEW NOODLE KUGEL

Years before everyone started to wring their hands over cholesterol, my mother was cutting back on butter and substituting yogurt for sour cream in baking. Here's her basic noodle pudding.

⌒ *Serves about 6*

¾	cup raisins
3	tablespoons amaretto
1	pound wide egg noodles
6	large eggs
1	cup ricotta or low-fat cottage cheese
1	cup plain yogurt
½	cup sugar
1½	teaspoons pure vanilla extract
1	teaspoon ground cinnamon
¼	teaspoon salt
1-2	apples (any type), peeled, cored and cut into short, thin slices (1-1½ cups)

TOPPING

¼	cup coarsely crushed corn flakes
1	teaspoon sugar
¼	teaspoon ground cinnamon
3	tablespoons unsalted butter, melted
3	tablespoons sliced almonds

1. Bring a large pot of salted water to a boil. Preheat the oven to 350 degrees F, with a rack in the center. Butter a 13-x-9-inch baking dish; set aside. In a small bowl, soak the raisins in the amaretto.

2. Cook the noodles in the boiling water until just tender, usually 9 to 10 minutes. Drain the noodles; rinse and set aside.

3. In a bowl, whisk together the eggs, ricotta or cottage cheese, yogurt, sugar, vanilla, cinnamon and salt. Add the drained noodles and the raisins with their soaking liquid; stir gently to combine. Transfer ½ of this mixture to the prepared pan. Scatter the apples over the noodles; top with the remaining noodle mixture.

4. **TOPPING:** In a small bowl, combine the corn flakes, sugar and cinnamon. Scatter the topping over the noodles; drizzle with the butter.

5. Bake the kugel for 20 minutes. Scatter the sliced almonds on top. Bake until the mixture is set and golden brown, about 25 minutes more. Cool to lukewarm on a wire rack, about 30 minutes, and serve cut into large squares.

HUNGARIAN CHEESE-NOODLE DESSERT
(*STIRIAI METÉLT*)

This Hungarian pudding, which is actually from Stiria, an area now in Austria, is made by baking tender homemade noodles made with cottage cheese in a souffléed batter, flavored with vanilla and lemon zest.

 *Serves 6*

CHEESE-NOODLE DOUGH
- 1 pound dry-curd cottage cheese, pressed through a sieve (discard any liquid)
- 3 large eggs, lightly beaten
  Pinch salt
- 2 cups less 1 tablespoon all-purpose flour

PUDDING BATTER
- 1½ tablespoons unsalted butter, softened
- ¼ cup plus 1 tablespoon sugar
- 3 large eggs, separated
  Grated zest of 1 lemon
- 1½ teaspoons pure vanilla extract
- 1½ cups sour cream
- ⅓ cup raisins
  Vanilla sugar (see Vanilla Bean, page 22) or confectioners' sugar, for sprinkling

1. **CHEESE-NOODLE DOUGH:** Combine the cottage cheese, eggs and salt in a bowl. Stir in the flour just until blended. Cover the bowl and chill well, at least 1 hour.

2. Bring a large pot of water to a boil. On a well-floured surface or between 2 sheets of wax paper, roll out the dough to an even ¼-inch-thick rectangle. Use a floured sharp knife to cut the dough into 2½-inch-wide strips. Cut each strip crosswise into

I've visited Hungary twice, and each time, I kept extending my visit, not wanting to leave. I spent a fall afternoon with István Lukács, chef at Budapest's Atrium Hyatt Hotel. His shiny pink face lit up when I asked him about his mother's desserts. As he showed me how to make the unusual cheese noodles, he served me a deep bowl of this warm pudding. I ate the whole thing.

207

¼- to ⅜-inch-wide noodles. Add the salt to the boiling water; add the noodles and cook until they rise to the surface; cook for 1 minute longer, until tender. Drain; rinse under cold water, and drain again. Set aside.

3. **PUDDING BATTER:** Preheat the oven to 400 degrees F, with a rack in the center. Butter and flour a 12-inch oval gratin dish or other shallow baking dish; set aside. With an electric mixer, beat the butter and ¼ cup of the sugar until smooth. Add the egg yolks and lemon zest and beat until smooth and light. With a large rubber spatula, gently fold in the vanilla extract, sour cream, raisins and the noodles; mix until all of the ingredients are combined.

4. In a bowl, beat the egg whites until they form soft peaks. Add the remaining 1 tablespoon sugar and beat until quite stiff but not dry. Fold a large spoonful of the meringue into the batter; gently fold in the rest. Spoon the batter into the buttered baking dish.

5. Bake the pudding for 20 minutes. Reduce the heat to 375 degrees and bake until golden and lightly set, 5 to 10 minutes longer. Cool on a wire rack for 15 to 20 minutes.

6. Sprinkle generously with vanilla sugar or confectioners' sugar. Serve warm, spooned out into serving dishes.

Czech Noodle and Apple Soufflé

(*Nudlový Nákyp*)

Some Czech noodle desserts are made with poppy seeds, sugar and butter, some with crumbled gingerbread. This one is soft, mostly noodles and apples bound with a bit of eggy batter. Serve it as you would a soufflé, warm, soon after baking.

Serves about 8

2⅔	cups milk
	Pinch salt
4	ounces wide egg noodles, broken into 1-inch pieces (about 1¾ cups)
5	tablespoons butter, softened
⅓	cup sugar
3	large eggs, separated
1½	teaspoons pure vanilla extract
2½	cups peeled, cored, sliced apples (any type; about 1 pound)
	Confectioners' sugar, for sprinkling

1. In a large saucepan, bring the milk and salt to a boil. Add the noodles and cook, stirring frequently, until tender, usually about 8 minutes. Set aside briefly to cool; do not drain.

2. Preheat the oven to 350 degrees F, with a rack in the center. Butter an 11-inch oval gratin dish or other large shallow baking dish. With an electric mixer, cream the butter and sugar in a large bowl, beating until light. Add the egg yolks and beat until light. Gently stir in the noodle-milk mixture and the vanilla.

3. In another bowl, beat the egg whites until nearly stiff. Fold the beaten whites into the noodle mixture. Pour ½ of the noodle mixture into the baking dish. Top with the sliced apples; cover with the remaining noodles.

4. Bake until the pudding is lightly golden and nearly set, but still slightly jiggly in the center, 30 to 35 minutes. Cool on a wire rack for about 10 minutes. Sprinkle with confectioners' sugar and serve warm.

"Meals Made from Flour"

Czech noodle desserts are part of a category called *mehlspeisen*, found throughout Eastern Europe.

To learn more about these desserts, I paid a visit to Mrs. Claire Fiala, who grew up in Bratislava, then in Czechoslovakia, and now lives in New York.

Over coffee and cakes, she told me, "*Mehlspeisen* was something we ate a lot. It means 'meals made from flour'—like pasta. We had a cook, but my mother made the dough with flour, water and eggs, rolling it out herself. There are lots of different types. In one dish, you make squares like ravioli and fill them with jam. Or in summer, you'd take a whole apricot or plum, replace the pit with a little cube of sugar and wrap it in a square of potato dough. You serve the boiled dumpling drizzled with sugar and poppy seeds or with bread crumbs and goose fat.

"Goose fat—can you imagine?" Claire bursts into laughter, her clear green eyes crinkling. "Now I eat very healthy, so I don't eat much fat."

ABOUT GRAIN PUDDINGS

*S*weetened puddings made with grains are staples throughout the world, with many cross-cultural parallels. Often, they are more tasty than you'd think on hearing their names. (After all, if you'd never tasted bread or rice pudding, would they excite you on a menu?)

Although oat-based puddings are much less familiar to us than rice or bread puddings, oats are among the oldest grains and have been used in puddings since ancient times.

Millet, a nutritious grain that is a staple in some parts of Africa, has been used to make puddings with surprising frequency. (We know millet mainly as bird seed.)

In Japan, red azuki beans are cooked, pureed, sweetened and sieved to form a mixture called *an*. It has a sweet taste and fudge-like texture and can be molded into various decorative confections.

Puddings of wheat berries (the whole wheat kernel, sometimes hulled) are made in the Middle East. A pudding of wheat berries and ricotta is the filling for *pastiera*, a Neapolitan tart also found in Sicily (page 510). An Armenian New Year's wheat-berry pudding is called *Anoush Abour* ("sweet soup") with the wheat suspended in a rose-water-scented sugar syrup that's garnished with dried fruits and almonds. It's a cool, refreshing celebration dish to get the new year off to a sweet start.

One of the most extravagant of all grain-based desserts is the *Cuscusu di Pistacchi* of Sicily, made with couscous and pistachios. Time-consuming and exacting to make, it repays the effort with a flavor at once subtle and headily perfumed. For those ready to put forth the effort required to make it, I direct you to Nicholas Malgieri's recipe, from the Santo Spirito Monastery, in *Great Italian Desserts* (Little, Brown, 1990). (Although the author will not confirm it publicly, rumor has it that Malgieri had to bribe a nun with a Cuisinart before she would part with the recipe.)

Spelt or Farina Pudding

*B*oil spelt with [pine] nuts and peeled almonds immersed in water and washed with white clay so that they appear perfectly white, add raisins, [flavor with] condensed wine or raisin wine and serve it in a round dish with crushed nuts, fruit, bread or cake crumbs sprinkled over it."

APICIUS
DE RE COQUINARIA
[ON COOKERY]
LATE 4TH TO
EARLY 5TH CENTURY A.D.

New England Oatmeal Pudding with Warm Maple Syrup

Oats permeate this warm pudding with their toasty grain flavor. Based on a New England recipe from the 1870s, this is a soothing indulgence on a cold day.

Serves about 8

2	cups old-fashioned or quick-cooking (not instant) oats
4	cups (1 quart) milk
3	large eggs
4	tablespoons (½ stick) unsalted butter, cut into pieces
½	cup sugar
½	teaspoon salt
¾	teaspoon fresh-grated nutmeg
½	cup golden or dark raisins
½	cup dried currants
	Pure maple syrup, for serving

1. Preheat the oven to 350 degrees F, with a rack in the center. Scatter the oats in a baking pan and toast, stirring now and then, until pale golden, usually 12 to 15 minutes. Meanwhile, scald the milk. Add the oats to the milk and stir to combine. Cover and let stand at room temperature until the oatmeal is very soft, about 30 minutes.

2. Increase the oven temperature to 375 degrees. Butter a 2-quart soufflé dish or other deep baking dish or casserole; set aside.

3. In a large bowl, beat the eggs; stir in the butter, sugar, salt, nutmeg, raisins and currants. Stir in the oatmeal mixture.

4. Pour the mixture into the baking dish; cover the dish with a sheet of buttered foil, buttered side down. Set the dish in a roasting pan and place in the oven. Pour in enough hot tap water to reach partway up the sides of the dish.

5. Bake until the pudding is set but still slightly wobbly in the center, about 45 minutes. (The timing can vary; do not overbake.) Cool to lukewarm on a wire rack, about 30 minutes.

6. Drizzle with maple syrup. Warming it is a nice touch.

To Make Oatmeal Puddings

Take a quart of oatmeal grotis [groats], pick them very clean, then let them soak all night in warm milk then bake a penny loaf and grate it, put it in . . . you must drayn the milk from the oatmeal, then take two pounds of boeuf suitt, or marrow, when you mix it, put in a pint of Creame, and season it with cloves mace and cinamon to yr taste, most cinamon, a little rosewater, a pound and halfe of currants, neer half a pound of sugar, five eggs the whites but of three, half an hower will boyle . . .

LADY ANNE MORTON
THE LADEY MORTONS
BOOKE OF RECEIPTS
HANDWRITTEN
MANUSCRIPT
ENGLAND, 1693

RECIPES

*Baked Pear (or Apple) Batter
  Pudding*
Custardy Prune Pudding
Sour Cherry Clafouti
Cranberry Duff
*Persimmon Buttermilk
  Pudding*
English Toffee Pudding
*Rum-Glazed Sweet Potato
  Pudding*
*Oven-Steamed Figgy Pud-
  ding*
*Steamed Pumpkin Pudding
  with Ginger-Lemon Cream*
*Tennessee Old Maid's Sweet
  Potato Pudding*
Big Berry Popover
*Reuben's Legendary Apple
  Pancake*
*Hungarian Walnut-Filled
  Crepes with Warm
  Chocolate Sauce*
Baked Apple Dumplings
Winter Fruit Dumplings

FRUIT PUDDINGS, SWEET PANCAKES AND DUMPLINGS

Hallo! A great deal of steam! A great deal of steam! The pudding was out of the copper. A smell like a washing-day! That was the cloth. A smell like an eating-house, and a pastry cook's next door to each other, with a laundress's next door to that! That was the pudding. In half a minute Mrs. Cratchit entered: flushed, but smiling proudly: with the pudding, like a speckled cannon-ball, so hard and firm, blazing in half a quartern of ignited brandy, and bedight with Christmas holly stuck into the top.

Oh, a wonderful pudding!

CHARLES DICKENS, *A CHRISTMAS CAROL*, 1843

arm fruit puddings—baked or steamed—are hallmarks in the world of rustic desserts, prime examples of the type of thing cooked at home rather than by professional pastry chefs. And when they're streamlined a bit (without the suet used in old English recipes and with a minimum of bread crumbs to bind), they can be lighter and tastier. But they still convey that homespun touch.

The word *pudding* was recorded as early as 1305 (and used, in some form, as far back as Homer's *Odyssey*) to describe a sausage-like dish in which the innards of an animal (or the skin of a fish) were stuffed with a savory mixture of minced grain and/or meat. The word derives from the Old French *boudin* ("sausage"), and, further back, from the Latin *botelinus.*

Early versions of puddings contained both meat and fruits, usually dried or candied. Even as late as the 17th century in England (and in the New England colonies), boiled puddings were served alongside meat and other main dishes.

But gradually, both pies and puddings separated into non-sweetened meat versions, containing chicken, steak and kidneys on one hand; and sweetened versions, with plum (meaning raisin) pudding, which once included meat, becoming a dessert.

While it is virtually universal, nowhere in the world has the pudding been raised to the level of national institution as in Britain, where the bone-chilling climate and the population's insatiable sweet tooth provided the perfect breeding conditions for pudding to emerge into full flower.

By Charles Dickens' day, hardly any proper English meal ended without one pudding or another (and many were centered around it; steak and kidney pud is still a favorite). Mrs. Beeton's *The Book of Household Management* (originally published in London in 24 monthly installments from 1859 to 1861, and then in book form in 1861) includes no fewer than 50 recipes for dessert puddings alone. (In a nod of acknowledgment to the country of origin, the French call all these desserts by their anglicized name, *le pouding.* So wide is the British repertoire that the term *pud* has come to be used generically in England to mean dessert.)

But don't think the British have cornered the market. Several French and American puddings are represented here, and those have become old favorites.

Fruit pancakes and dumplings are equally universal, found in wildly varying forms all over the world. Like fruit puddings, they begin with a simple batter. For pancakes, the batter is studded with fruit, then browned on a griddle or in a cast-iron skillet. (Fruit can also be served alongside or as a sauce.) A dumpling can include just about anything wrapped in dough: from small prune plums tucked into a potato-based dough and simmered until tender to Viennese *topfenknodl*—light cheese dumplings—to apple dumplings enclosed in pie dough and baked until golden.

The earliest of these dishes, pancakes, were among the first breads and began as a staple breakfast food. Buckwheat cakes, the most popular, were ubiquitous on American tables in the morning. Other kinds of pancakes were called variously griddle cakes, flapjacks or hominy cakes.

Spotted Dick

Aside from plum pudding, the many English puddings with which the Queen and her subjects still celebrate Christmas include:

≈ Spotted Dick (or Dog), a steamed suet pudding "spotted" with currants and raisins;

≈ Jam Roly-Poly, a suet-and-bread-crumb mixture spread with jam, then rolled and boiled (see page 568 for a lighter baked version);

≈ Thunder and Lightning, a rice pudding served with scalded cream (thunder) and golden syrup (lightning).

But like pie, which was often eaten for breakfast, pancakes evolved into a dessert, with sweet versions like Hannah Glasse's 18th-century Apple Fraze, in which sautéed apple slices are enveloped in pancake batter. Refine these a bit further, and you're in the realm of the thin, lacy crepe and such delicate desserts as crepes Suzette (crepes in orange-butter sauce) and Hungarian *palacsinta* (walnut-filled crepes, page 236).

Doughnuts, introduced by Dutch settlers to New Amsterdam (now New York) as *oly koeks* ("fried cakes"), and waffles, which were brought to America by the Germans and the Dutch, are also part of this family. I've chosen to omit them from this book, however, concluding that they are more breakfast breads than desserts. But you will find a fruit-studded popover that's perfect for brunch, and Reuben's Legendary Apple Pancake (page 234) not only lives up to the billing of its name but makes the best late-night snack ever.

"King Arthur"

When King Arthur first
did reign
He rul-led like a king.
He bought three sacks of
barley meal
To make a plum pud-ding.

The pudding it was made,
And duly stuffed with
plums,
And lumps of suet put in it
As big as my two thumbs.

The king and queen sat
down to it
And all the lords beside,
And what they couldn't eat
that night,
The queen next morning
fried.

ENGLISH SONG

BAKED PEAR (OR APPLE) BATTER PUDDING

Combining batter with fruit is one of the simplest ways to put together a warm pudding for dessert. A familiar one is bird's nest pudding, sometimes made with whole apples (the "eggs") baked in a nest of custard.

These batter puddings turn up, in one form or another, in virtually every American cookbook. Some are more like pancakes; others, like this one, surround the fruit with a creamier custard.

Serves about 8

⅓	cup raisins
2	tablespoons cognac or dark rum
3	tablespoons amaretto or other liqueur
2-3	cups peeled pear and/or apple wedges (about 4 whole fruits)
	Juice of ½ lemon
⅔	cup all-purpose flour
½	cup sugar
1½	cups milk
4	large eggs
1	tablespoon pure vanilla extract
2	tablespoons unsalted butter, cut into pieces
	Confectioners' sugar, for sprinkling
	Pure maple syrup, warmed, for serving (optional)

1. Soak the raisins in the cognac or rum and the amaretto for at least 30 minutes. Drain and reserve the raisins; the liquor is for the cook.

2. Preheat the oven to 375 degrees F, with a rack in the upper third. Butter a shallow casserole or baking dish. (I use a 12-inch round ceramic dish, but a large oval gratin dish would work fine, too. The point here is to bake the dessert in a container that has a lot of surface area.) Toss the pear and/or apple wedges with the lemon juice and the drained raisins; scatter in the prepared dish.

3. In a bowl, combine the flour and sugar until free of lumps. In a measuring cup or small bowl, whisk together the milk, eggs and vanilla until smooth. Make a well in the dry ingredients and add the liquid. Whisk gently just until smooth, no longer. Pour the batter over the fruit and dot the surface with the butter.

Rules to Be Observed in Making Puddings, &c.

In boiled Puddings, take great Care the bag or Cloth be very clean, and not soapy, and dipped in hot Water, and then well flowered. If a Bread-pudding, tye it loose; if a Batter-pudding, tye it close; and be sure the Water bolis [sic] when you put the Pudding in . . . then put in the Ingredients by degrees, and it will be smooth and not have Lumps; but for a plain Batter-pudding, the best way is to strain it through a coarse Hair Sieve, that it may neither have Lumps, nor the Treadels of the Eggs: And all other Puddings, strain the Eggs when they are beat. If you boil them in Wooden-bowls, or China-dishes, butter the Inside before you put in your Batter: And all baked Puddings, butter the Pan or Dish, before the Pudding is put in.

HANNAH GLASSE
THE ART OF COOKERY,
MADE PLAIN AND EASY
LONDON, 1747

215

Eve's Pudding

Pare 6 apples; chop them fine 6 ounces grated bread 6 ounces sugar 6 ounces currants sprinkled with flour. Mix all this together in a pan, with 6 ounces butter, 2 tablespoonfuls flour. Beat 6 eggs & add to the mixture nutmeg cinnamon. Bake 3 hours.

MRS. MATILDA ROGERS
RECIPE BOOK
MANUSCRIPT
NEW YORK, 1850

4. Bake the pudding until the custard sets, usually about 30 minutes. Transfer the dish to a wire rack.

5. Preheat the broiler with a rack 3 or 4 inches from the heat source. Sift confectioners' sugar over the surface of the pudding and broil, watching carefully to prevent burning, until the surface is glazed and golden, usually less than 1 minute. Cool the pudding briefly on a wire rack. Serve warm, drizzled with the optional warm maple syrup.

CUSTARDY PRUNE PUDDING
(*FAR BRETON*)

This is one of the best-loved traditional desserts from Brittany, on France's Atlantic coast. It's a thick custard with marinated prunes that is baked until spotted with gold. The word *far* means "pudding" in the Breton dialect.

On my first trip to France, a whirlwind Eurailpass adventure (when several hundred dollars could carry you—not lavishly, but comfortably, in a scruffy kind of way—for many weeks), I stopped in just about every pastry shop I saw, usually for a wedge of tart filled with a dense custard: *un flan*. The texture was irresistible: nothing but pastry cream, baked until firm. The custard in this hearty, flavorful dessert is nearly identical.

Try making it with prunes from Orchard Crest Farms in Oregon (see page 77 for mail-order information). They're incredibly moist, and when baked in this pudding, they emerge almost jam-like.

⟜ *Serves about 6*

12	moist pitted prunes
2	tablespoons dark rum, or a mixture of amaretto and brandy or whiskey
3	large eggs
½	cup sugar
	Pinch salt
½	teaspoon pure vanilla extract (optional, but good)
1	cup all-purpose flour
2	cups milk

1. Combine the prunes with the rum or other spirits in a small bowl. Set aside to soak for 1 hour or longer, stirring occasionally.

2. Preheat the oven to 350 degrees F, with a rack in the center. Generously butter a deep pie pan or other shallow baking dish 9½ to 11 inches in diameter. Arrange the prunes in the baking dish, avoiding the very center. Spoon any remaining soaking liquid over the prunes; set the dish aside.

3. In a bowl, whisk the eggs with the sugar, salt and optional vanilla until well blended. Sift in the flour a little at a time, whisking until smooth after each addition. Whisk in the milk until the batter is smooth. Pour the batter over the prunes.

4. Bake until the surface is spotted with gold and the custard is just set, usually about 1 hour (the timing can vary based on the size of the baking dish; do not overbake).

5. Cool to room temperature or lukewarm on a wire rack. Cut into wedges to serve.

SOUR CHERRY CLAFOUTI

A clafouti (the older spelling is clafoutis) is a French country dessert, with fruit baked in a batter that ends up being something between a custard and a pancake, puffed, golden and crisp. This is a version of the rustic original, an amalgam of several French recipes, including one from my friend, cookbook author Martha Rose Shulman.

Serves 6 to 8

2½ cups (about 1 pound) sour red cherries
1¼ cups milk
¼ cup sugar, plus more for sprinkling
3 large eggs
1 tablespoon pure vanilla extract or 2 teaspoons vanilla and 1 tablespoon cognac or kirsch
Pinch salt
½ cup sifted all-purpose flour
Sugar, for sprinkling

1. Preheat the oven to 350 degrees F, with a rack in the center. Butter the bottom and sides of an 8- or 9-inch round or oval gratin dish or pie pan.

2. Rinse, stem and pit the cherries, placing them in a colander set over a bowl to catch the juices.

3. In a blender or food processor, combine the milk, sugar, eggs, vanilla (or vanilla and cognac or kirsch), salt, flour and the reserved cherry juices. Process just until blended and smooth, no longer. (If you aren't using a machine, whisk together all the batter ingredients except the flour and cherry juices in a bowl. Whisk in the cherry juices, and then the flour; do not overmix.)

4. Place the cherries in the buttered dish. Pour the batter over the cherries (or strain it over, if it's slightly lumpy). Sprinkle the top with sugar.

5. Bake until the edges are dark golden and a toothpick inserted in the center emerges clean, usually 45 to 50 minutes. The clafouti will fall when it comes out of the oven; cool on a wire rack. Serve warm.

CRANBERRY DUFF

A favorite sailor's dish, a duff (the word is an old northern English pronunciation of "dough") was usually steamed in a cloth bag. Lighter than most steamed puddings and not too sweet, this version is baked in a fluted mold so that it emerges crunchy around the edges, its interior tender and warm.

This duff is based on an old recipe, originally made with blueberries, from Laura Barton of the Oregon Department of Agriculture. The cranberries give it a pleasant burst of tartness. Serve it warm, with Cider-Lemon Sauce (page 611), Foamy Sauce (page 616), Eggnog Custard Sauce (page 609), Ginger-Lemon Cream (page 228) or heavy cream.

Serves 8

2	cups all-purpose flour
1	tablespoon plus 1 teaspoon baking powder
1	teaspoon salt
1	teaspoon ground ginger
½	teaspoon fresh-grated nutmeg
4	cups (about 1 pound) fresh or frozen (not thawed) cranberries, picked over
2	cups sugar
3	large eggs
½	cup milk
1½	tablespoons unsalted butter, melted
1	teaspoon fresh lemon juice

1. Preheat the oven to 350 degrees F, with a rack in the center. Generously butter an 8- to 10-inch kugelhopf or tube pan. In a large bowl, sift together the flour, baking powder, salt, ginger and nutmeg. Stir in the cranberries and sugar.

2. In a small bowl, whisk together the eggs, milk, melted butter and lemon juice. Make a well in the dry ingredients; add the milk mixture. Stir together just until the dry ingredients are moistened and well combined, no longer. Pour the batter into the pan.

3. Bake until the top is golden brown and a toothpick inserted in the center emerges clean, about 1 hour and 25 minutes.

4. Cool in the mold on a wire rack for about 10 minutes. Unmold the pudding onto a serving plate. Serve warm.

Fresh pork once more,
once more plum duff,
take hold, take hold,
sure that's enough.
eat, eat your fill,
don't look forlorn,
here's roasted pig,
and there's cape horn.
so don't be making such a bother,
we'll eat up one and pass the other.

ATTRIBUTED TO
LANGSFORD W. HASTINGS
QUOTED IN
JOSEPH R. CONLIN'S
*BACON, BEANS, AND
GALANTINES—FOOD AND
FOODWAYS ON THE WESTERN
MINING FRONTIER*
1986

PERSIMMON BUTTERMILK PUDDING

Persimmons are best in the fall, and this pudding, loosely based on a recipe from chef Larry Forgione, owner of An American Place in New York City, New York, makes a fine Thanksgiving dessert. It's baked in a shallow baking dish until it puffs and the edges brown slightly; when cool, it sinks slightly and can be cut into neat squares. Topped with whipped cream, the creamy texture of this traditional American dessert is reminiscent of pumpkin pie, but the persimmons add a sweet-tart dimension, a melting quality all their own.

If you've never tried persimmons, this dessert will be a wonderful surprise. The trick with persimmons is to let them get so ripe that they're nearly collapsing.

⟿ *Serves about 8*

2	large dead-ripe persimmons (about 1¼ pounds)
3	tablespoons unsalted butter
2	cups buttermilk
3	large eggs
¾	cup packed light brown sugar
¼	cup sugar
1	teaspoon pure vanilla extract
1	cup all-purpose flour
1	teaspoon baking powder
1	teaspoon baking soda
1	teaspoon ground cinnamon
½	teaspoon fresh-grated nutmeg
	Pinch salt
	Whipped cream, for serving

1. Preheat the oven to 375 degrees F, with a rack in the center. Put the butter in an 8-inch square baking pan and place in the oven until melted; set aside. Leave the oven on.

2. Put the persimmons through a food mill, or peel and puree in a food processor. (You should have 1½ cups raw persimmon puree.) Scrape the pulp into a large bowl and add most of the melted butter, leaving a little in the baking pan. Add the buttermilk, eggs, brown and white sugars and vanilla; whisk until blended.

3. Sift the dry ingredients onto a sheet of wax paper; add to the persimmon mixture and mix just until combined. Scrape the mixture into the buttered baking dish.

4. Bake until the edges are lightly browned and the center is set, about 40 minutes.

5. Cool the pudding on a wire rack. Cut into squares and serve warm or at room temperature, topped with the whipped cream.

Persimmon Encounters

Encountering the wild persimmon (called *putchamin* by native Americans) for the first time, Captain John Smith found that an unripe fruit "will drawe a mans mouth awrie with much torment," but that, when ripe, "is as delicious as an Apricock."

That persimmon was the small variety native to America, but most persimmons you buy are the Asian variety, usually called Japanese persimmon (*kaki* in Japan) and originally native to China. In the Midwest and the South, persimmon is popular in puddings, is made into fudge and is used as a filling for rolled cakes.

Tilly's Pudding

Meantime Tilly attacked the plum-pudding. She felt pretty sure of coming out right, here, for she had seen her mother do it so many times, it looked very easy. So in went suet and fruit; all sorts of spice, to be sure she got the right ones, and brandy instead of wine. But she forgot both sugar and salt, and tied it in the cloth so tightly that it had no room to swell, so it would come out as heavy as lead and as hard as a cannon-ball, if the bag did not burst and spoil it all. Happily unconscious of these mistakes, Tilly popped it into the pot, and proudly watched it bobbing about before she put the cover on and left it to its fate.

LOUISA MAY ALCOTT
AN OLD-FASHIONED
THANKSGIVING
1882

222

ENGLISH TOFFEE PUDDING

A 10!" said my number-one taster. The recipe comes from Sheila's Cottage, Ambleside, in England's Lake District. The date-studded pudding base is baked in a shallow dish until set; it is then topped with a mixture of butter and brown sugar and baked again until it is glazed with a crunchy candy topping.

⤳ Serves 6 to 8

1   cup plus 1 tablespoon all-purpose flour
1   teaspoon baking powder
¾   cup (about 4 ounces) finely chopped dried pitted dates
7   tablespoons unsalted butter, softened
¾   cup sugar
1   large egg, lightly beaten
1   teaspoon baking soda
1   teaspoon pure vanilla extract
1¼   cups boiling water
¼   cup plus 1 tablespoon packed light brown sugar
2   tablespoons heavy cream
     Whipped cream, for serving

1. Preheat the oven to 350 degrees F, with a rack in the center. Butter a 9-to-10-inch pie pan or oval gratin dish; set aside.

2. Sift the 1 cup flour and the baking powder onto a sheet of wax paper or into a bowl; set aside. In a small heatproof bowl, toss the dates with the remaining 1 tablespoon of flour.

3. In a large bowl with an electric mixer at medium-high speed, beat together 4 tablespoons of the butter and the white sugar until light and fluffy. Lower the speed to medium-low; beat in the egg and about ¼ of the flour mixture; mix until smooth. Add the remaining flour mixture and mix just until incorporated.

4. Sprinkle the baking soda and vanilla over the dates; add the boiling water and stir to combine. Add the date mixture to the batter, beating until well blended. Pour the mixture into the prepared baking dish.

5. Bake until set and well browned on top, 30 to 40 minutes. Remove the pudding from the oven; preheat the broiler, with a rack about 4 inches from the heat source.

6. In a small saucepan over medium heat, bring the remaining 3 tablespoons butter, the brown sugar and the cream to a simmer. Simmer until thickened, about 3 minutes. Pour the topping over the hot pudding.

7. Broil the pudding until the topping bubbles, watching carefully to prevent burning, about 1 minute. Cool the pudding briefly on a wire rack. Serve warm, with whipped cream.

ABOUT VEGETABLE DESSERT PUDDINGS

*V*egetable dessert puddings may sound unappetizing at first, but sweet potatoes or carrots, parsnips or other root vegetables combined with brown sugar, spices, milk and eggs make surprisingly tasty desserts.

Carrot puddings and tarts abound in English cookery books, and given the vegetable's natural sweetness, the idea makes sense. Right alongside them, you can find plenty of English and American recipes for parsnip puddings and pies. Similarly, in Caribbean and African cooking, desserts are made with yucca, arrowroot and other starchy tubers. And in Indonesia, *kolak ubi* and *kolak labu* are desserts made by simmering cubes of sweet potatoes and pumpkins, respectively, in coconut syrup.

One of the oddest recipes for a vegetable pudding is a 1587 English version that details "how to make a pudding in a Turnip root." After the turnip is hollowed out, it's filled with a mixture of "sugar, sinamon and ginger, hard egg yolks, Claret wine, butter, vinegar, rosemarye, mace, and dates quartered." That recipe is followed by instructions for making "a pudding in a Caret root"—fiddly work.

Historically, though, the vegetable most often used for dessert-making is the potato. In nearly every bound recipe collection from the 17th century on, potato puddings appear as frequently as do apple, lemon, almond and bread puddings.

Carrot Puding

Take a large Carrot, boil it Tender then set it by to be cold and grate it through a hair sieve very fine, then put in half a pound of melted Butter beaten with Eight Eggs leaving out half the Whites, two or three Spoonfulls of Sack and Orange flower Water, half pint of good thick cream, a little grated Bread, a Nutmeg and a little salt, sweeten it to your tast, and make it of the thickness of an Orange Pudding.

HARRIOTT PINCKNEY
HORRY
*A COLONIAL
PLANTATION COOKBOOK*
SOUTH CAROLINA, 1770

RUM-GLAZED SWEET POTATO PUDDING

This is a simple baked pudding with a base of mashed sweet potatoes. It has a wonderfully rich flavor and is based on a recipe from Sarah Rutledge's *The Carolina Housewife* (Charleston, South Carolina, 1847), one of the landmark books of early Southern cooking. In colonial America, sweet potatoes were far more common than white ones. (Some recipes call for yams, with which sweet potatoes have become permanently confused. Virtually all of what we buy today, regardless of how they're labeled, are sweet potatoes. The confusion began when African-born slaves gave their native name—yam—to sweet potatoes.)

Essentially a pleasant variation on the Thanksgiving classic that is often topped with arc-welded marshmallows, this pudding is not cloyingly sweet and allows the sweet potatoes' own nice flavor to come through. Serve it warm, topped with whipped cream flavored with vanilla and dark rum.

⌒⌒ *Serves 6 to 8*

⅓	cup sweet or dry sherry or Madeira
⅔	cup raisins
2	pounds (about 6 medium) sweet potatoes, baked, boiled or steamed until tender
½	cup (1 stick) unsalted butter, melted
4	large eggs
2	cups milk
1	cup packed light brown sugar
½	teaspoon fresh-grated nutmeg
	Pinch salt
	Grated zest of 1 orange
2	tablespoons fresh lemon juice
¼	cup plus 1 tablespoon dark rum or bourbon

1. Pour the sherry or Madeira over the raisins in a small bowl; let stand for 30 minutes or longer.

2. Preheat the oven to 375 degrees F, with a rack in the center. Butter an 11-inch oval gratin dish, 8-inch square or other shallow baking dish; set aside.

3. Halve the cooked sweet potatoes; scoop out the flesh and place it in a large bowl. Add ¼ cup plus 1 tablespoon of the melted butter. Add the eggs, one at a time, and beat with an electric mixer

A Boiled Potatoe Pudding

Boil two pounds of potatoes, and beat them in a mortar fine; beat it in half a pd of melted butter, and boil it half an hour. Pour melted butter over it, with a glass of white wine, or the juice of a Seville orange, and throw sugar all over the pudding and dish.

SUSANNAH CARTER
THE FRUGAL HOUSEWIFE
PHILADELPHIA, 1802

into the sweet potato-butter mixture. Add the milk, ⅓ cup of the brown sugar, the nutmeg, salt and orange zest and beat until blended. Beat in the raisins and their soaking liquid. Scoop the mixture into the baking dish.

4. Warm the remaining 3 tablespoons melted butter in a small skillet. Stir in the remaining ⅔ cup brown sugar and the lemon juice; cook over medium-high heat, stirring occasionally, until bubbly, 3 to 5 minutes. Stir in the rum or bourbon and return the mixture to a boil. Drizzle the rum glaze randomly over the surface of the sweet potato mixture.

5. Bake until the pudding is set and the glaze is bubbly, about 45 minutes. Cool to lukewarm on a wire rack before serving.

TO MAKE INDIVIDUAL STEAMED PUDDINGS

You can oven-steam individual servings of the puddings that follow. Simply spoon the batter into well-buttered custard cups or ramekins, filling them about ⅔ full. (Glazed brown ceramic cups look great; you can also use miniature Bundt pans or muffin tins.)

Cover each with a small piece of buttered foil, buttered side down. Place the cups in a large roasting pan. Place the pan on the center rack of the oven and pour in about 1½ inches of hot tap water. Steam the puddings until set and a toothpick inserted in the centers emerges dry, usually 35 to 45 minutes (the timing can vary based on the depth of the cups; do not overcook).

The Rewards of Writing

What did I do in New York? I gave the fifteen pounds of typescript to my agent, and then went to lunch with him. This is one of the nicest parts of authorship. He sent the book around to the publisher, who asked me to lunch with him at his house in the country, on Sunday. This, too, was delightful, and I was especially charmed when the publisher's splendid lunch concluded with a figgy pudding, which is my favourite food, and what I strongly suspect the gods eat on Olympus. . . . Very harsh things have been said about publishers, but there can be nothing but good in the heart of a man who regales an author with figgy pudding.

ROBERTSON DAVIES
NEWSPAPER COLUMN,
1959
IN *THE ENTHUSIASMS OF ROBERTSON DAVIES*
1990

226

OVEN-STEAMED FIGGY PUDDING

For years," my friend Sue Crouse of Warren, Ohio, explains, "my mother always bought Crosse and Blackwell's fig pudding, and we had it for the holidays. We liked it better than plum pudding. Mother either steamed it right in the can or sometimes opened the can, put it on a cookie sheet and heated it up in the oven.

"Then Crosse and Blackwell stopped making the pudding. I wrote to them, and they told me it didn't have a very good shelf life. So then I fooled around with all the recipes I could find and changed them around and came up with this one. It's close to the one we always had, and I still make it now, at the winter holiday time."

Steamed fig puddings, heavy with suet, are old favorites in England. This one is in the same tradition as Christmas plum puddings, dark with spices and dried fruit, but mercifully lighter. Made with a small amount of melted butter instead of grated suet, it is drastically lower in fat than traditional puddings, but not at all dry. You can cut this pudding into neat slices; the figs and spirits keep it moist and heady.

Serves about 12

1	pound moist dried figs
1¾	cups milk
1½	cups all-purpose flour
1	cup sugar
2½	teaspoons baking powder
1	teaspoon fresh-grated nutmeg
1	teaspoon ground cinnamon
¾	teaspoon salt (optional)
3	large eggs
½	cup (1 stick) unsalted butter, melted and cooled slightly
1½	cups soft, fresh white or whole-wheat bread crumbs
3	tablespoons grated orange zest
2	tablespoons minced crystallized ginger (optional)
	Brandy or rum, for flaming the pudding (optional)
	Hard Sauce (page 615), vanilla ice cream or whipped cream, for serving

1. Preheat the oven to 350 degrees F, with a rack in the center. Generously butter a metal steamed pudding mold or a fluted tube pan; set aside.

2. With scissors, snip the stems off the figs; snip the figs into small pieces. Combine the figs and the milk in a saucepan. Cover and cook over medium heat for 15 minutes.

3. Meanwhile, sift together the flour, sugar, baking powder, nutmeg, cinnamon and optional salt on a sheet of wax paper.

4. Beat the eggs with an electric mixer at high speed until fluffy. Add the butter, bread crumbs, orange zest, optional crystallized ginger and the fig mixture. Add the flour mixture and mix just until blended, no longer. Spoon the fig mixture into the prepared mold, smoothing the top. (It shouldn't be more than about ⅔ full.) Cover the top with a sheet of buttered foil, buttered side down; it should be secure but leave a little room for expansion. (If your mold has a lid, butter the inside and forgo the foil.) Place the mold in a roasting pan and place on the oven rack. Pour in enough very hot tap water to reach partway up the sides of the mold.

5. Bake until the pudding is firm and pulls away from the sides of the mold, about 2 hours. Add more hot water to the roasting pan as needed.

6. Remove the pudding from the water bath; cool on a wire rack for about 5 minutes. Invert onto a serving plate; remove the mold. If desired, heat the brandy or rum, carefully ignite and pour over the pudding. Serve with hard sauce, vanilla ice cream or whipped cream.

Variation
STEAMED DATE PUDDING: Substitute 1 pound chopped dried pitted dates for the figs, or use a combination of the two.

First Figs

Adam and Eve had the material for the making of a fig pudding but it was not necessary to cook as everything was ready for them fresh from the Garden of Eden in the highest state of perfection.

MRS. MARY B. PEASE
THE PUDDING BOOK
ANOKA, MINNESOTA
1928

STEAMED PUMPKIN PUDDING WITH GINGER-LEMON CREAM

Though they hark back to the days when people had kitchen help, steamed puddings are convenient for entertaining, and they transport well. Steam the pudding up to 2 days ahead, loosen the foil and let it cool. At serving time, cover tightly and gently resteam just until heated through, usually about 30 minutes.

Try this with cinnamon or caramel ice cream.

⟋ *Serves 12 to 16*

PUDDING

⅔	cup coarsely chopped dried pitted dates
½	cup currants
2	tablespoons finely minced crystallized ginger, or more to taste
⅓	cup brandy
¼	cup bourbon or dark rum
1¼	cups soft, fresh bread crumbs, preferably whole-wheat
3	large eggs
½	cup sugar
¼	cup packed dark or light brown sugar
1	tablespoon molasses
3	cups pumpkin puree, fresh (page 496) or canned unsweetened
½	cup all-purpose flour
2	teaspoons baking powder
½	teaspoon ground allspice
¼	teaspoon fresh-grated nutmeg
¼	teaspoon salt
	Pinch ground cloves
3	tablespoons unsalted butter, melted

GINGER-LEMON CREAM

1½	cups heavy cream, chilled
2	tablespoons finely minced crystallized ginger, or more to taste
	Grated zest of 1 lemon

1. **PUDDING:** In a bowl, toss together the dates, currants, ginger, brandy and bourbon or rum. Set aside to macerate, tossing occasionally, for at least 1 hour, or overnight.

2. Generously butter a metal steamed pudding mold or a

10-inch fluted tube pan; set aside. Strain the liquid from the fruits and ginger into a mixing bowl; stir in the bread crumbs until moistened. Set aside the bread crumbs and the fruits.

3. In a bowl with an electric mixer, beat the eggs, white and brown sugars until very fluffy, about 4 minutes. Gently stir in the molasses and the pumpkin puree; stir in the crumb mixture.

4. Sift the flour, baking powder, allspice, nutmeg, salt and cloves onto a sheet of wax paper. Reserve about 3 tablespoons of the flour mixture. Add a bit of the remaining flour mixture alternately with some of the melted butter to the pumpkin mixture, folding gently. Quickly toss the reserved fruits with the reserved flour mixture; fold into the pudding batter. Pour the batter into the prepared mold; it shouldn't be more than about ⅔ full. Place a sheet of buttered foil, buttered side down, over the top of the mold; it should be secure but leave a little room for expansion. (If your mold has a lid, butter the inside and forgo the foil.)

5. Set up a steamer: Place a wire rack in a large pot with a tight-fitting lid. Choose a pot large enough to allow steam to circulate around the mold; I improvise a steaming rack by placing a flat wire cake rack on a small tart mold to allow room for a good inch of water. Add enough hot tap water to the pot to come up to the level of the rack; bring to a boil. Carefully place the pudding mold on the rack and cover the pot.

6. Steam, maintaining a steady but gentle boil, for 2 hours. You may have to add hot water to keep the level constant; be careful not to let the water boil away. After 2 hours, the pudding should be set but still slightly moist in the center. If a toothpick inserted in the center does not emerge clean, steam the pudding for another 15 minutes, or until done.

7. Remove the pudding to a wire rack. Remove the lid or foil. Cool until lukewarm. *(The pudding can be prepared up to 2 days in advance and resteamed until hot, about 30 minutes.)*

8. **Ginger-Lemon Cream:** Whip the cream until nearly stiff. Fold in the crystallized ginger and the lemon zest.

9. Unmold the warm pudding onto a platter; decorate if you wish (a sprig of holly is traditional). Serve warm, in slices, spooning a little of the whipped cream over each slice; pass the rest of the cream separately.

A Crookneck, or Winter Squash Pudding

Core, boil and skin a good squash, and bruize it well; take 6 large apples, pared, cored, and stewed tender, mix together, add 6 or 7 spoonsful of dry bread or biscuit, rendered fine as meal, half pint milk or cream, 2 spoons of rosewater, 2 do. [ditto] wine, 5 or 6 eggs beaten and strained, nutmeg, salt and sugar to your taste, one spoon flour, beat all smartly together, bake.

The above is a good receipt for Pompkins, Potatoes or Yams, adding more moistening or milk and rosewater and to the two latter a few black or Lisbon currants, or dry whortleberries scattered in, will make it better.

AMELIA SIMMONS
AMERICAN COOKERY
HARTFORD, CONNECTICUT
1796

229

"Tipsy Potatoes"

Show up at Miss Mary Bobo's Boarding House in Lynchburg, Tennessee, and you'll be greeted by a smiling Lynne Tolley, the great grand-niece of old Jack Daniel himself. You're seated at big tables for 12, and all the food is brought out in big platters and bowls just as it was in the old days.

"Miss Mary Bobo started the boarding house in 1908," Lynne explains, "and she ran it until her death in 1983—she was 102 when she died.

"What most people don't know is that this area, the birthplace of great American bourbon, is in a dry county. You can't buy a drink in the county—you have to go 15 miles to the nearest town that has liquor. But you can put it in desserts. One day, we had a film crew down here, and we had tipsy sweet potatoes that day, spiked with plenty of Jack Daniel's. One sweet lady had three helpings and just loved them. Finally, she figured it out and said, 'If my Baptist minister sees me eating these sweet potatoes, he'll just run me out of the church!'"

TENNESSEE OLD MAID'S SWEET POTATO PUDDING

Grated, not mashed, sweet potatoes make this very different from other puddings of its type. This is a wonderful old Southern dessert from Miss Mary Bobo's Boarding House in Lynchburg, Tennessee, home of Jack Daniel's whiskey.

Serves 8 to 10

¼	cup (½ stick) unsalted butter, softened
½	cup sugar
¼	cup packed light brown sugar
2	large eggs, beaten
1	teaspoon ground cinnamon
¼	teaspoon fresh-grated nutmeg
¼	teaspoon ground cloves
	Pinch salt
2½	cups coarsely grated raw peeled sweet potatoes (about 1 pound)
1½	cups milk
	Whipped cream, flavored with Jack Daniel's whiskey, if desired, for serving

1. Preheat the oven to 400 degrees F, with a rack in the center. Butter a 2-quart baking dish or an 8-inch square baking pan; set aside.

2. In a small bowl, with an electric mixer on high speed, cream together the butter, white and brown sugars until well blended and very light. Beat in the eggs; beat in the cinnamon, nutmeg, cloves and salt. Stir in the sweet potatoes; add the milk and mix thoroughly. Pour the mixture into the prepared pan.

3. Bake until set and golden on top, about 30 minutes. Cool to warm or room temperature on a wire rack. Serve, topped with whipped cream, if you like.

About Fruit Pancakes: the Fraze (Froise), Moise and Tansy

*B*efore there were baked fruit desserts like cobblers, fruits were incorporated into rustic pancakes and into egg dishes that resembled omelets. Three precursors of the fruit pancake, all now lost, are the *fraze* (or *froise*), the *moise* and the *tansy* (aka *tansey* or *tansie*). The fraze appears in many 18th-century English cookery books but goes back much further—the *Oxford English Dictionary* cites a use of the word in 1338 and indicates hazy French origins.

In her 1747 cookbook, *The Art of Cookery, made Plain and Easy*, Hannah Glasse gives a recipe for "Apple Frazes" that is grouped with several other pancake recipes. It includes blanched Jordan almonds and is made by dropping fritter-size portions of batter into a hot pan, topping them with apple slices and then with more batter. Like puddings, which included savory elements with sweet, fruit frazes sometimes included bacon.

At about the same time that I was searching out the origins of the fraze, my Sicilian-American friend Charlie, a mean cook and demon eater, asked me, "Have you ever heard of a *frosia*?" Within minutes, he was beating eggs with fresh bread crumbs and ricotta cheese and whipping up frittata-like egg pancakes with pieces of either fresh asparagus or cauliflower. This delicious Sicilian egg specialty, related linguistically, appears to be an earlier version of the fraze that traveled to the British Isles.

Similar, but more omelet than pancake, is something called a *moise* (or *mose*):

Roste your Apples very Faire, and when you have so done, peele them and strain them with the yolks of an Egge or twain and Rosewater, and boyle it on a Chafingdish with Coles with a piece of sweet Butter, put in Sugar and Ginger, and when you lay it into your dish cast Sinamon and Sugar on it.

A.W., *A Book of Cookrye*, London, 1587

A Fraze with Pippins [Apples]

Cut eight Pippins in pretty thick Slices, and fry them in Hog's Lard, or clarify'd Butter; when they are tender, lay them on a sieve to drain the Fat from them, then take four Eggs, keeping out two Whites, beat them up with some Flour, half a Pint of Cream, a little Salt and some Sugar; then put into your Batter a little Butter; fry half of it at a Time, and when it is fried a little, put your fried Pippins thick all over it. When enough, fry the other also, so serve them on small Dishes, strew'd over with some good Sugar.

ANONYMOUS
THE WHOLE DUTY
OF A WOMAN
LONDON, 1737

Another relative is the *tansy*, an omelet-like dish named for the bitter green juice of tansy leaves used to color it. "Green it with juce of Tansey and Juce of Spinedge, but mind you put not in too much tansey for makeing it too bitter . . ." a 1711 recipe advises.

Tansy dates from medieval times, when bitter herbs were eaten at Easter, a practice that recalls the bitter herbs served at Passover to represent the anguish of the Israelites' slavery in Egypt. Over time, as more bread, biscuit crumbs and sugar were added to the omelet-like mixture, the dish evolved into a warm pudding.

Although fraze, moise and tansy are all forgotten now, when you fry up apples in a pancake batter, you're making something virtually identical to these traditional desserts.

Big Berry Popover

A pie-size, not-too-sweet popover with fruit, this puffs up crisp and golden on the surface, remaining soft and eggy within. Popovers, a mainstay of ladies' lunches in the 1940s and 1950s, are made with a pancake-like batter and baked in the oven instead of fried in a pan. A Pyrex dish will work, but metal is preferable.

Serve this as you would a muffin, for brunch or breakfast. Try it with different berries or with sliced bananas or peeled pears.

❧ *Serves 6*

1	cup milk
1	tablespoon butter, melted
½	teaspoon pure vanilla extract
¼	cup plus 1 tablespoon sugar
¼	teaspoon salt
	Pinch fresh-grated nutmeg
1	cup sifted all-purpose flour
2	large eggs, beaten
¾-1	cup berries, picked over (sugared, if tart)
¼	teaspoon ground cinnamon

1. Preheat the oven to 450 degrees F, with a rack in the center. Thoroughly butter a 9-inch pie pan or other shallow baking dish, including the rim; set aside.

2. Whisk together the milk, butter, vanilla, the ¼ cup sugar, the salt and nutmeg. Whisk in the flour; do not overbeat. Whisk in ½ of the beaten eggs just until blended; whisk in the remaining eggs. Do not overbeat.

3. Place the berries in the pie pan or baking dish, leaving a wide border uncovered all around the sides of the dish, so the edges of the popover can crisp. Gently pour the batter over the berries. Mix the remaining 1 tablespoon sugar with the cinnamon; sprinkle over the batter.

4. Bake for 20 minutes. Lower the heat to 350 degrees without opening the oven door; continue to bake until the popover is puffed and golden, 15 to 20 minutes longer. Serve immediately, cut into wedges.

REUBEN'S LEGENDARY APPLE PANCAKE

Reuben's was the legendary Times Square after-theatre hang-out for generations of New Yorkers, the place where they tucked into Reuben's 12-inch apple pancake, along with the famed cheesecake, as a late-night snack. Researching the origins of this archetypal pancake, food journalist Marian Burros was directed to three very different recipes (all of which claimed to be the authentic original). Finally, she tracked down Arnold Reuben, Jr., the owner's son.

"We had a specialist make the pancakes," Mr. Reuben explained. "We had special, well-seasoned big iron skillets and we never washed them." After buying a 12-inch cast-iron skillet, learning how to caramelize the sugar properly and encountering the biggest hurdle of all, "trying to flip a 12-inch pancake," Ms. Burros concluded that the recipe would work better if halved and made in a smaller skillet.

She's right. I've streamlined it further by cooking the pancake in a nonstick skillet and by cutting back on butter and sugar. But it still tastes like Reuben's, glazed and gilded with caramel syrup—a great way to get your apple a day.

Try it for a late-night snack or a leisurely breakfast.

Serves 2

1	large green apple, such as Granny Smith
2	tablespoons raisins
9	tablespoons (½ cup plus 1 tablespoon) sugar
½	teaspoon ground cinnamon
3	large eggs
½	cup milk
1	teaspoon pure vanilla extract
½	cup all-purpose flour
4-6	tablespoons unsalted butter

1. Peel and core the apple; slice ¼ inch thick. Place in a bowl with the raisins, 1½ tablespoons of the sugar and the cinnamon. Mix well; cover and set aside, stirring occasionally, until needed.

2. In a bowl, beat the eggs with the milk and vanilla; whisk in the flour to make a smooth batter. Do not overmix.

3. Preheat the oven to 400 degrees F, with a rack in the center. In an 8-inch ovenproof nonstick skillet, heat 1 tablespoon of the butter over medium heat until it sizzles. Pour off any liquid that has accumulated, and add the apple and raisin mixture to the pan. Cook, stirring, until the apples soften, about 5 minutes.

4. Add 1 tablespoon butter and let it melt. Pour in the batter to cover completely. Cook over medium-high heat, pulling the set sides of the pancake away from the edges and allowing the runny batter to flow under and cook, shaking the pan occasionally to prevent sticking, until the pancake begins to firm, about 3 minutes. Sprinkle about 1½ tablespoons of the sugar evenly over the top.

5. You can either flip the pancake or invert it onto a plate and slide it back into the skillet. If you are brave enough to flip it, first add another 1½ tablespoons of butter, cut into pats, slipping it underneath the edges and center of the pancake. Flip the pancake. If you are inverting it onto a plate, do it decisively. Melt 1 tablespoon of butter in the empty pan, sprinkle with about 1 tablespoon sugar and slide the pancake back in.

6. Cook the second side, allowing the sugar to caramelize on the bottom. When it begins to brown (after 3 or 4 minutes), sprinkle the top with about 2 tablespoons of the sugar. If the pancake seems to stick, add a little more butter. Flip or invert the pancake again and allow the sugar to caramelize on the bottom, about 4 minutes.

7. Sprinkle about 2 tablespoons of sugar on top. Add more butter to the pan if needed. Flip or invert the pancake once again and continue to caramelize, shaking the pan occasionally, about 3 or 4 minutes longer.

8. Sprinkle the top of the pancake lightly with another tablespoon of sugar. Place the skillet in the oven and bake until the surface is golden brown, 8 to 15 minutes. Serve hot, dividing the pancake in the pan and transferring it to plates with a spatula.

"The Best Pancake I Ever Ate"

Recalling Reuben's apple pancake more than 30 years after she first tasted it on a snowy weekend visit to Manhattan, Marian Burros declared, "Others have made good cheesecakes. But who else has produced such a pancake—bursting with apples and raisins, encased in a coating of caramelized sugar. It remains in memory the best pancake I ever ate, surpassing more delicate crepes, even the Austrian raisin-filled extravaganza, *kaiserschmarren*."

HUNGARIAN WALNUT-FILLED CREPES WITH WARM CHOCOLATE SAUCE

This Old-World dessert is at once homey and elegant. Two friends and I enjoyed it as the conclusion of a totally unexpected but lavish Thanksgiving on a snowy night in Budapest during a year of wandering in the mid-1970s.

We were served a progression of wonders: half portions of a meat-stuffed pancake, stuffed mushrooms, a vegetable soup, filet of beef with Hungarian goose liver and paprika sauce, tenderloin of pork on Hungarian ratatouille, and finally, these crepes.

That night with a pang, we remembered Thanksgivings at home. But today when the holiday arrives, what invariably pops into my head is our warm welcome that night and that wonderful feast.

Makes 16 crepes; serves 6 to 8

CREPES
1½	cups all-purpose flour
1	teaspoon sugar
½	teaspoon salt
2	large eggs, beaten
¾	cup milk
¾	cup club soda or seltzer
	Vegetable oil

WALNUT FILLING
1½	cups (5½-6 ounces) ground walnuts
⅓	cup sugar
⅓	cup milk
	Pinch *each* ground cinnamon and ground cloves
2	teaspoons light rum

CHOCOLATE SAUCE
¾	cup heavy cream
¼	cup sugar
3	ounces semisweet chocolate, coarsely chopped
1	ounce unsweetened chocolate, coarsely chopped
2	tablespoons unsalted butter
	Fresh fruit, for garnish (optional)
½	cup light rum, for flaming (optional)

Hapsburg Crepes

Palacsinta are thin crepes, much loved in Hungary and also in Austria, where they are known as *palatcshinken*, in Czechoslovakia, where they are called *palacinky*, and in all the surrounding areas that were once part of the dessert-loving Hapsburg Empire. Hungarian expert George Lang notes that this sort of thin pancake seems to have originated in Romania. The oldest recorded source may be a Roman manuscript by Cato in *De Re Rustica*, which describes the complicated preparation of the *placenta*, a flat cake or pie made with wheat, rye cheese and honey, cooked slowly in a pan over live coals.

1. **CREPES:** Sift the flour, sugar and salt into a large bowl. Make a well in the center. Add the eggs, milk and club soda or seltzer to the well and stir, gradually mixing in the flour until all is incorporated. Cover the bowl; let stand for at least 1 hour.

2. Heat a 7- or 8-inch crepe pan or heavy skillet, preferably nonstick, over medium-high heat. Brush lightly with oil. Remove the pan from the heat. If necessary, thin the batter to the consistency of whipping cream with more club soda or seltzer. Stir the batter, ladle about 3 tablespoons into a corner of the pan and tilt the pan so the batter just coats the bottom. Pour the excess batter back into the bowl. Cook the crepe until the bottom is lightly golden, about 1 minute. Turn and cook until the second side is speckled brown, about 30 seconds. Slide it out onto a plate. Repeat with the remaining batter, stirring often. Adjust the heat and brush the skillet with oil, as needed. *(The crepes can be prepared up to 2 days ahead. Place wax paper between the layers and wrap tightly in plastic and refrigerate. Or wrap in plastic and then freezer paper and freeze.)*

3. **WALNUT FILLING:** Combine the walnuts, sugar, milk, cinnamon and cloves in a small, heavy saucepan over medium heat. Stirring constantly, bring to a simmer; simmer, stirring, for 2 minutes. Blend in the rum and add more milk, if necessary, until the mixture is the consistency of a thick paste.

4. Preheat the oven to 300 degrees F, with a rack in the center. Generously butter a shallow baking dish, such as an oval gratin dish or a 9-inch square pan. Arrange the crepes on a work surface, speckled sides up. Spread 1 tablespoon of the filling over the center of each crepe. Fold the crepes into quarters. Place in the prepared dish, overlapping slightly. Bake in the oven until heated through, about 10 minutes.

5. **CHOCOLATE SAUCE:** Meanwhile, combine the cream, sugar, both chocolates and 1 tablespoon of the butter in a small, heavy saucepan over medium-low heat. Stir constantly until the mixture comes to a boil. Boil, stirring constantly, for 4 minutes; remove from the heat. Stir in the remaining 1 tablespoon butter.

6. Arrange 2 crepes on each serving plate. Spoon some chocolate sauce over them. (If desired, fresh seasonal fruit can be a garnish.)

7. If you want to flambé, heat the optional rum in a small, heavy saucepan until just warm. Ignite the rum with a long match, carefully averting your face. Pour the flaming rum over each portion. Serve at once.

ABOUT FRUIT DUMPLINGS

*F*ruit dumplings, whether boiled fruit-studded dough or dough wrapped around whole fruits and baked until golden, figure large in cuisines all over the world. What could be more homey—and more homely—than a dumpling? Sometimes called a "pot-ball," the dumpling is synonymous with stick-to-the-ribs, grandmotherly nurturing.

Dumplings are a rich subworld of old-fashioned desserts, endlessly varied:

 "Drop biscuits," steamed over fruit in slumps and grunts (page 58).

 Boiled gnocchi-style dumplings, often wrapped around plums or other whole stone fruits, and drizzled with toasted bread crumbs and/or sugar.

 Pastry-wrapped whole apples, baked to a golden crisp (adjoining page).

 Sweet raviolis, including sweet *kreplach* (squares of dough filled with cheese or cherries); *vareniki* (half-moons filled with cheese or blueberries); *krafi* (ravioli filled with Parmigiano cheese sweetened with sugar, citrus zest and rum-soaked raisins, served at weddings in Istria, where Italy meets Croatia and Slovenia). According to my friend Lidia Bastianich, chef-owner of Felidia in New York City, the sweet filling augurs well for the happiness of a married couple.

"Why should Dumpling-Eating be ridicul'd, or Dumpling-Eaters derided?"

JOHN ARBUTHNOT
A LEARNED DISSERTATION ON DUMPLING
LONDON, 1726

Baked Apple Dumplings

This recipe is from my friend Florence Donovan, whose care keeps my baking teacher and "adopted godfather" Carlo Bussetti going strong. Florence keeps telling me that these dumplings are "nothing special," but the first time I made them, they disappeared before any other dessert. They're good-looking and tasty.

⌣ *Serves 4*

- 4 baking apples (Rome, Northern Spy, Baldwin or Jonathan)
- ¼ cup sugar
- ½ teaspoon ground cinnamon
- 1½ tablespoons unsalted butter
- ½ cup light corn syrup
- ⅓ cup molasses
  Ice cream or heavy cream, for serving (optional)

1. Preheat the oven to 375 degrees F, with a rack in the center. On a lightly floured surface, roll out the dough into a 12- to 14-inch square about ⅛ inch thick. With a sharp knife, cut the dough into 4 equal squares; reserve any trimmings.

2. Peel and partially core the apples from the top, leaving the bottoms intact. Combine the sugar and the cinnamon on a piece of wax paper; roll the apples in the cinnamon sugar. Place a lump of butter in each hollow.

3. Prick each square of dough in several places with a fork. Place an apple in the center of each square. Gather up the 4 corners of the dough around each apple, pinching the seams to seal, and overlapping the corners to seal on top. If you like, cut out leaves from the dough trimmings, tracing "veins" with the back of a knife blade. Gently place the apples in a 9-inch baking dish or pie pan. Combine the corn syrup and molasses; drizzle over the dough; pour the remainder into the baking dish around the apples.

4. Bake until the dough is golden brown and the apples are tender but not mushy, usually about 45 minutes. Cool to lukewarm in the pan on a wire rack. *(The dumplings can be reheated gently in a 325-degree oven for about 15 minutes if made in advance.)* Pour some of the juices over the apples and serve, topped with a little ice cream or cream, if you like.

"Coleridge holds that a man cannot have a pure mind who refuses apple dumplings. I am not certain that he is right."

Charles Lamb
ca. 1800

WINTER FRUIT DUMPLINGS

When Harlan "Pete" Peterson was growing up in North Dakota, his mother made individual dumplings, delicately folding the edges of a flat round of pie crust dough up and around the fruit. Pete is now chef-owner of Tapawingo, a converted shingled farmhouse in Ellsworth, Michigan, where he puts local products to imaginative use. But he still makes his mother's dumplings, combining fresh fruit with Michigan dried cherries. All sorts of fruit combinations are possible here; mix and match as you like.

In the restaurant, Pete serves these dumplings with his version of Warm Caramel Sauce (page 614) and Eggnog Custard Sauce (page 609). At home, they're fine on their own.

Makes 6 dumplings; serves 6

BUTTER PASTRY

1¼	cups all-purpose flour
2	teaspoons sugar
⅛	teaspoon salt
½	cup (1 stick) cold unsalted butter, cut into cubes
2-4	tablespoons ice water, as needed

FRUIT FILLING

3	ounces (about ½ cup) dried cherries or a combination of dried cherries and dried cranberries; or just raisins
3	tablespoons Calvados or other brandy
2	cups peeled, cored and thinly sliced apples, preferably Ida Red (about 2 apples) Grated zest and juice of 1 lemon
¼	cup packed light brown sugar
¼	teaspoon ground cinnamon Pinch *each* fresh-grated nutmeg and ground cloves
1½	tablespoons *each* coarsely chopped walnuts, almonds and pecans, all lightly toasted
⅓	cup (5⅓ tablespoons) unsalted butter, cut into small cubes

Milk and sugar, for glazing

1. **BUTTER PASTRY:** Combine the flour, sugar and salt in a large bowl. Cut in the butter until the mixture resembles coarse oatmeal. Add the ice water and toss until the dough begins to come together.

2. With lightly floured hands, gather the dough into a 6-inch-long cylinder. Wrap in plastic wrap and chill for at least 1 hour.

3. FRUIT FILLING: Meanwhile, place the dried fruit in a non-reactive saucepan and add the Calvados or other brandy. Cover and gently simmer the fruit until the liquid is absorbed, at least several minutes. Transfer to a large bowl, and stir in the apples, lemon zest and juice, brown sugar, spices and nuts.

4. Slice the chilled pastry dough into 6 equal pieces; roll out each piece on a lightly floured surface into a 5-inch circle about ⅛ inch thick.

5. Preheat the oven to 425 degrees F, with a rack in the center. Place a pastry round on a lightly buttered baking sheet. Top with some of the fruit-and-nut filling, mounding the filling in the center. Dot with some of the butter. Fold up the edges of the pastry, forming roughly folded "pleats" that leave about an inch of the filling uncovered in the center. Repeat with the remaining rounds and filling.

6. Brush the surface of the pastry with milk; sprinkle liberally with sugar. To prevent the filling from browning, place a small square of foil over the exposed fruit in each dumpling.

7. Bake for 10 minutes. Reduce the heat to 375 degrees. Continue baking until the tops of the dumplings are golden brown and the filling is bubbly, about 20 minutes longer. Cool on a wire rack. Serve warm.

Mysterious Dumpling

Now, to many a Royal Society, the Creation of a World is little more mysterious than the cooking of a Dumpling; concerning which last, indeed, there have been minds to whom the question, How the apples were got in, presented difficulties.

THOMAS CARLYLE
SARTOR RESARTUS
1831

RECIPES

Shrewsbury Cakes

Apees

Coconut Jumbles

*John Thorne's Lemon Icebox
    Crumbles*

Sand Tarts

Gingerbread Hermits

*M.F.K. Fisher's Ginger
    Hottendots*

Chocolate-Glazed Lebkuchen

*Real Scottish Petticoat Tail
    Shortbread*

Oatmeal Shortbread Squares

*Brown Sugar Shortbread
    Wafers*

*New Mexico Anise Christmas
    Cookies*

Tennessee Moonshine Cookies

*Canadian Molasses
    Leathernecks*

*Savannah Lace Christmas
    Cookies*

The Original Toll House Cookie

*All-American Fudge-Chunk
    Brownies*

*Pecan-and-Caramel-Glazed
    Brownies*

*White Chocolate–Macadamia
    Blondies*

Almond Brittle Cookies

Carlo's Cookie Dough

1950s Pecan Puffs

*Grandma's Poppy Seed
    Crescents*

Mary's Pignoli

Crumiri

Toasted Benne (Sesame) Wafers

Thin Almond Wafers

*Crunchy Almond and
    Hazelnut Cookies*

*Alsatian Christmas
    Cinnamon Stars*

Hungarian Nut Crescents

Greek Egg Biscuits

Armenian Egg Biscuits

Sicilian Fig-Filled Cookies

Cornmeal-Almond Biscotti

Quaresimale

242

CHAPTER 7

COOKIES

Any child who does not have a country grand-mother who keeps a cooky jar is as much to be pitied as one who grows up with protruding teeth. If it is impossible for a grandmother to live in or move to the country, solely to insure the proper spiritual start for coming generations, at least it is possible to have a cooky jar.

MARJORIE KINNAN RAWLINGS,
CROSS CREEK COOKERY, 1942

Everybody loves cookies. But especially Americans. While the British keep "biscuits" (their term for cookies) on hand for tea and Germans celebrate their Christmas traditions with lebkuchen (gingerbread cookies), only in America are milk and cookies such a key part of growing up. Where else in the world could you find a Cookie Monster?

Every American kid has his or her first experience in the kitchen baking—what else?—Toll House cookies. Chocolate chip cookies and brownies, both indigenous, are America's chief contributions to the world's baked goods. Both items are virtually unknown in the rest of the world—until recently.

Maida Heatter, who is this country's premier authority on desserts and author of several best-selling cookbooks, is obsessed with cookies—and hers are among the world's best. One night, as we were talking about restaurant desserts, she posed a question: "Why," she wondered, "don't more restaurants offer a plate of really great cookies?" (Actually, some now do just that.)

But possibly more than any other baked goods, cookies are the province of home bakers. And for me, the pleasures of home-baked cookies are unsurpassed. As with American cooking in general, the foundation for American cookies is English. Early American cookbooks always include a few English biscuit recipes, usually referring to them as "cakes" or "small cakes." The most frequent varieties are:

- macaroons (cookies made of ground nuts)
- jumbles (butter cookies, often cut into strips and twisted into knots or shaped into rings)
- rusks (crisp, twice-baked biscuits)
- sponge fingers or Naples biscuits (ladyfingers)
- apees (wine- and caraway-flavored butter cookies)
- Shrewsbury cakes (plain buttery cutouts, pronounced "shrows-bry")
- such various forms of crisp gingerbread as wafers, dots and gingerbread men

Cookies evolved from flat cakes or were fashioned from sweetened pie crust trimmings. From the beginning, they were eaten ritually or offered as part of celebrations and festivals in cultures all over the world. Stamped with images of gods and goddesses, animals or symbols, cookies often stood in for the real thing in animal or human sacrifices. German *springerle*, embossed anise-flavored cookies baked in special molds, are probably the best-known surviving example of this phenomenon. They date back to *Julfest*, a pagan midwinter festival. Their name is said to connote a jumping horse, a common motif on wooden *springerle* molds and the sacred animal of Wotan, king of the Nordic gods.

The word cookie comes from the Dutch *koekje* ("little cake") and was first used for only a couple of varieties. One of the earliest uses of the word in print that I've found is in an anonymous English *Memorandome Book* dating from 1783. American cookbooks from the same period also use the word, but infrequently.

As late as the Civil War period, most American cookbooks lumped cookies together with cakes, not differentiating between them. But by the time Fannie Farmer's *The Boston Cooking-School Cook Book* was published in 1896, cookies had earned their own chapter, "Gingerbreads, Cookies, and Wafers."

The cookies in this chapter offer a broad range, including some simple old-fashioned cutouts, drop cookies, bar and sheet cookies cut into squares, and a few choice international cookies.

Cookie Names from the Past

Courtships
Queries
Matrimony
Harmony
Wonders
Kisses and Secrets
Cocoanut Sweet-Hearts

243

ABOUT EARLY COOKIE FLAVORINGS

Vanilla, which we've come to expect as the basic flavoring for cookies, as well as for a host of other baked goods, was not used in most early American cookie recipes.

Thomas Jefferson introduced it into this country in 1789, when he returned from his stay as Minister to France to become George Washington's Secretary of State. Even when vanilla beans, which are native to Madagascar, began to be imported, they were expensive, used only by the few who could afford this exotic luxury. Vanilla is still costly—and with good reason—each plant must be pollinated by hand. Vanilla extract wasn't generally available until the late 1840s or 1850.

Instead, small cakes like jumbles and apees (not yet called cookies) were flavored with wine (most likely sherry, Madeira or Malaga), caraway seeds, nutmeg and other spices and rose water.

Ironically, today rose water tastes "foreign" to an American's palate, and we are more likely to associate its perfume with Middle Eastern sweets. This was not so in the 17th and 18th centuries. As you can see from the old English and American recipes that dot these pages, rose water at one time was a baking staple, used not only to flavor doughs and batters but to glaze cakes and pie crusts after baking.

SHREWSBURY CAKES

This recipe is almost unchanged from Amelia Simmons' version in *American Cookery* (Hartford, 1796). Shrewsbury cakes—pronounced "Shrows-bry"—are named after a borough in western England. This soft dough is delicate, and the cookies bake up crisp, with the pure flavor of butter, no vanilla. The dough is too soft and tricky to roll and so should be chilled and sliced (or it can be dropped from a spoon).

Hannah Glasse's Shrewsbury Cake recipe from 1744, grouped with "Maccaroons and yeasted Wigs" (a plain yeast-raised cookie), is flavored with rose water, but is otherwise identical to this simple recipe. Earlier English versions were often spiced with ginger or cinnamon.

Shrewsbury cakes appear again and again in early-American cookbooks, but once they made it here from England, they seem to have died out back home, a fate shared by pumpkin pie.

Makes about 30 cookies

- ½ cup (1 stick) unsalted butter, softened
- ½ cup plus 2 tablespoons sugar
- ⅛ teaspoon fresh-grated nutmeg or ground mace
- 1 large egg
- 1 cup all-purpose flour

1. In a small bowl, beat the butter until light. Gradually beat in the sugar and nutmeg or mace and mix until light and fluffy. Beat in the egg; beat in the flour just until blended. On a sheet of wax paper, roll the dough into a long, 2-inch-diameter log. Wrap in the wax paper and refrigerate until firm, at least 1 hour.

2. Preheat the oven to 350 degrees F. Butter 2 baking sheets.

3. Cut the log of dough into ¼-inch-thick slices. Place the slices about ½ inch apart on the prepared baking sheet. Bake until the cookies are lightly golden around the edges, about 8 minutes.

4. Cool the cookies on the baking sheets for 2 minutes; transfer to a wire rack and cool completely. Store in an airtight container.

Shrewsbury Cakes

2 eggs
6 oz butter
½ lbs sugar
½ cup milk
½ nutmeg
1 tea spoonful of Saleratus
A few caraway seeds & flour sufficient to make a soft dough.

FOUND WRITTEN ON THE ENDPAPER OF *THE KITCHEN DIRECTORY AND AMERICAN HOUSEWIFE* NEW YORK, 1844

Apees

APEES

*A pound of flour, sifted
Half a pound of butter.
A glass of wine, and a
tablespoon of rose-water,
mixed.
Half a pound of powdered
white sugar.
A nutmeg, grated
A tea-spoonful of beaten
cinnamon and mace.
Three table-spoonfuls of
carraway seeds.*

*Sift the flour into a
broad pan, and cut up the
butter in it. Add the
carraways, sugar, and spice,
and pour in the liquor by
degrees, mixing it well with
a knife. . . . Spread some
flour on your paste-board,
take out the dough, and
knead it very well with your
hands. . . . Roll it out in a
sheet about a quarter of an
inch thick. Cut it out in
round cakes, with the edge
of a tumbler, or a tin of
that size. Butter an iron
pan, and lay the cakes in it,
not too close together.
Bake them a few minutes in
a moderate oven, till they
are very slightly coloured,
but not brown. If too much
baked, they will entirely
lose their flavor. . . .*

ELIZA LESLIE
SEVENTY-FIVE RECEIPTS
BOSTON, 1828

This wine- and caraway-flavored butter cookie is a good example of how something from a kitchen of the past can be well worth rediscovering.

The cookie's name is the initials "A.P." spelled out, short for Anne Parmer, notes food historian William Woys Weaver; this is an American cookie.

The recipe has been adapted almost unchanged from Eliza Leslie's *Seventy-Five Receipts for Pastry, Cakes, and Sweetmeats*, published in 1828. In his preface to a recent facsimile edition of this book, Weaver points out that Miss Leslie's recipes were actually those of Mrs. Elizabeth Goodfellow and were available only to those attending lectures at Mrs. Goodfellow's Philadelphia cooking school.

Makes about 16 cookies

2	cups all-purpose flour
½	cup (1 stick) unsalted butter, cut into pieces
½	cup sugar
1	rounded teaspoon caraway seeds
½	teaspoon ground cinnamon
¼	teaspoon fresh-grated nutmeg
¼	cup dry white wine or dry sherry

1. Preheat the oven to 350 degrees F. Butter 2 baking sheets; set aside. In a bowl, cut the flour and butter together with a pastry blender or 2 knives until the mixture is crumbly. Mix in the sugar, caraway seeds, cinnamon and nutmeg; stir in the wine or sherry until the dough comes together and is somewhat stiff.

2. On a lightly floured surface, roll out the dough slightly less than ¼ inch thick. With a 3-inch round cookie cutter, cut out rounds and place about ½ inch apart on the prepared baking sheets (these cookies don't spread as they bake). Reroll the scraps.

3. Bake until the cookies are firm but still pale, not golden, about 14 minutes.

4. Transfer the cookies to a wire rack to cool completely. Store in an airtight container.

COCONUT JUMBLES

A simple butter cookie, with rich flavor and perfect crispness, this one is based on an 1824 "Jumbals" recipe from Mary Randolph's *The Virginia Housewife*.

Jumbles are among the oldest cookies around, still manufactured commercially. Regardless of variations in spelling and flavoring, jumbles are basic butter cookies, rolled out, cut into shapes and baked quickly. By the time American cookbooks in 1800 began to include recipes for these cookies, jumbles already had been popular for almost two centuries.

Makes 3 to 3½ dozen cookies

1	cup (2 sticks) unsalted butter, softened
1	cup sugar
½	teaspoon pure vanilla extract
2	drops almond extract
2	large eggs
2	cups all-purpose flour
2	cups shredded sweetened coconut
¼	teaspoon fresh-grated nutmeg
1	large egg white, lightly beaten, for glaze

1. With an electric mixer at medium speed, cream the butter and sugar until very light, about 5 minutes. Add the vanilla and almond extracts; add the eggs, one at a time. Lower the speed and beat in the flour, 1 cup of the coconut and the nutmeg; mix just until well blended, no longer. Gather the dough into a disk, wrap in plastic wrap and chill for at least 2 hours or overnight.

2. Preheat the oven to 350 degrees F. Lightly butter 4 baking sheets. Divide the dough into quarters. Keeping the remaining dough refrigerated, roll out 1 piece of the dough on a lightly floured surface to a thickness of ⅜ inch. Dip a 3- to 3½-inch fluted or plain round cookie cutter in flour and cut out circles. Place about 1 inch apart on the prepared baking sheets. Repeat with the remaining pieces of dough and scraps.

3. Brush the tops of the cookies with a light coating of the egg glaze; sprinkle with some of the remaining 1 cup coconut. Bake until the edges are lightly golden, about 11 minutes.

4. Transfer the jumbles to a wire rack to cool completely. Store in an airtight container.

Almond Jumballs

In the early to mid-1600s, English cookery books gave instructions on how "To make Sugar Cakes called Jumballs." At the end of that century, Mrs. Ann Blencowe, the wife of a member of Parliament, offers a complicated recipe for "Almond Jumballs" in her 1694 cookbook, *The Receipt Book of Ann Blencowe*.

It begins by grinding almonds with orange flower water or rose water, combining them with boiled sugar syrup, sugar and egg white and pounding the mixture to a paste. The mixture is then shaped. Mrs. Blencowe notes that it may be colored with chocolate or "cutchaneale" (cochineal—a red coloring naturally extracted from the dried bodies of cochineal insects, similar to mealybugs—still widely used in England). The cookies are then brushed with rose water or lemon juice and gently baked. Mrs. Blencowe adds that "it is best to sett them on something that they may not touch ye bottome of ye Oven."

JOHN THORNE'S LEMON ICEBOX CRUMBLES

This is from my friend, food writer John Thorne. The dough is shaped into balls by hand instead of being rolled out—an icebox method that makes doughs with a high butter content easier to handle. A crisp, crumbly cookie, it is tart with citrus and ferociously addictive.

Makes about 2 dozen cookies

½	cup (1 stick) unsalted butter, softened
1½	cups all-purpose flour, sifted
	Grated zest of 2 lemons
¾	cup sugar
2	large egg yolks
	Lemon juice or cold water, if needed

1. In a mixing bowl, combine the butter, flour and lemon zest with a pastry blender or 2 knives until the mixture is crumbly.

2. Add the sugar and egg yolks. With floured fingertips, quickly and gently work the mixture into a smooth dough, gathering it together in the bowl. If the mixture is too dry to cohere, add a few drops of lemon juice or cold water as needed. Cover the bowl with plastic wrap; chill until firm, about 30 minutes.

3. Preheat the oven to 350 degrees F. Lightly butter 2 baking sheets; set aside. Break off small pieces of dough and roll each into a 1-inch ball. Place the balls about 2 inches apart on the prepared baking sheets. Flatten each ball with the back of a fork, making a crisscross pattern with the tines. Bake the cookies until very pale gold, usually 12 to 15 minutes.

4. Cool the cookies on the baking sheets for 2 minutes; transfer to a wire rack and cool completely. Store in an airtight container.

SAND TARTS

These crisp, fragile wafers are rich with butter and have a high proportion of sugar that makes them crackle like glass. The recipe is loosely adapted from the handwritten manuscript of Mrs. Henry W. Darling, compiled from about 1882 to 1893 in Schenectady, New York.

Makes 3½ to 4 dozen cookies

½   cup (1 stick) unsalted butter, softened
1   cup sugar
2   large egg yolks
1   tablespoon hot water
1   teaspoon pure vanilla extract
1   cup all-purpose flour
     About 50 walnut halves
1   teaspoon ground cinnamon
1   large egg white, lightly beaten, for glaze

1. Beat the butter with an electric mixer at medium speed until fluffy. Add ¾ cup plus 1 tablespoon of the sugar and beat until light. Beat in the egg yolks, hot water and vanilla until combined. Lower the speed to slow, add the flour and mix just until incorporated, no longer. Gather the dough into a ball and wrap in plastic wrap; refrigerate until firm, 1 hour or overnight.

2. Preheat the oven to 375 degrees F. Lightly butter 2 baking sheets. Roll out ½ of the dough very thin on a lightly floured work surface. (This dough is rich and delicate; keep the surface, dough and rolling pin lightly floured as you work.) With a 2½-inch cutter (any shape you like), cut out cookies. Carefully transfer them to the prepared baking sheets, spacing them about ¾ inch apart. Continue rolling and cutting cookies with the remaining dough; reroll the scraps. Chill if not baking immediately.

3. Press a walnut half into each cookie. Mix the remaining 3 tablespoons sugar with the cinnamon. Brush the cookies with the egg white glaze; sprinkle with the cinnamon sugar. Bake until the edges are lightly golden, usually about 8 minutes (do not overbake).

4. Transfer the cookies to a wire rack to cool completely. Store in an airtight container.

A Swell Cook

Now the two friends had met again, and were seated side by side in the speeding train, talking and catching up on one another.

. . . He was silent while he thought about it, and embarrassed, not knowing what to say. Then, after a moment: "Gee!"—he shook his head—"your aunt was one swell cook! I never will fergit it! Remember how she used to feed us kids—every danged one of us in the whole neighborhood?" He paused, then grinned up shyly at his friend: "I sure wish I had a fistful of them good ole cookies of hers right this minute!"

THOMAS WOLFE
YOU CAN'T GO HOME
AGAIN
1940

GINGERBREAD HERMITS

Made since medieval times, gingerbread appeared in two main forms: as soft cake and as crisp or chewy cookies. Most ginger cookies are made by cutting a sheet of dough into rounds, strips or other shapes, including gingerbread men. Hermits, a gingerbread relative, are one of the best-loved old cookie varieties. These oversized ginger bar cookies are from my friend Mary Codola in Rhode Island.

Makes about 4½ dozen cookies

4	cups all-purpose flour
1½	teaspoons baking powder
1½	teaspoons baking soda
1½	teaspoons ground cinnamon
1	teaspoon ground ginger
1	teaspoon fresh-grated nutmeg
¼	teaspoon ground cloves
½	teaspoon salt
1	cup (2 sticks) unsalted butter, softened
2½	cups packed light or dark brown sugar
3	large eggs
⅓	cup molasses
1	cup raisins
1	cup coarsely chopped walnuts or pecans
3	tablespoons finely chopped crystallized ginger
1	large egg, beaten, for glaze

1. Preheat the oven to 375 degrees F. Butter and flour 3 baking sheets; set aside. Sift the flour, baking powder, baking soda, cinnamon, ground ginger, nutmeg, cloves and salt onto a sheet of wax paper; set aside.

2. Beat the butter with an electric mixer at medium speed until very smooth. Add the brown sugar and beat until light, about 3 minutes. Add the eggs, one at a time; beat in the molasses until smooth.

3. Lower the speed to slow and beat in the flour mixture just until blended. Add the raisins, nuts and crystallized ginger; do not overmix.

4. Divide the dough into 6 equal pieces. Shape each piece into a long rectangular log about 1 inch high and 1½ inches wide.

Place 2 logs on each prepared baking sheet, spacing them well apart; the cookies will spread as they bake. Brush the logs lightly with beaten egg glaze.

5. Bake until golden, but still quite soft; check carefully, the timing can vary from 10 to 14 minutes, but these cookies should not be overbaked.

6. Place the baking sheets on a wire rack and cool to room temperature. Slice into 2-inch-wide bars. Store in an airtight container. Hermits keep well for about a week.

M.F.K. Fisher's
Ginger Hottendots

These are tiny gingery rounds, baked crisp—homemade ginger snaps. Note that baking them for the time indicated results in crisp cookies with slightly chewy interiors, while a longer time in the oven will make them crisp throughout. Though the yield seems huge, these will go quickly (they keep well, too).

Makes about 15 dozen tiny cookies, a scant 1 inch in diameter

3¾	cups all-purpose flour
1½	teaspoons baking soda
2	tablespoons ground ginger
½	teaspoon ground cinnamon
¼	teaspoon ground cloves
¾	cup (1½ sticks) unsalted butter, softened
2	cups sugar
2	large eggs, well beaten
½	cup dark (not blackstrap) molasses
2	teaspoons cider vinegar or balsamic vinegar

1. Preheat the oven to 325 degrees F. Butter 2 baking sheets. Sift the flour, baking soda, ginger, cinnamon and cloves onto a sheet of wax paper; set aside.

2. Cream the butter and sugar with an electric mixer at medium speed. Stir in the eggs, molasses and vinegar. Add the sifted dry ingredients and mix just until blended, no longer.

Ginger Remedies

Not long before she died, M.F.K. Fisher, "the poet laureate of food writers," sent me her recipe for ginger cookies, adding a note that saying she liked to bake these cookies not only because they're tasty, but because they contain about three times the normal amount of ginger and so serve as a cure-all for digestive disorders. (Recent medical research confirms the folk-medicine belief that ginger does help relieve indigestion.)

"I thought they would be too hot for children, but only one child has ever complained about their being overspiced," she said.

"They are very good served at the end of a cocktail party," she added, "to evade trouble with the cops."

251

3. Roll the dough into ½- to ¾-inch balls. Place about 1 inch apart on the prepared baking sheets.

4. Bake until soft, about 7 minutes; don't overbake. The cookies will crisp as they cool.

5. Transfer the cookies to a wire rack and cool completely. Store in an airtight container.

CHOCOLATE-GLAZED LEBKUCHEN

Like many other elements of the Yuletide celebration, Christmas cookies began as a German tradition. Every year, I buy wonderful lebkuchen made by the German manufacturer Bahlsen. Called "Contessa," they are sold only at Christmastime—puffy little spice pillows, more soft cakes than cookies—their domed tops sugar-glazed, their flat undersides coated with dark chocolate.

This version is similar but is baked as a sheet, glazed with chocolate and cut into diamonds. Note that most lebkuchen doughs must ripen at least overnight before baking.

✎ *Makes 2 to 3 dozen small diamonds*

¾	cup sugar
½	cup plus 1 tablespoon honey
1	tablespoon water
¼	cup (½ stick) unsalted butter, cut into pieces
¾	cup chopped unblanched almonds
⅓	cup finely chopped candied or dried pineapple (or any other good candied fruit)
⅓	cup lightly beaten egg (slightly more than 1 large egg)
3	tablespoons fresh orange juice
½	teaspoon almond extract
1⅔	cups sifted all-purpose flour
1	teaspoon baking powder
½	teaspoon baking soda
1½	teaspoons ground cinnamon
1½	teaspoons ground cardamom
½	generous teaspoon ground cloves
½	teaspoon fresh-grated nutmeg
½	teaspoon ground ginger

Life Cake

The German word *lebkuchen* means "life cake," probably because of this baked good's superior keeping qualities. Swiss-born master pastry chef Albert Kumin says that he's "proud to serve four-year-old lebkuchen."

A forerunner of gingerbread, lebkuchen was originally baked in German monasteries. At Christmastime in Germany, lebkuchen is everywhere, in every window of every confectionery store—soft or crisp, in the shape of hearts, pigs (for good luck) or candleholders or constructed into elaborate gingerbread houses.

CHOCOLATE GLAZE
- 3 ounces semisweet chocolate, chopped
- 1½ teaspoons unsalted butter
- 1½ tablespoons boiling water

1. Make the dough 1 day before you plan to bake the lebkuchen. Combine the sugar, honey, water and butter in a large nonreactive saucepan over medium-high heat. Bring just to a boil, stirring to dissolve the sugar. The moment the mixture begins to boil, remove the pan from the heat. Stir in the almonds, candied fruit, beaten egg, orange juice and almond extract until smooth.

2. Resift the flour with the baking powder, baking soda, cinnamon, cardamom, cloves, nutmeg and ginger onto a sheet of wax paper. Add this mixture to the saucepan and stir just until well blended. Place a sheet of wax paper directly on the surface of the dough and cool thoroughly. Seal with plastic wrap or foil and let stand at room temperature overnight; do not refrigerate.

3. Preheat the oven to 350 degrees F. Butter and flour a 9-inch square baking pan. With a large rubber spatula or lightly floured fingertips, press the dough over the bottom of the pan, spreading it as smooth as possible. (The dough will be quite sticky.)

4. Bake until the surface is set, the edges shrink away from the sides of the pan and a toothpick inserted in the center emerges not quite clean, 27 to 29 minutes.

5. Cool to room temperature in the pan on a wire rack.

6. **CHOCOLATE GLAZE:** Melt the chocolate in the top of a double boiler or in a bowl set over hot water. Add the butter, and then the boiling water; stir until completely smooth. Spread the glaze over the surface of the cooled cookies. Let cool until the glaze is set.

7. Using a sharp knife and a ruler as a guide, cut the lebkuchen into neat diamonds or squares. Lebkuchen keep well, getting better as they age and are substantial enough to be sent as gifts through the mail.

Honey Cookeys

6 lb flour 2 lb sugar 3 lb honey 1 lb citron 2 oz of cinnamon 2 oz of ginger & some orange peel melt the honey & sugar then mix all together & make the rolls 2 fingers thick.

ANONYMOUS
MEMORANDOME BOOK
ENGLAND, 1783

GREAT MOMENTS
IN COOKIE HISTORY

5th century B.C.—Golden Age Greeks make mention of honey cakes, similar to cookies, sprinkled with spices. Also, early records of Assyrians, Babylonians, Greeks and Aztecs indicate that small, cookie-like cakes are used in religious ceremonies.

4th century B.C.—Dates are used in southern Mesopotamia to make sweetmeats, small confections similar to cookies. Even earlier, Egyptians use small cakes for live sacrifices to the gods. Later, Germanic tribes also use cookies sacrificially during hard times, when an ox cannot be spared.

Early 17th century—Known since medieval times, gingerbread rises in popularity. Made with bread crumbs and sweetened with honey and later with molasses, as it became available as a by-product of refined sugar, the gingerbread was frequently flavored with pepper as part of the spice blend.

1730—According to the *Oxford English Dictionary*, the word "cookie" is used in a Scottish reference to Dutch *koekje* (cookies)—a diminutive of *koek* (cake).

1796—In her newly published first American cookbook, *American Cookery*, Amelia Simmons, an "Orphan," includes a recipe for cookies flavored with coriander seed and leavened with pearl ash dissolved in milk. She also gives a recipe for a "Christmas Cookey," which, she says, "if put into an earthen pot, and dry cellar, or damp room, they will be finer, softer and better when six months old."

1870s—The wood-burning cast-iron range begins to be used, making it feasible to bake cookies at home. (Until the Civil War, all but wealthy housewives cooked over a fireplace.)

1897—The first mention of brownies appears in the Sears, Roebuck catalog. No one knows where they came from, but they are thoroughly American.

1902—Nabisco introduces Barnum's Animal Crackers, one of its all-time best-selling cookies.

1908—Hydrox cookies, an all-American classic, are introduced by Sunshine Biscuits. When searching for a name for this sandwich cookie, Sunshine thought of water "because water and sunshine are elements of purity and cleanliness." Water being a combination of hydrogen and oxygen, the name Hydrox was born.

March 6, 1912—Nabisco introduces Oreo sandwich cookies. Lorna Doone appears a week later, probably named for the heroine of a 19th-century Scottish romance by R.D. Blackmore.

For More Great Moments in Cookie History, see page 275.

Short and Sweet

The word *short* refers to the generous proportion of fat that makes this (and other cookies and pastries) so rich that it shatters into flaky layers. This recipe has 8 ounces of butter to 6 ounces of flour, with no eggs or leavening. That's 44 percent of the total ingredients by weight—proportionately double the amount of butter in ordinary cookies.

The characteristic fork-pressed edges mark shortbread as a home-baked product, rather than one baked professionally. Today, however, tins of commercially made British shortbread are exported to every corner of the globe.

REAL SCOTTISH PETTICOAT TAIL SHORTBREAD

Few things are better with a cup of tea or coffee than a wedge of butter shortbread. It's also the perfect thing when you want something crisp to serve with a soft dessert like custard or ice cream. Shortbread keeps well and makes an excellent gift.

Because this one tastes mainly of butter, use very fresh butter. Traditional Scottish recipes don't include salt—but they usually use salted butter. So I've added a tiny pinch of salt; without it, the flavor can be slightly flat.

This authentic Scottish recipe is from Nan Lang, who got the recipe from her mother, Mary Tennent, and sent it to Karyl Bannister's *Cook & Tell* newsletter.

Makes 2 dozen wedges

1	cup (2 sticks) best-quality unsalted butter, softened
½	cup sugar
1½	cups all-purpose flour, sifted
	Pinch salt

1. Preheat the oven to 300 degrees F. Lightly butter two 8-inch round cake pans; set aside.

2. In a large bowl, cream the butter and sugar with a large wooden spoon. (Nan Lang notes that "this recipe must be mixed by hand.") Work the mixture vigorously for about 5 minutes—this requires some muscle. Add the flour and salt, about ⅓ at a time, working in each addition thoroughly but gently. The last addition will make the mixture quite stiff; finish mixing with your hands, if you like.

3. Press ½ of the dough into each pan, patting it gently into an even round with smooth edges. With the back of a spoon handle, press indentations around the edge of each round of dough. With the tines of a fork, gently prick both rounds of dough at regular intervals, pressing all the way through to the bottom of each pan. With a sharp paring knife, score each round into 12 even wedges.

4. Bake until the shortbread is very pale gold—watch carefully, as it should not become too brown, 28 to 30 minutes.

5. Cool in the pans on a wire rack for about 5 minutes. While the shortbread is still very warm, gently cut through the score

marks with a sharp knife. Cool completely. Store the shortbread in the pans or in a tin, layered with wax paper and covered tightly. Shortbread keeps well and should be handled very gently to prevent shattering.

OATMEAL SHORTBREAD SQUARES
(GRASMERE GINGERBREAD)

This is a delicious shortbread-type cookie, cut into squares— moist, chewy, fragrant with ginger, with a slight oatmeal crunch. I got this recipe from Laura Barton of the Oregon Department of Agriculture, whose father bought this local specialty while he was bicycling through the town of Grasmere in northwest England's Lake District. This recipe can be doubled and baked in a 13-x-9-inch baking pan.

Makes 16 squares

- ¾ cup plus 2 tablespoons whole-wheat flour
- ¾ cup packed light brown sugar
- ¼ cup oats, preferably steel-cut; old-fashioned or quick-cooking oats (not instant)
- 1½ teaspoons ground ginger
- ¾ teaspoon cream of tartar
- ⅜ teaspoon baking soda
- ½ cup (1 stick) plus 1 tablespoon cold unsalted butter, cut into pieces

1. Preheat the oven to 325 degrees F. Lightly butter an 8-inch square baking pan. In a food processor, combine the flour, sugar, oats, ginger, cream of tartar and baking soda; pulse to combine. Add the butter and pulse on and off until the mixture is crumbly.

2. Pat the dough into the prepared pan, pressing the surface with a floured fork until even. Bake until the center is set and the top is pale golden brown, 20 to 30 minutes.

3. Cool to lukewarm in the pan on a wire rack. While still warm, very carefully cut into 16 two-inch squares. Cool completely in the pan. Store the squares in an airtight container.

Mary, Queen of Shortbread

Shortbread has been attributed to Mary, Queen of Scots, who, in the mid-1500s, was said to be very fond of this supernally buttery biscuit. It's been suggested that the name "petticoat tail" may be a corruption of the French *petites gatelles* ("little cakes").

Author Theodora Fitzgibbon offered another theory:

"... we rather think the name petticoat tails has its origin in the shape of the cakes, which is exactly that of the bell-hoop petticoats of our own ancient Court ladies!"

BROWN SUGAR SHORTBREAD WAFERS

This recipe is from Brooke Dojny and Melanie Barnard, authors of *Let's Eat In* and *Sunday Suppers*, and for many years co-columnists for *Bon Appétit* magazine.

This is a very rich dough, made in seconds in a food processor or by hand with a wooden spoon. You can bake it in a single round in a buttered tart pan or foil cake pan; it transports easily. Or, as I like to do, you can roll out the dough and cut it with cookie cutters. Because it's so buttery, this dough is tricky to roll out. For tips on rolling and baking, see the information at the end of the recipe.

Makes 12 to 16 wedges or about 2½ dozen cookies

½	cup (1 stick) cold unsalted butter, cut into pieces
¼	cup packed light brown sugar
1	teaspoon pure vanilla extract
	Pinch salt
¾	cup all-purpose flour
2	tablespoons cornstarch
2	teaspoons sugar
½	teaspoon ground cinnamon (optional)

1. Preheat the oven to 350 degrees F. If making shortbread wedges, place a 9-inch metal fluted tart pan or pie pan in the freezer to chill while preparing the dough. If baking cutouts, lightly butter 2 baking sheets.

2. In a food processor, combine the butter, brown sugar, vanilla and salt; process until light, about 20 seconds. Sprinkle the flour and cornstarch over the top and pulse 6 to 8 times, until the dough begins to clump together. (The dough can be made by hand or with an electric mixer using the same steps.)

3. **IF MAKING WEDGES:** Press the dough over the bottom of the chilled tart pan. Sprinkle with the sugar (mixed first with cinnamon, if you like) and prick the dough with the tines of a fork. Return to the freezer and chill for 5 minutes more.

IF MAKING CUTOUTS: Roll out the dough on a lightly floured surface, until it is about ¼ inch thick. Cut into the desired shapes with a cookie cutter. Place the cookies about ½ inch apart on the baking sheets. Sprinkle the tops lightly with the sugar (mixed first with cinnamon, if you like).

4. For wedges, bake until the edge of the shortbread round begins to brown and the center is firm, usually 25 to 28 minutes. For cutouts, bake until the edges and the bottoms of the cookies are pale gold, usually 8 to 10 minutes. Cut through the center of 1 cookie to check; when done, the center should be nearly baked through.

5. Cool the shortbread slightly on a wire rack. Cut the round into wedges while still warm using a small, sharp knife. Cool completely in the pan before serving. Let the cutouts cool on the baking sheet for about 2 minutes. Carefully transfer to the rack to cool completely. Store in an airtight container, with wax paper between the layers.

For Best Results

- Roll only a small portion of dough at a time, leaving the rest refrigerated. The dough should not become so cold that it cracks.
- Use just enough flour to keep the dough from sticking.
- As you work, use a dough scraper or metal spatula to lift the cut pieces of dough from the work surface.
- Reroll scraps gently, without incorporating too much flour from the work surface.
- Bake these cookies just until lightly browned at the edges— they'll still be soft when done. For melt-in-your-mouth texture, don't let the centers dry out completely.

Better Than Sex

Shortbread has beneficial effects on the soul. The warm glow it gives is better than alcohol, and more readily available than sex. Only 90p for a box (cardboard) of the best brand. Doesn't always work, though.

LUCY ELLMAN
SWEET DESSERTS
1988

Señá Martina's Anise Cookies

For *bizcochitos*, the traditional sugar cookies, Señá Martina liked to use native water ground whole wheat flour. She also preferred fresh hog's lard for the shortening; a large handful of lard and two handfuls of sugar went into a bowl. Señá Martina beat and beat with her hands until it was the consistency of whipped cream. Then she added a large pinch of anise seed. In another pan she mixed flour, salt, and baking powder (her mistress would have used *tequesquite*, sodium nitrate). "Very little water," thought Señá Martina, "or the *bizcochitos* will be hard." There was no need for cookie cutters; Señá Martina could shape the *bizcochitos* in any form desired and she prided herself on her artistic ability.

FABIOLA CABEZA
DE BACA GILBERT
THE GOOD LIFE:
NEW MEXICO TRADITIONS
AND FOOD
1949

NEW MEXICO ANISE CHRISTMAS COOKIES
(*BIZCOCHITOS*)

You find these delicious cookies everywhere you turn in Santa Fe. The characteristic anise flavor cuts through their richness, and they keep well. Try them with afternoon coffee or tea, or even for breakfast.

Makes about 4 dozen cookies

- 2 cups all-purpose flour
- 1 cup whole-wheat flour or whole-wheat pastry flour
- 1 teaspoon baking powder
- ½ teaspoon salt
- 1 cup solid vegetable shortening or fresh lard
- ¾ cup sugar, plus more for coating the cookies
- 1½ teaspoons anise seeds
- 4-6 tablespoons cold water

1. Preheat the oven to 350 degrees F. Lightly grease 3 baking sheets; set aside. Sift the flours, baking powder and salt onto a sheet of wax paper.

2. Beat the shortening or lard with an electric mixer on medium speed until soft. Add the sugar and anise seeds and beat until light and fluffy. Lower the speed to slow, add the flour mixture and beat just until combined. Turn off the machine and scrape down the sides of the bowl. Add the water gradually, using just enough to hold the dough together. You can roll out the dough now, or wrap in plastic and refrigerate for 1 to 2 hours to make it easier to handle.

3. Roll out the dough on a lightly floured surface to a thickness of about ⅜ inch. Cut into 1½-inch rounds or other shapes. Pour some sugar into a shallow bowl. Dip the tops of the cookies in the sugar to coat lightly; place them, sugar sides up, about ½ inch apart, on the prepared baking sheets.

4. Bake until the cookies are very lightly browned and nearly baked through, usually 20 to 22 minutes.

5. Cool completely on a wire rack. Store in an airtight container.

TENNESSEE MOONSHINE COOKIES

These are small, soft mouthfuls, like little fruitcakes with whiskey-soaked fruit. They're from Phila Hach (pronounced "Hah"), proprietress of Hachland Hill Inn in Clarksville, Tennessee.

Makes 6 to 7 dozen cookies

1½	cups (about 8 ounces) candied cherries, chopped
1½	cups (about 8 ounces) dried or candied pineapple, chopped
1½	cups (about 8 ounces) golden raisins
¾	cup chopped candied orange peel (about 4 ounces)
¾	cup chopped candied citron (about 4 ounces)
1	cup good whiskey, such as Tennessee whiskey or bourbon
3-4	cups chopped nuts (pecans, walnuts, almonds or a combination)
3	cups all-purpose flour
½	cup sugar
½	cup packed dark brown sugar
1	teaspoon ground cloves
1	teaspoon ground cinnamon
⅛	teaspoon salt
⅔	cup (1 stick plus 2⅔ tablespoons) unsalted butter, melted
3	large eggs, well beaten
1	teaspoon baking soda
1	tablespoon buttermilk or hot water

1. Combine the cherries, pineapple, raisins, orange peel and citron in a bowl. Pour in the whiskey and stir to combine. Cover and let soak overnight.

2. Preheat the oven to 325 degrees F. Butter 2 or 3 baking sheets. In a large bowl, stir together the nuts, flour, white and brown sugars, cloves, cinnamon and salt until blended. Stir in the melted butter and eggs just until combined. In a small cup, stir together the baking soda and buttermilk or hot water; stir into the batter. Stir in the fruits and their soaking liquid.

3. Spoon the mixture, by teaspoonfuls, onto the prepared baking sheets. (These cookies don't spread, so they can be placed

Nonstop Cook

Phila Hach has written 11 cookbooks—"and published every one of 'em myself." Her collection of Appalachian and Southern recipes for the 1982 World's Fair in Knoxville, Tennessee, has nearly 150,000 copies in print. "I'm an old TV personality," she told me. "I'm nonstop!" Of these cookies, she says:

"We love sweets in the South and always have loved them from Thomas Jefferson's days.

"Moonshine was illegal in lots of places. Even in wet counties, moonshining is still illegal because the old moonshiners don't pay their taxes.

"Moonshine cookies— they're butter cookies. Back on the farm, we had plenty of butter, and we milled our own flour, and we didn't have vanilla, so we used the corn whiskey [moonshine] to flavor the cookies. The ladies also make that same cookie and call it a thumbprint cookie. They make the batter up, and they put a thumbprint in the cookies, and fill it with whatever jam they have in the pantry."

fairly close together.) Bake until the bottoms are lightly browned, usually 15 to 20 minutes. Cool on the baking sheets on a wire rack for 5 to 10 minutes. Transfer to the rack to cool completely. "Keep in the cookie jar until mellow," Phila says.

CANADIAN MOLASSES LEATHERNECKS

There is no butter in this crisp, gingery molasses cookie—an old family recipe from Prince Edward Island, a lovely place tucked into the northern curve of Nova Scotia's coastline.

Makes about 5 dozen cookies

1	cup dark molasses
¾	cup packed light brown sugar
1	teaspoon cider vinegar or balsamic vinegar
1	large egg
2⅓	cups all-purpose flour
2	teaspoons baking soda
1½	teaspoons ground ginger
½	teaspoon salt

1. Preheat the oven to 350 degrees F. Generously butter 2 or 3 baking sheets; set aside. In a bowl, stir together the molasses, brown sugar, vinegar and egg. Sift the flour, baking soda, ginger and salt onto a sheet of wax paper; add to the molasses mixture and stir just until blended.

2. Spoon the batter by rounded teaspoonfuls onto the prepared baking sheets, spacing them about 1½ inches apart. Bake until the edges are golden but the cookies are still soft, 9 to 10 minutes.

3. Cool on the baking sheets on a wire rack for about 5 minutes. Transfer to the rack and let cool completely; they will crisp as they cool. Store in an airtight container.

SAVANNAH LACE CHRISTMAS COOKIES

These cookies, sheer lacy wafers glazed with dark chocolate, are based on a recipe from Meredith Frederick, pastry chef at Manhattan's Post House, one of the country's best steak houses.

Makes about 8 dozen cookies

¼ cup (½ stick) unsalted butter, softened
2 cups packed light brown sugar
2 large eggs, well beaten
1 teaspoon pure vanilla extract
1 teaspoon dark rum
½ cup all-purpose flour
1 teaspoon baking powder
2 cups (½ pound) coarsely chopped pecans
¼ cup chopped candied orange peel
¼ cup chopped candied lemon peel or additional candied orange peel
8 ounces semisweet chocolate, melted and kept warm

1. With an electric mixer on medium-high speed, cream the butter and sugar until fluffy. Add the eggs, one at a time, and beat until well blended. Stir in the vanilla and rum.

2. Combine the flour and baking powder in another bowl. Stir in the pecans and the candied peels until coated. Add to the butter mixture and mix just until blended; do not overmix. If you have time, chill the batter until firm, about 1 hour.

3. Preheat the oven to 375 degrees F. Butter and flour 3 baking sheets.

4. Drop the batter by half-teaspoonfuls onto the prepared baking sheets, spacing them about 3 inches apart. Bake until the cookies are bubbly, medium-golden brown and set, about 7 minutes.

5. Cool the cookies for about 3 minutes on the baking sheets on a wire rack. Transfer to the rack and cool completely.

6. With a small brush, paint ½ of the top of each cookie with melted chocolate. Put the cookies back on the rack until the chocolate is set.

THE ORIGINAL TOLL HOUSE COOKIE

The story of these cookies, more American than apple pie, has been told again and again: It starts at the toll house in Whitman, Massachusetts, built in 1709 at the halfway point between Boston and the port of New Bedford. Ruth Wakefield and her husband bought the Toll House Inn in 1930. Mrs. Wakefield cut up a chocolate bar to incorporate into a brown sugar cookie dough. Thinking that the chocolate would melt, she was surprised when the bits held their shape, softening just slightly. She named the cookies Toll House Cookies, and an American classic was born.

Then, in the 1930s, the Nestlé Company (which had purchased the rights to Ruth Wakefield's recipe) began manufacturing a prescored chocolate bar that could be broken into pieces of just the right size for Toll House Cookies.

The morsels were introduced in 1939, and the rest is history. Nestlé still owns the exclusive rights to the Toll House trademark, and this recipe is reprinted courtesy of the Nestlé Creative Kitchens. Once their original contract ran out, Nestlé changed the recipe very slightly. This is Mrs. Wakefield's original.

Makes about 30 cookies

1	cup plus 2 tablespoons sifted all-purpose flour
½	teaspoon baking soda
½	teaspoon salt
½	cup (1 stick) unsalted butter, softened
¼	cup plus 2 tablespoons packed dark or light brown sugar
¼	cup plus 2 tablespoons sugar
1	large egg
½	teaspoon pure vanilla extract
¼	teaspoon water
1	cup (6-ounce package) semisweet chocolate morsels
½	cup coarsely chopped walnuts or pecans

1. Preheat the oven to 375 degrees F. Lightly butter 2 baking sheets; set aside. Sift the flour with the baking soda and salt onto a sheet of wax paper.

2. With an electric mixer on medium speed, cream the butter with the brown and white sugars until light, about 3 minutes. Beat in the egg; add the vanilla and water and mix until blended.

3. Lower the speed to slow and beat in the flour mixture just until blended, no longer. Add the chocolate morsels and nuts; mix just until evenly distributed.

4. Drop well-rounded half-teaspoonfuls of the dough about 1 inch apart on the prepared baking sheets. Bake until the cookies are lightly golden, 10 to 12 minutes.

5. Transfer the cookies to a wire rack and cool completely. Store in an airtight container.

Primal Toll House

I planned to make Nestlé chocolate chip cookies. I felt a visceral pounding. I preheated the oven. The bag of chocolate bits had the original recipe on the back. Black letters on canary yellow. I had no interest in the variations. The original Toll House recipe in my experience was the best. I hung an oven thermometer from the baking rack. The thermometer read 350 degrees and the thermostat read 350 degrees. Hooray for truth and justice! The cookies were baked and came out as soft beige circles with a few raised pimples of chocolate. Miss Ruth Wakefield should be proud. Look what she did! The creator of chocolate chip cookies.

BETTE PESETSKY
MIDNIGHT SWEETS
1988

265

ALL-AMERICAN FUDGE-CHUNK BROWNIES

Brownies and chocolate chip cookies are arguably America's chief contributions to the dessert world. The first printed mention of brownies appeared in the Sears, Roebuck and Co. catalog of 1897, advertising "fancy crackers, biscuits, cakes, brownies . . . in 1 lb. papers."

Brownies were widely baked in the 1920s; by 1931, the first edition of *The Joy of Cooking* includes a recipe for "fudge squares." Both fudgy and cakey brownies have their partisans, with each camp claiming the one and only true brownie.

And when all of the flourless chocolate cakes and chocolate mousse or ganache cakes have come and gone, there will still be nothing like a fudgy brownie, dry and crackled on top, moist and dense within, with a glass of cold milk.

Makes 15 brownies

1¼	cups coarsely chopped pecans
2	ounces unsweetened chocolate, coarsely chopped
½	cup (1 stick) unsalted butter, cut into pieces
⅔	cup all-purpose flour
	Pinch salt
2	large eggs
1	cup sugar
1	teaspoon pure vanilla extract
4	ounces semisweet chocolate, cut into coarse chunks, or ⅔ cup semisweet chocolate morsels

1. Preheat the oven to 350 degrees F. Lightly butter an 8-inch square baking pan; set aside. Scatter the chopped pecans over a baking sheet and toast until fragrant and lightly colored, about 7 minutes. Set aside to cool slightly; leave the oven on.

2. Meanwhile, melt the unsweetened chocolate and butter in a heavy saucepan over low heat, stirring occasionally. Set aside to cool slightly.

3. Sift the flour and salt onto a sheet of wax paper; set aside. With an electric mixer at medium speed, beat the eggs until light and frothy, about 3 minutes. Gradually beat in the sugar; add the vanilla. Fold in the melted chocolate but don't incorporate it completely. Fold in the flour mixture until not quite incorporated. Add the pecans and chopped semisweet chocolate or morsels and fold

just until well blended, no longer. Transfer the batter to the prepared pan; smooth the top.

4. Bake until the top is dry but a toothpick inserted in the center emerges with some traces of melted chocolate and moist crumbs, about 25 minutes.

5. Place the pan on a wire rack and cool completely. Don't try to cut the brownies when warm. When cool, make 2 evenly spaced cuts in the brownies in one direction, 4 cuts in the other. Cover the pan with plastic wrap and store at a cool room temperature. The brownies can also be wrapped individually for lunch boxes and gifts.

PECAN-AND-CARAMEL-GLAZED BROWNIES

From Ron Popp's Garden Café in Omaha, this variation covers a dark brownie with an easy caramel pecan topping that recalls Turtles, the candies so popular in Chicago and throughout the Midwest. These make a good gift, wrapped individually or by the panful.

Makes about 16 brownies

      2   cups sugar
      1   cup (2 sticks) unsalted butter, softened
      4   large eggs
      1   cup unsweetened cocoa powder
      1   cup all-purpose flour, spooned lightly into a measuring
           cup
      2   teaspoons pure vanilla extract
      2   cups coarsely chopped pecans
     24   caramels (usually 7 or 8 ounces)
  36-48   pecan halves

1. Preheat the oven to 350 degrees F. Lightly butter a 13-x-9-inch baking pan. With an electric mixer at medium speed, mix the sugar, butter, eggs and cocoa just until blended. Lower the speed to slow and add the flour and 1 teaspoon of the vanilla; mix very briefly, just until the flour is partially blended in. Spread the batter evenly in the pan; scatter the chopped pecans over the top.

Hashish Fudge

This is the food of Paradise—of Baudelaire's Artificial Paradises: it might provide an entertaining refreshment for a Ladies' Bridge club or a chapter meeting of DAR.

Take 1 teaspoon black peppercorns, 1 whole nutmeg, 4 average sticks of cinnamon, 1 teaspoon coriander. These should all be pulverized in a mortar. About a handful each of stoned dates, dried figs, shelled almonds and peanuts: chop these and mix them together. A bunch of *canibus sativa* [hashish] can be pulverized. This along with the spices should be dusted over the mixed fruit and nuts, kneaded together. About a cup of sugar dissolved in a big pat of butter. Rolled into a cake and cut into pieces or made into balls about the size of a walnut, it should be eaten with care. Two pieces are quite sufficient.

THE ALICE B. TOKLAS
COOK BOOK
(RECIPE FROM
BRYON GYSEN)
1954

268

2. Bake until the edges are dry and a toothpick inserted near the center emerges covered with moist crumbs, usually about 25 minutes. Do not overbake, or the brownies will not be fudgy. Cool to room temperature on a wire rack.

3. When the brownies are cool, melt the caramels in a heavy saucepan over low heat, stirring until smooth. Remove from the heat and stir in the remaining 1 teaspoon vanilla. Drizzle parallel rows of the caramel mixture over the top of the brownies. (It's important to do this while the caramel is still warm, or it will be too difficult to spread. If necessary, return the saucepan to low heat to rewarm slightly.) Gently press the pecan halves into the caramel, forming neat rows. Let set for at least 10 minutes.

4. With a sharp serrated knife, cut the brownies into 4-x-2-inch bars. Cover the pan with plastic wrap and store at a cool room temperature. The brownies can also be wrapped individually.

WHITE CHOCOLATE–MACADAMIA BLONDIES

A blondie is a nonchocolate brownie. This one is a chewy brown sugar bar cookie crammed with chunks of white chocolate and macadamias or pecans. Use Tobler, Lindt or another high-quality white chocolate.

> ### Makes 15 bars

¾	cup coarsely chopped macadamia nuts or pecans
¾	cup plus 2 tablespoons sifted all-purpose flour
½	teaspoon baking soda
⅛	teaspoon salt
1	large egg
¾	cup plus 2 tablespoons packed light brown sugar
1½	teaspoons pure vanilla extract
½	cup (1 stick) unsalted butter, melted and cooled slightly
4	ounces best-quality white chocolate, coarsely chopped

1. Preheat the oven to 325 degrees F. Scatter the nuts on a baking sheet and bake until fragrant and lightly colored, about 7 minutes; set aside. Meanwhile, butter an 8-inch square baking pan. Resift the flour with the baking soda and salt onto a sheet of wax paper.

2. With an electric mixer at medium-high speed, beat the egg with the brown sugar until light and frothy, about 3 minutes. Beat in the vanilla and melted butter. Lower the speed to slow, add the flour and mix until not quite incorporated. Add the nuts and chopped white chocolate; fold just until well blended, no longer. Transfer the batter to the prepared pan; smooth the top.

3. Bake until the top is dry and golden and a toothpick inserted in the center emerges nearly dry, 27 to 30 minutes.

4. Place the pan on a wire rack and cool completely. Don't try to cut the blondies when warm. When cool, cut into 15 bars. Cover the pan with plastic wrap and store at a cool room temperature or wrap individually.

Variation
COCONUT BLONDIES: In step 2, stir in ⅔ cup shredded sweetened coconut with the nuts and the white chocolate.

ALMOND BRITTLE COOKIES
(MY ALL-TIME FAVORITE)

I've made these for about 20 years. A fragrant butter cookie base is brushed with a thin layer of jam, which shows as a delicate stripe under the topping of glazed almond slices—very tailored looking.

Because these addictive cookies are easy to make in quantity—a large sheet is cut into neat 1-inch squares—they are ideal for a large party or for giving as gifts.

Makes 5 dozen cookies

	Carlo's Cookie Dough (page 272)
½	cup jam, such as raspberry, black currant or apricot
1½	tablespoons brandy or any liqueur (optional)
9	tablespoons (1 stick plus 1 tablespoon) unsalted butter
½	cup plus 1 tablespoon sugar
¼	teaspoon salt
2	heaping tablespoons honey
¼	cup heavy cream
1	teaspoon pure vanilla extract
	Few drops fresh lemon juice
2	cups sliced blanched almonds (6 ounces)

1. Lightly butter a 15½-x-10½-inch jellyroll pan. Roll out the dough on a lightly floured surface until it is slightly larger than the pan. Carefully transfer the sheet of dough to the pan without stretching it, allowing the rough edges to hang over the sides. Chill for 20 minutes or longer. Meanwhile, preheat the oven to 400 degrees F.

2. Trim the edges of the chilled dough flush with the outside edges of the pan. Prick the dough all over with a fork. Bake just until slightly golden, 16 to 18 minutes, pricking any bubbles with a fork as they rise. Do not overbake; the dough will bake a second time. Remove the pan to a wire rack; leave the oven on.

3. In a small bowl, stir together the jam and the optional brandy or liqueur. Gently brush or spoon a thin, even layer of the jam mixture over the dough.

4. Melt the butter in a heavy saucepan. Add the sugar, salt and honey and cook, stirring over low heat, until the sugar dissolves. Add the cream, raise the heat and boil until the mixture is

smooth and thickened, 3 to 5 minutes. Remove from the heat; stir in the vanilla, lemon juice and almonds. Spoon the almond mixture over the dough; gently spread out to cover completely.

5. Return to the oven and bake until the topping is bubbly and golden brown, 17 to 20 minutes. (Watch carefully, as the topping can go beyond caramelized and burn quickly. You may want to rotate the pan, back to front, partway through the baking time to help it brown more evenly.)

6. Cool to room temperature in the pan on a wire rack. Use a yardstick to guide you as you cut the cookies into neat 1-inch squares; trim the rough edges and save for snacking. Tightly cover the cookies with plastic wrap, either in the pan or on a plate; store at room temperature for up to 3 days.

CARLO'S COOKIE DOUGH

This recipe comes from my friend and former baking teacher Carlo Bussetti. It's rich and buttery with vanilla and orange overtones, and because the butter is creamed, the baked pastry has a crisp cookie texture rather than flaky layers. This dough is also easy to handle, freezes well (make a double or triple batch) and always comes through.

I began using it years ago to line a baking sheet for Almond Brittle Cookies (page 270), but it also makes a crisp shell for virtually any tart and works beautifully for lining molds for individual tarts—it holds its shape and won't slip down as it bakes. Fill the miniature shells with fresh berries or with lemon curd.

Makes a 15½-x-10½-inch sheet or two 10-inch tart shells

1	cup (2 sticks) unsalted butter, softened
1	cup sugar
	Pinch salt
	Grated zest of 2 oranges
¼	cup lightly beaten egg (1 jumbo egg or 1 large egg plus one yolk)
2	tablespoons milk
2	teaspoons pure vanilla extract
2	cups cake flour (not self-rising)
1½	cups all-purpose flour

1. Cream the butter with an electric mixer at medium-high speed. Add the sugar, salt and orange zest; beat until fluffy. Beat in the egg, milk and vanilla. Lower the speed to slow, and add the flours; stop beating as soon as the flours are mixed in. This dough should be soft, but not sticky.

2. Gather the dough together. Dust with flour, wrap in plastic and chill for at least 1½ hours. Let the dough soften slightly before rolling out.

1950s Pecan Puffs

These rich confections are just ground nuts held together with butter and sugar, formed into balls and baked only until set, then rolled in confectioners' sugar. Similar nut cookies go by several aliases—Mexican wedding cakes, Russian tea cakes and others.

This cookie can be made with any of several nuts. The high fat content of pecans (over 70 percent) makes them especially melting and flavorful.

Makes about 32 cookies

½	cup (1 stick) unsalted butter, softened
2	tablespoons sugar
1	teaspoon pure vanilla extract
	Pinch salt
1	cup pecan pieces
1	cup sifted cake flour (not self-rising)
	Confectioners' sugar, as needed

1. Cream the butter with an electric mixer at medium speed until softened. Gradually add the sugar and continue beating until very light. Beat in the vanilla and salt.

2. In a food processor, pulse the pecans and flour until the nuts are ground and powdery. Add the nut mixture to the butter mixture and mix until blended. Wrap the dough in plastic wrap and chill for at least 30 minutes.

3. Lightly butter 2 baking sheets; set aside. Roll the dough into ¾- to 1-inch balls between the palms of your hands. Place the balls about 1 inch apart on the prepared baking sheets. Chill again while you preheat the oven to 300 degrees F.

4. Bake until the cookies are pale golden brown, about 35 minutes. While the cookies are still warm, roll them in confectioners' sugar sprinkled on a sheet of wax paper; handle them very carefully, as they're fragile. Place on wire racks to cool completely. Sprinkle with another layer of confectioners' sugar when cooled. Store in an airtight container, with sheets of wax paper between the layers.

Home on the Page

I used to bake cookies similar to these from my mother's worn copy of *The Joy of Cooking*, 1953 edition. I loved leafing through the book's index, flipping back and forth and reading the "Abouts" (chatty passages about ingredients, wild game, bread-baking and more). Captured on these pages, I felt I was visiting a real home, where the family knew food's rightful place and its potential for bringing people together.

273

GRANDMA'S POPPY SEED CRESCENTS
(*MOHN* MOONS)

I reconstructed this recipe from one that my grandmother had copied in a black-and-white-flecked composition book in the 1920s. Because they're *pareve* (neutral—containing no butter), they can be served with either meat or dairy meals by those who keep kosher. They're easy to make and not too sweet.

Makes about 7 dozen crescents

3	cups all-purpose flour
1	tablespoon baking powder
	Pinch salt
1	scant cup sugar
½	cup vegetable oil
4	large eggs
½	cup (2¼ ounces) poppy seeds

1. Sift the flour with the baking powder and salt into a large bowl. Make a well in the center of the flour. Add the sugar, oil, eggs and poppy seeds to the well. With an electric mixer, mix until the dough is well blended. At this point, the dough may look slightly grayish—that's OK.

2. Place the dough on a floured sheet of plastic wrap, sprinkle with a little flour, and wrap. Chill until quite firm, at least 2 hours or overnight.

3. Preheat the oven to 350 degrees F. Lightly grease 3 baking sheets; set aside. Divide the dough into 4 portions. Place 1 portion on a lightly floured work surface; refrigerate the remaining dough. Roll out the dough ⅜ inch thick. Cut out 2- to 2½-inch crescents with a floured cookie cutter. (You can find crescent-shape cutters in cookware stores; otherwise, form crescents by making 2 cuts with one side of a round biscuit cutter or a glass—the way my grandmother used to do it.) Transfer the cookies to the prepared baking sheets, spacing them about ½ inch apart. Repeat with the remaining dough, rerolling any scraps, too.

4. Bake the cookies until the edges and bottoms are lightly golden, 15 to 17 minutes. Transfer to a wire rack to cool. These cookies keep very well; store in an airtight container.

MORE GREAT MOMENTS IN COOKIE HISTORY

1930s—Ruth Wakefield introduces chocolate chip cookies by cutting a chocolate bar into chips and adding them to the cookie dough at her Toll House Inn in Whitman, Massachusetts (see page 264).

1939—The Nestlé Company introduces chocolate morsels, changing American cookies forever. Now, Nestlé manufactures 240 million morsels every day.

1956—Margaret Rudkin introduces her Pepperidge Farm line of "Distinctive Cookies." Her insistence on high-quality ingredients such as real butter was a rarity in commercially baked cookies of that time.

November 1969—A star is born: Cookie Monster appears on *Sesame Street*'s very first broadcast by Children's Television Workshop.

Early 1970s—Andy Warhol is photographed with his cookie jar collection for *New York* magazine. Viewed as corny for years, cookie jars become popular again, along with other folk crafts. After Warhol's death in 1987, his 175 jars fetched $250,000 when auctioned at Sotheby's.

1977—At a time when no one had ever heard of buying individual chocolate chip cookies, cookie stores start to appear in cities and malls from coast to coast. Mrs. Fields opens her first cookie store in Palo Alto, California. As of 1994, Debbie Fields' empire extends to over 600 stores in 7 countries.

June 1979—David Liederman opens the first David's Cookies store in New York City, bringing back the use of chocolate chunks instead of chips.

1985—Sales of several brands of "soft," "homestyle" cookies prove a major disappointment to their manufacturers. Cookie fans know that real cookies must be baked at home and that preservative-laden commercial versions are no substitute.

Presidential Macaroons

When President George Bush gave a White House luncheon for Queen Elizabeth, these macaroons, made from Thomas Jefferson's original recipe, were served:

Pour boiling water on your almonds and take off skin and put them in cold water. Wipe them well in a towel. Beat them in mortar.

Add whites of eggs from time to time, beating them always to prevent their turning into oil. Take them out of the mortar, add sugar. Beat them well with a wooden spoon. Taste the paste to see if it is not too bitter. Add sugar if you find too bitter.

Dresser les avec deux couteaux le grosseur d'un noix sur des feuilles de papier. [Using two knives, make pieces the size of a walnut on sheets of paper.]

Put them in an oven not too hot but hotter than after taking out the bread. You prove the proper heat of the oven by holding in it a little white paper. If it burns, it will burn your macaroons. If it just browns the paper, it is exact.

MARY'S PIGNOLI
(ITALIAN PINE NUT MACAROONS)

Macaroons are another basic cookie genre, found in most early Italian, French, English and American cookbooks. These pine nut macaroons are from Mary Alfano Codola, my beloved friend in Rhode Island.

They are crisp outside, rolled in a nubbly jacket of pine nuts, with a soft chewy interior.

If you can't get the pine nuts (or find them too expensive), these cookies are also good rolled in slivered or sliced almonds. I like to coat half the cookies in pine nuts, half in almonds.

⟿ *Makes about 5 dozen macaroons*

1	pound almond paste
1¼	cups sugar
4	large egg whites
1	pound (3½-4 cups) pine nuts

1. Preheat the oven to 350 degrees F. Line 2 or 3 baking sheets with parchment paper or lightly butter the sheets.

2. Break the almond paste into pieces; place in a mixing bowl with the sugar. Break up the almond paste with your fingers or an electric mixer, crumbling the ingredients together as you would for a pie crust, until evenly combined.

3. In a separate bowl, beat the egg whites to soft peaks. Stir a little of the egg whites into the almond mixture; it will be fairly dry. Fold in the remaining whites.

4. Place the pine nuts in a shallow bowl. Roll the almond paste mixture into 1-inch balls, keeping them as round as possible. Press each ball into the nuts and gently turn to coat evenly; they will look like little porcupines. Place on the prepared baking sheets, spacing them about 1 inch apart.

5. Bake the cookies until evenly pale gold, 15 to 17 minutes.

6. Cool the cookies in the pans on a wire rack for about 5 minutes. With a spatula, very carefully transfer the cookies to the rack to cool completely. These macaroons keep well; store in an airtight container.

CRUMIRI
(CORNMEAL BUTTER COOKIES)

This delectable cookie recipe is from my friend and former baking teacher Carlo Bussetti, who grew up in Cuneo, a village in the Piedmont region in northern Italy. Horseshoe-shaped, crisp and buttery, these have a pleasant cornmeal crunch.

Makes about 3 dozen cookies

¾	cup (1½ sticks) unsalted butter, softened
¾	cup sugar
	Pinch salt
	Grated zest of 1 lemon
1	large egg
1	large egg yolk, plus a little egg white, if needed
¾	cup plus 3 tablespoons all-purpose flour
⅔	cup cornmeal, preferably stone-ground

1. With an electric mixer at medium-high speed, cream the butter, sugar, salt and lemon zest until very light. Add the egg and then the egg yolk. Add the flour and cornmeal and mix just until incorporated; do not overmix. The batter should be cohesive but not too dry; add 1 teaspoon of egg white if necessary.

2. Preheat the oven to 350 degrees F. Line 2 baking sheets with parchment paper, or lightly butter the sheets. Place ½ of the dough in a pastry bag fitted with a large (½-inch wide, #4) star tip. Pipe the dough onto the baking sheets into horseshoe shapes about 2 inches wide, spacing them about ½ inch apart. (If you don't have a pastry bag, you can either roll walnut-size balls of dough into a rope and bend it into a horseshoe shape, or just flatten 1-inch balls of dough and bake them as round cookies.)

3. Bake until the cookies are crisp and the edges are beginning to turn lightly golden, 12 to 14 minutes.

4. Transfer the cookies to a wire rack and cool completely. Store in an airtight container.

TOASTED BENNE (SESAME) WAFERS

Benne (sesame) seeds were brought to the American South by slaves from Africa. This not-quite-sweet cookie is a hybrid—a combination of old South Carolina recipes for benne wafers and Italian sesame-coated biscotti. The crisp but tender biscuits bake to a pale gold and have the haunting, toasty flavor of sesame oil. They improve in flavor as they keep.

Makes 5 dozen cookies

2½	cups (about 12 ounces) sesame seeds
2	cups all-purpose flour
2	teaspoons baking powder
⅛	teaspoon salt
⅔	cup packed light brown sugar
½	cup sugar
½	cup (1 stick) unsalted butter, melted and cooled slightly
2	large eggs
2	large egg yolks
2	teaspoons toasted sesame oil (optional, available in Asian groceries and many supermarkets; do not substitute clear sesame oil)
½	teaspoon pure vanilla extract

1. Preheat the oven to 300 degrees F. Scatter the sesame seeds over a jellyroll pan and toast, stirring once or twice, until lightly golden, about 10 minutes. (Watch carefully to prevent burning.) Set aside to cool; increase the oven temperature to 350 degrees. Butter 3 baking sheets; set aside.

2. Combine all of the remaining ingredients in a large bowl. Add 1½ cups of the toasted sesame seeds and mix with an electric mixer at medium-low speed just until the dough comes together. Set aside at cool room temperature for about 10 minutes to firm up slightly.

3. Place the remaining 1 cup sesame seeds in a cake or pie pan. Measure a level tablespoon of the dough, drop it into the pan of sesame seeds, and gently turn to coat with seeds while you shape it into a 2-inch-long oval "log" with tapered ends. Gently place the cookie on one of the prepared baking sheets; repeat with the remaining dough, spacing the cookies about 1 inch apart.

4. Bake until lightly golden, 11 to 13 minutes.

5. Transfer to a wire rack to cool completely. These cookies improve on standing. Store in an airtight container.

THIN ALMOND WAFERS

This is a beautiful cookie—sheer and as pale gold as parchment, inlaid with almond slices. It's a family heirloom from Dottie McCulloch of Rhode Island.

Makes 5½ to 6 dozen cookies

1	cup (2 sticks) unsalted butter, softened
1	cup sugar
1	large egg
1	teaspoon pure vanilla extract
1¾	cups sifted all-purpose flour
1	teaspoon salt
2	cups sliced almonds

1. Preheat the oven to 325 degrees F. In a large bowl, with an electric mixer on medium speed, cream the butter and sugar until light. Add the egg and beat until very smooth; add the vanilla. Lower the speed and add the flour and salt, mixing just until incorporated.

2. Divide this batter in half; place each half on a large un-greased flat baking sheet (without raised sides). To do this, put most of the dough in the center of the baking sheet. Dip a spatula in warm water and, working back and forth as if you were icing a cake, carefully spread the batter to cover the entire baking sheet as evenly as possible, making as smooth a layer of dough as you can. Sprinkle the almonds evenly over the batter on each baking sheet; press very gently into the dough.

3. Bake each sheet until the edges are light brown but the center is not yet browned, usually about 12 minutes, but it can take as long as 14 or 15; watch carefully. Remove the pans from the oven; leave the oven on.

4. Quickly cut the hot cookies into neat 2-inch squares, cutting off the browned edges. ("The edges are the family batch.")

Secret Recipe

This is a secret recipe; it was willed to me by an old friend of my mother's. I don't think she would mind my sharing it. It is very special and always brings raves. Making the wafers is a bit tricky, but if you follow my directions carefully, you won't have a problem."

DOTTIE MCCULLOCH

5. Return the baking sheets to the oven and bake until lightly golden, about 5 minutes longer. Watch carefully to prevent over-baking.

6. Remove the sheets to a wire rack. Slide a spatula under the cookies to be sure they are loosened from the sheets. Cool completely on the pans. Pack in tins for storage, with sheets of wax paper between the layers.

"WE NEVER PAID ENOUGH ATTENTION"

*M*ary Alfano Codola is my adopted Italian mother in Rhode Island. Any time I stop by, Mary plies me with "a little something"—a bowl of soup, a freshly baked spinach pie, a few of her cookies. But for the Christmas season and to some extent on Easter, too, she pulls out all the stops. The activity starts just after Thanksgiving.

"I make my candies first and get them out of the way. I make the *torrone* [nougat], with filberts, toasted almonds and vanilla. They're cut in squares or little oblongs, and I wrap them. I keep them in a tin in the refrigerator so they don't soften up.

"Then I make my fudge and my chocolate almond brittle. Those you break up in irregular pieces. I make two or three batches a day. And then the things that last the longest, like almond bar cookies and fruit-filled cookies with prunes and raisins.

"Those are the only ones I freeze, but I don't cut them. I freeze them in strips. On the day before Christmas, my daughter Madelyne comes down and makes my cookie trays for me. We leave the cookies uncut, and only cut them on the day of the holiday. The last ones I make are the butter cookies and sugar cookies. I don't freeze any of those; I just put everything in tins.

"After the traditional Italian seafood dinner on Christmas Eve, we clear the table and all of the desserts come out—the candies, the cookies.

"At Christmas, Mamma would make her *mostacci-ol'*, this wonderful cookie that no one else learned how to make. When you've had them all your life, you don't appreciate them. And now that she's gone, we wish we'd learned how. We watched her but never paid enough attention to all the tricks. I wouldn't dare try them—wait 'til you hear how many steps are involved!

"On the day after Thanksgiving, she would make the dough, which was flour, brown sugar, white sugar, spices like mace, allspice, nutmeg—it smelled almost like a hermit. Then she'd mix it and knead it for a while and put it in a big earthenware mixing bowl and age it in the closet for three weeks. And it smelled so wonderful . . .

"For the filling, she'd start with her own peach preserves. In the summer, she'd buy half a bushel of peaches from an old peddler and make her preserves. She'd put the preserves in a mixing bowl and add plain unsalted chopped nuts, more spices and rinds of lemons, oranges and tangerines.

"Mamma would open up pieces of the dough with her fingers and put the preserves inside. Then she'd wrap the dough around the filling in a diamond shape and curve one little part of it around her thumb, so you could see the thumbprint in it. Then she'd put them on the baking sheet, and we'd flour the sheet really well, so the ends would be all coated.

"On one day you'd bake them, another day she'd dry them and brush every bit of flour off the cookies— the house would be coated with flour. And on another day she'd frost them. I don't know how she'd do it, but she would thin her frosting to a certain consistency with coffee. You'd paint the cookies on one side with the chocolate frosting and let them dry, then paint them on the other side and dry them again. She would sprinkle on a little of those candy confections, and that was it. Then they'd sit until Christmas, and you couldn't touch them or else!

"Those cookies were a real project—the chocolate had to be mocha-colored and dull, not shiny, and if you didn't get it right, forget it! Mamma taught my godmother to make them, but they were never as good.

"'They're good,' she would say, 'but they're not as good as your mother's.'"

CRUNCHY ALMOND AND HAZELNUT COOKIES
(*BRUTTI MA BUONI*)

This cookie is native to Piedmont in northern Italy, the regional fare of which has recently been "discovered" by Americans. The Italian recipe name translates as "ugly but good."

This recipe is from Andrea Purinan, who, with his father, runs Il Fornaio in Udine. It is his version of the classic cookie of the region: a rough cluster of sugared nuts, cooked first on top of the stove, then baked until crisp outside, slightly chewy within, with a haunting nut flavor. *Buono!*

Makes about 5 dozen cookies

1	cup egg whites (7-8 large eggs)
1¾	cups sugar
2½	cups (12-14 ounces) unblanched or blanched whole almonds, coarsely chopped
2½	cups (10 ounces) whole hazelnuts, preferably skinned, coarsely chopped

1. Preheat the oven to 325 degrees F. Butter 2 or more baking sheets; set aside.

2. In a large bowl, beat the egg whites with an electric mixer until frothy. Add the sugar and continue to beat until the mixture is white and thick, but has not yet formed soft peaks. Stir in the almonds and hazelnuts. Transfer the mixture to a heavy saucepan and cook over low heat, stirring with a large wooden spoon or paddle, until the mixture thickens slightly and turns pale beige, about 10 minutes.

3. Spoon the mixture by teaspoonfuls onto the prepared baking sheets, spacing them about 1 inch apart. Bake until the cookies are dry to the touch, about 20 minutes.

4. Transfer the cookies to a wire rack and cool completely. Store in an airtight container.

ALSATIAN CHRISTMAS CINNAMON STARS
(*HIMMELGESTIRN*)

From Jean Joho, chef of Chicago's Everest restaurant, an Alsatian specialty served on Christmas Eve. After a big family dinner and then midnight Mass, the family gathers back at home for warm mulled spiced wine and these cookies, the name of which means "little stars from the sky."

These are very fine cookies, buttery but light. This recipe makes a lot; you can wrap and freeze half of the dough and then roll it out and bake the rest of the cookies at another time.

Makes about 7 dozen cookies

1	cup (2 sticks) unsalted butter, softened
1	cup sugar
2¼	cups ground blanched or unblanched almonds
1	large egg
2½	teaspoons ground cinnamon
2	tablespoons minced candied orange peel or the grated zest of 1 orange
	Grated zest of ½ lemon
¼	cup kirsch, dark rum or brandy
3⅓	cups all-purpose flour
½	teaspoon baking powder
1	large egg, lightly beaten, for glaze

1. With an electric mixer at medium speed, cream the butter with the sugar just until well combined. Add the almonds and egg and beat until light. Add the cinnamon, candied orange peel or orange zest, lemon zest and kirsch or other spirit; beat until smooth.

2. In a small bowl, stir together the flour and baking powder. Add to the butter mixture and mix just until combined, no longer. Wrap the dough in plastic wrap and refrigerate until quite firm, at least 1 hour.

3. Preheat the oven to 350 degrees F. Lightly butter 2 or 3 baking sheets; set aside.

4. Working with about ¼ of the dough at a time and keeping the remainder refrigerated, roll out the dough on a lightly floured surface to a thickness of slightly less than ¼ inch. With a cutter, cut

out stars or other shapes. Place the cookies on the prepared baking sheets, spacing them about ½ inch apart; roll out the remaining dough, including the scraps, and cut out cookies.

5. Brush the cookies lightly with the egg glaze. Bake until lightly golden, usually 10 to 12 minutes.

6. Cool the cookies on the baking sheets on a wire rack for 5 to 10 minutes. Transfer to the rack to cool completely. Store in an airtight container.

HUNGARIAN NUT CRESCENTS
(*MANDULÁS KIFLI*)

No visit to Budapest is complete without a stop at Vörösmarty (which everyone calls Gerbeaud, after its original Swiss owner), a coffeehouse that has been popular since the mid-19th century. Sitting under a chandelier in one of its baroque salons, you can see why restaurateur George Lang calls this "The Taj Mahal" of coffeehouses in his book *The Cuisine of Hungary*. The glass cases are filled with dozens of precisely crafted pastries, including this macaroon-like crescent so typical of Austrian-Hungarian baking.

Makes about 1 dozen

DOUGH

1½	cups sugar
1	cup hazelnuts, with skins
3	tablespoons all-purpose flour
1	teaspoon grated lemon zest
1½	tablespoons apricot jam
2	large egg whites
¼	teaspoon almond extract

GLAZE AND DECORATION

1	large egg white, stirred with a fork
6	glacéed cherries, halved (optional)
¾	cup sliced almonds, coarsely chopped

1. **DOUGH:** Combine the sugar, hazelnuts, flour and lemon zest in a food processor and grind to a powder. Add the jam and 1 of the egg whites and process until mixed. Scrape down the sides of the bowl. With the machine running, gradually mix in enough of the second egg white to form a stiff paste.

2. Transfer the mixture to the top of a double boiler set over gently simmering water. Stir with a wooden spoon until the mixture softens and some of the sugar dissolves, about 6 minutes. Remove from the heat and stir in the almond extract.

3. Transfer the mixture to a shallow pan or platter. Press plastic wrap directly on the surface and refrigerate until cold, about 1 hour.

4. Preheat the oven to 350 degrees F. Butter and flour a baking sheet. Cut the dough into 12 pieces. Roll each piece into a 3-inch-long rope with tapering ends. Bend each rope into a crescent shape. Arrange the crescents about 2 inches apart on the prepared baking sheet.

5. **GLAZE AND DECORATION:** Brush the crescents lightly with the stirred egg white. Press a cherry half in the center of each crescent, if desired. Sprinkle with the almonds, pressing them gently into the dough.

6. Bake until the crescents are pale gold, about 15 minutes.

7. Set the baking sheet on a wire rack and let the crescents cool for about 10 minutes. Transfer to the rack and cool completely. Store in an airtight container.

A Plate of Cookies

I think I've earned the right to invite you to have a glass of tea with me," she said . . .

He followed her into the living room. The kettle in the kitchen began to whistle, and Tamara left to brew tea. Soon she carried in a tray with tea, lemon, and a plate of cookies—surely baked by Sheva Haddas. They were not uniform in shape, but crooked and twisted like the home-baked cakes in Tsivkev. They smelled of cinnamon and almonds. Herman chewed on a cookie. His tea glass was full and extremely hot and contained a tarnished silver spoon. In some odd way all the mundane characteristics of the Polish-Jewish past, down to the smallest details, had been transplanted to this place.

ISAAC BASHEVIS SINGER
ENEMIES, A LOVE STORY
1972

GREEK EGG BISCUITS
(KOULOURIAKA)

This is a delicate braided large egg biscuit, not too sweet—one of the best versions of its type. The recipe comes from Ellie Souvlis, who grew up in Athens but didn't begin to cook Greek specialties until she moved to this country to marry her husband, Harris, an Athenian who had started his medical practice in Connecticut several years earlier.

Keep these biscuits in a cookie jar, so you can dip them into morning coffee and have them on hand when you want to put out something with a cup of tea.

A tip: Keep the amount of flour in this dough minimal. The dough will be slightly sticky and a little tricky to braid, but the results—large and airy biscuits—are worth the trouble. This recipe can be halved.

Makes about 8 dozen biscuits

2	cups (4 sticks) unsalted butter, softened
1	cup sugar
4	large eggs
1	tablespoon pure vanilla extract
5½	cups all-purpose flour, or as needed
3	tablespoons baking powder
½	teaspoon salt
1	large egg, lightly beaten, for glaze
¼	cup sesame seeds, or as needed, for topping (optional)

1. With an electric mixer on medium speed, beat the butter until light. Add the sugar and beat for 10 minutes. Add the eggs, one at a time, beating well after each addition; beat in the vanilla.

2. Combine the flour, baking powder and salt on a sheet of wax paper. Add to the butter mixture and mix just until it comes together to form a soft, cohesive dough (add a little more flour if the dough is too soft to handle easily). I prefer to keep this dough very soft, for light biscuits, which means it must be handled very carefully.

3. Preheat the oven to 350 degrees F. Butter 3 baking sheets. Break off pieces of dough about the size of a jumbo olive. Lightly flour a work surface and the palms of your hands. Gently roll each piece of dough on the floured surface into a rope about 7 inches long and ¼ inch in diameter. Cross the ends of each rope, and

then twirl the loop of the dough in the opposite direction, forming a twist or braid. Transfer each twist to a prepared baking sheet. Repeat with the remaining dough, placing the twists about 1 inch apart.

4. Brush the twists lightly with the egg glaze; sprinkle with sesame seeds, if desired. Bake until the biscuits are a delicate pale gold color, 20 to 25 minutes.

5. Let cool in the pans on a wire rack for 10 minutes. Remove to the rack to cool completely. These biscuits keep well; store in an airtight container.

ARMENIAN EGG BISCUITS
(*KAHKE*)

These are extraordinary: a delicate, rich, but not-too-sweet cookie for teatime or breakfast. What makes them unique is the fragrant *mahleb* (also spelled *mahlab* or *mahaleb*)—a spice ground from wild cherry kernels, with a flavor reminiscent of fresh cherries—elusive, but fruity and very pleasant. It's used in Armenian, Greek and Arabic recipes. This version is Armenian, though similar biscuits are found throughout the Middle East. You can order *mahleb* by mail; see the end of the recipe for a source. (Even if you make it without the *mahleb*, this cookie is well worth trying.)

The dough, made with vegetable shortening and yogurt, is unusual but easy to handle. Like all cookies of this type, these keep very well, stored in an airtight jar.

Makes 4 to 5 dozen biscuits

1	cup (2 sticks) unsalted butter
¾	cup corn or other vegetable oil
¼	cup solid vegetable shortening
7-8	cups all-purpose flour
2	tablespoons sugar
1	teaspoon salt
2	teaspoons baking powder
3	tablespoons *mahleb* (optional; see page 288)
1	cup whole-milk plain yogurt
1	large egg, beaten, for glaze
	Black caraway or sesame seeds, for sprinkling

1. In a saucepan, heat the butter, oil and vegetable shortening just until melted; remove from the heat. Meanwhile, sift together 7 cups of the flour, the sugar, salt, baking powder and optional *mahleb* into a large bowl. Gradually add the melted fats and the yogurt and stir to form a cohesive dough. Add more flour if necessary to make a soft but not sticky dough.

2. Preheat the oven to 350 degrees F. Set out 2 or 3 nonstick baking sheets, or lightly butter regular baking sheets. Cut the dough into 4 equal parts. Divide each part into 12 to 15 walnut-size pieces; roll each piece into a rope about 6 inches long. Either pinch each rope at the center and twist the loose ends together, or form each rope into a ring and twist the loose ends into a topknot. Gently place the biscuits on the baking sheets, spacing them about 1½ inches apart; they will spread slightly as they bake.

3. Gently brush the egg glaze over the tops of the biscuits; sprinkle with caraway or sesame seeds. Bake until the biscuits are medium golden, usually 13 to 15 minutes.

4. Cool on the baking sheets on a wire rack for 5 to 10 minutes. Remove to the rack to cool completely. Store in an airtight container.

NOTE: *Mahleb* can be mail-ordered from Kalustyan's, 123 Lexington Avenue, New York, New York 10016; (212) 685-3451; (800) 352-3451; www.kalustyans.com.

SICILIAN FIG-FILLED COOKIES
(*CUCIDATI*)

This fig-filled pastry is not unlike a Fig Newton—but much better. Originally a Christmas specialty, *cucidate* is sometimes baked as one large pastry, or as individual cookies, with the top crust slashed to reveal the filling inside. This version is shaped very simply and cut into short individual segments.

Figs are traditional here, but you can also fill the cookies with a combination of figs and chopped dried apricots and/or dates.

Makes about 6 dozen cookies

PASTRY

2½	cups sifted all-purpose flour
½	cup sugar
2½	teaspoons baking powder
¼	teaspoon salt
½	cup (1 stick) unsalted butter
2	large eggs
½	teaspoon pure vanilla extract
¼	cup milk

FILLING

2	cups (1 pound) chopped dried figs or a mixture of figs and apricots and/or dates
1	cup seedless raisins
	Grated zest and juice of 1 orange
½	pound (about 2 cups) walnuts or hazelnuts, toasted briefly and chopped (rub off all hazelnut skins in a towel after toasting)
1	cup honey
½	cup dark rum or Marsala
1	teaspoon ground cinnamon

1. **PASTRY:** In a food processor, combine the flour, sugar, baking powder and salt; pulse to mix. Add the butter and pulse. Add the eggs, vanilla and milk and process to make a smooth dough. Remove the dough and shape into a disk; cut into 4 equal pieces. Wrap in plastic and chill until needed.

2. **FILLING:** Using the same bowl you made the pastry in (no need to wash it), pulse the figs or other dried fruits, raisins, orange zest and juice and nuts until the fruit is evenly chopped. Transfer

According to pastry chef and cookbook author Nick Malgieri, the name of these cookies is Sicilian dialect for *buccellati*, "little bracelets." Every Italian housewife or baker I asked had a slightly different version of them.

to a bowl. Stir in the honey, rum or Marsala and cinnamon; mix well and set aside.

3. Preheat the oven to 400 degrees F. Lightly butter 2 baking sheets; set aside. Working with 1 piece of the dough at a time, roll out the dough to a neat 8-inch-wide strip that is about ¼ inch thick. With a chef's knife, cut the strip lengthwise in half, forming 2 long strips, each about 4 inches wide.

4. Lay the strips horizontally on the work surface. Lightly brush the top inch of each strip with cold water. About ⅓ of the way up from the bottom of the dough, mound ¼ of the filling in a 1-inch-wide thick ribbon that runs from end to end. Carefully fold the moistened edge of the dough over the filling and press gently to seal the edges. Using a chef's knife and sharp downward strokes, cut each strip into 1-inch segments. Transfer them to the prepared baking sheets, placing the strips about 1 inch apart. Repeat with the remaining 3 pieces of dough and filling.

5. Bake until the tops are golden, 13 to 16 minutes.

6. Cool on the baking sheets on a wire rack for 10 minutes. Transfer to the rack to cool completely. Store in an airtight container.

ABOUT BISCOTTI

Biscotti means "twice cooked." These simple rusk-type biscuits (the English form of the same word, derived from the French *biscuit*, which also means "twice cooked") have been baked in Italy for centuries. Biscotti are generally made by cutting a baked strip of dough into slices and then returning the slices to the oven for a second baking until crisp. (Some biscotti, however, do crisp in only one baking.)

In Italy, the word *biscotti* is also used generically to refer to all sorts of small crisp cookies. Recently, biscotti have been riding something of a fashion wave. Their shape and sturdy twice-baked texture invite dunking into morning cappuccino or café au lait or into a sweet wine like Vin Santo.

CORNMEAL-ALMOND BISCOTTI

Judy Rodgers, chef-owner of San Francisco's Zuni Café, makes the best biscotti ever. This is her recipe.

⤳ *Makes about 4½ dozen biscotti*

1¼	cups whole unblanched almonds
½	cup (1 stick) cold lightly salted butter
1	cup sugar
2	large eggs
1	tablespoon anisette liqueur
1½	tablespoons anise seeds
1½	cups all-purpose flour, or as needed
½	cup cornmeal, preferably coarse-ground
1½	teaspoons baking powder
½	teaspoon salt

1. Preheat the oven to 325 degrees F. Line 2 or 3 baking sheets with parchment paper, or generously butter the baking sheets; set aside. Scatter the almonds over a baking sheet and toast until dark-medium brown, usually 12 to 15 minutes.

2. Cool slightly on a wire rack; leave the oven on. Chop enough of the almonds to measure ¼ cup. Set both the chopped and whole almonds aside.

3. Cream the butter with the sugar using an electric mixer just until combined, no longer. Add the eggs and mix until blended. Add the anisette liqueur, anise seeds, 1¼ cups of the flour, the cornmeal, baking powder, salt and all of the almonds; mix until combined and the nuts are distributed. Stir in enough of the remaining ¼ cup flour so the dough comes together, but is not sticky (the dough should pull away from the sides of the bowl).

4. Working on the prepared baking sheets, shape the dough into 4 or 5 long logs, each about 1 inch wide and ¾ inch high.

5. Bake until the dough is set and beginning to turn pale gold at the edges, about 13 minutes. Remove the baking sheets to a wire rack and cool for 5 to 10 minutes; leave the oven on.

6. Cut the biscotti into even slices about ½ inch wide. Arrange the slices, cut sides up, on the baking sheets. Return to the oven and bake the biscotti again until very lightly browned, about 10 minutes.

7. Transfer the biscotti to a wire rack and let cool completely. Store in an airtight container. (These biscotti keep well.)

QUARESIMALE
(MINIATURE HAZELNUT BISCOTTI)

I t took me months to track down this recipe for the cinnamon-nut biscotti that are traditional for Lent, and longer still to pry it from Veniero's, a pastry shop/café in New York City. Finally, baker Joe Fighera showed me how to make these cookies that are "crisp like glass."

The only trick was that the recipe required hard-to-get ingredients: pure cinnamon oil and ammonium carbonate, an old-time leavener that makes cookies incredibly crisp. It's the cinnamon oil that gives these biscotti their distinctive "red hots" cinnamon taste—a hot cinnamony flavor that's very different from that of ground cinnamon. You can now order it from Amazon.

Over the years, when I haven't had these special ingredients on hand, I've gradually worked out this tasty version of the same quaresimale biscuits, made with ordinary ingredients.

Makes about 6 dozen biscotti

1	pound (about 3½ cups) whole hazelnuts
1½	cups sugar
2	slightly rounded cups all-purpose or pastry flour
¼	teaspoon salt
1¼	teaspoons ground cinnamon
1	teaspoon baking powder
3	tablespoons unsalted butter, softened
5	drops pure cinnamon oil (optional)
½	cup plus 2 tablespoons egg whites (4-5 large egg whites)
1	large egg, beaten, for glaze

1. Preheat the oven to 375 degrees F. Line 2 baking sheets with parchment or wax paper; generously butter the paper. Scatter

the hazelnuts over another baking sheet and toast until medium-dark, usually 12 to 15 minutes. Cool slightly; wrap in a kitchen towel and rub off most of the skins.

2. Place the nuts in a large bowl. With an electric mixer at low speed, slowly beat in the sugar, flour, salt, cinnamon and baking powder; the nuts will get beaten up a bit, that's OK. Add the butter and optional cinnamon oil and mix until blended. Add the egg whites and mix until the dough is very slightly sticky when squeezed between 2 fingers; add a little more egg white or a spoonful of flour, if needed, to adjust consistency.

3. With palms lightly moistened with cold water, divide the dough into 4 parts. Shape each piece of dough into a long rope that's about ¾ inch in diameter. Place 2 ropes on each prepared baking sheet, spacing them well apart. Lightly brush the logs with the egg glaze.

4. Bake until the ropes of dough are medium gold and fairly firm, about 20 minutes.

5. Transfer the baking sheets to a wire rack and let cool for about 5 minutes. While still warm, cut the logs into ½-inch-thick slices using a large chef's knife and cutting with a firm downward motion. Cool completely on a wire rack. Store in an airtight container.

CAKES–PLAIN, FANCY AND BEYOND

> . . . Perhaps because of their humble and universal nature in the American diet, pies rarely appear in 19th-century paintings; cakes, on the other hand, abound. Then as now, cake was a special treat, and Champagne [then sweet] was an expensive and glamorous accompaniment.
>
> HELEN GUSTAFSON ET AL.,
> *ART WHAT THOU EAT—IMAGES OF FOOD IN AMERICAN ART*, 1990

Bring a cake to the table, and you've instantly created an occasion. It's with cakes that we mark off and celebrate the milestones as we pass through life—from birthdays to weddings and anniversaries. In many cultures, cakes console at times of death, too. In an earlier era in this country, those left behind would remember the departed over a funeral cake. Today, the coffee cake brought to the house of the bereaved may be store-bought, but the essential tradition remains.

Like other timeless circular symbols, the round form of a cake conveys a sense of wholeness. In cultures all over the world, cakes figure as part of sacrifices and other rituals. These celebratory and sacramental aspects take several forms.

At harvest festivals, cakes made of firstfruits, the earliest gathered grain or other fruits, are solemnly given to the deity in acknowledgment of the gift of fruitfulness—a cake of thanksgiving.

Among the Natchez Indians, women gathered the first sheaves of corn and used part of it to make the unleavened cakes that were presented to the setting sun and consumed later in the evening.

In some communities, cakes were eaten sacramentally, in order to obtain the divine life assumed to be present in them. In Denmark and Sweden, a cake is made in the form of a boar, which represents the corn-spirit. This practice of ingesting the spirit was carried over into Christianity in the ritual of Holy Communion.

Cakes were also used as a sacrifice in the spirit of propitiation or thanksgiving, a practice dating from ancient times. In India, ancient Vedic texts prescribed a sacrifice of cakes to the gods, and today in Indian villages, cakes, sweetmeats and parched or fried grain are still in evidence at village shrines.

Plato speaks of those who thought it impious to stain the altars of the gods with blood and instead sacrificed only cakes and fruits mixed with honey. In ancient Rome, ivy-crowned old women called *sacerdotes Liberi* sold cakes of oil and honey in the streets and carried with them a small altar to Liber (Bacchus, god of wine and revelry). Customers broke off pieces of the cake and offered them to the god. In Shinto ritual in Japan, rice cakes called *mochi* are presented at the tomb of Jimmu, the first Mikado.

Cakes were also offered ritually to the dead. The Egyptians, for example, laid cakes (or stone representations of them) beside the dead in the tomb, for *ka*, the human spirit, to feed on.

Clearly, many of our lingering cake traditions are what Professor J.A. McCulloch, in an essay called "Cakes and Loaves" in the *Encyclopædia of Religion and Ethics*, calls "folk-survivals" from sacrificial or sacramental practices. Cakes marked with symbols (hot cross buns) or figures (of Christ or the Virgin, used on Twelfth Night cakes) are obvious examples.

But if the symbolic significance of cakes has remained much the same as in ancient times, the experience of baking a cake at home has changed radically over the past two centuries. Today, even a made-from-scratch cake is a snap compared to the days when just getting the oven hot—by sweeping out coals in a brick oven or, later, by getting a wood fire going—was a major effort.

In colonial American kitchens, baking was done in small brick ovens built alongside the fireplace. The process was less exact—and more exacting—than today's, and home baking called for both skill and instinct. Cakes were a sometime luxury baked after the bread was finished, in the brick oven's lingering heat.

Before the days of clean, refined sugar, sweetening a cake or pudding wasn't just a matter of dipping into a canister. Some 17th- and 18th-century cookbooks give instructions for how "To Boyle and Clarify Sugar." (At that time, sugar was not a standard-

The Oven

Too much care cannot be given to the preparation of the oven, which is oftener too hot than too cool; however, an oven too cold at first will ruin any cake . . . A good plan is to fill the stove with hard wood . . . let it burn until there is a good body of heat, and then turn the damper so as to throw the heat to the bottom of the oven . . . In this way a steady heat to start with is secured . . . Many test their oven in this way: if the hand can be held in from twenty to thirty-five seconds . . . it is a "quick" oven, from thirty-five to forty-five seconds is "moderate," and from forty-five to sixty seconds is "slow". . . All systematic housekeepers will hail the day when some enterprising Yankee or Buckeye girl shall invent a stove or range with a thermometer attached to the oven, so that the heat may be regulated accurately. . . .

THE WOMEN OF FIRST
CONGREGATIONAL
CHURCH
MARYSVILLE, OHIO
*THE CENTENNIAL BUCKEYE
COOK BOOK*
MINNEAPOLIS, 1876

ized product and was cooked to remove impurities.) In the 18th century, refined sugar was sold in white cones called sugar loaves. An expensive luxury, sugar was used sparingly, scraped from an 8- to 10-pound loaf with special shears.

Chemical leaveners (today's baking powder and baking soda) were not yet available. Earlier cakes were leavened with pearl ash (potassium carbonate), made at home from wood ashes. It was an undependable product, for it could impart a bitter taste and ghoulish green streaks to the cakes.

In the 1820s and 1830s, stoves—mostly fueled by wood, some by coal—began to replace fireplace cooking in the homes of the well-to-do. But even these, considered newfangled, were labor-intensive. Still used by some of our grandmothers in many parts of the country a few decades ago, wood stoves demanded work but gave the cook a measure of control that good home bakers still miss.

Flipping a dial to preheat the oven is a taken-for-granted convenience, something bakers a few generations back couldn't have imagined.

CHAPTER 8

PLAIN CAKES AND CAKES WITH FRUIT

lain cakes are a varied group that includes easy-to-make butter cakes, spongecakes, pound cakes and a few favorite iced—but not fancy—cakes and gingerbread, which has perhaps the longest and most involved history of any baked good.

Many of these simple cakes have English origins. Brought over by the settlers, cakes baked in the colonies were likely to be plain, since the rigors of home life did not allow for elaborate sweets. Popular varieties in America's early days included pound cake, spongecake and gingerbread. Other cakes, like the simple but wonderfully buttery nut-topped *blitzkuchen* ("lightning cake"), show Germanic origins, as does gingerbread.

Only slightly more elaborate are cakes made with fresh fruit. When I asked cooks for their cherished family desserts, they inevitably had a favorite apple cake to share. In this chapter, you will also find a summer cake made with fresh peaches and blueberries, a spicy cake studded with moist prunes and an upside-down cake crowned with glistening whole cranberries.

RECIPES

Lightning Cake
Hot-Water Spongecake
Eliza Leslie's Indian
    Pound Cake
Currant-Orange Pound
    Cake
Little Round Pound Cakes
Whipped Cream Pound Cake
Sunshine Cake
Dick Witty's Angel Food
    Cake
Chef Andrea's Breakfast
    Polenta Cake
Patty's Cornmeal Butter
    Cake
Palio's Polenta Cake
Semolina Ring Cake from
    Friuli
Semolina Cake with Orange
    Flower Syrup
Karyl's Blueberry Cornmeal
    Loaf
John's Brown Sugar
    Raspberry Loaf
Rose's Legendary Honey Cake
Polish Honey Cake
Rich, Soft Spice Cake
Grandma's Banana Cake
Great St. Louis Orange Ring
    Cake with Orange Syrup
Edna Lewis's Sunday Night
    Cake
East-West Ginger Cake
Eliza Acton's Gingerbread
Marie's Rich Gingerbread
    with Candied Ginger and
    Lemon Glaze
Ligita's Quick Apple Cake
Hilda's Apple Cake
Margaret's Apple Cake
Prune Spice Cake
All-Time-Best Summer Fruit
    Torte
Cranberry Upside-Down
    Cake

297

LIGHTNING CAKE

Mrs. Farback's *Blitzen Kuchen*," said the spidery handwriting on an old recipe card handed down to my friend Sue Crouse by her grandmother. "Quicker than a mix!" said my assistant, Luli, popping this cake into the oven first thing one late-summer morning. Golden with eggs (about twice as many as in most yellow cakes, in ratio to the butter and flour), this is just about the best plain butter cake you can imagine.

Makes one 8- or 8½-inch single-layer cake; serves about 6

1	cup all-purpose flour
1	teaspoon baking powder
½	cup (1 stick) unsalted butter, softened
1	cup plus 1 tablespoon sugar
4	large eggs
	Grated zest and juice of ½ lemon
¼	cup chopped almonds or other nuts
	Confectioners' sugar, for sprinkling

1. Preheat the oven to 350 degrees F. Butter and flour an 8- or 8½-inch round cake pan; set aside. Combine the flour with the baking powder; set aside.

2. Cream the butter and the 1 cup sugar with an electric mixer at medium-high speed until very light. Beat in the eggs, one at a time; beat in the lemon zest and juice. Lower the speed to slow and add the flour mixture; beat just until combined, no longer. Scrape the batter into the prepared pan.

3. In a small bowl, combine the nuts with the remaining 1 tablespoon sugar; sprinkle over the batter.

4. Bake until the cake is lightly golden and a toothpick inserted in the center emerges clean, about 26 minutes.

5. Cool to room temperature on a wire rack. Sprinkle with confectioners' sugar. Unmold or serve from the pan, cut into wedges.

Hot-Water Spongecake

Hot-milk and hot-water spongecakes used to enjoy places of pride in the repertoires of good American home bakers. The difference between spongecake and other yellow cake layers (such as the 1-2-3-4 Cake, page 383) is the butter. Usually made without fat, spongecake is much lighter, with a pleasantly dry, spongy texture.

Spongecakes are leavened with air incorporated into the eggs—either whole eggs, or separated, with the whites beaten until stiff and folded into the batter. Some are made without fat, others have a little melted butter folded in. Adding hot liquid might seem to deflate all that air that you (or your electric mixer) have worked so hard to trap in the beaten eggs, but the liquid actually makes a light cake with a clean crumb. Some people swear by hot-milk spongecake, others by one made with hot water. If you bake one of each, side by side, you'll find that the cake made with water rises a full inch higher than the milk version and has a lighter, cleaner crumb—the hands-down winner.

Sprinkled with powdered sugar, this is a delicious plain cake on its own, with tea or coffee. Or you can split it first and sandwich the layers with berry, peach or apricot jam. You can use this spongecake as the basis of Boston Cream Pie (page 397), or in trifle, charlotte, tiramisù or any other dessert that calls for light cake as a component.

Makes one 9-inch single-layer cake; serves 6 to 8

1   cup all-purpose flour
1   teaspoon baking powder
¼   scant teaspoon salt
2   large eggs
1   cup sugar
1   teaspoon pure vanilla extract
⅓   cup boiling water

1. Preheat the oven to 350 degrees F. Butter the bottom only of a 9-inch round cake pan, or line the bottom of the pan with a round of parchment or buttered wax paper; set aside. Sift the flour onto a sheet of wax paper; resift it with the baking powder and salt; set aside.

2. Beat the eggs with an electric mixer at medium-high speed until light. Gradually add the sugar and beat until light, fluffy and lemon-colored. Beat in the vanilla.

Digestible Sponge

He took a knife out of his pocket and cut a slice. He started violently, and peered at the cake more closely. Then he looked reproachfully at Mary Poppins.

"This is your doing, Mary! Now don't deny it. That cake, when the tin was last open, was a plum cake and now—"

"Sponge is much more digestible," said Mary Poppins, primly. "Eat slowly please. You're not starving savages!" she snapped, passing a small slice each to Jane and Michael.

"That's all very well," grumbled Mr. Turvy bitterly, eating his slice in two bites. "But I do like a plum or two, I must admit. Ah, well, this is not my lucky day!"

P.L. TRAVERS
MARY POPPINS COMES BACK
1935

3. Fold the flour mixture into the egg mixture. Pour the boiling water down the side of the bowl and fold in very gently, deflating the batter as little as possible. Quickly but gently pour the batter into the prepared pan. Swirl the pan to smooth the top without deflating the batter.

4. Bake until the top of the cake is golden and springy when lightly pressed with a fingertip, 30 to 35 minutes.

5. Cool in the pan on a wire rack for 15 minutes. Run the tip of a knife around the sides of the cake to loosen it from the pan; invert onto the rack and turn right side up. Cool completely before serving.

Eliza Leslie's Indian Pound Cake

Pound cake made with cornmeal and spices—a "new American cuisine" creation? Think again. This is adapted only slightly from an 1837 recipe from Eliza Leslie, itself an early adaptation of an English cake incorporating the cornmeal native to the Americas. The addition of a small amount of baking powder, not available then, keeps the texture from becoming too close and dense.

Subtly spiced, this cake is light and not too sweet, with a pleasantly crunchy texture. (This recipe can be halved for 1 loaf.)

Makes two 9-x-5-inch loaves; each serves 8 to 10

1½	cups cornmeal, preferably Rhode Island jonnycake meal (see page 310)
1½	cups all-purpose flour
1	teaspoon baking powder
2	teaspoons ground cinnamon
¾	teaspoon fresh-grated nutmeg
¼	teaspoon salt
1	cup (2 sticks) unsalted butter, softened
1	cup packed light brown sugar
½	cup sugar
	Grated zest of 1 lemon
8	large eggs
½	cup milk
3	tablespoons brandy

1. Preheat the oven to 350 degrees F. Butter and flour two 9-x-5-inch loaf pans; set aside. Sift the cornmeal, flour, baking powder, spices and salt onto a sheet of wax paper; set aside.

2. Beat the butter with an electric mixer on medium-high speed until light. Add the brown and white sugars and the lemon zest and continue beating until very light. Add the eggs, one at a time, beating well. Add the milk and brandy. Lower the speed to slow, and add the sifted dry ingredients just until combined. Divide the batter between the prepared pans

3. Bake until each cake is golden and a toothpick inserted near the center emerges clean, about 45 minutes.

4. Cool the cakes in the pans on a wire rack for 15 minutes. Unmold and turn right side up; cool. Serve at room temperature.

Bake It Quickly . . .

The quicker most kinds of cake are baked, the lighter and better they will be; but the oven should not be of such a furious heat as to burn them. It is impossible to give any exact rules as to the time to be allowed for baking various kinds of cake, as so much depends on the heat of the oven. It should be narrowly watched while in the oven, and if it browns too fast, it should be covered with a thick paper. To ascertain when rich cake is sufficiently baked, stick a clean broom splinter through the thickest part of the loaf—if none of the cake adheres to the splinter, it is sufficiently baked.

Anonymous
The American Housewife
New York, 1839

CURRANT-ORANGE POUND CAKE

I f spongecake is all egg and air, pound cake is a showcase for butter. I'll take a plain, buttery pound cake or cookie over a cream-filled or thickly frosted cake any day.

Pound cake is named for the proportion of its ingredients, classically a pound each of butter, sugar, eggs and flour. The classic result is a dense cake, firm with butter and eggs, with a close, tight crumb (but not a soggy interior). While heavier than other cakes, a well-made pound cake has a delicacy all its own.

Recipes for pound cake diverge from the original equal proportions. Some cooks prefer pound cake leavened only by the air beaten into the eggs (and the butter, too). Some separate the whites and beat them stiff. I find that a very little baking powder (less than a teaspoon per pound of flour—about ¼ of the amount used in most cake batters) helps produce a clean crumb.

You can also put together a pound cake batter in a food processor (it will have a slightly closer texture), but for maximum airiness, I like to cream the heck out of the butter with an electric mixer.

During the Christmas-Chanukah season, I bake a triple or quadruple batch of this cake in miniature foil loaf pans (5¾-x-3¼-x-2 inches). Once the cakes cool, I wrap them well in plastic wrap, tie them with a red ribbon and return them to their original (rinsed and dried) pans to give as gifts.

All pound cakes improve when left overnight, well wrapped, before slicing.

~ *Makes two 8-x-4-inch loaves; each serves about 8*

1	cup dried currants
½	cup Cointreau or other orange liqueur
2¼	cups all-purpose flour
½	teaspoon salt
½	teaspoon baking powder
1¼	cups (2½ sticks) unsalted butter, softened
	Grated zest of 1 orange
1⅓	cups sugar
5	large eggs
¼	cup sour cream or plain yogurt
2	teaspoons pure vanilla extract
	Confectioners' sugar, for sprinkling

I knew a fine fly young man who used to spend the times we were together telling me about his girl friends. I was like his sister. Being a shy person I searched for a way to let him know that I was interested in an incestuous relationship. I invited him to dinner at my home but he arrived at 6 P.M. instead of 7 P.M. and I was scrubbing the floor, frying chicken, cutting collards and making pound cake.

VERTAMAE
SMART-GROSVENOR
VIBRATION COOKING
1970; 1986

1. Soak the currants in the liqueur for at least 1 hour; stir once or twice.

2. Preheat the oven to 325 degrees F. Butter two 8-x-4-inch loaf pans. Dust with flour, shaking out the excess; set aside. Sift together 2 cups of the flour, the salt and the baking powder onto a sheet of wax paper; set aside.

3. In a large bowl, beat the butter and orange zest with an electric mixer at medium-high speed until light. Gradually add the sugar and beat until the mixture is very fluffy, about 6 minutes. Lower the speed to slow and gradually add the sifted flour mixture; do not overbeat. Increase the speed to medium and beat in the eggs, one at a time. Add the sour cream or yogurt, vanilla and any unabsorbed liqueur from the currants, draining the currants well. Mix just until blended, but don't overmix.

4. Quickly toss the currants with the remaining ¼ cup flour; fold into the batter without overmixing. Divide the batter between the pans, tapping gently to settle the batter.

5. Bake until the cakes are golden and a toothpick inserted in the center emerges clean, about 1¼ hours. (The timing can vary; do not overbake.)

6. Cool the cakes in the pans on a wire rack for about 10 minutes. Run the tip of a knife around the sides of the cakes to loosen them from the pans. Invert the cakes onto the rack; turn right side up. Sprinkle the cakes with confectioners' sugar while they are still warm; cool the cakes completely. Return the cakes to the pans, tightly cover with plastic wrap and let stand at room temperature for at least 24 hours before serving. To serve, sprinkle the cakes with additional confectioners' sugar and cut into thin slices with a serrated knife.

To Make Little Fine Cakes

One pound of Butter beat to Cream, a Pound and a quarter of Flour, a Pound of fine Sugar beat fine, a Pound of Currans clean wash'd and pick'd, six Eggs, two Whites left out, beat them fine, mix the Flour and Sugar and Eggs by Degrees into the Butter, beat it all well with both Hands, either make it into little Cakes, or bake it in one.

HANNAH GLASSE
*THE ART OF COOKERY,
MADE PLAIN AND EASY*
LONDON, 1747

LITTLE ROUND POUND CAKES
(*QUATRE-QUARTS*)

"Four quarters," the French name of this recipe means, referring to the proportion of ingredients (one-quarter each butter, sugar, eggs and flour). In France, the cake is sometimes served with afternoon tea but rarely as dessert.

This recipe is from Michel Stroot, pioneering spa chef at The Golden Door in California. "When we were growing up in Belgium," Michel remembers, "my mother used to bake this cake in little molds, and we'd each take one with us to school."

❧ *Makes 8 small cakes or loaves; serves 8*

2	cups all-purpose flour, lightly spooned into measuring cups
1	cup (2 sticks) unsalted butter, softened
1	cup sugar
	Grated zest of 1 lemon
2	teaspoons pure vanilla extract
5	large eggs, separated
¼	teaspoon salt

1. Preheat the oven to 350 degrees F. Butter 8 small ramekins, custard cups or tiny loaf pans; sprinkle with sugar, shaking out the excess sugar to leave a very fine coating. Place the pans on a baking sheet; set aside. Sift the flour onto a sheet of wax paper; set aside.

2. Beat the butter with an electric mixer at medium-high speed until very creamy. Add the sugar and beat until very light, about 6 minutes. Beat in the lemon zest and vanilla; add the egg yolks and beat for about 2 minutes longer. Lower the speed to slow, add the flour and beat just until nearly blended, about 15 seconds, no longer. The mixture will be stiff and slightly hard to blend at this point; don't overmix.

3. In a bowl, beat the egg whites with the salt at high speed until nearly stiff, 3 to 4 minutes. Stir a large spoonful of the whites into the batter; fold in the remaining whites until blended. Again, you'll have to work and chop the somewhat stiff mixture slightly in order to blend in the whites, but don't overblend. Gently spoon the mixture into the prepared ramekins or pans, filling each about ⅔ full.

A Viennese Version

In Vienna, a similar cake is called *gleich gewicht*, my mother's dear friend Nada Neumann recalls, "which means 'the same amounts'—as much butter as flour, sugar and eggs. Our cook would throw in some cherries. It was baked in a square and then cut into small pieces, with powdered sugar on top. She served it for the *jause* [afternoon coffee and cake snack], with hot chocolate."

4. Bake until the cakes are golden brown and a toothpick inserted in the centers emerges clean, usually about 45 minutes (the timing can vary with the molds used).

5. Transfer to a wire rack and cool briefly. Run the tip of a knife around the sides of the cakes to loosen them from the ramekins; unmold and cool completely on the rack. You can either wrap the cakes in plastic, or return them to their ramekins and seal the tops with plastic.

WHIPPED CREAM POUND CAKE

Jean Bayrock, a fellow former summer student at the Culinary Institute of America in Hyde Park, New York, swears by this pound cake recipe, which is made without butter. Instead, a pint of cream is whipped and folded into the batter. Though it sounds wildly rich, this cake actually contains only half the fat and half the calories of a typical butter pound cake.

The finished cake has a much lighter texture and slightly looser crumb than a traditional pound cake. It's different and very fine.

Makes one 10-inch tube cake or two 8-x-4-inch loaves; serves 12 or more

2	cups all-purpose flour
2	teaspoons baking powder
1	teaspoon salt
1	cup heavy cream, well chilled
4	large eggs
1½	cups sugar
1	teaspoon pure vanilla extract
2-3	drops almond extract
2	tablespoons packed light brown sugar, for topping (optional)
	Grated zest of 1 orange, for topping (optional)
	Confectioners' sugar, for sprinkling

1. Preheat the oven to 350 degrees F. Butter a 10-inch tube pan or two 8-x-4-inch loaf pans; flour the pan(s), tapping out the excess; set aside. Sift together the flour, baking powder and salt onto a sheet of wax paper.

2. Beat the heavy cream with an electric mixer until just stiff; set aside.

3. In a large bowl, beat the eggs at high speed until they begin to fluff up. Slowly add the sugar and beat until pale and fluffy. Add the vanilla and almond extracts.

4. Lower the speed to slow and gradually add the flour mixture; beat just until blended, no longer. Gently fold in the whipped cream. Pour the batter into the prepared pan(s). If you like, sprinkle the tops of the loaves with the brown sugar and orange zest.

5. Bake until a toothpick inserted into the center of the cake(s) emerges clean, about 1 hour for the tube pan or 48 minutes for the loaves.

6. Cool in the pan(s) on a wire rack for 15 minutes. Run the tip of a knife around the sides of the cake(s) to loosen them from the pan(s). Carefully invert and turn right side up. Let cool completely on the rack. Sprinkle the top of the cake(s) with a light dusting of confectioners' sugar and serve at room temperature.

SUNSHINE CAKE

Adding egg yolks to angel food cake—but still no butter or shortening—turns angel food cake into Sunshine Cake, a golden winner. Slathered with caramel crunch and whipped cream, this is the basis for Peanut Brittle Crunch Cake (page 404).

⤙⤙ *Makes one 10-inch tube cake; serves 10 to 12*

1¼	cups cake flour (not self-rising)
1¼	cups sugar
6	large egg yolks
¼	cup water
1	tablespoon fresh lemon juice
1	teaspoon pure vanilla extract
8	large egg whites
1	teaspoon cream of tartar
½	teaspoon salt

1. Preheat the oven to 350 degrees F. Cut a circle of parchment or wax paper to fit the bottom of a 10-inch tube pan, preferably one with legs or a removable bottom. Lay the paper in the pan; do not grease the pan.

2. Sift the cake flour into a mixing bowl. Add ¾ cup of the sugar, the egg yolks, water, lemon juice and vanilla; mix until smooth. Do not overbeat.

3. In a large bowl, whisk the egg whites with the cream of tartar and salt until foamy; gradually add the remaining ½ cup sugar and beat constantly until the meringue is just stiff; do not overbeat. Pour the cake batter over the meringue and fold in gently just until blended. Transfer the batter to the cake pan. Run a knife through the batter a few times to deflate any air bubbles and smooth the mixture; don't overdo it.

4. Bake until the cake is golden and springs back when touched gently, about 50 minutes.

5. Remove the cake from the oven and invert it, still in the pan, onto its legs, or hang it over the neck of a funnel or bottle. Let the cake hang until cooled completely. Run the tip of a knife around the cake to loosen it from the sides and tube of the pan; unmold the cake. Cut the cake with a large serrated knife.

Sunshine Cake

This is made almost exactly like angel cake. Have the whites of eleven eggs and yolks of six, one and a half cupfuls of granulated sugar, measured after one sifting; one cupful of flour, measured after sifting; one teaspoonful of cream of tartar and one of orange extract. Beat the whites to a stiff froth, and gradually beat in the sugar. Beat the yolks in a similar manner, and add them to the whites and sugar and the flavor. Finally, stir in the flour. Mix quickly and well. Bake for fifty minutes in a slow oven, using a pan like that for angel cake.

MARIA PARLOA
*MISS PARLOA'S
NEW COOK BOOK
AND MARKETING GUIDE*
BOSTON, 1880

DICK WITTY'S
ANGEL FOOD CAKE

How many people remember watching or helping their mothers beat 10 or 12 egg whites with a scrupulously clean rotary egg beater—whirling, whirling, until the whites piled up like sweet snow? Others, from an even earlier time, remember egg whites beaten with a fork on a large platter.

Basically an egg-white-and-sugar meringue stabilized with a little flour, angel food cake is made without fat. Because of the cake's delicacy, follow the instructions below to the letter, and your angel food cake will be as lofty and tender as a cloud.

This tried-and-tried-and-always-true recipe is from Dick Witty, reprinted with thanks. Dick and his wife, cookbook author Helen Witty, eat very well indeed. Try this with crushed, lightly sugared strawberries.

In the old days, instructions always insisted on breaking angel food cake apart with a cake comb or with two forks— never a knife. If you use a gentle sawing motion, a serrated knife works fine.

☙ *Makes one 10-inch tube cake; serves 10 to 12*

1	cup sifted cake flour (not self-rising)
1⅓	cups (about 11 ounces) sugar, preferably superfine
	Pinch salt
1½	cups (about 12 large) egg whites
1	teaspoon cream of tartar
1	tablespoon fresh lemon juice
1	teaspoon cold water
1½	teaspoons pure vanilla extract
	Few drops almond extract
1½	pints ripe strawberries, hulled, halved or sliced, if large (optional)
	Sugar, for the berries, if using

1. Preheat the oven to 350 degrees F. Cut a sheet of parchment or wax paper to fit the bottom of a 10-inch tube pan, preferably one with legs or a removable bottom. Fit the paper into the pan; do not grease the pan; set aside.

2. Sift the flour, ⅓ cup of the sugar and the salt onto a sheet of wax paper. Sift the mixture 3 more times, working back and forth between 2 sheets of wax paper; set aside. Sift the remaining 1 cup sugar onto another sheet of wax paper; set aside.

3. Beat the egg whites with an electric mixer at medium-low speed until foamy. Add the cream of tartar, lemon juice, water and vanilla and almond extracts; increase the speed to slightly higher

than medium and beat until the whites are nearly stiff. Lower the speed to medium-low and beat in the 1 cup sifted sugar, 2 tablespoons at a time. Continue to beat until the peaks are stiff but not dry; turn off the mixer.

4. Sift about ¼ of the flour mixture onto the egg whites; fold in gently with a large rubber spatula. Repeat 3 more times, adding the remaining flour. Gently transfer the batter to the prepared tube pan. Run a knife through the mixture to eliminate any air pockets; smooth the top.

5. Bake until the top of the cake is lightly golden and the cake springs back when pressed lightly, about 45 minutes.

6. Remove the cake from the oven and invert it, still in the pan, onto its legs, or hang it over the neck of a funnel or bottle. Let the cake hang until cooled completely.

7. Meanwhile, combine ½ of the strawberries, if using, with sugar to taste. Crush gently with a potato masher or a large spoon. Stir in the remaining strawberries. Let stand at room temperature, stirring occasionally, for about 30 minutes. Cover and refrigerate.

8. Run the tip of a knife around the cake to loosen it from the sides and tube of the pan; unmold the cake. Cut wedges of cake with a serrated knife; spoon some of the crushed strawberries alongside, if you like.

⌒⌒ *Variation*
ORANGE ANGEL FOOD CAKE WITH TANGERINE GLAZE: Substitute 3 tablespoons fresh orange juice and the grated zest of 1 large orange for the lemon juice, water and vanilla in step 3; don't omit the almond extract, however. After unmolding the cake, make:

TANGERINE GLAZE
    1   cup sifted confectioners' sugar
    2   tablespoons plus 2 teaspoons frozen tangerine juice
        concentrate, thawed slightly
        Grated zest of ½ tangerine or orange

Combine the confectioners' sugar, tangerine juice concentrate and zest in a bowl and stir until smooth. Adjust the consistency, if necessary; the glaze should be fluid enough to spread over the cake, but thick enough to cling to the sides of the cake in drips. If the glaze is too thin, sift in a little more confectioners' sugar; if too thick, add more tangerine juice concentrate, a few drops at a time. With a flat spatula or table knife, spread some of the glaze over the top of the cooled cake, frosting the top smoothly. Push or spoon more of the glaze over the top edges of the cake so that it drips down the sides at intervals. Let the glaze set before serving the cake.

ABOUT CORNMEAL CAKES

*D*uring the past few years, desserts baked with cornmeal have been enjoying a new wave of popularity, with the grain lending its crunch to butter cakes, cookies, tart crusts and even puddings.

Cornmeal was introduced to Italy via Venice, probably around 1600, through commerce with the Orient. Thinking that this exotic grain was of Oriental origin, the Venetians called it *granoturco* (Turkish grain). The real origins of cornmeal, of course, are Mexican or Central American.

Cornmeal is used throughout Italy to make polenta and is also traditionally added to dessert cakes and other baked goods.

If you'd like to dress up these cornmeal cakes, follow the lead of restaurant pastry chefs and serve them topped with Warm Amaretto-Cognac Zabaglione (page 114).

FOR EXCELLENT CORNMEAL BY MAIL: Any of the recipes in this book will work with supermarket cornmeal. But if you want to taste the real thing, try the cornmeal made from white flint corn freshly ground between millstones (Rhode Island jonnycake meal) from Gray's Grist Mill, P.O. Box 364, Adamsville, Rhode Island 02801; (508) 636-6075; www.graysgristmill .com.

CHEF ANDREA'S BREAKFAST POLENTA CAKE

This simple cornmeal butter cake, with the double crunch of cornmeal and chopped almonds, will brighten the morning. For dessert at the restaurant, Andrea served this cake with berries and a touch of whipped cream. "I like it with a glass of milk," he once told me.

Makes one 8- to 9-inch tube cake; serves 6 to 8

½   cup (1 stick) unsalted butter, softened
½   cup plus ¼ teaspoon sugar
2   large egg yolks
    Grated zest of ½ orange
    Grated zest of ½ lemon
1   vanilla bean, split lengthwise, or 1 teaspoon pure vanilla extract
⅔   cup (about 4 ounces) unblanched almonds
¼   cup potato starch or cornstarch
½   cup cornmeal, preferably stone-ground
½   teaspoon baking powder
4   large egg whites
    Confectioners' sugar, for sprinkling

1. Preheat the oven to 325 degrees F. Generously butter an 8- to 9-inch kugelhopf or Bundt pan; set aside. Place the ½ cup butter, the ½ cup sugar, the egg yolks and the orange and lemon zests in a large bowl. If using the vanilla bean, scrape the seeds from the pod into the butter mixture, or add the extract. Beat with an electric mixer until light and creamy; set aside.

2. In a food processor, combine the almonds, potato starch or cornstarch, cornmeal and baking powder; process until powdery. Sift this mixture onto a sheet of wax paper (if bits of almond remain in the sifter, return them to the mixture); set aside.

3. In a bowl, beat the egg whites with the remaining ¼ teaspoon sugar until they form soft peaks. Gently fold the dry ingredients and ½ of the beaten egg whites into the butter mixture; fold in the remaining whites just until incorporated. Gently scrape the batter into the prepared pan.

4. Bake until the cake is golden and a toothpick inserted in

Grand Master

Andrea Hellrigl was chef-owner of Palio in New York City and of Villa Mozart in the Alpine Merano, Italy. When he died, in his early 60s, the world lost a great master in the Old-World artisan tradition. Many of Andrea's recipes were based on research into historic culinary texts.

the center emerges clean, usually about 40 minutes (the timing can vary with the pan used; do not overbake).

5. Cool the cake briefly in the pan on a wire rack. Run the tip of a knife around the sides of the cake to loosen it from the pan; invert onto the rack. Sprinkle with confectioners' sugar and serve lukewarm or at room temperature.

PATTY'S CORNMEAL BUTTER CAKE

This cake is a marvel of simplicity and, according to a friend who tasted her way through this book, one of the very best recipes. The cake's cornmeal crunch is in perfect counterpoint to its butter-and-egg richness. The recipe is adapted from one by Pat Tillinghast, chef-owner with her husband, Bruce, of Two Rivers in Providence, Rhode Island, an intimate restaurant at the downtown junction of the city's rivers. Pat serves the cake with mixed fresh berries tossed with crème de cassis and a little whipped cream.

Makes one 9- to 10-inch single-layer cake; serves about 10

1	cup cornmeal (sift first if using stone-ground meal)
½	cup all-purpose flour
1½	teaspoons baking powder
¼	teaspoon salt
1	cup (2 sticks) unsalted butter, softened
1	cup sugar
4	large eggs
¼	cup low-fat plain yogurt
	Grated zest of 2 lemons
1	tablespoon fresh lemon juice, strained
½	teaspoon lemon extract
	Fresh berries and whipped cream, for serving (optional)

1. Preheat the oven to 350 degrees F. Line a 9- to 10-inch round cake pan with a round of parchment or wax paper cut to fit. Butter the paper and the sides of the pan and sprinkle 2 tablespoons of the cornmeal over the bottom and sides; tap out any excess meal. Sift the remaining ¾ cup plus 2 tablespoons cornmeal with the flour, baking powder and salt; set aside.

2. In a large bowl, beat the butter with an electric mixer at medium-high speed until light. Gradually add the sugar and beat until light. Beat in the eggs, one at a time, but don't overbeat. Add the yogurt, lemon zest, juice and extract. Fold in the dry ingredients, a little at a time. Blend well, but don't overmix. Scrape the batter into the prepared pan.

3. Bake until the cake is golden and springs back when pressed lightly with a fingertip, about 50 minutes.

4. Cool the cake briefly in the pan on a wire rack. Run the tip of a knife around the sides of the cake to loosen it from the pan. Invert the cake, carefully peel off the paper, and turn it right side up. Cool completely. Tightly wrap the cake if not serving immediately. *(The cake keeps well for about 3 days.)*

5. Cut the cake into wedges, and serve at room temperature with fresh berries and whipped cream, if you like.

PALIO'S POLENTA CAKE

Buckwheat is the flour in this cake, a recipe from the late Andrea Hellrigl, a native of the Italian Alps and chef-owner of Palio restaurant in New York City. Because it is coarsely ground, buckwheat eventually became known in Italy as *polenta nera*, or black polenta.

This cake has a complex, rounded flavor, with elusive honey and spice notes. It's extraordinarily light—surprising, since the buckwheat flour, chocolate and nuts could easily render it leaden. At Palio, Andrea would split the finished cake in two or three layers, then fill it with cranberry marmalade and whipped cream. I find it moist and aromatic on its own, with just a sprinkling of powdered sugar.

> *Makes one 9- to 10-inch tube cake; serves about 12*

8	egg whites
¾	cup sugar
1⅓	cups (2 sticks plus 5⅓ tablespoons) unsalted butter, softened
6	large egg yolks
2	ounces bittersweet or semisweet chocolate, melted and cooled briefly
¼	cup honey
½	teaspoon ground cinnamon
½	teaspoon ground cloves
¼	teaspoon ground star anise (use a mortar or spice mill)
½	teaspoon pure vanilla extract
¼	teaspoon orange extract
2	cups ground unblanched almonds (about 1½ cups whole almonds; 7½ ounces)
¾	cup buckwheat flour (available in health food stores)
1	teaspoon baking powder
	Confectioners' sugar, for sprinkling

1. Preheat the oven to 325 degrees F. Butter a 9- to 10-inch tube, kugelhopf or Bundt pan; set aside.

2. In a bowl, beat the egg whites to soft peaks. Gradually add the sugar and beat until stiff; set aside.

3. In a large bowl, using the same beaters, beat the butter, egg yolks, chocolate, honey, cinnamon, cloves, star anise, vanilla and orange extracts until fluffy.

4. In a small bowl, combine the ground almonds, buckwheat flour and baking powder.

5. Fold ½ of the buckwheat flour mixture into the butter mixture. Gently fold in ½ of the beaten egg whites. Fold in the remaining buckwheat mixture, and then the remaining egg whites, just until blended. Scrape the batter into the cake pan.

6. Bake until the cake springs back lightly when pressed with a fingertip, usually about 45 minutes. (The timing can vary with the pan used; do not overbake.)

7. Cool the cake briefly in the pan on a wire rack. Run the tip of a knife around the cake to loosen it from the sides and tube of the pan; invert and cool completely. Sprinkle with confectioners' sugar before serving at room temperature.

NOTE: Andrea suggested letting this cake sit overnight, wrapped in plastic, to allow the flavors to develop.

I make this dessert with only semolina and ground almonds, no flour," said Giorgio Zuppio's grandmother, who lives in Friuli, Italy. "The recipe is over 100 years old, and I serve it with custard flavored with rum."

Best known for its role in making top-quality pasta, semolina is the flour milled from hard durum wheat, usually ground slightly coarse. It's available in health food stores and Middle Eastern markets. If you are serving the cake with rum-flavored custard, a few strawberries are a nice touch.

SEMOLINA RING CAKE FROM FRIULI

Food writer Corby Kummer pried this century-old family recipe from the grandmother of Giorgio Zuppio, the cook at Al Giardinetto, a restaurant in the town of Cormons in the Friuli region.

Though not as gritty as cornmeal, semolina flour gives this light spongecake a pleasant, delicate crunch.

⌐ *Makes one 9- to 10-inch tube cake; serves 8 to 10*

⅔ cup blanched or unblanched almonds
¾ cup (about 4 ounces) semolina flour
1 cup sugar
Grated zest of 1 lemon
6 large eggs, separated
Pinch salt
Confectioners' sugar, for sprinkling
Eggnog Custard Sauce (page 609), flavored with rum to taste, for serving (optional)
Sliced fresh strawberries, for serving (optional)

1. Preheat the oven to 350 degrees F. Generously butter and lightly flour a 9- to 10-inch kugelhopf, Bundt or tube pan; set aside.

2. In a food processor, grind the almonds with the semolina and sugar until powdery. Add the lemon zest and egg yolks and process just until blended. Transfer to a large bowl.

3. Beat the egg whites with the salt until they form nearly stiff peaks. Fold the whites into the semolina mixture just until combined. Scrape the mixture into the prepared pan; tap the pan on a surface to settle the mixture.

4. Bake until the cake is lightly golden and a toothpick inserted in the center emerges clean, about 40 minutes (the timing can vary with the pan used).

5. Cool the cake in the pan on a wire rack until lukewarm. Run the tip of a knife around the sides of the cake to loosen it from the pan; invert onto a serving plate. Sprinkle lightly with confectioners' sugar. Serve at room temperature, with rum-flavored custard and berries, if you like.

SEMOLINA CAKE WITH ORANGE FLOWER SYRUP

This is a wonderful Middle Eastern cake—simple to make, very different in composition from Western butter cakes, and low in fat. It's made with semolina and yogurt and infused with fragrant orange flower syrup after it's baked. Surprisingly, it isn't cloyingly sweet, perfect with tea for a midafternoon snack.

Makes one 8-inch single-layer cake; serves 16

SEMOLINA CAKE
- 1½ cups sugar
- 1½ cups plain yogurt
- 3 cups semolina flour (about 1 pound; available in health food stores and Middle Eastern markets)
- 1 teaspoon baking soda
- 1 teaspoon rose water (see page 148)
- 1 teaspoon orange flower water (see page 148)
- ¼ teaspoon ground cinnamon
- ⅛ teaspoon pure vanilla extract

ORANGE FLOWER SYRUP
- ½ cup sugar
- ¼ teaspoon orange flower water
- 3 tablespoons water
- 16 pine nuts

1. **SEMOLINA CAKE:** Preheat the oven to 325 degrees F. Lightly butter an 8-inch square baking pan; set aside.

2. In a large bowl, combine the sugar and yogurt; stir in the semolina, baking soda, rose water, orange flower water, cinnamon and vanilla just until combined. Pour the batter into the prepared pan.

3. Bake until the cake is set and the top is golden brown, 30 to 35 minutes. Remove from the oven to a wire rack; leave the oven on.

4. **ORANGE FLOWER SYRUP:** While the cake is baking, combine the sugar, orange flower water and water in a small saucepan. Bring to a boil over medium heat, stirring until the sugar dissolves. Continue to boil, uncovered, without stirring, until thickened, about 6 minutes.

"Eat More"

This recipe comes from pastry chef Sonia El-Nawal Malikian. I met her by accident, while spending an afternoon in the kitchen of the now-closed four-star restaurant at the Drake Swissôtel in New York City. A striking young woman who speaks perfect French, Sonia arrived in New York at age 12, from a Beirut torn by war.

"To start the new year off well, you go to someone's house, and you make homemade sweets and bring them over," Sonia said. "When I was growing up, it was always open house. You go to their home, and they feed you before they eat themselves. It's always, 'Take more, eat more. . . .'"

5. Lightly score the top of the cake into 16 two-inch squares; press a pine nut into the center of each square. Drizzle the syrup over the cake.

6. Return the cake to the oven, and bake until the syrup is absorbed, about 7 minutes longer. Cool the cake to room temperature in the pan on a wire rack. *(This cake can be wrapped and stored at room temperature for up to 2 days.)* Serve at room temperature.

KARYL'S BLUEBERRY CORNMEAL LOAF

The pairing of blueberries and cornmeal is a happy one; the tart berries burst through the cornmeal crunch. (Try adding a handful of blueberries to your favorite corn muffins for summer breakfast.)

This is a moist pound-cake-style loaf that slices clean and keeps well for several days. I like it best toasted—almost like an instant blueberry-cornmeal muffin. It's from Karyl Bannister's *Cook & Tell* newsletter.

Makes one 8-x-4-inch loaf; serves about 8

1½	cups all-purpose flour
⅓	cup cornmeal, preferably stone-ground
1½	teaspoons baking powder
½	teaspoon salt
½	cup plus 1 tablespoon low-fat plain yogurt
1	tablespoon fresh lemon juice
6	tablespoons (¾ stick) unsalted butter, softened
¾	cup sugar
1	teaspoon grated lemon zest
2	large eggs
⅔	cup fresh or frozen (not thawed) blueberries
	Sugar and cinnamon, for sprinkling

1. Preheat the oven to 350 degrees F. Butter an 8-x-4-inch loaf pan; set aside.

2. In a small bowl, stir together the flour, cornmeal, baking powder and salt; set aside. In a measuring cup, combine the yogurt and the lemon juice; set aside.

3. In a large bowl, cream the butter, sugar and lemon zest with an electric mixer on medium-high speed until light and fluffy. Beat in the eggs, one at a time, beating well after each addition. Lower the speed to slow. Reserve about 1 tablespoon of the dry ingredients. Add the dry ingredients alternately with the yogurt and mix just until blended, no longer.

4. Toss the reserved flour mixture with the blueberries; gently fold into the batter. Spoon the batter into the prepared pan. Sprinkle sugar and cinnamon over the top.

5. Bake the cake for 25 minutes. Cover loosely with foil and continue to bake until the cake is golden and a toothpick inserted in the center emerges clean, about 35 minutes longer.

6. Cool the cake in the pan on a wire rack. For best flavor, wrap the cake, still in the pan, and store overnight before cutting. Unmold or serve directly from the pan.

Real Food by Real People

Karyl Bannister's *Cook & Tell* is a "participatory" food newsletter in the fullest sense of the word. Each month, Karyl calls several of her readers to see what's cooking for dinner. She then shares some of their recipes interspersed with her own running commentary and thoughtful essays in a wonderfully stream-of-consciousness voice.

Karyl's food is real food, cooked by real people. Not surprisingly, good down-home dessert discoveries turn up frequently from both Karyl and her readers' kitchens. (For a year's subscription to *Cook & Tell*, send $16 to Karyl Bannister, 298 Hendricks Hill Road, Southport, Maine 04576; www.cook andtell.com.)

JOHN'S BROWN SUGAR RASPBERRY LOAF

This is a soft, fragile loaf cake, moist with brown sugar and heady with the scent of fresh raspberries. Cooking with raspberries is tricky—their fragrance can become overpowering when they are heated. In most cases, I prefer raspberries uncooked. But here, the cooking works, and the raspberries infuse the whole cake with their subtle perfume. The recipe is from John Thorne, publisher and editor of the newsletter *Simple Cooking*. "This cake is extravagant in its use of fresh raspberries, but you'll realize how worth the expense it is when, during the last ten minutes of baking, the kitchen is flooded with berry aroma," John wrote. "And the cake lives up to its advance billing with a deep, spicy berry flavor, marvelously set off by the butter and brown sugar."

Makes one 9-x-5-inch loaf; serves 8 to 10

¾ cup (1½ sticks) unsalted butter, softened
1 cup packed light or dark brown sugar
2 large eggs, beaten until frothy
2 tablespoons sour cream, buttermilk or plain yogurt
1 tablespoon grated lemon zest
⅛ teaspoon ground cinnamon
2 cups sifted all-purpose flour, sifted again after measuring
1 teaspoon baking soda
1 pint fresh raspberries
   Whipped cream, for serving (optional)

1. Preheat the oven to 325 degrees F. Generously butter a 9-x-5-inch loaf pan; set aside.

2. In a large bowl, beat the butter with an electric mixer at medium-high speed until light. Add the brown sugar and continue to beat until fluffy. Add the eggs and beat until the mixture is light and creamy. Lower the speed to slow and fold in the sour cream, buttermilk or yogurt, the lemon zest, cinnamon and flour to make a smooth batter. Beat just until the mixture comes together; turn off the machine.

3. Sift the baking soda over the batter, sprinkle on the raspberries and fold everything together with a large rubber spatula, mixing well, but breaking up the berries as little as possible. Gently spoon the batter into the prepared pan; smooth the top.

4. Bake until a toothpick inserted in the center emerges clean, about 55 minutes.

5. Let cool in the pan on a wire rack for about 15 minutes. Run the tip of a knife around the sides of the cake to loosen it from the pan. Carefully invert onto the rack; turn right side up. Cool completely. Slice and serve with whipped cream, if desired.

Wonderful and Wildly Biased

John Thorne's *Simple Cooking* is unique in the world of food writing— wildly biased, the voice of a singular person going his own merry way out there in the wilderness.

The newsletter contains some of the liveliest (and also some of the wackiest and most heartfelt) writing about food anywhere. (For a 5-issue subscription, $25, contact www.outlaw cook.com.)

Rose's Legendary Honey Cake

I found this recipe handwritten in my grandmother's recipe note-book. It's a traditional Jewish honey cake (*lekach*) from Eastern Europe, made with coffee and whiskey, but quite different from the usual Jewish holiday honey cake—lighter in color and texture, with a tender, spongy crumb—perfect with a cup of coffee. As with many Jewish holiday dessert recipes, it contains no dairy products, so it can be served after a meal containing meat.

⌒ *Makes one 9-inch tube cake; serves 12*

3	tablespoons sliced almonds
5	large eggs, separated
¾	cup sugar
2	cups all-purpose flour
½	teaspoon baking powder
½	teaspoon baking soda
½	cup honey, preferably buckwheat or other strongly flavored honey
¼	cup warm strong-brewed coffee
	Grated zest of 1 lemon
2	teaspoons fresh lemon juice
1	tablespoon Scotch, Irish or rye whiskey
	Pinch salt

1. Preheat the oven to 325 degrees F. Oil a 9-inch tube or Bundt pan. Scatter the sliced almonds in the bottom of the pan; set aside.

2. In a large bowl, beat the egg yolks and sugar with an electric mixer at medium-high speed until pale and thick, 5 to 7 minutes. Sift the flour, baking powder and baking soda onto a sheet of wax paper; set aside.

3. Stir together the honey and warm coffee; gradually whisk into the egg yolk mixture. Add the lemon zest, lemon juice and whiskey. Gently fold in the dry ingredients in 3 batches, just until incorporated.

4. Beat the egg whites with the salt until stiff but not dry. Fold a large spoonful of the beaten whites into the cake batter; gently fold in the rest. Pour the batter over the almonds in the prepared pan.

A Baker with "the Touch"

Even my grandmother, who turned out Sunday feasts and picnics to feed a large family of serious eaters, paid homage to Rose Macy as the legendary baker of our community. Like all great bakers, Rose "just had the touch." Her pastries, cookies and strudel were all fabled. But her honey cake was *it*. Rose was also the kind of baker who would give you a recipe, but accidentally leave out one ingredient.

Rose died at the age of 102, just before this recipe was published in a magazine article. But she lives on in the recipes still baked by her children and grandchildren and now, by you.

5. Bake until the cake is set and browned and the surface springs back when gently pressed, about 45 minutes.

6. Cool on a wire rack until lukewarm. Run the tip of a knife around the cake to loosen it from the sides and tube of the pan, unmold and cool completely. Serve at room temperature, cut into wedges.

POLISH HONEY CAKE
(*PIERNIK*)

This deep-mahogany colored cake has a melting, mellow honey flavor without being too sweet. Sometimes it's covered with chocolate icing, but I prefer it plain. Wrapped tightly, it keeps well for several days. "In fact," says my Polish friend Krystyna Mayer, who gave me the recipe, "the flavor will improve over time."

Makes two 8-x-4-inch loaves; each serves about 8

1⅓	cups honey
⅔	cup sugar
½	cup strawberry jam or thick prune puree (for homemade version, see page 367)
1	cup (2 sticks) unsalted butter, cut into pieces
1	tablespoon unsweetened cocoa powder
3½	cups all-purpose flour
2	teaspoons baking soda
1	scant teaspoon ground cloves
⅓	cup ground almonds or walnuts
⅔	cup chopped dates
⅓	cup raisins
⅓	cup milk
3	large eggs
2	tablespoons grated orange zest

1. In a large nonreactive saucepan, combine the honey, sugar, jam or prune puree, butter and cocoa over low heat. Cook, stirring, just until the sugar dissolves and the butter melts. Remove from the heat; cool to lukewarm.

2. Preheat the oven to 325 degrees F. Butter two 8-x-4-inch loaf pans; set aside. In a bowl, stir together the flour, baking soda

Festive Polish Desserts

When I lived in London for two years in the early 1980s, my closest friend was Krystyna Mayer, whose perfect Oxbridge accent belied the fact that she grew up in a Polish family, speaking both Polish and English as a young child.

"On practically every festive occasion," Krystyna said one afternoon over cappuccino, "I remember my family eating *Szarlotka* [apple tart, page 556], and also a coffee torte and *mazurek* [a nut cake cut in squares].

This cake, which we call *piernik*, a honey cake made with jam or thick prune puree, was a favorite, especially at Christmas."

and cloves. In another bowl, toss together the ground nuts, dates and raisins with 2 tablespoons of the flour mixture.

3. Add the milk and eggs to the cooled honey mixture and mix just until combined. Add the flour mixture, orange zest and dried fruits; mix together carefully. Divide the batter between the loaf pans; smooth the tops.

4. Bake until a toothpick inserted in the centers emerges clean, about 1 hour or slightly longer. If, after about 30 minutes, the cakes begin to brown too much, loosely cover with a sheet of foil.

5. Cool the cakes in the pans on a wire rack for 15 minutes. Invert to unmold, turn right side up, and cool to room temperature. Serve in slices.

RICH, SOFT SPICE CAKE

This is a simple and wonderfully light example of the spice cake genre. Fragrant with cardamom, it's based on a Finnish recipe passed down to playwright Karolyn Nelke by her great-aunt.

Makes one 8-inch single-layer square cake; serves about 8

	Fine, dry bread crumbs, for coating the pan (optional)
2	cups sifted all-purpose flour
2	teaspoons ground cinnamon
1	teaspoon ground cardamom
1	teaspoon baking powder
½	teaspoon baking soda
¼	teaspoon salt
2	large eggs
1¾	cups packed light brown sugar
½	cup (1 stick) unsalted butter, melted and cooled
1	cup sour cream or low-fat plain yogurt
	Confectioners' sugar, for sprinkling

1. Preheat the oven to 350 degrees F. Butter an 8-inch square cake pan and coat with the bread crumbs or flour, tapping out the excess; set aside.

2. Sift together the flour, cinnamon, cardamom, baking powder, baking soda and salt onto a sheet of wax paper; set aside.

3. In a large bowl with an electric mixer at medium-high speed, beat the eggs with the brown sugar until very light and fluffy, about 5 minutes. Stir in the cooled butter just until blended.

4. Lower the speed to slow and add the sifted dry ingredients, alternating with the sour cream or yogurt. Mix just until the batter is smooth. Pour the batter into the prepared pan.

5. Bake until the cake is set in the center and a toothpick emerges clean, 40 to 50 minutes.

6. Cool the cake completely in the pan on a wire rack. Sift a light layer of confectioners' sugar over the top. Cut into squares and serve from the pan.

Grandma's Banana Cake

When I began catering dinners and parties, my brochure, a study in overreach, was cluttered with the kinds of recipe titles guaranteed to let my clients know their guests would be "impressed" with the food. With one exception: There, among all the extravaganzas, was "Grandma's Banana Cake"—and everyone asked for it.

I often leave off the chocolate frosting and serve this cake with just a sprinkling of powdered sugar. But the chocolate-banana combination really makes it. Substituting plain yogurt for the sour cream works perfectly and cuts back considerably on fat.

Makes one 10-inch tube cake; serves 8 to 10

CAKE

2¼	cups cake flour (not self-rising), spooned lightly into measuring cups
1½	teaspoons baking powder
1½	teaspoons baking soda
¼	teaspoon salt
¾	cup (1½ sticks) unsalted butter, softened
1½	cups sugar
3	large eggs
2	teaspoons pure vanilla extract
¾	generous cup very ripe mashed bananas (about 2)
¼	cup plus 2 tablespoons sour cream or plain yogurt Confectioners' sugar, for sprinkling (optional)

CHOCOLATE FROSTING (OPTIONAL)

1½	cups sifted confectioners' sugar
3	ounces unsweetened chocolate, melted
2	tablespoons sour cream, or more as needed
2	tablespoons unsalted butter, softened
⅛	teaspoon salt
1	teaspoon pure vanilla extract

1. CAKE: Preheat the oven to 350 degrees F. Generously butter a 10-inch tube or Bundt pan. Flour the pan, shaking out the excess; set aside. Sift the flour with the baking powder, baking soda and salt onto a sheet of wax paper; set aside.

2. Beat the butter with an electric mixer at medium-high speed until very light. Gradually beat in the sugar and continue to beat until fluffy. Beat in the eggs, one at a time; beat in the vanilla.

3. Lower the speed to very slow; add ½ of the flour mixture in batches, alternating with the mashed bananas. Add the remaining flour mixture in batches, alternating with the sour cream or yogurt. Don't overmix; finish folding the ingredients together by hand, with a few strokes of a large rubber spatula. Pour the batter into the prepared pan.

4. Bake until a toothpick inserted in the center of the cake emerges clean, 50 to 55 minutes. Do not overbake.

5. Cool the cake in the pan on a wire rack for 10 to 15 minutes. Run the tip of a knife around the cake to loosen it from the sides and tube of the pan, and carefully unmold. Cool to room temperature. Dust with confectioners' sugar or frost; serve in slices or wedges.

6. **CHOCOLATE FROSTING** (optional): With an electric mixer, combine the confectioners' sugar and melted chocolate at medium-slow speed. Increase the speed slightly, add the sour cream, butter, salt and vanilla and mix until well blended. If the frosting is too stiff, add more sour cream until the frosting is of a spreadable consistency.

GREAT ST. LOUIS ORANGE RING CAKE WITH ORANGE SYRUP

If I feel like baking a cake "just to have around," this is likely to be the one. It is moist, tender and buttery, perked up with plenty of citrus flavor.

Aside from a couple of minor changes (I've replaced the original sour cream with yogurt and lightened the sugar syrup slightly), this is, as my friend Sue Crouse says, "a very old recipe indeed—and wonderful."

⌒ *Makes one 9-inch tube cake; serves 10 to 12*

CAKE

1¾	cups sifted all-purpose flour
1	teaspoon baking powder
1	teaspoon baking soda
1	cup (2 sticks) unsalted butter, softened
1	cup sugar
	Grated zest of 1 orange
3	large eggs, separated
1	cup low-fat plain yogurt
1½	teaspoons pure vanilla extract
	Pinch salt

ORANGE SYRUP

	Juice of 1 large orange
	Juice of 1 lemon
½	cup sugar
	Tiny pinch salt

1. **CAKE:** Preheat the oven to 325 degrees F. Butter and flour a 9-inch Bundt, kugelhopf or tube pan; set aside.

2. Working back and forth between 2 sheets of wax paper, sift together the flour, baking powder and baking soda 3 times; set aside.

3. In a large bowl, cream the butter until very light and fluffy. (Sue Crouse suggests doing this by hand; I use an electric mixer at medium-high speed.) Slowly add the sugar and orange zest and continue creaming until the sugar dissolves and the mixture is very light, about 8 minutes. Add the egg yolks, yogurt and vanilla; beat

until very light and fluffy. Lower the speed to slow, and carefully fold in the flour mixture, without overmixing.

4. Beat the egg whites with the salt until stiff but not dry. Fold the egg whites into the batter just until blended. Scrape the batter into the prepared pan; smooth the surface.

5. Bake until the cake is golden brown and a toothpick inserted in the center emerges clean, about 1 hour.

6. **ORANGE SYRUP:** Meanwhile, combine the orange juice, lemon juice, sugar and salt in a small nonreactive saucepan. Bring to a boil over medium heat; lower the heat and simmer the syrup very gently until thickened, about 8 minutes.

7. Cool the cake in the pan on a wire rack for 10 minutes. Run the tip of a knife around the cake to loosen it from the sides and tube of the pan. Invert the cake onto a plate with a rim. If the syrup is not hot, gently reheat it. Very slowly spoon or brush the hot syrup all over the surfaces of the hot cake. Serve the cake slightly warm or at room temperature.

When Sue Crouse sent me this recipe from her home in Warren, Ohio, she told me, "My grandmother always said this recipe came from St. Louis. She would not give it to anyone."

EDNA LEWIS'S
SUNDAY NIGHT CAKE

Cookbook author Edna Lewis grew up in Freetown, Virginia, a community started by freed slaves. Back when Edna was chef at Café Nicholson in New York City, regulars would drop by on Sunday nights "straight from the country or even from the airport," Edna remembers. Every Sunday, she'd bake a big panful of this deliciously plain yellow cake with burnt sugar icing.

The glaze recipe, typical of home baking early in this century, has been adapted slightly from Edna's original. Serve this cake right from the pan, with a glass of cold milk.

⌒ *Makes one 9-inch single-layer square cake; serves 9*

CAKE
1¾	cups plus 2 tablespoons all-purpose flour
2	teaspoons baking powder
¼	teaspoon salt
½	cup (1 stick) unsalted butter, softened
1½	cups sugar, preferably superfine
3	large eggs
⅔	cup milk
1	tablespoon pure vanilla extract

BURNT SUGAR GLAZE
1	tablespoon unsalted butter
1¼	cups packed dark brown sugar
⅓	cup milk
1¼	teaspoons pure vanilla extract

1. **CAKE:** Preheat the oven to 375 degrees F. Butter and flour the bottom only of a 9-inch square cake pan, shaking out the excess flour; set aside. Sift the flour onto a large sheet of wax paper. Resift it with the baking powder and salt; set aside.

2. In a large bowl, beat the butter with an electric mixer at medium speed until light and satiny. Gradually add the sugar and beat until well blended and very light. Add the eggs, one at a time, beating well after each addition. Add the flour mixture in 3 batches, alternating with the milk, beginning and ending with the flour. Each time you add the flour, mix just until incorporated. Add the vanilla and turn off the mixer. Finish folding the ingredients together by hand with a few strokes of a large rubber spatula. Pour the batter into the prepared pan.

3. Bake until a toothpick inserted in the center of the cake emerges clean, 35 to 40 minutes.

4. Remove the pan from the oven, run the tip of a knife around the edges of the cake, and invert immediately onto a wire rack. Remove the pan and carefully turn the cake right side up; cool for about 15 minutes. Cover the cake with a kitchen towel to prevent drying. Wait for about 1 hour before glazing.

5. **BURNT SUGAR GLAZE:** In a heavy saucepan, combine the butter, brown sugar and milk over medium heat. Stir to dissolve the sugar, and gradually bring to a boil. Boil, without stirring, until the mixture forms a soft ball (234 to 240 degrees F on a candy thermometer), usually about 12 minutes. (If you don't have a candy thermometer, test by dropping a spoonful of the boiling mixture into a cup of ice water and rolling it into a soft ball with your fingers.) Remove from the heat; stir until the glaze thickens and is spreadable. Stir in the vanilla.

6. Smooth the glaze over the cake with a spatula or table knife, letting it run down the sides of the cake. Let the glaze set for a few minutes before serving.

About Gingerbread

They sette him Roial spicerye And Gingebread.
Geoffrey Chaucer,
Sir Thopas, 1386

The history of gingerbread can be traced farther back than any other baked item except bread. German lebkuchen, a form of gingerbread originally made in monasteries, was first mentioned in print in 1320 and was spiced with honey, ginger and ground black pepper. Later, guilds were formed specifically for bakers of the various forms of lebkuchen.

Pepper was often included with the "warm spices" in medieval recipes, but the "pepper" in cookie names like German pfeffernüsse and the Swedish gingersnaps called *pepperkakor* refers to overall spiciness, and black pepper is not included as an ingredient.

Historian Karen Hess, whose wide-ranging and insightful research on gingerbread is included in the notes to *Martha Washington's Booke of Cookery*, which was compiled between 1749 and 1799, points out that medieval gingerbread comes from the field of medicine, not cookery. Cited in the *Oxford English Dictionary*, the word *Gingebrar*, from an English manuscript dated 1299, refers to preserved ginger, probably used as a digestive aid. But by the time Chaucer used the word in the late-14th century, it frequently indicated the edible cake.

Made with bread crumbs and honey, and later with treacle and molasses, gingerbread began to rise in popularity in England early in the 17th century. The French version, *pain d'épices* ("spice bread"), a centuries-old specialty of Dijon, is attributed to Chinese origins. Mrs. Hess hypothesizes that the Chinese were eating a spiced honey bread called *Mi-Kong* by the 10th century. It was said to be included among the rations for the followers of Genghis Khan. "The Arabs adopted it," Mrs. Hess continues, "and inevitably it came to Europe by way of the Crusaders."

Recipes recognizable to us as gingerbread appear in the 17th century, but the butter and eggs with which older, more bread-like gingerbreads were enriched don't show up in English recipe collections until the 18th century. By the time Amelia Simmons published her *American Cookery* in 1796, gingerbread was popular enough in this country to be included in some five different versions.

Early American gingerbreads took two basic forms:

- **Crisp gingerbread**, the dough rolled, cut and baked to the crisp (or chewy) cookies we know as ginger snaps, drops and gingerbread men
- **Soft gingerbread**, baked in a pan, is the cake-like product we know as gingerbread today.

Along with other plain cakes, gingerbread is a mainstay in the chapters on baking in every American cookbook from Amelia Simmons to the present.

"June, She don't yet know her letters ... but I will bring her the A B C in gingerbread."

TOBIAS SMOLLETT
THE EXPEDITION OF
HUMPHRY CLINKER
1771

EAST-WEST GINGER CAKE

This is from the cookbook author and popular blogger David Lebovitz. To use Shakespeare's phrase from *Twelfth Night*, fresh ginger makes it "hot i' the mouth."

Makes one 9-inch single-layer cake; serves 8 to 10

2½	cups all-purpose flour
½	teaspoon ground cinnamon
½	teaspoon ground cloves
¼	teaspoon freshly ground pepper
1	cup sugar
1	cup peanut oil or other bland oil
1	cup molasses
2	large eggs, lightly beaten
2	teaspoons baking soda
1	cup boiling water
¼	cup (about 2 ounces) minced, peeled fresh ginger, or to taste
	Lemon Cream (page 623, optional)

1. Preheat the oven to 350 degrees F. Butter a 9-inch spring-form pan; flour the pan, tapping out the excess; set aside. Sift together the flour, cinnamon, cloves and pepper onto a sheet of wax paper; set aside.

2. In a large bowl, combine the sugar, oil, molasses and eggs and beat with an electric mixer at medium-high speed until well blended. Add the sifted ingredients and mix just until blended.

3. Stir the baking soda into the boiling water; quickly add to the batter and mix just until blended. Stir in the minced ginger. Spread the batter in the prepared pan; smooth the top.

4. Bake until a toothpick inserted in the center of the cake emerges clean, about 1 hour. If the top of the cake browns too quickly during baking, loosely cover with foil.

5. Cool the cake in the pan on a wire rack for 15 minutes. With the tip of a knife, carefully loosen the sides of the cake from the pan; remove the sides of the pan. Cool to room temperature. Spoon a dollop of Lemon Cream alongside each wedge of cake, if you like, and serve.

ELIZA ACTON'S GINGERBREAD

Dark, moist and spicy, this recipe is fairly true to the original, from the mid-19th century.

◁ *Makes one 8-inch cake; serves 8*

2	large eggs
¾	cup molasses
1	scant cup packed light or dark brown sugar
1½-2	tablespoons ground ginger
	Pinch *each* ground allspice, cinnamon and freshly ground pepper
	Grated zest of 1 lemon
2	cups sifted all-purpose flour
6	tablespoons (¾ stick) unsalted butter, melted
½	cup buttermilk
¼	cup milk
1	teaspoon baking soda
	Applesauce, Cider-Lemon Sauce (page 611) or whipped cream, for serving

1. Preheat the oven to 350 degrees F. Butter and flour an 8-inch square cake pan or an 8- to 9-inch kugelhopf or Bundt pan.

2. In a large bowl, beat the eggs with an electric mixer at medium-high speed until light and frothy. Add the molasses and continue beating. Meanwhile, stir together the brown sugar, ginger, allspice, cinnamon, pepper and lemon zest. Gradually add to the egg mixture and beat until well blended.

3. Lower the speed slightly. Add about ⅓ of the flour, then the melted butter, and then another ⅓ of the flour. Quickly stir together the buttermilk, milk and baking soda; add to the batter and mix gently. Add the remaining flour and mix just until evenly blended, no longer. Pour the batter into the prepared pan.

4. Bake until the gingerbread shrinks slightly away from the sides of the pan and a toothpick inserted in the center emerges clean, about 45 minutes. If the gingerbread is browning too quickly, loosely cover it with foil halfway through the baking time.

5. Cool the gingerbread in the pan on a wire rack. Cut into large squares and serve directly from the pan, with applesauce, Cider-Lemon Sauce or whipped cream.

To Make Gingerbread

Take a pound and half of treacle, two eggs beaten, half a pound of brown sugar, one ounce of ginger beaten and sifted; of cloves, mace and nutmegs all together half an ounce, beaten very fine, coriander-seeds and carraway-seeds of each half an ounce, two pounds of butter melted; mix all these together, with as much flour as will knead it into a pretty stiff paste; then roll it out, and cut it into what form you please; bake it in a quick oven on tin-plates; a little time will bake it.

ELIZA SMITH
*THE COMPLEAT HOUSEWIFE:
OR, THE ACCOMPLISHED
GENTLEWOMAN'S
COMPANION*
16TH ED., LONDON
1758; 1727

MARIE'S RICH GINGERBREAD WITH CANDIED GINGER AND LEMON GLAZE

This is extraordinary gingerbread, moist and great-looking. Cookbook author (and great cook) Marie Simmons, my co-columnist for *Bon Appétit*, says she also likes to serve this cake with John's Mother's Lemon Sauce with Lemon Slices (page 612).

⌁ *Makes one 10-inch tube cake; serves 12 to 16*

1	tablespoon unsalted butter, melted, for the pan
1	cup (2 sticks) unsalted butter, softened
1	cup packed dark brown sugar
2	large eggs
2	cups dark molasses
3½	cups all-purpose flour
2	tablespoons ground ginger
2	teaspoons baking soda
½	teaspoon ground cloves
½	teaspoon salt
¼	cup minced crystallized ginger
1	cup boiling water

LEMON GLAZE

1	cup confectioners' sugar
1-2	tablespoons fresh lemon juice
½	teaspoon grated lemon zest

1. Preheat the oven to 350 degrees F. Generously brush the inside of a 10-inch Bundt or tube pan with the melted butter; sprinkle with a fine coating of flour and shake out the excess; set aside.

2. In a large bowl, beat the butter with an electric mixer at medium-high speed until light and fluffy. Add the sugar and beat until smooth. Beat in the eggs, one at a time, beating well after each addition. Gradually beat in the molasses in a slow, steady stream until blended.

3. Meanwhile, sift the flour, ginger, baking soda, cloves and salt together; stir in the crystallized ginger. Gradually beat the dry ingredients into the batter just until blended, no longer; turn off

the mixer. Add the boiling water to the batter, ⅓ cup at a time, stirring gently but thoroughly by hand with a large rubber spatula after each addition. Spoon the batter into the prepared pan.

4. Bake until the cake pulls away from the sides of the pan, 55 to 60 minutes.

5. Cool the gingerbread in the pan on a wire rack until warm, 20 to 30 minutes. The top of the cake may fall slightly upon cooling. Run the tip of a knife around the sides of the cake to loosen it from the pan. Invert the cake onto a platter.

6. **LEMON GLAZE:** In a small bowl, stir together the confectioners' sugar and lemon juice until smooth; add the lemon zest. Drizzle the glaze over the top of the cooled cake. The cake is delicious served slightly warm. But for neat cutting, let the glaze set before serving.

A FEW GOOD APPLES

A century ago, when setting out to make an apple cake, pie or brown Betty, you could choose from dozens of apple varieties. Today, supermarkets pretty much limit us to the same handful. Grown more for their shipping properties than for taste, today's apples look big, shiny and unblemished; they taste little more than "crisp and crunchy."

But there's hope. Varieties new to us, many of them actually "heirloom" apples that haven't been seen for decades, are turning up with more and more frequency at farmers' markets and well-stocked supermarkets, as growers respond to a more adventurous and food-conscious public.

- **Baldwin:** Tart with some sweetness.
- **Black Twig:** Sweet-tart; stays crisp in baking (better for cakes than pies).
- **Cox's (Orange) Pippin:** Sweet, with full, rounded flavor.
- **Golden Delicious:** Some from New York State farms are packed with sweet, juicy flavor—a far cry from the boring Golden Delicious supermarket apples we've become used to.
- **Gravenstein:** Tart, spicy, juicy. An old variety, grown on the East Coast.
- **Jonathan:** Sweet-tart, spicy, all-purpose.
- **Macoun:** Crisp, fresh, sweet-tart.
- **Mutsu (Crispin):** Sweet, tart, honey-like flavor. Becoming increasingly popular.
- **Northern Spy:** Full, robust flavor with some acidity.
- **Russet (also Roxbury Russet):** Sweet, complex character, rich flavor.
- **Winesap:** Firm, tart with slight sweetness.

"I fear that he who walks over these fields a century hence will not know the pleasure of knocking off wild apples. Ah, poor man, there are many pleasures which he will not know."

HENRY DAVID THOREAU
WILD APPLES
1862

LIGITA'S QUICK APPLE CAKE

Stick a bookmark right here, and leave it in. Sort of a "quick apple pie without the crust," this cake has become one of my all-time favorite, most-often-made recipes. It originally came from Karolyn Nelke, a friend in New York.

This is barely a cake at all—just a custardy batter quickly poured over apples and baked to a crusty gold. Browning the butter slightly adds a mellow flavor but isn't necessary. Serve this warm. It wants vanilla ice cream.

✒ *Makes one 10-inch single-layer cake; serves 8*

- 3 medium-size tart apples, such as Granny Smith, peeled, cored and thinly sliced (about 3 cups)
- 1 teaspoon fresh lemon juice
- ¾ cup plus 3 tablespoons sugar
- 2 teaspoons ground cinnamon
- ¾ cup (1½ sticks) unsalted butter, cut into pieces
- 2 large eggs, lightly beaten
- 1 cup sifted all-purpose flour
  Vanilla ice cream, for serving

1. Preheat the oven to 350 degrees F. Generously butter a 10-inch Pyrex pie pan.

2. Toss the apples in a bowl with the lemon juice, 2 tablespoons of the sugar and the cinnamon. Spread the apples evenly in the prepared pan.

3. Melt the butter in a small saucepan over medium heat; cook until lightly golden, about 7 minutes. Watch carefully to avoid burning. Pour the clear, browned butter into a bowl, leaving any sediment or foam in the pan.

4. Stir the ¾ cup sugar into the butter. Gently stir in the eggs; stir in the flour until blended. Spoon the batter evenly over the apples and spread into a layer. Sprinkle with the remaining 1 tablespoon sugar.

5. Bake until lightly golden and crusty, 40 to 45 minutes.

6. Cool in the pan on a wire rack. Cut into wedges and serve from the pan warm or at room temperature, with vanilla ice cream.

HILDA'S APPLE CAKE

This is one of the simplest apple cakes, and one of the best. A plain, buttery batter is poured over sliced apples, and the whole thing bakes up to a subtle cake that showcases the flavor of the fresh fruit. An excellent version of an old-fashioned genre, this tender cake is also good made with firm pears, peaches or plums.

Makes one 11-x-7-inch or 9-inch single-layer cake; serves 8

APPLES

1¼-1½	pounds (3-4) tart apples, such as Granny Smith or Greening, peeled, cored and thinly sliced (3-4 cups)
2	tablespoons unsalted butter, melted
¼	cup sugar
¾	teaspoon ground cinnamon

BATTER

¼	cup (½ stick) unsalted butter, softened
¾	cup plus 1½ tablespoons sugar
2	large eggs, separated
½	teaspoon pure vanilla extract
1	cup all-purpose flour
1	teaspoon baking powder
¼	cup milk
	Pinch salt
½	teaspoon ground cinnamon

1. **APPLES:** Preheat the oven to 350 degrees F. Butter an 11-x-7-inch Pyrex baking dish or a 9-inch square cake pan. Place the apples in the pan, drizzle with the melted butter and sprinkle with the sugar and cinnamon. Gently toss with your fingers; set aside. The pan should be about ¾ full.

2. **BATTER:** In a large bowl with an electric mixer on medium-high speed, cream the butter and the ¾ cup sugar until light. Beat in the egg yolks and vanilla. Sift in the flour and baking powder alternately with the milk and beat just until combined.

3. In a bowl, beat the egg whites with the salt until they form stiff, but not dry, peaks; fold into the batter. Pour the batter over the apples and spread out without deflating. Sprinkle the remaining 1½ tablespoons sugar and the cinnamon over the top.

Foolproof Cake

I think this cake is absolutely foolproof," says Bob Freedman, who gave me his mother's cake recipe. "A couple of times, I've tried to vary it, with more batter, more apples, whatever—but it always comes out best if you follow these instructions. It doesn't seem like enough batter when you put it into the pan, but it's just right. It's a great thing to make ahead for company."

4. Bake until the apples bubble up and the topping is golden, 35 to 40 minutes. If, after about 25 minutes, the cake is browning too quickly, loosely cover with foil.

5. Cool in the pan on a wire rack. Serve warm or at room temperature, directly from the pan.

MARGARET'S APPLE CAKE

This is the paragon of homey apple cakes—moist but not heavy, generous with apples, with a nut-and-spice crunch topping. The recipe comes from Margaret Stieber of Sheboygan, Wisconsin. Margaret is a great home baker, and she makes this cake with any baking apple, such as Cortlands, or with Golden Delicious. The cake keeps well for about 3 days. This recipe can be halved and baked in an 8-inch square pan.

Makes one 13-x-9-inch cake; serves 12 to 16

2½	cups all-purpose flour
1	teaspoon baking powder
1	teaspoon baking soda
2	teaspoons ground cinnamon
¾	teaspoon salt
1	cup (2 sticks) unsalted butter, softened
1	cup sugar
½	cup packed dark brown sugar
2	large eggs
1	cup buttermilk or a mixture of plain yogurt thinned with milk
2	cups peeled, cored, diced (½-inch) apples (about 4 small)

TOPPING

½	cup sugar
3	tablespoons all-purpose flour
1½	teaspoons ground cinnamon
3	tablespoons cold unsalted butter, cut into pieces
¾	cup coarsely chopped pecans or almonds

1. Preheat the oven to 350 degrees F. Butter a 13-x-9-inch baking pan; set aside. Sift the flour, baking powder, baking soda, cinnamon and salt onto a sheet of wax paper; set aside.

2. In a large bowl, beat the butter with an electric mixer at medium-high speed until creamy. Gradually add the white and brown sugars and beat until light and fluffy. Add the eggs, one at a time, and beat until smooth. Add the dry ingredients alternately with the buttermilk or yogurt mixture, beginning and ending with the dry ingredients. Stir in the apples just until blended; do not overmix. Pour the mixture into the prepared pan.

3. **TOPPING:** In a bowl or food processor, cut together the sugar, flour, cinnamon and butter until crumbly. Stir in the nuts; scatter over the cake batter in an even layer.

4. Bake the cake until a toothpick inserted in the center emerges clean, about 50 minutes.

5. Cool on a wire rack. Cut into large squares and serve luke-warm or at room temperature, directly from the pan.

Prune Spice Cake

A tall round of tender cake, gently spiced, moist with yogurt and generously studded with prunes. This is adapted from a recipe from Washington, D.C.'s Vista International Hotel.

For the plumpest, most flavorful prunes you've ever tasted, write to Orchard Crest Farms in Salem, Oregon (see page 77 for mail-order information). They make this cake something special.

Makes one 8½- to 9½-inch single-layer cake; serves about 8

1	cup pitted prunes
2	cups all-purpose flour
1	teaspoon ground cinnamon
1	teaspoon fresh-grated nutmeg
½	teaspoon ground allspice
½	teaspoon ground cloves
1	teaspoon baking powder
½	teaspoon baking soda
¾	cup (1½ sticks) unsalted butter, softened
1	cup sugar
3	large eggs
½	cup low-fat or nonfat plain yogurt
	Confectioners' sugar, for sprinkling

1. Preheat the oven to 350 degrees F. Butter an 8½- to 9½-inch springform pan; set aside. Place the prunes in a small bowl; cover with hot tap water and set aside.

2. Sift the flour, cinnamon, nutmeg, allspice, cloves, baking powder and baking soda onto a sheet of wax paper; set aside. In a large bowl with an electric mixer at medium-high speed, cream the butter and sugar until very light, 8 to 10 minutes. Add the eggs, one at a time, mixing for about 30 seconds after each. Lower the speed to slow, and add the flour mixture alternately with the yogurt, beginning and ending with the flour; do not overmix.

3. Drain the prunes well. Chop into rough pieces; they can be as small as ½ inch or as large as prune quarters. Fold the prunes into the batter just until blended. Transfer the batter to the prepared pan; smooth the top.

4. Bake the cake until lightly golden and a toothpick inserted in the center emerges clean, 50 to 55 minutes.

5. Cool briefly in the pan on a wire rack. Run the tip of a knife around the sides of the cake to loosen it from the pan; carefully remove the sides of the pan. Sprinkle the cake with confectioners' sugar while still warm. Serve at room temperature, cut into wedges.

ALL-TIME-BEST SUMMER FRUIT TORTE

The recipe for this fruit torte first appeared in 1960 in Marian Burros' *The Elegant But Easy Cookbook* (co-authored by Lois Levine), a book my mother swears by.

After trying every conceivable variant on cake-with-fruit, I can tell you that for summer fruit, this cake is *it*. There is no improving on its basic simplicity—tender yellow cake, put together in minutes (I usually mix the batter by hand with a wooden spoon) and topped with whatever fruit is best that week (see variations).

The cake is also sturdy enough to transport when you've volunteered to bring dessert. I usually double the recipe, baking two cakes in foil pans. They always get eaten.

> *Makes one 8- or 9-inch single-layer cake; serves 6 to 8*

½	cup (1 stick) unsalted butter, softened
¾	cup sugar
1	teaspoon pure vanilla extract
2	large eggs
1	scant cup all-purpose flour, spooned lightly into a measuring cup
1	tablespoon baking powder
	Pinch salt
2	peaches or nectarines, peeled, pitted and sliced
½	cup blueberries
	Sugar, for sprinkling
	Ground cinnamon, for sprinkling

1. Preheat the oven to 350 degrees F. Butter an 8- or 9-inch round cake pan.

2. With an electric mixer at medium-high speed (or in a mixing bowl with a large wooden spoon), beat the butter until light.

Beat in the sugar and vanilla until fluffy; beat in the eggs, one at a time.

3. In a small bowl, stir together the flour, baking powder and salt. Add to the butter mixture and stir just until combined, no longer.

4. Scrape the batter into the pan; smooth the top. Scatter the fruit over the batter. Sprinkle with sugar and cinnamon.

5. Bake until the cake is golden brown and baked through, about 45 minutes.

6. Cool in the pan on a wire rack. Serve at room temperature, cut into wedges.

⌒ *Variations*

Marian Burros' original recipe calls for 12 purple plums, halved, pitted and arranged skin side up. Raspberries also work well. In fall or winter, substitute sliced apples and fresh cranberries.

"Once More (Sigh) . . ."

Once, after endless reader requests, Marian Burros printed the recipe for this torte yet again, surrounded by a dotted line and a drawing of a chef clipping it with a pair of scissors, under the heading "Once More (Sigh), the Plum Torte."

"It is beyond understanding," Mrs. Burros wrote, "why fans of the recipe do not just save it from year to year, instead of depending on its appearance in this column."

CRANBERRY UPSIDE-DOWN CAKE

This cake is made with spongecake instead of yellow cake and is topped with sugar-glazed cranberries, for a lighter, not-too-sweet variation on the upside-down theme. The recipe also works nicely with peaches or nectarines and with brown sugar substituted for white in the topping.

⟜ *Makes one 9- or 10-inch single-layer cake; serves about 8*

CRANBERRY TOPPING
- ¼ cup (½ stick) unsalted butter
- ⅔ cup sugar
- ½ teaspoon ground cinnamon
- 2 cups (about ½ pound) fresh or frozen (unthawed) cranberries, rinsed and picked over

SPONGECAKE
- ¾ cup all-purpose flour, spooned very lightly into a measuring cup
- ¼ cup cornstarch
- 1 teaspoon baking powder
  Pinch salt
- 4 large eggs
- ¾ cup sugar
  Grated zest of 1 small lemon
- 1 tablespoon unsalted butter, melted and cooled
- ½ teaspoon pure vanilla extract

  Vanilla-flavored whipped cream, for serving (optional)

1. **CRANBERRY TOPPING:** Preheat the oven to 350 degrees F. Melt the butter in a saucepan over medium heat. Stir in the sugar and cinnamon and cook until the sugar begins to dissolve. Pour the mixture into a 9-inch square cake pan or a 9- or 10-inch oven-proof skillet and tilt to coat well. Add the cranberries in an even layer; set aside.

2. **SPONGECAKE:** Sift the flour, cornstarch, baking powder and salt onto a sheet of wax paper; set aside. Place the eggs, sugar and lemon zest in a large bowl and beat with an electric mixer at medium-high speed until the mixture is very pale and thick and almost tripled in volume, about 10 minutes. Turn off the mixer.

3. Spoon a large dollop of the beaten egg mixture into a small bowl. Add the melted butter and the vanilla and fold together until blended; set the bowl aside.

4. Working fairly quickly, sprinkle the flour mixture, a few tablespoons at a time, over the large bowl of beaten eggs and fold in very lightly, but thoroughly. Quickly fold in the reserved butter-egg mixture. Pour the batter over the cranberries in the pan; spread gently to even the top.

5. Bake until the cake is puffed and lightly golden and the center springs back when pressed lightly, about 35 minutes.

6. Remove the cake from the oven, run the tip of a knife around the sides of the cake to loosen it, and immediately invert the cake onto a serving plate. Leave the pan on top of the cake. After a few minutes, carefully remove the pan. Serve the cake lukewarm or at room temperature, with whipped cream, if you like.

American Cake

In the 1930s, the rage of home bakers was pineapple upside-down cake (also known as pineapple skillet cake). My friend, pastry chef-author Nick Malgieri, tells me that his Italian-speaking grandmother, who never learned English, knew how to make only one American dessert—pineapple upside-down cake. And my Russian-born grandmother had a friend teach her how to make it, too.

RECIPES

Quintessential Coffee Cake
Brown Butter Coffee Cake
Hotel Cipriani's Cocoa-
  Swirled Vanilla
  Breakfast Cake
Spiced Sandtorte
Shoo-Fly Cake
Coffee Coffee Cake with
  Espresso Glaze
Hawaiian Coconut Coffee
  Cake
Real Old-Fashioned Crumb
  Buns
Moravian Sugar Cake
Prune-Filled Pecan-Caramel
  Sticky Buns
Prune Lekvar
"Bee-Sting" Cake
Alsatian Cinnamon Cake
Helmstetter Kugelhopf
St. Louis Gooey Butter Cake
Coiled Yeast Coffee Bread
  with Nut Filling

CHAPTER 9

COFFEE CAKES

*M*y favorite definition of coffee cake comes from a magazine editor I've known for years, who pronounced definitively: "A coffee cake is anything that gets crumbs all over you when you eat it." The father of a friend of mine says that when it comes to coffee cakes, he looks for "good dunkability—if it soaks up half the cup of coffee, then you've got something."

Coffee cakes can be anything from barely sweet, yeast-raised breads to simple moist cakes to sugar-glazed pastries. The group includes yeast rolls (especially when spiraled with cinnamon and iced), crumb cakes, some plain butter cakes and various quick breads that go by such names as "tea cakes," "tea breads" and the like.

The category of coffee cakes is somewhat amorphous, defined more by function—you eat them with coffee or tea, usually on their own, rather than after a meal—than by type. But coffee cakes can be conveniently, if roughly, divided into quick (non-yeasted) and yeast-leavened versions.

The simplest coffee cakes are those that are leavened with baking powder and/or baking soda rather than with yeast, which requires kneading and long rising times. Originally, some of these, like Brown Butter Coffee Cake (page 352), were developed to approximate traditional yeast coffee cakes but require just a fraction of the time. Recipes for these quick coffee cakes proliferated as chemical leaveners became widely available.

Among the yeast-risen coffee cakes, the Alsatian kugelhopf is the prototype. Baked in its characteristic fluted mold, kugelhopf is similar to challah and brioche—made with a yeasted dough, usually with eggs, plus a little butter and sugar—although it's not as rich as most cakes. It's meant to be nibbled with a cup of something hot.

Other yeast-leavened coffee cakes, such as old-fashioned crumb buns (originally called *streuselkuchen*), moist Moravian sugar cake, with its dimpled butter-and-sugar surface, and "Bee-Sting" Cake (*bienenstich*) are of Germanic origin. Also included in this collection is a distinctive coffee cake from northeastern Italy that reflects the baking influences of Vienna and Budapest, the culinary centers from which the coffee-cake gospel spread throughout Eastern Europe. In America, cinnamon or "sticky" buns, developed in Philadelphia and currently riding a wave of popularity, are also prime examples of the yeast-raised coffee cake.

Not quite so hard to define is what makes a good coffee cake. Real butter, for one. Those wishfully named "butter horns," "Danish pastries" and "sweet rolls" (a Midwestern regionalism) frequently are made with fat you wouldn't allow anywhere near your kitchen. A good coffee cake should be freshly baked, preferably so fresh that you're enjoying it still warm from the oven.

Because coffee cakes are served on their own rather than as the conclusion to a meal, they signal a time for activity to stop. This, I suspect, is the real reason everyone loves them. Coffee cakes give us a chance to nibble something, to take a few moments to chat or just sit in peace.

Nada Neumann, a friend of my mother's who grew up in the former Yugoslavia, went to school in Geneva and now teaches French in northern New Jersey, remembers how coffee and cake provided a welcome respite when she was a child.

"My maternal grandmother was Austrian," Nada told me. "She entertained very frequently with coffee and cake in the afternoon. We had a cook, and all pastry was made from scratch—no mixes were ever used.

"The afternoon snack, called *jause* in German, was our family's favorite meal. The art of conversation was part of this delightful entertainment. It was loving, intelligent, informative and funny. I wish we had time for *jause* today."

Quintessential Coffee Cake

(Brown Sugar Buttermilk Crumb Cake)

Quick to put together, this cake has a lovely texture—moist and substantial but still pleasantly light, with a rich caramel-like flavor from the brown sugar. For ease, dependability and quick, homey goodness, there is no better coffee cake than this. The flour, butter and sugar are cut together until crumbly; then part of the mixture is set aside for a crumb topping. The rest is moistened with liquid and used as the base of the cake. The recipe comes from Susan Peery, an editor at *The Old Farmer's Almanac*, who got the recipe from her German grandmother.

⟜ *Makes one 13-x-9-inch cake or two 8-inch square cakes; serves about 12*

¾	cup (1½ sticks) unsalted butter, softened
1½	cups packed light brown sugar
2½	cups all-purpose flour
1	teaspoon baking soda
1	cup buttermilk, sour cream, or a mixture of plain yogurt thinned with milk
1	large egg, beaten
1	teaspoon pure vanilla extract
½	teaspoon salt

1. Preheat the oven to 350 degrees F. Butter a 13-x-9-inch baking pan or two 8-inch square pans.

2. In a medium bowl, cut the butter into the brown sugar and flour with a pastry blender or 2 knives until crumbly. Remove and reserve 1 cup of the mixture for the topping.

3. Beat the baking soda into the buttermilk, sour cream or thinned yogurt and add to the flour mixture. Add the egg, vanilla and salt and stir until smooth. Scrape the batter into the prepared pan; smooth the top. Sprinkle the reserved crumbs over the top.

4. Bake the cake until golden brown, about 30 minutes.

5. Cool to lukewarm on a wire rack. Cut into rectangles and serve warm or at room temperature, directly from the pan.

⌒ *Variation*

COFFEE CAKE WITH NUT STREUSEL: My friend Margaret
Fox, who owns Café Beaujolais in Mendocino, California, is
famous for a breakfast coffee cake that her regulars will not let her
take off the menu. It's almost identical to this crumb cake. Try
Margaret's addition of nuts to the streusel topping:

Remove and set aside ¾ cup of the crumb mixture (instead of
1 cup) in step 2. To this mixture, add 1 cup chopped walnuts or
pecans plus 1 teaspoon ground cinnamon. Proceed as directed.

BROWN BUTTER COFFEE CAKE

This moist, flavorful cake from Kim Anderson, former pastry chef at the spectacular Ritz-Carlton on the Gulf of Mexico in Naples, Florida, is one of the best in this collection. It's similar to a sour cream coffee cake but is made with yogurt instead, and with a small amount of whole-wheat flour. The brown butter glaze really makes it.

Because it's so moist, this cake keeps well. You can also bake it in 2 loaf pans; timing is included for both pan sizes.

Makes one 10-inch tube cake or two 8-x-4-inch loaves; serves 12 to 16

COFFEE CAKE

1½	cups all-purpose flour
1½	cups whole-wheat flour, or substitute all-purpose flour
1½	teaspoons baking powder
1½	teaspoons baking soda
¾	teaspoon salt
½	teaspoon ground cinnamon
¾	cup (1½ sticks) unsalted butter, softened
1½	cups sugar
3	large eggs
1½	teaspoons pure vanilla extract
1½	cups low-fat plain yogurt

FILLING

¾	cup coarsely chopped walnuts, pecans, hazelnuts (skins removed), almonds or black walnuts
½	cup packed light or dark brown sugar
1½	teaspoons ground cinnamon
½	teaspoon fresh-grated nutmeg

BROWN BUTTER GLAZE

¼	cup (½ stick) unsalted butter, softened
2	cups sifted confectioners' sugar
1	teaspoon pure vanilla extract
2	tablespoons milk

1. Preheat the oven to 350 degrees F. Butter and flour a 10-inch Bundt or tube pan or two 8-x-4-inch loaf pans; set aside.

2. **COFFEE CAKE:** Combine all of the dry ingredients in a bowl and stir to combine thoroughly; set aside. In a large bowl,

beat the butter and sugar with an electric mixer on medium-high speed until combined. Add 1 of the eggs and the vanilla and beat until very light. Add the remaining 2 eggs, one at a time, and beat until very smooth and creamy.

3. Lower the speed to slow and add the dry ingredients alternately with the yogurt, beginning and ending with the dry mixture. Don't overbeat.

4. **FILLING:** Combine all of the ingredients in a small bowl. Spread about ⅓ of the batter in each cake pan; sprinkle with ⅓ of the filling. Repeat the layering 2 more times.

5. Bake until the cake is golden brown and a toothpick inserted in the center emerges clean, usually 40 to 55 minutes, depending on the pan(s) used.

6. Cool in the pan(s) on a wire rack for 10 to 15 minutes. Run the tip of a knife around the cake to loosen it from the sides and tube of the pan and unmold. (Glaze while the cake is still warm.)

7. **BROWN BUTTER GLAZE:** While the cake is baking, melt the butter in a heavy saucepan over medium heat. Cook until the butter is nut-brown, 5 to 7 minutes; do not burn. Pour the brown butter into a bowl, leaving any dark sediment or foam behind.

8. Add the confectioners' sugar, vanilla and milk and stir until smooth. Add more milk, if needed, so the glaze will coat the cake evenly. (If the mixture becomes too thin, sift in a little more confectioners' sugar.) Brush the glaze over the surface of the cake, coating evenly. Or, if you like, spoon the glaze over the top of the cake and let it drip down the sides. Cut the cake with a serrated knife and serve at room temperature.

Always Delicious

If someone tells you, "I've got a great coffee cake recipe for you," chances are it's a sour-cream coffee cake, a rich dough layered in a deep tube pan with a cinnamon-nut filling. Everyone makes it, and it's always delicious. The cake may have Hungarian origins as *Szegedin* cake, from the city in southeast Hungary where sour cream is used prodigally.

HOTEL CIPRIANI'S COCOA-SWIRLED VANILLA BREAKFAST CAKE

(*TARALLO ABRUZZESE*)

In Italy, Greece and throughout the Mediterranean, housewives use olive oil in cake baking. It's important to use a mild-flavored type, not extra-virgin (several found in supermarkets are bland and work well for baking). The oil keeps the cake moist, but its flavor shouldn't intrude.

With its swirled vanilla and chocolate batters and sweet touch of orange, this is a nice, light cake to have with morning coffee. It's an adaptation of a cake served for breakfast at the Hotel Cipriani in Venice, one of the world's most luxurious resorts, where you breakfast on a sunny terrace overlooking a lagoon.

Makes one 10-inch tube cake; serves about 12

4	large eggs, separated
1	cup sugar
	Grated zest of 1 orange
½	cup bland olive oil
1	teaspoon pure vanilla extract
1⅓	cups milk
1	tablespoon baking powder
2¼	cups all-purpose flour, sifted
2	tablespoons unsweetened cocoa powder
	Confectioners' sugar, for sprinkling

1. Preheat the oven to 375 degrees F. Butter and flour a 10-inch tube or Bundt pan; set aside.

2. In a bowl with an electric mixer, beat the egg yolks, ¾ cup of the sugar and the orange zest until very pale and creamy, 4 to 5 minutes. Beat in the olive oil and vanilla. In a measuring cup, stir together the milk and the baking powder; add to the batter. Lower the speed to slow and mix in the flour; do not overbeat.

3. Beat the egg whites until frothy; gradually add the remaining ¼ cup sugar and beat until the whites are nearly stiff. Fold about ¼ of the whites into the batter; gently fold in the remaining whites.

4. In a small bowl, stir the cocoa with about ½ cup of the batter; set aside. Pour about half of the vanilla batter into the prepared pan; top with the cocoa batter. With a butter knife, swirl the batters together. Top with the remaining vanilla batter.

5. Bake until the cake is golden, shrinks away from the sides of the pan and springs back when pressed gently, 45 to 50 minutes.

6. Cool the cake in the pan on a wire rack for 10 to 15 minutes. Run the tip of a knife around the sides and tube to loosen the cake from the pan; unmold carefully. Sprinkle the cake with confectioners' sugar while still warm. Cool completely and sprinkle with sugar again. Cut the cake with a serrated knife.

SPICED SANDTORTE

In every *konditerei* (bakery-café) in Germany, you'll find buttery plain sandtorte, baked in fluted kugelhopf molds and sprinkled with a snowdrift of powdered sugar.

Similar to pound cake, this buttery cake is named for its sandy texture. It's one of the best unadorned cakes, the kind of thing people keep in the kitchen just to "have something around" in case people drop by.

This is a gently spiced variation. It keeps well and isn't too temperamental to travel on a picnic or a boat trip.

Makes one 8- or 9-inch tube cake; serves about 10

¼	cup chopped walnuts
1¼	cups sifted cake flour (not self-rising)
¾	cup sifted cornstarch
2	teaspoons baking powder
2	teaspoons ground cardamom
1	teaspoon ground ginger
1	teaspoon ground cinnamon
¾	teaspoon fresh-grated nutmeg
¼	teaspoon salt
1	cup (2 sticks) unsalted butter, softened
1	cup sugar
4	large eggs
2	teaspoons pure vanilla extract
	Confectioners' sugar, for sprinkling

1. Preheat the oven to 325 degrees F. Butter and flour an 8- or 9-inch kugelhopf, Bundt or tube pan. Scatter the walnuts in the bottom of the pan; set aside. Resift the cake flour and cornstarch with the baking powder, cardamom, ginger, cinnamon, nutmeg and salt onto a sheet of wax paper; set aside.

2. Beat the butter with an electric mixer at medium-high speed until light. Add the sugar and beat until very fluffy, about 5 minutes. Add the eggs, one at a time; add the vanilla and beat until smooth. Lower the speed to slow and add the dry ingredients all at once. Mix just until combined; do not overmix. Scrape the batter into the prepared pan; rap the pan on a surface to eliminate any air bubbles. Smooth the top.

3. Bake until the cake is pale gold and a toothpick inserted near the center emerges clean, about 55 minutes.

4. Cool the cake in the pan on a wire rack for about 5 minutes. Run the tip of a knife around the sides and tube to loosen the cake from the pan; invert onto the rack and lift off the pan. Cool to room temperature. To transport, return the cake to the pan. Sprinkle with confectioners' sugar before serving.

SHOO-FLY CAKE

This recipe is an ingenious adaptation of shoo-fly pie, the Pennsylvania Dutch favorite that has a soft molasses filling and a crumb topping. The moist cake is true to the flavors of the original, but because you don't have to roll out a crust, you can put it together in the time it takes to preheat the oven. This recipe can be halved and baked in an 8-inch square pan.

Makes one 13-x-9-inch cake; serves 12 to 16

4	cups all-purpose flour
2⅓	cups packed (1 pound) light brown sugar
1	cup (2 sticks) unsalted butter, cut into pieces, softened
2	cups boiling water
1	cup molasses
2	teaspoons baking soda

1. Preheat the oven to 350 degrees F. Butter a 13-x-9-inch baking pan; sprinkle with flour, tapping out the excess; set aside.

2. In a bowl with an electric mixer on low speed, combine the flour, brown sugar and butter and work into fine crumbs. Remove and reserve 1½ cups of the crumbs for the topping.

3. In a small bowl, combine the boiling water, molasses and baking soda; add to the mixing bowl and beat on medium speed until the batter is smooth and thin. Pour the batter into the prepared baking pan. Sprinkle the reserved crumbs over the top.

4. Bake the cake until a toothpick inserted in the center emerges clean, about 40 minutes.

5. Cool the cake to room temperature in the pan on a wire rack. Cut into big squares and serve directly from the pan.

This is my Aunt Anna's recipe," says Stephanie Richardson, a friend in the food business. "But my mother perfected it. She makes it for picnics and always for family gatherings."

COFFEE COFFEE CAKE WITH ESPRESSO GLAZE

I developed this cake, made with and meant to be served with coffee, a few years ago for a magazine article. After that, I forgot about it for quite a while. Years later, *Gourmet* included it in its collection of 50 dessert recipes to commemorate the magazine's 50th year.

Makes one 9-inch tube cake; serves 10 to 12

2	cups sifted all-purpose flour
1	teaspoon baking powder
½	teaspoon baking soda
¼	teaspoon salt
¾	cup (1½ sticks) unsalted butter, softened
1	cup sugar
2	large eggs
2	teaspoons pure vanilla extract
1	cup sour cream or plain yogurt
2	tablespoons instant coffee, preferably instant espresso powder
1	tablespoon hot water

ESPRESSO GLAZE

¾	cup confectioners' sugar
2-3	tablespoons strong-brewed coffee
1½	teaspoons instant espresso powder

1. Preheat the oven to 350 degrees F, with a rack at the center. Butter a 9-inch kugelhopf, Bundt or tube pan; set aside. Resift the flour with the baking powder, baking soda and salt onto a sheet of wax paper; set aside.

2. In a bowl, beat the butter with an electric mixer at medium speed until creamy. Gradually add the sugar and beat until light and fluffy. Add the eggs, one at a time, and mix until smooth; add the vanilla. Lower the speed to slow and add the flour mixture alternately with the sour cream or yogurt, beginning and ending with the dry ingredients. Do not overmix.

3. In a small bowl, stir together the instant coffee powder and hot water. Add about ⅓ of the cake batter and fold together until combined.

4. Pour ½ of the sour cream batter into the prepared pan. Carefully top with the coffee-flavored batter, spreading evenly. Spread the remaining sour cream batter on top; smooth the surface.

5. Bake until the cake is golden, the sides shrink away from the pan, and a toothpick inserted in the center emerges clean, about 50 minutes.

6. Cool the cake in the pan on a wire rack for about 30 minutes.

7. **ESPRESSO GLAZE:** Sift the confectioners' sugar into a medium bowl. Stir together 2 tablespoons of the brewed coffee and the instant espresso powder; stir into the confectioners' sugar. Add more brewed coffee, if necessary, to bring the glaze to a pourable consistency.

8. Run the tip of a knife around the sides and tube of the pan to loosen the cake; unmold. Brush the glaze over the top, letting some run down the sides. Let the glaze set. Serve cut into wedges. If not serving immediately, cover the cake with plastic wrap.

HAWAIIAN
COCONUT COFFEE CAKE

Yes, this really is from Hawaii. It's a moist cake, drenched with coconut milk. The recipe is adapted from one by Simon Waters, a former pastry chef at a resort on the big island. Try it for breakfast or brunch.

༄ *Makes one 9-to-10-inch cake; serves 8*

1¾	cups all-purpose flour, spooned lightly into measuring cups
¼	cup cornstarch
1	teaspoon baking soda
1	teaspoon baking powder
	Pinch salt
¾	cup (1½ sticks) unsalted butter, softened
1	cup sugar
3	large eggs
1½	teaspoons pure vanilla extract
1¼	cups low-fat plain yogurt
1¼	cups grated fresh or store-bought coconut, or more as needed (see page 396 for instructions on using fresh coconut)

COCONUT GLAZE

⅓	cup canned coconut cream, such as Coco López
2	teaspoons cold water

1. Preheat the oven to 350 degrees F. Generously butter a 9- to 10-inch springform pan; set aside. Sift the flour, cornstarch, baking soda, baking powder and salt onto a sheet of wax paper; set aside.

2. Cream the butter and sugar with an electric mixer at medium-high speed until very light, 6 to 8 minutes. Add the eggs, one at a time, and beat until smooth; beat in the vanilla. Lower the speed to slow and add the flour mixture alternately with the yogurt, beginning and ending with the flour. Gently pour the batter into the prepared pan; smooth the top. Evenly sprinkle with the coconut.

3. Bake until the cake is golden and a toothpick inserted in the center emerges clean, 50 to 55 minutes. If, after about 20 minutes, the cake is browning too quickly, loosely cover with foil.

4. Cool the cake on a wire rack for 10 to 15 minutes. Carefully run the tip of a knife around the sides and remove the sides of the springform pan.

5. **COCONUT GLAZE:** While the cake is cooling, heat the coconut cream and water in a saucepan over medium heat, stirring, just until the mixture is warm. Poke the entire surface of the cake gently with a fork or thin skewer. While the cake is still warm, slowly spoon the warm glaze over it and let it soak in. Cool the cake completely before serving.

REAL OLD-FASHIONED CRUMB BUNS

A good crumb bun is hard to find. Tipped off by a friend who is a devotee of this homey coffee cake, I tracked down Michael and Wendy London at Rock Hill Bakehouse in Gansevoort, New York. They are pioneer artisan bakers, who produce some of this country's best wood-oven-baked breads. Their crumb buns are light-years from the commercial variety; the yeast dough, rich with sweet butter and sour cream, is showered with plenty of crumbly streusel. Crumb buns—and coffee cakes in general—don't get much better than this.

These buns are best served warm and should be served on the day they are baked. Or freeze them, wrapped tightly, as soon as they are cool. Plan ahead: The dough needs to chill overnight.

⌇ Serves 20

DOUGH

2	packages active dry yeast
3	tablespoons lukewarm water
¼	cup plus 1 tablespoon sugar
1	cup (2 sticks) cold unsalted butter
4½	cups all-purpose flour
1½	teaspoons fine sea salt or kosher salt
3	large egg yolks
¾	cup sour cream
	Grated zest of 1 orange

STREUSEL

1⅓	cups all-purpose flour
2½	teaspoons ground cinnamon
⅔	cup sugar
1	teaspoon pure vanilla extract
11	tablespoons (1 stick plus 3 tablespoons) cold unsalted butter, thinly sliced
	Confectioners' sugar, for sprinkling

1. **DOUGH:** In a large bowl, stir together the yeast, water and the 1 tablespoon sugar. Let stand until the yeast bubbles, about 10 minutes.

2. Meanwhile, loosely wrap the butter in a large sheet of plastic wrap. Beat the butter, using a rolling pin as a bat, until the butter is malleable but still cold; set aside.

Choices

When I was growing up, my mother would take my little brother, Ken, and me into the bakery at the end of our street, and we could each choose one thing. For me, the choice was always between a sugar bun or a crumb bun.

Crumb buns are probably derived from German *streuselkuchen*. (Pronounced "stroy-sel," *streusel* means "litter" or "dust" in German.) A panful of yeast dough is topped with crumbs, baked in a large sheet and then cut into squares.

3. Add the remaining ¼ cup sugar, the flour, salt, egg yolks, sour cream and orange zest to the yeast mixture. With an electric mixer fitted with a dough hook or by hand with a wooden spoon, mix on low speed to blend; raise the speed to high and mix until well blended, several minutes.

4. Gradually add the butter and beat to form a soft, but not sticky, dough that just barely leaves the side of the bowl. Beat or knead until very smooth and elastic, 6 to 8 minutes. Transfer the dough to a buttered bowl; turn to coat all sides with butter. Lay a sheet of plastic wrap over the top and refrigerate overnight, until the dough is cold and has risen to double its volume.

5. STREUSEL: In a food processor, combine the flour, cinnamon and sugar. Add the vanilla and pulse to mix. Add the butter, a few pieces at a time, and pulse until the mixture crumbles into pieces about twice the size of peas. Refrigerate or freeze the streusel if not using it immediately.

6. Line the bottom of an 18-x-12-inch or 15½-x-10½-inch jellyroll pan with parchment or wax paper; butter the paper and the sides of the pan. Roll out the dough on a lightly floured surface to the size of the pan; fit the dough into the pan. With a sharp knife, cut the dough into 20 rectangles. Cover with a sheet of plastic wrap, and let rise in a warm place until halfway risen or about 1½ times its volume, usually 1 to 1½ hours.

7. Scatter about ⅓ of the streusel mixture over the half-risen dough. Cover again and let rise until fully doubled in volume, 1 to 1½ hours longer. When fully risen, scatter the remaining streusel over the dough.

8. Preheat the oven to 350 degrees F. Bake until the streusel is lightly browned and the edges are golden, usually 30 to 35 minutes. (The timing can vary with the pan used; do not overbake.)

9. Let cool briefly in the pan on a wire rack. Lightly dust with confectioners' sugar; the streusel should still show through. Serve warm. (Rewarm any buns that are not served soon after baking. The cooled buns can also be wrapped and frozen.)

NOTE: For information on ordering the Londons' extraordinary breads by mail, write to Rock Hill Bakehouse, 19 Exchange Street, Glens Falls, New York 12801; (518) 615-0777; www.rock hillbakehouse.com.

MORAVIAN SUGAR CAKE

This deliciously moist yeast-dough cake is baked in a sheet pan and cut into large squares or rectangles. Characteristically, the dimpled dough is topped with a generous blanket of spiced brown sugar and drizzled with melted butter.

The potato in the dough is the secret of the cake's moist texture—leftovers don't dry out the next day. This quickly put-together version is adapted from an old recipe unearthed by Karyl Bannister (see page 319 for information about Karyl's newsletter, *Cook & Tell*).

Makes twelve 3-inch-square servings

2	packages active dry yeast
¼	cup plus 1 tablespoon sugar
¼	cup lukewarm milk
3	cups all-purpose flour
½	cup cooked mashed potato (leftovers are fine)
6	tablespoons (¾ stick) unsalted butter, melted and cooled slightly
2	large eggs
½	teaspoon salt
¼	cup milk

TOPPING

½	scant cup packed light brown sugar
1½	teaspoons ground cinnamon
¼	cup (½ stick) unsalted butter, melted and cooled slightly

1. In a large bowl, stir together the yeast, the 1 tablespoon sugar and the lukewarm milk. Set aside in a warm place until bubbly, about 10 minutes.

2. Add the remaining ¼ cup sugar, 1½ cups of the flour, the potato, butter, eggs, salt and milk to the yeast mixture. Beat with an electric mixer fitted with a dough hook or by hand with a wooden spoon until the dough comes together; it will be very liquid. Mix for 2 minutes longer. Add the remaining 1½ cups flour and knead until the dough is very smooth, about 5 minutes longer. It will still be very sticky.

3. Place the dough in a buttered bowl; turn to coat on all sides. Cover loosely with plastic wrap. Let rise in a warm place until doubled in bulk, about 1 hour.

4. Butter the bottom and sides of a jellyroll pan or a 13-x-9-inch baking pan. Punch down the dough and set it in the prepared pan in a mass; don't fit it into the pan. Let rise in a warm place until partially risen but not doubled, about 30 minutes.

5. Pat out the dough with your fingertips to cover the pan evenly.

6. TOPPING: Combine the brown sugar and cinnamon and sprinkle all over the dough. Gently dimple the dough with a finger and drizzle the melted butter over the top. Let rise until doubled in volume, about 30 minutes. Meanwhile, preheat the oven to 375 degrees F. Place a large sheet of foil on the lower oven rack if you are using a baking pan with shallow sides to catch any butter that drips over the sides of the pan.

7. Bake the cake until deep golden brown and crisp around the edges, usually 15 to 16 minutes.

8. Cool briefly, cut into rectangles and serve warm. Once cool, this coffee cake keeps well, wrapped, and can be reheated, if you like.

Accidental Improvement

This cake has been a favorite of the Moravians since the German-born immigrants settled in Pennsylvania and North Carolina in the 18th century. As early as 1837, in fact, Eliza Leslie included a recipe for Moravian Sugar Cake in *Directions for Cookery*.

Out in Pennsylvania Dutch country, author-restaurateur Betty Groff recalls an accident that actually improved a friend's mother's sugar cake: "The dough was covered with linen cloths and set to rise overnight, and in the morning, it was discovered that the cat had apparently pranced across the cakes. Her mother filled the paw holes with extra butter and sugar and baked the cakes. They were the best ever!"

PRUNE-FILLED PECAN-CARAMEL STICKY BUNS

C innamon buns were first popularized in Philadelphia in the 19th century. When made well—with real butter, rarely found in commercial versions—a good cinnamon sticky bun can be among the most delicious and evocative of all baked goods. In this rendition, the dough is spiraled around a moist orange-scented prune filling.

Makes 12 buns; serves 12

DOUGH

¼	cup plus 2 tablespoons lukewarm water
1½	teaspoons active dry yeast (slightly more than ½ package)
2½	cups all-purpose flour
3	tablespoons sugar
½	teaspoon salt
¼	cup lukewarm milk
1	teaspoon pure vanilla extract
2	large eggs
¼	cup (½ stick) unsalted butter, cut into pieces, softened

TOPPING

¾	cup packed light brown sugar
6	tablespoons (¾ stick) unsalted butter, melted
2	tablespoons dark or light corn syrup
¾	cup pecan pieces
1	cup Prune *Lekvar* (recipe follows) or store-bought prune puree

1. **DOUGH:** In a large bowl, combine the 2 tablespoons lukewarm water and the yeast; let stand until bubbly, about 10 minutes.

2. Add the remaining ¼ cup lukewarm water, the flour, sugar, salt, milk and vanilla to the yeast mixture. Beat with an electric mixer fitted with a dough hook or by hand with a wooden spoon until combined. Beat in the eggs. Add the butter, a few pieces at a time, and beat on medium speed until the dough is silky and smooth, about 5 minutes. It will still be very sticky.

3. Lightly sprinkle the surface of the dough with flour. Cover

C innamon buns, sticky buns, "stickies," *schnecken* ("snails"), icing-topped "sugar buns"—all are similar.

the bowl with plastic wrap, and then with a kitchen towel; let rise in a warm place until doubled in bulk, about 1 hour.

4. **Topping:** In a bowl, whisk the brown sugar, melted butter and corn syrup until well combined. Pour into a 13-x-9-inch baking pan and spread over the bottom. Evenly scatter with the pecans; set aside.

5. Punch down the dough and turn it out on a well-floured surface. Pat or roll out into a 16-x-12-inch rectangle. Gently spread the dough with the prune *lekvar*. Beginning with a short end, roll up the dough into a neat, compact cylinder. Pinch the seams to seal. Cut the cylinder into 12 equal slices.

6. Arrange the slices, cut sides down, in the prepared pan, leaving a little space between them. Cover the pan with a kitchen towel. Let rise until doubled in bulk, 45 to 50 minutes.

7. Preheat the oven to 350 degrees F. Uncover the pan. Bake until the buns are golden brown, 25 to 30 minutes.

8. Invert the pan onto a serving platter; carefully lift off the pan. Cool the sticky buns to lukewarm. Pull apart and serve.

Prune *Lekvar*
(Thick Prune Puree)

Makes about 3 cups

1½	pounds (about 3 cups) pitted prunes
1¼	cups fresh orange juice
⅓	cup sugar

1. In a nonreactive saucepan, combine the prunes with 1 cup of the orange juice and the sugar. Cover and cook over medium-low heat until the prunes are very tender and have absorbed the liquid, about 20 minutes. Set aside to cool for 10 minutes.

2. Puree the mixture in a food processor or food mill until as smooth as possible. Stir in the remaining ¼ cup orange juice and a little more sugar to taste, if needed. Cover and refrigerate until needed. The *lekvar* will keep in the refrigerator for up to 1 month.

"BEE-STING" CAKE
(*BIENENSTICH*)

At the Allwood Bakery in Clifton, New Jersey, this cake used to be baked in huge sheets. The yeast dough was filled with custard and topped with a burnished nut glaze *bienenstich* ("bee-sting" glaze, in German). Now, the bakers there make it smaller and only on Saturdays. When I was 9, this was my idea of heaven.

This version has no custard filling; if you'd like to fill it, carefully split the cooled cake with a large serrated knife, and fill with Vanilla Pastry Cream on page 397.

Makes two 9-inch square cakes; each serves about 8

DOUGH
2	packages active dry yeast
¼	cup lukewarm water
¾	cup (1½ sticks) unsalted butter, softened
¾	cup sugar
2	large eggs
2	large egg yolks
½	teaspoon salt
1	teaspoon pure vanilla extract
½	cup lukewarm milk
½	cup sour cream or plain yogurt
3¾-4½	cups all-purpose flour
2	tablespoons unsalted butter, melted

BEE-STING GLAZE
⅔	cup packed light brown sugar
6	tablespoons (¾ stick) unsalted butter
¼	cup plus 2 tablespoons heavy cream
¼	cup plus 2 tablespoons honey
¼	teaspoon fresh lemon juice
1⅓	cups (about 5 ounces) sliced or slivered blanched almonds

1. **DOUGH:** In a small bowl, sprinkle the yeast over the lukewarm water. Let stand until foamy, about 10 minutes.

2. In a large bowl with an electric mixer fitted with a dough hook on medium speed or by hand with a wooden spoon, cream the butter and the sugar until light and fluffy. Beat in the whole eggs, one at a time, mixing well after each addition. Add the egg

yolks, salt, vanilla, milk, sour cream or yogurt and yeast mixture; beat until smooth, about 2 minutes.

3. Gradually beat in 3¾ cups of the flour until a very soft dough forms. Continue to beat, adding additional flour, if necessary, until the dough is smooth and elastic, 8 to 10 minutes. Place the dough in an oiled bowl, turn to coat and cover with a damp towel. Let rise in a warm place until doubled, about 45 minutes, or cover and refrigerate overnight.

4. Butter two 9-inch square cake pans. Punch down the dough and divide it in half. Press 1 piece of dough evenly over the bottom of each pan. Brush the top of each with 1 tablespoon of the melted butter. Cover and let rise in a warm place until doubled, 40 to 50 minutes.

5. **BEE-STING GLAZE:** In a small, heavy saucepan, stir together the brown sugar, butter, cream and honey over medium heat. Bring to a boil, stirring to dissolve the sugar; boil for 30 seconds. Remove from the heat and stir in the lemon juice and almonds. Let cool slightly, 8 to 10 minutes. Preheat the oven to 375 degrees F.

6. Drizzle the warm glaze evenly over both cakes. Bake until the nuts are golden brown, 30 to 35 minutes. Let cool to lukewarm or room temperature in the pans on a wire rack. Cut into squares and serve from the pans. *(The cakes can also be wrapped tightly in plastic and frozen for up to 2 weeks.)*

ALSATIAN CINNAMON CAKE
(*GÂTEAU À LA CANELLE*)

Unlike most traditional kugelhopfs, this dough contains no eggs, bringing the butter flavor forward. This cake is best eaten on the day it is baked; leftovers should be rewarmed or toasted. Offer sweet butter on the side.

⟿ *Makes one 10- to 11-inch or two 8-inch single-layer cakes; serves about 12*

KUGELHOPF DOUGH
⅓   cup golden raisins
2   tablespoons cognac or brandy
¼   cup plus 2 teaspoons sugar
1   package active dry yeast
1½   cups lukewarm milk
4   cups all-purpose flour
¾   teaspoon coarse (kosher) salt
½   cup (1 stick) unsalted butter, softened

FILLING
1   egg yolk, stirred together with 1 teaspoon cold water
⅔   cup crème fraîche (see note) or plain or vanilla yogurt (or use ⅓ cup heavy cream, whipped until not quite stiff)
¼   cup sugar
1   tablespoon ground cinnamon
⅓   cup sliced almonds
2   tablespoons cold unsalted butter, cut into small pieces

1. **KUGELHOPF DOUGH:** In a small bowl, combine the raisins, cognac or brandy and 1 teaspoon of the sugar; set aside. In another small bowl, combine the yeast with 1 teaspoon of the sugar and ¼ cup of the lukewarm milk. Set aside until foamy, about 10 minutes.

2. In large bowl with an electric mixer fitted with a dough hook, in a food processor or by hand with a wooden spoon, combine the remaining ¼ cup sugar, the flour and salt. Make a well in the center, and with the machine running, add the yeast mixture, ¼ cup of the milk and the butter, a few pieces at a time. Add just enough of the remaining 1 cup milk to make a dough that is quite moist but not sticky. Knead with the mixer for about 8 minutes, process for 1 full minute in a food processor or knead by hand for

10 to 15 minutes. Adjust the consistency of the dough with more milk or flour as needed.

3. Turn out the dough onto a lightly floured surface and knead by hand, working in the raisins and a little of their soaking liquid until the raisins are incorporated. Knead for 2 to 3 minutes longer, until the dough is quite moist but not sticky. The dough should be very smooth and elastic.

4. Place the dough in a buttered bowl and turn to coat with butter. Cover and let rise in a warm place until doubled in volume, about 2 hours or overnight in the refrigerator.

5. Generously butter a 10- to:11-inch fluted tart or quiche pan (or two 8-inch round cake pans). Punch the dough down and press it into the bottom and sides of the pan, forming an even edge. Cover with plastic wrap or a cloth and let rise until the dough has doubled and risen over the rim of the pan, 45 minutes or longer. Be sure to let the dough rise fully.

6. FILLING: Preheat the oven to 350 degrees F. Brush the edges of the dough with the egg yolk mixture. Spread the crème fraîche, yogurt or whipped cream over the dough, leaving a 1-inch border uncovered. Combine the sugar and the cinnamon in a small bowl; sprinkle a thick layer of cinnamon sugar over the surface of the dough. (You may need a little extra cinnamon sugar if you are making 2 smaller cakes.) Sprinkle the almonds on top; dot with the cold butter.

7. Bake until the cake is nicely browned on top, about 35 minutes.

8. Cool to lukewarm in the pan on a wire rack. Cut into wedges and serve warm, with sweet butter alongside. Rewarm or toast leftovers before serving.

NOTE: Crème fraîche is available in specialty food stores, or you can approximate your own (see page 624).

"Baking Is My Hobby"

Mrs. Jeanine Vongerichten and her husband, Georges, were visiting their son, celebrated New York chef Jean-Georges, from their tiny village near Strasbourg in Alsace. When I asked her for an old family dessert recipe, Jean-Georges piped up immediately: "*Oh, Maman, gâteau à la canelle!*" Mrs. Vongerichten happily agreed to share the old family recipe and insisted on making it for me herself.

"I make the dough on Saturdays," Mrs. Vongerichten said, kneading vigorously in her son's restaurant pastry kitchen, "and put it to rise. Then, I go out and do my shopping. I bake it Saturday night, for Sunday.

"I learned to bake when I was growing up," she says, "my uncle had a *boulangerie-pâtisserie*, and baking is my hobby."

371

ABOUT KUGELHOPF

*K*ugelhopf, the golden yeast coffee cake baked in its namesake decorative mold, is, to me, the embodiment of coffee cake: plain, not too rich, unfussy, undecorated—and heady with yeasty, buttery flavor.

For holidays, Alsatian bakers make kugelhopfs in special shapes: hearts or babies for an engagement or a wedding, bunnies and lambs for Easter, stars for Christmas. You can also find kugelhopf in Germany's Black Forest, in Vienna (where it is known as gugelhopf) and in every one of Budapest's still-thriving coffeehouses.

The history of this bread-cake is in doubt; some say that it existed as early as 1500. There are earthenware molds that date from the 18th century, and virtually all European cookbooks from the early 19th century on include a kugelhopf recipe.

Several sources say that when Marie Antoinette arrived in France from her native Austria in the late-18th century, she brought the kugelhopf with her across the Rhine and into Alsace before arriving in Paris. (Alsatian legend even holds that it was the Magi who left the kugelhopf in Alsace, en route to Bethlehem.)

Credit for it is also frequently given to Stanislas Lesczynski, once the King of Poland, who lived in exile in Lorraine. But kugelhopf is so basic that attributing it to a single source is probably futile.

In Alsace, kugelhopf pans are made of the local rustic earthenware pottery, traditionally painted with folk motifs. One Alsatian chef told me that you can't turn out a decent kugelhopf until the pan has been used steadily for at least 15 years.

Consider keeping a couple of different sizes of these fluted tube pans in your kitchen; all sorts of cakes look good baked in them. Heavy metal is preferred, and you must take care to butter those swirls well, to prevent unmolding disasters. If you don't have a kugelhopf pan, a Bundt pan works fine.

MAIL-ORDER SOURCE: Williams-Sonoma sells an 8½-inch (12-cup) nonstick kugelhopf pan and also a 6¼-inch (5-cup) pan. Contact www.williams-sonoma.com.

HELMSTETTER KUGELHOPF

This basic kugelhopf, light and fragrant, comes from the Boulangerie Helmstetter in the historic village of Colmar in Alsace. The shop and this recipe have passed from Helmstetter father to son for over 200 years. If you stop in, be sure to try their other specialty, a deliciously moist *pain aux noix* (walnut bread).

You can also serve this as a dessert, with syrup and ice cream (see the variation).

～～ *Makes one 8- to 9-inch kugelhopf; serves about 8*

SPONGE

1½	packages (about 1 rounded tablespoon) active dry yeast
1¼	cups all-purpose flour
½	cup lukewarm milk

KUGELHOPF

3	cups all-purpose flour
⅓	cup sugar
2	teaspoons salt
½	cup lukewarm milk
⅓	cup (5⅓ tablespoons) unsalted butter, softened
2	large eggs, lightly beaten
⅔	cup raisins
8	whole blanched almonds

1. **SPONGE:** Stir together the yeast, flour and lukewarm milk in a large bowl. Cover and set aside in a warm place until approximately doubled in volume, about 1½ hours.

2. **KUGELHOPF:** Combine the flour, sugar and salt in a large bowl. (I do not recommend making this dough in a food processor.) With an electric mixer fitted with a dough hook on low speed or by hand with a wooden spoon, add the sponge mixture, the milk, butter and eggs; mix until the dough comes together (it will be sticky). Increase the speed to medium-high and knead the dough until very smooth and elastic, about 10 minutes. As you knead, add a little flour, if necessary; the dough should still be somewhat sticky, but by the end of the kneading process, it should "clean the bowl" (not stick to the sides; this usually takes about ½ cup more flour). Turn off the mixer and knead in the raisins by hand until well distributed.

3. Generously butter an 8- to 9-inch kugelhopf or Bundt pan. Arrange the almonds in the bottom of the pan. Gather the dough into a ball, make a hole in the middle with your thumb, and fit the dough around the tube into the pan. The pan should be about ⅔ full; cover with plastic wrap. Set aside until the dough rises to the rim of the pan, generally 1 to 1¼ hours.

4. Preheat the oven to 375 degrees F, with a rack in the lower third. Uncover the dough. Bake until the cake is golden brown and sounds hollow when tapped, 40 to 45 minutes. Cover with a sheet of foil about halfway through the baking time if the surface begins to brown too quickly.

5. Cool in the pan on a wire rack for 10 minutes. Unmold the kugelhopf and cool thoroughly. Wrap well in plastic or a plastic bag to store. Serve at room temperature, cut into wedges.

⌒ *Variation*

DESSERT KUGELHOPF WITH EAU-DE-VIE SYRUP: Serve this as is, or with a few berries on the side. It combines beautifully with Alsatian Spiced Honey Ice Cream (page 599).

> ¾ cup cold water
> ⅓ cup sugar
> ⅔ cup eau-de-vie, such as pear, mirabelle or framboise

1. Combine the water and sugar in a small, heavy saucepan over medium heat. Bring to a boil, stirring to dissolve the sugar. Boil gently, without stirring, for 5 minutes. Stir in the fruit brandy; remove from the heat and set aside.

2. To serve, preheat the broiler or a toaster oven. Slice the kugelhopf with a serrated knife. Toast the slices, turning once, until lightly golden. Place each slice on a serving plate and brush the top generously with the syrup.

ST. LOUIS GOOEY BUTTER CAKE

Talk about unusual . . . St. Louis natives rave about this cake and are so loyal to it that they have it shipped from local bakeries when they move elsewhere. It originated during the Great Depression in the German section of south St. Louis.

Gooey butter cake usually starts with store-bought yeast coffee cake or Danish that's cut up and snugly fit into a buttered cake pan. The "gooey butter" is poured on top, and the whole thing arc-welds together to form a semimolten mass that's gilded and crusty.

My testing notes report that this is "sugary and delicious." Since then, I've tried several versions (some include yellow food coloring in the topping; this one does not). But none has the quintessentially gooey quality of this one, adapted from a recipe from Barbara Gibbs Ostmann, food editor at the *St. Louis Post-Dispatch*.

> *Makes two 9-inch square cakes; each serves about 8*

18-20	ounces store-bought yeast-raised coffee cake (icing or filling is OK here, as is frozen, day-old or a mixture of types)
1	cup (2 sticks) unsalted butter, softened
2½	cups sugar
	Pinch salt
1	large egg
¼	cup light corn syrup
¼	cup water
1	tablespoon pure vanilla extract
2¼	cups all-purpose flour
	Confectioners' sugar, for sprinkling

1. Generously butter two 9-inch square cake pans. Cut the coffee cake into wedges or rectangles. Fit ½ of the cake into each of the pans; press the pieces snugly together into a single layer.

2. In a bowl with an electric mixer on medium-high speed, beat the butter, sugar and salt until very smooth. Add the egg; beat in the corn syrup until smooth. Add the water and vanilla. Lower the speed to slow and mix in the flour.

3. Punch holes in the coffee cake with a fork. Pour the gooey butter batter all over the cake, dividing evenly between the 2 pans.

No Mistake

According to an account by Joyce Schwartz in *The Master Bakers Bulletin*, quoted by Ann Barry in *The New York Times*, "Usually, people in other cities said that [gooey butter cake] looked like a mistake, a flat gooey mess. Well, of course, that's what it is. No two recipes are the same," says Mrs. Schwartz.

Let stand for 20 minutes. Meanwhile, preheat the oven to 375 degrees F.

4. Bake until the gooey butter is bubbly and golden brown, about 30 minutes; do not overbake. (The topping will not be gooey if baked too long.) Cool the cakes to room temperature in the pans on a wire rack. Sprinkle with confectioners' sugar and serve directly from the pans.

ITALIAN COFFEE CAKES

The Friuli region of Italy northeast of Venice enjoys an amalgamated cuisine, reflecting the period before World War II when it was part of the Hapsburg Empire. I was lucky enough to visit this region with Lidia Bastianich, co-owner of Felidia Ristorante in New York City, which serves the traditional food of that part of the country.

Baking is of key importance in the food of Friuli and Trieste, the gateway port close to the border of what was Yugoslavia. Particularly notable are the yeast-raised coffee cake-breads, called *gubana*, *putiza* and *presniz*, which are coiled around rich nut fillings and sometimes served sprinkled with the local grappa (brandy made with grape skins). These regional breads are reminiscent of the baked goods of Vienna and Hungary, while their spices reflect Venice's former position as center of trade with the East.

Confusion between the breads is widespread, and a bread called by one name in one town may have another name just a few miles away. This refreshing (or confusing) lack of dogma is typical of the freewheeling Italian attitude toward food.

COILED YEAST COFFEE BREAD WITH NUT FILLING
(GUBANA)

*G*ubana is a luscious bread, with a rich yeast dough spiraled around a mixture of nuts and raisins moistened with grappa and/or other spirits. The time-honored formula calls for equal weights of dough and filling; one local baker told me he uses even more filling than dough for each round loaf. Frequently, slices of *gubana* are sprinkled with more grappa or slivovitz when served.

The filling comes from Andrea Purinan, who, with his father, runs Il Forniao di Mario Purinan, a bakery in the lovely town of Udine, capital of the Friuli region. The bakery makes *gubana* and *putiza* (a sweet yeast bread) year-round.

The dough follows a recipe from Simone Supanz, an ebullient former boxer who runs a bread bakery in Trieste.

Makes two 8- to 9-inch round loaves; each serves about 8

DOUGH

1½	cups lukewarm milk
2	packages active dry yeast
5¾-6	cups all-purpose flour
½	cup plus 3 tablespoons sugar
2	large eggs
2	large egg yolks
¼	cup heavy cream or half-and-half
2	teaspoons coarse (kosher) salt
	Grated zest of 1 large or 2 small lemons
¾	cup (1½ sticks) unsalted butter, cut into pieces, softened

FILLING

1⅓	cups (5-6 ounces) pine nuts, toasted and cooled
½	pound (about 2 cups) unblanched almonds
¼	pound biscotti or shortbread cookies (about 10 pieces Pepperidge Farm shortbread cookies)
½	cup sugar
1	cup (2 sticks) unsalted butter, melted
1	cup raisins
1½	tablespoons ground cinnamon
2	tablespoons pure vanilla extract
½	cup Marsala, or to taste

Bread of Easter

Lore has it that this coiled nut-filled yeast bread, the traditional Easter bread of Friuli, originated either in Gorizia or Cividale, nearby villages. The name, however, shows Slavic origins and probably derives from the Slavic *guba* (roughly, "folded"), which describes its characteristic snail shape. Others claim that the name is derived from *bubane*, Friulian dialect for "abundance."

When I visited Friuli one October, Andrea Purinan was starting a flour and water mixture that would ripen for two weeks. This "mother," which leavens the dough naturally without yeast, was the first step in making the bread for Christmas.

¼   cup plus 2 tablespoons Curaçao or other orange liqueur
¼   cup grappa or brandy

1   egg yolk mixed with 1 teaspoon cold water, for glaze
     Sugar, for sprinkling

1. **DOUGH:** To make the sponge, combine ¼ cup of the luke-warm milk and the yeast in a small bowl. Stir in 2 tablespoons of the flour and 1 tablespoon of the sugar. Set aside in a warm place until doubled, 20 to 30 minutes.

2. In a large bowl, with an electric mixer fitted with a dough hook or by hand with a wooden spoon, beat the eggs and egg yolks with the remaining ½ cup plus 2 tablespoons sugar until well blended. Beat in the remaining 1¼ cups lukewarm milk, the cream or half-and-half, salt and lemon zest. Mix in the butter; mix in the sponge mixture. Add the remaining flour, about ½ cup at a time, adding just enough to form a soft, moist and very slightly sticky dough, about 8 minutes with a mixer or 12 minutes by hand.

3. Transfer the dough to a lightly floured surface and knead by hand until it is springy, elastic and very smooth, about 8 minutes. If the dough becomes too sticky to handle easily, work in a little more flour as you knead. Transfer the dough to a buttered bowl and turn to coat with the butter; cover with plastic wrap or a kitchen towel. Let rise until doubled, usually about 1½ hours or overnight in the refrigerator.

4. **FILLING:** Meanwhile, in a food processor, combine the pine nuts, almonds, biscotti or shortbread cookies and the sugar; pulse until the nuts and cookies are the size of peas. Transfer the mixture to a bowl, and stir in the melted butter, raisins, cinnamon, vanilla, Marsala, Curaçao and grappa or brandy. Mix until all of the ingredients are moist and well combined. Add more seasonings and/or spirits to taste. Let the filling soak for at least 1 hour or overnight.

5. Punch down the dough and transfer it to a lightly floured surface. Form the dough into a smooth ball; cover and let stand for 10 to 15 minutes.

6. Divide the dough in half. Roll out ½ of the dough on a lightly floured surface to a 16-x-11-inch rectangle. Spread ½ of the filling evenly over the dough, leaving a 1-inch border on all sides. Starting from a long side, gently roll up the dough into a cylinder.

When you finish rolling, the seam should be on top; fold in the ends to enclose the filling.

7. Working very gently and beginning from the center of the cylinder, stretch the cylinder, so that it becomes even longer and narrower. Do this by picking it up at the center and elongating it as you move your fingers toward the ends. Starting with one end as the center, gently coil the cylinder of dough into a flat spiral shape. Transfer the coil, seam side down, to a buttered 8- to 9- inch round cake pan or springform pan; the coil should come to within an inch of the edges of the pan but should not touch the edges. Do not tuck the ends of the coil underneath.

8. Repeat steps 6 and 7 with the remaining dough and filling, placing the coil in a second buttered pan. Cover the pans with plastic wrap or a kitchen towel. Let rise in a warm place until nearly doubled, for about 1 hour.

9. Preheat the oven to 375 degrees F, with a rack at the center. Brush the coils gently with the egg yolk glaze. Let the dough stand for at least 10 minutes while the oven heats.

10. Lightly sprinkle the surface of the dough with sugar. Bake until the breads begin to turn golden brown, 20 to 25 minutes. Place a sheet of foil over the loaves and continue to bake until they are nicely golden brown and baked through (they should sound hollow when tapped), about 20 minutes longer.

11. Cool the breads in the pans on a wire rack for about 5 minutes. Carefully remove from the pans and cool completely on the rack. Serve warm or at room temperature.

RECIPES

1-2-3-4 Cake

*Jam Cake with Burnt Sugar
    Glaze*

Lemon-Molasses Marble Cake

*Lazy-Daisy Oatmeal Cake
    with Broiled Coconut-
    Pecan Icing*

*Applesauce-Carrot Cake with
    Lemon Cream Cheese
    Frosting*

*Dried Apple Gingerbread
    Stack Cake*

*Southern Coconut Layer Cake
    with Divinity Icing*

Orange Blossom Cake

Boston Cream Pie

Carolina Huguenot Torte

*Austrian Walnut Torte with
    Coffee Whipped Cream*

*Hazelnut Roll with Creamy
    Prune Filling*

Peanut Brittle Crunch Cake

Italian Skillet Cheesecake

*New York–Style Sour Cream
    Cheesecake*

*World War I Applesauce
    Cheesecake*

Quick Chocolate Candy Cake

Fudgy Chocolate Layer Cake

Low-Fat Chocolate Nut Torte

Chocolate Chiffon Loaf Cake

Chocolate Cloud Cake

CHAPTER 10

LAYER CAKES, FANCY CAKES, CHEESECAKES AND CHOCOLATE CAKES

Layer cakes and chocolate cakes figure large in birthday and other celebrations, often becoming family traditions. Many home bakers report that they bake a certain cake, such as a four-layer-high coconut cake, for their children's birthdays every year. If they dare experiment with another kind, the kids may eat it, but always grudgingly. "When it comes to birthdays, it has to be *that* cake," they told me.

With frosting between two, three or even more layers, these cakes are honest, homespun and brash, often concocted with more enthusiasm than finesse—quintessentially American. But while layer cakes are an American tradition, they are a fairly recent one, taking root only since the Civil War. Before that, in the early days of American cooking, cakes were fairly plain because baking at home was not an easy undertaking.

Several developments made cakes more feasible. By the 1840s to 1850s, brick-oven baking had been supplanted by the cast-iron wood-burning range. The gas range appeared in the 1850s but was considered extravagant and dangerous for the next 50 years. The development of cream of tartar in the 1850s, followed by baking powder in the late 1860s, also made home-baked cakes more manageable than those made with such earlier leaveners as pearl ash and saleratus.

By the time of the Civil War, layer cakes, which require more oven precision than gingerbread and other basic combinations, were coming into vogue. They are the most popular baked goods in handwritten recipe manuscripts of this period. Early layer cakes were sandwiched together with homemade jam or jelly.

In the South, the Northeast, the Midwest and wherever homemakers had butter and eggs, elaborate versions were created, including the following classics:

⌖ **Robert E. Lee Cake:** An extravagant cake—some recipes call for 15 eggs—with lemon-orange frosting. Records indicate that the cake itself, like many others, had been popular earlier and was rechristened with the name of the notable general who favored it.

⌖ **Lane Cake:** A showy white layer cake with a bourbon-spiked fruit-and-nut custard filling and white divinity frosting, named for Emma Rylander Lane, who first published a recipe for the cake in 1898 (without the frosting).

⌖ **Charleston's Lord and Lady Baltimore Cakes:** The latter was named for a fictional character in a novel by Owen Wister. Lord Baltimore is a yellow cake, while Lady is a white one; the layers of both are filled with a meringue mixture of pecans, raisins and figs, then iced with an egg-white frosting.

⌖ **Coca-Cola Cake:** Made with Coca-Cola in the batter and frequently with Coca-Cola-flavored marshmallow frosting.

Cakes in this chapter include layered and rolled European-style tortes (cakes made with ground nuts or bread crumbs instead of flour and spread with whipped cream and other fillings); cheesecakes, which have a long historical tradition of their own, and a carefully chosen group of chocolate cakes. To many people, cake isn't cake unless it's chocolate.

Meeting a Lady

I stepped forward to the counter, adventurous, but polite.

"I should like a slice, if you please, of Lady Baltimore," I said with extreme formality.

I thought she was going to burst; after a second she replied, "Certainly."

. . . I returned to the table and she brought me the cake, and I had my first felicitous meeting with Lady Baltimore. Oh, my goodness! Did you ever taste it? It's all soft, and it's in layers, and it has nuts—but I can't write any more about it; my mouth waters too much. . . .

OWEN WISTER
LADY BALTIMORE
1906

A Few Tips for Great-Looking Cakes

A good homemade layer cake has an appeal that even the most elaborate bakery cake cannot match. (Charm outshines perfection.) But here are a few professional tips to ensure that your cake will look as delicious as it tastes.

෩ **Cool the layers** in the pans on a wire rack for about 10 minutes. Then, run a knife blade around the edges, put the rack upside down over the pan and quickly invert the two. Cool the cake completely before frosting.

෩ **Dust off any loose crumbs** gently with a soft brush or the flat of your hand. Set aside the best-looking layer for the top. Place the bottom layer upside down on a serving plate, lining it first with a doily, if you like.

෩ **Before icing the cake,** slip strips of wax paper under the bottom layer all around the edges of the cake. They will keep the serving plate clean while you frost or decorate.

෩ **Spoon a generous amount of any icing** or filling between the cake layers and spread out with a palette knife or small spatula. Don't stint: The moisture will keep the cake soft.

෩ **Place the top layer right side up** on top of the first, and press it lightly into place.

෩ **With a palette knife or narrow metal spatula,** take up small globs of icing and spread them evenly around the sides of the cake. As you do this, gently steady the cake with the palm of your other hand.

෩ **Once the sides are done,** ice the top. Smooth the icing, or make lavish swirls with your knife. If the icing is smooth, finish it off by running the spatula around the sides one more time, to give a finished edge.

⤫ **If you like,** decorate the iced cake by pressing chopped nuts along the sides, strewing the cake with edible flowers (be sure they are edible) or strips of citrus zest, or piping a little of the icing through a pastry bag, forming rosettes, swirls or long, round ribbons over the cake.

⤫ **When you have finished,** carefully pull out the strips of wax paper. (Lick the bowl: cook's privilege.)

1-2-3-4 CAKE

The warhorse of layer cakes," the late author-cook Bill Neal called this cake in his book *Biscuits, Spoonbread, and Sweet Potato Pie.* Many people don't realize that the name refers to the quantities of its ingredients: 1 cup butter, 2 cups sugar, 3 cups flour, 4 eggs. (As actually handed down, the recipe usually strays from those proportions, though this one does not.) The original cake was made with sweet milk; this version calls for buttermilk, which adds flavor and helps keep the crumb tender.

Many of our mothers, grandmothers and great-grandmothers baked this cake from memory, measuring with a favorite tea cup—with perfect results every time. For those tired of stodgy cakes, returning to this classic is a revelation. It's moist and tender, with a light, even crumb, a golden color and a rich butter-and-egg flavor.

⤫ *Makes three 8-inch round layers or two 9-inch round layers or two 8-inch square cakes*

3	cups sifted cake flour (not self-rising)
1	tablespoon baking powder
1	teaspoon baking soda
½	teaspoon salt
1	cup (2 sticks) unsalted butter, softened
2	cups sugar
4	large eggs
1¼	cups buttermilk or a mixture of plain or lemon yogurt thinned with milk
1½	teaspoons pure vanilla extract

1. Preheat the oven to 350 degrees F. Butter and flour three 8-inch round cake pans, two 9-inch round pans or two 8-inch

Great Cake

Late one afternoon, a layer of 1-2-3-4 Cake sat unfrosted, cooling on a rack along with five or six more lavish desserts, when my number-one taster walked in. "What smells so great?" he sniffed, then headed right for the 1-2-3-4 and cut himself a big piece. "Great yellow cake," he said, reaching for the milk.

square pans; set aside. Resift the flour with the baking powder, baking soda and salt; set aside.

2. In a large bowl, cream the butter and sugar with an electric mixer at medium-high speed until very light. Beat in the eggs, one at a time. Lower the speed to slow and beat in the flour mixture alternately with the buttermilk or yogurt mixture, beginning and ending with the flour. Beat in the vanilla. Scrape the batter into the prepared pans, dividing gently.

3. Bake until the cakes are lightly golden and a toothpick inserted in the center emerges clean, 30 to 35 minutes.

4. Cool completely in the pans on wire racks. Run the tip of a knife around the sides of the cakes to loosen them from the pans; invert the cake layers and use as desired.

SUGGESTED FILLINGS: This is a basic cake, suitable for any occasion. Possible frostings include Glossy Dark Chocolate Frosting (page 414), Chocolate Frosting (page 326) or Divinity Icing (page 394).

JAM CAKE WITH BURNT SUGAR GLAZE

With jam in the batter, this moist, dense cake has a haunting berry aftertaste. Chunky with raisins and nuts, it is baked in a single thick layer and topped with a shiny burnt sugar glaze.

Makes one 9-inch square cake; serves about 9

- 2½ cups all-purpose flour
- 1 teaspoon baking soda
- ¾ teaspoon baking powder
- 1½ teaspoons ground cinnamon
- 1½ teaspoons ground allspice
- 1 teaspoon fresh-grated nutmeg
- ¾ teaspoon ground cloves
- ¾ cup (1½ sticks) unsalted butter, softened
- 1 cup sugar
- 4 large eggs
- 1 cup blackberry, raspberry or other fruit jam
- ¾ cup plus 2 tablespoons buttermilk or a mixture of plain or vanilla yogurt thinned with milk
- ⅔ cup raisins
- ⅔ cup coarsely chopped walnuts, black walnuts, hickory nuts or pecans
  Burnt Sugar Glaze (page 330)

1. Preheat the oven to 350 degrees F. Butter a 9-inch square cake pan. Sift the flour with the baking soda, baking powder, cinnamon, allspice, nutmeg and cloves onto a sheet of wax paper; set aside.

2. Cream the butter and the sugar with an electric mixer at medium-high speed until fluffy. Beat in the eggs, one at a time; beat in the jam. Lower the speed to slow, and add the flour mixture alternately with the buttermilk or yogurt mixture until just blended. Fold in the raisins and the nuts. Pour the batter into the prepared pan; smooth the top.

3. Bake until the cake is set and a toothpick inserted in the center emerges clean, about 30 minutes.

4. Cool the cake to room temperature in the pan on a wire rack. Spread with the glaze, and let stand until the glaze cools, about 5 minutes. Cut the cake into large squares and serve from the pan.

Traditions of Jam

Jam cakes are baked throughout the South, Appalachia and the Midwest. They typify "pantry baking"—making do with what's on hand through the winter, when there isn't much fresh fruit around.

As with several other basic cake genres, cakes with jam turn up in various guises in other parts of the world. In Denmark, for example, *brombaerkage*, blackberry jam cake, is made with raisins and spices and a coffee-flavored icing that's fluffier than the glaze here, but not unlike it in effect.

LEMON-MOLASSES MARBLE CAKE

Marble cake is among the most enduring of American cakes. In early recipes, the batter isn't made with chocolate, but with a spiced molasses batter offset by a pale lemon batter.

Marble cake begins to turn up in American cookbooks in the late 1800s. This one is adapted from an old recipe from Mary Leize Simons of Charleston, South Carolina. It's extraordinary—a big, dramatic-looking cake baked in a Bundt or tube pan—moist and full of flavor.

Makes one 9- to 10-inch tube cake; serves about 12

MOLASSES BATTER

6	tablespoons (¾ stick) unsalted butter, softened
¼	cup plus 2 tablespoons packed light or dark brown sugar
3	large egg yolks
¾	cup molasses
1⅔	cups all-purpose flour
½	teaspoon baking soda
½	teaspoon cream of tartar
½	teaspoon ground cinnamon
¼	teaspoon *each* ground mace, fresh-grated nutmeg and ground cloves
¼	cup plus 2 tablespoons plain yogurt

LEMON BATTER

6	tablespoons (¾ stick) unsalted butter, softened
1	cup sugar
	Grated zest of 1 lemon
1	teaspoon lemon extract
1⅔	cups all-purpose flour
½	teaspoon baking soda
½	teaspoon cream of tartar
¾	cup plain yogurt
3	large egg whites
	Pinch salt

Confectioners' sugar, for sprinkling

1. Preheat the oven to 350 degrees F. Butter and flour a 9- to 10-inch Bundt or tube pan; set aside.

2. **MOLASSES BATTER:** In a large bowl, cream the butter and brown sugar with an electric mixer on medium-high speed until very light. Beat in the egg yolks, one at a time; beat in the molasses. Sift the dry ingredients onto a sheet of wax paper; add to the batter alternately with the yogurt, beginning and ending with the dry ingredients. Do not overmix.

3. **LEMON BATTER:** In a large bowl, cream the butter, sugar and lemon zest with an electric mixer on medium-high speed until very light. Add the lemon extract. Sift the dry ingredients onto a sheet of wax paper; add to the batter alternately with the yogurt, beginning and ending with the dry ingredients (don't overmix). Beat the egg whites with the salt until nearly stiff. Fold about ¼ of the egg whites into the batter to lighten it; gently fold in the remaining whites.

4. Drop 3 or 4 large dollops of the lemon batter into the prepared pan. Top with 3 or 4 dollops of the molasses batter. Continue layering the batters. Gently rap the pan once against the countertop to settle the batters. With a butter knife, swirl the batters together a couple of times; don't overdo it.

5. Bake until the cake is golden brown and a toothpick inserted near the center emerges clean, about 1 hour. (The timing can vary with the pan used; do not overbake.)

6. Cool the cake in the pan on a wire rack for 10 to 15 minutes. Run the tip of a knife around the cake to loosen it from the sides and tube; unmold carefully. Cool completely on the rack. Sprinkle the top with confectioners' sugar, and serve in wedges.

Surprise!

Oh! How surprised their mother appeared when she was ushered out to the feast. Her delight in the cake was fully enough to satisfy the most exacting mind. She admired it on every side, protesting that she shouldn't have supposed Polly could possibly have baked it as good in the old stove; and then she cut it, and gave a piece to every child, with a little posy on top. Wasn't it good, though! For, like many other things, the cake proved better on trial than it looked, and so turned out to be really quite a good surprise all around.

MARGARET SIDNEY
*FIVE LITTLE PEPPERS AND
HOW THEY GREW*
1880

Lazy-Daisy Oatmeal Cake with Broiled Coconut-Pecan Icing

An old American favorite—a one-layer spiced oatmeal cake topped with a gooey nut-and-coconut icing that's quickly browned under the broiler.

This cake comes from Kerri Conan, my former editor at Simon & Schuster. The recipe is from Kerri's grandmother.

Makes one 9-inch single-layer cake; serves about 8

Cake
- 1¼ cups boiling water
- 1 cup old-fashioned or quick-cooking oats (not instant oatmeal)
- ½ cup (1 stick) unsalted butter, softened
- ¾ cup sugar
- ¾ cup packed light brown sugar
- 1 teaspoon pure vanilla extract
- 2 large eggs
- 1½ cups sifted all-purpose flour
- 1 teaspoon baking soda
- ¾ teaspoon ground cinnamon
- ½ teaspoon salt
- ¼ teaspoon fresh-grated nutmeg

Icing
- ¼ cup (½ stick) unsalted butter
- ¾ cup shredded sweetened coconut
- ½ cup chopped pecans
- ½ cup packed light brown sugar
- 3 tablespoons light cream or milk

1. **Cake:** Pour the boiling water over the oats; cover and let stand for about 20 minutes. Butter and flour a 9-inch square cake pan; set aside. Preheat the oven to 350 degrees F.

2. In a large bowl, cream the butter with an electric mixer on medium-high speed. Gradually add the white and brown sugars and beat until fluffy. Blend in the vanilla and eggs. Beat in the oatmeal mixture.

3. Sift together the flour, baking soda, cinnamon, salt and nutmeg. Add to the butter mixture and blend well. Pour the batter into the prepared pan; smooth the top.

4. Bake just until the cake springs back when pressed lightly with your fingertip and a toothpick inserted in the center emerges clean, 45 to 50 minutes.

5. ICING: While the cake bakes, melt the butter in a small saucepan. Remove from the heat and stir in the coconut, pecans, brown sugar and cream or milk until blended.

6. When the cake is done, preheat the broiler, with a rack about 4 inches from the heat source. Very gently spread the topping on the cake. Broil until bubbly and beginning to turn pale golden, usually about 2 minutes. Since the timing can vary, watch the cake carefully to avoid burning the topping.

7. Cool the cake completely on a wire rack. Cut into squares and serve directly from the pan.

C Was Once a Little Cake

Caky
Baky
Maky
Caky
Taky Caky
Little Cake

EDWARD LEAR
NONSENSE OMNIBUS
1943; CA. 1846

APPLESAUCE-CARROT CAKE WITH LEMON CREAM CHEESE FROSTING

The applesauce keeps this carrot cake moist, dense and richly flavored, and the lemon brightens the frosting nicely.

 Makes one 10-inch tube cake or two 8-x-4-inch loaves; serves 10 to 12

CAKE

2	cups all-purpose flour
2	teaspoons baking powder
2	teaspoons baking soda
¾	teaspoon salt
1	tablespoon ground cinnamon
1	teaspoon *each* ground allspice and fresh-grated nutmeg
½	cup drained canned crushed pineapple in unsweetened juice
¼	cup raisins
½	cup pecan or walnut pieces
1	cup sugar
3	large eggs
1	cup packed dark brown sugar
1¼	cups bland vegetable oil
½	cup applesauce
2	teaspoons pure vanilla extract
2	cups finely shredded peeled carrots (about 4)
⅔	cup shredded sweetened coconut

FROSTING

8	ounces cream cheese (regular or "light" but not nonfat), softened
¼	cup (½ stick) unsalted butter, softened
1	cup confectioners' sugar
	Grated zest and juice of 1 small lemon
½	teaspoon pure vanilla extract
¼	teaspoon lemon extract

1. **CAKE:** Preheat the oven to 350 degrees F. Lightly oil a 10-inch Bundt or tube pan, or two 8-x-4-inch loaf pans; set aside. Sift the flour, baking powder, baking soda, salt and spices onto a sheet of wax paper; set aside.

No Place for Economy

Wastefulness is to be avoided in every thing; but it is utterly impossible that cakes can be good (or indeed any thing else) without a liberal allowance of good materials.

Cakes are frequently rendered hard, heavy, and uneatable by a misplaced economy in eggs and butter; or tasteless and insipid for want of their due seasoning of spice, lemon, &c.

ELIZA LESLIE
DIRECTIONS FOR COOKERY
PHILADELPHIA
1848; 1837

2. In a food processor, pulse the pineapple, raisins, nuts and ¼ cup of the sugar until minced; do not overprocess or puree; set aside.

3. In a large bowl with an electric mixer on medium-high speed, combine the remaining ¾ cup sugar, eggs, brown sugar, oil, applesauce, vanilla and the minced pineapple-nut mixture; beat until well combined. Lower the speed to slow and gradually add the sifted dry ingredients. Stir in the carrots and coconut just until combined. Pour into the prepared pan(s).

4. Bake until the cake is golden brown, the edges shrink slightly away from the pan(s), and a toothpick inserted in the center(s) emerges clean, usually 50 to 60 minutes in a tube pan, about 45 minutes for loaves.

5. Cool the cake(s) to room temperature in the pan(s) on a wire rack.

6. **FROSTING:** Beat all of the ingredients together with an electric mixer until very smooth and light.

7. Run the tip of a knife around the cake to loosen it from the sides and tube of the pan; unmold and turn right side up if necessary. Split the cake(s) horizontally into 2 layers. Spread some of the frosting over the bottom layer; spread the remainder over the top. Chill if not serving immediately. Serve cool or chilled.

Dried Apple Gingerbread Stack Cake

Oance of the most interesting and unusual of traditional
American cakes, stack cakes are found in Appalachia and
throughout the Midwest, wherever apples were dried for winter
storage. This recipe, based on one from Indiana-based cookbook
author Marilyn Kluger, is a homey combination of warm spices
and rich apple flavor. It's not too heavy or cloyingly sweet.

Dried apples have concentrated flavor that is released when
they are simmered in liquid. Simmering in cider instead of water
adds another layer of apple flavor.

If four layers are too much, you can halve both the cake and
apple filling and bake the cake in a 9-inch round pan. Split it into
two layers and fill with the dried apples. Made this way, the cake is
still a good 2 inches high.

One 9-inch 4-layer cake; serves about 8

Filling
4   cups dried apples
2   cups apple cider or cold water, or as needed
½   cup sugar

Gingerbread Cake
1   cup vegetable shortening or ½ cup *each* vegetable
     shortening and unsalted butter (1 stick), at room
     temperature
1   cup sugar
1   large egg
1   cup sorghum syrup (see note) or molasses
1   cup buttermilk or a mixture of plain yogurt thinned
     with milk
1   teaspoon baking soda
3   cups sifted all-purpose flour
1   teaspoon ground ginger
¼   teaspoon ground cloves
½   teaspoon salt

Confectioners' sugar, for sprinkling on top

1. **Filling:** Gently boil the dried apples in the cider or water
to cover until they are very tender and form a chunky puree, about
20 minutes. Check the apples occasionally as they cook; if the
liquid is absorbed but the apples are still firm, add a little more

cider or water. Mash the apples slightly as they cook, and stir in the sugar when the apples are very tender. Mash well so the layers will be even and the cakes will stack easily. Set aside to cool to room temperature.

2. Preheat the oven to 375 degrees F. Butter and flour two 9-inch layer cake pans or two 9-inch cast-iron skillets; set aside.

3. **GINGERBREAD CAKE:** In a large bowl with an electric mixer on medium-high speed, cream the shortening or shortening and butter mixture with the sugar. Beat in the egg. Add the sorghum or molasses, buttermilk or yogurt, baking soda, flour, spices and salt; mix just until thoroughly combined. Divide the batter between the prepared pans.

4. Bake the cakes until a toothpick inserted in the centers emerges clean, 25 to 30 minutes.

5. Cool the cakes in the pans on a wire rack for 10 to 15 minutes. Run the tip of a knife around the sides of the cakes to loosen them from the pans; invert the cakes, turn right side up and cool completely.

6. Split each cake layer horizontally in half with a large serrated knife. Spread ⅓ of the dried apple filling between the layers and reassemble; the top of the cake will be plain. Loosely cover and let the stack cake stand for at least 2 hours so its flavors come together. Sprinkle the top with confectioners' sugar before serving.

NOTE: You can mail-order sorghum syrup from www.amazon.com.

Traditional Stack Cakes

The spicy layers of stack cake—as many as six—were often made with home-rendered lard and sorghum syrup and baked in cast-iron skillets. Sorghum syrup is made from a tropical grass similar to the stalks of Indian corn; it's less refined than cane sugar syrup and is frequently used in Southern baking.

SOUTHERN COCONUT LAYER CAKE WITH DIVINITY ICING

This recipe has been adapted slightly from the snowy white coconut cake that's long been served at Miss Mary Bobo's Boarding House in Lynchburg, Tennessee. Sprinkling the baked cake layers with coconut milk keeps them moist and adds another coconut dimension.

Makes one 9-inch 4-layer cake; serves about 8

CAKE

3¼	cups all-purpose flour
1	tablespoon plus 1 teaspoon baking powder
¼	teaspoon salt
1	cup (2 sticks) unsalted butter, softened
2	cups sugar
8	large egg whites
1	teaspoon pure vanilla extract
¼	teaspoon almond extract
1	cup milk

DIVINITY ICING

1½	cups sugar
2	tablespoons light corn syrup
⅓	cup cold water
3	large egg whites
½	teaspoon cream of tartar
	Pinch salt
1½	teaspoons pure vanilla extract
1	tablespoon fresh lemon juice
1½	tablespoons hot water
¼	cup coconut milk or 2½ tablespoons canned coconut cream thinned with 1½ tablespoons hot water
3	cups shredded or flaked fresh (see note) or store-bought coconut

1. CAKE: Preheat the oven to 350 degrees F. Butter and flour two 9-inch round cake pans; set aside. Sift the flour, baking powder and salt onto a sheet of wax paper; set aside.

2. With an electric mixer at medium-high speed, cream the butter and sugar until very light and smooth. Add all of the egg whites and the vanilla and almond extracts; beat until well com-

bined and smooth. Add ½ cup of the milk and mix well. Lower the speed to slow and add the sifted ingredients; mix just until blended, no longer. Fold in the remaining ½ cup milk. Divide the batter between the prepared pans; smooth the top.

3. Bake until the cake layers are golden brown, the edges shrink slightly away from the sides of the pans, and a toothpick inserted in the centers emerges clean, 40 to 45 minutes.

4. Cool the cake layers in their pans on a wire rack for 10 to 15 minutes. Run the tip of a knife around the sides of the cakes to loosen them; invert the cakes, turn right side up and cool to room temperature.

5. **DIVINITY ICING:** Combine the sugar, corn syrup and cold water in a small, heavy saucepan. Bring to a boil over medium heat, stirring to dissolve the sugar. Boil, uncovered, until the syrup reaches a temperature of 240 degrees F, usually 3 or 4 minutes. (This is the soft-ball stage. If you don't own a candy thermometer, drop a small spoonful of the hot syrup into a cup of ice water; the mixture will form a soft mass when pressed between your fingers.)

6. While the syrup is cooking, beat the egg whites, cream of tartar and salt with an electric mixer at medium-high speed until foamy. When the syrup reaches the soft-ball stage, slowly pour it into the beaten whites in a very slow, thin stream, beating all the time. (Try to pour the syrup into the center of the egg whites, so it doesn't spatter all over the sides of the bowl.) When all of the syrup has been added, add the vanilla and continue to beat until the mixture is fluffy and shiny and cools to room temperature, usually 7 to 8 minutes. Beat in the lemon juice and hot water.

7. With a long serrated knife, split each cooled cake layer horizontally into 2 layers. Sprinkle the cut side of each layer with 1 tablespoon of the coconut milk or thinned coconut cream.

8. Choose a layer with a flat surface and set it aside for the top. Place 1 of the layers, cut side up, on a serving plate. Spread it with a generous layer of icing; sprinkle on some coconut. Repeat with the remaining layers, spreading each with icing and coconut. Gently press the reserved layer, browned side up, on top.

9. Spread the top and sides of the cake with the remaining icing. Sprinkle the top of the cake with coconut, and gently press more coconut into the icing on the sides.

NOTE: Using a fresh coconut here makes a big difference—it's worth the trouble. To prepare fresh coconut:

1. Preheat the oven to 400 degrees F. With a clean nail, pierce the 3 eyes of the coconut; reserve the liquid, if you like, for cooking.

2. Place the coconut on a baking sheet. Bake until brittle, about 20 minutes.

3. Wrap the coconut in a towel and smack it with a hammer around its circumference. The shell will fall off in several pieces. Remove the thin layer of brown rind from the coconut flesh with a vegetable peeler.

4. Finely grate the coconut with the grater blade of a food processor or with a hand grater. Measure 3 cups grated coconut for this cake; set the rest aside for another use.

ORANGE BLOSSOM CAKE

A quick and simple cake, zingy with citrus. The Orange Curd (page 622) is an old favorite of mine; you can also use any store-bought lemon curd or preserves.

This is an American cousin of the Victoria Sandwich, one of the staples of the English tea table—spongecake split and sandwiched with raspberry jam, the top dusted with confectioners' sugar.

Makes one 9-inch 2-layer cake; serves 6 to 8

> Hot-Water Spongecake (page 299), or 1 layer of the 1-2-3-4 Cake (page 383), baked and cooled
> Orange Curd (page 622), Lemon Curd Filling (page 534) or 1-1½ cups any store-bought lemon curd
> Confectioners' sugar, for sprinkling

1. Brush off any excess crumbs from the cake. With a large serrated knife, split the cooled cake horizontally. Place the bottom layer on a cake plate or stand. Spread the curd evenly over the cake, gently spreading it nearly to the edges. Replace the top cake layer; gently press into place. Refrigerate if not serving immediately.

2. Sprinkle the cake with confectioners' sugar and serve.

There was an Old Man
of Berlin
Whose form was
uncommonly thin;
Till he once, by mistake,
Was mixed up in a cake,
So they baked the Old Man
of Berlin.

EDWARD LEAR
NONSENSE OMNIBUS
1943; CA. 1846

Boston Cream Pie

Not a pie at all. As a custard fan from way back, I love this simple combination of eggy yellow cake, custard and chocolate glaze.

Makes one 9-inch 2-layer cake; serves about 8

Vanilla Pastry Cream

1 cup milk
¼ cup plus 1 tablespoon sugar
Pinch salt
2 tablespoons cornstarch
2 large egg yolks
2 teaspoons cold unsalted butter
1 teaspoon pure vanilla extract

Hot-Water Spongecake (page 299), or 1 layer of 1-2-3-4 Cake (page 383), baked and cooled

Shiny Chocolate Glaze

3 ounces semisweet chocolate, finely chopped
¼ cup (½ stick) unsalted butter, cut into pieces
1½ tablespoons light corn syrup

1. **Vanilla Pastry Cream:** Rinse a heavy nonreactive saucepan with cold water; shake dry. Add ¾ cup of the milk and the 1 tablespoon sugar; bring to a boil over medium heat.

2. Meanwhile, in a bowl, whisk the remaining ¼ cup milk, the remaining ¼ cup sugar, the salt, cornstarch and egg yolks until pale and light, about 1½ minutes.

3. Remove the saucepan from the heat, and gradually whisk some of the hot milk into the egg yolk mixture. Scrape the warmed egg yolk mixture into the saucepan, and return to medium heat. Bring to a boil, whisking. Whisking constantly, boil for 1 minute. Remove from the heat and whisk in the butter and the vanilla.

4. Strain the pastry cream through a fine sieve into a clean bowl. Press a sheet of wax paper or plastic wrap directly on the surface to prevent a skin from forming. Refrigerate until cold, about 2 hours.

According to John Mariani's *The Dictionary of American Food & Drink*, the first printed mention of Boston Cream Pie was in *The New York Herald* in 1855. When the Parker House opened in Boston in 1856, this cake appeared on the menu as "Parker House Chocolate Pie." It's also been called "Boston Cream Cake."

5. Brush off any excess crumbs from the cake. With a large serrated knife, split the cooled cake horizontally. Place the bottom layer on a cake plate or stand. Spread the pastry cream evenly over the cake, reaching nearly to the edges. Replace the top cake layer; gently press into place.

6. **SHINY CHOCOLATE GLAZE:** Combine the chocolate, butter and corn syrup in a small, heavy saucepan over low heat. Stir until melted and smooth. Remove from the heat and set aside to cool until the glaze thickens slightly to a spreadable consistency.

7. Spread the chocolate glaze over the top of the cake. If you like, let some of the glaze drip down the sides. Let the glaze set for 10 minutes or so. Serve at cool room temperature. Store any leftovers in the refrigerator.

CAROLINA HUGUENOT TORTE

Huguenot torte is a pecan and apple cake layered with whipped cream. While most people think of this as an old Charleston dessert, it is actually much more recent, as is pecan pie.

Makes one 9-inch single-layer cake; serves about 8

1 cup mixed shelled nut pieces (pecans, walnuts, black walnuts)
¾ cup plus 2 tablespoons sugar, plus more for coating the pecans
2 large eggs plus 1 teaspoon egg yolk
¼ cup plus 2 tablespoons all-purpose flour
1 cup peeled, quartered, cored and finely chopped apple
8 perfect pecan halves
⅓ cup heavy cream, well chilled

1. Preheat the oven to 375 degrees F, and set a pan of water in the bottom of the oven. Lightly butter and flour a 9-inch springform pan, shaking out the excess flour; set aside.

2. Finely grind the nuts with the 2 tablespoons sugar in a nut grinder or food processor, until powdery but not oily. Set aside.

Tale of a Torte

My friend John Martin Taylor, owner of Charleston's cookbook shop Hoppin' John's and author of *Hoppin' John's Lowcountry Cooking*, sets the record straight on the history of Huguenot torte:

"I was put in touch with Evelyn Florance, whose recipe appears in Charleston Receipts [one of America's most successful community cookbooks] as the 'original Huguenot torte.' In the 1930s, she attended a church supper in

3. In a large bowl, beat the eggs and the egg yolk with an electric mixer on high speed until thick and doubled in volume, 5 to 10 minutes. Slowly add the remaining ¾ cup sugar, and beat until the eggs are very thick and light in color and the mixture has tripled in volume. Turn off the mixer.

4. Sift the flour over the egg mixture; sprinkle on the ground nuts and chopped apple. With a large spatula, fold together gently but rapidly, until well blended. Transfer the batter to the prepared pan.

5. Bake the cake until the top is golden brown and the sides begin to pull away from the pan, usually 25 to 30 minutes. Do not push on the meringue-like top, or it may cave in.

6. Cool the cake to room temperature in the pan on a wire rack.

7. While the cake is baking or cooling, scatter the pecan halves over a baking pan and toast in the oven until fragrant, about 8 minutes. While still hot, dip each nut in water and roll in sugar until lightly coated. Let dry on a wire rack.

8. When the cake has cooled completely, run the tip of a knife around the sides of the cake and remove the sides of the springform pan. Whip the cream until nearly stiff. Pipe or spoon 8 rosettes or dollops of the cream, evenly spaced, on top of the cake. Garnish each with a glazed pecan. Serve the cake immediately, or refrigerate until serving time.

Galveston, Texas, where she and her first husband ate something called Ozark pudding. 'The original was very gooey and sticky, and it had black walnuts,' she told me. 'I got a recipe for it and worked with it until it was the way I like it. I added some more eggs and some finely chopped pecans, and it puffed up, and I called it a torte. The name Huguenot Torte came in about 1942 when I was asked to make desserts for the Huguenot Tavern on the corner of Church and Queen Streets.'

"Ozark pudding, virtually the same dish, rarely appears in Arkansas cookbooks, though it seems to have originated in northwest Arkansas and southwest Missouri. It was served to Winston Churchill when he visited the Trumans in Fulton, Missouri, and made his famous 'Iron Curtain' speech."

AUSTRIAN WALNUT TORTE WITH COFFEE WHIPPED CREAM
(NUSSTORTE)

This very simple, very European nut torte with coffee whipped cream is from Nada Neumann, a Swiss-born friend of my mother's. It's one of the best.

Makes one 9-inch 3-layer torte; serves about 12

WALNUT TORTE

8	large eggs, separated
¾	cup plus 2 tablespoons sugar
1¾	cups (about 7 ounces) walnut pieces, toasted
2	tablespoons soft, fresh bread crumbs
1½	tablespoons strong-brewed coffee
1½	tablespoons dark or light rum

COFFEE WHIPPED CREAM

1½	cups heavy cream, well chilled
1½	tablespoons instant coffee powder
¾	cup confectioners' sugar

1. **WALNUT TORTE:** Preheat the oven to 350 degrees F. Line three 9-inch round cake pans with rounds of parchment or wax paper cut to fit. Butter and flour the paper and the sides of the pans; set aside.

2. In a large bowl, with an electric mixer at medium-high speed, beat the egg yolks with the ¾ cup sugar until very fluffy and at least doubled in volume, usually 5 to 6 minutes. The mixture should form a thick ribbon when the beaters are lifted; set aside.

3. Meanwhile, finely chop the nuts and set aside ¼ cup for the topping.

4. Add the ½ cup ground walnuts, bread crumbs, coffee and rum to the beaten egg mixture; fold together gently.

5. In a bowl, beat the egg whites until just stiff; do not over-beat. Fold a large spoonful of the whites into the egg yolk mixture; gently fold in the remainder. Divide the batter among the prepared pans; very gently smooth the tops.

6. Bake until the cake layers are lightly golden, pull away from the sides of the pans and spring back when pressed gently with a fingertip, about 24 minutes. Leave the oven on.

7. Cool the cakes in the pans on a wire rack for about 10 minutes. Meanwhile, in a small baking pan, toast the walnut halves in the oven until fragrant, about 8 minutes; set aside. Run the tip of a knife around the sides of the cakes to loosen them from the pans and carefully invert onto the rack. Gently peel off the paper; turn right side up. Let the cake layers cool completely.

8. **COFFEE WHIPPED CREAM:** In a bowl, stir ¼ cup of the cream with the coffee until smooth and the coffee dissolves. Add the remaining 1¼ cups cream and the confectioners' sugar and beat with an electric mixer until the cream is very fluffy and forms peaks that are just beyond soft, but not yet stiff. Do not overbeat.

9. Choose a cake layer with an even surface to serve as the top layer; set aside. Place 1 of the other layers on a cake stand or serving plate. Spread about ⅔ cup of the coffee whipped cream evenly over the layer. Repeat with a second layer, and another ⅔ cup cream. Place the remaining layer on top; gently press into place. With a spatula, smoothly frost the sides and top with the remaining coffee whipped cream. Arrange the toasted walnuts around the edges of the top of the cake. Chill for at least 1 hour before serving.

HAZELNUT ROLL WITH CREAMY PRUNE FILLING

Viennese and Hungarian repertoires offer a variety of fragrant nut sponge cakes, layered or rolled around apricot jam or whipped cream spiked with liqueurs, or sometimes spread with jam first, then with whipped cream.

This is a good, basic nut cake roll, filled with a deeply flavored prune *lekvar* lightened with whipped cream. *Lekvar* is an old Hungarian standby—a thick paste of prunes or apricots, used to fill all sorts of pastries. It's easy to make your own (page 367), but you can buy prune *lekvar* by mail-order from www.nutson line.com.

～ *Makes 1 long rolled cake; serves 12*

ROLL

1	cup finely ground hazelnuts (3½-4 ounces)
4	large eggs
3	tablespoons sugar
2	tablespoons honey
½	teaspoon pure vanilla extract
½	cup all-purpose flour
2	tablespoons unsalted butter, melted and cooled slightly

Confectioners' sugar, for sprinkling on top

FILLING

1	cup homemade thick prune puree (page 367) or store-bought
2	tablespoons Grand Marnier or Armagnac
½	cup heavy cream, well chilled

1. **ROLL:** Preheat the oven to 375 degrees F. Line the bottom of a 15½-x-10½-inch jellyroll pan with parchment or wax paper; set aside. Spread the ground hazelnuts over a small baking pan and toast in the oven, stirring once or twice, until fragrant and lightly colored, about 8 minutes. Set aside; leave the oven on.

2. In a large bowl with an electric mixer on high speed, beat the eggs and sugar until thick and fluffy. Add the honey and vanilla and beat until the mixture is very fluffy and has tripled in volume, about 7 minutes.

3. Combine the flour with the ground hazelnuts; gently fold into the beaten egg mixture. Spoon about 1 cup of the egg mixture into a small bowl; fold in the melted butter. Add this mixture to the batter and fold gently just until incorporated, no longer. Spread the batter evenly in the prepared pan.

4. Bake until the top of the cake is set and lightly golden, about 12 minutes.

5. Lay a clean kitchen towel on a work surface and sprinkle it with about 2 tablespoons confectioners' sugar. Run the tip of a knife around the sides of the cake to loosen it from the pan. Invert the cake onto the towel and carefully peel off the paper. Starting from a long side, using the towel to help you, roll up the cake into a neat cylinder. Cool completely on the towel.

6. **FILLING:** In a bowl, stir together the *lekvar* and Grand Marnier or Armagnac. Beat the cream until it forms soft peaks. Stir a few spoonfuls of the whipped cream into the *lekvar* to lighten it; gently fold in the remaining whipped cream just until smooth.

7. Carefully unroll the cake. If the edges have dried out, trim neatly with a serrated knife. Use a spatula to spread the filling over the surface of the cake. Use the towel to reroll the cake compactly; trim the ends with a serrated knife. Use the towel to transfer the cake roll, seam side down, to a long serving platter. Chill the roll until cold, at least 1 hour.

8. Sprinkle the cake roll with confectioners' sugar and serve in slices.

Watermelon Cakes

At the turn of the 20th century, Americans baked a trendy specialty called "Watermelon Cake." The cakes were baked in oval pans and assembled to look like the real thing:

FOR RED BATTER: Take the whites of 4 eggs, well beaten, and 1 cup red sugar, ½ cup butter, ½ cup sweet milk, 1 cup seedless raisins [for the "seeds," and vanilla, flour and baking powder] . . .

WHITE BATTER: Take the whites of 4 eggs, well beaten [sugar, butter, sweet milk, vanilla, flour, baking powder] . . . bake in an oval pan; using a plain oval tin ring . . . place the ring inside the pan to divide the batters; pour the red batter inside, and the white batter outside . . . and bake in a slow oven; when cut, you will have an exact imitation of a ripe watermelon.

ANNIE M. ZIMMERMAN
MY FAVORITE RECEIPT
ROYAL BAKING POWDER
COMPANY BOOKLET
IRWIN, PENNSYLVANIA
1898

PEANUT BRITTLE CRUNCH CAKE

People who grew up in San Francisco remember being taken as kids to Blum's and have fond recollections of the restaurant's signature Caramel Crunch Cake.

Famous for its chocolates, Blum's displayed rows of big, fluffy cakes to choose from; Caramel Crunch Cake was the best-known. This version, loosely suggested by a recipe of Chuck Williams (the founder of Williams-Sonoma), is true to the spirit of Blum's but different in details: The original was split into layers and lavishly filled with chopped caramel, without nuts. Tall, pale and tender, this cake is topped with whipped cream and crunchy pieces of peanut brittle.

Makes one 10-inch tube cake; serves 10 to 12

PEANUT BRITTLE TOPPING

1   cup sugar
¼   cup strong-brewed coffee, or 1 tablespoon instant coffee powder dissolved in ¼ cup hot water
3   tablespoons light corn syrup
2   teaspoons baking soda
1   cup dry-roasted peanuts, coarsely chopped

1   cup heavy cream, well chilled
1   tablespoon confectioners' or superfine sugar
1   teaspoon pure vanilla extract

1   Sunshine Cake (page 307), baked and cooled

1. PEANUT BRITTLE TOPPING: In a heavy saucepan, combine the sugar, coffee and corn syrup over medium-high heat. Bring to a boil, stirring to dissolve the sugar completely. Cook, without stirring, until the mixture reaches the hard-crack stage, about 310 degrees F on a candy thermometer, usually about 7 minutes. (If you don't own a candy thermometer, drop a small spoonful of the hot syrup into a cup of ice water; the mixture will immediately separate into hard, brittle threads.)

2. Remove the pan from the heat. Immediately sprinkle on the baking soda and stir carefully (do not splash this mixture; it's hot) until the mixture foams up, thickens and pulls away from the sides of the pan. Stir in the chopped nuts.

3. Carefully pour the mixture into an ungreased 9-inch cake or pie pan. Cool completely on a wire rack.

4. Place the cooled brittle between 2 large sheets of wax paper or in a heavy plastic bag; coarsely crush into uneven pieces with a rolling pin. The pieces should range in size from that of peas to small postage stamps.

5. Whip the cream with the sugar and vanilla until it forms nearly stiff peaks; do not overbeat. Brush any excess crumbs off the cake.

6. Spread the whipped cream over the top and sides of the cake. Carefully spread a little of the cream down into the central tube. Press the pieces of brittle into the cream on the top and sides. Refrigerate until cold, at least 1 hour.

7. Slice the cake with a long serrated knife and serve cold.

ABOUT CHEESECAKES

*C*akes and tarts baked with cheese are among the oldest of all baked goods, found wherever milk was transformed into simple, fresh-curd cheeses. In Roman times, sheep or goat cheeses were baked in cake-like breads. Other early forms of cheesecake, including one called *scriblita*, mentioned by the comic playwright Plautus, were fried in small cakes or baked on a hearth.

The oldest recorded cheesecake may be the *libum*, a flat cake or pie described by Cato in a Roman manuscript, *De Re Rustica*. "Crush two pounds of cheese," he begins, "mix with it a pound of rye flour, or, in order to render it lighter, throw in merely half a pound of wheat flour and an egg. Stir, mix, and work this paste; form of it a cake which you will place on leaves, and cook in a tart dish on the hot hearth."

More complex was the *placenta*, a cake made with sheep's milk cheese, rye and wheat flours and honey, slowly cooked in a pan on the hearth over live charcoals. This, according to eccentric 19th-century chef Alexis Soyer in *The Pantropheon*, was "the most celebrated of

White Torta

Prepare a pound and a half of best fresh cheese, chopped especially fine. Add twelve or fifteen egg whites, half a pound of sugar, half an ounce of white ginger, half a pound of pork liquamen and as much fresh butter. Blend in as much milk as you need. When you have blended this, put it into a pastry crust rolled thin and put it all in a pan and set it to bake on the hearth with a gentle flame. Then, to give it color, put coals on the lid. When it is cooked and taken from the pan, sprinkle ground sugar over it, with rosewater. This is very nourishing, slow to be digested; it warms the liver, brings on obstructions and causes stones and is bad for the nerves.

PLATINA
DE HONESTA VOLUPTATE
[OF HONEST INDULGENCE
AND GOOD HEALTH]
1475

ancient pies . . . which so delighted mankind, and by which the gods even allowed their fury to be appeased."

All cheesecakes spring from these simple beginnings: Basically, they are elaborations of sweetened fresh curds. Called "fresh cheese" by Elizabethans, these early desserts are virtually universal. They range from Little Miss Muffet's "curds and whey" to the sweetened soft ricotta eaten throughout the Mediterranean to the elegant French *coeur à la crème.*

In medieval times, concurrent with the simple cheese desserts discussed above, cheese curds were spiced and baked in tarts; these gradually evolved into what we know as cheesecakes. By the mid-17th century, *The Queens Closet Opened* (1655) gives instructions on how "To make a great Curd Loafe," a rich affair with 7 egg yolks, which, after baking, had its top sliced off and melted butter and sugar added.

If you followed a Robert May recipe published in 1660 in *The Accomplisht Cook*, you'd wind up with something slightly altered in flavor but not very different in substance from any number of today's "Authentic New York Style Cheesecakes." Common variations in books of the period include almond cheesecakes, lemon and orange cheesecakes and potato cheesecakes.

In 18th-century English recipes, cheese is lightly sweetened and flavored with cinnamon, nutmeg or rose water and eaten with fresh cream poured over. In Scotland, Hattered Kit is a dessert made by clabbering milk with buttermilk. The skimmed curds are left to drain, first in a sieve, and then in a "shape," to be sweetened and sprinkled with cinnamon, if desired, and eaten with fresh cream—directly parallel to *coeur à la crème.*

While cheesecake has its passionate fans, it should be conceded that many people find it too heavy as an after-dinner dessert. It's best on its own, with a cup of coffee—especially as a late-night treat.

ITALIAN SKILLET CHEESECAKE
(*CASSOLA*)

This is a beautifully light, not too sweet ricotta cheesecake, cooked by a unique method: baked in a skillet. It might be considered a direct descendant of the hearth-baked cheesecakes of ancient Rome.

For this recipe, you will need an 8-inch nonstick skillet with an ovenproof handle. (You can improvise with an 8-inch cake pan, if you handle it carefully.)

If at all possible, try this with freshly made ricotta, available at some cheese stores and Italian markets—its sweet milky flavor will surprise you.

Makes one 8-inch cake; serves 6

2	pounds ricotta cheese, preferably freshly made from whole milk
½	cup sugar
2	tablespoons cornstarch
3	large eggs, well beaten
1	large egg yolk
1	teaspoon extra-virgin olive oil
	Confectioners' sugar, for sprinkling
	Fresh raspberries or strawberries, for serving

1. Place the ricotta in a large bowl. With a wooden spoon, beat in the sugar and cornstarch. Add the eggs and the egg yolk and mix until smooth.

2. Preheat the oven to 350 degrees F. Brush a heavy 8-inch nonstick skillet with an ovenproof handle with the olive oil. Preheat the pan for a few seconds on the stovetop over low heat. Spoon in the ricotta mixture in a smooth layer. Cook on the stovetop until the outer inch of the mixture is set and the bottom is lightly golden, 15 to 20 minutes.

3. Place the pan in the oven and bake until the cheesecake is puffed and lightly golden, 10 to 15 minutes.

4. Remove the pan from the oven and run the tip of a knife around the sides of the cheesecake; invert onto a serving plate. Cool to lukewarm on a wire rack. Sprinkle the cheesecake with confectioners' sugar; serve in wedges, topped with ripe berries.

According to cookbook author Anna Teresa Callen, a native of Abruzzo, cheesecake is one of Italy's few truly classic desserts. "For me, the *torta di ricotta* was my favorite; my Aunt Cettina would make it for me. It can be made without a crust, but when you add a crust, it becomes a *crostata di ricotta*."

NEW YORK–STYLE
SOUR CREAM CHEESECAKE

For generations of New Yorkers, Lindy's cheesecake was and is the quintessence of the genre. The real thing is made with a pastry crust and heavy cream, not sour cream.

This cheesecake is a variation on Lindy's original. The flavor is mellow, with a lemony edge. It bakes up perfectly—no cracks, the palest gold edges. It's both substantial and creamy—a delicate balancing act.

Makes one 9-inch cake; serves 12 or more

CRUST
1	cup zwieback crumbs (about 18 pieces) or graham cracker crumbs (about 12 individual crackers)
1½	tablespoons sugar
2½	tablespoons unsalted butter, melted

FILLING
2½	pounds cream cheese, softened
1½	cups sugar
	Grated zest of 1 lemon and 1 small orange
½	teaspoon pure vanilla extract
3	tablespoons all-purpose flour
5	large eggs
2	large egg yolks
½	cup sour cream

1. CRUST: Preheat the oven to 375 degrees F. Butter the bottom of a 9-inch springform pan. Combine the crumbs with the sugar and butter and toss to moisten. Press the mixture onto the bottom of the pan.

2. Bake the crust until golden, about 8 minutes. Set aside on a wire rack to cool. Increase the oven heat to 500 degrees or more (without going all the way to broil). Butter the sides of the pan; set aside.

3. FILLING: In a large bowl, with an electric mixer, beat the cream cheese with the sugar, citrus zests and vanilla until creamy. Add the flour; beat in the eggs and yolks, one at a time, mixing well after each addition. Add the sour cream and mix until very smooth. Pour the mixture into the pan.

4. Bake the cheesecake for 12 minutes. Reduce the temperature to 200 degrees. Bake for 1 hour more.

5. Cool the cheesecake in the pan on a wire rack for about 15 minutes. While the cake is still warm, run the tip of a knife gently around the sides to loosen it from the pan. When cooled to room temperature, gently remove the sides of the pan. Chill until cold and firm, at least 3 hours.

6. Remove from the refrigerator about 20 minutes before serving. Cut the cheesecake with a knife dipped into hot water. Serve cold.

To Make Cheesecakes

Let your paste be very good, either puff-paste or cold butter paste, with Sugar mixed with it, then the whey being dried very well for the Cheese-Curds which must be made of new milk or butter, beat them in a mortar or tray, with a quarter of a pound of butter to every pottle of curds, and a good quantity of rose-water, 3 grains of amber griese or musk prepared, the crumbs of a small manchet [loaf] rubbed through a cullender, the yolks of 10 eggs, a grated nutmeg, a little salt, and a good store of sugar, mix all these well together with a little cream. . . . Instead of bread you may take almonds which are much better; bake them in a quick oven, and let them not stand too long in, least they should be too dry.

Robert May
The Accomplisht Cook
London, 1685

WORLD WAR I APPLESAUCE CHEESECAKE

This recipe is from World War I, when sugar was in short supply. It was given to my mother by Babs Riffin of Montclair, New Jersey, who last year celebrated her 50th wedding anniversary. Mrs. Riffin's mother made this cake during World War I, and Mrs. Riffin baked it herself during World War II, when sugar was scarce. There is neither cheese nor sugar in the recipe, but the applesauce and sweetened condensed milk combine with the eggs to give a cheesecake-like texture that's very light, with plenty of apple flavor.

⟶ *Makes one 9-inch cake; serves 8 to 10*

CRUMB CRUST
¾ cup zwieback crumbs (12-13 pieces) or graham cracker crumbs (9 individual crackers)
3 tablespoons sugar
½ teaspoon ground cinnamon
2½ tablespoons unsalted butter, melted

FILLING
3 cups smooth, thick, unsweetened applesauce
1 can (14 ounces) sweetened condensed milk
4 large eggs, separated
Grated zest and juice of 2 lemons

1. **CRUMB CRUST:** Preheat the oven to 425 degrees F. Butter the bottom of a 9-inch springform pan. Combine the crumbs, sugar, cinnamon and butter in a food processor or bowl; toss to moisten. Set aside about 1 tablespoon of the crumb mixture. Press the remainder over the bottom of the pan.

2. Bake the crust until set and slightly darker in color, about 8 minutes. Set aside to cool on a wire rack; leave the oven on. Butter the sides of the pan; set aside.

3. **FILLING:** In a bowl, combine the applesauce, condensed milk, egg yolks and lemon zest and juice. In another bowl, beat the egg whites until nearly stiff; gently fold into the applesauce mixture. Pour the filling into the cooled crust. Sprinkle the surface of the filling with the 1 tablespoon reserved crumbs.

4. Bake the cheesecake until a knife or toothpick inserted in the center emerges clean, 55 to 60 minutes.

5. Cool the cake to room temperature on a wire rack. Run the tip of a knife around the edge of the cake to loosen it from the pan; gently remove the sides. Chill the cake until cold, at least 2 hours. Serve cold.

ABOUT CHOCOLATE

*C*hocolate, which virtually conquered the rest of the globe, is one of the New World's most successful native products. Credit for it should go to the Aztecs, who combined the bitter cocoa bean with honey, cinnamon and other spices and vanilla to make a drink called *chocolatl*. When Spanish explorer Hernando Cortés arrived in Mexico in the early 1500s, the emperor Montezuma served him a nectar-like concoction of *chocolatl* made with sweetened ground cocoa that was chilled by dipping the vessels containing it into cold spring water canals that ran below his palace. The original version of this drink was made with beans toasted on a *metate* (stone) and ground with cornmeal, spices and chilies.

The Spanish conquistadores brought chocolate to Trinidad for cultivation, and it was carried back to the court of Spain, where it became a popular drink in the early 1600s. Sugar and vanilla, the latter also imported from the New World, were added to round out the flavor. Spain still consumed one-third of the world's production of cocoa until the early 19th century. From Spain, chocolate spread to France, where it was drunk in the court of Louis XIV, and then to England, where it was enjoyed as a beverage.

By 1765, Dr. James Baker had opened America's first chocolate mill in Dorchester, Massachusetts. It later became the company that produced Baker's Chocolate. In 1990, the average American consumed some 11 pounds of chocolate each year, up more than one-third from only a decade earlier.

QUICK CHOCOLATE CANDY CAKE

It was only 15 minutes before my dinner guests (including a chef) were due, and I dropped the finished dessert in smithereens all over the floor. In six minutes, I had a Quick Chocolate Candy Cake in the oven as a replacement, and the house smelled great when my friends arrived.

I've baked this moist, crunchy cake for years—it's the "little black dress of chocolate cakes," understated but always right. Made without flour but with fresh bread crumbs and ground nuts, it's loosely based on a recipe from the late Helen McCully, who edited the food pages for *McCall's* and *House Beautiful* magazines and who encouraged many young people in the food business, including me. A no-nonsense professional, Helen was endlessly, infectiously curious about food.

Don't overbake this cake, or you'll miss the moist chocolate center.

Makes one 8-inch single-layer cake; serves 8 to 10

½ cup (1 stick) unsalted butter, softened
½ cup sugar
1 tablespoon apricot preserves
1 tablespoon Grand Marnier or cognac
3 large eggs
4 ounces semisweet chocolate, melted and cooled slightly
1 cup blanched almonds, finely ground in a food processor
Grated zest of 1 orange
¼ cup soft, fresh bread crumbs
Confectioners' sugar, for sprinkling (see note)
Whipped cream or Eggnog Custard Sauce (page 609), for serving

1. Preheat the oven to 375 degrees F. Butter the sides of an 8-inch round cake pan. Line the bottom of the pan with parchment or wax paper; butter the paper and set aside.

2. With an electric mixer at medium-high speed, beat the butter and sugar until well blended and light. Beat in the preserves, Grand Marnier or cognac and 1 of the eggs. Add the remaining 2 eggs, one at a time, and beat until smooth. Stir in the melted chocolate, ground almonds, orange zest and bread crumbs until combined. Pour the batter into the prepared pan.

3. Bake until the cake is set but still slightly moist in the center, about 25 minutes; do not overbake.

4. Cool the cake in the pan on a wire rack for 15 minutes. Turn it out of the pan onto the rack and remove the paper. Turn the cake right side up; let cool to lukewarm or room temperature.

5. Sprinkle the top of the cake with confectioners' sugar. Serve in wedges with a spoonful of whipped cream, or surrounded by a pool of custard sauce.

Note: If you prefer a more finished look, top this cake with Shiny Chocolate Glaze (page 397).

About
German Chocolate Cake

German chocolate cake, that favorite American layer cake with coconut-pecan frosting, is not German. And it was not (as is sometimes reported) brought to the American Midwest by German immigrants.

The "German" in the name refers to German's Sweet Chocolate, named for Englishman Sam German, and now made by Baker's Chocolate.

The cake was first popular in either Texas or Oklahoma. After the recipe was published by a Dallas newspaper in 1957, German chocolate cake swept the country. But the cake had been around before that. One St. Louis woman recalled that she had been given the recipe by her mother-in-law in the late 1920s. During the Great Depression, she had stopped baking it because she couldn't afford the ingredients and lost the recipe. When it was published, she said it "was like meeting a long-lost friend."

FUDGY CHOCOLATE LAYER CAKE

Chocolate cake lovers tend to be very particular about what a chocolate cake should be. While working on this book, I baked and tasted one chocolate layer cake after another. But I wasn't satisfied until I tasted this one.

This is a down-home, all-American chocolate layer cake. It's chocolatey (cocoa makes the difference), without veering into the realm of fudge or a brownie. And while moist and light, this is a cake, not a mousse, not a fallen soufflé, not a flourless extravaganza (for that, see Chocolate Cloud Cake, page 420).

Makes one 9-inch 2-layer cake; serves about 8

CAKE

1¾	cups all-purpose flour
¾	cup plus 3 tablespoons unsweetened cocoa powder
1¼	teaspoons baking soda
⅛	teaspoon salt
¾	cup (1½ sticks) unsalted butter, softened
⅔	cup sugar
⅔	cup packed dark or light brown sugar
2	large eggs
2	teaspoons pure vanilla extract
1½	cups buttermilk

GLOSSY DARK CHOCOLATE FROSTING

½	cup (1 stick) unsalted butter, softened
1	cup confectioners' sugar, sifted
2	teaspoons pure vanilla extract
3	ounces unsweetened chocolate, melted and cooled slightly

1. **CAKE:** Preheat the oven to 350 degrees F. Butter the bottoms and sides of two 9-inch cake pans. Line the bottoms with rounds of parchment or wax paper cut to fit; butter the paper and set aside. Sift the flour, cocoa, baking soda and salt onto a sheet of wax paper; set aside.

2. In a bowl with an electric mixer on medium-high speed, cream the butter with the white and brown sugars until light. Add the eggs, one at a time, beating thoroughly after each addition. Add the vanilla.

3. Lower the speed to slow and add the dry ingredients alternately with the buttermilk, beginning and ending with the dry ingredients. Mix just until blended, no longer. Divide the batter between the prepared pans; smooth the tops.

4. Bake until the cakes shrink slightly away from the sides of the pans and a toothpick inserted in the centers emerges clean, usually 25 to 30 minutes.

5. Cool the cakes in the pans on wire racks for 10 minutes. Carefully loosen the cakes from the pans with the tip of a knife and invert onto the racks; carefully peel off the paper. Turn right side up and cool to room temperature.

6. **GLOSSY DARK CHOCOLATE FROSTING:** In a bowl with an electric mixer, cream the butter with the confectioners' sugar until very light. Add the vanilla and melted chocolate and beat until shiny and smooth.

7. Place 1 cake layer on a serving plate; spread with a small amount of the frosting. Top with the other layer; frost the sides and then the top, swirling the icing. Let the cake stand for at least 30 minutes before cutting. Serve at room temperature.

Chocolate Treat

Dorothy was looking with delighted absorption at the huge piece of chocolate cake that had been set before her and was already reaching for her fork . . . [Justine] felt a flash of repulsion at this sight of greed on automatic pilot, and then that was superseded by an odd feeling of tenderness based on her certainty that behind this mask of blind compulsion was a little girl in a state of solemn ecstasy over an extra-special treat—and then she was saddened by the . . . certainty that food was the only kind of treat this little girl ever got.

"It's good, isn't it?" she said.

"Very good," replied Dorothy. "Really tasty."

They ate in silence for a moment as Justine reflected on something a girlfriend had said once, that men bond when they drink and women bond when they eat dessert together.

MARY GAITSKILL
TWO GIRLS, FAT AND THIN
1990

Low-Fat Chocolate Nut Torte
(A Passover Recipe)

This light torte is from restaurant consultant and cookbook author Rozanne Gold. It's easy to put together, low in fat (made with cocoa instead of melted chocolate), pareve (containing no dairy products) and a good Passover recipe.

Makes one 9-inch single-layer cake; serves 8

½	cup walnut pieces
½	cup whole almonds
½	cup unsweetened cocoa powder
1	cup sugar
3	tablespoons vegetable oil
1	tablespoon dark rum or cognac (optional)
8	large egg whites
	Pinch salt
	Confectioners' sugar, for sprinkling

1. Preheat the oven to 350 degrees F. Scatter the walnuts and almonds in a pie pan and toast until fragrant, stirring once or twice, about 10 minutes. Remove from the oven (leave the oven on); transfer the nuts to a food processor; set aside to cool.

2. Lightly coat a 9-inch springform pan with butter, margarine or bland vegetable oil. Sprinkle with sugar; shake out any excess; set aside.

3. In a large bowl, combine the cocoa, ¾ cup of the sugar and the vegetable oil. In the food processor, combine the toasted nuts with the remaining ¼ cup sugar. Grind until powdery but not oily. Add the ground nut mixture and the optional rum or cognac to the bowl and stir until smooth.

4. In a separate bowl, with an electric mixer at medium-high speed, beat the egg whites with the salt until nearly stiff. Fold about ¼ of the egg whites into the cocoa-nut mixture; fold in the remaining whites. Do not overmix; the batter should be stiff and slightly hard to fold. Transfer the mixture to the prepared pan; smooth the top.

5. Bake until the cake is puffed, nearly set but still wobbly in the center and a toothpick emerges not quite clean, about 30 minutes.

6. Remove from the oven and cool in the pan on a wire rack for 10 to 15 minutes. Carefully run the tip of a knife around the sides of the cake and remove the sides of the pan. While the cake is still warm, sprinkle with confectioners' sugar. Sprinkle with a little more confectioners' sugar just before serving at room temperature.

Joyful Feast

During Passover, the eight days that mark the exodus of the Jews from Egypt, no flour or leavened bread products are eaten. At the joyful Seder feast on the first day, as the unleavened matzo is served, everyone recites together:

Let whoever is hungry come in and eat thereof;

let whoever is in need come in and celebrate.

CHOCOLATE CHIFFON LOAF CAKE

B illing it as "The Cake Discovery of the Century," General Mills introduced its Golden Chiffon Cake, made with vegetable oil instead of butter or solid shortening, in 1948. If you were around in the '40s, you may remember chiffon cakes sweeping the country, thanks to unflagging promotion. "Light as angel food," ads promised, "rich as butter cake and easy to make."

This chocolate loaf version of chiffon cake is made with cocoa; it's low in fat and cholesterol. It also keeps well, tightly wrapped in plastic.

Makes one 8-x-4-inch loaf; serves 8

⅓   cup unsweetened Dutch-process cocoa powder (see note)
½   cup boiling water
1   teaspoon instant coffee powder, preferably espresso
¾   cup cake flour (not self-rising)
¾   cup sugar
1   teaspoon baking powder
¼   cup bland vegetable oil
2   large egg yolks
1   teaspoon pure vanilla extract
4   large egg whites
    Pinch cream of tartar
    Raspberry Sauce (page 617; optional)
    Fresh raspberries, for garnish (optional)

1. Preheat the oven to 350 degrees F. Line the bottom of an 8-x-4-inch loaf pan with parchment or wax paper cut to fit; set aside.

2. Combine the cocoa, boiling water and instant coffee until blended; set aside. Sift the flour, ½ cup of the sugar and the baking powder into a large bowl. Stir in the cocoa mixture, oil, egg yolks and vanilla until combined.

3. In a separate bowl, beat the egg whites with the cream of tartar until they form soft peaks. Gradually beat in the remaining ¼ cup sugar and beat until the meringue forms stiff peaks. Vigorously fold about ¼ of the meringue into the batter; gently fold in the remaining whites. Scrape the batter into the prepared pan; smooth the top.

4. Bake until a toothpick inserted in the center of the cake emerges clean, about 55 minutes.

5. Cool the cake in the pan on a wire rack for 10 minutes. Invert the cake, remove the pan and carefully peel off the paper; let cool to room temperature. Serve with Raspberry Sauce and fresh raspberries, if you like.

NOTE: If not using Dutch-process (alkaline) cocoa powder, replace the baking powder with 1 teaspoon baking soda.

Birth of a Cake

Harry Baker, a California insurance salesman, first developed the chiffon cake in 1927 and guarded his secret recipe for 20 years. He then worked out an arrangement whereby Betty Crocker, then played by an actress on the radio show *Betty Crocker's Cooking School of the Air*, would introduce the cake to the public.

CHOCOLATE CLOUD CAKE

This flourless cake is crammed with chocolate (use only the best) and rich with butter and will fall slightly as it cools. The center is filled with softly whipped cream and sprinkled with cocoa powder—intensity, then relief, in each bite.

Makes one 8-inch single-layer cake; serves 8 to 12

CAKE

8 ounces best-quality bittersweet or semisweet chocolate, coarsely chopped
½ cup (1 stick) unsalted butter, cut into pieces, softened
6 large eggs: 2 whole, 4 separated
1 cup sugar
2 tablespoons cognac or Grand Marnier (optional)
Grated zest of 1 orange (optional)

WHIPPED CREAM TOPPING

1½ cups heavy cream, well chilled
3 tablespoons confectioners' sugar
1 teaspoon pure vanilla extract

Unsweetened cocoa powder, for sprinkling

1. **CAKE:** Preheat the oven to 350 degrees F. Line the bottom of an 8-inch springform pan with a round of wax paper; do not butter the pan. Melt the chocolate in a double boiler or in a bowl set over hot water. Remove from the heat and whisk in the butter until melted; set aside.

2. In a bowl, whisk the 2 whole eggs and the 4 egg yolks with ½ cup of the sugar just until blended. Whisk in the warm chocolate mixture. Whisk in the optional cognac or Grand Marnier and the optional orange zest.

3. In another bowl, with an electric mixer, beat the 4 egg whites until foamy. Gradually add the remaining ½ cup sugar and beat until the whites form soft mounds that hold their shape but are not quite stiff. Stir about ¼ of the beaten egg whites into the chocolate mixture to lighten it; gently fold in the remaining whites. Pour the batter into the pan; smooth the top.

4. Bake until the top of the cake is puffed and cracked and the center is no longer wobbly, usually 35 to 40 minutes. Do not overbake.

5. Cool the cake in the pan on a wire rack; the cake will sink as it cools, forming a crater with high sides.

6. **WHIPPED CREAM TOPPING:** At serving time, whip the cream with the confectioners' sugar and vanilla until not quite stiff. With a spatula, carefully fill the crater of the cake with the whipped cream, pushing it gently to the edges. Dust the top lightly with cocoa powder. Run the tip of a knife around the edges of the cake; carefully remove the sides of the pan and serve.

RECIPES

*Mother Church's Spirited
Dark Fruitcake*
*The Four Seasons' Christmas
Fruitcake*
Mr. Guinness's Cake
Election Cake
Tyrolean Christmas Fruitcake
*Mrs. Dalgairns' Scottish
Seed Cake*
*Nina's Fabulous Athenian
Nut Cake with Rum Syrup*
*Sephardic Walnut Cake with
Honey-Lemon Syrup*

CHAPTER 11

FRUITCAKES AND NUT CAKES

For a look at the Café
Beaujolais catalog—
more friendly letter than
advertisement—write to
Café Beaujolais, Box 1236,
Mendocino, California
95460.

P oor fruitcake. What other dessert has been so
ridiculed, so scorned, so vilified? Johnny Carson
used to joke that "there's only one fruitcake—it
just keeps getting passed around and around."
Unfortunately, the jokes are right in too many cases. What
could be worse than a dry cake, musty with garish candied fruit, and
weeks old. In her Café Beaujolais mail-order catalog, Margaret Fox
promised that in her fruitcake, she used "no green things—ever."

It's too bad that fruitcake has become the butt of jokes because made well, it can be delicious. Few foods are as festive, evok-
ing days when people were "at home" receiving on holidays, and
guests presented calling cards when they stopped by for a glass of
Madeira or sherry or a cup of punch.

One thing that helps improve fruitcake is using dried, not
candied, fruits. What's sold as candied fruit is usually chemically
embalmed beyond recognition. It's ironic that we've come to this
pass, because candying fruit is one of the highest and most complex forms of the confectioner's art, requiring repeated infusion of
the fruit in sugar syrups of increasing densities over 10 or more
days, until the cells of the fruit are saturated with sugar. It's one of
the oldest forms of preserving.

Before it became corrupted by ersatz mail-order atrocities,
fruitcake enjoyed a long and venerable history. Dried currants or
other dried fruits were added to bread dough, as were honey and

milk, when these extra luxuries were available. The fruitcake genre as we know it is the domain of the British, an outgrowth of their richly varied fruit-studded buns and fruited griddle breads, including "Singin' Hinny" and such Welsh griddle breads as *bara pyglyd*, whose name later became "pikelet."

Distinctions between early fruit-studded breads and fruit cakes were hazy. As C. Anne Wilson notes in *Food and Drink in Britain*, these breads were popular breakfast fare in 17th-century Britain, whether baked as loaves, cakes or small buns:

> The old heavy meal of ale, bread and meat or fish pottage was given up after the introduction of coffee and chocolate, and instead a lighter repast was taken . . . A recipe of 1727 for a well-fruited spice bread describes it as "an ordinary cake . . . good to eat with butter for breakfasts."

From such everyday breads to festive fruitcakes is but a small leap; both existed simultaneously. English fruitcakes are known by various names, sometimes by the names of the occasions they commemorate: Christmas Cake, Rich Plum (or "Plumb," an early term for raisin) Cake, Bride's Cake, Groom's Cake, Queen's Cake (for Queen Anne, then monarch not only of England but of her upstart American colonies, too), Scottish Dundee Cake and Madeira Cake.

So English is the fruitcake that it has come to be more than just a cake. In *Sweet Dishes*, Colonel Kenney-Herbert, writing in Madras in 1881, when the British Raj was at its height, observed that: "A good English plum cake . . . is a national institution."

German spice-and-fruit breads are a related northern European tradition. Tyrolean Christmas Fruitcake (page 432), made in the Alto Adige region of Italy and in adjacent southern Austria, is a delicious example, halfway between cake and confection.

Wherever they are found, fruitcakes seem to be associated with ritual. On Twelfth Night (January 5th), for example, a rich plum cake or pound cake (or, in France, *gâteau des rois*) is baked with a lucky token or a small figure inside; whoever gets the token enjoys good luck (and, in earlier times, may have been named king or queen of the holiday revels).

We think of fruitcake as a Christmas specialty, but the Scottish black bun, a festive cake studded with nuts, citrus rind and spices (including "Jamaica pepper," or allspice), is actually served on the last day of December (New Year's Eve), to mark the old Celtic festival called Hogmanay. On this day, also called "Cake-day," children would call out the holiday's name when visiting

Favorite Fruitcake

15 cups flour
Red thingies
Green thingies
Syrup
Glue

Mix ingredients. Bake. Spray with hairspray or lacquer.

friends and would be presented with the gift of some cake.

And then there is Scottish Dundee Cake, traditionally topped with cherries and almonds. This damp cake is said to be a holdover from the days when a sweet oat bannock, a flattish round or oval-shaped bread, was served to the women present at a child's birth. In a related old custom, a bannock with a ring baked in it would be given to a teething child. When the tooth came in, everyone was given a piece of the bread, and the child used the ring as a teething ring. Today, Dundee cake still marks christenings, weddings and Christmas.

MOTHER CHURCH'S SPIRITED DARK FRUITCAKE

This cake may make you rethink fruitcake. It's dark, very moist and soaked with plenty of spirits. What makes it distinctive is its lavish use of prunes, golden raisins and crystallized ginger instead of the ghoulish red and green stuff.

Mother Church isn't a religious institution—it's the Reverend Susan Campbell Church, vicar of the Episcopal Mission in Newport, Oregon, who developed this recipe. If you really want to taste something special, make this cake with prunes from Orchard Crest Farm in Oregon (see page 77 for mail-order information).

Prepare the cake a few weeks ahead of the holidays, and the flavors will perk up and ripen, nourished with more spirits from time to time. This confection-like cake also works nicely baked as small loaves for gift-giving.

◦⟿ *Makes two 9-x-5-inch loaves; each serves 8 to 10*

2	cups all-purpose flour
½	teaspoon baking powder
2	cups (4 sticks) unsalted butter, softened
2¼	cups sugar
6	large eggs, separated
2	tablespoons lemon extract
2½	cups (about 1 pound) golden raisins
1	cup chopped crystallized ginger
1	pound pitted prunes, coarsely chopped (about 2⅔ cups)
3½	cups (about 1 pound) chopped walnuts
	Pinch salt
2-3	cups brandy, dark rum or Scotch, as needed

1. Preheat the oven to 225 degrees F. Cut 2 sheets of wax paper each 9 inches wide and about 12 inches long. Fit each sheet of paper into a 9-x-5-inch loaf pan, with the ends overhanging the long sides of the pan. Butter the wax paper and the short ends of the pans; set aside. Sift 1½ cups of the flour with the baking powder; set aside.

2. In a large bowl, with an electric mixer on medium-high speed, cream the butter and sugar until light and fluffy. Beat in the egg yolks and lemon extract and blend well. Lower the speed to slow, and gradually beat in the sifted mixture; do not overmix. Toss the raisins, ginger and prunes with the remaining ½ cup flour; fold into the batter along with the walnuts.

3. In a bowl, beat the egg whites with the salt until nearly stiff. Fold a little of the egg whites into the batter; it will be very stiff. Fold in the remainder. Divide the batter between the prepared pans; smooth the tops.

4. Bake until a toothpick inserted in the center of the loaves emerges clean, 2¼ to 2½ hours.

5. Cool the cakes in the pans on a wire rack for 20 minutes. Unmold the cakes; peel away the wax paper and turn right side up. Cool completely on the racks.

6. Lay 2 large sheets of foil on a work surface. Cut a piece of cheesecloth large enough to wrap each cake; place each on top of a sheet of foil. Carefully place 1 cake on each piece of cheesecloth. Baste the top and sides of the cakes with ⅓ to ½ cup of your choice of liquor, brushing it on and letting it soak in for a few minutes. Brush again twice. Wrap the cakes in the cheesecloth; wrap in the foil. Refrigerate for 1 month to age and ripen, brushing them with more liquor through their cheesecloth about once a week.

Conversion

When I first baked this, a fruitcake-hating friend walked into the kitchen, tasted it and said, "I hate fruitcakes, because they're dense and dry. But this one is dense and moist, and I love it!"

The Four Seasons' Christmas Fruitcake
(Light Fruitcake Wrapped in Marzipan)

Four Seasons' pastry chef Patrick Lemblé, a native of Mulhouse in Alsace, wraps his holiday fruitcake in marzipan, an Old-World touch. This is a simple spiced cake, chock-full of fruits and nuts. It cuts into a precise cross-section, neatly enveloped in its marzipan wrapper.

For restaurant gifts, Patrick bakes over 300 pounds of this fruitcake over a period of five days. This is his recipe, downsized for home baking.

Makes three 8-x-4-inch loaves; each serves about 8

1	pound mixed dried fruits, such as prunes, apricots, apples, pears and figs
	Dark rum or brandy, as needed
2⅔	cups all-purpose flour
½	cup plus 1 tablespoon cornstarch
2½	teaspoons baking powder
¼	teaspoon salt
2½	teaspoons ground cinnamon
1½	teaspoons ground allspice
1½	teaspoons fresh-grated nutmeg
¾	teaspoon ground coriander (optional)
1	cup plus 6 tablespoons (2¾ sticks) unsalted butter, softened
1¾	cups plus 2 tablespoons confectioners' sugar
	Grated zest of 1 lemon
	Grated zest of 2 oranges
9	large eggs
2	cups (about ½ pound) chopped walnuts

Marzipan Wrapping

1½	pounds almond paste, preferably canned
3	cups confectioners' sugar
¼	cup plus 2 tablespoons light corn syrup
	Sugar, for sprinkling

1. Chop the mixed dried fruits into ½-inch dice. Place in a bowl and douse generously with rum or brandy. Soak overnight or longer, stirring occasionally. Drain, reserving the liquid; set aside.

2. Preheat the oven to 350 degrees F. Butter three 8-x-4-inch loaf pans; line the bottoms with rectangles of parchment or wax paper; butter the paper; set aside. Sift the flour, cornstarch, baking powder, salt and spices onto a sheet of wax paper; set aside.

3. In a large bowl, with an electric mixer on medium-high speed, cream the butter, confectioners' sugar and lemon and orange zests until pale and fluffy. Add the eggs, one at a time, mixing well between additions.

4. Lower the speed to medium-slow and fold in the flour mixture. Fold in the soaked fruits and the walnuts, along with 2 to 3 tablespoons of the soaking liquid. Divide the batter among the pans.

5. Bake until a toothpick inserted in the center of the loaves emerges clean, about 1 hour.

6. Remove the cakes from the pans and cool on wire racks for 15 minutes. Unmold, turn right side up and cool to room temperature.

7. **MARZIPAN WRAPPING:** In a food processor or with an electric mixer, combine the almond paste, confectioners' sugar and corn syrup until smooth and well blended. Alternately, knead together by hand. Divide the marzipan into 3 equal pieces. Neatly slice off any rough edges from each loaf; slice enough off the top of each loaf to level it.

8. On a work surface sprinkled with a little confectioners' sugar, roll out a piece of the marzipan to an even 11-x-8-inch rectangle. If you leave the marzipan somewhat tacky, it will stick to the cake by itself; if it does not, brush one side of the marzipan lightly with corn syrup. Drape the marzipan, syrup side down, covering the top and long sides, over 1 loaf. Tuck the edges under the bottom of the loaf and press gently so it adheres; don't worry about the short ends. Using a long serrated knife, cut a slice from both ends of the loaf, to expose the cake. Sprinkle sugar over the marzipan. Wrap tightly in plastic. Roll out the remaining pieces of marzipan, cover the remaining loaves, trim and wrap in the same fashion. Store at room temperature for up to 1 week.

A Pretty Cake

Take five Pounds of Flour well dried, one Pound of Sugar, half an Ounce of Mace, and as much Nutmeg, beat your Spice very fine, mix the Sugar and Spice in the Flour, take twenty-two Eggs, leave out six Whites, beat them, and put a Pint of Ale Yeast and the Eggs in the Flour, take two Pounds and half of fresh Butter, a Pint and half of Cream, set the Cream and Butter over the Fire, till the Butter is melted, let it stand till it is blood warm, before you put it into the Flour, set it an Hour by the Fire to rise, then put in seven Pounds of Currans, which must be plumped in half a Pint of Brandy, and three quarters of a Pound of candied Peels. It must stand an Hour and quarter in the Oven. You must put two Pounds of chopped Raisins in the Flour, and a quarter of a Pint of Sack. When you put the Currans in, bake it in a Hoop.

HANNAH GLASSE
*THE ART OF COOKERY,
MADE PLAIN AND EASY*
LONDON, 1747

MR. GUINNESS'S CAKE

This is a moist, light-textured, pale to medium gold cake, heady with spices and dried fruit, with a yeasty aroma. Guinness, the Irish family that founded the brewing company, has produced stout since 1759. This traditional Irish fruitcake recipe has been in the Guinness family for over 100 years.

Makes one 8-inch single-layer cake; serves about 10

1½	cups all-purpose flour
¾	teaspoon baking soda
¾	teaspoon ground cinnamon
½	teaspoon ground allspice
½	teaspoon ground ginger
¼	teaspoon fresh-grated nutmeg
¾	cup (1½ sticks) unsalted butter, softened
1	cup packed light brown sugar
4	large eggs
1	cup dark raisins
1	cup golden raisins
½	cup chopped candied orange peel, or grated zest of 2 oranges
½	cup chopped candied lemon peel, or grated zest of 2 lemons
½	cup chopped candied or dried pineapple or candied red cherries
1	bottle Guinness Stout, at room temperature
	Confectioners' sugar, for sprinkling
	Halved candied cherries, for decoration (optional)

1. Preheat the oven to 325 degrees F. Butter and lightly flour an 8-inch springform pan. Sift 1¼ cups of the flour, the baking soda, cinnamon, allspice, ginger and nutmeg onto a piece of wax paper; set aside.

2. In a large bowl, beat the butter with an electric mixer on medium-high speed until light and fluffy. Gradually beat in the brown sugar until thoroughly combined. Beat in the eggs, one at a time, beating well after each addition. Lower the speed to slow, add the flour mixture and beat just until blended.

3. In a small bowl, combine the dark and golden raisins, orange and lemon peels or zests, pineapple or cherries and the remaining ¼ cup flour. Toss to coat the fruit with the flour. Add to

Stout-Hearted Taste

World-renowned Guinness Stout, deep mahogany with a malty sweetness to its thick foam, flavors and moistens this cake. Beer and ale have long been used in bread- and cake-baking, for leavening as well as flavor.

the batter along with ⅓ cup of the Guinness. Beat until well blended. Pour the batter into the prepared pan.

4. Bake the cake for 45 minutes. Lower the oven temperature to 300 degrees. Continue baking until a toothpick inserted in the center of the cake emerges clean and the cake shrinks away from the sides of the pan, usually 25 to 30 minutes longer.

5. Cool the cake in the pan on a wire rack for 10 minutes. Carefully remove the sides of the pan; cool the cake to room temperature.

6. When the cake is at room temperature, prick the top surface all over, reaching about halfway through, with a fork or skewer. Transfer the cake to a large plate. Slowly and evenly pour about ¼ cup of the Guinness over the cake; let the liquid sink in for a few minutes. Invert the cake and remove the bottom of the springform. Prick the bottom of the cake all over, as you did the top. Slowly pour on about ¼ cup more Guinness. Allow the stout to be absorbed, about 10 minutes.

7. Turn the cake right side up and tightly wrap in plastic wrap. Wrap again in foil. Store in a cool place or in the refrigerator for at least 3 days. *(The cake can be stored for about 1½ weeks in the refrigerator; the flavors will improve.)*

8. Bring the cake to room temperature before serving. Just before serving, dust the top of the cake with confectioners' sugar. Decorate with a row of candied cherries, if you like.

Baker's Cakes

The Monday of the Feast—for it lasted two days—was kept by women and children only, the men being at work. It was a great day for tea parties; mothers and sisters and aunts and cousins coming in droves from about the neighbourhood. The chief delicacy at these teas was "baker's cake," a rich, fruity, spicy dough cake, obtained in the following manner. The housewife provided all the ingredients excepting the dough, putting raisins and currants, lard, sugar, and spice in a basin which she gave to the baker, who added the dough, made and baked the cake, and returned it, beautifully browned in his big oven. The charge was the same as that for a loaf of bread the same size, and the result was delicious. "There's only one fault wi' these 'ere baker's cakes," the women used to say, "they won't keep!" And they would not; they were too good and there were too many children around.

FLORA THOMPSON
LARK RISE TO CANDLEFORD
1939

ELECTION CAKE

Often called Old Hartford (or Salem) election cake, raisin-studded yeast cakes like this were originally served at Militia Day fairs after the American Revolution.

Food historian William Woys Weaver explains that the term *election cake* is a generic one (like wedding cake), applied to several different types of cakes. Some versions are glazed, but many of the oldest surviving recipes are not; some were baked in round earthenware pans rather than loaf pans. This is a moist election cake, with a tender, yeasty crumb.

Makes two 8-x-4-inch loaves; each serves about 8

SPONGE

1	package active dry yeast
½	cup packed light brown sugar
1½	cups lukewarm milk
3-3½	cups all-purpose flour

CAKE

¾	cup (1½ sticks) unsalted butter, softened
¾	cup packed light brown sugar
2	large eggs
½	cup all-purpose flour
1½	teaspoons ground cinnamon
¾	teaspoon fresh-grated nutmeg
½	teaspoon ground mace
1	cup raisins
⅔	cup (about 4½ ounces) chopped candied citron or dried pineapple (optional)
3	tablespoons brandy or dark rum (optional)

1. **SPONGE:** Dissolve the yeast and 2 tablespoons of the brown sugar in ¼ cup of the lukewarm milk; let stand until bubbly, about 10 minutes. Stir in the remaining ¼ cup plus 2 tablespoons brown sugar and the remaining 1¼ cups lukewarm milk; gradually add enough of the flour to form a soft dough. Knead in a food processor for 1 minute, or for 10 minutes by hand or with an electric mixer with a dough hook. Place in a buttered bowl, cover the top with a towel, and let rise until doubled in volume, usually 45 to 60 minutes. (You can also let it rise overnight in the refrigerator, punching it down once if it doubles during that time.)

2. **CAKE:** In a large bowl, cream the butter and brown sugar with an electric mixer until light. Beat in the eggs, one at a time. Punch down the risen sponge, break it up into pieces and add the pieces to the butter mixture; beat just until partially combined.

3. In a bowl, combine the flour with all of the spices; add the raisins and optional citron or pineapple and toss to coat. Add to the dough, along with the optional brandy or rum. Beat until well combined; the dough will be very soft.

4. Generously butter two 8-x-4-inch loaf pans. Divide the dough in half. On a lightly floured sheet of wax paper, with floured fingertips, press out each piece of dough into a long 8-inch-wide rectangle. Starting at a short end, roll up the dough as you would a jellyroll. Place each roll, seam side down, in one of the loaf pans. Cover and let rise in a warm place until fully doubled in volume, usually about 45 minutes. Meanwhile, preheat the oven to 350 degrees F.

5. Bake until the loaves are golden brown and sound hollow when tapped, usually about 45 minutes.

6. Cool the cakes in the pans on a wire rack for about 15 minutes. When cool enough to handle, invert the cakes onto the rack, unmold and turn right side up. Cool to room temperature. Wrap in plastic and store at room temperature for up to several days. Cut into slices to serve. These keep well and are delicious toasted.

Traveling Election

From New England, election cake traveled to the Midwest. "Old Hartford Election Cake" appears in *The Centennial Buckeye Cook Book,* originally collected in 1876 by the women of First Congregational Church in Marysville, Ohio.

Tyrolean Christmas Fruitcake
(*Zelten*)

A ndrea Hellrigl, the late chef-owner of Palio restaurant in New York City, was from Merano in Italy's Alto Adige region, near the Brenner Pass on the border with southern Austria. When I asked him what typifies Christmas baking in his region, he answered with one word: "*Zelten.*"

Somewhere between cookie and confection, this cake is made with so little batter that as you make it, you won't believe it will hold all the fruits and nuts together. It does. Note that you should start this about 1 week ahead. The recipe can be doubled. The cake is served in very small pieces.

Makes one 8-inch round cake; serves 10 to 12

FRUITS AND NUTS
- ¾ cup raisins
- ¾ cup dried currants
- ⅓ cup chopped dried figs
- 3 tablespoons chopped pitted dates
- ¼ cup pine nuts
- 1 tablespoon chopped candied orange peel
- 1 tablespoon chopped candied lemon peel or citron
- ½ cup ground almonds
- ¼ cup brandy
- 2 tablespoons dark rum
- 1 tablespoon fresh orange juice
- ½ teaspoon ground cinnamon
- ¼ teaspoon ground cloves
- ¼ teaspoon ground star anise (use a mortar or spice mill)

CAKE
- ½ scant cup rye or all-purpose flour
- ¼ cup plus 1 tablespoon lukewarm milk
- 1 teaspoon active dry yeast (about ⅓ package)
  Whole almonds or pine nuts, for decoration
  Dried or candied fruit, for decoration (optional)

GLAZE
- ¼ cup brewed espresso or other strong-brewed coffee
- 3 tablespoons honey

1. **FRUITS AND NUTS:** One week before baking, or at least the night before, chop the raisins, currants, figs, dates, pine nuts and candied peels with a knife (or pulse in a food processor) until they are the size of dried currants or tiny peas. Place the mixture in a container that can be sealed airtight. Add the ground almonds, brandy, rum, orange juice and spices; stir well to combine. Cover airtight and set aside at cool room temperature for up to 1 week. Stir the ingredients from time to time.

2. **CAKE:** In a large bowl, combine the flour, milk and yeast; stir vigorously. Cover and let rise in a warm place until doubled, usually 45 to 60 minutes.

3. Add the fruit and nut mixture and any soaking liquid to the dough. Stir vigorously to combine. Cover and let rise again, usually about 45 minutes.

4. Preheat the oven to 325 degrees F. Butter an 8-inch round cake pan. Scrape the dough into the pan and smooth the top; it should be about ¾ inch high. Gently press almonds or pine nuts into the dough, forming an attractive design. (If you like, arrange more dried or candied fruit on the surface, along with the nuts.)

5. Bake the cake until golden brown and a toothpick inserted in the center emerges clean, about 30 minutes.

6. Cool the cake in the pan on a wire rack until lukewarm.

7. **GLAZE:** While the cake is still warm, combine the espresso or coffee with the honey in a small cup. Brush the glaze over the surface of the warm cake. Let cool to room temperature. Cut the *zelten* into thin wedges for serving.

Smells of Home

This is a Christmas fruitcake, Tyrolean-style," Andrea Hellrigl told me, beaming. "It's made with dried figs, dates, citrus rind and pine nuts macerated for a week, with just enough yeasted rye dough to hold it together. It's glazed with espresso and honey. I can still smell the hot punch with tea, rum and orange—an orange was a big winter event then—and the warm atmosphere of home. *Zelten* means Christmas for me."

About Seed Cakes
and Caraway Comfits

*S*eed cakes are one of the mainstays of the British tea table. Though they may sound outmoded to our ears, they are still popular throughout Britain, with Scottish, Irish and English versions. American recipes for seed cakes were standard in books and manuscripts throughout the 19th century.

Before the days of commercial extracts, seeds and spices were the principal flavorings for desserts, along with fortified wines. The seeds, usually caraway, were used in two forms: Whole seeds were used to flavor cake batters and were glazed with sugar to decorate the cakes. The glazed seeds were known as comfits, and sometimes as "rising" or "kissing" comfits.

Comfits and other "sweetmeats" turn up frequently in old dessert recipes, as a decoration or garnish. In his penetrating study, *Sweetness and Power*, Dr. Sidney Mintz traces comfits to the 14th century, when they were served as a digestive aid at royal banquets with wine, as were such spices as cinnamon, cardamom and coriander.

The word *comfit*, he explains, is "cognate with French *confiture* and with English 'confection' and is still used generally to mean 'a confection with a firm (fruit, nut, seed) center, coated with sugars.'" Mintz traces comfits back still further to the candied sugars and spice trade of Venice, and "doubtless backward in time to North Africa and the Middle East."

He adds: "It is of incidental interest that, before confetti came to mean bits of colored paper, it meant bits of colored candy, and in some languages—such as Russian—it still does."

Comfits appear in American recipes, too, mostly in the 19th century. In *The Universal Receipt Book*, a fascinating little book published "by a Society of Gentlemen in New York" in 1814, the seeds play a leading role in "Delicate Little Caraway Puddings," made with Malaga wine, orange flower water and caraway comfits.

To Make Comfits of Various Colours

If you would have the comfits red, infuse some red saunders [sandalwood] into the water, till it is of as deep a colour as you desire it; or if you please, you may use cochineal or syrup of mulberries.

If green, boil some juice of spinage with the sugar;

If yellow, put saffron to the water you mix your sugar with.

Note: they must all be boiled to a candy height and then dried in your stove.

Hannah Glasse
The Compleat
Confectioner
Dublin, 1762;
London, 1760

MRS. DALGAIRNS' SCOTTISH SEED CAKE

This is a golden butter cake, beautifully domed, with the rich texture of a pound cake. It's generously flavored with candied citrus rind, ginger and nuts, though I've left out the comfits.

This recipe is adapted from one in Mrs. Dalgairns' seminal Scottish book published in Edinburgh in 1830. While it is by no means the oldest recipe in this book, I found something miraculous in taking the instructions written down by someone generations earlier, following them virtually as given and ending up with a perfectly risen golden cake. I felt Mrs. Dalgairns there over my shoulder, and with her to guide me, I completed a process she had set in motion during her lifetime.

Makes one 8-inch cake; serves about 12

1¾	cups all-purpose flour
¾	teaspoon baking powder
1	teaspoon fresh-grated nutmeg
1	cup (2 sticks) unsalted butter, softened
½	teaspoon rose water (optional)
1	cup sugar
4	large eggs, separated
¼	cup brandy
¾	cup whole blanched almonds
⅔	cup (about 4½ ounces) candied orange peel, cut into slivers
⅔	cup (about 4½ ounces) candied citron, cut into slivers (optional)
2-3	teaspoons caraway seeds, coarsely crushed in a mortar or spice mill
	Pinch salt
⅓	cup slivered or sliced almonds

1. Preheat the oven to 350 degrees F. Line the bottom of an 8-inch springform pan with parchment or wax paper. Generously butter the paper and the sides of the pan; set aside. Sift the flour with the baking powder and nutmeg onto a piece of wax paper; set aside.

2. In a large bowl, with an electric mixer on medium-high speed, beat the butter and optional rose water until very soft. Add the sugar and beat until very fluffy. Beat in the egg yolks, one at a time; beat in the brandy.

Scots Seed Cake

Take one pound and a half of dried and sifted flour, the same quantity of fresh butter washed in rose water, and of finely-pounded loaf sugar; six ounces of blanched sweet almonds, three quarters of a pound of candied orange-peel, half a pound of citron, all cut into thin narrow strips; one nutmeg grated, and a tea-spoonful of pounded caraway seeds, fifteen eggs, the yolks and whites separately beaten; then with the hand beat the butter to a cream, add the sugar, and then the eggs gradually; mix in the flour a little at a time, and then the sweetmeats, almonds, and spice, and lastly, stir in a glass of brandy; butter the hoop or tin pan, and pour in the cake so as nearly to fill it; smooth it over the top, and strew over it caraway comfits. Bake it in a moderate oven; it must not be moved or turned till nearly done, as shaking it will occasion the sweetmeats to sink to the bottom.

MRS. DALGAIRNS
THE PRACTICE OF COOKERY
EDINBURGH, 1830

435

3. Lower the speed to slow, add the flour mixture and beat until not quite blended. Add the whole almonds, the candied orange peel, optional candied citron and caraway seeds; beat until combined.

4. In a bowl, beat the egg whites with the salt until nearly stiff. Stir a large spoonful of whites into the batter (it will be quite heavy); fold in the remaining egg whites. Scrape the batter into the prepared pan and rap the pan on a surface to settle any air bubbles; smooth the top. The batter will almost fill the pan; that's fine. Sprinkle the slivered or sliced almonds around the edges of the batter.

5. Bake until the cake is golden brown and a toothpick inserted in the center emerges clean, usually 1½ hours or slightly longer; do not overbake. If, after 35 to 45 minutes, the top of the cake is browning too quickly, lay a sheet of foil on the surface and continue to bake until done.

6. Cool the cake completely on a wire rack. Run the tip of a knife carefully around the sides of the cake and remove the sides of the pan. Run a knife blade under the cake, lift it off the bottom and carefully peel off the paper. Transfer the cake to a serving plate. Cut the cake into thin wedges and serve 2 per person. Wrapped in plastic, the cake will keep for up to 5 days.

Comfit Prizes

. . . At last the Dodo said, "*Everybody* has won, and *all* must have prizes." The whole party at once crowded round her, calling out, in a confused way, "Prizes! Prizes!"

Alice had no idea what to do, and in despair she pulled out a box of comfits (luckily the salt water had not got into it), and handed them round as prizes. There was exactly one a-piece, all round.

. . . The next thing was to eat the comfits: this caused some noise and confusion, as the large birds complained that they could not taste theirs, and the small ones choked and had to be patted on the back.

LEWIS CARROLL
ALICE IN WONDERLAND
1865

NINA'S FABULOUS ATHENIAN NUT CAKE WITH RUM SYRUP
(*KARYTHOPITTA*)

This is one of the many Greek desserts made with nuts and syrup. Originally from Athens, it is a family recipe from Nina ("Nine-a") Karageorge, with whom I worked in a restaurant on Martha's Vineyard.

Makes one 9-inch single-layer cake; serves 9

Fine, dry bread crumbs, for coating the pan
1   box (6 ounces) zwieback biscuits, finely crushed or ground
2   teaspoons baking powder
1   teaspoon baking soda
1   teaspoon ground cinnamon
¼   teaspoon ground cloves
½   cup (1 stick) unsalted butter, softened
1   cup sugar
5   large eggs, separated
¼   cup milk
1   teaspoon pure vanilla extract
1   teaspoon almond extract
3   tablespoons dark rum
1   cup coarsely chopped walnuts
Pinch salt

RUM SYRUP
⅔   cup sugar
½   cup water
1   small lemon, halved
1   cinnamon stick
3   tablespoons dark rum, or to taste

1. Preheat the oven to 350 degrees F. Butter a 9-inch square cake pan; coat lightly with a layer of the bread crumbs, shaking out the excess. Set aside. In a bowl or on a sheet of wax paper, combine the crushed zwieback, baking powder, baking soda, cinnamon and cloves; set aside.

2. In a large bowl, cream the butter with an electric mixer on medium-high speed until fluffy. Add the sugar and beat until very

Sellout

Once the summer tourists had left the Vineyard, Nina Karageorge and I would experiment with new desserts for the restaurant's menu. When we started serving Nina's Fabulous Athenian Nut Cake, it was always the first dessert to sell out.

437

light. Add the egg yolks, one at a time. Add the milk, vanilla and almond extracts and the rum; beat until well combined.

3. Lower the speed to slow and beat in the dry ingredients. Stir in the walnuts until blended; do not overmix.

4. Beat the egg whites with the salt until stiff but not dry. Fold about ¼ of the beaten whites into the batter; gently fold in the remaining whites just until smooth. Pour the batter into the prepared pan.

5. Bake until a toothpick inserted into the center of the cake emerges clean, about 40 minutes.

6. Cool the cake to lukewarm in the pan on a wire rack.

7. **RUM SYRUP:** While the cake is baking or cooling, combine the sugar and water in a small, heavy saucepan over medium heat. Stir until the sugar dissolves, melting any crystals from the sides of the pan with a brush dipped in cold water. Squeeze in the juice of the lemon, add the 2 lemon halves and the cinnamon stick and bring the syrup to a boil. Boil, stirring occasionally, until syrupy, about 5 minutes. Add the rum and boil for 30 seconds longer.

8. Use a skewer or a large fork to poke holes all over the surface of the cake. Slowly strain some of the syrup over it. When the syrup has been absorbed, strain as much of the remaining syrup as you like on top and let the cake absorb it. Place the cinnamon stick on top of the cake. Cut the cake into large squares or diamond shapes and serve warm or at room temperature, from the pan.

SEPHARDIC WALNUT CAKE WITH HONEY-LEMON SYRUP
(TISHPISHTI)

These moist diamonds of ground walnut cake are the color of burnished mahogany and drenched with a fragrant honey-lemon syrup. The recipe is based on one from Salonika, Greece; similar versions are made in Turkey.

I like to combine the walnuts and honey with melted butter, rather than with the oil used in many traditional Middle Eastern recipes. There is also a version made with matzo meal for Passover, when no flour is consumed. The recipe can be halved and baked in an 8-inch square baking pan.

Makes about 4 dozen 1-inch diamonds

CAKE

1	cup (2 sticks) unsalted butter, cut into pieces, or a combination of butter and bland vegetable oil
2	cups water
1	cup honey
1	cup sugar
1½	teaspoons ground cinnamon
3	cups finely chopped walnuts
½	teaspoon salt
2½	cups all-purpose flour
1	teaspoon baking powder
1	teaspoon baking soda
4	dozen perfect walnut halves

SYRUP

1	cup honey
½	cup water
	Grated zest and juice of 2 lemons (about ½ cup juice)

1. **CAKE:** Preheat the oven to 350 degrees F. Butter a 13-x-9-inch baking pan; set aside.

2. In a large, heavy saucepan over medium-high heat, combine the butter or butter and oil, water, honey, sugar, cinnamon, walnuts and salt. Cook, stirring, until the butter melts and the mixture comes just to a boil; remove from the heat.

Family Resemblance

The resemblance between Sephardic *tishpishti* and other syrup-soaked Greek nut desserts is no accident. (The word *Sephardic* means "Spanish" in Hebrew.) When the Jews were expelled from Spain in 1492, they migrated into Portugal and eastward to Italy, Greece, Turkey and throughout the Mediterranean basin. Like Jews everywhere throughout history, the Sephardim adapted the foods of their new homes to their own dietary laws and to their rich heritage of customs for both everyday and festival meals.

3. Sift the flour, baking powder and baking soda onto a sheet of wax paper; stir the dry ingredients into the saucepan. Pour the mixture into the prepared pan; smooth the top. Arrange the walnut halves in even rows over the top of the cake.

4. Bake until the cake is golden brown and a toothpick inserted in the center emerges clean, usually 40 to 45 minutes.

5. Cool the cake to lukewarm in the pan on a wire rack.

6. **SYRUP:** While the cake is baking or cooling, combine the honey and water in a saucepan over medium-high heat. Add the lemon zest and bring the mixture to a boil. Simmer, stirring occasionally, until syrupy, about 5 minutes. Remove from the heat; stir in the lemon juice.

7. While the cake is still warm, pour the syrup over it, a little at a time, letting it all sink in. Let the cake stand for at least 4 hours, or preferably overnight, before serving.

8. Using a ruler as a guide, cut the cake at 1-inch intervals, parallel to the long edge of the pan. Now cut the cake crosswise on the diagonal into diamond shapes with a walnut in the center of each. Covered with plastic wrap placed directly on its surface, this cake keeps well for several days.

CHAPTER 12

RECIPES

Basic Pie Dough
Nick Malgieri's Flaky Butter
  Pie Dough
Rich Tart Dough

PIE BASICS

Pie really forms as important a factor in American
civilization as the *pot-au-feu* does in France.
GEORGE SALA, *AMERICA REVISITED*,
CA. EARLY 19TH CENTURY

*P*ies go back at least as far as ancient Rome. At first,
cooks wrapped simple flour-and-water pastes
around meats to seal in juices; these crusts were
not eaten. The word pie, though of obscure
origin, was "evidently a well-known popular word in 1362," says
the *Oxford English Dictionary*. From then on, pies and tarts in one
form or another are part of virtually every written record of food,
through the Middle Ages and into more recent centuries. What's
remarkable is how similar even very early pie recipes are to the pies
we bake today.

By the time they got from England to America, pies were
staples of home baking. Since they figured in every meal from
breakfast to supper, the American housewife was more likely to
bake a pie than a cake. Or to bake several pies, which could be
stored outside in cold weather (an early form of deep-freezing) or
stacked in a pie safe, a cupboard with a mesh or punched-tin panel
that allowed air circulation but kept the pies safe from pests.

A wedge of pie in a stoneware dish and a cup of coffee—this
was the essential early American breakfast. Food historian William
Woys Weaver notes that in the 17th century, "People got up early
in the morning and worked—then came back in for a breakfast of
cold meats, mutton chops, all sorts of bread—and pie. Pie was a

In 1900, Mrs. F.D.
Bergen of Ohio insisted
that the New England
"pie-belt" was outranked
by the Middle West, where
in farming areas, pie was a
necessity for two out of
three meals.

RECORDED IN THE
*JOURNAL OF
AMERICAN FOLKLORE*
1900

status symbol back then," he adds, "made when the American farmer became well off."

Today, the truck stop, diner or small-town café that takes pride in its home-baked pies is fast vanishing, but pie and coffee is still the morning start of choice for plenty of Americans on the go—a humble dessert admired the world over. When a New York restaurant and hangout, Joe Allen's, opened a branch in Paris in the 1970s, the Parisians, who can buy every conceivable type of pastry on any street corner, flocked to the place so they could taste the new sensation: "*les pies américains.*"

BAKING A PIE—STEP BY STEP

Cakes are fancy-ass, honey. Pie is *home*.
IDELLA JOHNSON, VETERAN PIE BAKER

While pie may be the great common denominator, many people find baking one more threatening than preparing any other dessert. And it's making and rolling out the crust that gets the Anxiety Devil going.

But pies aren't really difficult. The only way to do it, though, is to make a couple yourself, because you have to get the feel of the dough to know when it is right.

Every spring for the past several years, Crisco has sponsored a Great American Pie Celebration. Out of some 1,500 entries from all 50 states, judges select one finalist to represent each state. Then the winners all come together for a weekend of pie baking—a hot and heavy competition, and good fun.

In a way, this event is an updated, commercially sponsored version of the old county fair, when home bakers display their pride-and-joy baked goods under tents in hopes of taking a blue ribbon. While judging the contest a couple of years ago, I wandered among the contestants, marveling at their sure hands, their ingenuity at coming up with their own gimmicks and gadgets.

From these expert bakers' collective wisdom, the product of years of hands-on kitchen experience, I've put together a composite set of instructions for the entire process of baking a pie, from making the dough, through rolling it out and lining a pie pan, forming simple borders and lattice tops and prebaking a crust, to handling finished pies.

MAKING PERFECT PIE DOUGH

*C*ool fingertips make good pastry," an old adage goes. The general rule for all pie doughs is: *Handle them as little as possible and keep them cool as you work.* Otherwise, the fat can break down and become greasy, resulting in a leaden crust.

MAKING PIE DOUGH BY HAND

Measure the flour, sugar and/or salt into a large mixing bowl; sifting is optional but does help make a lighter, more thoroughly mixed dough. (I often measure the dry ingredients into a mixing bowl, without sifting, then give them a quick stir with a large spoon or whisk to aerate them.) Next, add the shortening and/or butter; it should be cold. Using 2 table knives, a wire pastry blender or just your fingertips, cut the shortening into the dry ingredients, rubbing the flour into the bits of shortening so that you form a crumbly mixture with pieces about the size of small peas. These flour-coated bits of fat will help keep the pie dough flaky as it bakes. Don't overblend—the mixture shouldn't be completely homogenous.

ADDING THE LIQUID

When the fat and flour have been cut together, sprinkle ice-cold water over the mixture—just enough to hold it together.

Many blue-ribbon winners swear by a teaspoon of vinegar in their pie dough, maintaining that this helps the dough come out perfect every time. The vinegar helps prevent the formation of gluten, the strands of protein that toughen the crust. (Conversely, forming gluten is precisely what you do want to do when kneading bread dough; the network of elastic strands supports the air pockets created as the dough rises.)

The amount of water needed in pie dough is variable, depending on the humidity in the atmosphere and the amount of moisture in the flour, so recipes can't be too exact. The trick: Add the water a little at a time. You can always add more, but once you've overmoistened the dough, you can't take it away. Add just enough water so that when you gather the dough together, it comes together in a cohesive mass. If it seems dry or there are floury patches, sprinkle with a few drops more water as you gather it together. Trust the feel of the dough, not the recipe.

Remember, the less you handle pie dough, at every stage, the lighter and flakier the finished result will be.

MIXING DOUGH IN A FOOD PROCESSOR

Making pie dough is one of the things a food processor does

best—provided that you don't overmix or overwork the dough. Because it is so powerful, the machine cuts together flour and fat in seconds, without heating up the fat.

Place the flour and the other dry ingredients in the food processor. Pulse on and off to combine and aerate them (this replaces sifting). Add the cold butter and/or shortening, cut into pieces. Pulse several times, just until the mixture is crumbly. Now, sprinkle on the minimum amount of liquid you think you'll need; pulse until the mixture starts to clump together. Add more liquid if the mixture is too dry to hold together.

In the early days of the food processor, people ran the machine steadily until the dough gathered itself into a ball on top of the steel blade. Now, I find that I like the dough better when I let it just begin to clump together, but remove it before it has gathered itself into a cohesive mass. I take the clumps of dough out of the work bowl and gather them together by hand. The texture comes out slightly less homogenous, and more flaky. You can also make pie dough with an electric mixer, cutting the flour and fat together with the beaters. I do this only when I'm making a quantity of dough and don't have access to a food processor; otherwise, it's easier to manage by hand.

GATHERING THE DOUGH TOGETHER

Whichever method you've used to make the dough, gather it into a ball. Place it on a lightly floured sheet of plastic wrap or wax paper and flatten it into a neat disk shape. Sprinkle very lightly with flour, wrap tightly and chill for at least 30 minutes before rolling out.

"As far as I'm concerned, you can roll that dough out as soon as you put it together," one blue-ribbon winner told me. And you can. But chilling the dough and giving it a rest lets the gluten relax a bit, making the dough more tender and preventing it from contracting as it bakes.

Pie dough can be refrigerated for about 3 days, or frozen for up to 3 months. If you've refrigerated the dough until it is very firm, take it out of the refrigerator and let it soften a little before rolling. (Obviously, frozen pie dough should be thoroughly defrosted.) You want dough that is cold enough not to stick when rolled, but malleable enough to roll easily. You'll know "by feel" when it's right.

MAKE-AHEAD STRATEGY FOR PIE CRUSTS

If you're going to the trouble of putting together a batch of pie dough, it's really no more trouble to make enough for 3 or 4 pies. That way, you can freeze the dough in 1- or 2-crust portions,

"Can you bake a pie? No! Neither can I."

IRVING BERLIN
"ANYTHING YOU CAN DO,
I CAN DO BETTER"
ANNIE GET YOUR GUN
1946

and you'll have it on hand whenever you want to bake a pie. This is especially helpful in the summer, when you don't want to spend more time than necessary in the kitchen.

You'll get the best results if you work with no more than 3 cups of flour at a time, whether you're cutting the ingredients together by hand or using a food processor. Divide the dough in 1- or 2-crust disks, tightly wrap in plastic and label each, noting the type of dough and the date, before freezing.

Rolling Out the Dough

When you watch a seasoned pie baker move with sure, fluid grace, rolling out pie dough looks easy. Some swear by a pastry cloth and/or a cloth cover for the rolling pin (the grandmother of a friend used to cut off one foot of a clean, thin white cotton knee sock, and use the tube part to cover the pin). I find that if you keep everything lightly floured—your board, your dough, even your rolling pin—you don't need to bother with the cloth or the sock. And while the coolness of a marble surface is helpful, I roll out all of my doughs on a butcher-block countertop.

First, lightly butter a pie pan. (This is not strictly necessary, as the high fat content in the dough itself will usually prevent sticking. But why tempt fate? You don't want a wedge of pie arc-welded to the pan as you're trying to serve it at the table.) Set the pan aside.

Lightly flour a large work surface, making sure to flour an area slightly larger than the pie pan. Have the flour cannister alongside your work area. Unwrap the dough and place it in the center of the floured area. Dust the dough and the rolling pin very lightly with flour.

The trick is: Always roll outward from the center of the dough—*not* back and forth. Always use a light touch so the dough doesn't stick to the board. Roll up from the center, then down from the center. Then rotate the dough 90 degrees, and roll again, first up from the center, then down. With every couple of rolls, pick up the dough slightly and turn it, in order to make sure that it isn't sticking to the work surface. If it begins to stick, sprinkle a little more flour underneath. (Not too much, or you'll make the dough dry and tough.) And if the rolling pin starts to stick to the dough, sprinkle the pin with a little more flour.

Keep rolling in this way, making the circle of dough larger and larger, and trying to keep the shape as evenly round as possible. Be sure to roll the edges to a thickness even with the center. Don't worry if the edges are a little ragged. For most pies, roll to a thickness of about ⅟₁₆ inch. Tarts or pies that need a sturdier crust can be closer to ⅛ inch thick.

LINING A PIE PAN
(FOR 1- AND 2-CRUST PIES)

*Y*ou're now going to transfer the round of dough to the buttered pan; you want to do this quickly and decisively, handling the dough gently, without stretching it. The easiest way is to fold the round of dough in half (to prevent tearing); quickly lift it and place it into the pie pan, with the fold in the center. Gently unfold and fit the dough, without stretching, over the surface of the pan. Be sure to fit the dough into the bottom edges of the pan, or it will contract as it bakes.

Trim the edges of the dough, leaving an overhang of about ¾ inch. If necessary, patch any holes in the dough with scraps.

For a 1-crust pie: Fold under the overhanging dough, pressing it onto the rim of the pie pan. Smooth the edge with your fingers, turning the pie pan as you go.

To flute or crimp the edge: Place your left forefinger on the inside of the pastry rim. With the thumb and forefinger of your right hand, push the pastry from the outside, forming a V-shape groove in the dough against the left forefinger inside. Continue around the edge of the pie, forming a zigzag pattern.

An easier method: Just press the back of the tines of a fork into the smooth pastry rim all around.

Chill the pie shell before filling and baking, if you have time. Even if you just pop it into the refrigerator for the time it takes to preheat the oven, it will firm up slightly and hold its shape better as it bakes.

For a 2-crust pie with a solid top: Leave the dough overhanging the rim of the pie pan once you've trimmed the edge. Roll out the top pie crust; the top crust can be slightly thicker than the bottom. If you're not baking the pie immediately, chill the pie shell; place the top round of dough on a wax-paper-lined plate and chill that, too. Chilling helps the dough relax, so that it won't shrink as it bakes.

To assemble a solid-topped 2-crust pie: Moisten the edges of the bottom crust with a fingertip dipped in cold water; this will help seal the edges of the two crusts. Place the filling into the bottom crust. Gently drape the top round of pastry over the filling; trim, leaving a ¾-inch overhang. Press both layers of dough together against the rim of the pie pan, sealing the edges of the top and bottom crusts. Fold under the overhanging crusts, pressing them onto the rim of the pie pan. Smooth the edge with your fingers, turning the pie pan as you go.

Form a fluted or fork-pressed edge, following the instructions above. Cut several slashes in the top to release steam.

Other decorative touches: You can reroll scraps of dough and cut out leaf shapes, tracing veins with the back of a paring knife, star (or other) shapes with a small cutter, or half circles, using a small fluted round cutter. Moisten the rim of a single-crust pie and arrange the pastry cutouts along the rim, overlapping them slightly. You can also arrange these cutouts on top of a 2-crust pie.

For a 2-crust pie with a lattice top: You may remember your grandmother weaving the strips of dough, first braiding them on a sheet of wax paper, then lifting the whole thing onto the pie. I cheat.

Here's how I do it: First, moisten the outer edge of the bottom crust (in the pan) with cold water, and have the top crust rolled out into a circle. Cut the top crust into strips using a fluted pastry wheel or sharp knife. When the strips are ready, spoon the filling into the bottom crust.

Now, lay ½ of the strips in one direction, parallel to each other, using the longest ones for the center of the pie. Then, just lay the rest of the strips in the other direction, parallel again, but at a sharp angle or right angle to the first set of strips.

It's not really braiding, but it looks just about as good. Once the strips are in place, press the ends into the overhanging edge of the bottom crust to seal, cut off any excess and make any kind of border you like.

I bake most of my pies with the oven rack in the lower third of the oven. That way, the heat crisps up the bottom crust as the pie bakes—you don't want a soggy-crusted pie. But get to know your oven. You don't want the bottom overbrowned, either.

To Partially Bake a Pie or Tart Crust

Crusts often are partially baked (or "blind-baked") so that soft fillings, such as custards or juicy fruits, won't make them soggy. (For more about prebaking crusts, see page 448.) Each pie and tart recipe gives detailed instructions on prebaking, but the general method is as follows:

Fit the dough into the pie pan and crimp the edge. Line the dough with a lightly buttered sheet of foil, buttered side down. (If you want to take the trouble, the traditional method is then to weigh down the foil with dried beans or rice; keep a canister of them on hand and reuse them indefinitely. You can also buy metal or ceramic "pie weights" made specifically for this purpose. Another practical solution is to fit an empty pie pan inside, on top of the foil.)

Simple Pretensions

When we started the restaurant we'd set out to simulate the kind of place we'd hoped to find on the drive back from Arizona—an eccentric little café that served honest food made by human hands . . . bread and hash browns made from scratch, soups and stews, two different pies every day. I sometimes felt we were deceiving them by pretending to be simple— we'd led convoluted, neurotic lives and now we were earning our living by arranging lattice crusts over apples from an orchard less than ten miles away and contracting with a local grandmother for homemade preserves.

MICHAEL CUNNINGHAM
A HOME AT THE END OF THE WORLD
1990

Bake the pie shell (usually at 400 degrees F, though the temperature can vary) until the edges are set, often about 8 minutes. Very gently remove the weights, if using, and foil; prick the dough lightly with a fork and bake the crust, pricking any air bubbles with a fork as they rise, until the surface is dry, but is not yet baked through, 5 to 7 minutes. In a partially baked pie crust, the edges will just begin to color to a pale gold.

Let the pie shell cool on a wire rack until needed.

TO FULLY BAKE A PIE CRUST

*P*ies crusts are fully prebaked when their fillings don't require baking or shouldn't be baked at all—as for some fresh fruit pies or a precooked filling. Line the dough with foil, as directed on page 447. Bake the pastry until the sides are set, 10 to 12 minutes. Gently remove the foil. Continue to bake, pricking any air bubbles gently with a fork, until the crust is lightly golden and just baked through, 8 to 12 minutes longer. Cool the baked pie shell on a wire rack.

The general rule is that once pastry has been baked, it shouldn't be refrigerated. Its texture and flavor will come through best at room temperature. Custard and cream pies are exceptions, as their fillings require refrigeration. But it's generally a good idea to take these pies out of the refrigerator 10 or 15 minutes before serving to restore their flavors.

Any pastry will work fine for just about any pie or tart. Other types of pie crusts, such as cookie crumb crusts, are explained in the recipes that use them.

Jolly Old Oven

Mrs. Harriet Beecher Stowe waxed romantic about her oven:

In the corner of the great kitchen, during all these days, the jolly old oven roared and crackled in great volcanic billows of flame, snapping and gurgling as if the old fellow entered with joyful sympathy into the frolic of the hour; and then, his great heart being once warmed up, he brooded over successive generations of pies and cakes, which went in raw and came out cooked, till butteries and dressers and shelves and pantries were literally crowded into jostling abundance.

QUOTED BY
DAVID HACKETT-FISHER
ALBION'S SEED
1989

Basic Pie Dough

The crusts for traditional fruit pies and other old-fashioned pies are usually made with lard or vegetable shortening, or a combination of butter (for flavor) and one of the other fats (for flakiness). This recipe is a modern version.

⌒ *Makes enough for one 9- or 10-inch pie*

1-Crust	2-Crust	
1½	2½	cups all-purpose flour
1	2	teaspoons sugar
½	¾	teaspoon salt
6	11	tablespoons cold unsalted butter, cut into small pieces
1½	2½	tablespoons cold solid vegetable shortening
3	5	tablespoons cold water, plus more as needed

1. Combine the flour, sugar, salt, butter and shortening in a food processor or in a mixing bowl. Pulse the machine on and off (or cut the ingredients together with 2 knives) until the mixture is crumbly.

2. Add the water and pulse (or toss with a fork) until the mixture begins to clump together. Gather it into a ball, sprinkling with a few more drops of water, if needed. Flatten slightly into a disk, wrap in plastic, and chill for at least 30 minutes before rolling out. (To roll out the dough and line the pie pan, see pages 445 to 446.)

Praise the Lard

Once upon a time and long ago B.C. (Before Cholesterol), when pigs were plump and pie crusts were short, lard was the fat of choice for many people.

Some people have never forgotten. Cooks in fancy restaurants and farm kitchens alike know that judicious use of lard in such products as pie crusts and biscuits produces a superior product. If you have a favorite biscuit, doughnut, or pie crust recipe using butter or another shortening and you wish to convert it to lard, remember this rule of thumb: use four-fifths as much lard as butter; use only three-fourths as much lard as solid vegetable shortening. Count the calories saved as another plus for lard. *Spend* those calories on your second piece of pie!

Susan Peery
"Praise the Lard and
Pass the Flaky Pie
Crust"
The Old Farmer's
Almanac
1991

NICK MALGIERI'S FLAKY BUTTER PIE DOUGH

This all-purpose pie dough is made with butter as its only fat. The small amount of cake flour keeps the crust tender, and the touch of baking powder, while not enough to make the dough puff, helps it cling to the pan. It's an excellent, richly flavored dough for all sorts of pies and tarts. Use it for any pie or tart in this book.

Makes enough for one 9-inch double crust

2	cups all-purpose flour
¼	cup cake flour
¼	teaspoon baking powder
¼	teaspoon salt
1	cup (2 sticks) cold unsalted butter
5-6	tablespoons ice water

1. In a mixing bowl, combine the all-purpose and cake flours, baking powder and salt. Stir well to blend.

2. Cut each stick of butter into 6 or 8 pieces. Using your fingertips, rub the butter into the dry ingredients until the mixture is mealy and no large pieces of butter are visible.

3. Sprinkle the water over the flour and butter mixture and toss with a fork to moisten. Add only enough water to make the dough hold together. Knead the dough into a ball and flatten into a 6- to 8-inch disk. Wrap in plastic or wax paper and refrigerate for about 1 hour, or until firm. (To roll out the dough and line the pie pan, see pages 445 to 446.)

NOTE: To make this pastry in a food processor, combine the dry ingredients and butter and pulse briefly until crumbly; do not overmix. Add the ice water gradually, and pulse just until the dough begins to clump together.

Rich Tart Dough

This dough is made with butter as its only fat, producing a slightly less flaky, but richer-tasting dough that's more like a cookie. It will work for any of the pies or tarts in this book.

Makes enough for one or two 9- to 10-inch pie shells

1 Shell	2 Shells	
1½	2½	cups all-purpose flour
2	4	tablespoons sugar
Pinch	¼	teaspoon salt
½	1	cup cold unsalted butter, cut into pieces
3	5	tablespoons ice water or cold orange juice, or as needed

1. If making the dough by hand, sift together the flour, sugar and salt into a large bowl. Cut in the butter with 2 knives or your fingertips, until the mixture is the texture of crumbly meal.

2. Sprinkle 3 tablespoons of the liquid over the flour mixture and toss with a fork until the pastry just comes together. Add more liquid if necessary, but do not moisten the dough too much. Gather the pastry together in a ball and flatten it into a disk. Wrap in plastic or wax paper and chill for at least 1 hour before rolling out. (To roll out the dough and line the pie pan, see pages 445 to 446.)

NOTE: To make this pastry in a food processor, combine the dry ingredients and butter and pulse briefly until crumbly; do not overmix. Add the liquid gradually and process just until the dough begins to clump together.

"Another day, another dollar; fourteen hours on snowshoes and wish I had pie."

FROM A
MAINE TRAPPER'S DIARY
QUOTED BY
ANNIE DILLARD IN
THE WRITING LIFE
1989

RECIPES

*Indiana Orchard Apple
    Crumb Pie*
*Down-East Cranberry Apple
    Pie*
*Dried Apple "Pour-Through"
    Pie*
*Rhode Island Chunky Pear
    Pie*
Double-Berry Lattice Pie
Country Peach Pie
*Lattice-Topped Peach-Berry
    Pie*
*Cape Cod Cranberry
    "Linzer" Pie*
Fresh Grape Pie
*Deep-Dish Rhubarb-
    Cherry-Berry Pie*
*Fried (or Baked) Apple
    "Half-Moon" Pies*
*Apple-Pecan Upside-Down
    Pie Baked in a Skillet*

FRUIT PIES

It is our firm conviction that the average pie of to-day is the direct cause of more ill-nature and general "cussedness" in mankind than anything else, and that there lurks more solid, downright dyspepsia in a square inch of baker's pie than in all the other dyspeptic-producing compounds known. The pie we desire to see upon the American table is one that is more the receptable [*sic*] for fruit than a blending of fruit with puff-paste so soggy that lead would digest almost as easily. When a top crust is used let there be but little of it, and so light and delicate that "fairy footfalls" would break through it.

THOMAS J. MURREY,
PUDDINGS AND DAINTY DESSERTS, 1886

*I*t's funny that along with Mom and the flag, apple pie has come to represent the quintessential American spirit because apple pie was brought over from England. The English love their apples, and their devotion to pies—meat pies, apple pies and other fruit pies—has carried on strong since the days when Shakespeare was still turning out a new play each year.

But the apple pie, baked in a deep earthenware dish, with top crust only, changed considerably as it crossed the Atlantic, with the eventual result that like much else that came over from abroad, it not only reinvented itself as all-American but eclipsed its English ancestor.

Often called "Pippin Pie" or "Codlin Pie" after their varieties, apple pies were common in England by the 16th and 17th centuries, as were pies made with quinces and pears. Sometimes the fruit was cooked first before being baked in a pie, a holdover from medieval times when uncooked fruit was feared as a source of disease. (In America, the fear of fresh fruit was perpetuated well into the 19th century.)

In virtually every English and American cookbook from the mid-17th century on, apple pie is the first fruit pie mentioned. One of the things noticeable about early pie recipes is their lack of detail; it was assumed that any cook who knew her way around the kitchen could put together a pie.

American colonists had no time or energy to gussy up their pies; pie-baking was simple and straightforward. Shaker apple pie, with apples memorably fragranced with rose water, is the embodiment of the Shaker spirit of "taking the ordinary and making it extraordinary." A popular early apple pie was the Marlborough pie, the apples sweetened and flavored with lemon juice, nutmeg and sometimes sherry; in a variation, the apples were combined with squash puree. The availability of apples and the sheer love of pie—for breakfast, lunch and supper—soon conspired to make apple pie even more popular here than in the mother country.

But let's not let our national love affair with apples overshadow the rainbow of other fruits that lend themselves to pie-making. Rhubarb has long been one of America's most popular ingredients (so much so that it was sometimes called "pie plant"), and strawberry-rhubarb pie is a welcome signal that spring has arrived. Grapes and plums both found their way into surprisingly delicious double-crust pies, while green tomatoes were combined with apples for a spicy "mincemeat" pie that remains a farmhouse favorite, providing an ingenious use for fruit that hasn't ripened before the frost. One of the traditional glories of high summer is peach pie, as is the varied realm of berry pies, which figure large in memory.

One afternoon in his kitchen, as James Beard reminisced about the beloved foods of his childhood, his eyes suddenly got a faraway look. With a sly smile creeping up the corners of his mouth, he murmured dreamily, "Wild huckleberry pies. . . ."

Taffety Tart

First, wet your paste with Butter, and cold water, roul it very thin, then lay Apples in Lays, and between every lay of Apples strew some fine Sugar, and some Lemon-peel cut very small; you may also put some Fennel-seed to them, let them bake an hour or more, then ice them with Rosewater, Sugar, and Butter beaten together, and wash them over with the same, strew more fine Sugar over them, and put them into the Oven again; this done, you may serve them hot or cold.

HANNAH WOOLLEY
THE GENTLEWOMAN'S COMPANION; OR, A GUIDE TO THE FEMALE SEX
LONDON, 1673

INDIANA ORCHARD APPLE CRUMB PIE

When I still owned a Fire Island house, we always welcomed the end of summer—and the departure of the summer crowds. So that's when we'd invite my friend Mick's sister, Nancy, for her annual visit from Indiana. Every year when we met her at the boat, she would be dragging two enormous canvas bags full of apples that she had picked the day before in an Indiana orchard.

Mick would unzip the bags and stick his face inside, inhaling deeply. Suddenly the house would fill with a winy apple fragrance, mingling with the cedar and pine cones crackling in the fireplace.

As the sky gradually lit up with stars, Nancy and I would peel apples, piling them high in a bottom crust, and then topping them with a dusting of streusel. What comes through in this pie is the flavor of apple—as clean and crisp as if picked right from the tree.

Makes 1 deep 9½-inch pie; serves about 8

FILLING

10-12	apples, such as Jonathans (and/or Northern Spies) and Golden Delicious
1	tablespoon fresh lemon juice
⅔-¾	cup sugar, or to taste
3	tablespoons cornstarch
2	teaspoons ground cinnamon
½	teaspoon fresh-grated nutmeg
	Pinch ground cloves (optional)

STREUSEL TOPPING

5	tablespoons cold unsalted butter
½	cup all-purpose flour
⅓	cup packed light brown sugar
1	teaspoon ground cinnamon
	Vanilla ice cream or Cheddar cheese, for serving (optional)

1. Preheat the oven to 375 degrees F, with a rack in the lower third. Roll out the pie dough on a lightly floured surface to a large circle about ⅛ inch thick. Fit it, without stretching, into a deep 9½-inch pie pan. Trim the edge, leaving a ¾-inch overhang forming a high fluted edge. Refrigerate while you prepare the filling.

"Thy breath is like the steame of apple-pyes."

ROBERT GREENE
ARCADIA
1590

2. **Filling:** Peel, core and thinly slice the apples into a large mixing bowl; toss with the lemon juice. In a small bowl, stir together the sugar, cornstarch, cinnamon, nutmeg and cloves, if using, until free of lumps. Toss with the apples and pile into the crust, mounding them in the center.

3. **Streusel Topping:** In a small bowl or in a food processor, pulse the butter, flour, brown sugar and cinnamon until well blended and crumbly. Evenly scatter the crumbs over the apples.

4. Place the pie on a foil-lined baking sheet. Bake until the topping is golden and the apples are tender and bubbling, 45 to 50 minutes.

5. Cool the pie on a wire rack. Serve lukewarm or at room temperature, with vanilla ice cream or Cheddar cheese, if you like.

Favorite Variations

Apple and Cheddar Pie
The Yankee way is to serve a slice of Cheddar alongside the pie. Or lay thin triangular slices of Cheddar around the rim of the top crust just before the pie finishes baking. Bake just long enough to melt the cheese.

Cheddar Crust or Crumb Topping
Toss about ⅓ cup grated sharp Cheddar cheese into your favorite recipe for a 2-crust pie, before adding the water. You can also add a small handful of grated Cheddar to a streusel crumb topping (see the topping for Indiana Orchard Apple Crumb Pie, page 454).

Apple and Quince Pie
A little quince will lend its perfume to an apple pie. Thinly slice a peeled, cored quince and add it to the filling. If you have preserved, cooked quince on hand, cut up about ½ cup of the fruit and add it to the filling.

For tips on apple varieties, see page 338.

"But I, when I undress me Each night upon my knees Will ask the Lord to bless me, With apple pie and cheese."

Eugene Field
"Apple Pie and Cheese"
ca. 1880

DOWN-EAST CRANBERRY APPLE PIE

This pie, made by the Kennebunk Inn in Kennebunk, Maine, won grand prize in *Yankee* magazine's Great New England Food Festival in the fall of 1989, beating out over 30 competing apple pies from inns all over New England. Bake one, and you'll see why—this is a big pie, with a layer of orange-scented cranberries tucked beneath Cortland apple slices, all piled high in a double crust.

Makes one 10-inch pie; serves about 8

Basic Pie Dough for a 2-crust pie (page 449)

CRANBERRY LAYER

2	cups (about 7 ounces) cranberries, picked over
1	cup sugar
½	cup orange juice, preferably freshly squeezed
½	cup water
	Grated zest of 1 orange
	Pinch fresh-grated nutmeg

APPLE LAYER

8-10	Cortland apples
⅓	cup all-purpose flour
1	cup sugar, or to taste
1¼	teaspoons ground cinnamon
¾	teaspoon fresh-grated nutmeg or apple pie spice
	Pinch salt
1½-2	tablespoons cold unsalted butter, cut into pieces
	Milk and sugar, for glaze
	Vanilla ice cream, for serving

1. Divide the dough into 2 slightly unequal portions. Roll out the larger piece on a lightly floured surface to a large circle slightly over ⅛ inch thick. Fit it, without stretching, into a buttered 10-inch (or deep 9½-inch) pie pan. Trim the edge, leaving a ¾-inch overhang. Roll out the other piece of dough to a circle ⅛ inch thick and transfer it to a foil-lined baking sheet. Chill the doughs while you prepare the fillings.

2. **CRANBERRY LAYER:** Place the cranberries, sugar, orange juice, water, orange zest and nutmeg in a nonreactive saucepan.

Partially cover and bring the mixture to a boil over medium heat, stirring occasionally. Uncover and boil gently until the mixture reduces by about ⅓, usually 20 to 25 minutes. (You should have about 1¾ cups of the cranberry mixture.) Set aside to cool.

3. **APPLE LAYER:** Preheat the oven to 400 degrees F, with a rack in the lower third. Peel the apples, quarter, core and thinly slice into a large bowl. In a smaller bowl, stir together the flour, sugar, spices and salt with a whisk or fork until completely free of lumps. Sprinkle this mixture over the apple slices and toss until the apples are evenly coated.

4. Moisten the edge of the bottom crust with cold water. Spoon the cranberry mixture in an even layer over the bottom of the dough. Top with the apples, mounding them in the center. Dot with the butter. Loosely drape the remaining dough over the top. Trim off the excess dough, leaving a ¾-inch overhang. Turn the edges of the top crust under the edges of the bottom crust, forming a smooth border on the rim of the pie pan. Crimp or flute the edge.

5. Brush the dough lightly with milk. If you like, cut out leaves from the trimmings and arrange them over the top, pressing gently to make them adhere. Sprinkle the dough with sugar to glaze lightly. Cut several slashes in the top crust to release steam.

6. Place the pie in the oven, with a sheet of foil underneath to catch any drips. Bake until the crust is golden brown and the juices are bubbling, about 50 minutes.

7. Cool the pie on a wire rack. Serve warm, with vanilla ice cream.

The Apple Pie ABC

A apple pie.
B bit it.
C curtsied for it.
D dreamed of it.
E eats of it.
F fought for it.
G grinned for it.
H hopped for it.
I illuminated it.
J jolted it.
K knocked it down.
L laughed at it.
M mourned for it.
N nursed it.
O opened it.
P peeped into it.
Q quartered it.
R rowed for it.
S sung to it.
T tumbled for it.
U uncovered it.
V viewed it.
W watched it.
X storm'd for a share.
Like a vixen so bold
You'd have thought you
had seen her
'Twas Xanthippe the
scold.
Y yeomaned it.
Z mounted his zebra
And said with a zest
though his share was
the last
Yet he liked it the best.

ANONYMOUS
"THE ADVENTURES OF
A, APPLE PIE"
1835

About Lears and Caudles

The American tradition of the "pour-through" pie, described in the recipe that follows, has old European roots. In the 17th and 18th centuries (and as early as the 14th), savory pies were moistened by a lear, a gravy-like mixture poured through an opening in the top crust of a pie or pastry with a funnel. Usually made with wine, meat gravy, vinegar, anchovies, oyster liquor and brown butter, the lear was added after baking, to moisten the filling.

For fruit and other sweet pies, a caudle—a mixture of wine, egg yolks and sugar thickened with butter kneaded with flour—was used. This one from *The Whole Duty of a Woman* (London, 1737) is typical:

A Caudle for Sweet Pies

Get half a Pint of white Wine, a little grated Nutmeg and Mace, and boil it; then beat up the Yolks of two Eggs, and put into it, with a Spoonful of refin'd Sugar, and a little Butter kneaded in Flour; shake it about and pour it in.

A similar recipe combined white wine with lemon juice, sugar and butter, and then directed the cook to "pour in your caudle as hot as you can, and shake it well in the pie and serve it up."

Caudles were also served from a bowl as warm egg-thickened drinks, the Elizabethan-era precursors of beverages like egg flip and milk punch.

DRIED APPLE "POUR-THROUGH" PIE

In the days before home refrigeration, apples and other fruits were dried and put by for the winter. Many old recipes from New England, the Appalachians and the Midwest show how the dried apples were then put to use in both sweet and savory dishes. Simmered into applesauce, dried apples were served as is, or used to fill Dried Apple Gingerbread Stack Cake (see page 392). Dried apple pie was a winter standby. Because drying concentrates the fruit's flavor and sweetness, this pie bursts with apple flavor—especially if you reconstitute the dried apples in cider instead of water.

"Pour-through" pies are an old American farm tradition, now just about forgotten. When the pie is almost finished baking, sweet cream is poured through a vent in the crust to moisten and enrich the filling, and the pie is returned to the oven for a few more minutes of baking.

> *Makes 1 deep 9- or deep 9½-inch pie; serves about 8*

	Basic Pie Dough for a 2-crust pie (page 449)
4	cups (1 quart) apple cider
1-1¼	pounds (about 5½ loosely packed cups) dried apples
¼	cup plus 1 tablespoon sugar, or more to taste
2½	tablespoons cornstarch
½	teaspoon ground cinnamon
¼	teaspoon fresh-grated nutmeg
1	tablespoon fresh lemon juice
2	tablespoons cold unsalted butter, cut into pieces
1	tablespoon milk
3	tablespoons heavy cream
	Vanilla ice cream or sharp Cheddar cheese, for serving

1. Divide the dough into 2 slightly unequal portions. Roll out the larger piece on a lightly floured surface to a thickness of ⅛ inch. Fit it, without stretching, into a buttered, 9- or deep 9½-inch pie pan. Trim the edge, leaving a ¾-inch overhang. Roll out the smaller piece of dough to a circle ⅛ inch thick and transfer it to a foil-lined baking sheet. Chill the doughs while you prepare the filling.

2. Bring the cider to a boil in a large saucepan. Add the dried apples, cover and simmer until softened but not mushy, 25 to 30

minutes (the timing may vary; add water, if necessary, to keep the apples covered with liquid). Drain the apples, reserving the cider.

3. Preheat the oven to 425 degrees F, with a rack in the lower third. Sift the ¼ cup sugar, cornstarch, cinnamon and nutmeg into a bowl. Add the drained apples and toss gently. Add ¼ cup of the reserved cider (chill the remainder for drinking) and the lemon juice, and toss again. Add more sugar, if necessary, to taste. Moisten the edge of the bottom crust with cold water. Pour the mixture into the pie pan, mounding the apples in the center. Dot with the butter. Loosely drape the remaining dough over the apples. Trim off the excess dough, leaving a ¾-inch border. Turn the edges of the top crust under the edges of the bottom crust, forming a smooth border on the rim of the pie pan. Crimp or flute the border.

4. Brush the pastry lightly with the milk; sprinkle with the remaining 1 tablespoon sugar to glaze lightly. Cut several wide slashes or holes in the top crust to release steam.

5. Place the pie on a foil-lined baking sheet and bake for 15 minutes. Lower the heat to 400 degrees and continue to bake until golden brown, about 30 minutes longer. About 5 minutes before the pie is done, dribble the cream into the slashes or holes in the top crust. Bake for 5 minutes longer.

6. Cool the pie on a wire rack. Serve warm with vanilla ice cream or wedges of sharp Cheddar.

Rhode Island Chunky Pear Pie

Why is apple pie everywhere and pear pie virtually unknown? In Tudor and Stuart times, English pies were made with pears and quinces nearly as often as with apples.

Baking with pears can be a little trickier than with apples; juicy varieties like Bartlett or Comice can release so much liquid that you need to adjust the amounts of other ingredients. Bosc pears, which are drier, can usually be substituted for apples without problems. Anjou pears are particularly fragrant.

This pie is so chunky with nuts and raisins that it's almost like a fresh fruit mincemeat. The recipe comes from Karen Lee, formerly a baker at Provender, a take-out shop and bakery in Tiverton, Rhode Island. I usually stop in and sit down for coffee and pie or a muffin when I'm on my way to Little Compton, one of the most beautiful places on this earth.

Makes 1 deep 9½-inch pie; serves about 8

	Basic Pie Dough for a 2-crust pie (page 449)
4	pounds (about 12) ripe pears (preferably Bosc or Anjou, which have a firm, dry texture)
2½	tablespoons orange liqueur, orange juice or amaretto
2½	tablespoons pure maple syrup, or more to taste
2	teaspoons grated orange zest
½	teaspoon ground cloves
⅔	cup walnut pieces
⅓	cup golden raisins
2	tablespoons quick-cooking tapioca
2	tablespoons cold unsalted butter, cut into pieces
1	egg yolk mixed with 1 teaspoon water, for egg wash

1. Preheat the oven to 425 degrees F, with a rack in the lower third. Divide the dough into 2 slightly unequal pieces. Roll out the larger piece on a lightly floured surface to a large circle ⅛ inch thick. Fit it, without stretching, into a buttered, deep 9½-inch pie pan. Trim the edge, leaving a ¾-inch overhang. Roll out the remaining dough and transfer it to a foil-lined baking sheet. Chill the doughs while you prepare the filling.

2. Peel, halve and core the pears; cut into coarse chunks, letting the pieces fall into a large bowl. You should have about 6 cups. Add the orange liqueur, orange juice or amaretto, the maple syrup, orange zest, cloves, walnuts, raisins and tapioca.

Toss gently to combine the ingredients. Place the filling in the pie shell, mounding it in the center. Dot with the butter.

3. Brush the edge of the pie crust with the egg wash. Loosely drape the remaining dough over the filling. Trim off the excess pastry, leaving a ¾-inch border. Turn the edges of the top crust under the edges of the bottom crust, leaving a smooth border on the rim of the pie pan. Crimp or flute the border. Brush the top of the pie with the egg wash. Make several slashes in the top of the dough.

4. Place the pie on a foil-lined baking sheet. Bake until the crust is golden brown and the juices begin to bubble up, about 50 minutes.

5. Cool the pie on a wire rack. Serve lukewarm or at room temperature.

DOUBLE-BERRY LATTICE PIE

On Fire Island, the highbush blueberries start to pop out in mid-July. You have to know where to look, and even then, after searching patiently, you're apt to come back with just a tiny bowl of berries. Not enough for a pie, but enough to start a pie. (A handful of berries does good things for a peach or nectarine pie.)

This is a basic formula for a two-crust berry pie; following these amounts, feel free to substitute other berries, or to combine berry varieties. (If you can find them in the wild, huckleberries make extraordinary pies.) This quantity of sugar makes a pie that's fairly tart but balanced in flavor; adjust to taste based on the fruit you're using.

Makes 1 deep 9½- or 10-inch pie; serves about 8

	Basic Pie Dough for a 2-crust pie (page 449)
4½-5	cups (2 pints) blackberries and blueberries, picked over
1	tablespoon fresh lemon juice
¾	cup sugar, or more, depending on the berries' sweetness
3	tablespoons cornstarch
	Pinch ground cinnamon
1	tablespoon cold unsalted butter, cut into pieces
1	tablespoon milk or cream, for glaze

1   tablespoon sugar, for glaze
     Vanilla ice cream, for serving

1. Preheat the oven to 425 degrees F, with a rack in the lower third. Divide the dough into 2 slightly unequal pieces. Roll out the larger piece on a lightly floured surface to a large circle ⅛ inch thick. Fit it, without stretching, into a buttered, deep 9½-inch or regular 10-inch pie pan. Trim the edge, leaving a ¾-inch overhang. Roll out the remaining dough into a large circle, and transfer it to a foil-lined baking sheet. Chill the doughs.

2. Toss the berries with the lemon juice in a large bowl. Stir together the sugar, cornstarch and cinnamon in a separate bowl. Quickly but thoroughly toss this dry mixture with the berries.

3. Pour the berry filling into the pie crust and dot with the butter. Moisten the edge of the crust with cold water. Cut the other circle of dough into 1-inch-wide strips, using a fluted pastry wheel or sharp knife. Lay ½ of the strips over the berries at even intervals, parallel to one another. Lay the remaining strips of dough across the top in the other direction, parallel again. Press the ends of the strips into the bottom crust. Trim off the excess dough. Fold the overhanging edges of the bottom crust onto the rim of the pie pan, pressing gently to form a smooth border. Crimp or flute the border, if you like. Brush the lattice with the milk or cream; sprinkle it with the sugar.

4. Cover the pie loosely with foil and place in the oven, with a sheet of foil underneath to catch any drips. Bake for 12 minutes. Remove the foil. Continue baking until the pie crust is golden brown and the filling is bubbly, 35 to 40 minutes longer.

5. Cool the pie on a wire rack. Serve warm or at room temperature, topping each wedge with vanilla ice cream.

Blueberries are one of only three fruits native to North America. (The others are cranberries and Concord grapes. Both make a mean pie, and both were more popular for pies in this country's early days than now.) According to the native Americans, blueberries are best when picked "before the dew is off."

COUNTRY PEACH PIE

Nothing says summer and home better than a freshly baked pie, a pie that, to quote a friend, "screams peaches."

Makes 1 deep 9½- or 10-inch pie; serves about 8

	Basic Pie Dough for a 2-crust pie (page 449)
8	large (3½-4 pounds) ripe peaches
1	tablespoon fresh lemon juice
⅓	cup packed light brown sugar
¼	cup plus 1 tablespoon sugar
3	tablespoons cornstarch
	Pinch *each* ground cinnamon, ground mace or fresh-grated nutmeg
	Pinch salt
2	tablespoons cold unsalted butter, cut into pieces
1	tablespoon milk, for glaze
	Vanilla ice cream, for serving (optional)

1. Preheat the oven to 425 degrees F, with a rack in the lower third. Divide the dough into 2 slightly unequal pieces. Roll out the larger piece on a lightly floured surface to a large circle no more than ⅛ inch thick; fit it, without stretching, into a buttered, deep 9½-inch or 10-inch pie pan. Trim the edge, leaving a ¾-inch overhang. Roll out the remaining dough into a large circle, and transfer it to a foil-lined baking sheet. Chill the doughs.

2. Dip the peaches in boiling water for 15 seconds; peel off their skins. Squeeze the lemon juice into a large bowl. Working quickly, stone and thickly slice the peaches, letting the slices fall into the bowl. You should have about 8 cups. Toss gently and discard any excess juices.

3. Sift together the brown sugar, the ¼ cup sugar, the cornstarch, cinnamon, mace or nutmeg and salt. Toss gently with the peaches, and pour the mixture into the pie pan, mounding the peaches in the center. Dot with the butter. Moisten the edge of the crust with cold water. Loosely drape the remaining dough over the filling. Trim off the excess dough, leaving a ¾-inch overhang. Turn the edges of the top crust under the edges of the bottom crust, forming a smooth border on the rim of the pie pan. Crimp or flute the border. Brush the pastry lightly with the milk; sprinkle with the remaining 1 tablespoon sugar. Cut several slashes in the top crust to release steam.

4. Cover the edges of the dough with strips of foil if you like, to prevent overbrowning. Place the pie in the oven, with a sheet of foil underneath to catch any drips. Bake until golden brown, usually 40 to 45 minutes, removing the strips of foil, if using, after 20 minutes.

5. Cool the pie on a wire rack. Serve warm or at room temperature, with vanilla ice cream, if desired.

TO THICKEN OR NOT TO THICKEN

Food writer John Thorne, author of the quarterly newsletter *Simple Cooking*, is adamant that fruit filling should never be thickened with flour:

Sometime in this century, professional food writers started slipping flour into their fillings, first in the berry ones, then in the apple ones, convincing us that there was something terribly vulgar about a runny pie. But flour makes it gummy and clouds the flavor.

I couldn't agree more about the joys of "a runny pie," with rivulets of juices that burst forth at the intruding touch of a fork, and I hate starchy, stodgy thickening.

But—a big but—you don't want soup. Pies with no thickener at all are awash in thin juices—filling the pan with a ½-inch-deep pool of liquid as soon as you remove the first slice. The rest of the pie is soggy before you've even started.

To prevent this, I thicken fillings in fruit pies very lightly with cornstarch—just enough to bind the clear juices, not enough to produce a floury, lifeless slice. Use only about 3 tablespoons cornstarch per 5 to 6 cups fruit, and the juices will flow, but just enough, not out of control.

As with all things in cooking, you've got to know your fruit. Apples that are dryish won't need cornstarch at all. Berries do, but just a little.

LATTICE-TOPPED PEACH-BERRY PIE

Peaches and berries marry well in a pie; the berries add a tart edge and deep color to the golden peach slices. Blackberries, blueberries or black or red raspberries all work nicely here. And if you can't get first-rate peaches, use nectarines.

This filling is not too sweet, with runny juices. For an interesting variation on a lattice crust, Wendy London of Rock Hill Bake House in Gansevoort, New York, brushes lattice strips of dough with milk and sprinkles them with a streusel mixture.

Makes one 9-inch pie; serves about 8

	Basic Pie Dough for a 2-crust pie (page 449)
7	large (3-3½ pounds) firm-ripe peaches or nectarines
	Juice of ½ lemon
½	pint blackberries, picked over
½	pint raspberries, picked over
2	tablespoons thick apricot or peach preserves
¼	cup packed light brown sugar, or more, depending on the berries' sweetness
2½	tablespoons cornstarch (or 3, if the fruits are especially juicy)
¾	teaspoon ground cinnamon
1	egg white, beaten until foamy
1	tablespoon milk, for glaze
1	tablespoon sugar, for glaze

1. Divide the dough into 2 slightly unequal pieces. Roll out the larger piece on a lightly floured surface into a large circle about ⅛ inch thick. Fit it, without stretching, into a buttered 9-inch pie pan. Trim the edge, leaving a ¾-inch overhang. Roll out the remaining dough into a large circle about ⅛ inch thick. Transfer it to a foil-lined baking sheet. Chill the doughs.

2. Dip the peaches or nectarines in boiling water for 15 to 20 seconds; peel off the skins. Squeeze the lemon juice into a large bowl. Working quickly, stone the peaches or nectarines and cut into wedges, letting them fall into the lemon juice. Toss gently and pour off any excess liquid, leaving the fruit somewhat moist. Add the blackberries, raspberries and preserves; toss gently to combine.

"The running blackberry would adorn the parlors of heaven."

WALT WHITMAN
SONG OF MYSELF
1855

3. In a small bowl, stir together the brown sugar, cornstarch and cinnamon with a fork or small whisk until free of lumps. Sprinkle over the fruit and toss gently until thoroughly mixed. Set the filling aside.

4. Preheat the oven to 425 degrees F, with a rack in the lower third. Brush all of the inside surface of the pie dough with a light coating of the egg white (this helps prevent sogginess). Spoon the fruit mixture into the pie shell. With a fluted pastry wheel or sharp knife, cut the remaining dough into strips about ¾ inch wide. Lay ½ of the strips over the fruit at even intervals, parallel to one another. Lay the remaining strips of dough across the top in the other direction, parallel again. Press the ends of the strips into the bottom crust. Trim off the excess dough. Fold the overhanging edges of the bottom crust onto the rim of the pie pan, pressing gently to from a smooth, high border. Brush the lattice with the milk; sprinkle it with the sugar.

5. Lightly cover the pie with foil and place it in the oven with a sheet of foil underneath to catch any drips. Bake for 10 minutes. Lower the heat to 400 degrees. When the fruit starts to bubble up (usually after about 10 minutes longer), gently remove the top sheet of foil. Continue to bake until the crust is golden brown and the fruit is bubbly, usually 35 to 40 minutes more.

6. Cool the pie on a wire rack. Serve warm or at room temperature.

⌒ *Variation*
PEACH- OR NECTARINE-BERRY PIE WITH ALMOND CRUMB TOPPING: Omit the lattice top. Sprinkle the fruit with streusel (see Indiana Orchard Apple Crumb Pie, page 454) tossed with ⅓ cup sliced almonds. Loosely cover with foil and bake at 400 degrees for 20 minutes. Remove the foil and continue to bake until golden, about 30 minutes longer.

CAPE COD CRANBERRY "LINZER" PIE

Dip into old American cookbooks and cranberry pies are right up there in popularity with apple, pumpkin, mincemeat and rhubarb. Combined with sweet apples in a filling, cranberries lend bright color and tart character to a pie. This recipe for autumn combines cranberries, apples, raisins and ginger. It's not made with an authentic linzer dough, but the look of the pie (or tartlets) is reminiscent of that Austrian classic. The filling looks great peeking through the lattice and makes beautiful individual tartlets.

〜 *Makes one 9- or 9½-inch pie to serve about 6 or 6 individual tartlets*

> Basic Pie Dough for a 2-crust pie (page 449)
> 1 orange
> 1¼ cups sugar
> 2 cups (7-8 ounces) fresh or frozen (not thawed) cranberries, rinsed and picked over
> 1½-2 sweet apples (Golden Delicious) or pears (Bosc or Anjou), peeled, cored and cut into ½-inch dice (about 1½ cups)
> 1 tablespoon minced crystallized ginger
> ¼ cup golden raisins
> Milk and cinnamon sugar, for glaze
> Vanilla ice cream, for serving

1. Divide the dough into 2 slightly unequal pieces. Roll out the larger piece on a lightly floured surface into a large circle ⅛ inch thick. Fit it, without stretching, into a well-buttered 9- or 9½-inch fluted tart or quiche pan with a removable bottom. (You can also make this in a 9-inch pie pan or 6 individual 3-inch tartlet pans.) Press the dough against the sides and trim the top edge even with the pan. Roll out the remaining dough into a circle about ⅛ inch thick; place the dough on a foil-lined baking sheet. Chill the doughs while you prepare the filling.

2. Remove the zest from the orange in strips with a vegetable peeler; squeeze the juice from the orange. Place the zest in a food processor with ½ cup of the sugar; process until the zest is finely chopped. Add about 1 cup of the cranberries and pulse until the berries are coarsely chopped. Transfer the mixture to a bowl and stir in the remaining 1 cup whole cranberries, the remaining ¾ cup sugar, the orange juice, apples, ginger and raisins.

3. Preheat the oven to 375 degrees F, with a rack in the center. Brush the edges of the bottom crust lightly with cold water. Pour the filling into the crust. With a fluted pastry wheel or sharp knife, cut the remaining round of dough into lattice strips about 1 inch wide. Lay ½ of the strips over the filling at even intervals, parallel to one another. Lay the remaining strips across the top in the other direction, parallel again. Press the ends of the strips into the bottom crust and trim off the excess dough. Fold the overhanging edges of the bottom crust onto the rim of the pan, pressing gently to form a smooth border. Brush the lattice lightly with milk; lightly sprinkle it with cinnamon sugar.

4. Place the pie on a foil-lined baking sheet. Bake until the pastry is golden and the filling is bubbly, about 1 hour.

5. Cool the pie on a wire rack. Carefully remove the sides of the pan. Serve warm or at room temperature, with vanilla ice cream.

Strange Tastes

We're so used to cranberries as sauce for turkey that we often forget that this native American berry adds plenty of flavor to pies, crumbles and all sorts of other desserts. When I apprenticed in a Paris kitchen some years ago, I was surprised to see a pastry chef pulling bags of imported Ocean Spray cranberries out of the freezer to make an open-face tart. As he spread the cooked whole berries on a base of almond cream and then napped them with red currant glaze, he called me over.

"You're American," he said, "what kind of desserts do Americans make with these *airelles*?" I told him that we don't use cranberries much for dessert. By this time, two or three other chefs had gathered around, curious about this strange sour American berry. "Well," they asked, "what *do* you use them for?"

"We cook them into a sort of relish and eat it with turkey."

"*Turkey?*" They were totally baffled.

469

FRESH GRAPE PIE

Grapevines grow wild in many parts of the United States, and their fruit often wind up in pies. You'll be surprised at how well grapes work. They are very juicy, with a texture that may remind you of a fresh cherry pie, but with a deep flavor all their own. This recipe is from Margaret Zaninovich, who grows grapes in Delano, California.

∾ *Makes one 9-inch pie; serves about 8*

Basic Pie Dough for a 2-crust pie (page 449)
5 cups (1½-1¾ pounds) Ribier, Concord or seedless red grapes, stemmed
1 tablespoon fresh lemon juice
1 cup sugar, plus more as needed
3 tablespoons cornstarch
½ teaspoon *each* ground cinnamon and salt
2 tablespoons cold unsalted butter, cut into pieces
Milk and sugar, for glaze
Vanilla ice cream, for serving (optional)

1. Divide the dough into 2 slightly unequal pieces. Roll out the larger piece on a lightly floured surface into a large circle ⅛ inch thick. Fit it, without stretching, into a buttered 9-inch pie pan. Trim the edge, leaving a ¾-inch overhang. Roll out the remaining dough into a large circle; place on a foil-lined baking sheet. Chill the doughs.

2. Preheat the oven to 425 degrees F, with a rack in the lower third. If using Ribier or Concord grapes (or other grapes with seeds), halve them and remove the seeds. Place the grapes in a food processor in 3 batches and pulse just until very coarsely chopped. Transfer the grapes to a colander and drain off the excess juice. Place the drained grapes in a large bowl and stir in the lemon juice.

3. In a small bowl, stir together the sugar, cornstarch, cinnamon and salt. Add this mixture to the grapes and toss to combine. Pour the mixture into the crust; dot with the butter. Moisten the edge of the crust with cold water. Loosely drape the remaining dough over the filling. Trim off the excess pastry, leaving a ¾-inch overhang; reserve the trimmings. Turn the edges of the top crust under the edges of the bottom crust, forming a smooth border on the rim of the pie pan. Crimp or flute the border.

4. Using a small knife or a leaf-shape cookie cutter, cut 6 leaf shapes from the pastry scraps. With the dull edge of a knife, lightly imprint leaf veins. Brush the top of the pie lightly with milk; arrange the pastry leaves on the surface, arching them slightly. Cut several steam vents. Sprinkle the pie lightly with sugar.

5. Place the pie on a foil-lined baking sheet. Bake until the pie is golden brown and the juices are bubbly, about 40 minutes.

6. Cool the pie on a wire rack. Serve warm or at room temperature, preferably with vanilla ice cream.

⌒ *Variation*

FRESH PLUM PIE: Small, tart purple prune plums work best. Substitute 5 cups stoned and sliced plums for the grapes, and eliminate the chopping and draining in step 2. Proceed as directed.

Grape Pie

Grapes make the best pies when very tender and green. If not very small, they should be stewed and strained, to get out the seeds, before they are made into pies— sweeten them to the taste when stewed. They do not require any spice. If made into a pie without steweing, put to each layer of grapes a thick layer of sugar, and a table-spoonful of water.

ANONYMOUS
THE KITCHEN DIRECTORY
AND AMERICAN HOUSEWIFE
1844

Favorite Pie

DEEP-DISH RHUBARB-CHERRY-BERRY PIE

Rhubarb pie is another old American favorite. Strawberry-rhubarb is the time-honored combination, and it makes sense. The two arrive in the garden at about the same time in spring, and the berries sweeten up the sour rhubarb.

This pie combines rhubarb with cherries and blueberries, a juicy mix with sweet-tart flavors and a deep ruby color. The trick is finding rhubarb and fresh cherries at the same time. I have found some late rhubarb in mid-June, when the cherries have started. If you can't find fresh cherries, substitute strawberries.

Makes one 8-inch square deep-dish pie; serves about 8

1	generous pint sweet or sour cherries, pitted and stemmed, or strawberries, hulled and halved or quartered, if large
1½	cups sugar, or as needed to taste
	Basic Pie Dough for a 2-crust pie (page 449)
1½	pounds rhubarb, trimmed and cut into ½-inch lengths (3½-4 cups)
1	generous pint blueberries, picked over
¼	teaspoon almond extract
⅓	cup quick-cooking tapioca or cornstarch
¼	teaspoon ground cinnamon or a blend of ground cinnamon, ground allspice and ground mace
	Pinch salt
1	egg white, beaten until foamy
	Sugar, for glaze

1. Toss the cherries or strawberries with ½ cup of the sugar and let stand until needed.

2. Divide the pie dough into 2 slightly unequal pieces. Roll out the larger piece on a lightly floured surface to a large square about ⅛ inch thick. Fit it, without stretching, into a buttered 8-inch square Pyrex or ceramic baking dish. Trim the edges of the dough, leaving a ¾-inch overhang. Roll out the remaining dough (including any trimmings) into a large, thin rectangle. Place it on a lightly floured sheet of wax paper; slide a plate or baking sheet underneath and chill the doughs.

3. Preheat the oven to 375 degrees F, with a rack in the lower third. In a large bowl, toss together the rhubarb, cherries or strawberries, blueberries and almond extract. In a small bowl, whisk the remaining 1 cup sugar with the tapioca or cornstarch, spices and salt until completely free of lumps. Sprinkle this mixture over the fruits and toss until blended.

4. Brush the dough-lined dish and the sheet of dough with a light coating of the egg white (this helps seal the dough, preventing sogginess), taking care to coat the dough at the edges of the baking dish. Spoon the fruit mixture into the pie shell. With a fluted pastry wheel or sharp knife, cut the rectangle of dough into strips about ¾ inch wide. Lay ½ of the strips over the fruit at even intervals, parallel to one another. Lay the remaining strips across the top, in the other direction, parallel again. Press the ends of the strips into the bottom crust. Trim off the excess dough. Fold the overhanging edges of the bottom crust onto the rim of the dish, pressing gently to form a smooth, high border. Sprinkle the lattice strips with sugar.

5. Gently lay a sheet of foil over the lattice crust (this helps heat the fruit filling). Place the baking dish in the oven, with another sheet of foil underneath to catch any drips. Bake for 20 minutes. Gently remove the top sheet of foil. Continue to bake until the crust is golden brown and the fruit juices are bubbling, usually 30 to 40 minutes longer.

6. Cool the pie on a wire rack. Serve warm or at room temperature.

FRIED (OR BAKED) APPLE "HALF-MOON" PIES

These are fried pies, made by folding a circle of dough over fresh or dried apples, a farm tradition of the Appalachians, the South (where they are called "applejacks") and the Midwest. The neat half-moon pies could then be packed in a lunchbox for mid-day eating in the fields or down in the mines.

The pies are virtually unchanged from the way they've been made in England for centuries. The adjoining recipe is nearly 350 years old and is pretty much the same as this one, which is partially based on one from cookbook author Marilyn Kluger.

While they are traditionally fried, I like these half-moon pies better when baked. I've included instructions for both.

Makes six 6-inch pies

FILLING

4   cups (about 1 pound) dried apples or dried peaches (about 1½ pounds)
    Cider (if using apples) or cold water (if using peaches), as needed
⅔   cup sugar, or to taste

DOUGH

3   cups all-purpose flour
½   teaspoon salt
1   cup cold lard or solid vegetable shortening
⅓   cup cold water

3   cups vegetable oil or shortening, or as needed, if frying
    Melted unsalted butter, as needed, if baking
    Confectioners' sugar, for sprinkling

1. **FILLING:** Cook the dried apples or peaches in cider or water to cover until they are tender, usually 15 to 20 minutes. Add more liquid, if necessary, if the fruit absorbs all of it before it is tender. Stir in the sugar until it dissolves; set the fruit aside to cool.

2. **DOUGH:** Sift together the flour and salt. Cut in the lard or shortening until the mixture resembles coarse cornmeal. Sprinkle the water, 1 tablespoon at a time, over the mixture, gently mixing with a fork until moistened. Gather the mixture into a ball. If you have time, wrap the dough in plastic or wax paper and chill for at least 30 minutes.

3. Divide the dough into 6 equal portions. Roll out and cut each portion into a neat 6-inch circle, using a saucer or plate as a guide and trimming away the excess dough. Put about ⅓ cup of the fruit onto each round of dough; moisten the edges with water, and fold over to make a half-moon shape. Press the edges together with the tines of a fork.

4. **IF FRYING THE PIES:** In a wide saucepan or a deep skillet, heat enough oil or shortening to measure ½ inch deep. Bring the fat to 375 degrees F. (If you don't own a frying thermometer, test the heat by throwing a cube of bread or a little flour or bread crumbs into the oil; it should sizzle gently but steadily and brown in about 45 seconds.) Adjust the heat as needed to maintain a steady frying temperature. Working in batches if necessary (don't crowd the pan), carefully slip the pies into the hot fat. Fry the pies, turning once with a skimmer or slotted spoon, until they are golden brown on both sides, usually 10 to 15 minutes total. Drain the pies on paper-towel-lined plates; cool to lukewarm or room temperature. Sprinkle the pies with confectioners' sugar before serving.

5. **IF BAKING THE PIES:** Preheat the oven to 375 degrees F, with a rack in the lower third. Place the pies on an ungreased baking sheet and lightly brush the tops with melted butter. Bake until lightly golden, usually about 25 minutes. Cool the pies on a wire rack. Sprinkle with confectioners' sugar before serving warm or at room temperature.

To Fry Apple-Pies

Take your paste, roul it thin, and make them up as big Pasties as you please, to hold a spoonful or a little lesse of your Apples [seasoned with cinnamon, ginger, sugar, and rosewater], and so fry them with Butter, not too hastily, lest they be burned.

A TRUE GENTLEWOMAN'S DELIGHT
LONDON, 1659

475

Apple-Pecan Upside-Down Pie Baked in a Skillet

This is an American version of the French Tarte Tatin, simplified to the point that it's easier than a basic apple pie. Inverted and dripping with bronze juices, the pie tastes like an apple sticky bun, but with a base of crisp butter pastry instead of yeast dough. Because no spices intrude on the clean fruit flavor, it's important to use a full-flavored apple. Northern Spy, Baldwin and Jonathan all work well here.

Though it holds up better than some versions, this pie should be baked shortly before serving for best texture and flavor.

✎ *Makes one 9- or 10-inch pie; serves about 8*

1	batch Galette Dough (page 532), Rich Tart Dough (page 451), or Basic Pie Dough (page 449)
1	whole egg, beaten for glaze
¼	cup (½ stick) unsalted butter
¾	cup sugar
1½	pounds (usually 4 or 5) apples, peeled, quartered, cored, and each quarter cut into 2 wedges
½	cup pecan halves
	Vanilla ice cream, for serving (optional)

1. On a lightly floured surface, roll out the pastry dough into a neat circle slightly larger than a 9- or 10-inch ovenproof skillet and no more than ⅛ inch thick. (A cast-iron skillet works well, but anything ovenproof is fine.) Transfer the round of dough to a plate lined with a sheet of wax paper or foil; brush it lightly with the beaten egg. Chill the dough while you prepare the apple wedges.

2. Preheat the oven to 400 degrees F, with a rack in the center. Melt the butter in the skillet over medium heat. Add the sugar and stir to combine it with the butter. Cook over medium heat, without stirring, until the sugar begins to caramelize, about 5 minutes. Add the apple wedges and toss to coat them with the caramel; remove the pan from the heat. Shake the skillet so the apples are evenly distributed—they don't have to be arranged too carefully. Tuck the pecans into the spaces between the apples.

3. Invert the dough over the skillet, draping it over the apples, without stretching, so that the egg-glazed side is down, against the apples. Trim the edges of the dough if more than about

½ inch hangs over; fold under the overhang and tuck it in against the sides of the skillet. Cut several short slits in the dough for steam vents.

4. Bake until the dough is well browned, crisp and baked through, 37 to 40 minutes.

5. Cool the pie in the skillet on a wire rack for about 10 minutes. Invert a serving plate over the skillet, hold it firmly in place and quickly invert the two. Remove the skillet and replace any apple pieces that stick to the pan. Cut the pie in wedges and serve warm, with ice cream, if you like. This pie can be reheated, but try to serve it as soon as possible after baking.

RECIPES

Indiana Sugar Cream Pie
Buttermilk Silk Pie
Midwestern Butterscotch
　　Cream Pie
Claremont Diner Coconut
　　Cream Pie
White Chocolate Banana
　　Cream Pie
Mile-High Caramel Cream
　　Pie
Lutz's Chocolate Cream Pie
Peanut Butter Pie with
　　Fudge Topping
Iowa's Favorite Custard Pie
Best-Ever Pumpkin Pie
Sour Cream Pumpkin
　　Chiffon Pie
Sweet Potato Pie
Dried Peach Pie with Cus-
　　tard and Meringue
Grandmother's Souffléed
　　Lemon Pie
Sour Cream Raisin Pie
Split-Level Lime Chiffon Pie
Mary's Rice Pie
Neapolitan Easter Pie
Hoover Toffee Ice Cream Pie

CUSTARD, CREAM AND ICE CREAM PIES

A custard pie which is curdled is a heart scald, a thin custard pie a disappointment. At a point between the two is the perfect custard, smoothly thickened, creamy, and delicate. True custard pies are thickened by eggs alone which act as a binder, leavener, thickener, stabilizer, and give texture as well as flavor. The temperature at which eggs coagulate is almost unbelievably low, and since we are accustomed to watching food bubble as it cooks, custard trouble is apt to happen now and then. Disastrous results follow too much heat . . .

LOUIS P. DE GOUY,
THE PIE BOOK, 1949

Pies cradled in what Shakespeare called "a custard coffin" are hardly new. It's the egginess—innocent, yet rich—that makes a well-made custard so elementally appealing. But the affection for "something soft and sweet in a crust" seems to be peculiarly American.

Baked both as large pies and individual tarts, custard pies had a place of pride in the repertoire of early-American homemakers. Pies with soft fillings like custard and pumpkin were called "puddings" in colonial days, but since the pudding dishes were first lined with a "paste," or pie crust, these puddings are what we now know as custard pies.

The American craze for cream pies, whether plain custard,

lemon, coconut, banana or chocolate and whether topped with whipped cream or meringue, seems to have taken hold in the latter days of the 19th century and come to full flower in the early 20th. Suddenly, popular cookbooks burst with cream pies of every description. Every drugstore lunch counter had its lemon meringue pie, gilded peaks standing tall and proud; the White Castle chain, founded in 1921 in Wichita, Kansas, still takes pride in its coconut custard. In a survey of home baking by *Farm Journal*, apple and cherry pie were America's favorites, closely followed by pumpkin, lemon, chocolate, pecan and coconut—nearly all custard or cream pies.

As is true with all popular phenomena, the custard and cream pie was and is often corrupted, made with ersatz ingredients and excess sugar or fake whipped cream: all sweetness and fluff, no substance.

But when made well—with crisp pastry, fresh eggs, real flavorings, quality chocolate, real cream—a home-baked cream or custard pie can be a baker's triumph.

This chapter showcases several types of pies with soft fillings, including ice cream pies. There are both true custard pies, in which an egg and milk filling is baked with the crust, and cream pies, with unbaked fillings poured into a baked pie shell.

LEAVE CUSTARD PIES SLIGHTLY WOBBLY . . .

Be sure to take any custard pie out of the oven when it's still slightly wobbly but not liquid in the center. The custard will set up further after you take it out. If overbaked, a custard-filled pie can crack as it cools.

In general, baked pies should not be chilled. But since most cream and custard pie fillings must be chilled, these pies are an exception. To bring up their flavor, take cream pies out of the refrigerator a few minutes before serving.

See also "Making Perfect Custards," page 137.

An Egg Pan-Pie

Take the Yolks of Eggs, a lump of Sugar, a little Butter and Orange-flower water; make as it were a kind of Cream; and put it into a piece of very thin fine Paste rais'd with a little Border from the Side-crust: then having grated some Lemmon-peel upon it, let it be baked and ic'd over with . . . rosewater butter and sugar, when ready to be brought to the table.

FRANÇOIS PIERRE DE LA
VARENNE
*LE VRAY CUISINIER
FRANÇOIS*
PARIS, 1682;
LONDON, 1653

479

INDIANA SUGAR CREAM PIE

This is a great favorite in Indiana farm country, where house-wives stake their reputations on a great sugar cream pie, frequently serving it as the conclusion to their traditional hearty Sunday dinner.

This custard is made without eggs; it's sweet, firm and tasty. It's based on an old recipe from Mary Durbin, who with her husband, Don, ran the Durbin Hotel in Rushville, Indiana, where Wendell Willkie set up his campaign headquarters.

Makes one 9- or- 9½-inch pie; serves about 8

	Basic Pie Dough for a 1-crust pie (page 449)
½	cup (1 stick) unsalted butter
1	cup sugar
1¼	cups milk
1	cup heavy cream
¼	cup cornstarch
2	teaspoons pure vanilla extract
	Fresh-grated nutmeg

1. Roll out the dough on a lightly floured surface into a large circle about ⅛ inch thick. Fit it, without stretching, into a buttered 9- or 9½-inch pie pan. Trim off the excess dough, leaving a ¾-inch overhang. Fold under the edge of the dough, pressing along the rim of the pan and forming a high, fluted border. Line the dough with a sheet of buttered foil, buttered side down, and chill while you pre-heat the oven to 375 degrees F, with a rack in the lower third.

2. Bake the pastry until the sides are set, 10 to 12 minutes. Gently remove the foil. Continue to bake, pricking any air bubbles with a fork, until the crust is pale golden and just baked through, 8 to 10 minutes longer. Cool the pie shell on a wire rack; leave the oven on.

3. While the crust is baking, combine the butter, sugar, 1 cup of the milk and the cream in the top of a double boiler (or in a heatproof bowl over a pan of simmering water). Heat the mixture, stirring occasionally, until very hot and the butter is melted.

4. In a cup, stir together the cornstarch and the remaining ¼ cup milk until smooth. Add to the mixture in the double boiler, and continue cooking, stirring constantly, until the custard thick-ens, about 5 minutes. Stir in the vanilla.

Sugar Cousins

A close relation to sugar cream pie is the brown sugar pie made by the Amish; brown sugar and a little flour are scattered in an unbaked pie crust, and evaporated milk is poured over, without mixing. The surface is strewn with bits of butter and cinnamon, and the whole thing comes together as it bakes.

5. Pour the custard mixture into the baked pie shell; sprinkle with nutmeg. Bake until the custard is set but still slightly wobbly in the center, about 10 minutes.

6. Cool the pie on a wire rack. Serve at room temperature or slightly chilled.

BUTTERMILK SILK PIE

Like chess pie and pecan pie, buttermilk pie can be baked in any season, when there's little fresh fruit in the larder. If you've never tried it, buttermilk pie is like custard pie, but with a gently mellow flavor that's almost like cheesecake. It's plain and wonderfully smooth. I like it best without the meringue that often tops it.

Makes one 9-inch pie; serves about 8

Basic Pie Dough for a 1-crust pie (page 449)
1 cup sugar
3 tablespoons cornstarch
1 large whole egg
3 large egg yolks
6 tablespoons (¾ stick) unsalted butter, melted
1½ cups buttermilk
1½ teaspoons pure vanilla extract
¼ teaspoon salt

1. Roll out the dough on a lightly floured surface into a large circle about ⅛ inch thick. Fit it, without stretching, into a buttered 9-inch pie pan. Trim the edge, leaving a ¾-inch overhang. Fold under the edge of the dough, pressing along the rim of the pan and forming a high, fluted border. Chill the pie shell while you preheat the oven to 350 degrees F, with a rack in the lower third.

2. Bake the pie shell, gently pricking any air bubbles with a fork until it is partially baked (it will not take on much color at this point), 8 to 10 minutes. Cool the pie shell on a wire rack; leave the oven on.

3. Meanwhile, in a bowl, whisk together the sugar and cornstarch until there are no lumps. Add the egg, egg yolks, melted

butter, buttermilk, vanilla and salt and mix well. Pour the filling into the partially baked pie crust.

4. Bake until the surface is a very pale golden color and the custard is set but still slightly wobbly in the center (the mixture will set up more as it cools; do not overbake), about 40 minutes.

5. Cool the pie to room temperature on a wire rack. Serve at room temperature or slightly chilled.

MIDWESTERN BUTTERSCOTCH CREAM PIE

This is an old-fashioned pie, with the golden flavors of brown sugar, butter and vanilla. The recipe is from the late Alberta Potts Violanti, who grew up in West Virginia, and then raised her kids on this pie in Michigan (her daughter, Nancy Hubbard, gave me the recipe). Mrs. Violanti topped this pie with meringue (see note); I like whipped cream—take your pick.

Makes one 10-inch pie; serves about 8

GRAHAM CRACKER CRUST
1¼-1½ cups (about 20 individual) finely crushed graham crackers
2 tablespoons sugar
6 tablespoons (¾ stick) unsalted butter, melted

BUTTERSCOTCH FILLING
¾ cup packed dark brown sugar
⅓ cup cornstarch
3 cups milk
4 large egg yolks
Pinch salt
1½ teaspoons pure vanilla extract
2 tablespoons unsalted butter

WHIPPED CREAM TOPPING
½-⅔ cup heavy cream, well chilled
1 tablespoon confectioners' sugar
½ teaspoon pure vanilla extract

1. **GRAHAM CRACKER CRUST:** Preheat the oven to 350 degrees F, with a rack in the center. In a bowl, combine the graham cracker crumbs, sugar and butter; toss to moisten the crumbs. Press evenly into a buttered 10-inch pie pan, reaching up to but not over the rim. Bake for 10 minutes. Cool the crust completely on a wire rack.

2. **BUTTERSCOTCH FILLING:** Meanwhile, stir together ½ cup of the brown sugar and the cornstarch in a bowl. Stir in ¼ cup of the milk and the egg yolks; set aside. Bring the remaining 2¾ cups milk, the remaining ¼ cup brown sugar and the salt to a boil in a nonreactive saucepan over medium heat.

3. When the milk is boiling, add a splash to the egg yolk mixture in the bowl and whisk well (this heats the yolks slowly, preventing curdling). Repeat the process 2 or 3 times. Scrape the mixture into the saucepan and bring to a boil, whisking constantly. Be sure to whisk around the edges of the pan. Boil, whisking, for 2 minutes. Strain the custard into a clean bowl. Whisk in the vanilla and butter until smooth. Place a sheet of wax paper or plastic wrap directly on the surface of the custard to prevent a skin from forming; refrigerate until cooled, about 2 hours.

4. Pour the cooled custard into the crust. Top with wax paper or plastic; chill.

5. **WHIPPED CREAM TOPPING:** Up to 1 hour before serving, whip the cream and confectioners' sugar until nearly stiff; stir in the vanilla. Using a pastry bag with a large star tip, pipe or spoon a wide border of the cream around the edge of the pie. If you prefer, the whipped cream can be spread over the surface of the pie and mounded in the center. Chill until needed and serve cold.

NOTE: If you prefer a meringue topping, follow the instructions in steps 4 and 5 of Dried Peach Pie with Custard and Meringue, page 500.

I lean forward over the oilcloth on the table so far my chin is almost on it. . . . The smell of the oilcloth reminds me of when I was a kid and I'd lean my chin on the table while my mother—God bless her and keep her—trimmed the crust off a pie.

ROBERT CAMPBELL
THE JUNKYARD DOG
1986

CLAREMONT DINER
COCONUT CREAM PIE

Anyone who grew up in northern New Jersey in the 1950s remembers the Claremont Diner, a landmark in the quintessential suburban cultural landscape. The creation of an Austrian-born tyrant named Morris Bauman, the Claremont had all the showy food you still find in glitzy diners everywhere—but done right, made from scratch with top-quality ingredients. More than three decades later, this is my approximation from memory of my favorite childhood pie.

To a lonely 5-year-old, the Claremont Diner was a wonderland of infinite possibilities. But the tough choice came when it was time for dessert. There were chocolate, lemon, coffee and Nesselrode cream pies, all made with a luscious Bavarian cream base, but I went for the coconut every time.

Makes one 9- or 9½-inch pie; serves about 8

	Basic Pie Dough for a 1-crust pie (page 449)
3½	ounces shredded sweetened coconut (about 1⅓ cups)
3	cups milk
1	envelope (about 2½ teaspoons) unflavored gelatin
½	cup sugar
¼	cup cornstarch
1	large whole egg
3	egg yolks
2	tablespoons unsalted butter
1	tablespoon plus 1 teaspoon pure vanilla extract
¾	cup heavy cream, well chilled (see note)

1. Roll out the dough on a lightly floured surface to a large circle about ⅛ inch thick. Fit it, without stretching, into a buttered 9- or 9½-inch pie pan. Trim off the excess dough, leaving a ¾-inch overhang. Fold under the edge of the dough, pressing along the rim of the pan and forming a high fluted border. Line the dough with a sheet of buttered foil, buttered side down, and chill while you preheat the oven to 375 degrees F, with a rack in the lower third.

2. Bake the pie shell until the sides are set, about 12 minutes. Gently remove the foil and continue to bake, pricking any air bubbles with a fork, until the crust is pale golden and just baked through, about 8 minutes longer. Cool the pie shell on a wire rack; leave the oven on.

3. Scatter the coconut over a baking pan and toast in the hot oven, stirring once or twice, until medium golden brown, about 9 minutes (watch carefully to prevent burning). Cool in the pan on a wire rack.

4. Place ⅓ cup of the cold milk in a mixing bowl or large measuring cup and sprinkle with the gelatin, stirring once or twice to moisten. Set aside to soften for about 5 minutes. Meanwhile, bring the remaining 2⅔ cups milk nearly to a boil in a heavy non-reactive saucepan over medium heat. When the gelatin is soft, add the sugar, cornstarch, egg and egg yolks and whisk until very well blended. Gradually whisk a little of the hot milk into the gelatin mixture; repeat this process once or twice. Pour the warmed gelatin mixture into the saucepan with the hot milk and bring the mixture to a boil, whisking. Boil, whisking constantly, for 2 minutes. Strain the pastry cream into a clean bowl; whisk in the butter and vanilla until smooth. Place a sheet of wax paper or plastic wrap directly on the surface of the pastry cream and refrigerate, stirring once or twice, until the pastry cream cools to room temperature.

5. Whip the cream until nearly stiff. Gently fold it into the pastry cream. Place the pie pan on a dinner plate (to catch any coconut that falls from the topping) and pour the filling into the cooled pie shell, mounding the filling in the center. Scatter the toasted coconut over the surface of the filling, covering it completely. Loosely cover and chill until the filling is set, at least 2 hours.

NOTE: At the Claremont Diner, the Bavarian cream filling was topped with a layer of whipped cream, then with the coconut. If you'd like to make it that way, increase the amount of cream to 1¼ cups. Whip as directed in step 5, adding 3 tablespoons of confectioners' sugar and ½ teaspoon vanilla to the cream. Fold slightly more than ½ of the whipped cream into the pastry cream. Pour the filling into the pie shell and chill the pie and the remaining whipped cream separately for about 20 minutes to firm up the filling slightly. With a spatula, gently spread the reserved chilled whipped cream over the filling, mounding it smoothly; top with the coconut and chill.

Variation

TOASTED COCONUT–BANANA CREAM PIE: To gild the lily, cut 2 ripe bananas lengthwise in half and then into slices. Fold the slices into the custard in step 5, just before the whipped cream. Proceed as directed. As with all desserts with sliced bananas, serve the pie on the day it is made, to prevent discoloration.

White Chocolate Banana Cream Pie

The Buckhead Diner in Atlanta, Georgia, is an updated, post-modern homage to the diner, a genuine American institution. In the same way, former chef-owner Gerry Klaskala's banana cream pie is a new reading of an old favorite—with its spirit kept intact.

Cocoa-dusted white chocolate curls dramatically top this pie. (If you'd like to simplify the recipe a little, leave out the chocolate curls, spread the custard with a thin layer of whipped cream and then sprinkle it lightly with cocoa powder.)

Fill the pie shell shortly before serving time. All of the components except the whipped cream can be prepared in advance.

Makes one 10-inch pie; serves about 8

Sugar Dough

- ½ cup (1 stick) cold unsalted butter, cut into pieces
- ¼ cup plus 1½ teaspoons sugar
- 2 teaspoons beaten egg (less than ½ of a large egg)
- 1 cup plus 2 tablespoons all-purpose flour

White Chocolate Pastry Cream

- 1 cup milk
- ½ vanilla bean, split lengthwise
- 3 large egg yolks
- ⅓ cup sugar
- 2 tablespoons cornstarch
- 1 tablespoon cold unsalted butter, cut into pieces
- 1½ ounces white chocolate, chopped

White Chocolate Curls (optional)

- 6 ounces white chocolate, chopped

- 1 cup heavy cream, well chilled
- 4 ripe bananas
  Juice of ½ lemon
- 1½ tablespoons banana liqueur or rum
- 1½ tablespoons white crème de cocoa or Amaretto
  Unsweetened cocoa powder, for sprinkling

1. **Sugar Dough:** In a food processor, combine the butter and sugar, pulsing just until blended (or cut the ingredients together with 2 knives). Add the egg, pulsing or tossing to combine. Add the flour and mix just until incorporated, no longer. Gather the dough

into a ball, flatten it into a disk, and wrap in plastic or wax paper. Chill for at least 30 minutes before rolling out.

2. Preheat the oven to 350 degrees F, with a rack in the lower third. Roll out the dough on a lightly floured surface to a large circle about ⅛ inch thick. Gently fit it, without stretching, into a buttered 10-inch tart pan with a removable bottom, preferably one with fluted sides. (Alternatively, you can bake this in a 10-inch or deep 9½-inch pie pan.) Trim off the excess dough, leaving a ¾-inch overhang. Tuck in the overhanging dough, pressing the edges of the crust against the sides of the pan and forming a high, fluted border. Line the dough with a sheet of buttered foil, buttered side down; weigh down with dried beans, rice or pie weights. Bake the shell until the sides are set, about 12 minutes. Carefully remove the weights and foil and gently prick the dough all over with a fork. Continue to bake until pale gold and baked through, about 5 minutes longer. Cool the pie shell completely on a wire rack.

3. **WHITE CHOCOLATE PASTRY CREAM:** Bring the milk and the vanilla bean to a boil in a heavy nonreactive saucepan. Meanwhile, whisk the egg yolks and sugar in a bowl until pale and light, about 1½ minutes. Whisk in the cornstarch until smooth. Remove the saucepan from the heat, and whisk about ¼ cup of the hot milk to the egg yolk mixture. Repeat once or twice. Scrape the warmed egg yolk mixture into the saucepan with the remaining milk and return to a boil, whisking. Whisking constantly, boil for 1 minute. Remove the pastry cream from the heat, and whisk in the butter and white chocolate until smooth. Strain the custard into a clean bowl. Place a sheet of wax paper or plastic wrap directly on the surface of the pastry cream and refrigerate until cooled.

4. **WHITE CHOCOLATE CURLS** (optional): Melt the white chocolate in a double boiler set over hot water until smooth. Pour the chocolate onto a marble slab or the back of a smooth baking sheet. With a spatula, spread out the chocolate into an even ⅛-inch-thick layer. Set aside at cool room temperature or refrigerate until the chocolate is firm but not brittle (8 to 10 minutes in the refrigerator).

5. Push a chef's knife blade or palette knife away from you through a 4-inch width of the chocolate, forming a loose curl. Continue to form chocolate curls with the remaining chocolate. (The chef likes them "big and thin.") With a large spatula, very gently transfer the curls to a baking sheet and refrigerate until needed. *(The recipe can be prepared in advance to this point.)*

6. Shortly before serving time, whip the cream until nearly stiff. Thinly slice the bananas and toss with the lemon juice to prevent darkening. Fold the bananas and the liqueurs into the chilled pastry cream; gently fold in the whipped cream until blended. Fill the cooled pie shell with the filling. Gently scatter the chocolate curls over the filling, covering the tart completely. Very lightly dust the chocolate curls with cocoa powder and serve.

MILE-HIGH CARAMEL CREAM PIE

This is sort of a grown-up version of Midwestern Butterscotch Cream Pie (page 482). The filling is a light mousse with a caramel flavor, piled high in a crust.

~~~ *Makes one 9- or 9½-inch pie; serves about 8*

	Basic Pie Dough for a 1-crust pie (page 449)
3	cups milk
2	cups sugar
3	tablespoons cold water
¼	cup boiling water
⅓	cup cornstarch
1	envelope plus 1 teaspoon (about 3½ teaspoons) unflavored gelatin
	Pinch salt
5	large egg yolks
2	tablespoons unsalted butter, cut into pieces
2	teaspoons pure vanilla extract
1	cup heavy cream, well chilled

1. Roll out the dough on a lightly floured surface to a large circle about ⅛ inch thick. Fit it, without stretching, into a buttered 9- or 9½-inch pie pan. Trim off the excess dough, leaving a ¾-inch overhang. Fold under the edge of the dough, pressing along the rim of the pan and forming a very high fluted border. Chill while you preheat the oven to 400 degrees F, with a rack in the lower third.

2. Prick the dough lightly with a fork. Line the dough with buttered foil, buttered side down; weigh down the foil with dried beans, rice or pie weights. Place the pan on a heavy baking sheet.

Bake until the sides are set, usually 6 to 8 minutes. Carefully remove the weights and foil. Continue to bake, pricking any air bubbles with a fork, until cooked through and lightly golden, 8 to 12 minutes longer. Cool the pie shell thoroughly on a wire rack.

3. Scald 2⅔ cups of the milk in a heavy nonreactive saucepan. Set aside over low heat.

4. In a large, heavy skillet over medium-high heat, combine 1⅔ cups of the sugar with the cold water, stirring until the mixture begins to boil. Stir until the sugar dissolves. Boil, without stirring, until the mixture caramelizes to a medium amber color. Remove the skillet from the heat and carefully stir in the boiling water until smooth. Add the caramel to the scalded milk, stirring over low heat until the caramel dissolves and the mixture is smooth.

5. Meanwhile, in a large heatproof bowl, whisk together the remaining ⅓ cup sugar, the cornstarch, gelatin and salt until blended. Whisk in the egg yolks and the remaining ⅓ cup cold milk until smooth. Whisk the hot milk mixture into the egg yolk mixture in a thin stream; return the mixture to the saucepan. Whisk constantly over medium heat until the custard boils and thickens. Boil, whisking constantly, for 1 minute. Remove from the heat and whisk in the butter and vanilla. Strain the custard into a clean bowl. Place a sheet of wax paper or plastic wrap directly on the surface of the custard to prevent a skin from forming, and refrigerate, stirring occasionally, until the mixture is barely tepid.

6. Whip ½ cup of the heavy cream until nearly stiff. Give the custard a quick stir, and fold in the whipped cream. Pour the custard into the cooled pie shell. Loosely cover and refrigerate until set, about 2 hours.

7. Shortly before serving, whip the remaining ½ cup cream until nearly stiff. Transfer to a pastry bag fitted with a large star tip and pipe rosettes or shells around the edge of the pie, or spoon on the cream in soft mounds.

LUTZ'S CHOCOLATE CREAM PIE

More than one generation of Chicago food lovers remembers Lutz Olkewicz's wonderful baking for the Cape Cod Room in the Drake Hotel. His chocolate pie has double the quantity of chocolate usually used for custard fillings. It's dense, dark and deeply flavored.

While chocolate cream pie seems like 20th-century Americana, tarts with chocolate have been around for centuries.

❧ *Makes one 9- or 9½-inch pie; serves about 8*

	Basic Pie Dough for a 1-crust pie (page 449)
2	cups milk
1	cup heavy cream
½	cup sugar
2	large eggs
3	tablespoons cornstarch
10	ounces semisweet chocolate, chopped
¼	cup (½ stick) unsalted butter
1½	teaspoons pure vanilla extract
¾	cup heavy cream

1. Roll out the dough on a lightly floured surface to a large circle about ⅛ inch thick. Fit it, without stretching, into a buttered 9- or 9½-inch pie pan. Trim off the excess dough, leaving a ¾-inch overhang. Fold under the edge of the dough, pressing along the rim of the pan and forming a very high fluted border. Chill while you preheat the oven to 400 degrees F, with a rack in the lower third.

2. Prick the dough lightly with a fork. Line with a sheet of buttered foil, buttered side down; weigh down the foil with dried beans, rice or pie weights. Place the pan on a heavy baking sheet. Bake until the sides are set, usually 6 to 8 minutes. Carefully remove the weights and foil. Continue to bake, pricking any air bubbles with a fork, until cooked through and lightly golden, 8 to 12 minutes longer. Cool the pie shell thoroughly on a wire rack.

3. Scald 1½ cups of the milk and all of the cream in a heavy nonreactive saucepan over medium heat.

Pie to Die for

I think black bottom pie [a cream pie with a chocolate bottom layer] is the most delicious pie I have ever eaten. . . . I hope to be propped up on my dying bed and fed a generous portion. Then I think that I should refuse outright to die, for life would be too good to relinquish.

MARJORIE KINNAN
RAWLINGS
CROSS CREEK COOKERY
1942

4. Meanwhile, in a bowl, whisk the remaining ½ cup milk with the sugar, eggs and cornstarch until smooth. Add a little of the hot milk mixture to the bowl, and whisk well. Repeat with more hot milk. Return the warmed mixture to the saucepan and bring to a boil, whisking. Boil, whisking constantly, for 2 minutes. Turn off the heat and add the chocolate, butter and 1 teaspoon of the vanilla; continue whisking until the mixture is smooth. Strain the custard into a clean bowl. Place a sheet of wax paper or plastic wrap directly on the surface of the custard to prevent a skin from forming, and refrigerate until cooled to room temperature.

5. Pour the custard into the cooled pie shell. Loosely cover and chill for at least 2 hours.

6. Whip the cream with the remaining ½ teaspoon vanilla until nearly stiff. Spread it over the pie with a spatula, swirling attractively. Chill before serving.

PEANUT BUTTER PIE WITH FUDGE TOPPING

Peanut butter and chocolate are an immortal combination; the archetype is Reese's Peanut Butter Cups. This is an easy pie to make, with kids' flavors that adults never outgrow.

Peanut butter, that staple of every American pantry, is a fairly recent invention, having just celebrated its 100th birthday in 1990. According to author John Egerton (his lively, affectionate *Southern Food* is a must for anyone who loves food), peanuts originated in South America at least 3,500 years ago. Eventually, they were brought to Asia and Africa, and then to North America by African slaves. But until late in the 19th century, peanuts were strictly a local crop. It was George Washington Carver who was responsible for the peanut's domestication—and for peanut butter.

Makes one 9-inch pie; serves about 8

GRAHAM CRACKER CRUST
1   cup graham cracker crumbs (about 15 individual crackers)
¼   cup sugar
¼   cup (½ stick) unsalted butter, cut into pieces, softened

Peanut Butter Pie

. . . When I come home
from school at three,
My mother is waiting there
for me.
I have chores that I must
do.
(I'll bet that you have
some, too.)
First I have a little treat;
She gives me a little bite to
eat.
I chew and I pretend that I
Am eating peanut butter
pie.

Try, try some peanut
butter pie,
If you don't think it's
wonderful,
I want to know why,
It'll stick to your mouth
Till you can't say "Hi!"
Try, try some peanut
butter pie.

TOM PAXTON
"PEANUT BUTTER PIE"
ALCAZAR RECORDS

FILLING

8	ounces cream cheese, softened
1	cup creamy peanut butter (do not use old-fashioned or freshly ground)
1	cup confectioners' sugar
2	tablespoons unsalted butter, softened
1	tablespoon pure vanilla extract
½	cup heavy cream, well chilled

FUDGE TOPPING

½	cup heavy cream
6	ounces semisweet chocolate, chopped

1. **GRAHAM CRACKER CRUST:** Preheat the oven to 350 degrees F, with a rack in the lower third. In a medium bowl, combine the graham cracker crumbs, sugar and butter until well blended. Press evenly into a buttered 9-inch pie pan, reaching up to but not over the rim. Bake until lightly browned, about 10 minutes. Cool the crust completely on a wire rack.

2. **FILLING:** Beat the cream cheese and peanut butter with an electric mixer at medium speed until well blended. Add the confectioners' sugar, butter and vanilla and continue beating until fluffy.

3. Whip the cream until not quite stiff. Fold a large spoonful of the whipped cream into the peanut butter mixture to lighten it; gently fold in the remainder. Carefully spoon the filling into the cooled crust, spreading evenly. Loosely cover the pie and refrigerate until firm, about 3 hours. (You can put it in the freezer, if you'd like to speed it up.)

4. **FUDGE TOPPING:** Bring the cream to a simmer in a small, heavy saucepan. Add the chocolate and stir until smooth. Set aside to cool to lukewarm. Gently spread the topping over the cooled pie. Refrigerate until firm, about 3 hours. *(This pie can be made 1 day ahead; cover it loosely with wax paper or plastic wrap and refrigerate.)*

5. Cut the pie into wedges and serve cold.

IOWA'S FAVORITE CUSTARD PIE

This is an Iowa farm recipe from my mother's own cookbook," says Ron Popp, who grew up in Dow City, Iowa, and now owns The Garden Café in Omaha, Nebraska. "Many of our best restaurant desserts come right from her recipes. Most of what she baked came from her German heritage. Her baking wasn't 'fancy gourmet,' it just wowed everybody with its great flavor."

This basic custard pie cuts into clean slices; the high proportion of eggs and real cream makes it rich and smooth.

Makes one 10-inch or deep 9½-inch pie; serves about 8

Basic Pie Dough for a 1-crust pie (page 449)
1⅔ cups heavy cream
1 cup milk
4 large eggs
¾ cup sugar
¼ teaspoon salt
Sprinkling of fresh-grated nutmeg
1½ teaspoons pure vanilla extract

1. Preheat the oven to 375 degrees F (or 350 degrees, if you are using Pyrex), with a rack in the lower third. Roll out the dough on a lightly floured surface into a large circle about ⅛ inch thick. Fit it, without stretching, into a buttered deep 9½- or 10-inch pie pan. Trim off the excess dough, leaving a ¾-inch overhang. Fold under the edge of the dough, pressing along the rim of the pan and forming a high fluted border. Refrigerate the pie shell.

2. In a heavy saucepan, scald the cream and milk. In a bowl, whisk together the eggs, sugar, salt, nutmeg and vanilla. Quickly add the hot milk mixture and whisk constantly until thoroughly mixed; do not overmix.

3. Place the pie shell on the oven rack and pour in the custard mixture. Bake until the custard is spotted with gold and set, but still slightly wobbly in the center, usually 40 to 45 minutes. (The timing can vary based on the depth of the pie pan; do not overbake.)

4. Cool the pie on a wire rack. Serve lukewarm. (It's also good cold.)

Old-Fashioned Cream

Cream that has not been ultrapasteurized is quickly becoming a thing of the past. Some supermarkets still carry it, as do small local dairies. If you can get your hands on it, or on extra-high-butterfat cream from a local dairy, grab it. Cholesterol be damned, it makes a beautifully silky custard.

In ultrapasteurizing, cream is heated to 280 degrees F for at least 2 seconds, extending its shelf life by at least 4 times—to as long as 2 months. Unfortunately, it takes away the cream's fresh flavor and also makes it harder to whip.

Torta from Gourds

Grind up gourds that have been well cleaned. . . . Then let them boil a little, either in rich juice or in milk. When they are half-cooked and have been passed through a strainer into a bowl, add as much cheese as I said before. Take a half a pound of belly or fat udder boiled and cut up or, instead of this, if you wish, take the same amount of either butter or liquamen, add half a pound of sugar, a little ginger, some cinnamon, six eggs, two ladles of saffron, and blend thoroughly. Put this preparation in a greased pan or in a pastry shell and cook it over a slow fire. There are those who add strips of leaves, which they call lagana, instead of the upper crust. When it is cooked and set on a plate, sprinkle it with sugar and rosewater. It is likewise difficult to digest and of poor nourishment.

PLATINA
DE HONESTA VOLUPTATE
[OF HONEST INDULGENCE
AND GOOD HEALTH]
1475

494

ABOUT PUMPKIN PIE

Like most things American, pumpkin pie has its roots somewhere else. The pie was originally English. Before that, it was probably of earlier Italian origin, brought to England by French chefs. In Platina's recipe for a torta of pumpkin from the Renaissance, the saffron and fat may seem alien, but the family resemblance to our pumpkin pie is almost astounding.

In the Po Valley of northern Italy, where *zucca* (pumpkin) is used to fill tortellini and other pastas, pumpkin puree is used in a *crostata di zucca* (pumpkin pie or tart), the filling flavored with almonds, cornmeal and candied orange rind—reminiscent of Platina's recipe. Known variously as *potiron* or *citrouille*, pumpkin is also used to make rustic desserts in France.

English recipes for pumpkin pie are found in several cookbooks of the 17th and 18th centuries, mostly in books that reflect the dining habits of the well-to-do. But according to food historian C. Anne Wilson, after pumpkin pie was introduced to America by early colonists, it went out of fashion in England during the course of the 18th century.

Like other open-face pies with soft fillings, early-American pumpkin pie was called a pudding. If you served Amelia Simmons's recipe for "pompkin pudding" on page 496 with pumpkin custard poured into a pudding dish lined with puff pastry, no one would suspect that you had used a recipe over 200 years old.

BEST-EVER PUMPKIN PIE

One autumn while cooking at a restaurant on Martha's Vineyard, I became obsessed with pumpkin pie, testing one recipe after another, making yet a few more adjustments each time, in search of the perfect pie. I could "taste" this one in my head— simple and custardy, light but with some body to cut through, the flavor subtly rounded with vanilla and complex spicing, but with the pumpkin, not the spice, predominant.

Makes one deep 9½-inch pie; serves about 8

Basic Pie Dough for a 1-crust pie (page 449)
2   cups pumpkin puree, preferably homemade (page 496; if you use canned pumpkin, be sure it's unsweetened puree, not pie filling)
⅔   cup packed dark or light brown sugar
⅓   cup sugar
1   tablespoon all-purpose flour
½   teaspoon salt
1½   teaspoons ground cinnamon
½   teaspoon fresh-grated nutmeg
½   teaspoon ground ginger
¼   teaspoon ground allspice
    Pinch freshly ground pepper
1   cup heavy cream
⅓   cup milk
2   large eggs, lightly beaten
3   tablespoons bourbon or rum
1½   teaspoons pure vanilla extract
    Whipped cream flavored with pure maple syrup or pure vanilla extract, for serving

1. Roll out the dough on a lightly floured surface to a large circle about ⅛ inch thick. Fit it, without stretching, into a buttered deep 9½-inch pie pan. Trim off the excess dough, leaving a ¾-inch overhang. Fold under the edge of the dough, pressing along the rim of the pan and forming a fairly high fluted border. Chill the dough while you preheat the oven to 400 degrees F, with a rack in the lower third.

2. Line the dough with a lightly buttered sheet of foil, buttered side down. Bake the pie shell for about 8 minutes. Very gently remove the foil; prick the dough all over with a fork. Bake the crust until the surface of the dough is dry, but has not yet

Perfect Pie

Once I got it right, I've baked this pie every year at Thanksgiving. When I first met my friend Mick, as autumn was livening up New York City, he told me that when he was a kid, he always ate pie for breakfast. Ever the cook-provider, I baked him a pumpkin pie and carried it downtown to Bleecker Street in a shopping bag.

Every year after that, I would bake this pie for our Thanksgiving dinner, even if—especially if—it was just two for the holiday feast. Now that it's just me, this pie will always remind me of feeding him.

495

baked all the way through, about 5 minutes longer. Set the pie shell aside until needed; leave the oven on.

3. Meanwhile, whisk together the pumpkin puree, brown and white sugars, flour, salt, spices, pepper, cream, milk, eggs, spirits and vanilla in a large bowl. Taste and correct the seasonings. Pour the mixture into the pie shell.

4. Bake until the filling is set but still slightly wobbly in the center, usually about 45 minutes.

5. Cool the pie on a wire rack. Serve with the flavored whipped cream.

⌒ *Variations*

If you like, substitute about 3 tablespoons pure maple syrup for an equal amount of the white sugar. A tablespoonful of minced crystallized ginger (in addition to the other spices) gives the flavor a nice edge, too, but don't let it take over.

EASY FRESH PUMPKIN PUREE

*M*any people think that making fresh pumpkin puree is a huge pain in the neck. But it doesn't have to be. If you bake the pumpkin in halves, you eliminate all the peeling and strenuous scraping. And the flesh comes out firmer, with a fuller flavor than when boiled or steamed. Bake 2 or 3 pumpkins once in the fall, and freeze the puree in pint containers (each is enough for 1 pie), so you'll have it on hand when you need it. Sugar pumpkins, found at many farmers' markets, are the sweetest and best.

Here's how:
1. Preheat the oven to 375 degrees F. Halve the pumpkins crosswise and place them, cut sides down, on a foil-lined baking sheet. Cover the entire sheet with foil, tenting it over the pumpkins and crimping the edges.

2. Bake until the flesh is very tender, usually about 1½ hours.

Pumpkin Pudding

. . . One quart stewed and strained [pumpkin], 3 pints cream, 9 beaten eggs, sugar, mace, nutmeg and ginger, laid into paste . . . and with a dough spur [a jagged-edged wheel, used to cut pastry], cross and chequer it, and bake in dishes three quarters of an hour.

No. 2. One quart of milk, one pint pumpkin, 4 eggs, molasses, allspice and ginger in a crust, bake 1 hour.

AMELIA SIMMONS
AMERICAN COOKERY
HARTFORD, 1796

3. Remove the foil and let the pumpkin halves cool. Remove the seeds, scrape the flesh into a food processor and puree (or strain) until smooth. Pack the puree into 1-pint containers; label and date. Refrigerate or freeze the puree until using. Frozen pumpkin puree keeps well for about 6 months.

SOUR CREAM PUMPKIN CHIFFON PIE

Here's a luscious unbaked pumpkin pie, with layers of light pumpkin chiffon alternating with whipped cream. This recipe is from Normand le Claire, chef-owner of the Red Rooster Tavern in North Kingstown, Rhode Island.

Makes one 9- or 9½-inch pie; serves about 8

    Basic Pie Dough for a 1-crust pie (page 449)
½   cup chopped pecans
¼   cup cold water
1   envelope (about 2½ teaspoons) unflavored gelatin
3   large eggs, separated (for a note on egg safety, see page 23)
⅓   cup plus ¼ cup sugar
1¼ cups fresh (preceding page) or canned unsweetened pumpkin puree
½   cup sour cream or plain yogurt
½   teaspoon salt
½   teaspoon ground cinnamon
¼   teaspoon *each* ground ginger, ground cloves and fresh-grated nutmeg
    Pinch freshly ground pepper (optional)
2   cups heavy cream, well chilled
1   cup sifted confectioners' sugar
2   teaspoons pure vanilla extract

1. Roll out the dough on a lightly floured surface to a large circle about ⅛ inch thick. Fit it, without stretching, into a buttered 9- or 9½-inch pie pan. Trim off the excess dough, leaving a ¾-inch overhang. Fold under the edge of the dough, pressing along the rim of the pan and forming a high fluted border. Chill briefly while you preheat the oven to 375 degrees F, with a rack

in the lower third. Lightly toast the pecans until fragrant, about 5 to 7 minutes; set aside.

2. Prick the dough lightly with a fork and line it with a lightly buttered sheet of foil, buttered side down. Weigh down the foil with dried beans, rice or pie weights; set the shell on a heavy baking sheet. Bake until the sides are set, 10 to 15 minutes. Carefully remove the weights and foil. Continue to bake, pricking any air bubbles with a fork, until the shell is lightly golden and baked through, 10 to 15 minutes longer. Cool the pie shell on a wire rack.

3. Place the cold water in a small bowl and sprinkle the gelatin over it; set aside. In the top of a double boiler over simmering water, beat the egg yolks and ⅓ cup of the sugar with a whisk or an electric mixer until warm to the touch and very light and fluffy, about 5 minutes. Add the gelatin mixture and whisk constantly until it dissolves, about 1 minute longer. Remove from the heat, and transfer the egg mixture to a large metal bowl.

4. Whisk in the pumpkin puree, sour cream or yogurt, salt, cinnamon, ginger, cloves, nutmeg and optional pepper. Cover and chill the mixture, stirring frequently, until it begins to thicken, but is not set, about 30 minutes. (If you'd like to hasten the process, place the bowl in a larger bowl of ice water and stir constantly until the mixture begins to thicken but not set, about 6 minutes.)

5. Beat the egg whites until they form soft peaks. Gradually add the remaining ¼ cup sugar and beat constantly until the whites are stiff and shiny. Gently fold the meringue into the pumpkin mixture; set aside at room temperature.

6. Whip the cream until slightly stiff (do not overbeat). Gently whisk in the confectioners' sugar and vanilla, and whisk just until nearly stiff. Pour ½ of the pumpkin mixture into the cooled pie shell. Top with ½ of the whipped cream mixture, spreading gently with a spatula. Top with the remaining pumpkin mixture, and then with the remaining whipped cream, mounding it in the center. (If you prefer, you can save some of the whipped cream and pipe it around the edges, using a pastry bag with a star tip.) Loosely cover and chill the pie for at least 2 hours.

7. Just before serving, sprinkle the edges with the toasted pecans.

SWEET POTATO PIE

This is the basic Southern-style sweet potato pie—smooth, subtle and with plenty of sweet potato flavor. It has been freely adapted from a recipe in *Cookery of the Old South*, a handwritten book "translated from Southern lore" by Kay Burdette in 1938.

In the original recipe, the egg whites were beaten and then folded into the filling. I've simplified the recipe, using whole eggs for a smoother, more custardy texture.

Makes one 9- or 9½-inch pie; serves about 8

	Basic Pie Dough for a 1-crust pie (page 449)
2	cups cooked sieved sweet potatoes (usually 3-4 medium-size, about 1¼ pounds; see note)
4	large eggs
1	cup packed dark or light brown sugar
	Juice of 1 orange
	Juice of ½ lemon
1	cup heavy cream, or a mixture of cream and milk
¼	cup (½ stick) unsalted butter, melted
½	teaspoon ground cinnamon
½	teaspoon ground allspice
¼	teaspoon fresh-grated nutmeg
	Whipped cream, flavored with sherry and chopped pecans, if you like, for serving

1. Roll out the dough on a lightly floured surface to a large circle about ⅛ inch thick. Fit it, without stretching, into a buttered 9- or 9½-inch pie pan. Trim off the excess dough, leaving a ¾-inch overhang. Fold under the edge of the dough, pressing along the rim of the pan and forming a high fluted border. Line the pie shell with a sheet of buttered foil, buttered side down, and chill while you pre-heat the oven to 400 degrees F, with a rack in the lower third.

2. Bake the pie shell until the sides are set, about 8 minutes. Gently remove the foil. Continue to bake, pricking any air bubbles with a fork, until the crust is just beginning to color but has not yet baked all the way through, 8 to 10 minutes longer. Set the pie shell aside; leave the oven on.

3. With an electric mixer at medium speed or with a whisk, combine the sweet potatoes, eggs, brown sugar, citrus juices, cream, butter and spices until very smooth. Pour the mixture into the warm, partially baked shell.

499

4. Bake the pie for 15 minutes. Lower the heat to 350 degrees, and continue to bake until the pie is set but the center is still slightly wobbly, 20 to 30 minutes longer. (The timing can vary based on the depth of the pie pan; do not overbake.)

5. Cool the pie on a wire rack. Serve at room temperature, with the flavored whipped cream.

NOTE: Baking sweet potatoes in their jackets, as you would a baked potato, results in dense, flavorful flesh. Scrub the skins, pat dry, prick in a few places with a fork, and bake the sweet potatoes in a pie pan or shallow pan in a preheated 400-degree oven for about 1 hour, or until the flesh is very tender. Cool, halve lengthwise and scrape the flesh from the skins. Mash and press through a sieve or puree in a food processor.

DRIED PEACH PIE WITH CUSTARD AND MERINGUE

Just a small amount of dried peaches perfumes this whole pie, which is composed of a layer of dried peaches, then custard and then meringue. This recipe is from Holmes Café, a "meat-and-three-veg café" in Alabama, famed for its pies.

Makes one 9- or 10-inch pie; serves about 8

Basic Pie Dough for a 1-crust pie (page 449)

PEACH FILLING
½   cup (about 3 ounces) dried peaches (use dried fruit that is moist)
½   cup cold water

CUSTARD
⅓   cup sugar
3   tablespoons unsalted butter
2   tablespoons all-purpose flour
1   cup milk
3   large egg yolks
1   teaspoon pure vanilla extract
    Pinch salt

MERINGUE

- 3 large egg whites
- ¼ cup plus 2 tablespoons sugar
- 1 teaspoon pure vanilla extract

1. Roll out the dough on a lightly floured surface to a large circle about ⅛ inch thick. Fit it, without stretching, into a buttered 9- or 10-inch pie pan. Trim off the excess dough, leaving a ¾-inch overhang. Fold under the edge of the dough, pressing along the rim of the pan and forming a high fluted border. Chill the pie shell until needed.

2. **PEACH FILLING:** Place the peaches and the water in a small saucepan, cover and simmer until the peaches are tender, about 10 minutes. Mash the peaches with a potato masher or in a food processor until pureed. Set aside to cool while you preheat the oven to 350 degrees F, with a rack in the lower third.

3. **CUSTARD:** In a large bowl, mix the sugar, butter and flour with an electric mixer. Add the milk, egg yolks, vanilla and salt and mix until blended. Spread the peach filling over the bottom of the pie shell. Pour the custard over the peaches. Bake until the custard is just set and pale golden, about 40 minutes.

4. **MERINGUE:** Toward the end of the baking time, use an electric mixer to whisk the egg whites until foamy. Gradually add the sugar and then the vanilla, and continue beating until the meringue forms stiff, but not dry, peaks. When the custard is done, spread the meringue over it, swirling attractively and making sure it touches the edges of the pie shell all around.

5. Continue baking until the meringue is browned lightly, 10 to 15 minutes.

6. Cool the pie on a wire rack. Serve lukewarm, at room temperature or slightly chilled.

⌒ *Variation*

QUINCE MERINGUE PIE: Substitute 1 to 1½ cups Honey-Stewed Quinces (page 75) for the dried peaches, omitting the cooking in step 2. Proceed as directed.

ABOUT LEMONS AND LEMON PIE

*L*emon pie is one of the cornerstones of home baking. Lemon and orange pies (and puddings, which they were called early on) are among the most frequently found baked goods in old cookbooks, whether Italian, French, English or American.

Citrus fruits have long been an expensive luxury. Native to northern India, lemons were not used in the Mediterranean until after the time of Christ. In European recipes, lemons were frequently put up as marmalade and other sugared preserves, as well as being used for a host of medicinal purposes, for everything from "curing" freckles and pimples to soothing colds and tonsillitis. The ancient Romans considered lemons an antidote for all poisons.

An early example of a lemon tart appeared in 1653, in La Varenne's *Le Vray Cuisinier François*. Made with "green Lemmons" and "some candy'd Lemmon-peel grated," the tart is served sprinkled with sugar and pomegranate kernels.

Except for its lack of meringue, Eliza Leslie's 1828 American recipe for Lemon Pudding is identical to the lemon meringue pie we know today. But while we think of lemon meringue pie as a perennial favorite, lemon pies didn't appear in American cookbooks with any frequency until about the 1840s.

One of the most interesting American versions is the Shaker lemon pie, made by slicing lemons very thin—rind and all—layering them with sugar in a deep bowl and letting the mixture stand overnight. The sugar helps pull the juices from the lemons and softens and almost lightly candies the rinds. Then the whole thing is piled between two crusts and baked—nothing wasted, in true Shaker spirit. It's very tart and very tasty. A similar Shaker lemon pudding is topped with meringue.

But the classic, of course, is lemon meringue pie. The conventional filling is made with water, cornstarch, sugar and lemon juice and zest. The filling in Grandmother's Souffléed Lemon Pie (recipe follows), on the other hand, is thickened with just egg yolks and no starch. The result is essence-of-lemon flavor, tart and true, in a fluffy golden custard.

To Make Two Lemon Pies

The juice of 2 lemons & the rind grated 2 soda biscuits broke up in a dish with ¼ pound butter & a tea cup of fine sugar, & 1 pint of *boiling water* poured over all. Cover, and let stand to cool. Beat up 5 eggs keeping out 3 whites & add them in when the custard is cold, with the grated rind of 2 lemons. Wash the butter *well*, in two waters. Make the pastry.

MRS. MATILDA ROGERS
RECIPE BOOK
MANUSCRIPT
NEW YORK, 1850

GRANDMOTHER'S SOUFFLÉED LEMON PIE

I think this recipe beats the cornstarch version all to pieces," says Sue Crouse, my good friend in Warren, Ohio, whose grandmother's recipe this is. "My grandmother always said this pie was her mother's original." It takes its place with the best lemon pies ever.

Sue Crouse's last word: "Truthfully, I am not too crazy about meringue topping and think the pie is excellent without it." (She's right.) See the note on the next page if you want to try it.

∽ *Makes one 9-inch pie; serves about 8*

Basic Pie Dough for a 1-crust pie (page 449)
6   large egg yolks
¾   cup sugar
     Grated zest and juice of 1 large lemon
3   large egg whites

1. Roll out the dough on a lightly floured surface to a large circle about ⅛ inch thick. Fit it, without stretching, into a buttered 9-inch pie pan. Trim off the excess dough, leaving a ¾-inch overhang. Fold under the edge of the dough, pressing along the rim of the pan and forming a neat fluted border. Chill while you preheat the oven to 350 degrees F, with a rack in the lower third.

2. Prick the dough lightly with a fork. Bake the pie shell, pricking any air bubbles that rise, until it is lightly golden and just baked through, usually about 15 minutes. Cool on a wire rack; leave the oven on.

3. Meanwhile, in the top of a double boiler over simmering water, whisk the egg yolks until foamy. Whisk in the sugar in a slow stream; whisk in the lemon zest and juice. Cook, whisking constantly, until the filling thickens, usually about 10 minutes. Remove from the heat and set aside.

4. With an electric mixer, beat the 3 egg whites until nearly stiff but not dry. Gently fold them into the lemon filling, just until blended. Gently pour the filling into the pie shell.

5. Bake until the filling is puffed, set and pale golden, about 15 minutes. Cool on a wire rack. Serve, preferably while still lukewarm.

503

Note on Meringue Topping: If you'd like to top this pie with meringue, here are Sue's instructions: "Beat the 3 leftover egg whites until they form soft peaks, then slowly add ½ cup sugar, beating until very stiff." Increase the oven heat to 400 degrees, and spread the meringue over the baked filling, making sure the filling is completely covered all the way to the edges. Bake just until lightly browned; watch carefully, as the meringue can burn easily.

Sour Cream Raisin Pie

Both sour cream and buttermilk raisin pies are old Midwestern favorites. Sour cream pies were also popular in California (before the days of "California cuisine"), sometimes made with locally grown chopped dates. There are also Southern incarnations: "Belle of New Orleans Pie" (also known as "Famous Amber Pie") is made with sour cream, raisins, vinegar and pecans, spiced and topped with whipped cream.

Two-crust raisin pies, such as the Pennsylvania Dutch version called *rosina*, are sometimes known as "funeral pies," brought to console the grieving.

This cool chiffon-style pie is refreshing in warm weather.

Makes one 9-inch pie; serves about 8

	Rich Tart Dough (page 451), or Basic Pie Dough for a 1-crust pie (page 449)
½	cup fresh orange juice
1	envelope (about 2½ teaspoons) unflavored gelatin
½-⅔	cup raisins
2	large eggs
½	cup sugar
2	cups (1 pint) sour cream
½	teaspoon pure vanilla extract
⅓	cup heavy cream, well chilled
	Long strands of orange zest, for garnish (use a zester or vegetable peeler)

1. Roll out the dough on a lightly floured surface to a large circle about ⅛ inch thick. Fit it, without stretching, into a buttered 9-inch pie pan. Trim off the excess dough, leaving a ¾-inch overhang. Fold under the edge of the dough, pressing along the rim of the pan and forming a high fluted border. Chill while you preheat the oven to 400 degrees F, with a rack in the lower third.

W hat you and I need to do is bake a raisin cream pie," twangs the rangy woman who owns a Reno boarding house for divorcing wives in the film *Desert Hearts.*

Written and Directed by
Donna Deitch
1985

2. Prick the dough lightly with a fork and line it with a sheet of buttered foil, buttered side down. Weigh down the foil with dried beans, rice or pie weights; place the pie pan on a heavy baking sheet. Bake until the sides are set, usually 6 to 8 minutes. Remove the weights and foil. Continue to bake, pricking any air bubbles with a fork, until the dough is baked through and lightly golden, 8 to 12 minutes longer. Remove the pie shell from the oven and cool thoroughly on a wire rack.

3. Place the orange juice in a small nonreactive saucepan and sprinkle on the gelatin; set aside. Place the raisins in a small bowl and add warm water to cover; set aside.

4. In the top of a double boiler or heatproof bowl over simmering water, whisk the eggs and sugar until combined. Continue whisking until the mixture is warm to the touch, light, fluffy and tripled in volume, about 10 minutes.

5. Meanwhile, place the gelatin mixture over low heat until dissolved and smooth. Remove the beaten egg mixture from the double boiler, add the gelatin mixture, and whisk or beat with an electric mixer until cooled to room temperature, about 5 minutes.

6. Place the sour cream in a bowl and stir once or twice to smooth it out. Gently fold the egg mixture and the vanilla into the sour cream. Whip the heavy cream until nearly stiff; fold it gently and quickly into the sour cream mixture, until not quite combined. Place the bowl in the refrigerator, giving it a quick fold once or twice, until the mixture begins to thicken slightly, about 30 minutes.

7. Drain the raisins thoroughly; fold into the sour cream mixture until blended. Pour the mixture into the cooled pie shell. Loosely cover and chill until set, at least 2 hours.

8. Garnish the pie with strands of orange zest before serving.

Pie Share

She reached across the table and took my fork from my hand and cut a bite off my slice of raisin pie and popped it into her mouth. "Sorry. I love Nick's raisin pie. Let me get you another fork." She laughed. "I can't help myself."

"No, that's okay, we can share . . ."

RUSSELL BANKS
AFFLICTION
1989

SPLIT-LEVEL
LIME CHIFFON PIE

Originally made with the tart juice of Florida Key limes, key lime pie became popularized in a recipe that uses sweetened condensed milk, egg yolks and regular lime juice. Dense and creamy, it was (and is) usually served in a graham cracker crust.

This is a rethinking of that pie. It's made with lime juice and plain yogurt and is very light and low in fat, bursting with lime tartness. It separates into neat layers as it chills.

Makes one 9-inch pie; serves about 8

GINGERSNAP CRUMB CRUST
1½ cups fine gingersnap crumbs (about 18 two-inch cookies)
3 tablespoons sugar
⅓ cup(5⅓ tablespoons) unsalted butter, melted

FILLING
1½ envelopes (3¾ teaspoons) unflavored gelatin
1 cup cold milk
3 large eggs, separated (for a note on egg safety, see page 23)
¾ cup plus 2 tablespoons sugar
1 cup fresh lime juice (usually 4-6 limes)
1 cup low-fat plain yogurt

Thin lime slices, halved, for garnish

1. **GINGERSNAP CRUMB CRUST:** Preheat the oven to 350 degrees F, with a rack in the center. In a bowl, combine the gingersnap crumbs, sugar and butter; toss to moisten the crumbs. Press evenly into the bottom and sides of a buttered 9-inch pie pan, reaching up to but not over the rim. Bake until the crumbs are set and slightly darker brown, about 9 minutes. Cool the crust completely on a wire rack.

2. **FILLING:** Sprinkle the gelatin over the milk in a nonreactive saucepan, whisk until combined and set aside for 5 minutes. Pour 2 to 3 tablespoons of the milk mixture into a bowl, and bring the remaining milk in the saucepan nearly to a boil. Add the egg yolks and the sugar to the bowl; whisk to combine. Whisk in the hot milk, a little at a time. Return the mixture to the pan.

3. Cook the custard over low heat, stirring almost constantly, until it thickens enough to coat the back of a spoon, about 7 minutes. Do not allow to boil. Immediately strain the custard into a clean bowl, and whisk in the lime juice and yogurt.

4. Beat the egg whites until not quite stiff. Thoroughly but gently fold the whites into the still warm custard mixture. Pour into the cooled pie crust. Loosely cover and chill until set, about 2 hours.

5. Garnish with the halved lime slices and serve cool.

NOTE: If you'd rather have a smooth custard instead of one that separates into layers, refrigerate the mixture at the end of step 3, stirring now and then, until it begins to thicken. Then proceed to fold in the beaten egg whites as directed.

MARY'S RICE PIE

This is one of the best recipes in this book. When I brought a few pieces of this wonderfully creamy pie to the kitchen where I used to cook as a volunteer, it was devoured instantly, and I had half a dozen requests—which became demands—for the recipe. Baked in a rectangular pan, it is sturdy and travels well. The recipe is from Mary Codola of Rhode Island, who has been baking it for her family at Easter for many years.

This recipe can be halved and baked in an 8-inch square pan.

⌒ *Makes one 13-x-9-inch pie; serves about 12*

1½	cups long-grain white rice
	Pastry Dough (page 510), Carlo's Cookie Dough (page 272) or Basic Pie Dough for a 2-crust pie (page 449)
5	cups milk
1	teaspoon salt
6	large eggs
1	pound (about 2 cups) ricotta cheese, drained in a cheesecloth-lined sieve or colander for a few hours or overnight
1½	cups sugar, or less to taste
2	cups heavy cream
2	teaspoons pure vanilla extract
1	teaspoon ground cinnamon, for sprinkling

1. Bring a large pot of salted water to a boil. Meanwhile, place the rice in a large sieve and rinse under cold water; drain. Gently boil the rice for 15 minutes; drain well.

2. Meanwhile, preheat the oven to 350 degrees F, with a rack in the center. Butter a 13-x-9-inch baking dish. Roll out the dough on a lightly floured surface to a large rectangle about ⅛ inch thick. Gently fit the dough into the baking dish, without stretching; cut the edges even with the top of the dish. Carefully line the dough with a sheet of buttered foil, buttered side down. Bake until the sides are set, usually about 8 minutes. Carefully remove the foil. Continue baking, pricking any air bubbles with a fork, until the dough begins to turn very pale gold, usually another 6 to 8 minutes. Cool on a wire rack; leave the oven on.

3. Combine the drained rice with 4 cups of the milk and the salt; simmer until tender, usually about 20 minutes.

4. In a bowl, beat the eggs with the remaining 1 cup milk. Add the ricotta, sugar, cream and vanilla. Stir in the rice and milk mixture and mix well. Pour into the pie shell and sprinkle the cinnamon on top.

5. Bake until the filling is firm and set, about 50 minutes.

6. Cool the pie on a wire rack to room temperature. Serve at cool room temperature. To store, cover and refrigerate but let come to room temperature for about 20 minutes before serving.

Easter Pie

Every Easter, my mother would get started early," says Mary Codola, my adopted Italian mother, as we sit (eating, of course) in her Rhode Island kitchen.

"I make this only once a year, at Easter," Mary says. "I'd like to make it more, but these days with cholesterol problems, I don't. The recipe comes from my older sister, Phyllis. Sometimes I also make *pasticciot'*, a yellow cream pie. And little tarts with yellow cream with pineapple and a lattice crust."

In Rhode Island, southern Italian cooking still survives, usually learned from the mother-in-law.

509

NEAPOLITAN EASTER PIE
(*PASTIERA NAPOLETANA*)

Also called *pizza grana* and "grain pie" by Italian-Americans, *pastiera* starts with cooked wheat berries embedded in a ricotta custard, perfumed with candied fruit and orange flower water. That custard is then enclosed in a crust of *pasta frolla*, a sweet Italian pastry dough made with eggs.

This recipe, adapted from one Nick Malgieri brought back from Naples, appears in slightly different form in his *Great Italian Desserts* (Little, Brown, 1990). I've tried many versions of this traditional pie, but this is the best—the components come together perfectly.

The recipe looks complicated, but the steps aren't difficult. In New York's Little Italy, containers of hulled wheat kernels labeled "Easter grain" are sold every spring. (The grain is available canned, already cooked, in Italian neighborhoods.) Wheat berries are also sold in Middle Eastern grocery stores and in stores that sell whole grains. Be sure to buy hulled wheat berries.

Makes two 9-inch pies; each serves about 8

WHEAT

4	ounces hulled wheat berries (kernels, about ⅔ cup)
¼	teaspoon salt
2	tablespoons butter

PASTRY DOUGH

3	cups all-purpose flour
¾	cup sugar
1	teaspoon baking powder
	Pinch salt
½	cup (1 stick) cold unsalted butter, cut into pieces
3	large eggs, well beaten

RICOTTA FILLING

1½	pounds (3 cups) ricotta cheese
1½	cups sugar
7	large eggs
1½	teaspoons orange flower water (for a mail-order source, see page 148)
1	cup mixed candied fruit, rinsed and finely chopped
1	large egg, beaten, for egg wash

Pastiera is traditional in Naples and also can be found in other parts of Southern Italy, as well as in Sicily. The wheat is a sign of spring's rebirth. In Sicily, a similar wheat-berry-and-ricotta pudding called *cuccia di Santa Lucia* is served on St. Lucy's Day in December, the shortest day of the year.

1. **WHEAT:** Soak the wheat berries in cold water to cover, preferably overnight, or for at least 6 hours. Drain and rinse the wheat. Place in a saucepan with the salt, butter and enough water to cover by several inches; bring to a boil. Partially cover and simmer until tender, 1½ to 2 hours. As the wheat simmers, stir occasionally to prevent sticking and add water, if needed, to keep the wheat covered. Drain, rinse if the wheat is sticky, and allow to cool. Cover and refrigerate until needed.

2. **PASTRY DOUGH:** Mix the flour, sugar, baking powder and salt in a bowl. Rub in the butter by hand, until finely crumbled. Add the beaten eggs and stir until well combined. Gather the dough together, kneading gently, until it pulls together into a mass; divide the dough into 3 equal pieces. Wrap separately in plastic and chill until firm.

3. **RICOTTA FILLING:** Beat the ricotta in a bowl to soften it slightly; beat in the sugar. Add the eggs, orange flower water and candied fruit and mix until blended. Stir in the cold cooked wheat.

4. Preheat the oven to 350 degrees F, with a rack in the lower third. Roll out each of 2 pieces of the dough into a large circle about ⅛ inch thick. Fit each, without stretching, into the bottom and up the sides of a buttered 9-inch pie pan, a 9-inch straight-sided cake pan, or a springform pan. (I like this best in the springform pan.) Trim the edge of the dough just below the rim of the pans.

5. Roll out the remaining piece of dough into a large rectangle about ⅛ inch thick. Cut this dough into 20 half-inch-wide strips. Brush the pastry strips and the top edge of each pastry shell with the egg wash. Pour ½ of the ricotta filling into each pie shell. Gently arrange the strips of dough over the filling, crisscrossing them in a diagonal lattice with 5 in each direction over each pie. Trim off the excess dough and gently press the end of each strip into the sides of the bottom crust.

6. Bake until the pastry is lightly browned and the center of the filling is set but still slightly wobbly, about 45 minutes.

7. Cool on a wire rack; remove the sides of the springform pan, if using. Serve at room temperature.

HOOVER TOFFEE ICE CREAM PIE

O wner David Cohen of the Old Mexico Grill in Santa Fe, New Mexico, says that this outstanding ice cream pie with its Oreo cookie crust is the restaurant's best-selling dessert. It's made in a springform pan, filled all the way to the top. At the Old Mexico Grill, the filling is made with chocolate ice cream; I like layers of coffee and vanilla.

The ice cream filling is generously studded with crunchy toffee, homemade by caramelizing sugar with butter (a *lot* of butter) and then glazing the toffee with dark chocolate. Be warned: The crumbled toffee kept disappearing from the kitchen before I could get the pie assembled.

This pie is big, bold and dramatic.

Makes 1 deep 10-inch pie; serves 12 or more

5	cups (about 15 ounces) sliced blanched almonds

COOKIE CRUST

½	pound (about 21) Oreo or Hydrox cookies
1	cup all-purpose flour
½	cup (1 stick) unsalted butter, melted

BUTTER TOFFEE

1	cup (2 sticks) plus 5 tablespoons unsalted butter
1½	cups sugar
⅓	cup cold water
1	tablespoon fresh lemon juice
¼	teaspoon salt
½	teaspoon pure vanilla extract
½	teaspoon almond extract
6	ounces semisweet chocolate, melted

2	quarts premium-quality chocolate ice cream (or 1 quart *each* coffee and vanilla, or your own choice)

1. Preheat the oven to 350 degrees F, with a rack in the center. Scatter the sliced almonds in a jellyroll pan and toast until pale golden, about 10 minutes. Set aside; leave the oven on.

2. **COOKIE CRUST:** Butter the bottom of a 10-inch springform pan (leave the sides unbuttered); set aside. In a food processor, grind the cookies until they form coarse crumbs. Transfer to a

bowl and stir in the flour; stir in the melted butter and toss to moisten evenly. Press the mixture onto the bottom of the prepared pan. Bake until the crumb mixture is set, usually 12 to 15 minutes. Transfer the pan to a wire rack and let cool to room temperature. Place the pan in the freezer for 30 minutes or longer.

3. **Butter Toffee:** In a large, heavy saucepan, combine the butter, sugar, water, lemon juice and salt. Bring to a boil, stirring to dissolve the sugar. Once the mixture comes to a boil, cook, uncovered and without stirring, over medium heat until it caramelizes, about 8 minutes.

4. Meanwhile, butter a 13-x-9-inch baking pan or a jellyroll pan and set aside. When the caramel is ready, remove it from the heat and stir in the vanilla and almond extracts and about 3 cups of the toasted almonds. Pour the toffee mixture into the buttered pan and set aside to cool.

5. With a spatula, spread the melted chocolate over the cooled toffee. Immediately sprinkle the chocolate with about 1 cup of the remaining toasted almonds. Freeze for 1 hour, or until firm.

6. Turn the toffee out onto a work surface and break it into chunks or pieces about ½ inch in size; set aside. *(The toffee can be made in advance and stored in a plastic bag or an airtight container.)*

7. Let the ice cream soften very slightly. In a large bowl with an electric mixer or with a large wooden spoon, stir the ice cream briefly, just until malleable. Fold in the chunks of toffee. (If using vanilla and coffee ice cream, do the coffee first, folding in about ½ of the toffee.) With a large rubber spatula, spread the ice cream over the crust. Place in the freezer. If you are using vanilla ice cream, soften it, fold in the remaining toffee, and spread it over the layer of coffee. Smooth the top and sprinkle with the remaining 1 cup toasted almonds.

8. Place the pan in the freezer. When the mixture has firmed up slightly, cover the surface with plastic wrap and freeze until the pie is firm, usually about 6 hours.

9. Place the pie in the refrigerator to let it soften slightly for about 20 minutes before serving. Run the tip of a knife around the sides of the pie; carefully remove the sides. Cut the pie into wedges with a knife dipped into hot water and serve.

RECIPES

John Thorne's Best-Ever
Pecan Pie
Maine Maple Sugar Pie
New England Boiled Cider
Pie
French Canadian Maple
Sugar Pie
Orleans Sweet Potato–Pecan
Pie
Dried-Fruit Mincemeat Pie
with Lattice Cream Cheese
Crust
Green Tomato and Apple
Mincemeat Pie

CHAPTER 15

NUT, SUGAR AND MINCEMEAT PIES

*T*raditionally, before all foods were available in all seasons, home bakers had to rely on the pantry when winter arrived, cobbling together pies from the nuts and dried fruits that were always on hand. In many of these pies, a leading role was played by sugar in its various forms: molasses, maple syrup, sorghum or corn syrup.

Though these "pantry pies" are still made in many places, they have earned a special place of distinction in the American South. Southerners, who love pie—especially pecan pie—above all other desserts, "secretly consider dessert the real main course," quips *Washington Post* food writer Phyllis Richman. Some truck stops down South still serve home-baked pies for breakfast.

Pecan pie, sweet potato pie, chess pie (a traditional mixture of eggs, butter and sugar or brown sugar)—all are Southern favorites. Not as well known is Old Dominion Pie, a Virginia pie with pineapple, apricots, walnuts and meringue topping. Derby Pie, the trademark dessert of Kentucky, is similar to chess pie but studded with nuts and chocolate chips.

While pecan pie is the prime pie in the South, it is not the old Southern dessert most of us think it is. Look through key sources, and it is conspicuously absent—until the 1920s or so, that is. Food writer John Thorne, whose wonderful pecan pie recipe is included in this chapter, hypothesizes that pecan pie dates from the development of commercial corn syrup. "By the 1940s, a generation later," he says, "it had become a grand old Southern dessert."

But pantry pies are not limited to the South. In New England and in Quebec, boiled cider (apple cider reduced to an essence) and maple syrup (also boiled down until concentrated) are used to make pies.

Mincemeat, another "keeping" ingredient, originated in England long before refrigeration was available in the home. Originally, the mincemeat process was used to preserve freshly butchered meat through the winter. Like confit, mincemeat was put in crocks or jars, in which it would keep for months without danger of spoilage. Once on hand, the mincemeat could be turned into a batch of pies that would hold up for some time. Made from stewing beef, beef tongue or venison, mincemeat pie had its roots in necessity. Over time though, it became synonymous with celebration. My meatless rendition, made from a combination of fresh and dried fruits (page 524), retains the traditional flavors, while lightening the dessert considerably.

JOHN THORNE'S BEST-EVER PECAN PIE

This pie has a firm yet yielding texture, a rich pecan presence and real depth of flavor, not just sweetness. In fact, one taster called it "the only pecan pie I ever had that wasn't too sweet."

The secret of this pie is Lyle's Golden Syrup, which John Thorne, in his *Simple Cooking* newsletter, says offers "the taste of sugar without its mouth-deadening sweetness; the rich, thick syrupy texture of molasses without its coarse pungency."

Lyle's Golden Syrup is made from sugar cane, not corn syrup. It's a British staple, used in Bakewell tarts, treacle tarts and other traditional baked goods. (See note for mail-order information.) This pie also uses muscovado sugar, a less refined brown sugar. You can substitute light corn syrup for the Golden Syrup and use light brown sugar for the muscovado with complete success.

When buying all nuts, but particularly pecans, whose high fat content speeds rancidity, seek out a source with a high turnover, to ensure perfect freshness.

Makes one 9-inch pie; serves about 8

An Old Friend

I was happy to find my old friend, mince pie, in the retinue of the feast; and finding him to be perfectly orthodox, and that I need not be ashamed of my predilection, I greeted him with all the warmth wherewith we usually greet an old and very genteel acquaintance.

WASHINGTON IRVING
OLD CHRISTMAS
CA. 1820

Basic Pie Dough for a 1-crust pie (page 449)
1   cup packed natural raw cane dark muscovado sugar, turbinado or light brown sugar
⅔   scant cup Lyle's Golden Syrup or light corn syrup
2   tablespoons full-flavored dark rum, such as Haitian rum
¼   cup (½ stick) unsalted butter, softened
3   large eggs
1   teaspoon pure vanilla extract (not in Thorne's original, but I like it)
¼   teaspoon salt
2   cups (about ½ pound) broken pecan meats
     Slightly sweetened whipped cream or vanilla ice cream, for serving

1. Roll out the dough on a lightly floured surface to a large circle about ⅛ inch thick. Fit it, without stretching, into a buttered 9-inch pie pan. Trim off the excess dough, leaving a ¾-inch border. Fold under the edge of the dough, pressing along the rim of the pan and forming a high, fluted border. Chill the pie shell until needed.

2. In a large saucepan, combine the sugar, Golden Syrup or corn syrup, rum and butter. Bring to a boil over medium heat. Boil for about 1 minute, stirring constantly and scraping back any foam that clings to the sides of the pan. Remove the pan from the heat; set aside to cool to lukewarm, at least 15 minutes. Meanwhile, preheat the oven to 350 degrees F, with a rack in the lower third.

3. In a small bowl, beat the eggs until creamy. Beat the eggs into the cooled syrup; stir in the vanilla, salt and pecans. Pour the filling into the pie shell.

4. Bake until the filling is set but still slightly wobbly in the center, about 50 minutes. Cool the pie completely on a wire rack.

5. Serve the pie at room temperature with plenty of slightly sweetened whipped cream. (Vanilla ice cream isn't bad, either.)

NOTE: Both Lyle's Golden Syrup and turbinado sugar can be found in many specialty food stores. Both can be ordered from www.amazon.com.

◔ *Variation*

BLACK WALNUT PIE: Substitute shelled black walnut meats for the pecans; proceed as directed.

MAINE MAPLE SUGAR PIE

In 1890, the maple trees in the state of Vermont alone produced 1,445,000 gallons of maple syrup. By 1941, that figure had dwindled to 775,000. And in 1991, Vermont's maple syrup production was down to only 440,000 gallons—a fraction of what it had been a century earlier.

Why? According to Henry Marckres of the Vermont Department of Agriculture, it's because fewer people are "sugaring off" and also because there are now far fewer maple trees, since land has been cleared and developed. (A maple tree must be at least 40 years old before it can be tapped for syrup.) Much of what's sold as "pancake syrup" has no more than a trace of real maple in it.

Whatever the use, buy only pure maple syrup. Grade A, pale and subtle, is usually preferred, but if you can find it, Grade B—darker, fuller in flavor and less "refined"—carries the maple flavor through nicely in baking.

This is a lovely pie from Karyl Bannister, author-creator of the *Cook & Tell* newsletter, a custardy chess-type pie with true maple flavor, not blaring sweetness.

◔ *Makes one 9-inch pie; serves about 8*

       Basic Pie Dough for a 1-crust pie (page 449)
3   large eggs, lightly beaten
1   cup pure maple syrup
2   tablespoons unsalted butter, melted
½   cup packed brown sugar, preferably dark brown
2   tablespoons all-purpose flour
1   teaspoon pure vanilla extract
       Squeeze of fresh lemon juice
       Pinch salt
½   cup chopped walnuts or pecans
       Whipped cream, for serving

1. Roll out the dough on a lightly floured surface to a large circle about ⅛ inch thick. Fit it, without stretching, into a buttered 9-inch pie pan. Trim off the excess dough, leaving a ¾-inch border.

Jack Wax

"Why," wrote Lois W. Campbell of Tombstone, Arizona, "do good New Englanders in your various letters and stories call what I was brought up on as 'Jack Wax' . . . 'maple syrup on snow'? It seems a shame to have that fun name die out. Jack Wax was no simple syrup on snow, but rather had to be carefully boiled down to just the right stage, then trickled over pans of fresh snow. It was wonderfully chewy."

YANKEE MAGAZINE

Fold under the edge of the dough, pressing along the rim of the pan and forming a high, fluted border. Chill the pie shell while you preheat the oven to 350 degrees F, with a rack in the lower third.

2. With a whisk or electric mixer, beat the eggs, maple syrup, butter, brown sugar, flour, vanilla, lemon juice and salt until smooth. (Strain the mixture if it is lumpy.) Stir in the nuts. Pour the mixture into the pie shell.

3. Bake until the pie is almost set, but still slightly wobbly in the center, about 35 minutes.

4. Cool the pie on a wire rack to room temperature. Serve with whipped cream.

ABOUT BOILED CIDER

Boiled cider, a time-honored New England tradition, is to sweet cider what maple syrup is to sweet sap. When sweet cider is boiled down to a fraction of its original volume, it reaches a syrup that is roughly the same density as maple syrup. Boil it further, and you'll have apple jelly.

Eric Chittenden, owner of Cold Hollow Cider Mill in Waterbury Center, Vermont, explains that boiled cider was developed by early settlers to Vermont. Kept on hand, it was used as a multipurpose sweetener to sweeten and flavor mince pies, to spread, jelly-like, on bread and to provide pectin and sweetness when making jellies with other fruits. (Many of today's so-called no-added-sugar jams, supposedly revolutionary, are sweetened with apple juice concentrate.) Boiled cider was also reconstituted to make fresh apple juice in the wintertime.

To order the fascinating *American Cider Book* (with Yankee recipes), contact www.amazon.com.

How To Make Boyled Sider

Lay your apples a month a sweatinge . . . then take out yr eyes and yr tales, and cutt out yr worme eaten . . . and when it is very fine bottle it out and cool it very well; golden rennets are yr best aples to make this sort of syder.

COLLECTION OF MEDICAL AND COOKERY RECEIPTS HANDWRITTEN FOLIO ENGLAND, 17TH CENTURY

New England Boiled Cider Pie

When I went up to New Hampshire to interview cookbook author Ken Haedrich, I spent two days with Ken, his wife, Karen, and their three kids (now four), breathing clean air, walking along wooded roads and by the creek that runs alongside their house.

It was Ken who first told me about boiled cider, sold in bottles, and he gave me one to take along with me. Fresh apple cider is boiled in modified maple syrup evaporators until it is reduced to about one-tenth of its original volume. It has a very sweet and concentrated apple flavor. In northern New England, boiled cider is used to make a two-crust pie filled with a very sweet, pale-tan custard.

This is a new version of boiled cider pie, with grated apples suspended in a cider custard with a jolt of lemon—apple-on-apple flavor.

⌒ *Makes one 8- or 9-inch pie; serves about 8*

      Basic Pie Dough for a 1-crust pie (page 449)
- ⅔   cup boiled cider or 2 cups apple cider, boiled down to ⅔ cup
- 2   tablespoons sugar, or to taste
- 2   tablespoons plus 1 teaspoon unsalted butter, melted
- 2   tablespoons fresh lemon juice
      Pinch salt
- 3   large eggs, well beaten
- 2   tart apples, such as Granny Smith, peeled, cored and coarsely grated
- 3   tablespoons packed light or dark brown sugar
- ⅛   teaspoon fresh-grated nutmeg
      Vanilla ice cream or whipped cream, for serving (optional)

1. Roll out the dough on a lightly floured surface to a large circle about ⅛ inch thick. Fit it, without stretching, into a buttered 8- or 9-inch pie pan. Trim off the excess dough, leaving a ¾-inch border. Fold under the edge of the dough, pressing along the rim of the pan and forming a high, fluted border. Chill the pie shell while you preheat the oven to 375 degrees F, with a rack in the lower third.

Pungent Pie

When I was a boy and visited my grandparents on a northern Vermont farm, where my grandfather had a good apple orchard . . . my grandmother made a dish the memory of which even today makes my mouth water. It was called dried-apple-boiled-cider pie. In Vermont farmhouses in the early days, apples were peeled, cored and quartered, and then strung on twine string . . . Kept there for long winter weeks with the kitchen fire going, the slices of apple dried and darkened and when used in pies gave a flavor that no fresh apples ever did or could. . . . The principal reason for the superb taste of my grandmother's pie was the boiled cider that she made on the kitchen stove. It was tangy, pungent, rich, tart and wonderful. I suspect that the generous amount of soft maple sugar she used with the apples did not hurt the pie any. Ever since those far-off days, all apple pies I have eaten have tasted insipid.

Vrest Orton
The American Cider Book
1973

519

2. In a bowl, whisk together the boiled cider, sugar, melted butter, lemon juice, salt and eggs. Add the grated apples and stir to blend well. Pour the filling into the pie shell; sprinkle the brown sugar and nutmeg over the top.

3. Bake until the mixture is just set in the center, usually about 50 minutes.

4. Cool the pie on a wire rack. Serve warm, and top the pie with vanilla ice cream or whipped cream, if you like.

NOTE: To order boiled cider by mail, contact King Arthur Flour, 58 Billings Farm Road, White River Junction, Vermont 05001; (800) 827-6836; www.kingarthurflour.com. Boiled cider is available in glass jars (called "pure cider syrup"); write or call for current prices.

FRENCH CANADIAN MAPLE SUGAR PIE
(*TARTE AU SUCRE*)

This is similar to pecan pie, but the touches of tea and vinegar give it a nice tart edge. The recipe is from the late Regina Menard of Plaisance, Quebec, a cousin of my friend, first-class baker and cook Ruth Cousineau.

Makes one 9-inch pie; serves about 8

      Basic Pie Dough for a 1-crust pie (page 449)
3   large eggs
¾   cup plus 2 tablespoons packed light brown sugar
¾   cup pure maple syrup
6   tablespoons (¾ stick) unsalted butter, melted
¼   cup brewed tea
2   tablespoons plus ½ teaspoon cider vinegar
      Pinch salt
¾   cup coarsely chopped walnuts
      Lightly whipped cream or vanilla ice cream, for serving

1. Roll out the dough on a lightly floured surface to a large circle about ⅛ inch thick. Fit it, without stretching, into a buttered 9-inch pie pan. Trim off the excess dough, leaving a ¾-inch border. Fold under the edge of the dough, pressing along the rim of the pan and forming a high, fluted border. Chill the pie shell while you preheat the oven to 450 degrees F, with a rack in the lower third.

2. In a bowl, whisk together the eggs and brown sugar. Add the maple syrup, butter, tea, vinegar and salt and whisk until smooth. Stir in the walnuts. Set the pie shell on a heavy baking sheet; pour in the filling.

3. Bake for 10 minutes. Reduce the heat to 350 degrees and continue to bake until the center is just set, about 25 minutes longer.

4. Cool the pie on a wire rack. Serve warm or at room temperature, with lightly whipped cream or vanilla ice cream.

ORLEANS SWEET POTATO–PECAN PIE

If sweet potato pie is good, and pecan pie is good, the reasoning goes, how much better to put the two together? In this recipe from Ginger Walsh, a Nashville food stylist and an excellent baker, the brown sugar bubbles up with the butter and pecans to form a caramelized glaze.

Makes one 9-inch pie; serves about 8

Basic Pie Dough for a 1-crust pie (page 449)

SWEET POTATO FILLING
1½	cups cooked sieved sweet potatoes (usually from 2-3 baked sweet potatoes, about 1 pound)
½	cup packed light brown sugar
3	large eggs
1	teaspoon ground cinnamon
1	teaspoon ground ginger
½	teaspoon salt
1	cup chopped pecans

PECAN GLAZE
⅔	cup packed light brown sugar
¾	cup chopped pecans
¼	cup (½ stick) unsalted butter, melted

Whipped cream or vanilla ice cream, for serving (optional)

1. Roll out the dough on a lightly floured surface into a large circle about ⅛ inch thick. Fit it, without stretching, into a buttered 9-inch pie pan. Trim off the excess dough, leaving a ¾-inch overhang. Fold under the edge of the dough, pressing along the rim of the pie pan and forming a high, fluted border. Line the dough with a sheet of foil. Chill while you preheat the oven to 350 degrees F, with a rack in the lower third.

2. SWEET POTATO FILLING: Mash the sweet potatoes with an electric mixer until smooth. Add the brown sugar, eggs, cinnamon, ginger and salt, mixing until well blended. Remove the foil lining from the pie shell. Scatter the chopped pecans in an even layer over the bottom of the pie shell. Carefully pour the filling over the pecans.

Hypocrite Pies

This kind of "double-decker" pie represents an old Southern baking tradition. The pies can be composed of two fillings baked in a single crust, as here, or they can be two pies baked separately, then stacked one on top of the other, crust and all. Author Sarah Belk says that they are also called "hypocrite pies" (one filling "hides" the other), "stacked pies" or "two-story pies."

522

3. Bake for 20 minutes (the filling will be only partially set); leave the oven on.

4. **PECAN GLAZE:** Meanwhile, combine the brown sugar, pecans and butter in a bowl and blend well. With 2 teaspoons, drop the mixture carefully over the partially baked filling, without disturbing the filling. Loosely cover the edges of the crust with foil, if necessary, to prevent them from getting too brown.

5. Bake the pie until the glaze is golden brown and bubbly, about 20 minutes longer.

6. Cool the pie briefly on a wire rack. Serve warm, with whipped cream or ice cream, if you like.

ABOUT MINCEMEAT

Though they are now made less frequently, mince pies of all types were much-loved festive desserts, first in England, then in America, principally in New England.

The tradition of simmering meat—beef, corned beef, venison—then macerating it slowly with copious amounts of suet, dried fruits and a healthy spiking of spirits has its roots in Elizabethan times, when meats were potted under a layer of butter in order to preserve them. This method became more popular in the 17th century; mincing the meat began early in the 18th century. Hence its popularity in the early days of the American colonies, where mincemeat was often made with game such as venison, rabbit or whatever could be taken in the wild.

One night, on the popular 1960s television show *I've Got a Secret*, when the panelists were asked to come up with the mystery hidden in their midst, the secret turned out to be that the pie they were munching on was made from mincemeat that had been preserved for over 100 years. When the panelists discovered this, they didn't look too amused.

"Lay pretty long in bed, and then rose, leaving my wife desirous to sleep, having sat up till four this morning seeing her mayds make mince pies . . ."

SAMUEL PEPYS
DIARY
DECEMBER 25, 1666

To Make Minst Pyes

Take your Veale and perboyle it a little, or mutton, then set it a cooking: and when it is colde, take three pound of suit to a legge of mutton, or fower pound to a fillet of Veale, and then mince them small by them selves, or together whether you will, then take to season them halfe an once of Nutmegs, halfe an once of Cloves and Mace, halfe an once of Sinamon, a little Pepper, as much Salt as you think will season them, either to the mutton or to the Veale, take fiv yolkes of Egges when they be heard, halfe a pinte of Rosewater full measure, halfe a pound of Suger, then straine the Yolkes with the Rosewater and the Suger and mingle it with your meate, if ye have any Orenges or Lemmans you must take two of them, and Make the pilles very thin and mince them very finalle, and put them in a pound of currans, six dates, have a pound of prunes laye Currans and Dates upon the top of your meate, you muste take two or three

DRIED-FRUIT MINCEMEAT PIE WITH LATTICE CREAM CHEESE CRUST

A modern adaptation of mincemeat with no meat at all, and no suet. Instead, the tender crust enfolds a lightened mixture of apples and dried fruits, gently spiced and liberally doused with spirits. This recipe is based on one in Marion Harland's *Common Sense in the Household* (New York, 1871).

~ *Makes one 9- or 9½-inch pie; serves about 8*

CREAM CHEESE DOUGH

1	cup (2 sticks) unsalted butter, softened
8	ounces cream cheese, softened
3	tablespoons sugar
	Pinch salt
½	teaspoon pure vanilla extract
2	cups all-purpose flour

DRIED-FRUIT MINCEMEAT FILLING

2	tart apples, peeled, cored and cut in ¼-inch dice
1	firm-ripe pear, peeled, cored and cut in ¼-inch dice
1	cup dried currants
½	cup chopped dates
½	cup chopped dried figs
½	cup golden raisins
3	tablespoons chopped candied citron (optional)
6	gingersnap cookies, coarsely crushed
	Grated zest and juice of 1 orange
1	tablespoon fresh lemon juice
1	cup packed light brown sugar
¼	cup brandy, or more as needed
1	tablespoon dry white wine
1	teaspoon ground cinnamon
½	teaspoon ground mace
½	teaspoon ground allspice
¼	teaspoon ground cloves
¾	teaspoon salt
1	tablespoon cold unsalted butter, cut into pieces
	Sugar, for sprinkling
	Vanilla ice cream or whipped cream, for serving (optional)

1. **Cream Cheese Dough:** With an electric mixer or a food processor, cream together the butter, cream cheese, sugar and salt until light and fluffy. Add the vanilla and mix briefly; lower the speed and mix in the flour just until blended. Gather the dough into a ball. Flatten slightly, dust with flour and wrap in plastic or wax paper. Chill for at least 30 minutes, or until the dough is just firm.

2. Divide the chilled dough into 2 slightly unequal portions. On a lightly floured surface (or between 2 sheets of wax paper), roll out the larger piece to a large circle about ⅛ inch thick. Fit it, without stretching, into a buttered 9- or 9½-inch pie pan. Roll out the remaining dough into a circle ⅛ inch thick; transfer it to a foil-lined baking sheet. Chill the doughs.

3. **Dried-Fruit Mincemeat Filling:** In a bowl, combine the apples, pear, currants, dates, figs, raisins, optional citron, gingersnaps, orange zest and juice, lemon juice, brown sugar, brandy, wine, spices and salt. Stir gently until uniformly combined and moistened. If the mixture seems dry, stir in another splash of brandy.

4. Preheat the oven to 350 degrees F, with a rack in the lower third. Cut the chilled circle of dough into 1-inch-wide strips, using a fluted pastry wheel or sharp knife. Moisten the edge of the pie crust with cold water. Transfer the filling mixture to the pie shell and dot with the butter.

5. Lay ½ of the dough strips across the top of the pie at even intervals, parallel to one another, pressing the edges of the strips into the edges of the bottom crust. Lay the remaining strips of dough across the top in the other direction, parallel again. Press the ends of the strips into the bottom crust. Trim off the excess dough. Fold the overhanging edges of the bottom crust onto the rim of the pie pan, pressing gently to form an even border. Crimp or flute the border, if you wish. Sprinkle the top of the pie with sugar.

6. Bake the pie until the filling is bubbly and the crust is golden brown, about 1 hour (the timing can vary).

7. Cool the pie to room temperature on a wire rack. Serve with ice cream or whipped cream, if you like.

Pomewaters [a variety of cooking apple] or Wardens [pears] and mince with your meate . . . if you will make good crust put three or foure yolkes of egges a litle Rosewater, & a good deale of suger.

Anonymous
The Good Hous-wives Treasurie
London, 1588

525

Green Tomato and Apple Mincemeat Pie

Tomatoes are a fruit and make a tart, flavorful pie. (Other tomato desserts, such as tomato puddings, were popular in this country around the turn of this century.)

According to Phyllis Richman, food writer for *The Washington Post*, green tomato pie is "not just a way to get rid of green tomatoes; it is good enough to be an excuse for growing [them] in the first place."

This green tomato "mincemeat" plays the tomatoes against apples for a pleasant sweet-tart tang.

✑ *Makes one 9-inch pie; serves about 8*

1	pound (about 3 medium) green tomatoes cored, halved, seeded and coarsely chopped (about 3 cups)
1	cup boiling water
	Kosher or table salt
1	small orange
1¼	pounds sweet apples, such as Golden Delicious
¾	cup raisins
¾	cup packed light brown sugar, or more to taste
¾	teaspoon salt
½	teaspoon ground cinnamon
¼	teaspoon ground cloves
¼	teaspoon fresh-grated nutmeg
⅛	teaspoon ground ginger
2	tablespoons cider vinegar or white-wine vinegar
2	teaspoons finely chopped crystallized ginger
	Basic Pie Dough for a 2-crust pie (page 449) or Cream Cheese Dough (page 524)
1	tablespoon milk, for glaze
1	tablespoon sugar, for glaze
	Vanilla ice cream, for serving (optional)

1. In a food processor, combine the tomatoes and boiling water. Pulse until the tomato is chopped into small pieces. Drain into a colander and sprinkle lightly with the salt; let stand for 1 hour. Press down firmly to expel nearly all of the liquid. Transfer the tomatoes to a nonreactive saucepan.

2. Grate the orange zest into the saucepan. Discard the thick orange rind and seeds, chop the orange pulp and add it, along with any accumulated juice, to the tomatoes. Peel, core and chop

the apples; add them to the tomatoes along with the raisins, brown sugar, salt, spices, vinegar and crystallized ginger. Cover the pan and bring to a boil. Reduce the heat and simmer gently, partially covered, until tender, usually 12 to 15 minutes. Set aside to cool before assembling the pie.

3. Preheat the oven to 350 degrees F, with a rack in the lower third. Roll out the pie crust on a lightly floured surface to a large circle about ⅛ inch thick. Fit it, without stretching, into a lightly buttered 9-inch pie pan. Trim the edges of the dough, leaving a 1-inch overhang. Roll out the top round of pastry. With a cookie cutter, cut 5 or 6 round holes in the top pastry, or use a paring knife to cut tomato-shaped cutouts. Moisten the edge of the bottom crust with cold water. Pour the filling into the pie pan. Loosely drape the remaining dough over the filling. Trim off the excess dough, leaving a 1-inch border. Turn the edges of the top crust under the edges of the bottom crust, forming a smooth border on the rim of the pan. Press the back of a fork all around the edge. Brush the top of the dough with the milk. Cut a cross in the center, fold each flap back and press it into the surface of the pie. Sprinkle with the sugar.

4. Place the pie on the oven rack, with a sheet of foil underneath to catch drips. Bake until the top is golden brown and the filling is bubbly, about 1 hour (the timing can vary).

5. Cool on a rack to room temperature. Serve with ice cream, if you like.

Fresh Mince

This is new cider," said Mrs. Larrabee, busily filling glasses. "We just got it home this week." She set cookies before us, and then, as a climax, brought a huge wedge of fresh mince pie and a generous chunk of yellow cheese and put these before my father.

"I'm not giving Delly any," she explained kindly, "because I don't want to spoil her supper."

"No danger spoiling my supper, I s'pose," chuckled my father, neatly fitting a slice of cheese to a piece of the pie with his knife. "Not with mince pie, anyhow."

DELLA T. LUTES
HOME GROWN
1937

RECIPES

Breakfast Pear Tarte Tatin
Free-Form Pear Galette
The World's Best Lemon Tart
Long Island Double Blue-
*   berry Tart*
Alsatian Pear Tart with
*   Macaroon Crunch Topping*
Cranberry-Raspberry Tart
*   Pastiche*
Gingered Carrot Custard
*   Tart*
Cornmeal Pear Tart with
*   Frangipane*
The Coach House Quince and
*   Almond Tart*
Belgian Sugar Tart
Caramel-Walnut Tart
Ray's Holiday Nut Tart
Hungarian Cheese Tart
Warm Rice Pudding Tart
*   with Dried Fruit*
Polish Apple Tart

CHAPTER 16

TARTS

There was an Old Person of Pett
Who was partly consumed by regret;
He sat in a cart
And ate cold Apple Tart
Which relieved that Old Person of Pett
EDWARD LEAR,
NONSENSE OMNIBUS, 1943; CA. 1846

When is a pie a tart? Both pies and tarts are known as *les tartes* in French. But today, the general understanding is that a tart is open-face, with a single bottom crust, and usually (though not always) baked in a shallow pan with straight sides.

These kinds of tarts were among the first pies and originated as savories, filled with meat or fish. By the time of the Renaissance, sweet tarts had appeared; Platina's recipes for pumpkin and rice torta, which date from 1475, are remarkably similar to the contemporary ones in this chapter.

Leaf through old French and English cookbooks, and you'll come across a profusion of *tartes*, *tourtes*, *pastes* and "pyes," as well as elaborately designed top-crust constructions called "florentines" or "florendynes," also known as "flories." These were usually meat or fish, though fruit was often included in meat pies. During the 16th century, when the final course of formal banquets emerged as a distinct dessert course, fruit tarts were served, along with sweet wines, marmalades and other preserved fruits, marchpane (marzipan), wafers and other sweetmeats. In 17th-century French-influenced English cookbooks, "flawn of apples" and "Cheese Tart, Flawn, or Custard"—tarts by another name—were standard preparations of their time.

While some tarts, such as the pear galette baked free-form on a baking sheet (page 532), can be rustic, I generally think of them as being somewhat more delicate than pies, which are often hearty, deep-dish affairs. (In practice, though, these distinctions are hard to draw with precision; there is a good deal of overlap between the two categories.)

Because of its refined appearance, there is something particularly festive about a tart. Bring one to the table or take one along with you to a dinner party—they transport well—and you've brought a celebration. They look impressive, but they aren't hard to make. In fact, because they have just a single crust, tarts often are easier to put together than pies. To further simplify the process, you can make several batches of dough at once, freeze them separately, and transfer the frozen disk to the refrigerator to thaw the night before you need it. From there, it's just a matter of rolling out the dough and assembling a filling. Bake the tart shortly before the meal, so the pastry stays crisp and light.

The tarts collected in this chapter range from the very simple—a Tarte Tatin made with pears and biscuit dough and a blueberry tart with both uncooked and cooked blueberries—to the height of elegance: an Alsatian fruit tart topped with custard and a sheer layer of macaroon; a gleaming red tart that combines cranberries and fresh raspberries; and a luxurious nut tart.

The lemon tart and the caramel-walnut tart are two old favorites that I've been making for years. For birthdays and other festive dinners, I sometimes bake one of each and serve a small wedge of both on the same plate. The clean astringency of the lemon offsets the almost bitter edge of the caramel and walnuts, and both are mellowed by softly whipped cream—a glorious indulgence.

Breakfast Pear Tarte Tatin

This upside-down fruit-and-biscuit tart is loosely adapted from a recipe from food stylist Anne Disrude. When you invert the skillet, the fat pear wedges are glazed with nuts and syrup, which drip down over the spiced biscuit base. To ease things in the morning, the dough can be partially made the night before; it's just spooned on top—no rolling required.

Serves 4

Spiced Cornmeal Biscuit Dough

¾	cup plus 2 tablespoons all-purpose flour
¼	cup plus 2 tablespoons cornmeal
3	tablespoons sugar
1	teaspoon baking powder
1	teaspoon baking soda
½	teaspoon salt
¾	teaspoon ground cinnamon
3	tablespoons cold unsalted butter, cut into pieces
⅓	cup low-fat plain yogurt
⅓	cup cold water
2	tablespoons unsalted butter
⅓	cup packed light brown sugar
3	tablespoons coarsely broken walnuts (optional)
2	ripe pears, such as Bosc or Bartlett, peeled, cored, quartered; each quarter cut into 2-3 wedges

1. **Spiced Cornmeal Biscuit Dough:** In a food processor or bowl, combine the flour, cornmeal, sugar, baking powder, baking soda, salt and cinnamon. Pulse or cut in the butter. Combine the yogurt and water and add to the dough, pulsing or stirring with a fork just until it comes together. *(If you are not using the dough immediately, place it on a lightly floured plate, cover with plastic wrap, and refrigerate.)*

2. Preheat the oven to 425 degrees F, with a rack in the center. Heat the butter in a 7- or 8-inch ovenproof skillet, preferably cast-iron or nonstick. Add the brown sugar and cook over medium heat until the sugar has nearly melted. Remove from the heat, scatter the optional walnuts over the sugar mixture, and arrange the pears in the pan, with most of the rounded sides down

and the narrow tops toward the center. Scatter clumps of the dough over the pears in the skillet, roughly covering them.

3. Place the pan in the oven and bake until the dough is nicely browned and a toothpick inserted in the dough emerges clean, usually about 25 minutes.

4. Remove from the oven and let stand in the pan for about 2 minutes. Run the tip of a knife around the edges and invert onto a plate. (Replace any pears that stick to the pan.) Cut into large wedges and serve warm.

PREBAKING TART CRUSTS

*I*n many of the recipes in this chapter, tart crusts are partially baked before the filling is added. This requires a little extra effort, but the results are worth it. Partially baking the crust means that any soft, moist fillings, such as custard mixtures and juicy fruits, won't soak into the crust.

It's best to use a lightly buttered pan with a removable bottom, so the finished tart can be lifted away from the sides of the pan. The traditional method for prebaking is to line the shell with foil or parchment paper, and to weigh down the crust with dried beans or rice—keep a full canister of these for indefinite reuse. (You can also use metal or ceramic pie weights, if you want to invest in another kitchen gimmick.)

Weighing down the crust helps prevent the sides from sagging before they set in the oven's heat. For most pastry doughs, a sheet of buttered foil tucked into place against the bottom and sides will work just as well without extra weight.

In prebaking, the crust should be just partially baked—not all the way through. When the surface looks dry and the edges just begin to color, that's enough.

Each recipe gives specific instructions whenever prebaking is called for.

The Oldest Pastry

A galette is a thin, flat round, "the oldest of all pastries," according to the French edition of *Larousse Gastronomique.* Galettes can be traced back to the Neolithic period, to round cakes made with various grains and honey, baked over hot coals.

The best-known galette is the *galette des Rois,* similar to Pithiviers (see page 572), served at Epiphany (12 days after Christmas), with a small porcelain doll baked inside for good luck. Whoever finds the doll (or sometimes a bean) is crowned King, and he then names his Queen.

There are both sweet and savory galettes, and the term is used for baked goods—always round—ranging from the buckwheat crepes of Brittany to Normandy's crisp *sablé* butter cookies.

FREE-FORM PEAR GALETTE

A galette is a rustic French country dessert, less formal than the precisely fluted tart. This one is an adaptation of a superb recipe from Diana Sturgis, test kitchen director at *Food & Wine* magazine.

The fruit is arranged atop a flat round of pastry, which is formed directly on a baking sheet. Because galettes are baked free-form, you can make them in any shape you like. Bake the galette shortly before serving dinner (not more than a couple of hours ahead, if possible), and then rewarm slightly just before serving.

Glazed with a pinwheel of sheer pear slices, this one is nothing short of heavenly, especially if you serve it warm, with a chilled dessert wine. Make it for a gathering of close friends—there's something communal about cutting big wedges from the huge round on a big wooden board.

Serves 6

GALETTE DOUGH

1	cup all-purpose flour
1	teaspoon sugar
½	teaspoon salt
5	tablespoons cold unsalted butter, cut into small pieces
1	large egg
1	teaspoon milk
2	tablespoons apricot preserves, strained, or as needed

PEARS

2-3	firm-ripe Bosc pears (6-7 ounces each)
2	tablespoons unsalted butter, melted
2	teaspoons sugar

Vanilla ice cream, whipped cream or crème fraîche, for serving (optional)

1. **GALETTE DOUGH:** In a food processor or a bowl, toss together the flour, sugar and salt. Pulse or cut in the butter until the mixture is crumbly. Beat the egg with the milk in a measuring cup. Sprinkle 2 tablespoons of the egg mixture over the flour mixture and pulse or stir it in with a fork (reserve the remainder). Working quickly, gather the dough into a smooth mass. On a lightly floured surface, pat out the dough into a 5-inch disk. Wrap in plastic or wax paper and refrigerate until cold but not too hard,

about 30 minutes. *(The dough can be prepared a day or two ahead. Let soften at room temperature until malleable, about 15 minutes, before rolling out.)*

2. Preheat the oven to 425 degrees F, with a rack in the center. On a lightly floured surface, roll out the dough into a 9½-inch circle, turning it clockwise an inch or two each time you roll, to maintain an even shape. Transfer the dough to a lightly buttered heavy baking sheet. Fold in about ¼ inch of the dough all around, forming a neat, smooth rim. With the back of a knife, score decorative diagonal indentations around the rim. Brush the rim with a little of the reserved beaten egg. Brush 1 tablespoon of the apricot preserves over the bottom of the tart shell. Refrigerate while you prepare the pears.

3. **PEARS:** Peel, quarter and core the pears. Slice each quarter lengthwise into 5 thin wedges. Arrange all but about 6 of the pear slices on the dough in a spoke pattern, overlapping them slightly. Trim the remaining slices and arrange them in the center of the tart.

4. Gently brush the pear slices with the melted butter and sprinkle with the sugar. Bake until the dough is crisp and golden and the pears are tender, 25 to 30 minutes.

5. Thin the remaining 1 tablespoon of the apricot preserves with about ½ teaspoon hot water and brush over the pear slices. If you like, slide the galette onto a large wooden cutting board for serving. Serve the galette warm, cutting it into large wedges and topping with a little ice cream, whipped cream or crème fraîche, if you like. (The galette can be rewarmed for 8 to 10 minutes at 350 degrees, if baked ahead.)

THE WORLD'S BEST LEMON TART
(*TARTE AU CITRON NÉZARD*)

After tasting my way through just about every *tarte au citron* in Paris, I came back again and again to the simple version baked at Nézard, a tiny unknown pâtisserie on the Left Bank near Montparnasse. Nowhere else did the lemon burst with such sharp citrus zing in each mouthful. No other tart cut so cleanly, each slice standing neat and trim on the plate, its unadorned surface of baked lemon curd glazed with gold.

There's still no dessert more refreshing after dinner, whether in winter, when there's little other fruit around, or in summer, served with a few fresh berries on the side.

Makes one 9- or 10-inch tart; serves about 8

Rich Tart Dough for 1 shell (page 451)

LEMON CURD FILLING

Juice of 2 lemons
6 large eggs
1 scant cup sugar
10 tablespoons (1 stick plus 2 tablespoons) cold unsalted butter, cut into pieces
Finely grated zest of 3 lemons

3 tablespoons apricot preserves or orange marmalade
1 paper-thin lemon slice

1. Roll out the dough on a lightly floured surface into a large circle; the crust for this tart should be very thin. Gently fold the dough in half, and fit it, without stretching, into a lightly buttered 9- or 10-inch fluted tart or quiche pan with a removable bottom. Trim off the excess dough, leaving a ¾-inch overhang. Tuck in the overhang, pressing the edges of the dough against the sides of the tart pan to form a high, smooth border. Chill the tart shell while you preheat the oven to 400 degrees F, with a rack in the center.

2. Line the tart shell with a sheet of lightly buttered foil, buttered side down. Weigh down with dried beans, rice or pie weights; place the shell on a heavy baking sheet. Bake until the edges are set, 8 to 10 minutes. Very carefully lift out the weights

and foil; prick the dough lightly with a fork. Continue to bake until the pastry is very pale gold, about 8 minutes longer. Cool slightly on a wire rack; leave the oven on.

3. **LEMON CURD FILLING:** In the top of a double boiler or a heatproof bowl, whisk together the lemon juice, eggs and sugar until blended. Add the butter, and set over simmering water. Whisk the mixture constantly until thick and smooth, about 8 minutes. Do not let the mixture boil; be sure to scrape the bottom as you whisk. Remove from the heat. Strain the mixture into a clean bowl; whisk in the lemon zest. (If you are not going to use the custard immediately, lay a sheet of wax paper or plastic wrap directly on the surface and refrigerate.)

4. Pour the custard into the tart shell. Bake until the filling is set and lightly golden, about 30 minutes. Cool the tart to room temperature on a wire rack, 1 to 2 hours.

5. Strain a thin layer of the preserves directly over the surface of the tart (if you are using a stiff marmalade, it may need to be warmed before straining). Gently brush it over the surface of the tart, glazing evenly (brush gently so you don't tear the custard). Lay the thin slice of lemon in the center of the tart; glaze the lemon slice with the preserves. Remove the tart from the rim of the pan and serve at room temperature.

Variation
FRESH ORANGE TART: For the lemon zest and juice, substitute the zest of 1 orange and 1 lemon, ¼ cup fresh orange juice and the juice of ½ lemon.

"Tomorrow, Monsieur . . ."

I started stopping in regularly at Nézard to eat a little lunch, and once the owners started getting used to seeing my face, I asked for the lemon tart recipe, always being told, "Certainly, *Monsieur*— tomorrow." This went on for weeks: lots of "tomorrows," lots of smiles, but still no recipe.

Finally, when I explained that I was returning to America, the proprietor broke down and let me talk to the pastry chef, who explained the recipe to me in great detail—on one condition: that I *never* bake this tart anywhere in Paris. I've kept that promise.

535

Long Island Double Blueberry Tart

This tart bursts with the flavor of high summer. Raw and cooked blueberries counterpoint one another, offering a refreshing change from the usual two-crust berry pie.

⸻ *Makes one 9-inch tart; serves about 8*

> Rich Tart Dough for 1 shell (page 451) or Basic Pie Dough for a 1-crust pie (page 449)
> 3 pints fresh blueberries, picked over
> ¼ cup cold water
> ⅔ cup sugar, or less, depending on the berries' sweetness
> 3 tablespoons cornstarch
> ½ teaspoon ground cinnamon
> 1 lemon
> Small pinch freshly ground pepper (optional)
> Lightly sweetened whipped cream, flavored with pure vanilla extract, for serving

1. Roll out the dough on a lightly floured surface into a large circle about ⅛ inch thick. Fit it, without stretching, into a lightly buttered 9-inch fluted tart or quiche pan with a removable bottom. Trim off the excess dough, leaving a ¾-inch overhang. Tuck in the overhang, pressing the edges of the dough against the sides of the tart pan to form a high, smooth border. Chill the tart shell while you preheat the oven to 400 degrees F, with a rack in the center.

2. Line the pastry with a sheet of lightly buttered foil, buttered side down. Weigh down the foil with dried beans, rice or pie weights; place the tart pan on a heavy baking sheet. Bake until the sides are set, 8 to 10 minutes. Carefully remove the weights and foil. Continue to bake the shell, pricking any air bubbles with a fork, until the dough is golden and baked through, 10 to 13 minutes longer. Cool the tart shell on a wire rack.

3. Combine about 2 cups of the blueberries with the cold water in a heavy nonreactive saucepan. Cover and bring to a boil. Meanwhile, in a small bowl, use a fork to stir together the sugar, cornstarch and cinnamon. Use a zester or vegetable peeler to remove the zest from the lemon; reserve a few long, thin strands of zest for garnish. Finely chop the remaining zest and add it to the sugar mixture. Juice the lemon, and stir the juice into the

sugar mixture; add this mixture to the berries. Boil gently, uncovered, stirring constantly, until thickened, about 5 minutes. (Adding a hint of pepper is a nice touch.) Remove from the heat, place a sheet of wax paper or plastic wrap directly on the surface, and chill, stirring occasionally, until completely cooled, about 1 hour.

4. Set aside about 1 cup of the nicest uncooked blueberries. Stir the remaining uncooked berries into the cooled berry mixture. Shortly before serving, pile the blueberry mixture into the tart shell, mounding it carefully. Top with an even layer of the reserved uncooked blueberries and garnish with a few strands of the reserved lemon zest. Chill, if not serving immediately.

5. If the tart was chilled longer than 30 minutes, remove it from the refrigerator a few minutes before serving. Gently remove the tart from the rim of the pan. Top each slice with a large spoonful of lightly whipped cream, and pass the remaining cream separately.

ALSATIAN PEAR TART WITH MACAROON CRUNCH TOPPING

A lsatian fruit tarts nestle the fruit in a layer of custard. They're made with pears, raspberries and yellow and blue plums—all the fruits used to make the eaux-de-vie that are the region's pride. This is a terrific tart, the mantle of almond macaroon providing crunchy contrast to the soft custard below.

Makes one 9- or 10-inch tart; serves about 8

Rich Tart Dough for 1 shell (page 451)

PEARS

2	firm-ripe pears, such as Bosc, peeled, cored and cut into ¼-inch slices
	Pear eau-de-vie or fresh lemon juice

CUSTARD

2	large eggs
1	large egg yolk
½	cup crème fraîche, sour cream or heavy cream
¼	cup milk
2	tablespoons sugar
¼	teaspoon grated lemon zest
¼	teaspoon pure vanilla extract

MACAROON CRUNCH TOPPING

¾	cup (about 3 ounces) thinly sliced blanched almonds
¼	cup sugar
3	tablespoons dried currants
1	egg white, or more if needed

1. Roll out the dough on a lightly floured surface into a large circle about ⅛ inch thick. Gently fold the dough in half, and fit it, without stretching, into a lightly buttered 9- or 10-inch fluted tart or quiche pan with a removable bottom. Trim off the excess dough, leaving a ¾-inch overhang. Tuck in the overhang, pressing the edges of the dough against the sides of the tart pan to form a high, smooth border. Chill the tart shell while you preheat the oven to 400 degrees F, with a rack in the center.

2. Line the dough with a sheet of lightly buttered foil, buttered side down. Weigh down with dried beans, rice or pie weights; place on a heavy baking sheet. Bake until the edges are set, usually about 8 minutes. Very carefully lift out the weights and foil; prick the dough lightly with a fork. Continue to bake until the dough is very pale gold, 6 to 8 minutes longer. Cool slightly on a wire rack; lower the oven temperature to 350 degrees.

3. **PEARS:** Arrange the pear slices in the tart shell, overlapping them slightly in a circular pattern. Fill in the center with the remaining slices. Sprinkle the pears with the eau-de-vie or lemon juice. Bake, still on the baking sheet, until the pears just begin to become tender, about 12 minutes. Do not overcook the pears; they will bake further. Leave the oven on.

4. **CUSTARD:** In a bowl, whisk together the eggs, egg yolk, crème fraîche or sour or heavy cream, milk, sugar, lemon zest and vanilla until smooth. Carefully pour the custard over the pears, filling the tart nearly up to the edge. Bake until the custard is barely set in the center, 17 to 20 minutes. Remove from the oven; leave the oven on.

5. **MACAROON CRUNCH TOPPING:** Stir together the almonds, sugar, currants and egg white until the ingredients are very lightly coated with egg white. If it is too dry, stir in a few drops more egg white. Carefully spoon the topping onto the surface of the tart in a thin, even layer, smoothing it very gently with a palette knife or the back of a spoon. Bake until the topping is lightly golden, 15 to 20 minutes.

6. Cool the tart on a rack. Remove the tart from the rim of the pan; serve slightly warm or at room temperature.

⌒ *Variations*
Substitute 3 McIntosh apples, peeled, cored and sliced; or 1 cup raspberries; or 10 small plums, halved and stoned, for the pears.

"Mmm, Almond Tarts"

Poised on steady legs
First your poet begs
Several eggs.
Froth them to a mousse,
And then introduce
Lemon juice.
Simmering like silk,
Aromatic milk
Of almonds will
come next, and next
prepare
Pastry light as air
to coat with care
Each pretty pastry mould.
Which sweetly will enfold
The liquid gold.
Smile, a father, fond,
Wave your fiery wand,
Bake till blond.
Melting mouths and
hearts,
Mmmmmm, saliva starts—
Almond Tarts.

EDMOND ROSTAND
CYRANO DE BERGERAC
TRANSLATED BY ANTHONY
BURGESS
1897; 1971

CRANBERRY-RASPBERRY TART PASTICHE

A glistening jewel box of a tart, with pureed raspberries and whole cranberries combined over a pure cream custard that just holds its shape.

The secret to this tart: Baking the custard at a low temperature results in a luscious consistency.

⁓ *Makes one 10- or 11-inch tart; serves about 10*

PASTICHE TART DOUGH

2   tablespoons plus 2 teaspoons lukewarm water
½   teaspoon salt
2   scant cups (8 ounces) all-purpose flour
1½   teaspoons sugar
½   cup plus 2 tablespoons plus 2 teaspoons (1 stick plus 2 tablespoons plus 2 teaspoons) cold unsalted butter, cut into pieces
2   tablespoons well-beaten egg (about ½ of a large egg)

CUSTARD

1½   cups heavy cream
½   vanilla bean, split lengthwise, or 1 teaspoon pure vanilla extract
4   large egg yolks
½   cup sugar

FRUIT TOPPING

¾   scant cup fresh raspberries, picked over and loosely packed (5 ounces)
¾   cup sugar
3⅔   cups fresh or frozen (not thawed) cranberries (12 ounces), rinsed and picked over
   Thin strands of orange zest, for garnish

1. **PASTICHE TART DOUGH:** In a small bowl, stir together the water and the salt until the salt dissolves. Place in the refrigerator until cold. In a food processor or bowl, combine the flour and sugar. Add the butter and pulse or cut in until the mixture is crumbly. Turn off the machine. Stir the beaten egg into the cold water mixture; add it, pulsing or stirring with a fork, until the ingredients are combined and the dough comes together; do not overmix. Gather the dough into a ball; flatten into a disk. Wrap the dough in wax paper or plastic and refrigerate for several hours or overnight.

Picture-Perfect

In Providence, Rhode Island, tucked behind the Italian markets of Atwells Avenue, you'll find Pastiche, a pastry shop-café, where the gleaming glass cases are filled with cakes and picture-perfect tarts, including this one.

2. Roll out the dough on a lightly floured surface into a large circle about ⅛ inch thick. Gently fold the dough in half, and fit it, without stretching, into a buttered plain or fluted 10- or 11-inch tart pan with a removable bottom. Trim off the excess dough, leaving a ¾-inch overhang. Tuck in the overhang, pressing the edges of the dough against the sides of the pan, to form a high, smooth border. Freeze the pastry shell for about 15 minutes while you preheat the oven to 350 degrees F, with a rack in the center.

3. Line the tart shell with a lightly buttered sheet of foil, buttered side down. Weigh down with dried beans, rice or pie weights. Bake until the edges are set, about 20 minutes. If the foil sticks, bake slightly longer. Carefully remove the weights and foil. Continue to bake, pricking any air bubbles with a fork, until baked through and golden, 8 to 15 minutes longer.

4. **CUSTARD:** Meanwhile, scald the cream with the vanilla bean in a nonreactive saucepan (if using vanilla extract, do not add it now). Off the heat, in the top of a double boiler or in a heat-proof bowl, whisk together the egg yolks and sugar. Very gradually whisk in the hot cream. Set over simmering water and cook the custard, stirring constantly, until it thickens very slightly and coats the back of a spoon, 7 to 10 minutes; do not allow to boil. Remove from the heat, and stir in the vanilla extract, if using. (If using the vanilla bean, remove it from the custard and scrape the seeds from the pod into the custard.)

5. The custard should be ready by the time the tart shell is golden brown (the custard should be hot when it goes into the oven). Pour the hot custard mixture into the tart shell and lower the oven temperature to 225 degrees. Bake until the custard is set but still soft to the touch (it should not jiggle when the pan is shaken gently), 15 to 20 minutes.

6. Cool the tart on a wire rack for 30 minutes. Loosely cover and refrigerate until the custard is firm.

7. **FRUIT TOPPING:** Puree the raspberries in a food processor or blender; you should have nearly ⅔ cup puree. (At Pastiche, the puree is left unstrained.) In a large nonreactive sauté pan, combine the raspberry puree with the sugar and bring to a boil over medium-high heat. Boil until slightly reduced, 2 to 3 minutes. Stir in the cranberries and cook over high heat, stirring, until some of the cranberries pop but the remainder are still whole, about

4 minutes. Immediately remove from the heat, transfer to a bowl and chill for 20 minutes, stirring occasionally.

8. Spoon the fruit mixture over the tart and chill for about 20 minutes. Garnish with the strands of orange zest. Remove the tart from the rim of the pan and serve.

GINGERED CARROT CUSTARD TART

A long with desserts made from parsnips, turnips, potatoes and other root vegetables, carrot tarts and puddings were fairly common in earlier centuries. Except for carrot cake, these desserts have been lost over time. This tart will be a pleasant surprise.

Makes one 10-inch tart; serves 8 to 10

	Basic Pie Dough for a 1-crust pie (page 449) or Rich Tart Dough for 1 shell (page 451)
1	pound carrots, peeled, trimmed and coarsely chopped
2	large eggs
¼	cup packed light brown sugar
2	tablespoons sugar
1½	teaspoons all-purpose flour
¾	cup heavy cream
½	cup milk
2½	tablespoons finely chopped crystallized ginger
	Pinch *each* fresh-grated nutmeg and freshly ground pepper
	Grated zest of 1 lemon
1	tablespoon bourbon or rum (optional)

1. Roll out the dough on a lightly floured surface into a large circle about ⅛ inch thick. Gently fold the dough in half, and fit it, without stretching, into a lightly buttered 10-inch fluted tart or quiche pan with a removable bottom. Trim off the excess dough, leaving a ¾-inch overhang. Tuck in the overhang, pressing the edges of the dough against the sides of the tart pan to form a high, smooth border. Chill the tart shell while you preheat the oven to 400 degrees F, with a rack in the center.

2. Line the dough with a sheet of lightly buttered foil, buttered side down. Weigh down with dried beans, rice or pie weights; place the shell on a heavy baking sheet. Bake until the edges are set, usually about 8 minutes. Very carefully lift out the weights and foil; prick the dough lightly with a fork. Continue to bake until the dough is very pale gold, 6 to 8 minutes longer. Cool the tart shell on a wire rack; lower the oven temperature to 350 degrees.

3. In a large saucepan, cook the carrots in boiling water to cover until they are very tender; drain thoroughly. Return the carrots to the empty pan over medium heat and toss constantly until all of the excess moisture evaporates. Puree the carrots in a food processor or blender until very smooth. Transfer the puree to a mixing bowl; there should be about 1¼ cups.

4. Add the eggs, brown and white sugars and flour and whisk until smooth. Add the cream, milk, crystallized ginger, nutmeg, pepper, lemon zest and optional bourbon or rum and whisk until smooth. Pour the carrot mixture into the tart shell. Place the tart on a heavy baking sheet.

5. Bake until the filling is set in the center, about 30 minutes.

6. Cool the tart on a wire rack to room temperature. Remove the tart from the rim of the pan. Serve at room temperature.

To Make a Carrot Pudding

Take a pint of Cream a penny loaf grated take the same quantity of Carrot grated as you do your bread raw out of ye ground only scraped or par'd mix these with the cream 12 Eggs half of the whites nutmeg sugar and salt according to Your taste when you are ready to set it to the Oven melt half a pd of Butter & mix in your pudding you must butter your dish you put it in if you please you may put Crust at the bottom let your oven be very quick & 3 quarters of an hour will bake it.

LADY ANNE MORTON
THE LADEY MORTONS
BOOKE OF RECEIPTS
HANDWRITTEN
MANUSCRIPT
ENGLAND, 1693

CORNMEAL PEAR TART WITH FRANGIPANE

The crust of this tart is made slightly crunchy with cornmeal and filled with pears cradled in a layer of almond and macaroon frangipane. The dough is based on a recipe from Joyce Goldstein, chef-owner of Square One restaurant in San Francisco.

Makes one 9-inch tart; serves about 8

CORNMEAL TART DOUGH

1	cup all-purpose flour
⅔	cup sieved cornmeal
½	cup sugar
1½	teaspoons grated lemon zest
½	teaspoon salt
½	cup plus 2 tablespoons (1¼ sticks) cold unsalted butter, cut into pieces
2	large egg yolks
1	tablespoon honey
1	tablespoon pure vanilla extract

PEARS

4	firm-ripe Bosc pears, peeled, halved and cored
	Fresh lemon juice
2	tablespoons dry white wine or water

ALMOND-MACAROON FRANGIPANE

¾	cup (4½-5 ounces) almonds, with or without skins
½	cup (about 1 ounce) amaretti (crisp Italian macaroons)
½	cup sugar
2	tablespoons all-purpose flour
½	cup (1 stick) unsalted butter, softened
2	large eggs
1	teaspoon pure vanilla extract
2	tablespoons pear eau-de-vie (pear brandy) or other liqueur

1	large egg, beaten
	Sugar, for sprinkling

1. **CORNMEAL TART DOUGH:** In a food processor or bowl, combine the flour, cornmeal, sugar, lemon zest and salt. Add the butter and pulse or cut in until the mixture resembles coarse meal.

2. In a cup, combine the egg yolks, honey and vanilla. Slowly add the liquids to the flour, pulsing or mixing with a fork until the mixture forms a cohesive dough. Gather the dough together and divide in half; form each half into a flattened disk. Wrap each half in wax paper or plastic; set one aside to rest for about 10 minutes. (Refrigerate or freeze the remaining ½ of the dough; use it for another tart.)

3. Butter a 9-inch fluted tart or quiche pan with a removable bottom. This pastry is tricky to roll, so it's easier to do with your fingers. Press it evenly into the bottom and up the sides of the pan. Form a neat, even rim. Chill the dough while you preheat the oven to 375 degrees F, with a rack in the center.

4. Line the tart shell with a lightly buttered sheet of foil, buttered side down, pressing to cover the bottom and sides evenly. Weigh down the shell with beans, rice or pie weights. Bake until the sides are set, about 8 minutes. Carefully remove the weights and foil; prick the dough lightly with a fork. Continue to bake until the dough begins to turn pale gold but has not yet baked through, 5 to 6 minutes longer. Cool the tart shell on a wire rack; leave the oven on.

5. **PEARS:** Meanwhile, place the pear halves in a shallow buttered baking dish or pie pan. Sprinkle the pears with lemon juice; spoon the wine or water around the pears. Cover with foil and bake (along with the crust is fine) until the pears are firm-tender, usually 10 to 15 minutes (the timing can vary based on the ripeness of the fruit; do not overbake). Remove from the oven and set aside to cool; leave the oven on.

6. **ALMOND-MACAROON FRANGIPANE:** Place the almonds, amaretti, sugar and flour in a food processor. Grind until powdery. Add the butter, eggs, vanilla and eau-de-vie or other spirit and process until smooth.

7. Brush the inside of the tart shell lightly with the beaten egg. Spread a thin layer of the frangipane over the bottom of the shell, using just enough to cover. Drain the pears on paper towels; blot up any excess liquid. Cut the pear halves in half again, making long quarters. Arrange them in the shell in a spoke pattern, thinner ends toward the center. Spoon the remaining frangipane between the pears; sprinkle the entire surface with a light coating of sugar.

8. Bake the tart until the frangipane is set and pale gold in color, about 20 minutes.

9. Cool the tart briefly on a wire rack. Remove the tart from the rim of the pan and serve at room temperature.

THE COACH HOUSE QUINCE AND ALMOND TART

Quince is one of the most-often-included fruits in old English books, in which recipes are as likely to be for preserving the fruit itself as for tarts and pies.

If you're lucky enough to have access to fresh quinces, do not miss this perfumed tart, which glistens with rose-colored fruit. This is a favorite recipe of Leon Lianides, owner of the Coach House in New York City, now closed.

Fresh quinces aren't easy to find, but they do turn up at local farmers' markets—especially if you let growers know that you're interested. The Kent family, whose orchards are in Milton, New York, have them every fall at New York City's Greenmarkets.

Makes one 9- or 10-inch tart; serves about 8

Rich Tart Dough for 2 shells (page 451)
3½ cups Honey-Stewed Quinces (page 75)
2 tablespoons chopped almonds, toasted until fragrant, about 7 minutes
Lightly whipped cream or vanilla ice cream, for serving

1. Roll out ⅔ of the dough on a lightly floured surface into a 12-inch circle. Fit the dough, without stretching, into a lightly buttered 9- or 10-inch fluted tart or quiche pan with a removable bottom. Trim the edge, leaving a ¾-inch overhang. Tuck in the overhang, pressing the edges of the dough against the sides of the tart pan to form a high, smooth border. Chill the tart shell. Roll out the remaining dough between 2 sheets of wax paper to a 10-inch circle. Chill while you preheat the oven to 375 degrees F, with a rack in the center.

2. Line the tart shell with a lightly buttered sheet of foil, buttered side down. Bake for 6 minutes. Remove the foil. Continue to bake for 4 minutes longer, pricking the dough lightly with a fork if

it bubbles up. Remove from the oven and set the tart shell on a wire rack. Leave the oven on.

3. Remove the top sheet of the wax paper from the remaining dough. Use a fluted pastry wheel or a sharp knife to cut the dough into ¾-inch-wide strips. Spoon the quinces into the tart shell. Lay ½ of the strips over the quinces at even intervals, parallel to one another. Lay the remaining strips of pastry across the top in the other direction, parallel again. Press the ends of the strips into the sides of the tart and trim any excess pastry.

4. Bake the tart until lightly golden, about 25 minutes.

5. Remove the tart to a wire rack. Sprinkle the almonds over the top. Cool to room temperature. Remove the tart from the rim of the pan. Serve with whipped cream or vanilla ice cream.

To Make a Quince Pye

Take eight or ten faire Quinces, pare them without and wipe them within then take an once of Sinamon, a pounde and a halfe of Sugar, a little Saunders [sandalwood], and in every one of them a clove or two, then heate your oven resonablye, and let it stand in six howers, this pie is not to be made after Easter then they be out of season . . . with your sugar put in five or six spoonefulls of Rose water.

Anonymous
The Good Hous-wives
Treasurie
London, 1588

BELGIAN SUGAR TART
(*TARTE AU SUCRE*)

When I asked chef Pierre Wynants, the celebrated 3-star chef-owner of Comme Chez Soi in Brussels, who is capable of celestially sophisticated desserts, for a recipe from his childhood in Belgium, this tart is what immediately came to his mind. It's rustic and homey, the custard filling crusted with butter and sugar.

If you'd like to make this in a 9- or 9½-inch pie pan instead of a quiche pan, multiply the filling ingredients by 1½ (3 eggs, and so forth).

Makes one 9-inch tart; serves about 8

	Rich Tart Dough for 1 shell (page 451) or Basic Pie Dough for a 1-crust pie (page 449)
2	large eggs
¾	cup packed dark brown sugar
¾	cup sugar
½	cup ground almonds
1½	tablespoons all-purpose flour
½	cup plus 1 tablespoon crème fraîche (page 624) or heavy cream
1	teaspoon pure vanilla extract (not traditional, but good)
2	tablespoons unsalted butter, cut into small pieces

1. Roll out the dough on a lightly floured surface to a large circle about ⅛ inch thick. Fold the dough in half, and fit it, without stretching, into a buttered 9-inch quiche or tart pan with a removable bottom. Trim off the excess dough, leaving a ¾-inch overhang. Tuck in the overhang, pressing the edges of the dough against the sides of the tart pan and forming a high, smooth border. Chill the shell while you make the filling.

2. Preheat the oven to 350 degrees F, with a rack in the center. In a mixing bowl, whisk the eggs, brown and white sugars, ground almonds and flour until combined. Whisk in the crème fraîche or cream and the vanilla until blended. Place the tart shell on a baking sheet, and pour in the filling. Dot the filling with the butter.

3. Bake until the filling is puffed, lightly golden and nearly set; the center will still be slightly liquid, about 30 minutes.

4. Cool the tart on a wire rack. Serve lukewarm or at room temperature.

Lucky Accident

Originally, this tart was made by first scattering the dry ingredients for the filling into the crust, then pouring the egg-and-cream mixture over and dotting it with butter. When I once whisked everything together by accident, I liked the texture even better.

CARAMEL-WALNUT TART

Nut tarts are a rich indulgence with a long pedigree. From the earliest recorded recipes, endless variations on sweetened nuts in pastry figure in the cookery collections of virtually every culture in the world.

Think of this tart as a sort of lightened pecan pie, but with a slightly bitter edge from the caramel and the walnuts that cuts through the sweet richness. This is a house favorite that I've been baking for years.

Makes one 9- or 10-inch tart; serves about 10

	Rich Tart Dough for 1 shell (page 451)
⅔	cup sugar
¼	cup cold water
1¼	cups heavy cream
1	teaspoon pure vanilla extract
1	tablespoon unsalted butter
2	large eggs, lightly beaten
3	tablespoons sugar
1½	cups coarsely chopped walnuts, plus 10 walnut halves
	Unsweetened whipped cream, for serving

1. Roll out the dough on a lightly floured surface into a large circle about ⅛ inch thick; the crust for this tart should be as thin as possible. Gently fold the dough in half, and fit it, without stretching, into a lightly buttered 9- or 10-inch fluted tart or quiche pan with a removable bottom. Trim off the excess dough, leaving a ¾-inch overhang. Tuck in the overhang, pressing the edges of the dough against the sides of the tart pan and forming a high, smooth border. Chill the tart shell while you preheat the oven to 400 degrees F, with a rack in the center.

2. Line the dough with a sheet of lightly buttered foil, buttered side down. Weigh down with dried beans, rice or pie weights; place the tart on a heavy baking sheet. Bake until the edges are set, 8 to 10 minutes. Very carefully lift out the weights and foil; prick the dough lightly with a fork. Continue to bake until the pastry is very pale gold, about 8 minutes longer. Cool on a wire rack; leave the oven on.

3. Make caramel by combining the sugar and water in a small, heavy saucepan over medium heat and stirring until the sugar dissolves. Use a brush dipped in cold water to wash down

---

Aliter Dulcia
[Other Sweets]

Mix pepper, [chopped] nuts, honey, rue, and raisin wine. Cook in milk and pastry. Thicken with a little egg and bake. Pour honey on top, sprinkle [with filberts], and serve.

APICIUS
DE RE COQUINARIA
[ON COOKERY]
TRANSLATED BY
JOHN EDWARDS
1ST CENTURY A.D.; 1984

any sugar crystals that form around the sides of the pan. Be sure the sugar dissolves completely before the mixture comes to a boil. Boil the mixture, without stirring, until it turns medium amber in color, 5 to 8 minutes; watch carefully to avoid burning.

4. Remove the pan from the heat and very carefully add the cream; the mixture will sputter violently. Return the pan to medium heat and stir to dissolve the caramel. Boil gently, stirring, until lightly thickened, 7 to 8 minutes. Remove the pan from the heat; stir in the vanilla and butter.

5. Whisk the eggs and sugar in a bowl until blended; gradually whisk in the caramel mixture. Stir in the chopped walnuts. Pour the filling into the tart shell. Arrange the walnut halves around the edge. Place the tart on a baking sheet.

6. Bake until set, but still slightly wobbly in the center, about 20 minutes. (A toothpick inserted near the center will emerge not quite clean.)

7. Cool the tart on a wire rack. Remove the tart from the rim of the pan, and serve slightly warm or at room temperature, with unsweetened whipped cream.

RAY'S HOLIDAY NUT TART

This is spectacular—walnuts, hazelnuts and almonds traced with a filigree of glossy, midnight-black chocolate. There's no egg in the filling: The generous quantity of nuts is held together with a toffee-like mixture of honey, cream, butter and sugar. Believe it or not, this isn't killingly sweet; the bourbon cuts through it all. This filling also works beautifully as individual tartlets; see instructions on the next page.

The recipe is from Chris Wissmar, one of the cooks at Ray's Boathouse on Puget Sound, a must for visitors to Seattle.

Makes one 10- to 12-inch tart; serves 10 to 12

Rich Tart Dough for 1 shell (page 451)

FILLING
½	cup packed light brown sugar
1½	tablespoons sugar
¼	cup honey
½	cup (1 stick) unsalted butter
¼	cup heavy cream
1½	cups very coarsely chopped walnuts
¾	cup very coarsely chopped hazelnuts
¾	cup very coarsely chopped almonds
2	tablespoons bourbon
1	teaspoon pure vanilla extract

CHOCOLATE DRIZZLE
1½	ounces semisweet chocolate, chopped (¼ cup)
2	tablespoons heavy cream
1	tablespoon unsalted butter

1. Roll out the dough on a lightly floured surface into a large circle about ⅛ inch thick. Gently fold the dough in half, and fit it, without stretching, into a lightly buttered 10- to 12-inch fluted tart or quiche pan with a removable bottom. Trim off the excess dough, leaving a ¾-inch overhang. Tuck in the overhang, pressing the edges of the dough against the sides of the tart pan and forming a high, smooth border. Chill the tart shell while you preheat the oven to 375 degrees F, with a rack in the center.

2. Line the dough with a sheet of lightly buttered foil, buttered side down. Place the tart shell on a heavy baking sheet. Bake for about 6 minutes. Carefully remove the foil. Continue to bake,

A Chocolate-Tart

Put two Spoonfuls of fine Flour in a Stew-pan, with the Yolks of six Eggs, reserve their White, and mix these with some Milk; add a Quarter of a Pound of rasped Chocolate with a Stick of Cinnamon, some Sugar, a little Salt, and some rasped green Lemon-peel, and let them be a little While over the Fire. After which, put in a little preserved Lemon-peel cut small, and, having tasted whether it has a fine Flavour, let it cool. When cold, mix this with the reserved White of Eggs, beat up to Snow; doing the rest as directed in the other Articles.

This Composition, as also the Marmelade made either with Apples or with Apricocks, may be used with *Tarts, Feuillantines, Genoises, Cakes, &c.*

VINCENT LA CHAPELLE
THE MODERN COOK
LONDON, 1744; 1733

pricking any air bubbles with a fork, until the edges are pale golden, 6 to 8 minutes more. Cool the tart shell on a wire rack; lower the oven temperature to 350 degrees.

3. **FILLING:** In a small saucepan, combine the brown and white sugars, honey and butter. Bring slowly to a boil over low heat. Add the cream and stir in the walnuts, hazelnuts, almonds, bourbon and vanilla. Pour the filling into the partially baked tart shell; it should not be completely full or the mixture may bubble over.

4. Bake until the filling is set, about 15 minutes. Cool the tart on a wire rack.

5. **CHOCOLATE DRIZZLE:** In a heavy saucepan, combine the chocolate, cream and butter over low heat. Heat, stirring often, until the chocolate and butter melt and the mixture is smooth. Remove from the heat. With a teaspoon, drizzle thin lines of the chocolate mixture over the tart. Let stand for about 30 minutes or until set. Serve at room temperature.

⌁ *Variation*

TO MAKE INDIVIDUAL TARTLETS: This amount of filling will fill about twelve 4-inch tartlet molds or a standard muffin tin, with twelve 2½-inch cups. In either case, first line the buttered pans with rounds of the dough. If you roll the dough fairly thin, you can fill the pans without prebaking. Reduce the baking time in step 4 as needed, so that the filling bakes just until set. Drizzle with the chocolate as directed in step 5.

HUNGARIAN CHEESE TART

This simple cheese tart is based on a 19th-century recipe from Károly Gundel, the "father of Hungarian gastronomy." Gundel's restaurant, which he opened in the center of Budapest's City Park in 1910, was recently revitalized by restaurateur George Lang.

Makes one deep 9½-inch tart; serves 8 to 10

	Carlo's Cookie Dough (page 272) or Rich Tart Dough for 1 shell (page 451)
1	pound dry-curd cottage cheese, pressed through a sieve (discard any excess liquid)
¾	cup heavy cream
4	large egg yolks
½	cup plus 2 tablespoons sugar
	Grated zest of 1 lemon
½	teaspoon pure vanilla extract
6	large egg whites
½	cup raisins
1	tablespoon all-purpose flour

1. Roll out the dough on a lightly floured surface into a large circle about ⅛ inch thick. Carefully fold the dough in half, and fit it, without stretching, into a lightly buttered deep 9½-inch pie pan. Trim off the excess dough, leaving a 1-inch overhang. Tuck in the overhang, pressing the edges of the dough against the sides of the pie pan and forming a high, smooth border. Chill the tart shell while you preheat the oven to 400 degrees F, with a rack in the center.

2. Line the dough with a sheet of lightly buttered foil, buttered side down. Weigh down with dried beans, rice or pie weights; place the tart shell on a heavy baking sheet. Bake until the edges are set, about 8 minutes. Very carefully lift out the weights and foil; prick the dough lightly with a fork. Continue to bake until the dough is very pale gold, about 8 minutes longer. Cool the tart shell on a wire rack; lower the oven temperature to 350 degrees.

3. Combine the strained cottage cheese, cream, egg yolks, ½ cup of the sugar, lemon zest and vanilla in a large bowl until blended.

4. Beat the egg whites until they form soft peaks, gradually add the remaining 2 tablespoons sugar and continue beating until stiff but not dry. Stir a large spoonful of the whites into the cottage cheese mixture to lighten it; fold in the remaining whites until nearly combined.

5. Quickly toss the raisins with the flour and add to the cheese mixture; fold gently just until combined. Pour the filling into the tart shell.

6. Bake until the filling is golden and set in the center, about 45 minutes.

7. Cool on a wire rack. Serve warm or at room temperature.

WARM RICE PUDDING TART WITH DRIED FRUIT

At first I thought that this creamy rice pudding in a cookie crust might be an effort to over-refine an old-fashioned childhood favorite. But the pudding puffed to a wonderfully delicate texture and seemed true to the original spirit. Serve it warm.

Makes one 9-inch tart; serves about 8

2½	cups whole milk
⅓	cup sugar
¼	teaspoon salt
⅓	cup long-grain white or Arborio (Italian short-grain) rice
1	tablespoon unsalted butter
1	teaspoon pure vanilla extract
	Carlo's Cookie Dough (page 272; you will need only about ½ of the dough)
2	large egg yolks
¼	cup dried currants or raisins
¼	cup chopped dried pitted dates
2	tablespoons thick apricot jam
⅓	cup heavy cream
1½	tablespoons sugar
1	teaspoon ground cinnamon

1. In a saucepan, combine 2 cups of the milk with the sugar and salt and bring to a boil. Stir in the rice. Lower the heat, cover and simmer gently until the rice is quite tender, about 45 minutes. Stir from time to time as the rice cooks, and adjust the heat as needed to maintain a gentle simmer.

2. Transfer the rice to a bowl, and stir in the butter and vanilla; fluff the rice with a fork. Set aside briefly to cool. *(The rice can be prepared to this point up to 1 day in advance.)*

3. Roll out the dough on a lightly floured surface into a large circle about ⅛ inch thick. Gently fold the dough in half, and fit it, without stretching, into a lightly buttered 9-inch fluted tart or quiche pan with a removable bottom. Trim off the excess dough, leaving a ¾-inch overhang. Tuck in the overhang, pressing the edges of the dough against the sides of the tart pan and forming a high, smooth border. Chill the tart shell while you preheat the oven to 400 degrees F, with a rack in the center.

4. Line the dough with a sheet of foil; weigh down with dried beans, rice or pie weights. Place on a heavy baking sheet. Bake until the edges are set, 8 to 10 minutes. Very carefully lift out the weights and foil; prick the dough lightly with a fork. Continue to bake until the dough is baked through and golden, usually 10 to 13 minutes more. Cool the tart shell on a wire rack. *(The shell can be baked up to 6 hours in advance.)*

5. Shortly before serving time, preheat the oven to 400 degrees. With a fork, gently stir the remaining ½ cup milk, the egg yolks, currants or raisins, dates and apricot jam into the cooled rice. Whip the cream until not quite stiff; fold into the rice mixture. Pour the filling into the tart shell. Combine the sugar and cinnamon and sprinkle over the surface.

6. Bake until the filling is lightly golden and puffed, but still slightly jiggly in the center, about 15 minutes.

7. Cool the tart briefly on a wire rack. Remove the tart from the rim of the pan and serve warm.

Rice Torta

When you have cooked rice well, either in milk or in rich juice, spread it on a table until the moisture has been forced from it; then to this in a bowl blend in a little cheese, well grated, ten well beaten egg whites, sugar with rosewater and one ladle of milk, if you wish. Having dissolved all this in a plate, cook it, observing what we said about the white torta. . . . This is very nourishing and helps the liver. It increases fertility, causes stones, and brings on obstructions.

PLATINA
DE HONESTA VOLUPTATE
[OF HONEST INDULGENCE
AND GOOD HEALTH]
1475

POLISH APPLE TART
(*SZARLOTKA*)

This lovely, homey-looking Polish tart with its fragrant cooked-apple compote filling is topped with a cookie-like dough that's woven into a lattice. It's an old family recipe from my friend Krystyna Mayer in London.

Traditionally, this dessert is served cut into squares. If you are baking it in a tart or springform pan, cut it into wedges.

Makes one 9-inch tart; serves about 8

DOUGH

1⅔	cups all-purpose flour
⅔	cup sugar
½	teaspoon ground cinnamon
	Pinch salt
1	large egg
2	tablespoons vegetable oil or unsalted butter, melted
¼	cup milk
1	teaspoon pure vanilla extract

FILLING

6	large apples (3 McIntosh and 3 tart apples, such as Granny Smith, about 2 pounds total), peeled, cored and cut into 1-inch chunks
¼	cup sugar, plus more for sprinkling
1	teaspoon mixed spices (ground cinnamon, ground mace, ground allspice, fresh-grated nutmeg and/or cloves)

Confectioners' sugar, for sprinkling

1. **DOUGH:** Sift the flour, sugar, cinnamon and salt into a large bowl; make a well in the center. Combine the egg, oil or zbutter, milk and vanilla in a cup; pour into the well. Stir with a fork, pulling in the flour from the sides of the well, until the mixture forms a soft dough. Transfer the dough to a sheet of wax paper and form into a disk; wrap and refrigerate for at least 1 hour while you prepare the filling.

2. **FILLING:** Place the apples in a large skillet over medium heat. Cover and cook until the apples start to sizzle. Lower the heat and cook, stirring frequently, until the apples are very tender,

usually 20 to 25 minutes. Stir in the sugar and spices. Remove the pan from the heat; mash the apples with the side of a large spoon to make a chunky puree. Set aside to cool.

3. Preheat the oven to 350 degrees F, with a rack in the center. Butter a 9-inch fluted quiche or tart pan. (Alternatively, you can use a 9-inch springform pan or a square baking pan.) Pat about ⅔ of the chilled dough into the buttered pan, making an even bottom layer and pressing the dough about 1 inch up the sides of the pan. Spread the filling over the dough.

4. Place a sheet of wax paper on a work surface; flour lightly. Pat out the remaining dough into an even circle about ⅛ inch thick. (This dough is too sticky and delicate to roll easily.) Cut the dough into ¾-inch-wide strips. Carefully lift the strips of dough with a spatula or dough scraper and arrange them in a lattice pattern over the filling, pressing the ends of the strips into the dough on the sides of the pan. Sprinkle the lattice with white sugar.

5. Bake until the pastry is golden, usually 45 to 50 minutes.

6. Cool the tart in the pan on a wire rack. Sprinkle the tart with confectioners' sugar. Serve lukewarm or at room temperature, cut into wedges.

RECIPES

*Fruit-Filled Lattice Torte
with Four Fillings*
Ricotta Strudel from Trieste
*Paul Kovi's Poppy Seed
Strudel*
*Dried Fruit Strudel with
Pear-Brandy Custard
Sauce*
Baked Jam Roly-Poly
*Jack Daniel's Raisin Roll
with Whiskey Sauce*
Quick Puff Pastry Dough
*Carême's Hazelnut Pithiviers
with Orange*
*Greek Custard-Filled Phyllo
Pastry*
Crisp Apple Kolachy
*Pennsylvania Dutch Butter
Semmels*
Hamantaschen
"Mouthfuls" from Abruzzo
*Jewish Honey-Nut Puff
Clusters*
*Apple (or Other Fruit)
Fritters*
French Fruit Puffs

CHAPTER 17

THE WORLD OF PASTRIES

It was also baking day. He loved seeing his mother bent over the enormous kitchen table, elbow-deep in dough, moving to the measured rhythm of making bread. . . . Before, in times of plenty, she had put aside a bit of the dough, added milk, eggs, and cinnamon, and made buns that she stored in a tin—one for each child for each day of the week.

ISABEL ALLENDE, *EVA LUNA*, 1988

When you start to explore strudel, Danish and all of the other baked goods that are neither pie nor cake, you're opening the door to the entire world of pastry. From simple yeast-raised kolachy—buns filled with fruit or cheese—to ethereally flaky puff pastry creations like mille-feuilles (Napoleons) and pithiviers; from Greek and Middle Eastern phyllo desserts (baklava, galaktaboureko) to Wienerbrod, the real Danish pastry made with a yeast dough folded with butter, pastry displays intricate and glorious variations from culture to culture.

Some of these specialties lie outside the realm of this book. Because of the skills required to make them, certain pastries are not baked at home but are purchased from professional chefs (or, in Italy, South America and other Latin-influenced countries, from nuns in convents). Some pastries, such as Wienerbrod or hand-rolled strudel dough, while within the expertise of the experienced cook, are too involved to be included in a homespun collection.

But many other pastries are at the heart of home baking. This small but varied selection from many parts of the world focuses on simple baked items. Also included are the fried pastries that are often the cornerstones of festival celebrations.

With pastry, more than with any other area of baking, it's crucial to get a feel for working with doughs. But as with kneading bread dough, once you've done it once or twice, making pastry becomes easy—or at least manageable. The important thing is to get your hands in the dough—*mettre les mains à la pâte.*

FRUIT-FILLED LATTICE TORTE WITH FOUR FILLINGS
(*MÜRBETEIG*)

This deliciously buttery pastry is from my friends Florence and Walter Heilbronner in New Jersey. The recipe has been in the Heilbronner family for over 100 years.

"*Mürbeteig* is a rich tart pastry, and the fillings depend on the season," Florence says. "I make it with apples in winter, rhubarb in spring, blueberries or peaches in summer and plums in the fall." Instructions for each fruit follow the recipe. (You can double this recipe and bake it in a 13-x-9-inch baking pan.)

⤳ *Makes one 11-x-7 inch pastry, or one 9-inch square; serves 6 to 8*

2	cups all-purpose flour
⅓	cup sugar
1	teaspoon baking powder
	Pinch salt
⅛	teaspoon ground cinnamon
½	cup (1 stick) unsalted butter, softened
1	large egg
1	tablespoon sour cream or yogurt
1	tablespoon grated lemon zest
	Fruit Filling (recipes follow)

1. Place all of the dough ingredients in a food processor and pulse until they start to come together. Gather the pastry on a sheet of wax paper or plastic wrap; wrap and chill for at least 1 hour, or preferably overnight.

Survival Torte

When the Heilbronner family left Nazi Germany just before the outbreak of World War II, this torte was a key element in the family's survival. "In the beginning," Walter Heilbronner explains, "when we didn't have the proverbial pot 'to do anything in,' my mother sold her baked goods to the local old-fashioned grocery store in our Detroit neighborhood.

"She baked her own challah, which I and our kids still bake today, and fruit tortes like this. I worked in another grocery store, and my brother had a newspaper route."

This recipe, says Florence, was "handed down to Walter's mother from her mother. Our children now make it for their families."

2. Preheat the oven to 375 degrees F, with a rack in the center. Generously butter an 11-x-7-inch or 9-inch square baking pan. Divide the dough into 2 equal pieces. Press 1 piece of the dough into the baking pan, forming an even layer over the bottom of the pan and reaching about 1½ inches up the sides.

3. Top the dough with 1 of the fruit fillings below. Roll out the remaining dough slightly less than ⅛ inch thick (this is easiest if you roll it between 2 sheets of wax paper). Cut the dough into ¾-inch-wide strips. Arrange the strips diagonally over the fruit filling, making a crisscross lattice pattern. Mrs. Heilbronner braids the lattice strips; you can simply lay ½ of the strips in one direction, and the remainder across diagonally in the other. Press the ends of the strips into the pastry on the sides of the pan to seal; trim off any excess pastry.

4. Bake until the pastry is golden brown, about 30 minutes.

5. Cool on a wire rack. Serve warm or at room temperature, cut into large squares or rectangles.

Fruit Fillings

PLUM FILLING

1	pound Italian prune plums (about 14)
½	cup sugar
⅛	teaspoon ground cinnamon
1	tablespoon butter, cut into pieces

Cut the prune plums in quarters, leaving them attached at one end. Remove the stones. Arrange the plums, skin sides down, over the pastry in step 3. Sprinkle with the sugar and cinnamon; dot with the butter.

APPLE FILLING

5	tart apples (add a little lemon juice if the apples aren't very tart)
½	cup sugar
	Pinch salt
1	tablespoon cornstarch
⅛	teaspoon fresh-grated nutmeg or ¼ teaspoon ground cinnamon
1	tablespoon butter, cut into pieces

Peel, core and thinly slice the apples. Toss in a bowl with the sugar, salt, cornstarch and spice. Transfer to the pastry-lined pan in step 3; dot with the butter.

PEACH FILLING

5	large ripe peaches (2¼-2½ pounds)
1	tablespoon fresh lemon juice
⅓	cup packed light or dark brown sugar
¼	cup sugar
2	tablespoons cornstarch
	Pinch *each* ground cinnamon and ground mace or fresh-grated nutmeg

Peel the peaches by dipping them into boiling water for 15 seconds; rinse under cold water in a colander and slip off the skins. Halve, stone and slice the peaches into a bowl. Toss with the lemon juice, brown and white sugars, cornstarch and spices. Arrange the peaches over the pastry in step 3.

RHUBARB OR BLUEBERRY FILLING

Use 4 cups fruit (trim and slice the rhubarb; pick over the blueberries), using the ingredients and following the instructions for the peach filling above. Adjust the amount of sugars to taste.

⌒ *Variation*

ALTERNATE SHAPING METHOD: Florence notes that "mürbeteig is also a delicious cookie dough, and I always make a few cookies with leftover scraps, rolling out 2 thin circles, spreading jam in between them and then baking them." (Bake them at 350 degrees, just until the edges are lightly golden.)

RICOTTA STRUDEL FROM TRIESTE
(*STRUCOLO DI RICOTTA*)

A lthough strudel is a Viennese pastry, this one is a specialty of the Jewish community in Trieste, the port near Italy's eastern border. Until World War I, Trieste was within Austria, and the area was the summer retreat of the Austro-Hungarian monarchs.

The cheese filling is scented with lemon and raisins, a characteristic flavor combination of the region. The pastry, simplified by using phyllo dough instead of hand-stretched strudel dough, is dusted with powdered sugar. Strudels can also be drizzled with a mixture of bread crumbs, sugar and melted butter.

⌒ *Makes 2 strudels; serves about 8*

1½	cups (¾ pound) ricotta cheese, preferably fresh (available at Italian markets and some cheese shops)
2	large eggs, separated
½	cup sugar
	Grated zest of 1 lemon
¼	cup golden raisins
3	tablespoons dark raisins
¼	cup (½ stick) unsalted butter, melted
6	sheets frozen phyllo dough, thawed in the refrigerator Confectioners' sugar, for sprinkling

1. Place the ricotta in a dampened cheesecloth-lined sieve set over a bowl; drain in the refrigerator for at least 1 hour.

2. In a bowl, combine the egg yolks, ¼ cup of the sugar and the lemon zest and stir just until blended. Add the drained ricotta; gently fold together without beating or liquefying the cheese. Gently stir in all of the raisins.

3. Beat the egg whites until foamy; gradually add the remaining ¼ cup sugar and continue to beat until the whites form peaks that are almost but not quite stiff. Fold the whites into the ricotta.

4. Preheat the oven to 375 degrees F, with a rack in the center. Line a baking sheet with parchment paper, or lightly brush the sheet with a little of the melted butter. Set the butter and the baking sheet near a work surface. Gently unfold the phyllo dough. Carefully place 1 sheet of phyllo on the baking sheet, covering the

remaining sheets with plastic wrap or a damp kitchen towel (keep the sheets covered as you work to prevent them from drying out). Brush the sheet of phyllo with some of the melted butter. Repeat with 2 more sheets of phyllo, stacking the leaves of dough on top of the first.

5. Gently spoon ½ of the filling along one short side of the dough, mounding it in a line about 1 inch from the short end and 2 inches in from each of the long sides. Gently fold the short end over, covering the filling; brush lightly with butter. Loosely roll up the strudel, ending with the seam down. (It is important not to fold and roll it too tightly to allow room for expansion as the filling bakes.) Gently press the filling toward the center at both ends of roll so the edges of the dough can be folded under. Fold each end as you would wrap a gift, making 2 diagonal folds that form a triangular point, and tucking the point underneath the end of the strudel. Again, don't make the roll too tight.

6. Brush the dough lightly with butter and cut several steam holes on top with the point of a sharp knife. Make another roll, using the remaining phyllo, filling and melted butter. Carefully transfer the strudels to the baking sheet, spacing them a couple of inches apart.

7. Bake until the strudels are lightly golden brown and crisp, 35 to 40 minutes.

8. Transfer the baking sheet to a wire rack; sprinkle the strudels lightly with confectioners' sugar while still warm. Serve warm or at room temperature, sprinkling the strudel with a little more confectioners' sugar. To serve, cut off the ends, and serve two 1-inch-thick slices per portion.

NOTE: The strudel can be rewarmed in a 350-degree oven for 10 to 15 minutes before serving.

Strudel Variations

This strudel is a good example of a Jewish dish that became assimilated into the larger Italian culinary culture. (Other examples are fried artichokes and various eggplant dishes.)

Strucolo can be made in several ways, with a number of fillings. Fried bread crumbs are sometimes scattered over the dough before spooning on the filling, to absorb the filling's moisture and keep the dough crisp. Another strudel is made using a dough based on mashed potatoes, similar to gnocchi dough. And *strucolo* can also be wrapped in a cloth and steamed or simmered in boiling water, instead of being baked.

"Her Magic Hand"

A former professional soccer player, Paul Kovi waxes poetic when the subject turns to his native cooking, specifically that of Transylvania (the region east of Budapest, now part of Romania). But few foods inspire his passion like his mother's poppy seed strudel.

"I have always loved poppy seed strudel," he begins. During Kovi's frugal years as a university student away from home in Kolozsvár, his mother would send him parcels of food. "Every one of those weekly parcels contained several feet of poppy seed strudel, the sole request on my part.

"All my life I have been watching strudel-making," he says. He explains the procedure at length, recalling how he would watch his mother mix the dough, shape it into small loaves and spread melted butter or fat on the tops with "a tiny brush made out of goose feathers." After the dough had rested for 30 minutes, the delicate stretching procedure began.

PAUL KOVI'S POPPY SEED STRUDEL

I have always loved poppy seed strudel," says Paul Kovi, the Hungarian-born co-owner of the Four Seasons restaurant in New York City. "My mother was known to make the *very* best— really it was more of a candy than a strudel."

You can enjoy Kovi's mother's strudel without his mother's magic by making it with purchased phyllo dough. Sprinkling the dough with a mixture of bread crumbs and sugar incorporates a little air between the leaves, keeping them separate.

⟞⟞⟞ *Makes 3 strudels; serves 12 to 14*

POPPY SEED FILLING
1	cup milk
1	large egg yolk
½	cup (1 stick) unsalted butter
½	cup vanilla sugar (see Vanilla Bean, page 22) or ½ cup sugar plus 1½ teaspoons pure vanilla extract Grated zest of 1 lemon
6	ounces ground poppy seeds (about 2⅓ cups; some spice merchants will grind poppy seeds for you; otherwise, you can grind them in a spice mill)
¼	cup minced raisins
1	tablespoon cognac
1	tablespoon dark rum
2	tablespoons honey
1	teaspoon unsweetened cocoa powder
2	egg whites
1	teaspoon sugar

PHYLLO
½	cup unsalted butter, or as needed, melted
¾	cup soft fresh bread crumbs, or as needed
¾	cup sugar, plus more for sprinkling on top
15-18	sheets frozen phyllo dough, thawed in the refrigerator
1	egg, lightly beaten (optional)

1. **POPPY SEED FILLING:** In a nonreactive saucepan, combine the milk, egg yolk, butter, vanilla sugar and lemon zest over low heat. Stir constantly until the mixture comes nearly to a boil. Add the poppy seeds and bring to a full boil. Remove from the heat; set aside to cool for 10 minutes. Stir in the raisins, cognac, rum, honey and cocoa powder.

2. Beat the egg whites with the 1 teaspoon sugar until nearly stiff. Gently fold into the poppy seed mixture.

3. **PHYLLO:** Preheat the oven to 375 degrees F, with a rack in the center. Cover a table or work surface with a clean cloth or large kitchen towel and dust with flour. Line 2 baking sheets with parchment paper or lightly butter them. Set the melted butter and the baking sheets near the work surface. Combine the bread crumbs and sugar. Gently unfold the phyllo dough. Carefully place 1 sheet of phyllo on the cloth, covering the remaining sheets with plastic wrap or a damp kitchen towel (keep the sheets covered as you work to prevent their drying out). Lightly brush the sheet of dough with melted butter; sprinkle lightly with some of the bread crumb mixture. (This keeps the leaves separated during baking.) Repeat the layering, until you have 5 or 6 layers.

4. Spread about ⅓ of the filling along the long edge of the pastry. Gently fold over that side of the dough to cover the filling; brush the exposed pastry with a little more melted butter. Grasp the edge of the cloth and roll up the strudel without making it too tight. Cut the ends of the pastry if necessary to fit the length of the baking sheet; brush with butter to seal. Push down the edges of the pastry with the sides of your palms, keeping the filling inside. If you like, brush the top of the strudel with a little of the beaten egg to make a crisper crust. Sprinkle generously with sugar.

5. Repeat the process, forming 3 strudels. Place them on the baking sheets, spaced slightly apart.

6. Bake the strudel until it is crisp and lightly golden, usually 35 to 40 minutes.

7. Cool on a wire rack to lukewarm before slicing. The strudel can be rewarmed at 350 degrees for 10 to 15 minutes.

"To get ready for this maneuver, she covered our big, rectangular kitchen table with a clean, white oversized tablecloth, which she again floured with abandon. Then she began rolling and pulling the dough carefully, stretching it until it was hanging off the four corners. Circling the table innumerable times, with her hand under the thinning dough, endlessly manipulating, she never made a hole. I stood there mesmerized by the incredible dexterity of her magic hand, admiring the technique, as her wrist rapidly continued its spiral movements in stretching the dough layer farther and ever thinner. Her arms moved like a rotating machine. In the end, the dough was so light and translucent that one could blow it off the table or even read a newspaper placed under it."

Dried Fruit Strudel with Pear-Brandy Custard Sauce

This strudel is not an Old-World specialty, but it's in that spirit. It's made with a flaky sour cream dough that's easy to handle; the filling is a blend of fresh and dried fruits—almost a mince-meat—perfumed with pear brandy. Serve the strudel warm, with a pool of cool custard surrounding each portion.

∽ *Serves 10*

Sour Cream Dough

3	cups all-purpose flour
3	tablespoons sugar
½	teaspoon salt
1	cup (2 sticks) cold unsalted butter, cut into pieces
¼	cup cold solid vegetable shortening, cut into pieces
¼	cup sour cream
⅓	cup cold water, plus more as needed

Filling

¾	cup golden raisins
⅔	cup coarsely chopped pitted prunes
⅔	cup coarsely chopped dried pitted dates
½	cup dried currants
	Grated zest of 1 orange
	Grated zest of 1 lemon
⅓	cup eau-de-vie, such as pear, prunelle, mirabelle or framboise, or dark rum or brandy
2	large firm-ripe pears, such as Bosc (about 1¼ pounds)
1	tablespoon fresh lemon juice
2	tablespoons honey
3	gingersnap cookies, coarsely crumbled (use 4, if the pears are very juicy)
1	teaspoon ground cinnamon
½	teaspoon ground allspice
¼	teaspoon ground cardamom
¼	teaspoon fresh-grated nutmeg
	Tiny pinch freshly ground pepper

Cream or milk and sugar, for glaze
Confectioners' sugar, for sprinkling

"It's your grandma's strudel that's kept this family together."

Grandpa to Peggy Sue
In Francis Ford
Coppola's
Peggy Sue Got Married
1986

Eggnog Custard Sauce (page 609), with 3 tablespoons
pear eau-de-vie or other brandy, or to taste

1. **Sour Cream Dough:** Combine the flour, sugar and salt
in a food processor and pulse to mix. Add the butter and shortening and pulse briefly until the mixture is crumbly. Stir together the
sour cream and cold water; add to the flour mixture and process
just until combined. Add just enough extra cold water, a spoonful
at a time, until the dough begins to clump together but doesn't
yet form a ball.

2. Gather the mixture together (it will be rough at this
point), and transfer it to a lightly floured surface. Roll out into a
12-x-8-inch rectangle. Fold in thirds, as you would a business letter. Rotate the dough 90 degrees; repeat the rolling and folding
once more. Wrap the dough in plastic and chill for at least 1 hour.
(The pastry can be refrigerated or frozen at this point.)

3. **Filling:** In a bowl, combine the raisins, prunes, dates,
currants and orange and lemon zests. Pour the eau-de-vie or other
spirits over the mixture and stir to combine. Set aside to soak for at
least 30 minutes.

4. Peel the pears, quarter, core and cut into ½-inch dice,
tossing with the lemon juice to prevent browning. Add the pears
to the dried fruit mixture, along with the honey, gingersnaps,
cinnamon, allspice, cardamom, nutmeg and pepper. Stir gently to
combine.

5. On a lightly floured surface, roll out the pastry to a
16-x-14 inch rectangle about ⅛ inch thick. Trim off the rough
edges. Divide the rectangle in half, forming two 14-x-8-inch rectangles. Brush the short edges of each rectangle lightly with cold
water. Spoon ½ of the filling in a narrow strip down the center of
each rectangle, leaving about 2 inches uncovered at the short ends.
Bring 1 long side of the pastry up and over the filling. Brush that
edge lightly with cold water; bring the other side up, overlapping
slightly; press gently to seal. With the sides of your palms, press the
filling toward the center to keep it compact. Trim off the ends of
the pastry if necessary, leaving about 1½ inches at each end. Bring
the ends of pastry up and press gently onto the top surface.

6. Place a buttered baking sheet next to the pastry. Gently
ease the strudel onto the sheet, inverting it so that the seam is
down. Repeat with the other strudel, spacing them apart slightly.

Chill while you preheat the oven to 375 degrees F, with a rack in the center.

7. Glaze the pastry lightly by brushing the surface with the cream or milk; sprinkle with a light coating of sugar. Bake until the pastry is golden brown, about 45 minutes.

8. Cool the strudel on the baking sheet on a wire rack until warm. (If you are baking the strudel in advance, rewarm gently at serving time.) To serve, sprinkle the strudel with confectioners' sugar and cut into slices about 2½ inches wide. Surround each slice with a little of the cold custard sauce and pass the remaining sauce separately. (The strudel can be rewarmed at 350 degrees for 10 to 15 minutes.)

BAKED JAM ROLY-POLY

This version, a radically lightened version of English roly-poly, with a buttermilk biscuit dough, bakes until crisp and golden; it's almost like a jam-filled cookie.

⌒ *Serves 6*

1¼	cups all-purpose flour
3	tablespoons sugar
1	teaspoon baking powder
1	teaspoon baking soda
½	teaspoon salt
3	tablespoons cold unsalted butter, cut into pieces
⅔	cup buttermilk or ⅓ cup *each* plain yogurt and low-fat milk, or more as needed
1	large egg
1	teaspoon pure vanilla extract
⅓-½	cup jam, such as raspberry, blackberry or cherry
	Milk, for glaze
	Cinnamon sugar, for sprinkling

1. In a food processor or bowl, combine all of the dry ingredients; pulse or stir to combine well. Cut in the butter until crumbly. In a small cup or bowl, beat the buttermilk or yogurt-milk mixture with the egg and vanilla until smooth. Add to the flour mixture and pulse just until combined, no longer. *(The dough*

*can be made several hours in advance; flour lightly, wrap in plastic
and refrigerate until needed.)*

2. Preheat the oven to 350 degrees F, with a rack in the
center. Line a baking sheet with parchment paper or butter it
lightly. Lay a sheet of wax paper on a work surface; flour lightly.
Pat or gently roll out the biscuit dough to a 9-x-6-inch rectangle
about ¼ inch thick. Beat the jam once or twice in a small bowl,
and spoon it gently over the dough, leaving a ½-inch border all
around. Starting with a long side, roll up the dough, so that the
jam forms a spiral pattern. Transfer the roly-poly to the baking
sheet, seam side down. Brush the dough lightly with the milk;
sprinkle with the cinnamon sugar.

3. Bake until golden brown and baked through, 30 to 35
minutes.

4. Cool on the pan on a wire rack. Serve warm or at room
temperature, slicing with a serrated knife. (The ends are reserved
for the cook.)

JACK DANIEL'S RAISIN ROLL WITH WHISKEY SAUCE

Filled with nuts and raisins, this pastry roll is served with a smooth, warm sauce flavored with Jack Daniel's whiskey. The recipe comes from Miss Mary Bobo's Boarding House in Lynchburg, Tennessee. "This is a wonderful old Tennessee dessert that we still serve," says the proprietress, Lynne Tolley.

Serves 8 to 10

1	cup raisins
⅓	cup (5⅓ tablespoons) unsalted butter, melted
1	cup sugar
1	teaspoon ground cinnamon
½	cup chopped pecans
	Basic Pie Dough for a 1-crust pie (page 449)

WHISKEY SAUCE

¾	cup sugar
¼	rounded teaspoon baking soda
¼	cup plus 2 tablespoons buttermilk
2	teaspoons light corn syrup
6	tablespoons (¾ stick) unsalted butter
3	tablespoons Jack Daniel's whiskey, or to taste

1. In a small saucepan, combine the raisins with water to cover and bring to a simmer over medium heat. Remove from the heat and drain thoroughly. Transfer the raisins to a small bowl, add the butter, sugar, cinnamon and pecans and mix until blended. Set the mixture aside to cool completely.

2. Preheat the oven to 375 degrees F, with a rack in the center. Roll out the dough on a lightly floured surface into a 10-x-7-inch rectangle. Spread the raisin filling evenly over the entire surface of the dough. Starting with a short end, roll up, jellyroll-style. Press the seams to seal; fold under the ends to enclose the filling. Place the roll, seam side down, on a buttered baking sheet.

3. Bake until golden brown, about 30 minutes. Cool on a wire rack.

4. **WHISKEY SAUCE:** Meanwhile, in a small saucepan, combine the sugar, baking soda, buttermilk, corn syrup and butter. Bring to a boil over medium heat. Continue boiling until the

mixture reaches the soft-ball stage, 235 degrees F, usually about 5 minutes. (If you don't own a candy thermometer, drop a small spoonful of the hot syrup into a cup of ice water; the mixture will form a soft mass when pressed between your fingers.) Remove from the heat. Cool to lukewarm, about 15 minutes. Stir the whiskey into the sauce.

5. Cut the raisin roll in slices, and serve warm, with the sauce.

QUICK PUFF PASTRY DOUGH

This puff pastry is made in a flash. Because there is more butter than flour by weight, it rises beautifully, even though it's made without all of the traditional rests between turns. It freezes well.

Makes about 3 pounds

3½	cups all-purpose flour
½	cup cake flour (not self-rising)
1	teaspoon salt
2¾	cups (5½ sticks) cold unsalted butter, cut into ½-inch cubes
1	cup cold water, or as needed

1. Sift the flour and salt into a large bowl. Cut in the butter, using a pastry blender, 2 knives or your fingers. Leave the butter in large chunks (about ¼ inch). Stir in just enough cold water to hold the dough together. At this point, the dough will look lumpy and not blended.

2. Transfer the dough to a floured surface and roll it out to a 16-x-12-inch rectangle. Use a pastry scraper to fold the dough in thirds, as you would fold a business letter. Rotate the dough 90 degrees, so the open side is to your right; this is called a single turn. Give the dough 3 more single turns, rolling it out to a 16-x-12-inch rectangle, folding it in thirds, and rotating 90 degrees for each turn. The dough will become smoother and more homogenous with each turn.

3. Divide the dough into 3 equal portions, cutting straight through the dough with a sharp knife. Wrap each portion individually in plastic wrap. Chill for at least 2 hours or overnight before rolling out.

Swan of Cream Puff

Listen and I'll tell you what Miss Nell served at the party," Loch's mother said softly, with little waits in her voice. She was just a glimmer at the foot of his bed . . .

"An orange scooped out and filled with orange juice, with the top put back on and decorated with icing leaves, a straw stuck in. A slice of pineapple with a heap of candied sweet potatoes on it, and a little handle of pastry. A cup made out of toast, filled with creamed chicken, fairly warm. A sweet peach pickle with flower petals around it of different-colored cream cheese. A swan made of a cream puff. He had whipped cream feathers, a pastry neck, green icing eyes. A pastry biscuit the size of a marble with a little date filling." She sighed abruptly.

"Were you hungry, Mama?" he said.

EUDORA WELTY
GOLDEN APPLES
1949

571

CARÊME'S HAZELNUT PITHIVIERS WITH ORANGE

Glamorous and very professional-looking, this traditional mainstay of French pâtisserie is actually a cinch to put together. It's nothing but two scallop-edged disks of puff pastry sandwiched around a rich nut paste filling. This version is based on Antonin Carême's recipe for *Gâteau de Pithiviers aux Avelines* from his monumental *Le Pâtissier Royal Parisien*, which first appeared in 1815.

Makes one 10-inch cake; serves about 12

5	ounces (about 1 generous cup) hazelnuts, with skins
½	cup sugar
	Grated zest of 1 orange
3	tablespoons unsalted butter, softened
1	large egg
1	large egg yolk
2½	tablespoons Grand Marnier or other orange liqueur
¼	teaspoon almond extract
	Pinch salt
⅓	recipe Quick Puff Pastry Dough (page 571), or 1 pound store-bought puff pastry, preferably all-butter
1	egg yolk, beaten with 1 tablespoon water, for glaze Confectioners' sugar, for sprinkling

1. Preheat the oven to 350 degrees F. Scatter the hazelnuts over a baking sheet and toast until fragrant, about 10 minutes. Cool slightly; rub off most of the hazelnut skins with a kitchen towel.

2. In a food processor, combine the nuts, sugar and orange zest; process until powdery. Add the butter, egg, egg yolk, Grand Marnier, almond extract and salt and process until smooth. Scrape the filling into a bowl; cover with plastic wrap and chill until fairly firm, at least 30 minutes.

3. Divide the puff pastry into 2 pieces, one slightly larger than the other. Roll out the smaller piece on a lightly floured surface to a neat round about ¹⁄₁₆ inch thick. Using a 10-inch plate or a tart pan bottom as a guide, cut out a 10-inch circle of pastry; reserve the trimmings. Roll out the larger piece of pastry ⅛ inch thick and cut out an 11-inch circle.

4. Place the smaller circle of pastry on an ungreased baking sheet. Spoon the filling into the center of the pastry, forming a neat 5-inch disk. Lightly brush the outer rim of the pastry with cold water. Carefully place the larger round of pastry on top, centering it and gently pressing down at the edges, around the mounded filling to seal it in compactly. Cut a hole in the center of the pastry with a sharp knife. Cut a decorative piece of pastry from the trimmings to surround the hole; you can also cut out shapes such as leaves. (Reserve the trimmings, stacking them together, for another use.) Use the tip of a sharp knife to score the top decoratively, without cutting through. Cut the edges in a scallop pattern. Brush the pastry with a thin layer of the egg yolk mixture, without letting any drip over the edges. Chill the pastry for 15 minutes or longer.

5. Preheat the oven to 450 degrees F, with a rack at the center; remove the top rack and keep nearby. Brush the pastry again with the egg yolk wash. Place the pastry in the oven and immediately lower the heat to 400 degrees. Bake for 15 minutes.

6. Lower the heat to 350 degrees and continue to bake until the pastry is golden brown, 20 to 25 minutes longer.

7. Remove the baking sheet from the oven and raise the heat to 450 degrees. Position the cool oven rack in the top third of the oven. Sprinkle the Pithiviers with confectioners' sugar and return it to the oven. Bake just until the sugar melts and forms a shiny golden glaze, 3 to 4 minutes (watch carefully to prevent burning).

8. Cool the Pithiviers briefly on a wire rack, then serve warm or at room temperature (do not refrigerate).

Lucky Pastry

Seen in pâtisserie windows throughout France, Pithiviers is named for its town of origin, in the Orléans region. To celebrate Twelfth Night, a bean is baked in the filling; whoever finds it will be blessed with good luck all year long.

Ground nut fillings like this one date back to the Middle Ages, when ground almonds and sugar were used to make marzipan (or marchpane, as it was also known), which probably originated in Italy.

In France, La Varenne's seminal *Le Vray Cuisinier François* (Paris, 1653) includes *tourtes* (open tarts) of pistachios, *massepin* and *franchipanne*—all similar to the mixture here. By the time Carême developed his recipe in 1815, this type of nut mixture was already old-fashioned.

GREEK CUSTARD-FILLED PHYLLO PASTRY

(*GALAKTABOUREKO*)

This Greek family dessert, with farina-thickened custard between layers of buttered phyllo leaves, can be linked in spirit to both American custard pies and French mille-feuilles (Napoleons).

The thin sheets of phyllo dough look as though they're difficult to work with. But once you set out your ingredients neatly and get the system down, things move quickly and smoothly. The recipe can be halved and baked in an 8-inch square pan.

Makes about 2 dozen pieces

8	cups (2 quarts) milk
¾	cup sugar
	Grated zest of 1 orange
⅔	cup farina (Cream of Wheat)
4	large eggs
1	tablespoon pure vanilla extract
2	tablespoons fresh orange juice
½	cup (1 stick) unsalted butter, or as needed, melted
1	pound (1 package) frozen phyllo dough, thawed in the refrigerator

SPICED LEMON SYRUP

1	cup sugar
1	cup water
	Zest of 1 large lemon (grated or in strips)
2	cinnamon sticks
4	whole cloves
	Juice of 1 large lemon

1. Rinse a large, heavy saucepan or casserole with cold water; shake dry (this helps prevent the milk from sticking). Bring the milk, sugar and orange zest to a boil over medium heat. Whisking constantly, add the farina in a thin stream. Cook, stirring constantly, until thickened slightly, about 3 minutes. Remove from the heat and cool the custard mixture, stirring from time to time to prevent a "skin" from forming. (If you like, hurry the cooling along by placing the pan in a large bowl of ice water.) If making ahead, cover, pressing wax paper or plastic wrap directly on the surface, and chill for up to 2 days.

2. Add the eggs, one at a time, whisking to blend well. Stir in the vanilla and orange juice.

3. Brush a large 13-x-9-x-3-inch baking dish with a little of the melted butter. Carefully unfold the phyllo dough and place the stack on a work surface. (Don't worry if some sheets tear as you work.) Cover with a slightly dampened kitchen towel. Carefully arrange a layer of phyllo dough over the bottom and sides of the pan. If necessary, place the sheets alternately at one end, then at the other, overlapping slightly so that the bottom of the pan is evenly covered and the dough overhangs the edges of the pan slightly. Lightly brush the layer of dough with melted butter. Repeat, stacking 6 or 7 layers on top, buttering each sheet lightly before adding the next.

4. Preheat the oven to 350 degrees F, with a rack in the center. Pour the cooled custard over the phyllo. Repeat the layering, using 7 or 8 layers of the phyllo over the filling and brushing each layer with melted butter. Any phyllo trimmings can be tucked between 2 of the top layers. The very top layer should be smooth and even. With scissors, trim the edges neatly. Brush the edges lightly with cold water to seal. Brush the surface with a final coating of melted butter. With a sharp knife, score the top layer of pastry into diamond shapes, without cutting through to the filling.

5. Bake until the top is golden brown, about 45 minutes. Transfer the pan to a wire rack.

6. **SPICED LEMON SYRUP:** While the pastry is baking, combine the sugar and water in a nonreactive saucepan. Add the lemon zest, cinnamon sticks and cloves and bring mixture to a boil. Reduce the heat and simmer for 5 minutes. Remove from the heat; stir in the lemon juice.

7. Strain ⅓ of the syrup slowly over the baked pastry while it is still hot. Wait for the syrup to be absorbed and strain ½ of the remaining syrup on top. When absorbed, strain the remaining syrup on top. Set aside to cool to room temperature.

8. Cut the cooled pastry into diamond shapes and serve at a cool room temperature.

CRISP APPLE KOLACHY

Kolachy (also called *kolacy* or *koláčky*), fruit-filled buns or pastries with many variations, are a Czech specialty. The dough can be leavened with yeast or baking powder, or it can be rolled and folded to make a pastry.

This kolachy is made with a flaky cottage-cheese dough filled with apples. The recipe is from cookbook author Beatrice Ojakangas, who lives in Duluth, Minnesota, where German, Scandinavian and Czech baking traditions still thrive. Beatrice is a first-rate baker and has introduced many Americans to Scandinavian specialties.

 Makes 16 pastries

FLAKY COTTAGE-CHEESE PASTRY
1 cup (2 sticks) cold unsalted butter
2 cups all-purpose flour
½ teaspoon ground mace or fresh-grated nutmeg
1 cup creamed-style cottage cheese
Ice water, if needed

APPLE FILLING
4 medium-size tart apples, such as Granny Smith
¼ cup (½ stick) unsalted butter
½ cup sugar
½ teaspoon ground cinnamon

1 egg, beaten with 2 tablespoons milk, for glaze
Pearl sugar (see note) or coarsely crushed sugar cubes, for sprinkling

1. **FLAKY COTTAGE-CHEESE PASTRY:** In a bowl, cut the butter into the flour until the mixture resembles coarse crumbs. Add the mace or nutmeg and toss together. Add the cottage cheese and mix until blended, pressing the dough into a ball. If the mixture does not cohere, add 1 to 2 tablespoons ice water.

2. Dust the dough lightly with flour and turn out onto a pastry cloth or a lightly floured surface. Working on a pastry cloth is the traditional way; you can also work with the dough on a lightly floured sheet of wax paper. This dough is slightly sticky, but be patient, and don't add too much flour, or the finished product will be less delicate. Using a rolling pin as a bat, pound out the dough as flat as possible; roll out into a 16-inch square. Fold into thirds, as you would fold a business letter.

3. Pound the dough again to flatten it. Roll out again into a 12-x-7-inch rectangle and fold in thirds as above, starting from a short side and tucking in the uneven edges, if necessary (the edges should be fairly even at this point). Wrap the dough in plastic and refrigerate for 30 minutes.

4. **APPLE FILLING:** Meanwhile, peel, core and slice the apples ¼ inch thick. Melt the butter in a large skillet over medium heat. Add the apples and sauté until tender-crisp, about 3 minutes. Sprinkle with the sugar; remove from the heat and cool to room temperature. Sprinkle with the cinnamon.

5. Roll out the dough to a 16-inch square. Cut into 16 four-inch squares. Place the squares on a baking sheet and chill again until the dough is firm enough to handle.

6. Preheat the oven to 350 degrees F. Lightly butter 2 baking sheets.

7. Divide the apple filling among the pastry squares, leaving any syrup in the bowl. For each square, lift 2 opposite corners of the pastry over the filling and overlap them by ½ inch; pinch to make a packet with 2 open ends. Place the packets on the baking sheets. Brush the top of each pastry packet with the egg and milk mixture; sprinkle with the sugar.

8. Bake until the kolachy are golden, 15 to 20 minutes.

9. Remove the kolachy from the pans and cool on wire racks. Serve lukewarm or at room temperature.

NOTE: Pearl sugar, a coarse-grained sugar that holds its shape when baked, can be ordered by mail from Kitchen Krafts, (800) 298-5389; www.kitchenkrafts.com.

Kolachy and Coffee

Variations on kolachy are found in Vienna, Czechoslovakia, Germany and Scandinavia, as well as in Pennsylvania Dutch country, the parts of the eastern and middle United States settled by Germans.

"I've had these kolachy served to me by my longtime friend Marie Mihelick, who is of Czech background," Beatrice Ojakangas says. "She serves them with coffee, either around 4 o'clock in the afternoon or in the morning at a *kaffeeklatsch*. They're also sold in bakeries in Minnesota."

PENNSYLVANIA DUTCH BUTTER SEMMELS

These Pennsylvania Dutch specialties are puffy pillows of light, yeasty dough kept moist by the addition of potato. This version is adapted from a recipe from Sue Hoffman, a cooking teacher in Carlisle, Pennsylvania.

Begin making the pastry the night before, so it can rise overnight. For the lightest, most delicate texture, be sure to let the shaped pastries rise fully.

Makes about 2 dozen pastries

1	package active dry yeast
½	cup lukewarm water
3	tablespoons solid vegetable shortening
10	tablespoons (1 stick plus 2 tablespoons) unsalted butter
½	cup plus ⅓ cup sugar
1	large egg
2¾	cups all-purpose flour
1	teaspoon kosher salt or ¾ teaspoon table salt
1	small potato (about 3 ounces), cooked, peeled and mashed or grated
2½	teaspoons ground cinnamon

1. Dissolve the yeast in the warm water; set aside until foamy. In a food processor or a bowl, combine the shortening, 3 tablespoons of the butter, the ½ cup sugar, the egg, 1 cup of the flour and the salt; process for 15 seconds or mix until smooth. Add the yeast mixture and the potato and process for 20 seconds, or stir vigorously with a wooden spoon for about 2 minutes. Cover the bowl with an oiled sheet of plastic wrap, oiled side down (if using a food processor, just cover the work bowl with the plastic), and let rise at room temperature overnight. (If the mixture rises to more than 2½ times its volume, you can stir it down and refrigerate it until needed.)

2. The next day, stir down the batter. Return it to the food processor, if you are using one. Add the remaining 1¾ cups flour and process for 20 seconds, or beat with a wooden spoon until the dough is smooth and slightly sticky, 3 to 4 minutes.

3. On a lightly floured surface, roll out the dough to a neat 12-x-8-inch rectangle ½ inch thick. Cut the dough into 24 neat 2-inch squares. Butter 2 baking sheets. Place each square of dough

on a baking sheet and bring the 4 corners into the center, pinching the corners together and twisting them into a topknot.

4. Place a thin pat of butter (about ½ teaspoon) over the center of each pastry. Cover the baking sheets with plastic wrap and let rise until nearly doubled in bulk, usually 1¼ to 1½ hours.

5. About 15 minutes ahead, preheat the oven to 400 degrees F. Bake the semmels until lightly golden, 10 to 12 minutes (don't overbake). Transfer the baking sheets to wire racks to cool. Melt the remaining 3 tablespoons butter; brush the warm pastries with the butter. Combine the remaining ⅓ cup sugar with the cinnamon; sprinkle it over the pastries. Serve warm.

HAMANTASCHEN
(JAM-FILLED "HAMAN'S POCKETS")

These three-corner pastries, originally served to celebrate Purim and now baked year-round in Jewish bakeries, are filled with thick prune or apricot preserves, with poppy seeds, or sometimes in New York, with chocolate. Thick raspberry jam is tasty and looks good, too.

Many recipes for hamantaschen are made with a pareve dough (that is, without meat or dairy ingredients), usually using oil instead of butter. The cream cheese dough used here is flaky and buttery, with the flavor of a good cookie, not just a bland wrapper.

Makes about 2 dozen pastries

¼	cup (½ stick) unsalted butter, softened
4	ounces (½ cup) cream cheese, softened
½	teaspoon pure vanilla extract
	Grated zest of 1 orange
¾	cup sugar
1	large egg
2	cups all-purpose flour
1	teaspoon baking powder
	Pinch salt
1	cup thick raspberry jam or other filling, or as needed

1. With an electric mixer, cream together the butter, cream cheese, vanilla and orange zest. Slowly beat in the sugar; beat in the egg. Add the flour, baking powder and salt and beat just until incorporated; do not overmix. Pat the dough into a disk; wrap in plastic or wax paper. Chill the dough for at least 30 minutes.

2. Preheat the oven to 350 degrees F. Lightly butter 2 baking sheets; set aside.

3. Roll out the dough on a lightly floured surface to a thickness of slightly more than ⅛ inch. Using a cutter or a saucer as a guide, cut the dough into 4-inch rounds. With a pastry brush or a fingertip, brush the edges of each round lightly with cold water. Mound 2 level teaspoons of jam or other filling in the center of each circle of dough. The folding is easy if you picture an equilateral triangle within each circle of dough. Fold up about ¾ inch of dough at the bottom of the round, forming a straight, horizontal bottom to the triangle. Fold in about ¾ inch of dough on each side, forming a triangle with a point at the top. The dough will not meet in the center; the filling will show. Pinch together the edges of the dough at the 3 points of the triangle. Transfer the filled rounds carefully to the baking sheets.

4. Bake just until the hamantaschen are pale gold on top, 30 to 35 minutes.

5. Cool on a wire rack. Serve at room temperature. These will keep well for up to 3 days.

Free-for-All

This Eastern European Jewish pastry (the name may actually be a variation on *mohntaschen*, or poppy seed pockets) is the best-known food of the free-for-all Purim celebration, which commemorates the last-minute saving of Persian Jews from destruction. The pastries are supposed to represent the hat worn by Haman, counselor to the king and the villain in the Purim story. Purim is a time to take gifts of food to the homes of friends and to drink wine—according to the Talmud, "until you no longer know the difference between the names of Mordecai and Haman."

"MOUTHFULS" FROM ABRUZZO
(*BOCCONOTTI ABRUZZESI*)

Bocconotti ("mouthfuls") were a specialty of my grandmother," explains Abruzzo native Anna Teresa Callen, author of several cookbooks. The nut-and-wine-filled pastry is traditionally baked in a tallish fluted mold similar to a brioche mold. You can bake the pastries in brioche molds or in a muffin tin.

~ *Makes about 12 pastries*

DOUGH
- 2 cups all-purpose flour
- ½ cup sugar
- ½ cup (1 stick) cold unsalted butter, cut into pieces
- 2 large eggs
  Cold water, if needed

TOASTED ALMOND FILLING
- 1 cup (about 6½ ounces) whole almonds, skins on
- ⅓ cup sugar
- ¼ cup plus 2 tablespoons unsweetened cocoa powder
  Grated zest of 1 orange or lemon
  Pinch ground cinnamon
- ⅔ cup sweet Marsala, Vin Santo or sweet sherry, or as needed

  Cinnamon sugar or cinnamon confectioners' sugar, for sprinkling

1. **DOUGH:** In a food processor, pulse the flour, sugar and butter until crumbly. Add the eggs and pulse until the dough begins to come together. Gather the dough into a ball (adjust the consistency if necessary, adding a little cold water if the dough is dry, or sprinkling it with a little more flour if it is too sticky). Press into a disk, wrap in plastic or wax paper and chill for at least 30 minutes.

2. **TOASTED ALMOND FILLING:** Preheat the oven to 375 degrees F. Scatter the almonds over a pie pan or shallow baking dish and toast until fragrant and the skins have darkened slightly, 8 to 10 minutes. Set aside briefly to cool for 5 to 10 minutes; leave the oven on.

"This Habit of Visiting"

In Italy," Anna Teresa Callen explains, "there is this habit of visiting, when people come to wish you well. So you serve this pastry with tea or coffee or chocolate. In wintertime, it's always chocolate.

"My grandmother made these *bocconotti* when I would come back from wherever I was because they were a favorite of mine. She taught me how to cook. On a rainy afternoon, she'd say, 'Let's make 6 eggs of pasta.' I'd ask her, 'How much flour do you use?' and she'd say, 'All the flour the eggs want to drink.' And if you make it that way, you'll never make a mistake."

3. In a food processor, grind the almonds with the sugar until powdery. Add the cocoa, citrus zest, cinnamon and enough of the wine to make the mixture creamy but not too wet.

4. Generously butter 12 small fluted brioche or a 12-cup muffin tin. Roll out the pastry on a lightly floured surface to an even thickness of ⅛ inch. Using a cutter or a saucer as a guide, cut out 12 rounds of pastry large enough to line the bottom and sides of the molds you're using. Gently fit the pastry rounds into the molds. Pour the filling into the shells, dividing evenly and filling the shells to a little below the rims of the molds.

5. Roll out the remaining dough. Cut out 12 rounds of pastry large enough to top each pastry shell. Set the tops in place and pinch the rims of each pastry to seal. (Leftover dough can be saved for another use.)

6. Place the *bocconotti* on a baking sheet or place the muffin tin in the oven and bake until the pastry is lightly golden brown, about 25 minutes.

7. Cool the pastries on a wire rack. Sprinkle the tops with cinnamon sugar or cinnamon confectioners' sugar and serve at room temperature.

JEWISH HONEY-NUT PUFF CLUSTERS
(*TAIGLACH*)

One of the most unusual Jewish pastries, this consists of nuts and dozens of tiny baked puffs of dough, simmered in honey and glued into mounds, crowns or pyramids. The honey sets so that it's no longer sticky.

Taiglach are served at Jewish New Year in the fall or to break the Yom Kippur fast. *Taiglach* (or *taygleh*), "little bits of dough" in Yiddish, is the Ashkenazic (Eastern European) name; Sephardic Jews call this *pinyonati*, derived from the name for pine nuts.

At Jewish bakeries, *taiglach* are made in a large ring or pyramid shape. For easier serving at home, form them into 3-inch balls, as recommended by the late Jennie Grossinger, whose kitchen advice was taken on faith by two generations of Jewish-American homemakers.

Makes about 18 clusters

1¼	cups all-purpose flour
½	teaspoon baking powder
	Pinch salt
2	large eggs, well beaten
2	tablespoons vegetable oil
⅔	scant cup honey, preferably dark
¼	cup plus 2 tablespoons packed light brown sugar
½	teaspoon ground ginger
¼	teaspoon fresh-grated nutmeg
¼	teaspoon ground cinnamon
1	cup hazelnuts, walnuts or blanched whole almonds or a combination
¼	cup candied cherries (optional)

1. Preheat the oven to 350 degrees F, with a rack in the center. Sift the flour, baking powder and salt into a bowl. Make a well in the center, and add the eggs and oil. Gradually work the flour into the eggs, mixing until the dough holds together.

2. Break off pieces of the dough and roll into ropes about as thick as pencils. Cut the dough into ½-inch lengths and place on a lightly oiled baking sheet.

3. Bake until the pieces of dough are lightly browned, about 20 minutes. Cool the puffs on the pan on a wire rack.

4. In a wide skillet or a casserole, bring the honey, brown sugar, ginger, nutmeg and cinnamon to a boil over medium heat. Reduce the heat and simmer, uncovered, for about 8 minutes. Drop the puffs into the simmering syrup and simmer, turning them with a slotted spoon once or twice as they cook, for 5 minutes. Stir in the nuts and simmer, stirring frequently, for 5 to 10 minutes longer. To test for doneness, drop a spoonful of the mixture onto a wet plate; if it holds together, it's done. If not, cook further until it coheres. Stir in the cherries, if using.

5. Turn out the mixture onto a wet baking sheet. Let cool until the mixture can be handled easily. With palms moistened in cold water, shape the mixture into 3-inch balls. Serve at room temperature. To store or give as gifts, wrap each ball in a square of wax paper or cellophane and twist to close or tie with a ribbon.

The Many Forms of Taiglach

This pastry has close relatives. Very similar are the *strufoli* made by Neapolitan-Americans at Christmas, little puffs (*chiacchiere*, "chatters") that are baked or fried and studded with candied fruit and colored sprinkles. Even the French dessert *croquembouche* (literally, "crunches in the mouth"), cream-filled puffs glued with caramel into a monumental pyramid, is in the same tradition.

ABOUT FRIED PASTRIES

To the delight of children all over the world, homemakers break off small pieces of dough, drop them into sizzling hot fat, fry them to a crisp golden frizzle, drain them and sprinkle the crusty morsels with a snowdrift of confectioners' sugar. Made with bread dough or cream puff dough, these fried pastries are universal. Call them what you like, these loops, twists or puffs of fried dough are essentially the same:

- *chrustchiki* (loops; Poland)
- *fritelle* (puffs or strips; Italy)
- *crostoli* (flat strips; Friuli, Alto Adige and throughout the Veneto in Italy)
- *bugie* ("rags"; Piedmont region, Italy)
- *zacarelle* ("strips of paper"; Abruzzo, Italy)
- *zeppoli* (served on the feast day, San Giuseppe, on March 19th; Naples, Italy)
- *guanti* ("gloves"; Naples, called *wandi* in Rhode Island's Italian-American community)
- *sfingi* (Sicily)
- *heizenblozen* (Yiddish, from Eastern Europe)

All these pastries are part of Carnival, of which the last day is Mardi Gras or Shrove Tuesday, sometimes known as "pancake day," when foods rich in oil are consumed wildly before the weeks of Lenten austerity to come.

On the feast days, Italian-Americans still stage traditional festivals in the streets of New York's Little Italy. And they still fry mountains of dough in vast cauldrons, (though today's vendors are more likely to be non-Italian entrepreneurs). These feasts have introduced fried pastries to a wide audience—though unfortunately, most are not at their best, which is why many people associate them with indigestion.

Greaseless frying requires care. When done well, crisply fried food—whether fruit fritters or French fries—is hard to resist.

Follow the detailed tips in these recipes to ensure perfect fried pastries.

APPLE (OR OTHER FRUIT) FRITTERS

This recipe is virtually intact from the 1655 original (see next page). Fry these fritters carefully, and they'll come out crisp, greaseless and delicious. Try making them with other fruits, too; just about any fruit works well. Plan to serve them as soon as possible after frying.

Makes about 1½ cups batter, enough for about 4 cups fruit; serves about 8

- ⅔ cup ale or beer
- 2 large eggs, separated
- 1½ teaspoons melted butter or vegetable oil
- 3 tablespoons sugar
- ¾ teaspoon ground ginger
- ½ teaspoon pumpkin pie spice (or a mixture of ground cinnamon, fresh-grated nutmeg and ground allspice)
- ⅜ teaspoon salt
- 1 cup all-purpose flour
- 4 cups sliced trimmed apples, or any combination of banana slices, diced mango or papaya, grapes, fresh figs, pineapple
  Vegetable oil, for deep-frying
  Cinnamon confectioners' sugar, for sprinkling

1. In a small bowl, whisk together the ale or beer, egg yolks, melted butter or oil, sugar, ginger, pumpkin pie spice and salt; whisk in the flour just until blended. Cover the bowl with a kitchen towel and let the batter rest for about ½ hour.

2. Cut the fruit into bite-size pieces. For best results, drain on paper towels to absorb any excess moisture.

3. Pour oil into a large, deep casserole, heavy sauté pan or electric deep-fryer to a depth of 1 inch. With an electric mixer, beat the egg whites until stiff but not dry; fold the beaten whites into the batter.

4. Preheat the oven to 250 degrees F, to keep the fritters warm. Have the batter and the prepared fruit near the stovetop or deep-fryer. Alongside, set out a platter or jellyroll pan lined with a double thickness of paper towels, for draining the fritters.

5. Heat the oil over medium heat to about 365 degrees F. (If you don't own a frying thermometer, test by throwing a cube of bread or bread crumbs into the oil; the bread should sizzle gently but steadily and brown in about 45 seconds.) Adjust the heat as needed to maintain a steady frying temperature. Be sure to let the oil reheat before adding each new batch.

6. Begin dipping each piece of fruit in the batter, coating lightly and slipping it into the fat. Fry the fritters, a few at a time (don't crowd or they won't cook properly), turning them halfway through, until golden brown, usually about 30 seconds. Remove with a slotted spoon, spatula or a mesh skimmer to the paper-towel-lined platter, draining all possible oil back into the pan. Transfer the fritters to the oven while preparing the remaining batches.

7. Sprinkle the hot fritters with cinnamon confectioners' sugar and serve at once.

To Make Fritters

Take halfe a Pint of Sack, a pint of Ale, some Aleyeast, nine Eggs, yelks and whites, beat them very wel, the Eggs first, and then altogether, put in some Ginger and Salt, and fine flower, then let it stand an houre or two, then shred in the Aples when you are ready to fry them, then suet must be all Beef suet or halfe Hoggs suet tried out of the leaf.

W.M.
A Servant to Queen
Henrietta Maria,
Wife of Charles I
of England
*The Queens Closet
Opened*
London, 1655

French Fruit Puffs
(*Beignets Soufflés*)

These French puffs of dough (choux paste) are made with any of several fruits and quickly deep-fried in oil, where they instantly expand to airy nothings. They also can be served with warm apricot jam or Raspberry Sauce (page 617).

This classic pastry is a cinch to make. The detailed instructions below may look complicated. They aren't.

Makes about 3½ dozen small puffs; serves 6 to 8

Choux Pastry
- ½ cup water
- ¼ cup (½ stick) unsalted butter, cut into pieces
- 1 teaspoon sugar
- ¼ rounded teaspoon salt
- ½ cup all-purpose flour
- 2-3 eggs, as needed

Fruit

Fresh ripe fruit alone or in combination (pineapple, mango, banana, papaya, apples, pears), trimmed and cut into bite-size pieces
Sugar, if needed
Cognac or eau-de-vie (optional)

Vegetable oil, for deep-frying
Confectioners' sugar or cinnamon confectioners' sugar, for sprinkling

1. **Choux Pastry:** In a heavy saucepan, heat the water, butter, sugar and salt over medium heat until the water is boiling and the butter is melted. Add the flour all at once and stir vigorously with a wooden spoon; the mixture will come together to form a smooth paste that resembles mashed potatoes. Cook, stirring, to dry out the mixture slightly, about 3 minutes. Remove from the heat; scrape the mixture into a bowl.

2. With an electric mixer, beat the paste at medium speed for a few moments to cool slightly. Add 2 eggs, one at a time, and beat until blended. Turn off the machine. Test the consistency by lifting a spoonful of the mixture; it should form a peak that stands and then droops slightly. Add more egg, a bit at a time, to reach

this consistency; the mixture usually takes about 2½ eggs, but the amount can vary. Cover and refrigerate, if not using immediately.

3. FRUIT: If the fruit is very juicy, drain the excess juices on paper towels. Sprinkle with sugar and/or a little cognac or eau-de-vie, if you like.

4. Preheat the oven to 250 degrees F, to keep the puffs warm as they are fried. Place the bowl of batter and the bowl of fruit near the stovetop or the deep-fryer. Alongside, set out a jellyroll pan lined with a double thickness of paper towels, for draining the puffs.

5. Pour oil into a wide, heavy sauté pan or an electric deep-fryer to a depth of about 1 inch. Heat over medium heat to a temperature of 365 to 375 degrees F. (If you don't own a frying thermometer, test by throwing a cube of bread or bread crumbs into the oil; the bread should sizzle gently but steadily and brown in about 45 seconds.) Adjust the heat as needed to maintain a steady frying temperature. Be sure to let the oil reheat before adding each new batch.

6. Lift a piece of the fruit with a teaspoon, and dip it into the batter, using a second teaspoon to envelop the fruit in about ½ teaspoonful of the batter. Gently slip the batter-coated fruit into the oil and form more puffs, frying just enough at a time so they are not crowded. Turn the puffs over once halfway through with a slotted spoon or skimmer, until golden on all sides, usually 2 to 3 minutes total. Lift them from the oil as they are done, draining all possible oil back into the pan; drain on the paper-towel-lined pan. Keep the puffs warm in the oven as you fry the remaining batches.

7. Sprinkle the puffs with confectioners' sugar or cinnamon confectioners' sugar and serve warm.

RECIPES

*Ice Cream Social Peach Ice
    Cream*
*Grandmother's Lemon
    Custard Ice Cream*
*Espresso-Cinnamon Ice
    Cream*
*English Brown Bread Ice
    Cream*
*Alsatian Spiced Honey Ice
    Cream*
*Slushy Melon Ice with
    Cointreau*
Classic Italian Coffee Ice
*Coarse-Crystal Wine Ice
    with Sangría Granita
    Variation*
Hazelnut Semifreddo
Cappuccino Semifreddo
Frozen Cappuccino
*Trumps Peanut Brittle
    Sundae*

CHAPTER 18

FROZEN DESSERTS

People went straight for the meat, of course [in a grab-all-you-can supermarket contest]. But once they had it in their baskets they allowed themselves some long-ago forgotten pleasures like peaches. Or ice cream. There is food that fills you up and then there is food that tastes so good in the mouth it makes a person feel human again. It brings back memories. It reminds a guy of other things.

SARAH SCHULMAN,
PEOPLE IN TROUBLE, 1990

Because freezing ice cream requires special equipment—or snow, which often had to be hauled at great expense—it has always been considered a "special treat" dessert.

The "frigid niceties" served by Procope Cultelli, an Italian, at his coffeehouse in the Rue de l'Ancienne Comédie in Paris in the 1660s, are said to have paved ice cream's way to worldwide popularity. (More than 300 years later, you can still visit the Café Procope today.)

Here in America, Dolley Madison is generally credited with introducing ice cream at her husband's second inaugural ball in 1812. Actually, ice cream had already been enjoyed half a century earlier. In 1744, a "curious" dessert called strawberry ice cream was served at the Governor's mansion in Annapolis, Maryland. And records show that George Washington bought a "cream machine for ice" in 1784 to use at Mount Vernon and that Thomas

Jefferson brought back an ice cream recipe from France in 1789—well before Dolley Madison's days as first lady.

In the days before electric freezers, making ice cream and keeping it cold involved both ice and machinery—not an easy process. As it freezes, ice cream must be kept moving, or it will take on a rock-hard rather than a creamy texture. Before the crank machine was patented in 1848, ice cream was made in various contraptions in which the cream mixture was placed in an ice pail, where it was stirred by hand within a larger container of ice. Some early machines consisted of nested pewter basins—tall cylinders placed one inside the other. The cream was placed in the smaller cylinder, ice and salt in the larger. Periodically, the cylinder containing the cream was opened and stirred. Sometimes actual snow was packed around the cylinder.

In the late 1700s, French immigrants sold ice cream—still a curiosity for the American public—at shops in New York and Philadelphia. After visiting New York City, Jean Anthelme Brillat-Savarin wrote in *The Physiology of Taste*:

> Women in particular found so novel a taste irresistible, and nothing could be more amusing than the little grimaces they made when eating [ices]. They were utterly at a loss to conceive how a substance could be kept so cold in a temperature of ninety degrees.

At the turn of the 19th century, ice cream was still a rare luxury. But by the 1820s and 1830s, it had become a democratic treat for all levels of American society. The ice cream social of the late 1800s was a genteel gathering, where ice cream was served with cookies, fruits, cakes and lemonade. By the time the sundae acquired its name in 1899, the soda fountain had become an American institution; today, we can hardly imagine its place in small-town American life. How many dreams, plans, flirtations and crushes were launched gazing across the tops of a tall ice cream soda? As the drugstore soda jerk puts it in the children's book *Soda Jerk*, "Tips are okay. But the secrets are better."

Today, each one of us eats nearly 17 quarts of ice cream and frozen yogurt each year, whether licking a dripping cone in the summer, tucking into a sundae piled high with hot fudge and whipped cream, or spooning it right from the Häagen-Dazs container while watching late-night television or movies on the VCR. But despite its wide availability, ice cream, perhaps more than any other dessert, continues to be an out-of-the-ordinary treat, connoting instantaneous happiness. In many rural households, churning ice cream in a hand-cranked freezer packed with ice and rock salt remains a summer ritual, and a family outing to get ice cream cones still makes an occasion of a hot summer night.

One change from the past is evident, however: making homemade ice cream is now a snap—both faster and easier than in the days when cranking was an arduous chore, however fun the results may have been. Thanks to a new generation of machines, particularly the electric kind that do the churning for you, the range of ice creams has expanded dramatically to include innumerable combinations of fresh fruits at their peak, unusual flavors like guava and gianduja (chocolate-hazelnut) and low-fat variations like ice milk, frozen yogurt and sorbets.

International influences, too, are apparent: Frozen desserts no longer mean just ice cream. Sorbets, which were rediscovered when nouvelle cuisine became the vogue, are among the most refreshing of these, bursting with fruit flavors, with no fat at all. The Italian granita, a coarser ice, is easy to make. A semifreddo (literally, "half-cold" in Italian) is between an ice cream and a mousse in texture—frozen, but still soft enough to spoon. Semifreddi are made in the traditional flavors (vanilla, chocolate, coffee, various fruits), but also veer off into wonderful variations: hazelnut, zabaglione, Marsala, cappuccino. Many of these frozen desserts are made without any equipment more special than a mixing bowl and a whisk.

Choosing the Right Machinery—or None at All

*Y*ou can now buy home ice cream makers ranging from simple plug-in machines to the chilled canister type to self-refrigerating home churners that turn out frozen desserts in minutes. All of them work fine, and you should follow the manufacturer's instructions for the specifics.

I don't make ice cream often, so I am happy with a small Waring machine. I like it because it uses ice cubes rather than crushed ice, and table or kosher salt instead of rock salt. Friends rave about the expensive Simac Gelateria machine, which they say is worth it.

But if you don't want to invest in an ice cream machine, you can still make your own frozen desserts at home. Just use the **still-freezing method:**

1. Place the prepared ice cream or frozen dessert mixture in 1 or 2 shallow metal pans, such as cake pans or ice-cube trays without the dividers. Place in the freezer and freeze until firm around the edges, but still slushy in the middle, usually 20 to 45 minutes.

2. Remove the pans from the freezer and stir the firm and liquid portions of the mixture together with a wooden spoon. Return to the freezer until the mixture is again firm around the edges. Repeat 1 or 2 more times, freezing the mixture until it is uniformly frozen the last time. Let the dessert soften briefly in the refrigerator before serving, if necessary.

Ice cream and sherbets made this way won't be quite as smooth as those that are churned continually by machine. But you'll still be able to enjoy refreshing homemade frozen desserts, with the full flavors of ingredients you choose yourself.

ICE CREAM SOCIAL PEACH ICE CREAM

"Like eating a frozen peach," said the little boy, licking it off the spoon as I brought this ice cream, just churned, out onto our sunny deck one summer.

When the peaches start to ripen, it's a signal to get out the ice cream maker. What better way to get through the summer heat than to cool off with hand-cranked ice cream, bursting with chunks of ripe peaches?

This formula is based on a recipe from my old friend Barbara Tropp, owner of China Moon Café in San Francisco and cookbook author extraordinaire. The ice cream is made with an uncooked, no-egg base, for a smooth, light texture. It's clean-tasting and not too sweet—like spooning up frozen peaches and cream.

✐ Makes about 1 quart

3	medium-size fully ripe peaches, peeled, stoned and chopped (about 1½ cups)
¼	cup plus 2 tablespoons sugar
1½	teaspoons pure vanilla extract
2	cups (1 pint) half-and-half, or 1½ cups whole milk plus ½ cup heavy cream

1. In a bowl using a potato masher or wooden spoon, break up the peaches with the sugar and vanilla until coarsely mashed. Stir in the half-and-half or milk and cream. Taste and add more sugar if needed.

2. Pour the mixture into an ice cream maker and freeze according to the manufacturer's directions. (You can also still-freeze this ice cream, though it will not be as smooth; see instructions, page 593.)

3. When the ice cream is thickened and frozen, scrape it into a plastic container, cover and freeze for at least 1 hour. Let the ice cream soften slightly in the refrigerator before serving.

GRANDMOTHER'S LEMON CUSTARD ICE CREAM

This recipe was served at the church ice cream festival in Sunbury, Pennsylvania, in the 1800s," Dorothy McCulloch told me, as we walked through her garden along the east banks of Narragansett Bay in Rhode Island. "It's my grandmother's recipe," she said, "and has been a favorite of my family for many years."

Why has lemon ice cream disappeared? What could be more refreshing than cool citrus? This is a good example of old-fashioned ice cream made with a cooked custard base.

Makes 1½ to 2 quarts

Finely grated zest of 3 lemons
½ cup fresh lemon juice
¾ cup sugar
2 cups (1 pint) half-and-half, or 1½ cups whole milk plus ½ cup heavy cream
4 large egg yolks
Pinch salt
2 cups (1 pint) heavy cream

1. In a small bowl, combine the lemon zest and lemon juice; stir in the sugar with a fork. Let stand for at least 30 minutes. The sugar helps release the flavor of the zest.

2. Scald the half-and-half or milk and cream in a large non-reactive saucepan over medium heat; set aside.

3. In a nonreactive bowl, whisk the egg yolks and salt with an electric mixer until well blended. Slowly add about ½ of the scalded half-and-half to the eggs and stir gently; return the mixture to the saucepan.

4. Cook the custard over medium-low heat, stirring constantly, until thick enough to coat the back of a spoon (do not let the custard boil, or it will curdle). Immediately remove the pan from the heat; strain the custard into a large bowl. Stir in the lemon mixture and the heavy cream. Lay a sheet of wax paper or plastic wrap directly on the surface to prevent a skin from forming, and refrigerate until thoroughly chilled.

Lemon Ice Cream

Pare the yellow rind from three lemons, put it into a porcelain skillet, with the beaten yolks of eight eggs, a quart of rich sweet cream, and simmer it gently till the flavor of the lemons is extracted: then strain it into a bowl, and stir in it while warm three quarters of a pound of powdered loaf sugar. When it is cold, stir gradually into it the juice of the three decorticated lemons, and freeze it as directed. . . . As much of the sweetness is lost by the process of freezing, ice creams require more sugar than the common cold creams.

LETTICE BRYAN
THE KENTUCKY HOUSEWIFE
CINCINNATI, 1839

5. Pour the custard into an ice cream maker, and freeze according to the manufacturer's directions. (You can also still-freeze this ice cream, though it will not be as smooth; see instructions, page 593.)

6. When the ice cream is thickened and frozen, cover it and place it in the freezer until nearly firm. Let soften slightly in the refrigerator before serving.

ESPRESSO-CINNAMON ICE CREAM

The Italians love their ice cream. In fact, they could be considered responsible for its arrival (via the French) in the United States. Every village in Italy has its gelateria, where locals line up for gelato, granita, sorbetto or semifreddo.

This is a simple but rich ice cream, intense with dark-roasted coffee bean flavor that is infused into the cream.

Makes about 1½ quarts

¾	cup espresso coffee beans
2¼	cups milk
1	cup heavy cream
2	cinnamon sticks
1	vanilla bean, split lengthwise, or 1½ teaspoons pure vanilla extract
4	large egg yolks
⅔	cup sugar

1. Scatter the coffee beans in a dry skillet and set over medium heat. Roast, stirring constantly, until the beans begin to release their oils, about 10 minutes (do not let the beans darken). Cool the beans briefly. Grind them coarsely in a coffee grinder or an electric spice mill.

2. In a heavy saucepan, combine the coffee, milk, cream, cinnamon sticks and vanilla bean (if using vanilla extract, do not add it now). Bring to a simmer; turn off the heat. Cover and let the mixture steep for at least 30 minutes.

3. Strain the mixture through a fine sieve into the rinsed-out saucepan. Bring the liquid nearly to a boil over medium heat.

4. Meanwhile, in a bowl, whisk together the egg yolks and sugar until blended. Very gradually whisk the hot milk mixture into the egg yolks. Return the mixture to the saucepan and cook the custard over medium-low heat, stirring almost constantly, until it thickens lightly and coats the back of a spoon, about 8 minutes (do not boil). Strain the custard into a clean bowl. Scrape the seeds out of the vanilla bean into the custard or stir in the vanilla extract. Lay a sheet of wax paper or plastic wrap directly on the surface to prevent a skin from forming and refrigerate until chilled.

5. Pour the mixture into an ice cream maker, and freeze according to the manufacturer's directions. (You can also still-freeze this ice cream, though it will not be as smooth; see instructions, page 593.) Pack the ice cream into a plastic container and freeze at least 1 hour before serving. If necessary, let the ice cream soften slightly in the refrigerator before serving.

ENGLISH BROWN BREAD ICE CREAM

This ice cream is tastier than it might sound. After a long stay working in England, I brought back the recipe, handwritten in an elegantly spidery backhand by an English friend. What I did not realize is how old the idea is, dating back more than a century.

Toasting the bread crumbs and brown sugar (the original recipe calls for coarse Demerara sugar) in a hot oven until caramelized is what gives the ice cream its spectacular flavor. The toasted crunch holds up even after freezing—similar to today's "cookies and cream," but with a deeper caramel flavor and more texture. This is closer to a frozen mousse than a true ice cream.

⟿ *Makes 1 generous quart*

2	cups loosely packed cubed whole-wheat bread, with crusts
¼	cup plus 2 tablespoons packed light brown sugar or Demerara sugar
2	large eggs, separated (for a note on egg safety, see page 23)
6	tablespoons superfine or regular sugar
1⅔	cups heavy cream
2	teaspoons pure vanilla extract

1. Preheat the oven to 450 degrees F. In a food processor, grind the bread to fine crumbs. Add the brown sugar and pulse once or twice to combine. Spread the mixture over a baking pan and bake, stirring several times, until the sugar is lightly caramelized and the bread crumbs are toasted, about 6 minutes. Set aside to cool.

2. With an electric mixer at medium-high speed, beat the egg whites until frothy. Gradually add 3 tablespoons of the sugar and beat until the whites form soft peaks; set aside. In a separate bowl, with the electric mixer still at medium-high speed, beat the egg yolks, the remaining 3 tablespoons sugar, the cream and the vanilla until the mixture is fluffy but not stiff.

3. Stir the crumb-sugar mixture into the cream mixture until combined. Fold in the meringue mixture just until blended. Transfer the mixture to a large plastic container, cover tightly and freeze for at least 2 hours. Let the ice cream soften slightly in the refrigerator before serving.

In 1807, Maria Eliza Rundell included a "Brown Bread Ice" in *A New System of Domestic Cookery*, directing her readers to soak "a small proportion" of stale brown bread, grated "as fine as possible," in cream for "two or three hours, sweeten and ice it."

ALSATIAN SPICED HONEY ICE CREAM

Flavoring cream with honey and spices is at least as old as the ancient Greeks, for whom honey was the principal sweetener. This ice cream is fragrant and mellow; try it with a slice of toasted Helmstetter Kugelhopf moistened with eau-de-vie syrup (page 374).

Makes about 1 quart

1	cup milk
½	cup fragrant honey, such as lavender honey
4	large egg yolks
1	cup heavy cream or crème fraîche (page 624)
1	teaspoon ground cinnamon, or to taste
	Large pinch fresh-grated nutmeg, or to taste
	Pinch ground cloves, or to taste

1. In a heavy nonreactive saucepan, scald the milk with the honey. The mixture may begin to curdle; that's OK, but do not boil hard. Meanwhile, in a bowl, whisk together the egg yolks, cream or crème fraîche, cinnamon, nutmeg and cloves.

2. Very gradually whisk the hot milk-honey mixture into the egg yolk mixture; correct the seasonings, if necessary. Pour the mixture back into the saucepan and set over medium-low heat. Cook the custard, stirring almost constantly, until it thickens slightly and coats the back of a spoon, about 8 minutes (do not boil). Strain the custard into the rinsed-out bowl. Lay a sheet of wax paper or plastic wrap directly on the surface to prevent a "skin" from forming and refrigerate until chilled.

3. Pour the mixture into an ice cream maker and freeze according to the manufacturer's directions. (You can also still-freeze it, though it will not be as smooth; see instructions, page 593.) Pack the ice cream into a plastic container and freeze at least 1 hour before serving. If necessary, let it soften briefly in the refrigerator before serving.

Variation

HALVAH ICE CREAM: My friend Helen Mayer suggests adding a bar of crumbled halvah to any basic ice cream recipe, such as the one above, and steeping a vanilla bean in the milk— "amazingly delicious," she says.

On Honey

There is among the bees great care and solicitude about making honey . . . The best and sweetest honey is made from thyme. . . . As for the honey from the region of the Black Sea . . . which, according to some authorities contains some poisonous quality, it is pointless to discuss it, since we are concerned with that which makes for pleasure.

PLATINA
DE HONESTA VOLUPTATE
[OF HONEST INDULGENCE
AND GOOD HEALTH]
1475

599

Cold Comfort

SLUSHY MELON ICE WITH COINTREAU

A quick, easy fruit refresher for a hot summer's night, whether made in an ice cream freezer or still-frozen by hand. Use whatever type of melon you like; just make sure that they are verging on overripe.

Makes 3 to 4 cups

⅔ cup sugar
1¾ cups cold water
2 very ripe cantaloupes, halved and seeded
    Juice of 1 lime
2 tablespoons Cointreau or other orange-flavored liqueur, or more to taste

1. Combine the sugar and water in a small saucepan. Bring to a boil, stirring to dissolve the sugar. Boil gently, uncovered, without stirring, for 5 minutes. Pour the syrup into a bowl and chill until cold.

2. Scoop the melon flesh into a food processor or blender. Add the lime juice and puree until nearly smooth. Transfer to a 9-inch square metal baking pan (or other shallow pan) and stir in the syrup and Cointreau. Cover and place the pan in the freezer.

3. Freeze until the edges are frozen but the center is still soft, usually about 45 minutes. Beat the crystals into the soft center with a wooden spoon. Return to the freezer.

4. Repeat the stirring process 2 more times (at 30- to 45-minute intervals), or until the ice has crystallized uniformly into a slushy mixture. Transfer to a plastic container, cover and store until needed. (This ice can also be frozen in an ice cream maker, following the manufacturer's directions.)

5. To serve, soften the ice, if necessary, in the refrigerator for about 20 minutes. Serve in wine glasses or dessert bowls.

CLASSIC ITALIAN COFFEE ICE
(*GRANITA DI CAFFÈ CON PANNA*)

This ice tastes like crystalline frozen espresso, eaten with a spoon, and it's very easy to make. The coffee is brewed strong, sweetened to taste and then frozen into chunky, flavor-packed crystals.

～ *Makes about 3 cups*

3	cups hot strong-brewed espresso
½-⅔	cup sugar
	Whipped cream, for serving

1. Sweeten the coffee with the sugar to taste while hot, stirring to dissolve the sugar. Cover and chill thoroughly in the refrigerator.

2. Pour the coffee into a pie pan or ice-cube trays without the dividers. Carefully place in the freezer until the mixture is firm around the edges (usually after about 45 minutes).

3. Cut it into coarse crystals with 2 knives, blending the firm and liquid portions. Return to the freezer. Repeat the cutting and blending 1 or 2 more times.

4. The last time, the mixture should be crystallized throughout. Cut the ice into coarse, even crystals (you can also scrape it with a fork); spoon it into wine glasses, top with a spoonful of whipped cream, and serve.

COARSE-CRYSTAL WINE ICE WITH SANGRÍA GRANITA VARIATION

This is a basic method for making wine-flavored ices. Use a fork to scrape off long, thin crystals and gently pile them into wine glasses just before serving. Though you can use any white wine, slightly fruity ones work best. The recipe is followed by a more "pop" version with the refreshing red-wine and citrus flavors of Spanish sangría.

Makes about 1 quart

⅔ cup sugar
¾ cup cold water
   Zest of 1 lemon, removed in strips with a vegetable peeler
   Juice of 1 lemon
   Juice of ½ orange
1 bottle (750 ml) slightly fruity white wine, such as Gewürtztraminer, Riesling, Chenin Blanc or Champagne

1. Combine the sugar, water and lemon zest in a small saucepan over medium-low heat, stirring until the sugar dissolves. Bring the syrup to a boil. Pour the syrup into a bowl and chill until cold. Discard the zest.

2. Combine the cold syrup with the citrus juices and wine. Transfer the mixture to shallow metal baking pans or ice-cube trays; the mixture should be no deeper than about ½ inch. Freeze until the edges are firm, but the center is still liquid, usually 1 to 1½ hours.

3. With 2 forks, cut together the firm and liquid portions of the ice, forming large crystals. Freeze again until firm.

4. At serving time, cut the ice into coarse, even crystals (you can also scrape it with a fork). Gently spoon into tall wine glasses or goblets. Serve immediately.

⌒⌒ *Variation*

SANGRÍA GRANITA

¾	cup sugar
¾	cup cold water
	Zest of 1 orange, removed in strips with a vegetable peeler
2	cinnamon sticks
	Juice of ½ orange
1	bottle (750 ml) dry red wine, such as Spanish Rioja, Beaujolais or Merlot
	Very thin orange slices, for garnish

Follow the instructions for the Coarse-Crystal Wine Ice, adding the orange zest and cinnamon sticks to the syrup with the lemon zest in step 1. Discard the zests and cinnamon sticks before adding the orange juice and wine. Serve the granita garnished with the orange slices.

HAZELNUT SEMIFREDDO

Semifreddo—literally "half-cold"—is a type of Italian gelato with a texture somewhere between ice cream and mousse. It's frozen enough to refresh but yields readily to the touch of the tongue—suave, sublime sensuality.

Semifreddi can be flavored with fruits, nuts, caramel and characteristic creamy flavors, such as eggs and Marsala, crushed amaretti (almond macaroons), or chocolate and hazelnuts.

For this nut-flavored semifreddo, milk is infused with roasted hazelnuts until they give up all their flavor.

⌒⌒ *Makes about 1 quart*

1¾	cups (about 7 ounces) hazelnuts, with skins
2½	cups milk, or as needed
6	large egg yolks
½	cup sugar
⅔	cup heavy cream, well chilled

1. Preheat the oven to 375 degrees F. Spread the hazelnuts in a single layer in a large baking pan. Roast until fragrant and just beginning to brown, about 10 minutes. Set aside to cool slightly. Rub the hazelnuts gently in a kitchen towel to remove some of the loosened skins.

2. Coarsely chop and set aside a few hazelnuts for the topping, if desired. Finely grind the remaining nuts with 2 tablespoons of the sugar in a food processor, being careful not to overprocess them, or they will become oily.

3. Bring the milk to a boil in a heavy saucepan over medium-high heat. Stir in the ground hazelnuts and simmer over very low heat, stirring occasionally, for 3 minutes. Remove from the heat; cover and let stand for about 1 hour.

4. Line a colander with dampened cheesecloth and place it over a large bowl. Strain the nut milk through the colander. Gather the edges of the cheesecloth and carefully squeeze the hazelnuts to extract as much liquid as possible. Discard the hazelnuts. Measure the hazelnut milk. You should have 2 cups; add milk, if necessary. Transfer the milk to a nonreactive saucepan, and bring to a boil over medium heat.

5. Whisk the egg yolks and the remaining 6 tablespoons sugar in a bowl just until blended. Gradually whisk in the hot milk; return the mixture to the saucepan. Cook over low heat, stirring constantly, until the custard thickens enough to coat the back of a spoon; do not boil. Strain the custard into a clear bowl. Lay a sheet of wax paper or plastic wrap directly on the surface and refrigerate until cold.

6. Pour the custard into a shallow metal 8- or 9-inch square baking pan. Freeze, uncovered, until the mixture is set around the edges but still partially liquid in the center, 45 minutes to 1 hour.

7. Scrape the custard into the bowl of a food processor and process briefly until the mixture is nearly smooth. Return it to the shallow pan. Repeat the freezing and processing procedure 1 or 2 more times.

8. Beat the cream until it forms soft peaks. Fold the custard into the whipped cream; return the mixture to the metal pan. Cover and freeze again until very cold but still light and smooth, about 45 minutes. The mixture should be soft enough to spoon out easily. Serve, topped with the reserved chopped toasted hazelnuts, if desired.

CAPPUCCINO SEMIFREDDO

Freezing coffee is a deft way to savor after-dinner coffee and a refreshing dessert, all in one. This luscious two-layered frozen coffee semifreddo is from cookbook author Michele Scicolone. Michele lightly cooks the whipped egg mixture by whisking in hot sugar syrup. "It makes a smoother semifreddo," Michele explains, "and prevents it from getting grainy when frozen."

⌒ *Serves 8*

½	cup sugar
¼	cup water
4	large eggs
⅛	teaspoon ground cinnamon
¾	cup heavy cream, well chilled
¼	cup confectioners' sugar
1	tablespoon instant espresso powder dissolved in 1 teaspoon warm water
	Chocolate-covered coffee beans (available at specialty food shops), for garnish (optional)

1. Line a 9-x-5-inch metal loaf pan with a large sheet of plastic wrap, leaving a 2-inch overhang at the short ends. Chill the pan in the freezer.

2. In a small saucepan, combine the sugar and water; simmer, stirring, until the sugar dissolves.

3. While the syrup simmers, beat the eggs in a bowl with an electric mixer at medium-high speed until they are thick and pale, 3 to 4 minutes. Continue beating, adding the hot syrup in a very thin stream (try to pour it into the middle of the egg mass). Beat until the mixture has doubled in volume and is cool to the touch, 5 to 8 minutes. Stir in the cinnamon.

4. Whip the cream with the confectioners' sugar until not quite stiff. Gently fold the whipped cream into the egg mixture. Pour ½ of the mixture into the chilled pan; freeze for 45 minutes.

5. Meanwhile, stir the dissolved espresso into the remaining egg mixture. Cover and chill while the paler mixture is in the freezer. Gently fold the espresso mixture together if it has separated; pour it over the frozen cream mixture. Cover the pan with plastic wrap and return it to the freezer. Freeze for 8 hours or overnight.

6. Unmold the semifreddo onto a serving platter; carefully peel off the plastic wrap. Arrange the optional chocolate-covered coffee beans decoratively on top. Slice and serve.

FROZEN CAPPUCCINO
(A BLENDER DRINK)

Wandering around the Italian-American neighborhood that is Boston's North End one June afternoon when the temperature was 98 degrees, I stopped in at Caffè dello Sport. Sitting there in the cool of the café, listening to quiet conversations in Italian, I could have been in any village in southern Italy. I asked if they could make an iced cappuccino. They could and did, and it was the best anywhere. Based on my watching the counterman as I drank two tall ones, here is the recipe.

⌁ **Serves 2**

1	cup hot strong-brewed coffee, preferably espresso or another dark roast
	Sugar or superfine sugar, to taste
⅔	cup whole milk
6	ice cubes
	Unsweetened cocoa powder, for sprinkling

1. Sweeten the coffee to taste while it's still hot. (If the coffee has cooled, sweeten it with superfine sugar, which dissolves instantly.) Pour the coffee into a heatproof container and refrigerate until cold. Chill 2 tall glasses, about 12 ounces each, in the refrigerator.

2. Remove the glasses from the refrigerator, and pour ½ cup of the coffee in each. Place the milk and ice cubes in a blender and blend at high speed until frothy. Top each glass with the milk mixture, dividing it evenly and shaking the froth on top of each drink as you pour. Sprinkle with cocoa and serve immediately.

TRUMPS PEANUT BRITTLE SUNDAE

Michael Roberts, cookbook author and chef-owner of Trumps Restaurant in Los Angeles (now closed), has devised the sundae of your dreams.

Makes about 4 cups peanut brittle, enough for 16 sundaes—if it lasts that long

PEANUT BRITTLE

1½	cups sugar
¼	cup cold water
½	pound raw shelled peanuts
½	teaspoon baking soda
¼	teaspoon salt

Warm Caramel Sauce (page 614)
Premium vanilla ice cream
Whipped cream (optional)

1. **PEANUT BRITTLE:** Butter a baking sheet; set aside. Combine the sugar and water in a heavy saucepan over medium heat. Cook, stirring and brushing any sugar crystals from the sides of the saucepan with a brush dipped in cold water, until all of the sugar is dissolved but before the syrup comes to a boil. Boil the syrup gently, without stirring, until it turns amber, 8 to 10 minutes. Immediately turn off the heat. Carefully stir in the peanuts, baking soda and salt (the mixture will foam up). Quickly pour onto the buttered baking sheet and spread out evenly. Set aside to cool.

2. When cool, break the brittle into coarse pieces. Transfer to a plastic bag and break into ½-inch pieces with a hammer or other heavy object. Cover and store at room temperature.

3. Rewarm the caramel sauce slightly, if necessary.

4. For each sundae, spoon about 2 tablespoons of the caramel sauce into the bottom of a deep wine goblet or sundae glass. Top with a scoop of the ice cream; sprinkle with 2 tablespoons of the peanut brittle. Spoon 1 tablespoon of caramel sauce over the brittle; top with a second scoop of ice cream, 2 tablespoons more peanut brittle and a dollop of the optional whipped cream. Drizzle with 1 tablespoon of caramel sauce. Serve at once.

Ice Cream Thoughts

There was a shop in my little town that made its own ice cream, hand-dipped chocolates, nonpareils and peanut brittle. I remember being taken in for a sundae on a Friday night when I was about 6. I silently watched packs of teenagers troop in after a basketball game, thinking that I'd never get to be as big as those breezy, confident 16-year-olds.

RECIPES

Eggnog Custard Sauce
Low-Fat Custard Sauce
Cider-Lemon Sauce
John's Mother's Lemon Sauce
    with Lemon Slices
Schrafft's Hot Fudge Sauce
Warm Caramel Sauce
Hard Sauce
Foamy Sauce
Raspberry Sauce
Chunky Double-Berry Sauce
Southern Wine Sauce for
    Spongecake
Spiced Sour Cherry Compote
    for Ice Cream
Pot-au-Feu Praline Sauce
Nesselrode Sauce
Orange Curd
Lemon Cream
Sweet Muscat Sabayon
Crème Fraîche

CHAPTER 19

DESSERT SAUCES

". . . melt butter, sack and sugar for sauce."
ELIZA SMITH,
THE COMPLEAT HOUSEWIFE, LONDON, 1758

When I was about 4 years old, I would agonize for hours about how to spend a dime at the Breslows' candy store/soda fountain down at the end of our small-town street. Just behind the marble counter, each of the fountain's gleaming knobs promised a different syrup to flavor an ice cream soda or drizzle over ice cream: chocolate, strawberry, cherry, butterscotch, "wet nuts" (walnuts in syrup) and vanilla syrup for cream soda. A separate metal compartment held my favorite—hot fudge.

Spooned over ice cream, a slice of plain cake or fresh fruit, a luscious homemade sauce can transform a humdrum dessert into something special. Today, some of the stars of the contemporary dessert sauce world are actually old-fashioned favorites: crème anglaise, the smooth English custard; caramel sauce, made by simmering caramelized sugar with cream until smooth; and the ubiquitous raspberry puree, now joined by sauces made from mango, passion fruit and other fruit exotica. And chocolate and hot fudge sauce will always be a welcome topping to just about anything.

While many traditional toppings for puddings, such as hard sauce, were little more than flavored and sweetened softened or melted butter, today's sauces tend to be lighter in fat and more pronounced in flavor. Many of the sauces in this chapter are based on fruit rather than butter and cream.

EGGNOG CUSTARD SAUCE

This is the classic boiled custard sauce, lightened and slightly less sweet than traditional recipes. Unmatched for versatility, it is delicious on warm puddings. For an even simpler dessert, pass a pitcher of cool custard sauce along with a bowl of assorted fresh fruits. The English serve this sauce on virtually everything, including chocolate cake: No wonder the French call it crème anglaise.

Makes about 2½ cups

- 2   cups whole milk
- 1   vanilla bean, split lengthwise, or 1½ teaspoons pure vanilla extract
- 6   tablespoons sugar
- 5   large egg yolks
- 2   teaspoons *each* cognac and amaretto, or 1½ tablespoons dark rum (optional)

1. Rinse a heavy nonreactive saucepan with cold water; shake dry (this helps prevent sticking). Add the milk, vanilla bean (if using vanilla extract, do not add it now) and 3 tablespoons of the sugar and bring the mixture nearly to a boil over medium heat. If you have time and are using the vanilla bean, remove from the heat, cover and set aside to steep for about 1 hour.

2. Return the milk to a simmer on low heat. Meanwhile, in a bowl, whisk the egg yolks with the remaining 3 tablespoons sugar until blended but not fluffy. Gradually whisk in about ½ of the milk to warm the eggs. Pour all of the egg mixture into the simmering milk. Cook, stirring constantly, until the custard thickens enough to coat the back of a spoon, usually about 7 minutes; do not boil.

3. Immediately pour the custard through a fine sieve into a clean bowl. Scrape the seeds from the vanilla bean into the sauce or stir in the vanilla extract, if using. Stir in the optional cognac and amaretto or the rum to taste. Cool briefly in the refrigerator, stirring once or twice. When chilled, cover the bowl until needed.

Variations

Add bourbon, Grand Marnier, pear eau-de-vie or another eau-de-vie instead of the cognac and amaretto in step 3.

Flavor the custard with 1 to 2 strips of orange zest, infusing it in the milk with the vanilla bean in step 1.

Good Enough to Drink

I once served this sauce to a crowd, alongside a huge glass bowl of pitted sour cherries, blackberries, blueberries, tiny strawberries and fresh red currants. The custard sauce was gone before the fruit—I found one guest drinking it straight from a glass.

Flavor the sauce with hazelnuts (see instructions for roasting and infusing in Hazelnut Semifreddo, page 603, steps 1 to 3) in step 1.

Flavor the custard with coffee or espresso (add 2 teaspoons instant coffee or espresso dissolved in 1 teaspoon hot water) in step 1.

LOW-FAT CUSTARD SAUCE

By using low-fat milk and whole eggs instead of yolks, you can cut back substantially on the amount of fat in custard sauce, while retaining the traditional flavor and body. Note that because this sauce contains egg whites, which curdle before yolks, it should be watched very closely.

Makes about 2¾ cups

2½	cups low-fat (1%) milk
1	vanilla bean, split lengthwise, or 2 teaspoons pure vanilla extract
1	strip orange zest
2	large eggs
⅓	cup sugar

1. Rinse a heavy nonreactive saucepan with cold water; shake dry (this helps prevent sticking). Add the milk, vanilla bean (if using vanilla extract, do not add it now) and orange zest to the pan and bring the mixture nearly to a boil. Remove from the heat, cover and set aside to steep for at least 30 minutes.

2. Return the milk to a simmer. Meanwhile, in a bowl, whisk the eggs and sugar until smooth but not fluffy. Gradually whisk in about ½ of the hot milk to warm the eggs. Pour all of the egg mixture into the simmering milk. Cook the custard over low heat, stirring constantly, until the mixture thickens enough to coat the back of a spoon, usually 7 to 8 minutes; do not allow the sauce to boil.

3. Strain the custard into a clean bowl. Scrape the seeds from the vanilla bean into the custard or stir in the vanilla extract. Cool briefly in the refrigerator, stirring once or twice. When chilled, cover the bowl until needed.

Cider-Lemon Sauce

L emon sauces are traditional over warm gingerbread and puddings; cookbook author Sallie Williams' touch of using fresh apple cider instead of water mellows this sauce beautifully. Aside from its perfect marriage with gingerbread (pages 334 to 337), try this sauce over poached pears, a baked apple, Oven-Steamed Figgy Pudding (page 226), or fresh figs, halved, sprinkled with sugar and warmed in the oven.

Makes about 1¼ cups

⅓ cup sugar
1 tablespoon cornstarch
½ teaspoon ground cinnamon
1 cup apple cider
   Pinch salt
¼ cup fresh lemon juice
   Grated zest of 1 lemon

1. In a heavy nonreactive saucepan, whisk the sugar, cornstarch and cinnamon until free of lumps. Place over medium heat and whisk in the cider and salt; bring to a boil. Boil gently, whisking, until smooth and lightly thickened, about 5 minutes.

2. Remove from the heat; pour the sauce into a bowl. Whisk in the lemon juice and zest. Cool to lukewarm. Taste and add more lemon juice, if needed. This sauce keeps well, tightly covered and refrigerated. Rewarm before serving, if necessary.

Apple Pudding Sauce

P reserve clean parings & cover with best apples, and put them on & stew in a porcelain pan with some slices of apple, and enough water to cover them. Cover closely and stew 15 or 20 minutes. Drain in a colander and return to the saucepan, sweeten, flavor with lemon juice, and thicken with sifted Graham flour or cerealine.

Mrs. Henry W. Darling
Handwritten
Manuscript
Schenectady, New York
ca. 1882-93

JOHN'S MOTHER'S LEMON SAUCE WITH LEMON SLICES

My friend, *Bon Appétit* column collaborator and cookbook author Marie Simmons, got this recipe from her mother-in-law, Mrs. Beatrice Simmons. Try it, instead of the lemon glaze, over Marie's Rich Gingerbread with Candied Ginger and Lemon Glaze (page 336) or on any gingerbread or steamed pudding.

Makes about 1⅓ cups

½ cup sugar
1 tablespoon cornstarch
1 cup cold cider or water
Grated zest and juice of 1 lemon
1 lemon, thinly sliced (about 8 slices)
2 tablespoons unsalted butter
Pinch salt

1. In a small nonreactive saucepan, stir together the sugar and cornstarch. Add the cider or water in a slow stream and stir until smooth.

2. Set the pan over medium heat and bring the mixture to a boil. Stir in the lemon zest and juice, lemon slices, butter and salt until the butter melts. Serve immediately.

SCHRAFFT'S HOT FUDGE SAUCE

This recipe has been adapted slightly from Schrafft's original for the home kitchen. Combining both melted chocolate and cocoa results in complex flavor: Use only the best of both here (Swiss Lindt or Tobler, French Valrhona and Belgian Callebaut are all excellent chocolates; Droste, Valrhona and Williams-Sonoma's Pernigotti cocoa are also good). This sauce has the full body and consistency of true hot fudge, firming up slightly as it hits the cold ice cream.

Makes about 2 cups

¼	cup unsweetened cocoa powder
½	cup sugar
	Pinch salt
½	cup whole milk
1	cup heavy cream
1	cup light corn syrup
3	ounces best-quality semisweet chocolate, finely chopped
	Few drops of malt vinegar or cider vinegar
2	tablespoons unsalted butter, thinly sliced
1	teaspoon pure vanilla extract

1. In a heavy saucepan, whisk together the cocoa, sugar, salt and milk until the mixture forms a smooth paste. Place over medium heat and stir in the cream, corn syrup, ⅔ of the chocolate and the vinegar. Bring the mixture to a boil, whisking or stirring frequently. Boil, whisking frequently, until the sauce reaches 220 to 225 degrees F on a candy thermometer, about 8 minutes.

2. Remove from the heat; whisk in the butter, vanilla and the remaining chocolate until the sauce is smooth. Set aside for a few minutes before serving.

3. Store the sauce in the refrigerator in a tightly covered jar or container. Rewarm before serving, either by spooning a little into a small skillet or by heating the entire jar, uncovered, in a microwave oven. You can also place the jar in a saucepan of cold water and bring it slowly to a bare simmer. This sauce keeps well, refrigerated, for 3 weeks or longer.

Small-Town Soda Fountain

Just as every small town had its soda fountain, New York City kids of all ages had Schrafft's, founded in 1861. Although the chain has closed, you can still enjoy the sauce that many New Yorkers remember as their primal hot fudge experience, thanks to food journalist Florence Fabricant, who tracked down the Schrafft's formula.

Warm Caramel Sauce

This sauce is a sleek, glossy bronze color, intense with real caramel flavor. Keep it on hand, warm briefly and serve over ice cream, broiled pears or a brownie.

The recipe can be doubled or tripled; it makes a great holiday gift, packed in jars.

Makes about 1⅔ cups

¾	cup plus 2 tablespoons sugar
3	tablespoons cold water
2	cups heavy cream
1	teaspoon pure vanilla extract
1½	teaspoons cold unsalted butter

1. Combine the sugar and cold water in a small, heavy saucepan over medium heat. Cook to dissolve the sugar, stirring, and brushing down any crystals on the sides of the pan with a brush dipped in hot water. Raise the heat and bring the syrup to a boil. Boil, without stirring, until the mixture caramelizes to a medium-dark amber color, 5 to 10 minutes; the timing can vary.

2. Remove the pan from the heat and gradually add the cream. Take care; the mixture will bubble up violently.

3. Return the sauce to medium heat and boil gently until thickened and smooth, 5 to 6 minutes. Remove from the heat. Stir in the vanilla; swirl in the butter.

4. Rewarm the sauce before serving, either by spooning a little into a small skillet or by heating the entire jar, uncovered, in a microwave oven. This sauce keeps well, refrigerated, for 3 weeks or longer.

Variation

Rusty Nail Caramel Sauce: To flavor the sauce with the components of the classic Rusty Nail cocktail, stir in 2 tablespoons Scotch, or more to taste, and 2 tablespoons Drambuie or Grand Marnier just before removing the sauce from the heat in step 3. This sauce can also be spiked with either bourbon or cognac.

HARD SAUCE

Ubiquitous on old-fashioned desserts, this sauce is basically nothing more than creamed butter that is sweetened and spiked with spirits. One old cookbook calls this "Soft, Hard Sauce."

⸻ *Makes about ½ cup*

¼	cup (½ stick) unsalted butter, softened
	Grated zest of ¼ orange
¾	cup confectioners' sugar
2	tablespoons cognac, brandy, rum or bourbon, or to taste
½	teaspoon pure vanilla extract

1. Combine the butter, orange zest and confectioners' sugar in a small bowl and cream together until well incorporated and very light. Stir in the cognac or other spirit and the vanilla.

2. Spoon the mixture into a glass serving dish or a small bowl; cover with plastic wrap. Chill at least overnight before serving. Or, as Florence B. Jack advises in *Cookery for Every Household* (London, 1934), "This sauce should be served piled up in a little fancy glass or china dish . . . Serve lightly sprinkled with grated nutmeg."

Cold Sweet Sauce

Take equal portions of fresh sweet butter and powdered loaf sugar; work them thoroughly together, and flavor it with grated nutmeg and a few drops of essence of lemon. This is an excellent sauce, and may be eaten with almost any kind of boiled puddings, also baked batter, plum and bread puddings, dumplings, rolls, fritters, pancakes, &c. It should be sent to table in a small glass plate, provided with a tea-spoon or butter knife.

LETTICE BRYAN
THE KENTUCKY HOUSEWIFE
CINCINNATI, 1839

FOAMY SAUCE

Once widely known in New England and in the South, foamy sauce has all but disappeared. Whip this warm froth just before serving over steamed puddings and fruit desserts. This is based on a late 19th-century recipe from Mrs. Mary J. Lincoln, author of *Mrs. Lincoln's Boston Cook Book* (*What to Do and What Not to Do in Cooking*, 1896), and the first principal of the Boston Cooking School.

Makes about 1 cup

- 6 tablespoons (¾ stick) unsalted butter, softened
- ½ cup confectioners' sugar
- 1 teaspoon pure vanilla extract
- 2 tablespoons cream sherry or other spirit (Madeira, brandy, rum or a liqueur)
- ¼ cup boiling water
- 1 large egg, well beaten

1. Bring a kettle of water to a boil. Meanwhile, in a small heatproof bowl, cream the butter with the confectioners' sugar and vanilla until very light. Half fill a small skillet with boiling water from the kettle; maintain at a simmer.

2. Just before serving the sauce, whisk the sherry or other spirit and the ¼ cup boiling water into the butter mixture. Whisk in the beaten egg. Place the bowl into the simmering water and whisk vigorously until the sauce thickens slightly and is foamy, 2 to 3 minutes. Transfer the sauce to a sauceboat and serve immediately.

Foamy Sauce

Beat the butter to a cream, then add gradually the sugar, and beat until white; then add the white of one egg unbeaten, beat again, then add the remaining white and beat the whole until *very, very* light. When ready to serve, add [1 gill of] sherry or vanilla, boiling water, stand the bowl in a basin of boiling water over the fire, and stir until frothy—no longer. Take from the fire, and serve immediately, or it will lose its lightness.

SARAH TYSON RORER
MRS. RORER'S
PHILADELPHIA COOK BOOK
PHILADELPHIA, CA. 1886

Raspberry Sauce

This brightly colored sauce has a tart, lively flavor because the berries aren't cooked. Serve it over ice cream, cakes or fresh fruits. It keeps well, refrigerated, for about 3 days.

ᴄ✑ *Makes about 2 cups*

1 generous pint fresh raspberries, picked over, or
   2 packages (10 ounces each) frozen raspberries, thawed
   and drained, with juices reserved
   Sugar, to taste
   Fresh lemon juice, to taste
   Framboise or crème de cassis, to taste (optional)

1. Puree the raspberries in a food processor or blender until smooth. Strain to eliminate the seeds. Add sugar, lemon juice and optional spirit to taste. (If using frozen raspberries, thin the sauce, if necessary, with a little of the reserved berry juices.)

2. Cover and chill until needed.

Chunky Double-Berry Sauce

This sauce features whole berries bathed in crimson puree. You can also make this with 2 pints of raspberries or with blueberries and blackberries.

ᴄ✑ *Makes 2 generous cups*

1 pint ripe strawberries, hulled
1 pint ripe raspberries, picked over
   Sugar, to taste
   Few drops fresh lemon juice
1-2 tablespoons crème de cassis, framboise or other berry
   eau-de-vie or liqueur (optional)

1. Puree the strawberries and slightly less than ½ of the raspberries in a food processor until smooth. Strain to eliminate the seeds. Add sugar to taste, plus the lemon juice and optional spirit. Stir in the reserved whole raspberries.

2. Cover and refrigerate the sauce. It will keep for up to 3 days.

SOUTHERN WINE SAUCE FOR SPONGECAKE

This warm sauce is adapted from a Charleston recipe; its winy flavor is characteristic of colonial desserts. It tastes warm and mellow when made with dry Madeira (Rainwater or Sercial, the driest), but sweeter Malmsey, sherry or port works well here, too.

Serve over plain cake or with fresh fruit or a steamed pudding.

Makes about 1⅓ cups

¼ cup (½ stick) unsalted butter, softened
⅓ cup sugar, or less, if using a sweet wine
1 cup Madeira, sherry or port
Pinch fresh-grated nutmeg

1. Cream the butter and sugar in a bowl until light.

2. Pour the Madeira, sherry or port into a nonreactive saucepan and set over low heat. Warm the wine briefly, just a minute or two; watch carefully so it does not ignite. Add the warm wine and nutmeg to the butter mixture and beat until smooth.

3. Serve the sauce warm, over spongecake or other plain cakes.

Wine Sauce for Rum or Batter Pudding

Have ready some drawn butter—the moment you take it from the fire, stir 2 glasses of white wine or alcohol, 2 Tablespoonsful of sugar and 1 grated nutmeg.

MATILDA L. ROGERS
RECIPE BOOK
MANUSCRIPT
NEW YORK, 1850

SPICED SOUR CHERRY COMPOTE FOR ICE CREAM

This chunky sauce is good spooned over not only ice cream, but also over a slice of spongecake, pound cake or angel food cake. Better yet, serve the cake à la mode, then spoon on this sauce, warmed slightly.

Makes about 3 cups

3	cups (1 generous pint) sour cherries
3-4	allspice berries
1	cinnamon stick
⅔	cup sugar, or to taste
¼	cup light corn syrup
2	tablespoons cold water
1	teaspoon fresh lemon juice, or to taste
	Few drops almond extract

1. Stem and pit the cherries, reserving the juices and a few of the pits. Place the cherries and their juices in a small nonreactive saucepan.

2. Tie a piece of cheesecloth around the reserved pits, the allspice berries and the cinnamon stick. Add to the pan with the sugar, corn syrup and water. Cover and bring to a boil over medium-high heat. Lower the heat, cover and simmer, stirring occasionally, until the cherries are just tender, about 5 minutes.

3. Remove the cherries with a skimmer or slotted spoon to a bowl; drain all of the syrup back into the pan. Gently boil the syrup, uncovered, until reduced by about ½, usually 10 to 15 minutes. Watch carefully toward the end of the simmering time, so the sugar does not become jelly-like or caramelize.

4. Add the lemon juice and almond extract to taste. Pour the syrup over the cherries, leaving the spice bag in the bowl to infuse. Cool until lukewarm.

5. Remove the spice bag, squeezing all possible juices into the bowl. Serve the compote warm or cold.

POT-AU-FEU PRALINE SAUCE

At Pot-au-Feu Restaurant in Providence, Rhode Island, pastry chef Lori Nadeau Richardson serves this chunky caramel-nut sauce over a vanilla mousse. There's little it wouldn't taste good on: ice cream or frozen yogurt, fresh peaches, angel food cake or spongecake.

Makes about 2 cups

3	cups sugar
1	cup cold water
	Pinch cream of tartar
1	cup coarsely chopped pecans
1	cup coarsely chopped blanched almonds
1½	cups hot water
⅓	cup bourbon

1. Place ½ cup of the sugar in a saucepan with ½ cup of the cold water. Bring to a boil, stirring to dissolve the sugar completely. Remove from the heat and set aside.

2. In a heavy saucepan or skillet, combine the remaining 2½ cups sugar with the remaining ½ cup cold water and the cream of tartar. Cook over medium heat, stirring to dissolve the sugar completely, and wiping down any crystals from the sides of the pan with a brush dipped in cold water. When the sugar is completely dissolved, bring the mixture to a boil.

3. Cook over medium-high heat, without stirring, until the sugar caramelizes to a medium amber color, 10 to 15 minutes; the timing can vary. Add all of the nuts and swirl the pan until they are well coated. Carefully add the hot water and bourbon (the mixture will sputter); remove from the heat.

4. Stir in the reserved sugar-water mixture until smooth. Set aside to cool. Cover and chill. Stir to recombine before serving.

NESSELRODE SAUCE

This rich but easy-to-make sauce is named after Count Karl Nesselrode, who was a Russian diplomat in the 1860s. The original sauce was created by his chef, M. Morey, for the Count's entertainment. (Little did Nesselrode know what he'd be remembered for.)

Makes about 2 cups

- ½ cup golden raisins
- ½ cup dried currants
- ¼ cup chopped candied citron or candied orange peel, or the grated zest of 1 small orange
- ¾ cup cooked chestnuts, drained and rinsed, crumbled into coarse pieces (see note, page 112)
- ½ cup dark or light rum or a mixture of rum and amaretto or Frangelico liqueur
- 1 cup chestnut puree (1 small can, about 8 ounces; or use pureed cooked fresh chestnuts; see note, page 113)
- 1 teaspoon pure vanilla extract (or to taste, if the chestnut puree is already flavored with vanilla)
  Sugar, if needed

1. In a bowl, combine the raisins, currants, citron or orange peel or zest, crumbled chestnuts and rum and/or liqueur. Stir in the chestnut puree and vanilla until smooth. Sweeten with sugar to taste if you are using unsweetened chestnut puree. Cover and refrigerate at least overnight. If possible, let the sauce mellow and ripen for a week or two.

2. Bring the sauce to room temperature before serving over ice cream. Time improves this sauce; it will keep well for 2 months.

ORANGE CURD

Though the juice of any orange works well here, see if you can find blood oranges. Their deep red juice and dark zest contribute a brilliant red-orange color to this tasty recipe. Serve a spoonful over spongecake or pound cake, or spread it on toast, brioche or a muffin. This curd makes a great gift, and the recipe can be multiplied. It is from Susan Stegner, former pastry chef at Coco Pazzo in New York City.

⌒ *Makes 1 generous pint*

12   large egg yolks (8 egg yolks and 2 whole eggs can be substituted)
1   cup sugar, or to taste, depending on the oranges' sweetness
¾   cup fresh orange juice, preferably blood orange juice
¼   cup fresh lemon juice
1   cup (2 sticks) cold unsalted butter, cut into pieces
       Grated zest of 2 oranges, preferably blood oranges

1. In a nonreactive saucepan over low heat (or in the top of a double boiler over simmering water), cook the egg yolks, sugar, lemon juice and orange juice, whisking constantly, until thickened, usually about 10 minutes.

2. Remove from the heat; whisk in the cold butter, a few pieces at a time. Whisk in the zest. Taste and add more sugar, if necessary (the mixture should be tart but nicely balanced). Place a sheet of wax paper or plastic wrap directly on the surface of the curd to prevent a skin from forming and cool to room temperature on a wire rack.

3. When cool, pour the curd into jars or containers, tightly cover and refrigerate for up to 1 month.

Lemon Cream

This is a smooth lemon curd lightened with whipped cream— light, suave and luxurious. The recipe is from the cookbook author David Lebovitz. Originally devised to accompany East-West Ginger Cake (page 334), the cream can be served on any plain cake; it's also delicious on ripe berries.

Makes about 3 cups

Grated zest of 1 lemon
½ cup fresh lemon juice
½ cup sugar
½ cup (1 stick) unsalted butter
2 teaspoons water
3 large eggs
4 large egg yolks
1 cup heavy cream, well chilled

1. Place the lemon zest and juice, sugar, butter and water in a heavy nonreactive saucepan over medium heat. Cook, stirring, until the butter melts.

2. In a bowl, beat the eggs and egg yolks with a whisk, just until blended. Whisk in about ⅓ of the hot lemon-butter mixture to warm the eggs; return the mixture to the saucepan. Cook over low heat, whisking constantly, just until the mixture thickens, usually about 3 minutes.

3. Remove from the heat and strain into a large heatproof container. Press a sheet of wax paper or plastic wrap directly on the surface of the curd to prevent a skin from forming. Refrigerate until cold. *(The curd can be prepared up to 2 days ahead. Chill until needed.)*

4. Up to 20 minutes before serving, beat the cream until it forms soft peaks. Fold the cream into the lemon mixture. Cover and chill until needed.

SWEET MUSCAT SABAYON

Enjoying a dessert wine in a whipped egg sabayon may be one of the best ways to enjoy its nectar-like intensity. Serve this sabayon over a combination of seasonal fruits in light syrup. In summer, try red currants, raspberries, sour cherries and strawberries or blueberries, tossed with a little sugar and left to stand until the berries give off some of their juices. In winter, try the sabayon over a compote of poached pears and dried fruits, moistened with a little orange juice.

Makes about 3 cups

> Warm Amaretto-Cognac Zabaglione (page 114)
> ⅔   cup Quady Essencia, Muscat de Beaumes-de-Venise or other Muscat or late-harvest wine
> ⅓-½   cup heavy cream, well chilled (optional)

Prepare the zabaglione according to the instructions on page 114, substituting the wine for the cognac and amaretto in step 2, and reducing the sugar to ¼ cup. For a thicker sabayon, whip the heavy cream until not quite stiff. Fold in the whipped cream just before serving.

CRÈME FRAÎCHE

This simulates the thick, slightly sour cream that graces desserts in France.

Makes about 2⅓ cups

> 2   cups heavy cream
> ⅓   cup buttermilk

1. Combine the cream and buttermilk in a saucepan and heat just until warm, about body temperature (just under 100 degrees F). Do not let the mixture get hot.

2. Pour the mixture into a clean plastic or glass container; cover the container and place it in a larger container of warm

water. The water should come up to the level of the cream. Allow to stand in a warm place until the cream thickens, 12 to 36 hours. Replace the water every now and then to keep it warm.

3. Refrigerate the cream. It will keep for about 1 week.

ROBERTSON DAVIES' PUNCHBOWL
(A SPIRITED FINALE)

Robertson Davies, one of my favorite novelists, once mentioned an alcoholic punch that was traditionally served by his family at celebrations. After repeated badgering, Mr. Davies was kind enough to send it to me. We made a bowl of this punch as this book was being finished.

Here is his recipe:

1   large lemon
1   quart of boiling China tea (teabags won't do; must be freshly brewed and strong without being black)
1   teacup of brandy—Spanish is very good
1   teacup rum—Jamaican rum, not a white rum
1   quarter pound lump sugar

1. Rub all the yellow of the skin of a big lemon with some of the sugar lumps. Put these ingredients together in a metal bowl—silver for preference.

2. If the tea is boiling, you should be able to light the fumes with a match, which is very pretty.

3. Pour the burning punch into glasses or cups; a china bowl may be used if necessary, but the punch does not flame so well as in metal.

"This is a strong punch and should be treated with discretion."

ROBERTSON DAVIES

625

HISTORICAL SOURCES

NOTE: ALL MANUSCRIPTS ARE FROM THE HELEN HAY WHITNEY COLLECTION,
NEW YORK PUBLIC LIBRARY.

A.W. *A Book of Cookrye*. London, 1587.

Acton, Eliza. *Modern Cookery*. London: Longmans, Green, Reader, and Dyer, 1878. (1st ed., 1857.)

Agulló i Vidal, Ferrán. *LLibre de la Cuina Catalana*. Barcelona, 1933.

The All-New Fannie Farmer Boston Cooking School Cook Book. Ed. Wilma Lord Perkins. Boston: Little, Brown, 1959.

Allen, [Mrs.] Ida [Cogswell] Bailey. *Ida Bailey Allen's Modern Cook Book*. Garden City, New York: Garden City Publishing, 1924.

The American Heritage Cookbook. New York: American Heritage, 1964.

The American Housewife. (By "An experienced lady"). New York: Collins, Keese, 1839.

Apicius. *De Re Coquinaria* [On Cookery]. Trans. Joseph Dommers Vehling. New York: Dover, 1977. (Reprint of Chicago: Walter M. Hill, 1936.)

Apicius. *De Re Coquinaria*. (*The Roman Cookery of Apicius*. Trans. John Edwards. Washington: Hartley & Marx, 1984.)

Artusi, Pellegrino. *La Scienza in Cucina e L'Arte di Mangiar Bene*. Firenze: A. Vallardi, 1983. (1st ed., ca. 1890.)

Ayrton, Elisabeth. *The Cookery of England*. London: André Deutsch, 1975.

Beecher, Catherine E. *Miss Beecher's Housekeeper and Healthkeeper*, 1874.

Beeton, Mrs. Isabella. *The Book of Household Management*. London: S.O. Beeton, 1861. (Facsimile ed., New York: Farrar, Straus & Giroux, 1969.)

Beeton. Mrs. Isabella. *Mrs. Beeton's Cookery Book*. Blackpool: J.S. Doidge, 1902. (Facsimile ed., London: Rigby, 1981.)

Better Homes Lifetime Cook Book. Des Moines, Iowa, 1935.

Bitting, Katherine. *Gastronomic Bibliography*. London: The Holland Press, 1981. (Facsimile of 1st ed., San Francisco, 1939.)

Blencowe, Ann. *The Receipt Book of Ann Blencowe*. (England, 1694.) Reprint, London: Guy Chapman, 1925.

Brillat-Savarin, Jean Anthelme. *The Physiology of Taste*. Trans. M.F.K. Fisher. New York: Heritage Press, 1949. (Originally written 1825.)

Brown, Marion. *Marion Brown's Southern Cook Book*. Chapel Hill: The University of North Carolina Press, 1968. (First published 1951.)

Bryan, Lettice. *The Kentucky Housewife*. Cincinnati, Ohio: Shepard & Stearns, 1839. (Facsimile ed., ed. Bill Neal. Columbia, South Carolina: University of South Carolina Press, 1991.)

The Buckeye Cook Book. New York: Dover, 1975. Facsimile of *Practical Housekeeping: A Careful Compilation of Tried and Approved Recipes*. Minneapolis, Minnesota: Buckeye Publishing, 1876.

Burdette, Kay. *Cookery of the Old South*. In calligraphy, with woven covers. Glendale, California, 1938.

Byron, May. *May Byron's Pudding Book*. London: Hodder Stoughton, 1917.

Cardella, Antonio. *Sicilia e le Isole in Bocca*. Palermo, Sicily: Edikronos, 1981.

Carême, Marie Antonin. *Le Cuisinier Parisien, ou L'art de la Cuisine Française au Dix-Neuvième Siècle*. Paris, 1854.

Carter, Susannah. *The Frugal Housewife*. Philadelphia, 1802. (First published London, 1772.)

Child, Mrs. Lydia Maria. *The American Frugal Housewife*. Boston: Carter, Hendee, 1833.

Choice Recipes. Dorchester, Massachusetts: Walter Baker, 1914.

A Closet for Ladies and Gentlewomen, or The Art of Preserving, Conserving, and Candying. London, 1656.

Collection of Medical and Cookery Recipes. English manuscript, 17th century.

The Compact Edition of The Oxford English Dictionary. Oxford: Oxford University Press, 1981.

The Complete Cook. London, 1658. (Large portions are verbatim from *The Queens Closet Opened*.)

Crowen, Mrs. Thomas J. *Every Lady's Cook Book*. New York: Kiggins & Kellogg, 1854.

Curnonsky [Sailland, Maurice Edmond], ed. *Recettes des Provinces de France*. Paris: P.E. Lamaison, 1959.

Dainty Desserts for Dainty People. Johnston, New York: Charles B. Knox Co., 1915.

Dalgairns, Mrs. *The Practice of Cookery*. Edinburgh, 1830.

Darling, Mrs. Henry W. *Recipe Book*. Manuscript. Schenectady, New York, ca. 1882-93.

Dawson, Thomas. *The Good Huswifes Iewell [Jewel]*. London, 1587.

de Pomiane, Edouard. *Cuisine Juive: Ghettos Modernes*. Paris: Albin Michel, 1929.

The Dessert Book. (By "A Boston Lady"). Boston: J.E. Tilton, 1872.

Directions for Cookery. Philadelphia, 1837; 1898.

Emerson, Lucy. *The New England Cookery*. Montpelier, Vermont, 1808. (Much is verbatim from Amelia Simmons' *American Cookery*.)

Escoffier, Auguste. *Le Guide Culinaire*. Trans. H.L. Cracknell and R.J. Karmann. New York: Mayflower Books, 1979. (First published 1902.)

Every Day Cookery, Table Talk, and Hints for the Laundry. Chicago, 1884.

Farmer, Fannie Merritt. *The Boston Cooking-School Cook Book*. Boston, 1896.

Farmer, Fannie Merritt. *The Boston Cooking-School Cook Book*. Toronto: McClelland & Stewart, 1932.

Farmer, Fannie Merritt. *Rumford Cook Book*. Providence, Rhode Island: Rumford Chemical Works, 1906.

Fast, Mady. *I Dolci a Trieste*. Trieste: Edizione "Italo Svevo," 1989.

Fettiplace, Elinor. *Elinor Fettiplace's Receipt Book*, 1604. Ed. Hilary Spurling. New York: Viking, 1986.

Filippini, Alessandro. *The Table*. New York: Merriam, 1889.

Finck, Henry Theophilus. *Food and Flavor*. New York: The Century Company, 1913.

Fitzgerald, Mrs. Charles. Irish manuscript, 1796.

Forde, Maria. *Memorandum Book Containing Cookery Recipes*. English manuscript, ca. late 18th to early 19th century.

Francatelli, Charles Elmé. *The Modern Cook*. London: Richard Bentley, 1865.

Gilbert, Fabiola Cabeza de Baca. *The Good Life: New Mexico Traditions and Food*. Santa Fe: The Museum of New Mexico Press, 1986. (First published 1949.)

Glasse, Hannah ("A Lady"). *The Art of Cookery, made Plain and Easy*. London, 1747. (Facsimile ed., London: Prospect Books, 1983.)

Glasse, Hannah. *The Compleat Confectioner*. Dublin, 1762. (First published London, 1760.)

Good Housekeeping's Book of Menus, Recipes, and Household Discoveries. New York, 1922.

The Good Hous-wives Treasurie. London, 1588.

Green, Olive. *Everyday Desserts*. New York: G.P. Putnam, 1911.

Grigson, Jane. *Jane Grigson's British Cookery*. New York: Atheneum, 1985.

Hale, Sarah Josepha. *The Ladies' New Book of Cookery*. New York: H. Long & Brother, 1852.

Hale, Sarah Josepha. *Mrs. Hale's New Cook Book*. Philadelphia: T.B. Peterson, 1857.

Harland, Marion. *Cookery for Beginners*. Boston: D. Lothrop, 1884.

Hewitt, Jean. *The New York Times Heritage Cook Book*. New York: G.P. Putnam, 1972.

Hooker, Richard J. *Food and Drink in America: A History*. Indianapolis/New York: Bobbs-Merrill, 1981.

Horry, Harriott Pinckney. *A Colonial Plantation Cookbook* (1770). Facsimile ed., ed. Richard J. Hooker. Columbia, South Carolina: University of South Carolina Press, 1984.

"*It Whips!*" Irradiated Carnation Milk, 1940.

Jack, Florence B. *Cookery for Every Household*. London: Thomas Nelson, 1934.

Jones, Evan. *American Food: The Gastronomic Story*. 2nd ed. New York: Random House, 1981. (First published 1975.)

Josselyn, John. *New-England's Rarities Discovered* (1672). Boston: Massachusetts Historical Society, 1972. (First published 1672.)

Junior League of Charleston. *Charleston Receipts*. Charleston, South Carolina, 1950.

Kander, Mrs. Simon (Lizzie Black) and Mrs. Henry Schoenfeld. *The Settlement Cook Book*. Milwaukee: "The Settlement," 1903. (Facsimile ed., New York: Hugh Lauter Levin, 1984.)

Kent, Countess of. *Manual of Physic and Preserving*. London, 1659.

Kimball, Marie. *Thomas Jefferson's Cook Book*. Charlottesville: University Press of Virginia, 1976.

The Kitchen Directory and American Housewife. New York: Mark H. Newman, 1844. (1st ed., 1841.)

Kitchiner, William. *The Cook's Oracle*. 2nd ed. London, 1818.

La Chapelle, Vincent. *The Modern Cook*. 3rd ed. London, 1744 (1st ed., 1733.)

Ladies of the Congregational Society. *The Calender Club Cook Book*. Bridgeton, Maine, 1902.

La Varenne, François Pierre de. *Le Cuisinier François*. Paris, 1654. (1st ed., Lyon: Pierre David, 1651.)

La Varenne, François Pierre de. *Le Vray Cuisinier François*. Paris, 1682. (1st ed., 1653.)

Lea, Elizabeth E. *Domestic Cookery*. Baltimore, 1866.

Lee, Mrs. N.K.M. *The Cook's Own Book*. Boston, New York, and Philadelphia, 1832.

Leslie, Eliza. *Directions for Cookery*. Philadelphia: Carey & Hart, 1848. (1st ed., 1837; facsimile ed., New York: Arno Press, 1973.)

Leslie, Eliza. *Miss Leslie's New Receipts for Cooking*. Philadelphia, 1874.

Leslie, Eliza. *Seventy-Five Receipts*. Boston: Monroe and Francis, 1828.

Leyel, Mrs. C.F. and Miss Olga Hartley. *The Gentle Art of Cookery*. London: Chatto & Windus, 1983. (1st ed., 1925.)

Lincoln, Mrs. D.A. (Mary Johnson Bailey.) *Frozen Dainties*. Nashua, New Hampshire: The White Mountain Freezer Company, 1897; also 1905.

Lincoln, Mrs. D.A. *Mrs. Lincoln's Boston Cook Book (What to Do and What Not to Do in Cooking)*. Boston, 1896.

Lowenstein, Eleanor. *Bibliography of American Cookery Books 1742-1860*. Worcester, Massachusetts: American Antiquarian Society; New York: Corner Book Shop, 1972.

Lowinsky, Ruth. *Lovely Food*. London: Nonesuch Press, 1931.

Maldonado, Diego Granado. *Libro del Arte de Cocina*. Madrid, 1609. (1st ed., 1599.)

Malone, Ruth M. *Where to Eat in the Ozarks; How It's Cooked*. Little Rock, Arkansas: Pioneer Press, 1961.

Manuscript Recipe Book [in three different hands]. English manuscript, 17th century.

Markham, Gervase. *The English Hus-wife*. 1615. (Facsimile ed., *The English Housewife*, Kingston, Ontario: McGill-Queens University Press, 1986.)

Marnette, Monsieur. *The Perfect Cook*. London, 1686.

Massialot, François. *Le Cuisinier Royal et Bourgeois*. Paris, 1698. (1st ed., 1691.)

Massialot, François. *The Court and Country Cook*. London, 1702. (Trans. of *Le Cuisinier Royal et Bourgeois*.)

May, Robert. *The Accomplisht Cook*. London: Nathaniel Brook, 1671. (1st ed., 1660.)

May, Robert. *The Accomplisht Cook*. London: O. Blagrave, 1685.

McNeill, F. Marian. *The Scots Kitchen*. London and Glasgow: Blackie & Son, 1942. (1st ed., 1929.)

Memorandome Book. England, 1783.

Menon. *La Cuisinière Bourgeoise*. Brussels, 1774; 1790. (1st ed., 1759.)

Morton, Lady Anne. *The Ladey Mortons Booke of Receipts, most of which she hath experimented her selfe and are verey good*. England, 1693.

My Favorite Receipt. New York: Royal Baking Powder Co., 1898.

Oswald, Ella. *German Cookery for the American Home*. New York: Baker and Taylor, 1907.

Paddleford, Clementine. *How America Eats*. New York: Charles Scribner's Sons, 1960.

Parloa, Maria. *Miss Parloa's New Cook Book and Marketing Guide*. Boston: Dana Estes, 1880.

Pease, Mrs. Mary B. *The Pudding Book*. Anoka, Minnesota, 1928.

Pennypacker family. *Cookery Recipe Book*. Manuscript, West Chester, Pennsylvania, 1880-1935.

Platina, *De Honesta Voluptate* [Of Honest Indulgence and Good Health]. Originally written Venice: Mallinckrodt Chemical Works, 1475. Latin facsimile with English translation, 1967.

Price, Mrs. Elizabeth. *The New, Universal, and Complete Confectioner*. London, ca. 1780. (Much of this material is similar or identical to Hannah Glasse's *The Compleat Confectioner*, 1760.)

Putnam, Mrs. Elizabeth H. *Mrs. Putnam's Receipt Book*. Boston: Ticknor, Reed, and Fields, 1849.

Raffald, Elizabeth. *The Experienced English Housekeeper*. Philadelphia: James Webster, 1818. (First published London, 1773.)

Rand, Abigail. *Domestic Cookery*. English manuscript, 17th century.

Randolph, Mary. *The Virginia Housewife*. Washington: Davis and Force, 1824. (Facsimile ed., ed. Karen Hess. Columbia, South Carolina: University of South Carolina Press, 1984.)

Rogers, Matilda L. *Recipe Book*. Manuscript, New York, 1850.

Rombauer, Irma. *Joy of Cooking*. St. Louis: A.C. Clayton Printing Co., 1931. (1st ed.)

Rombauer, Irma. *Joy of Cooking*. St. Louis: A.C. Clayton Printing Co., 1936.

Rombauer, Irma and Marion Rombauer Becker. *Joy of Cooking*. New York: Bobbs-Merrill, 1953.

Rombauer, Irma and Marion Rombauer Becker. *Joy of Cooking.* New York: Bobbs-Merrill, 1979.

Rorer, Sarah Tyson. *Mrs. Rorer's Key to Simple Cookery.* Philadelphia: Arnold, 1917.

Rorer, Sarah Tyson. *Mrs. Rorer's New Cook Book.* Philadelphia, 1902.

Rorer, Sarah Tyson. *Mrs. Rorer's Philadelphia Cook Book.* Philadelphia, ca. 1886.

Rosický, Marie. *Bohemian-American Cook Book.* Omaha, Nebraska: National Printing, 1925.

Rundell, Maria Eliza. *A New System of Domestic Cookery.* Boston: William Andrews, 1807.

Rutledge, Sarah. *The Carolina Housewife.* Charleston: W.R. Babcock, 1847. (Facsimile ed., Columbia, South Carolina: University of South Carolina Press, 1979.)

Salmon, William. *The Family Dictionary or Household Companion.* 2nd ed. London, 1696.

Simmons, Amelia. *American Cookery.* Hartford, Connecticut: Hudson & Goodwin, 1796. (Facsimile ed., Boston: Rowan Tree Press, 1982.)

Smith, E. [Eliza]. *The Compleat Housewife: or, The Accomplished Gentlewoman's Companion.* London, 1758, 16th ed.; 1st ed., 1727. (Facsimile ed., Kings Langley, Herts.: Arlon House, 1983.)

Smith, Mary. *The Complete House-Keeper, and Professed Cook.* Newcastle: T. Slack, 1772.

Soyer, Alexis. *The Gastronomic Regenerator.* 5th ed. London, 1848.

Soyer, Alexis. *The Pantropheon.* New York and London: Paddington Press, Ltd., 1977. (1st ed., London: Simpkin, Marshall, 1853.)

Tannahill, Reay. *Food in History.* (Rev. ed.) New York: Crown, 1989.

Two Hundred Years of Charleston Cooking. Eds. Blanche S. Rhett and Lettie Gay. Columbia, South Carolina: University of South Carolina Press, 1976.

Tyree, Marion Cabell, ed. *Housekeeping in Old Virginia.* Louisville, Kentucky: John P. Morton & Co., 1879.

W.M., A Servant to Queen Henrietta Maria, Wife of Charles I of England. *The Queens Closet Opened.* London: Nathaniel Brook, 1655. (12 eds. published between 1655 and 1698.)

Wainwright, Elizabeth. *The Receipt Book of a Lady of the Reign of Queen Anne.* English manuscript, 1711. (Reprint Medstead, Hampshire: The Az Press, 1931.)

Washington, Martha. *Martha Washington's Booke of Cookery.* (1749-1799.) Facsimile ed., ed. Karen Hess. New York: Columbia University Press, 1981.

Weaver, William Woys. *Additions and Corrections to Lowenstein's Bibliography of American Cookery Books, 1742-1860.* Worcester, Massachusetts: The American Antiquarian Society.

Webster, Mrs. A.L. ("A Married Lady"). *The Improved Housewife.* Hartford, 1846; 1854. (First published 1844).

The Whole Duty of a Woman. London, 1737.

Wilson, C. Anne. *Food and Drink in Britain.* Aylesbury, Bucks.: Penguin, 1976. (First published 1973.)

Wilson, Elizabeth. *Cookery Manuscript.* England, 1824.

Winthrop, John Jr. *Letter to the Royal Society, 1662.* Reprinted in full in *New England Quarterly*, Vol X, No. 1, 1937.

Wolcott, Imogene. *The Yankee Cook Book.* Brattleboro, Vermont: Stephen Greene Press, 1971. (1st ed., 1939.)

The Women of First Congregational Church, Marysville, Ohio. *The Centennial Buckeye Cook Book.* 1876.

Woolley, Hannah. *The Gentlewoman's Companion; or, a Guide to the Female Sex.* London, 1673.

PERMISSIONS

ACKNOWLEDGMENTS

 book of this scope owes much to the contributions of many people besides its author. The spark for the project was a casual conversation with editor extraordinaire Roy Finamore, then at Stewart, Tabori and Chang. Roy has been unstintingly generous with invaluable editorial advice and has since become a treasured friend.

Conversations with Carole Lalli and Nach Waxman made me realize that I wanted to make this a comprehensive book with expansive text. Kerri Conan picked up the ball and kept the faith, even though all she ever saw was a detailed outline. Both Carole and Kerri were important midwives in what may have been one of the longest births in contemporary cookbook publishing.

My dear friend Nick Malgieri, one of America's outstanding pastry chefs and a fine baking teacher who not only has an encyclopedia of knowledge at the tip of his tongue but can explain technique in a way that's clear and hilarious, was always there— to answer questions, offer advice or kvetch with me.

Maida Heatter is a treasure; I am blessed to have her as a loving, supportive friend.

Susan Lescher, my agent for some 15 years, went through more effort on behalf of this book than on any half-dozen others and always believed in it. Carolyn Larson and Wes Bazin, thank you for the many things you did. Naomi Uman helped with early recipe testing; Barbara Prisco was her amazing self at transcribing tapes. At Chapters Publishing, Cristen Brooks somehow consolidated several drafts, plus hundreds of queries and comments—and made all clear.

Evie Righter's keen editorial eye clarified a long, involved manuscript.

This book finally provided me the opportunity to work with Lisa Ekus; publicist Merrilyn Siciak was a joy.

Mardee Haidin Regan brought her unique blend of food expertise, impeccable grasp of detail and welcome sense of humor under pressure, making this a clearer, better book throughout.

Alan Richardson's photographs have an artistry all their own, and Anne Disrude, whose food styling I've admired for years, is one of the few people I would trust implicitly to make my food look wonderful.

Two women were crucial to the work on this book, which went on (and on) for years. Ceri Hadda helped me steadily for over three years, not only typing and organizing but offering valuable editorial and baking advice at every step.

Luli Gray was by my side throughout, testing most of the recipes, helping with research and writing, chasing down mail-order ingredients, deciphering confusing notes from repeated recipe tests and offering her food and writing talents, loving support and sardonic wit. Just by being there, Luli kept me going.

So many others were there when times were rough: David Ricketts, Sandy Gluck, Joel Kanoff and Elizabeth Schneider. And my loving brother and sister, Ken and Diana; my nephew and niece, Jeremy and Erica; and all my cousins. And especially my mother, Fran Sax—sometimes life provides angels when we most need them.

Most important, Rux Martin and Barry Estabrook took on this project wholeheartedly from our first conversation about it. Rux reorganized sections and chapters radically, tightened and trimmed and always managed to find the essence of what I was trying to express.

Finally, I wish to thank all the home cooks and chefs who shared their recipes and reminiscences so generously. They are the soul of this book.

"You've got to be thankful for everything," my Grandma Mollie used to say, her bright eyes flashing.

INDEX

A

Aliter Dulcia (other sweets), old recipe, 549

Almond(s)
Alsatian Christmas Cinnamon Stars, 283
Alsatian Pear Tart with Macaroon Crunch Topping, 538
Blancmange, Modern, 106
Brittle Cookies (My All-Time Favorite), 270
Chef Andrea's Breakfast Polenta Cake, 311
Chocolate-Glazed Lebkuchen, 252
Coiled Yeast Bread with Nut Filling, 377
-Cornmeal Biscotti, 291
Cornmeal Pear Tart with Frangipane, 544
The Four Seasons' Christmas Fruitcake (Light Fruitcake Wrapped in Marzipan), 426
and Hazelnut Cookies, Crunchy, 282
Hoover Toffee Ice Cream Pie, 512
Hungarian Nut Crescents, 284
Jumballs, old recipe, 247
Lekvar (Thick Prune Puree), 367
Low-Fat Chocolate Nut Torte, 416
Mary's Pignoli (Italian Pine Nut Macaroons), 276
"Mouthfuls" from Abruzzo, 581
Mrs. Dalgairns' Scottish Seed Cake, 435
Palio's Polenta Cake, 314
Pot-au-Feu Praline Sauce, 620
Quick Chocolate Candy Cake, 412
and Quince Tart, The Coach House, 546
Ray's Holiday Nut Tart, 551
Semolina Ring Cake from Friuli, 316
Wafers, Thin, 279
Alsatian Christmas Cinnamon Stars, 283

Alsatian Cinnamon Cake, 370
Alsatian Pear Tart with Macaroon Crunch Topping, 538
Alsatian Spiced Honey Ice Cream, 599
Amaretto-Apricot Fool, 92
Amaretto-Cognac Zabaglione, Warm, 114
Angel Food Cake
Dick Witty's, 308
Orange, with Tangerine Glaze, 309
Sunshine, old recipe, 307
Sunshine Cake, 307
Anise Christmas Cookies, New Mexico, 260
Anise Cookies, Señá Martina's, old recipe, 260
Apees, 246
Apees, old recipe, 246
Apple(s)
Batter Pudding, Baked, 215
Boiled Cider Pie, New England, 519
boyled sider, old recipe, 518
Bread Pudding, 186
Brown Betty with Cake Crumbs, 48
Cake, Hilda's, 340
Cake, Ligita's Quick, 339
Cake, Margaret's, 341
Cape Cod Cranberry "Linzer" Pie, 468
Carolina Huguenot Torte, 398
cider, boiled, about, 518
and Cookie Crumb Dessert, Danish ("Peasant Girl with Veil"), 57
Cranberry Pie, Down-East, 456
Crumb Pie, Indiana Orchard, 454
Dried, Gingerbread Stack Cake, 392
Dried, "Pour-Through" Pie, 459
Dried-Fruit Mincemeat Pie with Lattice Cream Cheese Crust, 524
Dumplings, Baked, 239
Fraze with Pippins, old recipe, 232
Fritters, 586

Fruit-Filled Lattice Torte with Three Fillings, 559
and Green Tomato Mincemeat Pie, 526
"Half-Moon" Pies, Fried (or Baked), 474
heirloom, about, 338
Kolachy, Crisp, 576
with Macaroon Soufflé and Cool Custard, Warm Baked, 82
Marie's Fall Fruit Compote, 74
Mom's New Noodle Kugel, 206
Mush, 53
and Noodle Soufflé, Czech, 209
Pancake, Reuben's Legendary, 234
Pandowdy, 48
-Pecan Upside-Down Pie Baked in a Skillet, 476
Pie, about, 452–453
Pie, variations on, 455
"Pie," Swedish, with Vanilla Sauce, 55
pies, frying, old recipe, 475
Pudding Sauce, old recipe, 611
Ruby Baked, 78
Rye 'n Injun, old recipe, 46
Tart, Polish, 556
varieties, 338
varieties of, 78
Winter Fruit Dumplings, 240
Applesauce
-Carrot Cake with Lemon–Cream Cheese Frosting, 390
Cheesecake, World War I, 410
Apricot(s)
-Amaretto Fool, 92
Madeira Dried Fruit Compote, 77
Sponge, 99
Armenian Egg Biscuits, 287
Arroz con Leche (Luli's Simplest Rice Pudding), 172
Asian-Style Coconut Tapioca Pudding, 134
Atholl Brose, Frozen Scottish, 113
Austrian Walnut Torte with Coffee Whipped Cream, 400

B

Bakeware. *See* Cookware and bakeware
Banana
  Cake, Grandma's, 326
  Pudding, 126
  Pudding with Vanilla Wafers, 127
  –Toasted Coconut Cream Pie, 485
  White Chocolate Cream Pie, 486
Bavarian, Ricotta, 110
"Bee-Sting" Cake, 368
Beignets Soufflés (French Fruit Puffs), 588
Belgian Sugar Tart, 548
Benne (Sesame), Toasted, Wafers, 278
Berry(ies). *See also* Blueberry(ies); Cranberry(ies); Raspberry(ies); Strawberry(ies)
  Black and Blueberry Grunt (or Slump), 58
  bringing out flavor of, 63
  Buckle, Lightened Down-East, 62
  Double- , Lattice Pie, 462
  Double- , Sauce, Chunky, 617
  The Finamore Shortcake, 65
  -Peach Lattice-Topped Pie, 466
  Popover, Big, 233
  Raylene's Blackberry Cobbler, old recipe, 35
  Shortcakes with Buttermilk-Almond Biscuits, 66
  Summer Pudding of Four Red Fruits, 202
  Two- , Buckle, Traditional, 60
  Virginia Blackberry Roll, 44
Bienenstich ("Bee-Sting Cake"), 368
Biscotti
  about, 290
  Cornmeal-Almond, 291
  Hazelnut, Miniature (Quaresimale), 292
Biscuits, Egg, Armenian, 287
Biscuits, Egg, Greek, 286
Bizcochitos (New Mexico Anise Christmas Cookies), 260
Black and White Cannoli Cream, 89
Blackberry(ies)
  Black and Blueberry Grunt (or Slump), 58
  Cobbler, Raylene's, old recipe, 35
  Double-Berry Lattice Pie, 462

Lattice-Topped Peach-Berry Pie, 466
Lightened Down-East Berry Buckle, 62
Roll, Virginia, 44
Summer Pudding of Four Red Fruits, 202
Black Walnut Pie, 517
Blancmange, about, 107
Blancmange, Almond, Modern, 106
Blintz "Soufflé," 164
Blondies, Coconut, 269
Blondies, White Chocolate–Macadamia, 269
Blueberry(ies)
  All-Time-Best Summer Fruit Torte, 344
  and Black(berry) Grunt (or Slump), 58
  Cornmeal Loaf, Karyl's, 318
  Deep-Dish Rhubarb-Cherry-Berry Pie, 472
  Double, Tart, Long Island, 536
  Double-Berry Lattice Pie, 462
  Fruit-Filled Lattice Torte with Three Fillings, 559
  in North American culinary history, 50–51
  Shortcakes with Low-Fat Cornmeal-Yogurt Biscuits, 68
  Traditional Two-Berry Buckle, 60
Bocconotti Abbruzzesi ("Mouthfuls" from Abruzzo), 581
Boiled Loaf, old recipe, 188
Boiled Potatoe Pudding, old recipe, 224
Bon Ton's New Orleans Bread Pudding with Whiskey Sauce, 188
Boston Cream, old recipe, 204
Boston Cream Pie, 397
Boyled Sider, old recipe, 518
Brandy
  The Four Seasons' Christmas Fruitcake (Light Fruitcake Wrapped in Marzipan), 426
  Mother Church's Spirited Dark Fruitcake, 424
  Robertson Davies' Punchbowl (A Spirited Finale), 625
Brazilian Coconut Custards, 148
Bread. *See also* Bread Puddings
  Brown, Ice Cream, English, 598
  Easter bread of Friuli, about, 378

Yeast Coffee, Coiled, with Nut Filling, 377
Bread Puddings
  about, 183
  Apple, 186
  Boiled Loaf, old recipe, 188
  Bon Ton's New Orleans, with Whiskey Sauce, 188
  Boston Cream, old recipe, 204
  Bread-and-Butter, The Coach House, 184
  Buttermilk Corn Bread, 187
  Caramel, Omaha, 190
  Challah, with Raisins, 185
  Chocolate, Italian, 196
  Chocolate Silk, 194
  Gingerbread Custard, 204
  Green Pudding, old recipe, 200
  history of, 170–171
  Muffin Pudding, old recipe, 187
  Panettone, Caramelized, 198
  Soufflé, Commander's Palace, 192
  Summer Pudding of Four Red Fruits, 202
  Warm Pear Charlotte, 200
  with Wine and Cheese, Santa Fe, 195
  Yr Custard Puddinge, old recipe, 191
Breakfast Pear Tarte Tatin, 530
Breakfast Polenta Cake, Chef Andrea's, 311
Broiled Pears with Warm Caramel Sauce, 81
Brown Betty, defined, 34
Brown Betty, Pear or Apple, with Cake Crumbs, 48
Brown Butter Coffee Cake, 352
Brownies, Fudge-Chunk, All-American, 266
Brownies, Pecan-and-Caramel-Glazed, 267
Brown Sugar
  Buttermilk Crumb Cake (Quintessential Coffee Cake), 350
  pie, about, 480
  Raspberry Loaf, John's, 320
  for recipes, 21
  Shortbread Wafers, 258
Buckle
  Berry, Lightened Down-East, 62
  defined, 34
  Two-Berry, Traditional, 60
Budino di Ricotta (Italian Ricotta Pudding), 129

Budino Nero (Italian Chocolate Bread Pudding), 196
Burnt Cream, old recipe, 149
Butter
  for recipes, 21
  softening quickly, 25
Buttermilk
  -Almond Biscuits, Berry Shortcake with, 66
  Brown Sugar Crumb Cake (Quintessential Coffee Cake), 350
  Corn Bread Pudding, 187
  Pudding, Persimmon, 220
  Silk Pie, 481
Butterscotch Cream Pie, Midwestern, 482
Butterscotch Pudding, 124

C
Cabinet Pudding, 158
Cake flour, for recipes, 21
Cakes. *See also* Cheesecakes; Chocolate Cakes; Coffee Cakes; Fruitcakes; Gingerbread; Pound Cakes
  All-Time-Best Summer Fruit Torte, 344
  Angel Food, Dick Witty's, 308
  Angel Food, Orange, with Tangerine Glaze, 309
  Apple, Hilda's, 340
  Apple, Ligita's Quick, 339
  Apple, Margaret's, 341
  Applesauce-Carrot, with Lemon–Cream Cheese Frosting, 390
  Austrian Walnut Torte with Coffee Whipped Cream, 400
  baking, old cookbook rules for, 301
  Banana, Grandma's, 326
  Blueberry Cornmeal Loaf, Karyl's, 318
  Boston Cream Pie, 397
  Brown Sugar Raspberry Loaf, John's, 320
  Carolina Huguenot Torte, 398
  Cinnamon, Alsatian, 370
  classic American cake names, 381
  Coconut Layer, Southern, with Divinity Icing, 394
  cornmeal, about, 310
  Cornmeal Butter, Patty's, 312
  Cranberry Upside-Down, 346
  Edna Lewis's Sunday Night, 330
  Hazelnut Roll with Creamy Prune Filling, 402

Honey, Polish, 323
Honey, Rose's Legendary, 322
Icebox, Magic, old recipe, 118
Icebox (Charlotte Russe), 118
Jam, with Burnt Sugar Glaze, 385
Kugelhopf, 372
layer cakes, about, 380–381
layer cakes, preparing, 382–383
Lemon-Molasses Marble, 386
Lemon Pudding Cake, 128
Lightening, 298
made with fruit, about, 297
Nut, Nina's Fabulous Athenian, with Rum Syrup, 437
Oatmeal, Lazy-Dazy, with Broiled Coconut-Pecan Icing, 388
1-2-3-4, 383
Orange, Ring, with Orange Syrup, Great St. Louis, 328
Orange Blossom, 396
Peanut Brittle Crunch, 404
plain cakes, about, 297
Polenta, Breakfast, Chef Andrea's, 311
Polenta, Palio's, 314
Prune Spice, 343
Semolina, with Orange Flower Syrup, 317
Semolina Ring, from Friuli, 316
Spice, Rich, Soft, 325
Spiced Sandtorte, 356
Spongecake, Hot-Water, 299
Spongecake, Marie's Vanilla, 117
stack, about, 393
Stack, Dried Apple Gingerbread, 392
Sunshine, 307
Sunshine, old recipe, 307
symbolic significance and traditions, 294–296
Walnut, Sephardic, with Honey-Lemon Syrup, 439
Watermelon, old recipe, 404
Canadian Molasses Leathernecks, 262
Cannoli Cream, Black and White, 89
Cannoli Cream, Light, for Fresh Fruit, 89
Cape Cod Cranberry "Linzer" Pie, 468
Capirotada (Santa Fe Bread Pudding with Wine and Cheese), 195
Cappuccino, Frozen (A Blender Drink), 606
Cappuccino Semifreddo, 605

Caramel
  -and Pecan-Glazed Brownies, 267
  Bread Pudding, Omaha, 190
  Cream Pie, Mile-High, 488
  Custard, Cuban, 147
  Pôts de Crème, 141
  Pudding, South American, 125
  Sauce, Rusty Nail, 614
  Sauce, Warm, 614
  -Walnut Tart, 549
Caramelized Panettone Bread Pudding, 198
caraway comfits, about, 434
Carême's Hazelnut Pithiviers with Orange, 572
Carlo's Cookie Dough, 272
Carolina Huguenot Torte, 398
Carrot
  -Applesauce Cake with Lemon–Cream Cheese Frosting, 390
  Custard Tart, Gingered, 542
  Pudding, old recipes, 223, 543
Cassola (Italian Skillet Cheesecake), 407
Caudles and lears, about, 458
Challah Bread Pudding with Raisins, 185
Charlotte, Warm Pear, 200
Charlotte Russe (Icebox Cake), 118
Cheese. *See also* Cheesecakes; Ricotta
  Apple and Cheddar Pie, 455
  Blintz "Soufflé," 164
  Cheddar, adding to apple pie, 455
  Cream, –Lemon Frosting, Applesauce-Carrot Cake with, 390
  Mom's New Noodle Kugel, 206
  -Noodle Dessert, Hungarian, 207
  Tart, Hungarian, 553
  Tiramisù, 160
  and Wine, Santa Fe Bread Pudding with, 195
Cheesecakes
  about, 405–406
  Applesauce, World War I, 410
  Italian Skillet, 407
  old recipe, 409
  Sour Cream, New York–Style, 408
  White Torta, old recipe, 406
Cherry(ies)
  -Berry-Rhubarb Pie, Deep-Dish, 472

Dried, or Cranberries, and Honey, Wild Rice Pudding with, 178
and Nectarine Cobbler with Rich Pastry Dough ("Summer Riches"), 40
removing pits from, 41
Sour, Clafouti, 218
Sour, Compote, Spiced, for Ice Cream, 619
Tennessee Moonshine Cookies, 261
Winter Fruit Dumplings, 240
Chestnut(s)
and Cream Dessert (Mont Blanc), 112
Nesselrode Sauce, 621
Chiffon Pie, Lime, Split-Level, 506
Chiffon Pie, Sour Cream Pumpkin, 497
Chocolate. *See also* Chocolate Cakes; White Chocolate
All-American Fudge-Chunk Brownies, 266
Bread Pudding, Italian, 196
Cream Pie, Lutz's, 490
-Glazed Lebkuchen, 252
-Hazelnut Pudding, Warm, 130
history of, 411
Hoover Toffee Ice Cream Pie, 512
Mexican, Flan with Kahlúa, 145
Mocha Pôts de Crème, 141
Molten, Thomas Keller's, 162
The Original Toll House Cookie, 264
Peanut Butter Pie with Fudge Topping, 491
Pecan-and-Caramel-Glazed Brownies, 267
Pôts de Crème, 141
Pudding, Double, 122
Ray's Holiday Nut Tart, 551
Sauce, Dark, Pears Poached in Mint Tea with, 80
Sauce, Warm, Hungarian Walnut-Filled Crepes with, 236
Savannah Lace Christmas Cookies, 263
Schrafft's Hot Fudge Sauce, 613
Silk Bread Pudding, 194
Soufflé, Edna Lewis's, 168
-Tart, old recipe, 551
Chocolate Cakes
Chocolate Chiffon Loaf, 418
Chocolate Cloud, 420
Fudgy Chocolate Layer, 414
German chocolate, about, 413

Low-Fat Chocolate Nut Torte, 416
Quick Chocolate Candy, 412
Christmas
Cinnamon Stars, Alsatian, 283
Cookies, Anise, New Mexico, 260
Cookies, Savannah Lace, 263
English puddings (Spotted Dick, etc.), old recipes, 213
Fruitcake, The Four Seasons' (Light Fruitcake Wrapped in Marzipan), 426
Fruitcake, Tyrolean, 432
Cider
boiled, about, 518
Boiled, Pie, New England, 519
Boyled Sider, old recipe, 518
-Lemon Sauce, 611
Cinnamon
Cake, Alsatian, 370
-Espresso Ice Cream, 596
Stars, Alsatian Christmas, 283
Citrus Wine Jelly, 102
Citrus zest, working with, 25
Clafouti, Sour Cherry, 218
Claremont Diner Coconut Cream Pie, 484
Classic Crème Brûlée, 150
Classic Italian Coffee Ice, 601
The Coach House Bread-and-Butter Pudding, 184
The Coach House Quince and Almond Tart, 546
Cobblers and crisps. *See also* Shortcake(s)
about, 32–34
Apple Mush, 53
Apple Pandowdy, 48
Black and Blueberry Grunt (or Slump), 58
cobblers and crisps, defined, 33–34
Cranberry Crumble with Fall Fruits, 50
Danish Apple and Cookie Crumb Dessert ("Peasant Girl with Veil"), 57
Lightened Down-East Berry Buckle, 62
make-ahead strategy for, 41
Mixed Fruit Cobbler, 35
New Hampshire "Plate Cake," 42
Peach Pot-Pie, old recipe, 38
Pear or Apple Brown Betty with Cake Crumbs, 48
Pear Pandowdy, 47
preparing, tips for, 37

Raylene's Blackberry Cobbler, old recipe, 35
Rhubarb-Strawberry Crisp with Cinnamon-Walnut Topping, 52
Rye 'n Injun, old recipe, 46
Southern-Style Peach and Raspberry Cobbler with Pecan-Crunch Topping, 38
"Summer Riches" (Cherry and Nectarine Cobbler with Rich Pastry Dough), 40
Swedish Apple "Pie" with Vanilla Sauce, 55
Traditional Two-Berry Buckle, 60
Virginia Blackberry Roll, 44
Warm Plum Crisp, 53
Cocoa-Swirled Vanilla Breakfast Cake, Hotel Cipriani's, 354
Coconut
Applesauce-Carrot Cake with Lemon–Cream Cheese Frosting, 390
Blondies, 269
Coffee Cake, Hawaiian, 360
Cream Pie, Claremont Diner, 484
Custards, Brazilian, 148
Jumbles, 247
Layer Cake, Southern, with Divinity Icing, 394
-Pecan Icing, Broiled, Lazy-Dazy Oatmeal Cake with, 388
Tapioca Pudding, Asian-Style, 134
Toasted, –Banana Cream Pie, 485
Coffee
Cappuccino Semifreddo, 605
Coffee Cake with Espresso Glaze, 358
Cup Crème Caramel, 142
Espresso-Cinnamon Ice Cream, 596
Frozen Cappuccino (A Blender Drink), 606
Ice, Classic Italian, 601
Mocha Pôts de Crème, 141
Pôts de Crème, 141
Tiramisù, 160
Whipped Cream, Austrian Walnut Torte with, 400
Coffee Cakes
about, 348–349
Alsatian Cinnamon Cake, 370
"Bee-Sting" Cake, 368
Brown Butter, 352
Coffee, with Espresso Glaze, 358

Coffee Cakes (*cont.*)
  Coiled Yeast Bread with Nut Filling, 377
  Dessert Kugelhopf with Eau-de-Vie Syrup, 374
  Easter bread of Friuli, about, 378
  Hawaiian Coconut, 360
  Helmstetter Kugelhopf, 373
  Hotel Cipriani's Cocoa-Swirled Vanilla Breakfast Cake, 354
  Italian coffee cakes, about, 376
  kugelhopf, about, 372
  Moravian Sugar Cake, 364
  with Nut Streusel, 351
  Prune-Filled Pecan-Caramel Sticky Buns, 366
  Quintessential (Brown Sugar–Buttermilk Crumb Cake), 350
  Real Old-Fashioned Crumb Buns, 362
  Shoo-Fly Cake, 357
  Spiced Sandtorte, 356
  St. Louis Gooey Butter Cake, 375
Cold Sweet Sauce, old recipe, 615
Colonial Cup Custard, 139
Commander's Palace Bread Pudding Soufflé, 192
Compotes and baked fruit
  about, 70–71
  Broiled Pears with Warm Caramel Sauce, 81
  Chilled Citrus Platter, 73
  Crinkly Baked Pears, Trattoria-Style, 79
  Dutch Mennonite Dried Fruit Compote in Creamy Syrup, 76
  Forgotten Pudding, 85
  Honey-Stewed Quinces, 75
  Madeira Dried Fruit Compote, 77
  Marie's Fall Fruit Compote, 74
  Pavlova, 83
  Pears Poached in Mint Tea with Dark Chocolate Sauce, 80
  Poached Plum and Raspberry Compote in Late-Harvest Wine Syrup, 72
  Ruby Baked Apples, 78
  Spiced Sour Cherry Compote for Ice Cream, 619
  Warm Baked Apples with Macaroon Soufflé and Cool Custard, 82

Cookie Crumb and Apple Dessert, Danish ("Peasant Girl with Veil"), 57
Cookies. *See also* Shortbread
  about, 242–243
  All-American Fudge-Chunk Brownies, 266
  Almond and Hazelnut, Crunchy, 282
  Almond Brittle (My All-Time Favorite), 270
  Almond Jumballs, old recipe, 247
  Almond Wafers, Thin, 279
  Alsatian Christmas Cinnamon Stars, 283
  Anise, Señá Martina's old recipe, 260
  Anise Christmas, New Mexico, 260
  Apees, 246
  Apees, old recipe, 246
  Armenian Egg Biscuits, 287
  biscotti, about, 290
  Canadian Molasses Leathernecks, 262
  Carlo's Cookie Dough, 272
  Chocolate-Glazed Lebkuchen, 252
  Christmas, Savannah Lace, 263
  Coconut Blondies, 269
  Coconut Jumbles, 247
  Cornmeal-Almond Biscotti, 291
  Cornmeal Butter (*Crumiri*), 277
  early flavorings for, 244
  Fig-Filled, Sicilian, 289
  Gingerbread, old recipe, 250
  Gingerbread Hermits, 250
  Grandma's Poppy Seed Crescents, 274
  great historical moments, 254–255, 275
  Greek Egg Biscuits, 286
  history of, 243, 244, 254–255, 275
  Honey Cookeys, old recipe, 253
  Hungarian Nut Crescents, 284
  John Thorne's Lemon Icebox Crumbles, 248
  Mary's Pignoli (Italian Pine Nut Macaroons), 276
  M.F.K. Fisher's Ginger Hottendots, 251
  1950s Pecan Puffs, 273
  The Original Toll House, 264
  Pecan-and-Caramel-Glazed Brownies, 267

Quaresimale (Miniature Hazelnut Biscotti), 292
Sand Tarts, 249
Shrewsbury Cakes, 245
Shrewsbury Cakes, old recipe, 245
Tennessee Moonshine, 261
Thomas Jefferson's macaroon recipe, 276
Toasted Benne (Sesame) Wafers, 278
types of, 243
White Chocolate–Macadamia Blondies, 269
Cook & Tell newsletter, 319
Cookware and bakeware
  baking pans, 28–29
  baking pan sizes and equivalents, 31
  knives, 27
  parchment paper, 29
  saucepans, 27–28
  skillets, 28
Cornmeal
  -Almond Biscotti, 291
  Blueberry Loaf, Karyl's, 318
  Butter Cake, Patty's, 312
  Butter Cookies (*Crumiri*), 277
  buying, 310
  cakes, about, 310
  Chef Andrea's Breakfast Polenta Cake, 311
  Durgin-Park's Indian Pudding, 136
  Eliza Leslie's Indian Pound Cake, 301
  Pear Tart with Frangipane, 544
  Rye 'n Injun, old recipe, 46
  -Yogurt Biscuits, Low-Fat, Blueberry Shortcakes with, 68
Cranberry(ies)
  Apple Pie, Down-East, 456
  Crumble with Fall Fruits, 50
  Dried, or Cherries, and Honey, Wild Rice Pudding with, 178
  Duff, 219
  "Linzer" Pie, Cape Cod, 468
  in North American culinary history, 50–51
  -Raspberry Kissel, 95
  -Raspberry Tart Pastiche, 540
  Upside-Down Cake, 346
Cream
  buying, for recipes, 21–22
  old-fashioned, buying, 493
  whipping, 24
Cream Pies
  about, 478–479

Butterscotch, Midwestern, 482
Chocolate, Lutz's, 490
Coconut, Claremont Diner, 484
Mile-High Caramel, 488
Peanut Butter, with Fudge Topping, 491
Sour Cream Pumpkin Chiffon, 497
Toasted Coconut–Banana, 485
White Chocolate Banana, 486
Creams, fools, and jellies. *See also* Fool(s); Jellies; Syllabubs
about, 86–88
Apricot Sponge, 99
Black and White Cannoli Cream, 89
Charlotte Russe (Icebox Cake), 118
Cranberry-Raspberry Kissel, 95
Frozen Scottish Atholl Brose, 113
Jefferson's Tea Cream, 103
Light Cannoli Cream for Fresh Fruit, 89
Magic Icebox, old recipe, 118
Modern Almond Blancmange, 106
Mont Blanc (Chestnut and Cream Dessert), 112
Panna Cotta and Poached Pears in Merlot Syrup, 108
Peach Sponge, old recipe, 99
Pear Snow, 96
Raspberry Flummery, 98
Raspberry Flummery, old recipe, 98
Ricotta Bavarian, 110
Sack Creame, old recipe, 104
Sherry Velvet Cream, 104
Snow Eggs, old recipe, 87
Spanish Cream (Snow Cream), 105
Strawberry Nonsense, 115
Warm Amaretto-Cognac Zabaglione, 114
Crema Catalana, old recipe, 150
Crème anglaise (custard sauce), about, 121
Crème Brûlée
about, 121
Classic, 150
origins of, 149
Pumpkin, Bert Greene's, 151
Crème Caramel
about, 121
Coffee Cup, 142
Maple Sugar, Jasper White's, 143

Crème Fraîche, 624
Crepes
Hapsburg, about, 236
Hungarian Walnut-Filled, with Warm Chocolate Sauce, 236
Crinkly Baked Pears, Trattoria-Style, 79
Crisps. *See* Cobblers and Crisps
Crookneck or Winter Squash Pudding, old recipe, 229
Crumb Buns, Real Old-Fashioned, 362
Crumble, Cranberry, with Fall Fruits, 50
Crumble, defined, 34
Crumiri (Cornmeal Butter Cookies), 277
Cuban Caramel Custard, 147
Cucidati (Sicilian Fig-Filled Cookies), 289
Curd, Orange, 622
Currant(s)
Dried-Fruit Mincemeat Pie with Lattice Cream Cheese Crust, 524
Molded Rice Pudding with Caramel Sauce, 181
Nesselrode Sauce, 621
New England Oatmeal Pudding with Warm Maple Syrup, 211
-Orange Pound Cake, 302
Steamed Pumpkin Pudding with Ginger-Lemon Cream, 228
Tyrolean Christmas Fruitcake, 432
Custard Pies
about, 478
baking, 479
brown sugar pie, about, 480
Buttermilk Silk, 481
Dried Peach, with Custard and Meringue, 500
Egg Pan-Pie, old recipe, 479
Indiana Sugar Cream, 480
Iowa's Favorite, 493
Lemon, Grandmother's Souffléed, 503
Lime Chiffon, Split-Level, 506
Neapolitan Easter, 510
Pompkin Pudding, old recipe, 496
pumpkin, about, 494
Pumpkin, Best-Ever, 495
Quince Meringue, 501
Rice, Mary's, 508
Sour Cream Raisin, 504
Sweet Potato, 499

Custard(s). *See also* Pôts de Crème
about, 120–121
Bert Greene's Pumpkin Crème Brûlée, 151
Burnt Cream, old recipe, 149
Cabinet Pudding, 158
Caramel, Cuban, 147
Classic Crème Brûlée, 150
Coconut, Brazilian, 148
Coffee Cup Crème Caramel, 142
Crema Catalana, old recipe, 150
Cup, Colonial, 139
Floating Island, 155
Luli's Trifle, 156
Maple Sugar Crème Caramel, Jasper White's, 143
Mexican Chocolate Flan with Kahlúa, 145
Oeufs à la Neige with Raspberries, 153
old recipes, 138, 140
preparing, tips for, 137–138
Sauce, Eggnog, 609
Sauce, Low-Fat, 610
Tiramisù, 160
Whim Wham, old recipe, 157
Custardy Prune Pudding, 216
Czech Noodle and Apple Soufflé, 209

D
Danish Apple and Cookie Crumb Dessert ("Peasant Girl with Veil"), 57
Date(s)
Dried-Fruit Mincemeat Pie with Lattice Cream Cheese Crust, 524
Dried Fruit Strudel with Pear-Brandy Custard Sauce, 566
English Toffee Pudding, 222
Polish Honey Cake, 323
Pudding, Steamed, 227
Steamed Pumpkin Pudding with Ginger-Lemon Cream, 228
Della Lutes' Mother's shortcake, old recipe, 66
Dessert(s)
about the recipes, 16–18
home desserts, memories of, 12–13
ingredients for, 21–22
kitchen equipment for, 26–31
measuring ingredients for, 19–20

Dessert(s) (*cont.*)
  pure flavors for, 18–19
  rise of, around the world,
    13–15
  techniques and tips for, 24–25
Diplomat pudding, about, 159
Doughnuts, history of, 214
Down-East Berry Buckle,
  Lightened, 62
Down-East Cranberry Apple Pie,
  456
Dried fruit. *See* Fruit, Dried
Drinks
  Frozen Cappuccino (A Blender
    Drink), 606
  Robertson Davies' Punchbowl
    (A Spirited Finale), 625
Dulce de Leche (South American
  Caramel Pudding), 125
Dumplings
  about, 213
  Apple, Baked, 239
  fruit, types of, 238
  Winter Fruit, 240
Durgin-Park's Indian Pudding,
  136
Dutch Mennonite Dried Fruit
  Compote in Creamy Syrup, 76

E

Easter
  bread of Friuli, about, 378
  eggs (with blancmange), family
    recipe for, 106–107
  Pie, Neapolitan, 510
East-West Ginger Cake, 334
Eggnog Custard Sauce, 609
Egg(s). *See also* Meringue
  buying, for recipes, 21
  food safety and, 23
  Pan-Pie, old recipe, 479
  whites, beating, 24
Election Cake, 430
English Brown Bread Ice Cream,
  598
English Christmas puddings, types
  of, 213
English Toffee Pudding, 222
Equipment, kitchen. *See also*
  Cookware and bakeware
    cooling racks, 27
    electric mixers, 26
    essential gadgets, 30
    food processors, 26
    large work surface, 27
    nonstick-coated baking sheets,
      26–27
Espresso-Cinnamon Ice Cream,
  596
Eve's Pudding, old recipe, 216

F

Far Breton (Custardy Prune
  Pudding), 216
Farina or Spelt Pudding, old recipe,
  210
Fig(s)
  Dried-Fruit Mincemeat Pie with
    Lattice Cream Cheese Crust,
    524
  -Filled Cookies, Sicilian, 289
  Madeira Dried Fruit Compote,
    77
  Oven-Steamed Figgy Pudding,
    226
The Finamore Shortcake, 65
Flan de Chocolate con Kahlúa
  (Mexican Chocolate Flan with
  Kahlúa), 145
Floating Island, 155
  about, 152–153
  old recipe, 155
Flour
  adding to batters and doughs,
    25
  for recipes, 21
  sifting, 24
Flummery
  about, 97
  Raspberry, 98
  Raspberry, old recipe, 98
Foamy Sauce, 616
Foamy Sauce, old recipe, 616
Fool(s)
  about, 86, 90
  Apricot-Amaretto, 92
  Norfolk-Fool, old recipe, 92
  Plum, 91
Forgotten Pudding, 85
The Four Seasons' Christmas
  Fruitcake (Light Fruitcake
  Wrapped in Marzipan), 426
The Fraze (Froise), Moise and
  Tansy (Fruit Pancakes), about,
  231–232
Fraze with Pippins (Apples), old
  recipe, 232
French Canadian Maple Sugar Pie,
  521
French Fruit Puffs, 588
Fritters, Apple (or other fruit), 586
Fritters, old recipe, 587
Frozen Cappuccino (A Blender
  Drink), 606
Frozen Desserts. *See* Ice; Ice
  Cream; Semifreddo
Frozen Scottish Atholl Brose, 113
Fruit, Dried. *See also* Fruitcakes;
  specific dried fruits
  Compote, Dutch Mennonite, in
    Creamy Syrup, 76

Compote, Madeira, 77
Dried-Fruit Mincemeat Pie with
  Lattice Cream Cheese Crust,
  524
mincemeat, about, 523
Strudel with Pear-Brandy
  Custard Sauce, 566
Fruitcakes
  about, 422
  caraway comfits, about, 434
  Dark, Mother Church's
    Spirited, 424
  Election Cake, 430
  The Four Seasons' Christmas
    (Light, Wrapped in
    Marzipan), 426
  history of, 422–424
  Mr. Guinness's Cake, 428
  Mrs. Dalgairns' Scottish Seed
    Cake, 435
  old recipe, 427
  Scots Seed Cake, old recipe,
    435
  seed cakes, about, 434
  Tennessee Moonshine Cookies,
    261
  Tyrolean Christmas, 432
Fruit Pies
  Apple Crumb, Indiana Orchard,
    454
  Apple Crumb, variations on,
    455
  Apple "Half-Moon," Fried (or
    Baked), 474
  Apple-Pecan Upside-Down,
    Baked in a Skillet, 476
  apple pies, frying, old recipe,
    475
  Cranberry-Apple, Down-East,
    456
  Cranberry "Linzer," Cape Cod,
    468
  Double-Berry Lattice, 462
  Dried Apple "Pour-Through,"
    459
  Grape, Fresh, 470
  Grape, old recipe, 471
  history of, 452–453
  lears and caudles, about, 458
  Peach, Country, 464
  Peach-Berry, Lattice-Topped,
    466
  Peach- or Nectarine-Berry, with
    Almond Crumb Topping, 467
  Pear, Chunky, Rhode Island,
    461
  Plum, Fresh, 471
  Rhubarb-Cherry-Berry, Deep-
    Dish, 472
  Taffety Tart, old recipe, 453

thickening, 465
Fruit Puddings. *See also*
Dumplings; Pancake(s)
Baked Pear (or Apple) Batter
Pudding, 215
Boiled Potatoe Pudding, old
recipe, 224
Carrot Puding, old recipe, 223
Cranberry Duff, 219
Crookneck or Winter Squash
Pudding, old recipe, 229
Custardy Prune Pudding, 216
English Toffee Pudding, 222
Eve's Pudding, old recipe, 216
history of, 212–214
individual steamed puddings,
preparing, 225
old rules for, 215
Oven-Steamed Figgy Pudding,
226
Persimmon Buttermilk
Pudding, 220
Sour Cherry Clafouti, 218
Steamed Date Pudding, 227
Steamed Pumpkin Pudding
with Ginger-Lemon Cream,
228
Tennessee Old Maid's Sweet
Potato Pudding, 230
Tilly's Pudding, old recipe, 222
Fruit(s). *See also* Compotes and
baked fruit; *specific fruits*
Apples (or other fruit) Fritters,
586
dumplings, types of, 238
exotic fruits, about, 71
Fall, Compote, Marie's, 74
-Filled Lattice Torte with Three
Fillings, 559
Forgotten Pudding, 85
Four Red, Summer Pudding of,
202
Fresh, Light Cannoli Cream
for, 89
Mixed, Cobbler, 35
native to North America, 50–
51
New Hampshire "Plate Cake,"
42
Puffs, French, 588
Summer, Torte, All-Time-Best,
344
Winter, Dumplings, 240
Fudge, Hashish, old recipe, 268

G

Galaktaboureko (Greek Custard-
Filled Phyllo Pastry), 574
Galette, Pear, Free-Form, 532
galettes, about, 532

Gâteau à la Canelle (Alsatian
Cinnamon Cake), 370
German chocolate cake, about, 413
Ginger. *See also* Gingerbread
Candied, and Lemon Glaze,
Marie's Rich Gingerbread
with, 336
Dried Apple Gingerbread Stack
Cake, 392
Gingerbread Custard, 204
Gingerbread Hermits, 250
Gingered Carrot Custard Tart,
542
Hottendots, M.F.K. Fisher's,
251
Mother Church's Spirited Dark
Fruitcake, 424
Oatmeal Shortbread Squares,
257
Gingerbread
East-West Ginger Cake, 334
Eliza Acton's, 335
history of, 332–333
old recipes, 250, 335
Rich, Marie's, with Candied
Ginger and Lemon Glaze,
336
Grains. *See also* Cornmeal; Oats;
Rice
grain-based puddings, about,
210
Neapolitan Easter Pie, 510
Spelt or Farina Pudding, old
recipe, 210
Granita di Caffè con Panna
(Italian Coffee Ice), 601
Grape-Nuts Pudding, 127
Grape Pie, Fresh, 470
Grape Pie, old recipe, 471
Grasmere Gingerbread (Oatmeal
Gingerbread Squares), 257
Greek Custard-Filled Phyllo Pastry,
574
Greek Egg Biscuits, 286
Green Pudding, old recipe, 200
Green Tomato and Apple
Mincemeat Pie, 526
Grunt, Black and Blueberry, 58
Grunt, defined, 34
Gubana (Coiled Yeast Coffee
Bread with Nut Filling), 377

H

"Half-Moon" Pies, Apple, Fried
(or Baked), 474
Halvah Ice Cream, 599
Hamantaschen, about, 580
Hamantaschen (Jam-Filled
"Haman's Pockets"), 579
Hapsburg Crepes, about, 236

Hard Sauce, 615
Hashish Fudge, old recipe, 268
"Hasty pudding," about, 135
Hawaiian Coconut Coffee Cake,
360
Hazelnut(s)
and Almond Cookies, Crunchy,
282
Biscotti, Miniature
(Quaresimale), 292
-Chocolate Pudding, Warm,
130
Hungarian Nut Crescents, 284
Pithiviers with Orange,
Carême's, 572
Ray's Holiday Nut Tart, 551
Roll with Creamy Prune Filling,
402
Semifreddo, 603
Helmstetter Kugelhopf, 373
Hermits, Gingerbread, 250
Himmelgestirn (Alsatian Christmas
Cinnamon Stars), 283
Honey
Cake, Polish, 323
Cake, Rose's Legendary, 322
Cookeys, old recipe, 253
Ice Cream, Alsatian Spiced, 599
-Lemon Syrup, Sephardic
Walnut Cake with, 439
-Nut Puff Clusters, Jewish, 583
-Stewed Quinces, 75
Hoover Toffee Ice Cream Pie, 512
Hotel Cipriani's Cocoa-Swirled
Vanilla Breakfast Cake, 354
Hot-Water Spongecake, 299
Huguenot Torte, Carolina, 398
Hungarian Cheese-Noodle
Dessert, 207
Hungarian Cheese Tart, 553
Hungarian Nut Crescents, 284
Hungarian Walnut-Filled Crepes
with Warm Chocolate Sauce, 236
Hypocrite pies ("stacked pies,"
"two-story pies"), 522

I

Ice
Coffee, Classic Italian, 601
Slushy Melon, with Cointreau,
600
Wine, Coarse-Crystal, with
Sangría Granita Variation, 602
Icebox Cake, Magic, old recipe,
118
Icebox Cake (Charlotte Russe),
118
Ice Cream
Alsatian Spiced Honey, 599
English Brown Bread, 598

Ice Cream (*cont.*)
  Espresso-Cinnamon, 596
  Halvah, 599
  history of, 590–592
  ice cream makers, choosing,
    593
  Lemon, old recipe, 595
  Lemon Custard,
    Grandmother's, 595
  Peach, Ice Cream Social, 594
  Pie, Hoover Toffee, 512
  preparing, without ice cream
    machine, 593
  Spiced Sour Cherry Compote
    for, 619
  Trumps Peanut Brittle Sundae,
    607
Indiana Orchard Apple Crumb Pie,
  454
Indiana Sugar Cream Pie, 480
Indian pudding, about, 135
Indian Pudding, Durgin-Park's,
  136
Iowa's Favorite Custard Pie, 493
Italian Chocolate Bread Pudding,
  196
Italian coffee cakes, about, 376
Italian Coffee Ice, Classic, 601
Italian Pine Nut Macaroons
  (Mary's Pignoli), 276
Italian Ricotta Pudding, 129
Italian Skillet Cheesecake, 407

J
Jack Daniel's Raisin Roll with
  Whiskey Sauce, 570
"Jack Wax," about, 517
Jam
  Almond Brittle Cookies (My
    All-Time Favorite), 270
  cakes, about, 385
  Cake with Burnt Sugar Glaze,
    385
  -Filled "Hamen's Pockets"
    (Hamantaschen), 579
  Roly-Poly, about, 213
  Roly-Poly, Baked, 568
Jasper White's Maple Sugar Crème
  Caramel, 143
Jefferson, Thomas, recipes, 87,
  103, 276
Jefferson's Tea Cream, 103
Jellies
  alcoholic Jell-O, story about,
    102
  Citrus Wine, 102
  Jell-O, history of, 101
  molded, about, 100–101
  molded, history of, 87

old recipe for, 100
  Rum Jelly, old recipe, 88
Jewish Honey-Nut Puff Clusters,
  583

K
Kahke (Armenian Egg Biscuits),
  287
Karythopitta (Nina's Fabulous
  Athenian Nut Cake with Rum
  Syrup), 437
Kissel, Cranberry-Raspberry, 95
Kitchen equipment. *See*
  Equipment, kitchen
Kolachy, Apple, Crisp, 576
Koulouriaka (Greek Egg Biscuits),
  286
Kugel, about, 205
Kugel, Mom's New Noodle, 206
Kugelhopf
  about, 372
  Alsatian Cinnamon Cake, 370
  Dessert, with Eau-de-Vie Syrup,
    374
  Helmstetter, 373

L
Lard, about, 449
Lazy-Dazy Oatmeal Cake with
  Broiled Coconut-Pecan Icing,
  388
Lears and caudles, about, 458
Lebkuchen, Chocolate-Glazed,
  252
Lekvar, Prune (Thick Prune
  Puree), 367
Lemon(s)
  about, 502
  -Cider Sauce, 611
  Cream, 623
  Custard Ice Cream,
    Grandmother's, 595
  Icebox Crumbles, John
    Thorne's, 248
  Ice Cream, old recipe, 595
  lemon juice, for recipes, 22
  -Molasses Marble Cake, 386
  Pie, Grandmother's Souffléed,
    503
  pies, about, 502
  Pies, old recipe, 502
  Pudding Cake, 128
  Sauce with Lemon Slices, John's
    Mother's, 612
  Syllabub, 94
  Tart, World's Best, 534
Lewis, Edna, 168–169, 330
Life cake (lebkuchen), history of,
  252

Light Cannoli Cream for Fresh
  Fruit, 89
Lightened Down-East Berry
  Buckle, 62
Lightning Cake, 298
Lime Chiffon Pie, Split-Level, 506
Lime Syllabub, 94
Loaf Cake
  Blueberry Cornmeal, Karyl's,
    318
  Brown Sugar Raspberry, John's,
    320
  Chocolate Chiffon, 418
Long Island Double Blueberry
  Tart, 536
Low-Fat Chocolate Nut Torte,
  416
Low-Fat Cornmeal-Yogurt
  Biscuits, Blueberry Shortcakes
  with, 68
Low-Fat Custard Sauce, 610
Luli's Simplest Rice Pudding, 172
Lutz's Chocolate Cream Pie, 490

M
Macadamia(s)
  Coconut Blondies, 269
  –White Chocolate Blondies,
    269
Macaroons, Italian Pine Nut
  (Mary's Pignoli), 276
Macaroons, Thomas Jefferson's
  original recipe, 276
Macaroon Soufflé and Cool
  Custard, Warm Baked Apples
  with, 82
Madeira Dried Fruit Compote, 77
Maine Maple Sugar Pie, 517
Mandulás Kifli (Hungarian Nut
  Crescents), 284
Maple Sugar
  Crème Caramel, Jasper White's,
    143
  in food history, 143
  Pie, French Canadian, 521
  Pie, Maine, 517
  on snow (Jack Wax), 517
Maple Syrup
  Marie's Brown Rice Pudding
    with, 179
  Warm, New England Oatmeal
    Pudding with, 211
Marble Cake, Lemon-Molasses,
  386
Mary's Pignoli (Italian Pine Nut
  Macaroons), 276
"Meal Made from Flour," 209
Melon Ice, Slushy, with Cointreau,
  600

Meringue
and Custard, Dried Peach Pie
with, 500
Floating Island, 155
floating island, about, 152–153
Floating Island, old recipe, 155
Forgotten Pudding, 85
oeufs à la neige, about, 152–153
Oeufs à la Neige with
Raspberries, 153
Pavlova, 83
pie topping, note about, 504
snow eggs, description of, 121
Snow Eggs, old recipe, 87
Mexican Chocolate Flan with
Kahlúa, 145
M.F.K. Fisher's Ginger
Hottendots, 251
Midwestern Butterscotch Cream
Pie, 482
Mincemeat
about, 523
Dried-Fruit, Pie with Lattice
Cream Cheese Crust, 524
Green Tomato and Apple, Pie,
526
Minst pyes, old recipe, 524
Mocha Pôts de Crème, 141
Modern Almond Blancmange, 106
Mohn Moons (Grandma's Poppy
Seed Crescents), 274
Molasses
East-West Ginger Cake, 334
Eliza Acton's Gingerbread, 335
Gingerbread Hermits, 250
Leathernecks, Canadian, 262
-Lemon Marble Cake, 386
Marie's Rich Gingerbread with
Candied Ginger and Lemon
Glaze, 336
M.F.K. Fisher's Ginger
Hottendots, 251
Shoo-Fly Cake, 357
Mont Blanc (Chestnut and Cream
Desserts), 112
Moonshine cookies, about, 261
Moonshine Cookies, Tennessee,
261
Moravian Sugar Cake, 364
Mother Church's Spirited Dark
Fruitcake, 424
"Mouthfuls" from Abruzzo, 581
Mr. Guinness's Cake, 428
Mrs. Dalgairns' Scottish Seed
Cake, 435
Muffin Pudding, old recipe, 187
Mürbeteig (Fruit-Filled Lattice
Torte with Three Fillings), 559
Mush, Apple, 53

N
Neapolitan Easter Pie, 510
Nectarine(s)
All-Time-Best Summer Fruit
Torte, 344
-Berry Pie with Almond Crumb
Topping, 467
and Cherry Cobbler with Rich
Pastry Dough ("Summer
Riches"), 40
Nesselrode Sauce, 621
New England Boiled Cider Pie,
519
New England Oatmeal Pudding
with Warm Maple Syrup, 211
New Hampshire "Plate Cake," 42
New Mexico Anise Christmas
Cookies, 260
New York–Style Sour Cream
Cheesecake, 408
Nick Malgieri's Flaky Butter Pie
Dough, 450
1950s Pecan Puffs, 273
Noodle Puddings
about, 205
Czech Noodle and Apple
Soufflé, 209
history of, 170–171
Hungarian Cheese-Noodle
Dessert, 207
Mom's New Noodle Kugel,
206
Norfolk-Fool, old recipe, 92
Nudlovy' Nákyp (Czech Noodle
and Apple Soufflé), 209
Nusstorte (Austrian Walnut Torte
with Coffee Whipped Cream),
400
Nut(s). *See also* Almond(s);
Hazelnut(s); Pecan(s); Walnut(s)
Brown Butter Coffee Cake, 352
Coconut Blondies, 269
Filling, Coiled Yeast Bread
with, 377
grinding, 25
-Honey Puff Clusters, Jewish,
583
Italian Pine Nut Macaroons
(Mary's Pignoli), 276
Mont Blanc (Chestnut and
Cream Dessert), 112
Nesselrode Sauce, 621
Peanut Brittle Crunch Cake,
404
Peanut Butter Pie with Fudge
Topping, 491
Santa Fe Bread Pudding with
Wine and Cheese, 195
storing, 22

Streusel, Coffee Cake with, 351
Tart, Ray's Holiday, 551
Tennessee Moonshine Cookies,
261
toasting, 22
Trumps Peanut Brittle Sundae,
607
White Chocolate–Macadamia
Blondies, 269

O
Oats
Cranberry Crumble with Fall
Fruits, 50
Frozen Scottish Atholl Brose,
113
Lazy-Dazy Oatmeal Cake with
Broiled Coconut-Pecan Icing,
388
New England Oatmeal Pudding
with Warm Maple Syrup, 211
Oatmeal Pudding, old recipe,
211
Oatmeal Shortbread Squares
(Grasmere Gingerbread), 257
Oeufs à la neige, about, 152–153
Oeufs à la Neige with Raspberries,
153
Omaha Caramel Bread Pudding,
190
1-2-3-4 Cake, 383
Orange(s)
Angel Food Cake with
Tangerine Glaze, 309
Blossom Cake, 396
Chilled Citrus Platter, 73
Citrus Wine Jelly, 102
Curd, 622
-Currant Pound Cake, 302
Ring Cake with Orange Syrup,
Great St. Louis, 328
Sandy's Citrus Rice Pudding,
176
Tart, Fresh, 535
The Original Toll House Cookie,
264
Orleans Sweet Potato–Pecan Pie,
522
Ovens, circa 1880, 296
Oven-Steamed Figgy Pudding, 226
Ozark pudding, about, 399

P
Palacsinta (Hapsburg Crepes),
about, 236
Palio's Polenta Cake, 314
Pancake(s)
Apple, Reuben's Legendary,
234

Pancake(s) (*cont.*)
Big Berry Popover, 233
Fraze with Pippins (Apples), old recipe, 232
fruit: The Fraze (Froise), Moise and Tansy, about, 231–232
Hapsburg crepes, about, 236
history of, 213–214
Hungarian Walnut-Filled Crepes with Warm Chocolate Sauce, 236
Pandowdy
Apple, 48
defined, 34, 46
origins of, 46
Pear, 47
Panettone Bread Pudding, Caramelized, 198
Panna Cotta and Poached Pears in Merlot Syrup, 108
Parchment paper, about, 29
Passover recipe (Low-Fat Chocolate Nut Torte), 416
Pastiera Napoletana (Neapolitan Easter Pie), 510
Pastry(ies)
about, 558–559
Apples (or other fruit) Fritters, 586
Baked Jam Roly-Poly, 568
Carême's Hazelnut Pithiviers with Orange, 572
Crisp Apple Kolachy, 576
Dough, Quick Puff, 571
Dried Fruit Strudel with Pear-Brandy Custard Sauce, 566
foreign names for, 585
French Fruit Puffs, 588
fried, about, 585
Fritters, old recipe, 587
Fruit-Filled Lattice Torte with Three Fillings, 559
Hamantaschen (Jam-Filled "Haman's Pockets"), 579
Jack Daniel's Raisin Roll with Whiskey Sauce, 570
Jewish Honey-Nut Puff Clusters, 583
"Mouthfuls" from Abruzzo, 581
Paul Kovi's Poppy Seed Strudel, 564
Pennsylvania Dutch Butter Semmels, 578
Phyllo, Greek Custard-Filled, 574
Ricotta Strudel from Trieste, 562
strudel variations, 563
Pavlova, 83

Peach(es)
All-Time-Best Summer Fruit Torte, 344
-Berry Lattice-Topped Pie, 466
-Berry Pie with Almond Crumb Topping, 467
Dried, Pie with Custard and Meringue, 500
Dutch Mennonite Dried Fruit Compote in Creamy Syrup, 76
Fruit-Filled Lattice Torte with Three Fillings, 559
Ice Cream, Ice Cream Social, 594
Melba Shortcakes, 68
Pie, Country, 464
Pot-Pie (old recipe), 38
and Raspberry Cobbler, with Pecan-Crunch Topping, Southern-Style, 38
Sponge, old recipe, 99
Peanut Brittle Crunch Cake, 404
Peanut Brittle Sundae, Trumps, 607
Peanut Butter Pie with Fudge Topping, 491
Pear(s)
Batter Pudding, Baked, 215
-Brandy Custard Sauce, Dried Fruit Strudel with, 566
Broiled, with Warm Caramel Sauce, 81
Brown Betty with Cake Crumbs, 48
Charlotte, Warm, 200
Cornmeal Tart with Frangipane, 544
Crinkly Baked, Trattoria-Style, 79
Dried-Fruit Mincemeat Pie with Lattice Cream Cheese Crust, 524
Galette Free-Form, 532
Marie's Fall Fruit Compote, 74
Pandowdy, 47
Pie, Chunky, Rhode Island, 461
Poached, and Panna Cotta in Merlot Syrup, 108
Poached in Mint Tea with Dark Chocolate Sauce, 80
Snow, 96
Soufflés, Little, 165
Tart, Alsatian, with Macaroon Crunch Topping, 538
Tarte Tatin, Breakfast, 530
Pecan(s)
All-American Fudge-Chunk Brownies, 266

-and-Caramel-Glazed Brownies, 267
-Apple Upside-Down Pie Baked in a Skillet, 476
-Caramel Sticky Buns, Prune-Filled, 366
Carolina Huguenot Torte, 398
-Coconut Icing, Broiled, Lazy-Dazy Oatmeal Cake with, 388
-Crunch Topping, Southern-Style Peach and Raspberry Cobbler with, 38
Margaret's Apple Cake, 341
Pie, Best-Ever, John Thorne's, 515
Pot-au-Feu Praline Sauce, 620
Puffs, 1950s, 273
Savannah Lace Christmas Cookies, 263
–Sweet Potato Pie, Orleans, 522
Pennsylvania Dutch Butter Semmels, 578
Persimmon Buttermilk Pudding, 220
persimmons, about, 221
Phyllo
Pastry, Greek Custard-Filled, 574
Paul Kovi's Poppy Seed Strudel, 564
Ricotta Strudel from Trieste, 562
Pie Dough
Basic, 449
Flaky Butter, Nick Malgieri's, 450
fully baking, 448
lining pie pan with, 446–447
make-ahead strategy for, 444–445
partially baking, 447–448
perfect, preparing, 443–445
Rich Tart, 451
Piernik (Polish Honey Cake), 323
Pies. *See also* Cream Pies; Custard Pies; Fruit Pies; Pie Dough; Tarts
baking, step by step, 442–445
Black Walnut, 517
Boiled Cider, New England, 519
Dried-Fruit Mincemeat, with Cream Cheese Crust, 524
Dried Peach, with Custard and Meringue, 500
Green Tomato and Apple Mincemeat, 526
history of, 441–442
Ice Cream, Hoover Toffee, 512
lemon, about, 502
lemon, old recipe, 502

lining pans for, 446–447

Maple Sugar, French Canadian, 521

Maple Sugar, Maine, 517

Minst pyes, old recipe, 524

nut, sugar, and mincemeat, about, 514–515

Pecan, Best-Ever, John Thorne's, 515

Sweet Potato–Pecan, Orleans, 522

Torta from Gourds, old recipe, 493

Pine Nut(s)

Coiled Yeast Bread with Nut Filling, 377

Macaroons, Italian (Mary's Pignoli), 276

Pithiviers, about, 573

Pithiviers, Hazenut, with Orange, Carême's, 572

Pluma Mooss (Dutch Mennonite Dried Fruit Compote in Creamy Syrup), 76

Plum(s). *See also* Prune(s)

Crisp, Warm, 53

Fool, 91

Fruit-Filled Lattice Torte with Three Fillings, 559

Pie, Fresh, 471

and Raspberry Compote, Poached, in Late-Harvest Wine Syrup, 72

and Raspberry Compote in Late-Harvest Wine Syrup, Poached, 72

Polenta Cake, Breakfast, Chef Andrea's, 311

Polenta Cake, Palio's, 314

Polish Apple Tart, 556

Polish Honey Cake, 323

Popover, Big Berry, 233

Poppy Seed Crescents, Grandma's, 274

Poppy Seed Strudel, Paul Kovi's, 564

Potato. *See* Sweet Potato

Pot-au-Feu Praline Sauce, 620

Pôts de Crème, 140

about, 121

Caramel, 141

Chocolate, 141

Coffee, 141

Mocha, 141

Pound Cakes

Currant-Orange, 302

Indian, Eliza Leslie's, 301

Little Round, 304

old recipe, 303

Viennese version, 304

Whipped Cream, 305

Praline Sauce, Pot-au-Feu, 620

Prune(s)

Dried Fruit Strudel with Pear-Brandy Custard Sauce, 566

Dutch Mennonite Dried Fruit Compote in Creamy Syrup, 76

-Filled Pecan-Caramel Sticky Buns, 366

Filling, Creamy, Hazelnut Roll with, 402

Madeira Dried Fruit Compote, 77

Marie's Fall Fruit Compote, 74

Mother Church's Spirited Dark Fruitcake, 424

Pudding, Custardy, 216

Spice Cake, 343

Puddings. *See also* Bread Puddings; Custard(s); Fruit Puddings; Noodle Puddings; Rice Puddings; Soufflés

Banana, 126

Banana, with Vanilla Wafers, 127

Butterscotch, 124

Caramel, South American, 125

Chocolate, Double, 122

Chocolate-Hazelnut, Warm, 130

Coconut Tapioca, Asian-Style, 134

English Christmas puddings, types of, 213

Eve's, old recipe, 216

grain-based, about, 210

Grape-Nuts, 127

hasty puddings, about, 135

Indian, Durgin-Park's, 136

Indian puddings, about, 135

Lemon Pudding Cake, 128

Oatmeal, old recipe, 211

Oatmeal, with Warm Maple Syrup, New England, 211

Prune, Custardy, 216

Ricotta, Italian, 129

ricotta, made in Italy, 129

simple, description of, 120–121

Spelt or Farina, old recipe, 210

Sponge, old recipe, 128

steamed, individual, preparing, 225

Sweet Potato Pudding, Rum-Glazed, 224

Tapioca, Fluffy Baked, 133

Tapioca, old recipe, 132

vegetable, about, 223

Puff Pastry Dough, Quick, 571

Pumpkin

Chiffon Sour Cream Pie, 497

Crème Brûlée, Bert Greene's, 151

pie, about, 494

Pie, Best-Ever, 495

(Pompkin) Pudding, old recipe, 496

Pudding, Steamed, with Ginger-Lemon Cream, 228

puree, about making, 496

Punch, Robertson Davies' Punchbowl (A Spirited Finale), 625

Q

Quaresimale (Miniature Hazelnut Biscotti), 292

Quatre-Quarts (Little Round Pound Cakes), 304

Quince(s)

and Almond Tart, The Coach House, 546

and Apple Pie, 455

Honey-Stewed, 75

Meringue Pie, 501

Pye, old recipe, 547

Quindin de Ya-Ya (Brazilian Coconut Custards), 148

Quintessential Coffee Cake (Brown Sugar–Buttermilk Crumb), 350

R

Raisin(s)

Apple Bread Pudding, 186

Baked Custard-Style Rice Pudding, 174

Bon Ton's New Orleans Bread Pudding with Whiskey Sauce, 188

Buttermilk Corn Bread Pudding, 187

Challah Bread Pudding with, 185

Dried Fruit Strudel with Pear-Brandy Custard Sauce, 566

Dutch Mennonite Dried Fruit Compote in Creamy Syrup, 76

Election Cake, 430

Gingerbread Custard, 204

Gingerbread Hermits, 250

Helmstetter Kugelhopf, 373

Hungarian Cheese-Noodle Dessert, 207

Jam Cake with Burnt Sugar Glaze, 385

Mom's New Noodle Kugel, 206

Raisin(s) (*cont.*)
 Mother Church's Spirited Dark
  Fruitcake, 424
 Mr. Guinness's Cake, 428
 Nesselrode Sauce, 621
 New England Oatmeal Pudding
  with Warm Maple Syrup, 211
 Pie, Sour Cream, 504
 Roll with Whiskey Sauce, Jack
  Daniel's, 570
 Rum-Glazed Sweet Potato
  Pudding, 224
 Santa Fe Bread Pudding with
  Wine and Cheese, 195
 Sicilian Fig-Filled Cookies, 289
 Tennessee Moonshine Cookies,
  261
 Tyrolean Christmas Fruitcake,
  432
Raspberry(ies)
 Brown Sugar Loaf, John's, 320
 Chunky Double-Berry Sauce,
  617
 -Cranberry Kissel, 95
 -Cranberry Tart Pastiche, 540
 Flummery, 98
 Flummery, old recipe, 98
 Lattice-Topped Peach-Berry
  Pie, 466
 Lightened Down-East Berry
  Buckle, 62
 Luli's Trifle, 156
 and Peach Cobbler, with Pecan-
  Crunch Topping, Southern-
  Style, 38
 Peach Melba Shortcakes, 68
 and Plum Compote, Poached,
  in Late-Harvest Wine Syrup,
  72
 Sauce, 617
 Summer Pudding of Four Red
  Fruits, 202
 Traditional Two-Berry Buckle,
  60
Raylene's Blackberry Cobbler, old
 recipe, 35
Reuben's Legendary Apple
 Pancake, 234
Rhode Island Chunky Pear Pie,
 461
Rhubarb
 -Cherry-Berry Pie, Deep-Dish,
  472
 Fruit-Filled Lattice Torte with
  Three Fillings, 559
 -Strawberry Crisp with
  Cinnamon-Walnut Topping,
  52
Rice. *See also* Rice Puddings
 Pie, Mary's, 508

Pudding Tart, Warm, with
 Dried Fruit, 554
 Torta, old recipe, 555
Rice Puddings
 Baked Custard-Style, 174
 Brown Rice, with Maple Syrup,
  Marie's, 179
 choosing rice for, 171
 Citrus, Sandy's, 176
 as comfort food, 172
 Creamy Diner-Style, 173
 history of, 170–171
 Lady Leicester's Spanish Pap,
  old recipe, 173
 Molded, with Caramel Sauce,
  181
 Rice Creame, old recipe, 177
 Simplest, Luli's, 172
 Thunder and Lightning, about,
  213
 Wild Rice, with Honey and
  Dried Cherries or Cranberries,
  178
Ricotta
 Bavarian, 110
 Black and White Cannoli
  Cream, 89
 Italian Skillet Cheesecake, 407
 Light Cannoli Cream for Fresh
  Fruit, 89
 Mary's Rice Pie, 508
 Neapolitan Easter Pie, 510
 Pudding, Italian, 129
 puddings, in Italy, 129
 Strudel from Trieste, 562
Riz à l'Impératrice, Lightened
 (Molded Rice Pudding with
 Caramel Sauce), 181
Robertson Davies' Punchbowl (A
 Spirited Finale), 625
Roly-Poly, Baked Jam, 568
Rose's Legendary Honey Cake,
 322
Rose water, about, 244
Ruby Baked Apples, 78
Rum
 -Glazed Sweet Potato Pudding,
  224
 Jelly, old recipe, 88
 Nesselrode Sauce, 621
 Robertson Davies' Punchbowl
  (A Spirited Finale), 625
 Syrup, Nina's Fabulous
  Athenian Nut Cake with, 437
Rusty Nail Caramel Sauce, 614
Rye 'n Injun, old recipe, 46

S

Sabayon, Sweet Muscat, 624
Sack Creame, old recipe, 104

Salzburger Nockerl (Saltzburg
 Little Mountain Soufflé), 166
Sand Tarts, 249
Sandtorte, Spiced, 356
Santa Fe Bread Pudding with Wine
 and Cheese, 195
Sauces
 about, 608
 Apple Pudding, old recipe, 611
 Caramel, Rusty Nail, 614
 Caramel, Warm, 614
 Cider-Lemon, 611
 Cold Sweet, old recipe, 615
 Crème Fraîche, 624
 Custard, Low-Fat, 610
 Double-Berry, Chunky, 617
 Eggnog Custard, 609
 Foamy, 616
 Foamy, old recipe, 616
 Hard, 615
 Hot Fudge, Schrafft's, 613
 Lemon, with Lemon Slices,
  John's Mother's, 612
 Lemon Cream, 623
 Nesselrode, 621
 Orange Curd, 622
 Pot-au-Feu Praline, 620
 Raspberry, 617
 Spiced Sour Cherry Compote
  for Ice Cream, 619
 Sweet Muscat Sabayon, 624
 Wine, for Rum or Batter
  Pudding, old recipe, 618
 Wine, Southern, for
  Spongecake, 618
Savannah Lace Christmas Cookies,
 263
Schrafft's Hot Fudge Sauce, 613
Scots Seed Cake, old recipe, 435
Scottish Atholl Brose, Frozen, 113
Scottish Petticoat Tail Shortbread,
 Real, 256
Scottish Seed Cake, Mrs.
 Dalgairns', 435
seed cakes, about, 434
Semifreddo
 about, 592
 Cappuccino, 605
 Hazelnut, 603
Semolina Cake with Orange Flower
 Syrup, 317
Semolina Ring Cake from Friuli,
 316
Señá Martina's Anise Cookies, old
 recipe, 260
Sephardic Walnut Cake with
 Honey-Lemon Syrup, 439
Sesame (Benne), Toasted, Wafers,
 278
Sherry Velvet Cream, 104

Shoo-Fly Cake, 357
Shortbread
    butter quantities in, 256
    dough, handling, 259
    Petticoat Tail, Real Scottish,
        256
    Squares, Oatmeal, 257
    Wafers, Brown Sugar, 258
Shortcake(s)
    about, 64
    Berry, with Buttermilk-Almond
        Biscuits, 66
    Blueberry, with Low-Fat
        Cornmeal-Yogurt Biscuits, 68
    Della Lutes' Mother's, old
        recipe, 66
    The Finamore, 65
    make-ahead strategy for, 41
    Peach Melba, 68
Shrewsbury Cakes, 245
Shrewsbury Cakes, old recipe, 245
Sicilian Fig-Filled Cookies, 289
Simple Cooking newsletter, 320,
    321
Slump, Black and Blueberry, 58
Slump, defined, 34
Snow Cream (Spanish Cream), 105
Snow Eggs. *See also* Oeufs à la
    Neige
    description of, 121
    old recipe, 87
Snows (fruit-based)
    about, 87, 96
    Pear, 96
Soufflés
    about, 163
    Blintz, 164
    Blintz, old recipe, 164
    Bread Pudding, Commander's
        Palace, 192
    Chocolate, Edna Lewis's, 168
    description of, 121
    Pear, Little, 165
    Saltzburg Little Mountain, 166
    Thomas Keller's Molten
        Chocolate, 162
Sour Cream Pumpkin Chiffon Pie,
    497
Sour Cream Raisin Pie, 504
South American Caramel Pudding,
    125
Southern Coconut Layer Cake
    with Divinity Icing, 394
Southern-Style Peach and
    Raspberry Cobbler with Pecan-
    Crunch Topping, 38
Southern Wine Sauce for
    Spongecake, 618
Spanish cream, about, 105
Spanish Cream (Snow Cream), 105

Spelt or Farina Pudding, old
    recipe, 210
Spice Cake, Prune, 343
Spice Cake, Rich, Soft, 325
Spiced Sandtorte, 356
Spiced Sour Cherry Compote for
    Ice Cream, 619
Spices, for recipes, 21, 22
Sponge
    Apricot, 99
    Peach, old recipe, 99
    Pudding, old recipe, 128
Spongecake, Hot-Water, 299
Spongecake, Vanilla, Marie's, 117
Spotted Dick (or Dog), about,
    213
Squash. *See also* Pumpkin
    Crookneck or Winter, Pudding,
        old recipe, 229
St. Louis Gooey Butter Cake, 375
Stack Cake, Dried Apple
    Gingerbread, 392
Stack cakes, about, 393
Steamed Pumpkin Pudding with
    Ginger-Lemon Cream, 228
Sticky Buns, Prune-Filled Pecan-
    Caramel, 366
Stiriai Metélt (Hungarian Cheese-
    Noodle Dessert), 207
Strawberry(ies)
    Berry Shortcakes with
        Buttermilk-Almond Biscuits,
        66
    Chunky Double-Berry Sauce,
        617
    Nonsense, 115
    -Rhubarb Crisp with
        Cinnamon-Walnut Topping,
        52
    Summer Pudding of Four Red
        Fruits, 202
Strudel
    Dried Fruit, with Pear-Brandy
        Custard Sauce, 566
    Poppy Seed, Paul Kovi's, 564
    Ricotta, from Trieste, 562
    variations on, 563
Stucolo di Ricotta (Ricotta Strudel
    from Trieste), 562
Sugar, 21. See also Brown Sugar;
    Maple Sugar
Summer Pudding of Four Red
    Fruits, 202
"Summer Riches" (Cherry and
    Nectarine Cobbler with Rich
    Pastry Dough), 40
Sundae, Peanut Brittle, Trumps,
    607
Sunshine Cake, 307
Sunshine Cake, old recipe, 307

Swedish Apple "Pie" with Vanilla
    Sauce, 55
Sweet Potato
    –Pecan Pie, Orleans, 522
    Pie, 499
    Pudding, Rum-Glazed, 224
    Pudding, Tennessee Old
        Maid's, 230
Syllabubs
    about, 93
    Lemon, 94
    Lime, 94
    old recipe, 93
    Tangerine, 94
Szarlotka (Polish Apple Tart), 556

T

Taffety Tart, old recipe, 453
Taiglach, many forms of, 584
Taiglach (Jewish Honey-Nut Puff
    Clusters), 583
Tangerine(s)
    Chilled Citrus Platter, 73
    Syllabub, 94
Tapioca
    old recipe, 132
    Pudding, Coconut, Asian-Style,
        134
    Pudding, Fluffy Baked, 133
    types of, 132
Tarallo Abruzzese (Hotel Cipriani's
    Breakfast Cake), 354
Tart Dough
    partially baking, 447–448
    prebaking, 531
    Rich, 451
Tarte au Citron Nézard (The
    World's Best Lemon Tart), 534
Tarte au Sucre (Belgian Sugar
    Tart), 548
Tarte au Sucre (French Canadian
    Maple Sugar Pie), 521
Tarts. *See also* Tart Dough
    about, 528–529
    Apple, Polish, 556
    Caramel-Walnut, 549
    Carrot Pudding (tart), old
        recipe, 543
    Cheese, Hungarian, 553
    Chocolate-Tart, old recipe, 551
    Cornmeal Pear, with
        Frangipane, 544
    Cranberry-Raspberry Tart
        Pastiche, 540
    Double Blueberry, Long Island,
        536
    Gingered Carrot Custard, 542
    Lemon, The World's Best, 534
    Nut, Ray's Holiday, 551
    Orange, Fresh, 535

Tarts (*cont.*)
    Pear, Alsatian, with Macaroon
      Crunch Topping, 538
    Pear Galette, Free-Form, 532
    Pear Tarte Tatin, Breakfast, 530
    prebaking crusts for, 531
    Quince and Almond, The
      Coach House, 546
    Quince Pye, old recipe, 547
    Rice Pudding, Warm, with
      Dried Fruit, 554
    Sugar, Belgian, 548
Tea
    Cream, Jefferson's, 103
    Mint, Pears Poached in, with
      Dark Chocolate Sauce, 80
    Robertson Davies' Punchbowl
      (A Spirited Finale), 625
Tennessee Moonshine Cookies,
  261
Tennessee Old Maid's Sweet
  Potato Pudding, 230
Thomas Keller's Molten
  Chocolate, 162
Thunder and Lightning, about,
  213
Tilly's Pudding, old recipe, 222
Tiramisù, 160
Tishpishti (Sephardic Walnut Cake
  with Honey-Lemon Syrup), 439
Tocino del Cielo (Cuban Caramel
  Custard), 147
Tomato, Green, and Apple
  Mincemeat Pie, 526
Torta, Rice, old recipe, 555
Torta from Gourds, old recipe,
  493
Tortes
    Carolina Huguenot, 398
    Chocolate Nut, Low-Fat, 416
    Fruit-Filled Lattice, with Three
      Fillings, 559
    Spiced Sandtorte, 356
    Summer Fruit, All-Time-Best,
      344
    Walnut, Austrian, with Coffee
      Whipped Cream, 400
Traditional Two-Berry Buckle, 60
Trifle, Luli's, 156
Trifles, about, 121
Trumps Peanut Brittle Sundae, 607
Tyrolean Christmas Fruitcake, 432

U

Upside-Down Cake, Cranberry,
346

V

Vanilla
  about, 244
  beans, working with, 22
  extract, buying, 22
  history of, 121
Vanilla Wafers, Banana Pudding
  with, 127
Vegetable dessert puddings, about,
223
Virginia Blackberry Roll, 44

W

Walnut(s)
  Black, Pie, 517
  Cake, Sephardic, with Honey-
    Lemon Syrup, 439
  -Caramel Tart, 549
  -Cinnamon Topping, Rhubarb-
    Strawberry Crisp with, 52
  Coffee Cake with Nut Streusel,
    351
  -Filled Crepes with Warm
    Chocolate Sauce, Hungarian,
    236
  The Four Seasons' Christmas
    Fruitcake (Light Fruitcake
    Wrapped in Marzipan), 426
  French Canadian Maple Sugar
    Pie, 521
  Gingerbread Hermits, 250
  Jam Cake with Burnt Sugar
    Glaze, 385
  Low-Fat Chocolate Nut Torte,
    416
  Mother Church's Spirited Dark
    Fruitcake, 424
  Nina's Fabulous Athenian Nut
    Cake with Rum Syrup, 437
  The Original Toll House
    Cookie, 264
  Ray's Holiday Nut Tart, 551
  Rhode Island Chunky Pear Pie,
    461
  Sicilian Fig-Filled Cookies, 289
  Torte, Austrian, with Coffee
    Whipped Cream, 400
Watermelon Cake, old recipe, 404

Whim Wham, old recipe, 157
Whipped cream, preparing, 24
Whipped Cream Pound Cake, 305
Whiskey
  Sauce, Bon Ton's New Orleans
    Bread Pudding with, 188
  Sauce, Jack Daniel's Raisin Roll
    with, 570
  Tennessee Moonshine Cookies,
    261
White Chocolate
  Banana Cream Pie, 486
  Coconut Blondies, 269
  -Macadamia Blondies, 269
White Torta, old recipe, 406
Wild Rice Pudding with Honey
  and Dried Cherries or
  Cranberries, 178
Wine
  and Cheese, Santa Fe Bread
    Pudding with, 195
  Crinkly Baked Pears, Trattoria-
    Style, 79
  Ice, Coarse-Crystal, with
    Sangría Granita Variation, 602
  Jelly, Citrus, 102
  Late-Harvest, Syrup,
    and Raspberry Compote in, 72
  Madeira Dried Fruit Compote,
    77
  "Mouthfuls" from Abruzzo,
    581
  Panna Cotta and Poached Pears
    in Merlot Syrup, 108
  Sauce, Southern, for
    Spongecake, 618
  Sauce for Rum or Batter
    Pudding, old recipe, 618
  Sweet Muscat Sabayon, 624
World War I Applesauce
  Cheesecake, 410

Y

Yr Custard Puddinge, old recipe,
  191

Z

Zabaglione, about, 86
Zabaglione, Amaretto-Cognac,
  Warm, 114
Zelten (Tyrolean Christmas
  Fruitcake), 432